P9-BHX-594

THE POLITICS AND MANAGEMENT OF CANADIAN ECONOMIC POLICY

The Politics and Management of Canadian Economic Policy

Richard W. Phidd
G. Bruce Doern

Macmillan of Canada

Canadian Cataloguing in Publication Data

Phidd, Richard W.
The politics and management of Canadian economic policy

Bibliography: p.
Includes index.
ISBN 0-7705-1611-4

1. Canada — Economic policy. I. Doern, G. Bruce, 1942- II. Title.

HC115.P43 338.971 C77-001830-0

Printed in Canada for
The Macmillan Company of Canada Limited,
70 Bond Street,
Toronto M5B 1X3

CONTENTS

PREFACE

As one of Canada's political leaders has said, "The universe is unfolding as it should." While this may or may not be true, it certainly presents problems for people wanting to write books, particularly on the politics and management of Canadian economic policy. The analysis in this book treats events to about the end of 1976 but undoubtedly more "unfolding" will have occurred by the time it appears in printed form.

This book is written for a fairly diverse audience, including students taking academic courses in the political economy of the Canadian state, government-industry relations, Canadian politics and public administration, and economic management. Since there are far more "students" of economic management outside the universities than there are inside, we hope that the book will be useful, both as a source of information and to facilitate a more complete understanding of political and economic-management processes, for other such readers in government, industry, labour, and the Canadian community at large.

Because of the expected diversity of the audience, we have tried to organize our material with the expectation that it will be used in a variety of different ways. Thus, although the book will be read by many as a complete entity, there will be some whose interest will be limited to the more particular, or to only the more general, aspects of the analysis. We have therefore felt it necessary to include a reasonable amount of repetition of key parts of the analysis to accommodate the different ways in which we expect the book will be used.

Our analysis is the joint product of about seven years' work. At various stages, this work has been encouraged, challenged, criticized, and hence greatly improved, by numerous colleagues, government, industrial, and union officials, students, and other fellow-travellers.

We have learned much in the process. In particular we are indebted to J. W. Grove, Dr. David Slater, and the late

Dr. John J. Deutsch, all of Queen's University, who especially helped in the early stages of research. Later we profited from the commentary of Arthur Smith, André Raynauld, and Peter Aucoin, as well as that of our colleagues and students at the University of Guelph, and at the School of Public Administration at Carleton University, particularly Gilles Paquet, Ian Macdonald, Vince Wilson, and O. P. Dwivedi. The financial support of Carleton University, and a Sabbatical Leave Fellowship from the Canada Council are also gratefully acknowledged.

We thank Jocelyn Barrett, Phyl Anderson, Lee McPherson, Trish Donnelly, Diane Perozzo, and June Hubert for the typing of the manuscript at various stages of drafting, as well as for much cheerful administrative support. The editorial work of Beverley Beetham of Macmillan of Canada is also much appreciated.

To Iskah and Joan and our two families we owe our greatest debt. They will be encouraged and relieved to know that the book is indeed finally finished.

The value of the book derives from what we have learned from the above-mentioned persons and from the numerous other people whom we have interviewed. Any weaknesses remaining in the book are our responsibility.

Richard W. Phidd and G. Bruce Doern
1978

To Iskah and Joan

PART ONE

Introduction

Part I introduces the scope and boundaries of the book by locating it in the evolution of the disciplines of Canadian political science, economics, and public administration and by linking it to the recent rediscovery of the need to analyse economic policy in the context of a political-economy approach.

Chapter 1 defines and analyses the concept of economic management in the general context of the interface between politics, public policy, and public administration, and in relation to the general historical evolution of government organization in Canada.

Chapter 2 presents a general discussion of the politics of Canadian economic policy through an analysis of the role of the Canadian state, the conflicting and competing goals of economic policy, and efforts to articulate these goals. It also ties these central political dimensions to the choices among the exhortative, expenditure, and regulatory instruments of governing available to Canadian politicians and economic managers.

Introduction

The academic analysis of Canadian economic policy has been largely the preserve of economists whose focus, naturally enough, has been on substantive economic questions. This book is about the politics, management, and organization of economic policy and policy processes in the Government of Canada. It will describe and evaluate the political, managerial, and organizational structures and processes which significantly affect how economic policy works, or fails to work, in practice.

In many political systems the task of conducting such an analysis has been immeasurably aided by the published works of governmental practitioners in the art of economic policy-making. Since this publishing tradition has been much less well established in Canada, it makes the task of outside researchers both more difficult, and more necessary.

Accordingly, this book is based on the elementary view that our understanding of economic policy-making in Canada can benefit from the examination of political and organizational analysis as a complement to the analysis provided by economists, be they of the academic or governmental variety. The making of economic policy in Canada occurs in the executive-bureaucratic arena of the Canadian political system and hence, economic-policy analysis is intellectually incomplete until it incorporates political, managerial, and organizational variables. The basic intent of this book is to describe the political and organizational roles, structures, and processes, and to evaluate and explain the making of Canadian economic policy in those contexts.

We hope that the book can serve a useful integrative function academically and in other more practical ways as well. In the context of literature on Canadian politics we hope that the book will help integrate some of our knowledge about central public-policy and budgetary processes. Economic policy forces a consideration of these processes in the total context and fabric of governing. The central cycle and rhythm of economic-policy processes greatly influences other policy processes, and other policy options and outcomes. Existing analyses of public policy have tended to centre on particular cases or issues, or on parts of the central structures of policy-making. In the context of public-administration literature, we hope that the book will help build on the work of J. E. Hodgetts and others in developing an understanding of important components of government organization. In this regard, because of the absence of very basic published analyses and information on such important federal departments as Finance, Industry, Trade and Commerce, Regional Economic Expansion, Consumer and Corporate Affairs, and Manpower and Immigration, we have presented, especially in Part III of the book, a considerable amount of detail about their policy mandates and their organization.

In one important sense we provide this detail for the reader without any apologies or remorse. It is our conviction that economic-policy processes cannot be honestly assessed in an intellectual way by naively hoping that the burdensome details will go away. The management of the economy, in both its political and administrative senses, involves action through organizations and navigation through an intricate web of past and present legislative and non-legislative values, commitments, and constraints. It is essential to understand economic management not only at the macro or Keynesian level but also at the micro level. The departments analysed in Part III are not dry, sterile appendages of a mythical bureaucracy; they have been given tasks by the political process and are the custodians of important political and economic values and programs. Moreover, it is at the micro level that the politics and management of Canadian economic policy are increasingly played out. Agency and interdepartmental behaviour is an important dimension of politics. Organizational roles and behaviour are the micro-politics of economic policy. They are to macro-politics what micro-economics is to macro-economics.

We view this book to be a part of the recently rediscovered traditions of Canadian political economy.[1] The fact that politics and economics are inextricably linked in governmental economic-policy processes will strike the lay reader of this book as being obvious and elementary. This elementary fact is somewhat less apparent when one considers the development of the academic disciplines of political science and economics. In earlier times, these disciplines were more closely linked, both intellectually and organizationally, through a political-economy approach. The need to study political and economic power together was the basis of the tradition established by Innis and others. During the past twenty-five years the disciplines have tended to drift apart both intellectually and organizationally. The separation was fortunately never complete since certain segments of both disciplines held the political-economy linkage to be essential. In recent years there has been a growing recognition of the need for a renewed political-economy focus.

Politics is the process through which a society authoritatively allocates values and resolves conflict. It therefore involves both the process of choosing goals and priorities and the selection of various instruments of governing through which legitimate support and/or compliance is secured.

Political science investigates the ways in which societies govern themselves. It is concerned with the goals of the political system, the structural relationships in that system, the patterns of individual and group behaviour which explain how that system functions, and the policy outcomes. The focus of political science on goals, processes, and governing instruments inevitably requires an analysis of organizations. The study of political science has involved a varied commitment to different areas of subject matter.[2] Some scholars are more inclined to restrict their emphasis to such areas as voting behaviour, interest groups, or legislative behaviour as the crucial dimensions of politics. Other political scientists are more inclined to see politics everywhere. Thus, the internal politics of organizations, social class conflict, intergovernmental relations, and general analyses of political culture are examined.

Whatever the items listed as the primary variables with which politics is concerned, rationality and control are usually involved. Political actors must be able to control others whose responses and/or support are needed to bring about the desired state of affairs. Moreover, political actors in a democratic state must secure support and compliance in a legitimate way. These considerations lead naturally to forms of political organization and to changes in the organization of policy formulation and governmental management.

In the context of the Canadian cabinet system of government this demands that a major focus be placed on the executive-bureaucratic arena.[3] The analysis of the making of public policy, therefore, requires a greater intellectual understanding of what might traditionally be called "public administration" or what more accurately ought to be identified as "political administration and public-sector management and organization."[4] Intrabureaucratic organization and management are the focal points of micro-politics, requiring a more explicit analysis of the role of government and the state, and of the intellectual developments in management, budgeting, and the behaviour of organizations. Because of this essential requirement the study of Canadian politics has to concern itself more with the impact of both management and economics.

The reorientation toward a political-economy approach also stems from divergent viewpoints in the study of economics. In the contemporary setting economists are primarily concerned with applying their analytical tools to facilitate the problems of choice. Economics is concerned with the production and distribution of goods where resources are scarce and choices must be made. Hence, economists engage in theoretical and empirical research on macro-economic subjects such as reaching and maintaining full employment, avoiding inflation and deflation, understanding and promoting economic growth, analysing fiscal and monetary policies, defining balance and imbalance in international payments, and on micro-economic subjects such as marketing, pricing, monopolies, manpower, labour markets, union movements, farm issues, and problems resulting from inequalities in income-distribution and poverty. The areas studied and the approach adopted depend also on the nature of the problems to be solved by society at a given period of time.[5]

In some respects Canadian economists have demonstrated a stronger recognition of the role of government than have Canadian political scientists. This is especially true in the area of macro-economics where the Keynesian concepts were centred on counter-cyclical activity carried out by governments. In general terms, however, the understanding of actual decision-making processes in organizations, particularly public organizations, has not been a central feature of Canadian economic analysis. Economists, moreover, when they address themselves to organizational and political questions, often tend to treat these variables as being merely *means* or techniques, necessary to achieve so-called real economic objectives.[6] Political and organizational analysis cannot afford to make the same assumption. Political and organizational processes are valued ends in themselves, especially in a democratic, and in an increasingly bureaucratic, state. Greater recognition of these issues has brought some economists closer to the discipline of political science and to an applied understanding of the processes of economic management.[7]

Despite the slow progress of the above process of mutual intellectual interdependence and recognition in academic circles, the political economies of all states have increasingly reflected the reality of the interdependence between politics, economics, and management. Industrial and post-industrial societies have developed highly differentiated structures and accordingly have witnessed an increased number of private and public organizations all participating in, or attempting to influence, the decision-making process. Many will claim that this differentiation means that power is more widely distributed among a large number of organizations both public and private thus greatly complicating societal management. Others will claim that power is more concentrated.

Regardless of these conflicting interpretations, it is now clear that, at any point in time, existing organizational structures act as important constraints on the development of new initiatives in government since policy is never formulated in a vacuum or *de novo*. In this respect economic policy, like any other area of governmental policy, is concerned with both continuity and change. The reorganization of Finance departments or the creation of new structures such as the departments of Manpower and Immigration, and Consumer and Corporate Affairs reflect the continuing demands for innovation and reorganization. These initiatives have been taking place in response to new problems to be solved.

In pragmatic terms the structure of government reflects a changing commitment to goals or to the reordering of governmental priorities.

The conflict and co-operation which take place between the departments and agencies concerned with policy formulation constitute a significant domain which must be studied. The aggregate managerial dimensions of economic-policy formulation, as well as the political influences within the Cabinet, have been largely ignored in Canadian analysis.[8]

This book stresses the management of economic policy, that is, the process through which the increasingly complex and competing goals, instruments, agencies, and research needs of economic policy are co-ordinated and controlled. The emphasis on management arises precisely because of the growing complexity of goals, instruments, and agencies, and hence the need for the processes to be "managed".

The goals include the usual so-called primary (Keynesian) goals of full employment, economic growth, price stability, and international balance-of-payments equilibrium, but they obviously also include the welfare goals of both class and regional redistribution; hence economic management shades into so-called social policy. The latter embodies the government's provision of public goods and hence cannot be divorced from the goverment's role as producer through such vehicles as state enterprise. As if the above Keynesian and welfare goals were not enough, there has been, in recent years, a further layering of goals, many of which are centred on the qualitative structural regulation of the economy in such areas as foreign investment, competition, technology transfers, and the environment.

The managerial necessities are evident both in the narrower sense of the economic management processes *within* the federal government, and on the broader public sector-private sector, intergovernmental, and international, dimensions of economic management as well. Thus in the broadest sense economic management involves the processes of developing a consensus, or otherwise resolving the economic conflicts that inherently arise among sectors of the political economy including government, business, labour, and agriculture.

The boundaries of the concept of economic management obviously cannot be defined with absolute precision. Chapter 1 will outline the principal features in greater detail. It is sufficient to say at this stage, however, that this book will define economic policy and management to include not only the narrower field of fiscal and monetary policy but also the broader implications of aggregate governmental expenditures and programs which impinge on, and significantly influence, economic behaviour. The boundaries of economic management are also partly defined by the specific departments and agencies which are viewed to be a part of the economic-policy machinery. Hence the processes of co-ordinating and controlling the goals, instruments, and activities of the departments of Finance, Industry, Trade and Commerce, Regional Economic Expansion, Consumer and Corporate Affairs, Manpower and Immigration, as well as the Treasury Board, Bank of Canada, Privy Council Office, Prime Minister's Office, and the Economic Council of Canada, are part of economic management.

There is obviously some inevitable arbitrariness in the selection of the departments listed above. A wider definitional net could include such departments as Labour, Health and Welfare, Energy, Mines and Resources, Transportation, Agriculture, and Science and Technology. While we have confined our focus in this book to the departments and agencies listed in the previous paragraph, we will refer constantly to the roles and changing influence of other departments as well as Crown corporations.

Some of the difficulties in defining economic management can also be seen in the context of economists' efforts at classifying economic phenomena in terms of demand and supply. Demand management is traditionally viewed to be the aggregate short-term management of demand to counteract and compensate for the changes in the business cycle. Supply management tends to be tied to the medium or even longer term and involves the management of the supply of factors of production including labour, resources, and research and development. The complex interrelationships between demand and supply and between the short run and the medium and long runs are increasingly evident and thus also constitute a central part of economic management.[9]

The concept of economic management obviously does not imply that the competing goals, agencies, and instruments are fully or necessarily well co-ordinated. It does imply that the growing complexity imposes the need to attempt to co-ordinate and control the process and hence to "manage" it. The processes and structures of economic management therefore deserve careful, critical analysis and understanding.

The overall management dimensions are of course inextricably linked to politics and to political and bureaucratic norms and behaviour. As Chapter 2 will point out more thoroughly, politics involves both the allocation of values and goals and also the selection of various governing instruments through which political authorities seek to secure compliance and/or support. This book will stress the need to view politics both in terms of goals and governing instruments.

For businessmen, students of economics, and others who might tend to treat both politics and bureaucracy as being merely unfortunate aberrations of human behaviour which we could better do without, we hope that the book will help develop a more complete understanding of the important rationalities of political and organizational behaviour. We think it is important that the Cabinet, central policy processes, and interdepartmental relations in complex bureaucracies be understood, at least in part, on their own terms. This is not to suggest that as authors or as readers we ought to accept or tolerate all that we find there, but it is important, we think, to attempt to view economic-policy processes, at least in part, in terms of the rationalities of politics and management and in terms of the complex and conflicting demands placed upon economic policy-leaders in the Government of Canada. In particular it is absolutely essential to disabuse those who adopt the notion (usually, but not exclusively, found in the corporate world) which simplistically suggests that cabinets and cabinet decision-making processes are, or ought to be, essentially similar to private-sector decision-making and policy processes. While the focus of the book on the management of economic policy bears witness to the growing importance of developments in government management concepts, many of which were in turn based on business management practices, it is nonetheless true that governmental processes have been, are, and must be fundamentally different in nature.[10]

Although the focus of the analysis is on the Canadian Federal Cabinet and bureaucracy, the book also treats the political and managerial aspects in a comparative perspective. There are very few political and organizational issues and reforms that have not been tried somewhere else. Hence, we will refer to the comparative experiences of Britain, France, the United States, and other countries.

Our analysis is based on an assessment of numerous published and unpublished reports and documents as well as on confidential interviews with over two hundred officials, politicians, businessmen, and officials of labour unions conducted over the past several years. Needless to say, one way to find out about how economic policy is made is to talk to those who are involved in the making of it. Hence, we are indebted to many public servants and industrial and union officials for their co-operation and information, and for their insights into the process. Our task as academic analysts is to describe the processes and organization and to attempt to explain and critically analyse the patterns and processes of behaviour discovered there.

It will be readily apparent that there are many parts of the total economic-policy process which the book does not and could not fully explore. Our focus is on the Government of Canada; hence, we do not *fully* describe and assess the structure of Canadian industry, labour, and market mechanisms, nor the organization of economic policy in provincial governments, in the total intergovernmental domain, and in the international sphere. Nonetheless, the central links with these critical sectors cannot help but emerge when one examines, as this book does, the economic departments and their several clienteles. Although we strongly relate the making of economic policy to the budgetary process of the Government of Canada we have left unexplored many details of the budgetary process. Moreover, not all of the departments with economic policy roles have been analysed with the same degree of detail.

As authors we are also products of certain intellectual and academic orientations and have approached the development of this book from two complementary perspectives. The book in part reflects work originally done by Richard Phidd for a doctoral thesis on the role of the Economic Council of Canada. This work, in turn, reflected Phidd's previous background and interest in comparative economic planning and economic management. In other respects the analysis builds on previous analysis by Bruce Doern on the structures of policy-making in Canada and on the organization and functioning of the Cabinet. Needless to say the collaboration of two authors with these somewhat different, though complementary, perspectives still leaves many weaknesses. We hope, nonetheless, that a political and organizational analysis centred on the management of economic policy in the executive-bureaucratic arena will help shed some light on this central issue of contemporary Canadian government.

Our research and analysis leads us to the firm view that economic policy processes and outcomes can be and should be reformed but that such reform must be more fully cognizant of the political and organizational questions that will inevitably influence such reforms. The tendency to treat organizational and political variables as being irrational intrusions into an otherwise rational economic world fails totally to comprehend the rationality of both politics and organization.

In general the book is organized into four parts, progressing from the general to the relatively more specific and ending with some general concluding observations. Part I provides an introduction to the evolution of issues in the politics and management of Canadian economic policy. Part II describes and evaluates the central structures and processes of economic-policy formulation in the Government of Canada. Part III describes and evaluates the more detailed operation of economic-policy formulation in the major departments concerned. Part IV offers some concluding comments on selected issues in the politics and management of Canadian economic policy, and on organizational reform.

Thus, in Chapter 1, we place the analysis of economic management in the general context of the interface between politics, public policy, and public administration, and in the context of the general evolution of central policy organization in the Government of Canada. Chapter 2 examines the values and goals and hence the politics of Canadian economic policy in the context of the Canadian political economy, and in relation to the basic governing instruments available to politicians. Chapter 3 relates the making of economic policy to the central structures and processes of cabinet government, including the fiscal and budgetary process, cabinet committees, central agencies, cabinet policy processes, and the political characteristics of cabinet portfolios. Chapter 4 then relates these aggregate organizational variables to the dynamics of executive-bureaucratic processes, and Chapter 5 relates them to the roles of economic policy-leaders in the Government of Canada.

Chapters 6-12 carry the analysis into the even more specific domains of economic management, including the major departments on both the so-called demand and supply sides of economic policy, and assessments of the efforts made to secure economic policy consensus and co-ordination between the public and private sectors, and between levels of government.

Chapter 6 presents a brief historical overview of the evolution of economic-management departments. Chapter 7 focusses on the Department of Finance but also deals with its relationships to the Treasury Board and the Bank of Canada, and thus with the relationships between fiscal policy, monetary policy, and the general management of the government and the government expenditure process. Chapter 8 examines the government-industry interface as it has been reflected in the organization of the Department of Industry, Trade and Commerce, and Chapter 9 examines regional development policy through the evolution of the Department of Regional Economic Expansion. The analysis of specific departments continues in Chapter 10 with an examination of the Department and Commission of Employment and Immigration which emerged both as a response to, and as an influence on, the concern for the qualitative and human side of labour-market and employment policies. Finally, the emergence of the Department of Consumer and Corporate Affairs with its focus on restructuring the legal framework of the Canadian marketplace is analysed in Chapter 11. Part III concludes with an analysis of how these several and evolving departments, mandates, goals, and programs reflect, and seek to influence, the processes of conflict and consensus in Canadian economic management.

Finally, in Chapters 13 and 14 we present two forms of summary analysis. Chapter 13 selects a few contemporary issues in the politics and management of Canadian economic policy and assesses them in the light of the central themes discussed in the book. These issues include: the growing complexity of economic variables and processes and their impact on future reform processes; the relationship between economic research and knowledge and reform processes; the emergence of new economic portfolios as a reflection of reform processes; the openness of Canadian economic-policy processes; the role of political and organizational variables as a factor in the explanation of the growth of government expenditure; the political relationship between macro- and micro-economic management; and the evolving and future roles of central Finance and Treasury ministries.

In Chapter 14 we relate our entire analysis to the evolving debate about tripartism in Canada in the so-called post- (incomes) control period and to the major competing liberal, pluralist, and corporatist characterizations of the modern Canadian political economy.

NOTES

1. On the important traditions and evolution of Canadian political economy see Daniel Drache, "Rediscovering Canadian Political Economy". Paper presented to the Canadian Political Science Association meetings in Edmonton (June 1975); Robin Neill, *A New Theory of Value: The Canadian Economics of H. A. Innis* (Toronto, 1972); and K. J. Rea and J. T. McLeod, eds., *Business and Government in Canada,* second ed. (Toronto, 1976). For a comparative view see Robert Eyestone, *Political Economy* (Chicago, 1972), and Robert A. Dahl and Charles E. Lindblom, *Politics, Economics and Welfare* (New York, 1956).

2. For the most succinct review of Canadian political science see Allan C. Cairns, "Alternative Styles in the Study of Canadian Politics", *Canadian Journal of Political Science,* Vol. VII, no. 1 (March 1974), pp. 101-27; see also Donald Smiley, "Must Canadian Political Science be a Miniature Replica?" *Journal of Canadian Studies,* Vol. IX (February 1974), pp. 31-42; for comparative views see O. R. Young, *Systems of Political Sciences* (Englewood Cliffs, N. J., 1968), and David Easton, *A Systems Analysis of Political Life* (New York, 1965).

3. See G. Bruce Doern and Peter Aucoin, eds., *The Structures of Policy-Making in Canada* (Toronto, 1971), pp. 1-7, and Thomas Hockin, ed., *Apex of Power* (Toronto, 1971).

4. See Hugh Heclo and Aaron Wildavsky, *The Private Government of Public Money* (London, 1974). Heclo and Wildavsky consistently use the phrase "political administration" in their excellent analysis of the British budgetary and expenditure process.

5. An illustration of the range of concerns in Canadian economic analysis can be found in L. J. Officer and L. B. Smith, eds., *Issues in Canadian Economics* (Toronto, 1974). For comparative views see Robert Heilbroner, ed., *Economic Means and Social Ends* (Englewood Cliffs, N. J., 1969), and Kenneth Boulding, *Economics as a Science* (New York, 1970).

6. There are, of course, some notable exceptions. See Dahl and Lindblom, *Politics, Economics and Welfare*; Albert Breton, *The Economic Theory of Representative Government* (Chicago, 1974); and J. C. H. Jones, "The Bureaucracy and Public Policy: Canadian Merger Policy and the Combines Branch, 1960-71", *Canadian Public Administration*, Vol. XVIII, pp. 269-96. The work of Breton and of Acheson and Chant, Canadian economists who have utilized bureaucratic theory, will be assessed in Chapter 4.

7. For an analysis of these trends and issues see Eyestone, *Political Economy*, chapters 4 and 5, and R. L. Heilbroner, *Between Capitalism and Socialism* (New York, 1970).

8. The closest we have come to published analyses of the politics and management of Canadian economic policy is in the areas of budgeting and financial management. See, for example, W. L. White and J. C. Strick, *Policy, Politics and the Treasury Board in Canadian Government* (Don Mills, 1970); J. C. Strick, *Canadian Public Finance* (Toronto, 1973); A. W. Johnson, "The Treasury Board of Canada and the Machinery of Government in the 1970s", *Canadian Journal of Political Science*, Vol. VI, no. 9, pp. 346-66; and M. Hicks, "The Treasury Board of Canada and Its Clients", *Canadian Public Administration*, Vol. XVI, no. 2, pp. 182-205. For comparative analyses of other states, however, see Lawrence Pierce, *The Politics of Fiscal Policy Formation* (Pacific Palisades, Ca., 1971); Heclo and Wildavsky, *The Private Government of Public Money*; and Robert D. Lee and R. W. Johnson, *Public Budgeting Systems* (Baltimore, 1973).

9. Ely Devons, *Planning and Economic Management*, edited by Sir Alec Cairncross (Manchester, 1970), pp. 123-220.

10. For excellent comparative and Canadian analyses see Peter Self,

Administrative Theories and Politics (Toronto, 1973), and J. E. Hodgetts, *The Canadian Public Service, 1867-1967: A Physiology of Government* (Toronto, 1973).

CHAPTER ONE

Economic Management, Public Policy, and Public Administration

The political economy of the modern Canadian state is determined by a wide variety of general forces and variables including the general acceptance of a mixed-capitalist market economy, the existence of a federal system of government, the centrifugal imperatives of a bilingual, and multi-cultural population, the existence of economic classes, the reality of extensive foreign ownership of Canadian industry (both manufacturing and primary resource industry), a dependence on foreign trade, and the increasing concentration of population in urban centres. These features of the Canadian political economy have been analysed extensively and constitute the aggregate environment within which Canadian economic policies have been, and are, developed. In the final analysis, the determination and management of Canadian economic policy are profoundly influenced by these general forces.

Less well known, and certainly less understood, are the more specific political, managerial, and organizational dynamics of Canadian economic-policy formulation. These dynamics can only be intellectually understood by examining the economic-policy processes and organizations as they exist in the executive-bureaucratic arena of the Government of Canada, and by relating these processes and organizations to the evolving processes of economic management.

This book will stress the extent to which the politics of Canadian economic-policy formulation is increasingly influenced by the development of concepts related to public management in general, and economic management in particular. Since the rest of the book will deal extensively with the detailed intragovernmental management, organization, and politics of economic policy, this chapter will define the concept of economic management and place the analysis in the general context of public decision-making processes and recent changes in the relationships between public policy, public administration, and government structure. Chapter 2 will then present an analysis of the broad political dimensions of economic policy in Canada.

This chapter is organized into four sections. The first section will define and set out the basic dimensions of economic management. The second section will identify the political and managerial context of economic decision-making. The third section will relate the politics and management of economic policy to the general conceptual problems of differentiating policy from management and administration. Our introduction to the broad relationships between policy, administration, and economic management will then be completed in section four with a brief introduction to recent efforts to restructure the federal policy-making and administrative machinery.

ECONOMIC MANAGEMENT

Economic management is the process through which the increasingly complex and competing goals, instruments, agencies, and research needs of economic policy are co-ordinated and controlled. Contained within this broad definition are a number of factors which require a more detailed discussion in order that the boundaries of our analysis may be established as clearly as possible.[1]

In traditional economic terms economic management involves the fiscal policy co-ordination of both aggregate expenditure and particular taxation and expenditure decisions and programs which have an important economic impact. It involves the processes of debt management and borrowing as well as the regulation of the supply of money and credit. It consequently involves the management of both demand and supply and the increasing problems of differentiating supply from demand. In organizational terms it involves co-ordinating the relationships between economic research and intelligence and the ongoing needs of policy and program officials on the one hand, and the general public on the other hand. It involves the process of delegating economic policy functions, instruments, and programs to different Cabinet portfolios, governmental departments, and agencies. This in turn involves problems of horizontal co-ordination among departments and vertical co-ordination between departments and central agencies. Finally, and in its most important and political context, economic management involves a continuing process of determining and co-ordinating the shifting economic-policy goals and priorities. It involves the selection of the voluntary, expenditure and regulatory instruments of governing through which economic-policy objectives must ultimately be achieved. In Canada's federal, liberal, democratic political system the pursuit of goals and the selection of governing instruments obviously requires the development of economic-management institutions and processes through which both public sector-private sector and intergovernmental and regional consensus can be achieved or conflicts can be resolved. Thus the intricate balancing of traditional stabilization goals with welfare and redistributive goals must ultimately be achieved through bargaining between governments and labour, business, agricultural, and consumer interests.

The importance of using a concept of economic management as a conceptual basis for understanding economic-policy processes in the Government of Canada is perhaps best symbolized by the description, given in 1975 by Michael Pitfield, Secretary to the Cabinet. Pitfield described the Department of Finance as the "court of last resort" for economic policy.[2] No such description would have accompanied the Finance department's role ten years earlier. The metaphorical reference to the court of last report is an important reflection of how the processes of economic-policy formulation have evolved. It is simply no longer as plausible as it once might have been to speak of a single department "making" policy. The widening complexity of goals, instruments, agencies, and research needs means that a broader managerial requirement has become necessary. The promotion and control of economic activity has become a highly important and pervasive governmental function. Economic policy-making becomes, therefore, an important part of both politics and public administration.

Economic management deals with the most basic issues of the politics and economics of taxing and spending. The most critical problem in economic management arises from the fact that, as total governmental expenditure levels increase, financing becomes more difficult because the revenue which must be raised usually increases as a percentage of national income, thereby squeezing taxpayers harder every year. The basic redistributive issues of society also emerge in that taxing choices involve the selection of which classes will bear which proportion of both the aggregate tax load and of the marginal increases in tax rates. In addition to these redistributive issues, counter-cyclical policy constraints on aggregate taxation and spending levels have added more problems for policy-makers.

Budgetary principles, on the one hand, require expenditures to be determined by program needs and tax levels to be set so as to cover expenditures, irrespective of the state of the economy. Counter-cyclical fiscal policy, on the other hand, requires a net budget surplus of revenues over expenditures when economic conditions are inflationary and a net deficit when the economy is sluggish. These two standards often conflict with each other, and this conflict gives rise to the intense political battles every year within the Cabinet, the bureaucracy, and the House of Commons. These battles over taxing and spending constitute, moreover, the central component of federal-provincial relations.

The management of economic policy, therefore, involves intricate conflicts affecting decisions on taxing and spending which further impinge on the level and utilization of the public debt, the capital requirements of both the public and private sectors, and government cash flows. These in turn have an impact on the government's efforts, through the Bank of Canada and the banking system, to control the aggregate supply of money and credit, through both direct regulation and moral suasion.

The concept of economic management involves an analytical distinction between demand management and supply management. While such a distinction is frequently made, it is important to keep in mind the considerable overlap between the demand and the supply dimensions. Demand management is usually related to the short-term manipulation of aggregate demand to even out business cycles and to insure more stable economic conditions. Supply management is usually related to influencing, over the medium or long term, the supply of the several factors of economic production and hence involves such areas as manpower policy, education, and research and development. In recent years it has increasingly involved energy, agriculture, and food policies as well. The distinctions between demand and supply management are somewhat similar but not identical with those distinctions that are frequently made between fiscal policy and economic policy. Fiscal policy usually is used to imply the financial actions of government which operate in the short run to facilitate stable growth. It is usually related to the aggregate management of total expenditure and to the manipulation of personal, corporate, and sales taxes to facilitate short-term economic activity. Economic policy, on the other hand, tends to be equated with the broader economic implications of government expenditures and programs and hence embraces many of the supply and longer-term aspects of economic policy.

The principal cast of characters in federal economic-policy formulation includes several executive agencies, legislative committees, and a host of private economic interest groups. This book will critically examine the Department of Finance, the Bank of Canada, the Treasury Board, the departments of Industry, Trade and Commerce, Regional Economic Expansion, Consumer and Corporate Affairs, Manpower and Immigration, and the Economic Council all performing different but complementary roles. These roles must be integrated into a more comprehensive system through the cabinet committee system, the Cabinet as a whole, and ultimately through Parliament.

The mere mention of the several departments and agencies listed above is a reflection of other important dimensions. Economic management is intricately related to questions of delegation, horizontal co-ordination among departments, and vertical co-ordination between central agencies and economic departments. While specific policy-making instruments have been, and can be, delegated to different ministers, the ultimate co-ordination of economic policy must be carried out at the cabinet level. The critical problem is that of deciding which minister should have primary responsibility for the managerial and administrative aspects of economic-policy co-ordination.

The need to achieve concurrently an ever-widening list of economic and social objectives has increased the number of agencies participating in the economic-policy formulation process. The Treasury Board deals with broad managerial questions affecting the government as a whole. The Department of Finance deals with "economic affairs", i.e., with stabilization policies affecting public- and private-sector spending decisions. Even more selective aspects of the management of economic policies have been delegated to the departments of Industry, Trade and Commerce, Regional Economic Expansion, Manpower and Immigration, and Consumer and Corporate Affairs, to name only a few.

From a more hierarchical perspective, economic-management responsibilities are conducted through the Cabinet Committee on Priorities and Planning and the Cabinet Committee on Economic Policy. These committees are supported by a complex system of departmental and interdepartmental committees. The mandate of the Priorities and Planning Committee includes the establishment of broad objectives of the government and major questions of policy having long-term implications. In theory this committee performs, essentially, a normative planning function. As such it is not exclusively concerned with economic management but it can impose severe constraints on the economic-planning process.

Economic management also encompasses the increasingly complex relationships between research and economic policy. The causal connection can work in both directions. Developments in emerging economic problems point to the need for research; research leads to demands for new organizations and programs. These relationships will be examined both in a historical context and in terms of the role of such policy advisory bodies as the Economic Council of Canada. Economic management also involves the problems of acquiring, organizing, and analysing data both as a basis for making decisions and as a basis for evaluating whether these decisions have had their intended effects.

Finally, and most importantly, economic management encompasses the determination and co-ordination of economic goals and policies affecting government and business, government and labour, government and agriculture, and government and welfare. We cannot examine all of these areas in this volume, but our analysis will demonstrate, nevertheless, the pervasiveness of economic policy-making. Recent efforts to gain a general consensus on anti-inflationary policies are illustrative of the fact that economic policy, particularly in times of turbulence, cannot be formulated without societal support and compliance.

The support enjoyed by political leaders is partly reflected in their ability to influence various organizations, which, in a pluralistic society, impose constraints on the formal political structures. Accordingly, an adequate explanation of the concept of economic management should also encompass the institutional level from which the more specific objectives of given organizations are derived. The recongition of these aspects is important in bridging the micro-macro gap in both political and economic analysis.

At the broadest level of economic analysis we are concerned with institutional change. Economic stabilization instruments operate within a broader system of social values which make their utilization legitimate. Economic management impinges on the foundation of economic institutions. Thus major changes in the institutional structure of the economy will alter the basic system in which the more specific instruments of economic policy such as discretionary fiscal and monetary instruments, exchange-rate instruments, and direct-control instruments are used. Although it is difficult to determine when a change is large enough to constitute a major change in the institutional structure of the economy, recent attempts to reform anti-inflation policy, competition policy, foreign-ownership policy, regional-development policy, and social policy should be considered as attempted changes in the institutional structure of the Canadian system.

Economic-policy formulation encompasses many policy-formulation instruments which will be discussed at greater length in Chapter 4. Economists tend to speak of instruments and goals as if they were always in a "means-end" relationship. However, it is very difficult in political terms to draw clearcut lines between means and ends because policy is not necessarily made in that way. In fact, policy formulation involves several hierarchical value systems with conflicting value components. Processes and instruments become ends in themselves especially in a democratic state.

Economic management becomes a central aspect of governmental decision-making when it is realized that governmental direction is intended not just to supplant or supplement private production, but to provide goods or services to a segment of the population that would not otherwise have them. Governmental economic management seeks to make up deficiencies in the normal distribution of economic rewards by going outside the market to provide goods and services directly to consumers.

Economic management in a liberal, democratic state and in a mixed economy involves the establishment and development of processes to resolve business-government relationships. Some critics of the liberal, democratic state will argue that these relationships are already too cosy. Others will cite the absence of reliable consultative mechanisms and encourage a movement towards "indicative planning" or even "corporatism", the latter concept implying more formal, even statutory, relationships between governments, industry, and organized labour, where the three parties collectively allocate the economic pie.[3]

In effect, the management of economic policies is concerned with economic planning. The possibility of a parallel growth in government planning is suggested almost inevitably by successful business planning. Co-ordination of the activities of large businesses becomes itself an object of government planning and policy-making. Economic planning in Canada, however, has not until recently been *openly* espoused in the political arena by either the Liberal or Progressive-Conservative parties. We are left rather with a gradual evolution toward economic management which ultimately carries with it enormous planning implications. The evolving mix and complexity of economic goals and processes has generated an increasing concern. The statements of Prime Minister Trudeau early in 1976, and the resultant debate on creating new tripartite institutions has raised the issue of economic planning to its highest level of political visibility. We will examine this issue in Chapters 2 and 14.

Because of the interrelatedness of economic activities the Minister of Finance possesses an umbrella function in the policy-making system. This responsibility has led many critics to question the feasibility of a single minister performing this broad managerial role. It may increasingly be suggested by some that this role should be delegated to a Board on Economic Management, analogous in form to the Treasury Board. The use of collective boards has precedence not only in the existence of the Treasury Board but also in the existence of the Bank of Canada which is directed by a board of directors. The imposition of formal collective boards linked, but largely separate, from the Finance minister has been a historic issue. For example, as a result of the Coyne Affair in the late 1950s, the Bank of Canada was made less independent of the minister. Central banks were created partly on the belief that questions regarding the supply of money should not be left in the hands of politicians. When James Coyne, then the Governor of the Bank of Canada, attempted to take an independent course, the Minister of Finance sought to dismiss him. Satisfaction with the degree of independence for various economic authorities varies over time. More recently concern has been expressed that the Governor of the Bank of Canada has been perhaps too willing to follow the dictates of government policy and has been too reluctant to strike an independent position.

THE POLITICAL AND MANAGERIAL CONTEXT OF ECONOMIC DECISION-MAKING

Decisions concerning economic policy are the product of a complex political and organizational process. The decisions may be dealt with on a narrow as well as on a broad front. In the narrower context, emphasis may be placed on fiscal policy as the most important component of the policy-formation process. Organizationally this would require that we focus on the Department of Finance. In the broader context emphasis may be placed on the overall concerns of economic management such as monetary policy, debt-management, government expenditure, and supply-management policies, all viewed in a comprehensive manner.

The various governmental departments may be regarded as agencies performing primary roles. Each has different inclinations toward the utilization of various governing instruments. The instruments used can involve minimum, moderate, or maximum degrees of coercion and they may be used in a sequential order depending on the facility with which they can be deployed.[4] Voluntary instruments, especially monetary and debt-management policy, may tend to be used first, to solve most small and relatively unimportant problems. Changes in taxes and transfers are usually saved for large problems; they are used when the political costs of not controlling inflation or not  increasing employment are likely to be large—at least large enough to counterbalance the political costs of compelling the public to pay more taxes. In short, monetary and debt-management instruments may be tried for controlling inflation or increasing employment before government expenditures are adjusted, which in turn may be used before taxes and transfers are employed.

Inherent in the process is the fact that economic policy-making encompasses inputs from economic advisers and from several organizational and decision-making processes. Several governmental agencies participate in the policy-making process, each of which is responsible for a different set of activities necessary for the formulation of the government's economic policy. While there is general agreement among these participants that government policy should promote goals such as full employment, price stability, economic growth, balance-of-payments equilibrium, and the reduction of regional and other income disparities, the participants in each agency often disagree about the operational meaning of these objectives and about the priority that should be given to each of them. For example, the Governor of the Bank of Canada was very concerned between 1965 and 1967 that the full-employment policy espoused by the Economic Council would lead to rising prices. The Department of Labour, with its strong trade-union clientele, and the Department of Manpower and Immigration were concerned about the high rate of unemployment since it imposed new pressures on their policies and programs. Between 1969 and 1973 the Department of Finance generally adopted an expansionary policy and reduced the level of unemployment. However, it subsequently had to pursue anti-inflationary policies as well as policies to maintain reasonably acceptable levels of employment. Each component of the economic policy-making machinery evaluates the effect of its environment on its policies. These interorganizational relationships influence the policy which is formulated. Hence it is important to ascertain and understand the roles performed by the Department of Finance, the Treasury Board, the Privy Council Office, and the major economic-policy departments in the formation of economic policy as well as the dynamics of the relationships among them.

Economic-policy processes must be understood in a more *sequential* manner as well. Thus an understanding of economic-policy processes requires an identification of the economic forecasting procedures followed by Statistics Canada, the departments of Finance, and Manpower and Immigration, among others, and the constraints under which they operate. It involves an identification of the key cabinet ministers involved in the process of setting general governmental priorities and expenditure priorities, as well as in economic-policy formation, and an evaluation of legislative scrutiny reflected in the parliamentary committee system. The various structures specialize in particular aspects as the problem under consideration moves through the process.

Economic policy can also be visualized, as Bertram Gross has suggested, in the context of roles such as: i) general leadership roles;

ii) general staff roles; iii) special staff roles; iv) financial management roles; and v) critical problem roles.[5]

General leadership roles are performed by the Prime Minister and Minister of Finance and are institutionalized through the Cabinet Committee on Priorities and Planning. General leadership roles involve filling key posts, the provision of overall perspectives, policy formation, and the mediation of disputes. General staff roles are performed by the Privy Council Office, the Department of Finance, and the Treasury Board, and include co-ordinating, expediting, and bargaining. Special staff roles are necessary to improve the decision-making process. The information and analysis which come from agencies like the Economic Council of Canada, Statistics Canada, the Planning Branch in the Treasury Board, and the Bank of Canada must be included in this category. Financial-management roles are provided by the Treasury Board, the Department of Finance, and the Bank of Canada. Accordingly these roles include budget policy, tax policy, and money and credit. Critical problem roles emerge because of the periodic crises which the government has faced from time to time. These would include the establishment of the Prices and Incomes Commission, the Food Prices Review Board, the Anti-Inflation Board, and the various references which have been submitted to the Economic Council of Canada.

It is essential to stress the different requirements and conflicting demands made on actors who perform these different roles. The attempts in recent years to reorganize the Prime Minister's Office (PMO) and the Privy Council Office (PCO) were aimed at coping with the general leadership role problem. Attempts to reorganize the Department of Finance and the granting of a more specialized role to the Treasury Board represented an effort to reconcile financial-management roles. Finally, the role of the Economic Council of Canada represented an attempt to introduce economic-policy advice not only in a more public fashion but also in the context of a time frame (the so-called medium term) which conflicted with the short-term time frame of the Finance Department.

The general leadership, general and special staff, financial-management, and critical-problem roles need careful examination. It can be argued that the Prime Minister needs an increased general and economic-policy capability if he is to perform the central leadership function in the Cabinet. The problem, however, is not only the need for central leadership, but how it should be done. In a cabinet system of government what approach should be used to improve the capability of central co-ordination?

The establishment in the United Kingdom of a Central Policy Review Staff was an attempt to aid the Cabinet in looking collectively into important issues that used to be the special preserve of individual ministers or of no one at all.[6] The strengthening in recent years of the Canadian PMO and the PCO were designed to achieve similar objectives. However, it is clear that politicians and administrators may easily come to resent and fear a man or an organization whose business it is to take the larger view of their departmental business, to do so with the Prime Minister's special favour, and without hard responsibility for executing it. Policy may need better "intelligence", but other participants demand that it not be acquired at their expense. Thus, when attempts were made to strengthen the intelligence capability of the economic secretariat in the PCO, the Deputy Minister of Finance threatened to resign.

The creation of a Department of Economic Affairs (DEA) in the United Kingdom was an attempt to separate long-term growth decisions from short-term financial-management decisions.[7] It led to competition and duplication between the two agencies and the Treasury was subsequently strengthened with the abandonment of the DEA. It became apparent that one was never out of the short-term. The important was invariably compromised by the urgent. Decisions taken immediately involved long-term considerations but necessarily had to work with the raw material of the present. The DEA wanted to be in on the present and the Treasury wanted to get in on the future. In Canada, the Economic Council was established in 1963 to look more explicitly at medium- and long-term problems in contrast to the short-term orientation of the Department of Finance. Despite the fact that it frequently took at least a medium-term view of economic policy, the Council became embroiled in controversy because its recommendations could frequently be seen to be conflicting with the Finance Department's actions, the latter usually conceived for a short-run time frame.[8]

Even in the realm of critical problem roles we find controversy and overlapping activities. The Economic Council of Canada has, from time to time, been assigned the responsibility of searching for new solutions to a number of critical problems such as inflation, competition policy, and price increases in the construction industry. The PCO has performed a major role in the scanning of critical problems. Still more recently, the Ministry of State for Science and Technology, the Ministry of State for Urban Affairs, and the Ministry of State for Small Business have been assigned the investigation of some critical problems. All of these agencies have encountered operational problems and it is now questioned whether critical problem roles can be performed by anything more than *ad hoc* agencies or "fire-fighting units".[9]

The political and managerial context of economic decision-making within the Government of Canada can thus be viewed in a variety of ways. This book will analyse the politics and management of Canadian economic policy primarily by focussing on particular departmental and agency roles. The importance of visualizing the economic-management process both sequentially, and in terms of general leadership, general and special staff, financial-management, and critical problem roles will also be utilized, however, as a secondary but complementary way of viewing economic-management process.

POLICY, PUBLIC ADMINISTRATION, AND MANAGEMENT

A thorough understanding of the evolution towards economic management cannot be developed unless economic management is linked to the concepts of policy, public administration, and management generally, and to recent efforts at restructuring the central machinery of policy-making in Canada. These links are not easily or simply traced, but it is essential that the definitional and conceptual arguments about policy, administration, and management be analysed before examining Canadian economic-policy processes in further detail. The links are the products of decades of evolution reflected in a series of public studies of government organization, the development of private-sector management concepts and their importation into government, the development of principles regarding public budgetary and financial accountability, the development of Keynesian economics, the emergence of systems-oriented management concepts, and the general evolution of government from its *laissez-faire* origins to its contemporary interventionist roles and functions. These evolving links must be seen both in a comparative and in a Canadian context.[10]

In the comparative context the evolution can be seen in the succession of British and American studies of government organization which treated government management in an ever-broadening sense. The early concepts of management stressed financial management in the sense of strict accountability and control geared toward the preservation of honesty and probity in government. Later, the concern gradually shifted to the broader integration and "management" of people and resources and to the need to differentiate management of the economy on broad Keynesian grounds, from the more routine features of financial management.[11] Philosophical concern shifted from the negative aspect of financial control to the more positive aspect of overall program efficiency and effectiveness. Throughout this period there was also much discussion and analysis about the theoretical, democratic, and practical linkages between policy and administration.

In the Canadian context the evolution toward economic management can be seen in largely similar ways. The Glassco Commission traced the early forms of "honesty and probity" management concepts that had been characteristic of federal management until the late 1950s and recommended a broader concept of governmental management.[12] This included the identification of a broader "general manager" role for the Treasury Board which was to be separated from the Finance Department's implicit role as economic manager. It also envisaged broader policy co-ordination roles for the PCO. These concepts were quickly followed by the development in the late 1960s and early 1970s of planning, programming, and budgeting systems and by the reorganization of cabinet committees, and cabinet support organizations, all intended to support a more integrated concept of public policy and public management. At the same time, the Canadian system was experimenting with its own version of economic-policy advisory and consultative bodies such as the Economic Council of Canada.[13]

The intellectual understanding of the formulation and management of economic policies cannot be separated from important arguments and controversies about the relationships between policy and administration and hence about the relationships between elected politicians and public servants.

Woodrow Wilson argued early in this century that government administrators should concern themselves with the execution of plans as laid down by the law and accordingly they should not engage in political strife. This doctrine became known as the "politics- or policy-administration dichotomy". At a later stage it was suggested that the practice of politics and administration leads inevitably to involvement in politics by bureaucrats. The reasoning was that policies made by politicians express the general will of the state but that administrators were inevitably concerned with the further, more detailed discretionary choices involved in giving effect to that general will.[14] Arguments about the reality and desirability of the politics-administration dichotomy resurface continually. For example, these arguments reappear in more recent analyses which have attempted to reconcile the tenets of democracy with the efficiency criteria from management science. Can efficiency and sound management be intertwined with the public and its elected politicians? In 1964 the Royal Commission on the Organization of the Government of Canada (the Glassco Commission) articulated a management ideology and implied that the two principles could be reconciled.[15] The Glassco Commission and its managerial ideology was an important reflection of the emergence of the administrative state.

The emergence of the administrative state has brought with it the need to consider and conceptualize several sub-systems of behaviour and several levels of complexity in the relationships between public servants and politicians. The need for effective means of delegating increasingly complex roles and tasks, and the need by political authorities to deal with an increasingly complex array of changing demands from a very turbulent environment has resulted in an ambivalent concern about the capacity of public bureaucracies to innovate, on the one hand, and to be controlled, on the other.

Thus, contemporary theories of organization have emphasized the need for more flexible and adaptive organizations involving more horizontal than vertical communication and control processes in modern organizations.[16] The need to foster greater innovation has been viewed from both the macro and micro perspectives. At the micro-cosmic level greater attention has been placed on the conditions in organizations which facilitate change such as psychological security and freedom, great diversity of inputs, commitment to search for solutions, certain amounts of structure which limit the search for solutions, and moderate amounts of benign competition. At the broader societal, or macro-cosmic level concern has been expressed about the capacity to achieve *social change* including the application of science and technology to the solution of human problems. In the latter context, for example, governments have been concerned with expediting the process through which new technological discoveries and brought into the governmental and industrial process.

While greater efforts have been made to foster innovations at both the macro and micro levels these efforts have been invariably accompanied by a growing concern about the power of public bureaucracies and of public servants. The efforts to restructure central policy machinery (discussed in the final section of this chapter) were intended both to facilitate change and to establish better political control over senior public servants. The relationships between cabinet ministers and senior public servants represent one central dimension of the policy-administration dichotomy to be explored more fully in Chapter 5.

The central dilemmas in the policy-administration dichotomy are further revealed in the various academic assessments and definitions of policy. Sir Geoffrey Vickers defines policy as a "set of standards or norms" which is closely associated with "normative planning".[17] Policy also encompasses, however, "the setting of governing relations" or norms, rather than the mere setting of goals, objectives, or ends. Vickers speaks of an appreciative system: "A national ideology, a professional ethic, an individual personality, resides not in a particular set of images but in a set of readiness to see and value and respond to its situation in particular ways." He concludes "... our appreciative system grows and changes with every exercise of image formation, a process normally gradual and unconscious; and like all systems it is resistant to changes of a kind or at a rate which might endanger its own coherence."[18]

Governmental ministers and officials clearly do have different appreciative systems and they view policy from different perspectives. The same individuals will perform different roles if they are relocated from departments such as Industry, Trade and Commerce, to Finance, the Treasury Board, or the PCO. In addition, conflict arises from disagreement between agencies over the desirable action to be taken.

Vicker's effort to link policy not just to goals but to "governing relations" is in accord with the political emphasis given to public policy by authors such as Theodore Lowi.[19] In Lowi's view, policy is related not just to goals but also to the exercise of different degrees of legitimate coercion. These degrees of coercion, e.g., exhortation, financial incentives, and direct regulation, help define different political arenas.

A brief sampling of other authors and governmental reports further illustrates the difficulties and yet the necessity of making some distinctions between policy, administration, and management. For example, Desmond Keeling considers policy to be a "set of interrelated and consistent objectives, plans and decision rules".[20] Management, in his view, "refers to the search for the best use of resources in pursuit of objectives subject to change."[21] Hence, management is the process of organizing the elements of productive enterprise—money, materials, equipment, people — in the interest of economic and organizational ends. Keeling views administration to be the making of rules, the adjudicating of cases, and the issuing of orders affecting the rights and obligations of private citizens and parties by public officials other than judges or legislatures. With regard to administrative systems, Keeling suggests that administrative systems lie at the end of the spectrum closest to judicial systems and are linked by a variety of quasi-judicial or administrative-judicial systems within the public service:

> It is, I believe, from the criteria and attitudes of mind appropriate to a judicial system that public service administration systems have derived many of their characteristic features: it is a fact which can most readily be observed by studying the processes of government in European countries where there is no pretence that any rigid boundary separates legal from administration processes.[22]

Keeling has also surveyed the arrival of management concepts and definitions in government. In a comparative reference he noted that the Brownlow Committee in the United States (1937) spoke of administrative management:

Good management will promote in the fullest measure the conservation and utilization of our national resources and spells this out plainly in social justice, security, order, liberty, prosperity, in material benefit and in higher values of life.[23]

"Management" was used here in regard to broad societal management. Management in government was also emphasized by the Committee on the Control of Public Expenditures in Britain (Plowden Committee). In this regard the use of the term was restricted to financial management. The Plowden Committee observed:

We now talk of the Management side of the Treasury as distinguishable from the economic and financial side. Much is comprehended in this classification of Treasury business—the label attaches to a kind of hold-all containing within a variety of assorted subject matter.[24]

In 1968 the British Fulton Report provided another interpretation:

Four aspects... make up the total management task of the Civil Service:
(a) Formulation of policy under political direction
(b) Creating the machinery for implementation of policy
(c) Operation of the administrative machine
(d) Accountability to Parliament and the Public.[25]

The federal Glassco Commission in the early 1960s and the Ontario Government's Committee on Government Productivity in the early 1970s are important Canadian examples in which the notion of management systems was viewed in very catholic terms as encompassing virtually all of government activity.[26]

The Glassco Commission, as noted earlier, formulated a general plan of management which encompassed the Cabinet and the PCO, a new and strengthened Treasury Board with its own secretariat, and the Department of Finance, all performing important co-ordinative functions for the system as a whole. The Department of Finance was to be concerned with the fiscal capability of the system while the Treasury Board was to be concerned primarily with the expenditure side and with management. Thus, there was an attempt to separate management of the public service from management of the economy.

It is important to note, however, that the Glassco Commission report did not directly concern itself with economic policy and, as such, merely implied that the Department of Finance should be concerned with the management of economic policy. This fact should be assessed against the suggestions made and attempted in other states where it has been argued that it is difficult for a single department to effectively handle the complex objectives of economic policy.[27] The complexities involved in the formulation of economic policy have brought about the establishment of new departments such as Manpower and Immigration concerned with training and mobility programs, and Regional Economic Expansion concerned with removing regional economic disparities.

In addition to the above developments and discussions, the analysis of organizations and their management has been aided in recent years by the development of a systems approach to management. Such systems approaches have emerged both from management-science circles and from those studying the sociology of organizations.[28] Systems analysis alerts both analysts and practitioners to the vertical and horizontal dimensions of organizations. Thus, from a systems perspective, organizations can be conceived to include a broad institutional system, a managerial system, and a technical system. The technical function is performed at lower levels of the organization. The management sub-system mediates between the technical sub-systems and integrates them, in some respects, with the institutional level. Managers work within the specifications given by the technical sub-system.

The broader "institutional system" links a large number of organizations at the societal level. The broader values of the society impose constraints on what organizations can do. Thus, universities, hospitals, and even business corporations are considered to be responsible to and constrained by the society. Managers, therefore, must integrate the management system with the broader societal system and accordingly they are represented in the institutional realms such as Boards of Directors of large corporations. The Board of Governors of the Bank of Canada, and the Treasury Board of Canada operate on the same principle of linking broader institutional elements with their more specific organizational needs.

The identification of institutional, managerial, and technical sub-systems is important in both analytical and practical ways for several reasons. It assists in understanding the continuing needs in government for delegation of functions and of the mutual interdependence of the sub-systems. It points out the need for different levels of governmental effectiveness, and it draws attention to both the horizontal and vertical dimensions of policy co-ordination and implementation. The manner in which departments and sub-systems may be integrated into the overall policy organization of the government represents, moreover, a microcosm of how various organizations in the larger society are regulated, though not necessarily controlled, by the state.

It is, therefore, especially important to analyse economic management not in terms of a simplistic or monolithic conception of "bureaucracy" but rather in terms of real processes and in relation to observed systems of behaviour.

Our analysis in Part III will indicate how bureaucratic agencies can evolve over time, frequently resisting change, but also often reflecting and causing change. Some economic departments have grown larger, but at a later stage have undergone a form of debureaucratization through the shedding or reallocation of certain less essential functions. Others may go through a process of decentralization only to be halted partly because the controlling elements of the government or the department feel themselves to be losing control of the decentralized elements. The evolution of the Finance Department as well as other economic departments illustrate the need to avoid simplistic views of bureaucratic structure and behaviour.

Contemporary public organization tends to suggest the presence of several centres of power and co-ordination. Hence, the separate decisions of various organizations must be accommodated. This view suggests that the initiating authority has reasonable freedom of action subject to the necessity of co-operating with other authorities at appropriate points. Governmental administrative systems are so complex and interrelated that conflicts between "poly-centricity" and "planning" or between "autonomy" and "control" are often subtle questions of degree. The foregoing means that many levels of conflict resolution must be accommodated in attempts to improve policy formulation in general and economic management in particular.

Comprehensive policy-making requires that priorities be set and that managers and administrators synchronize their roles to facilitate the attainment of the objectives sought. It is clearly not an easy or a tidy process. It is for these reasons that attempts have been made to establish planning branches in the Treasury Board, the PCO, the PMO, and the Finance Department. The public service has elements which both respond to change as well as inhibit it, and both of these alternative forces will be examined. Decisions which authorize action for one social group must be distinguished from the negative decisions which effectively block action proposed by another group.

Decision-making for economic management must accordingly be viewed as a continuous series of choices made over time rather than as an exceptional and infrequent event which occurs only at certain points in time. Different attitudes toward risk, the uncertainty of policy consequences, and the inadequacy of information make flexible incremental processes a necessity. At the same time, however, a comprehensive approach is acknowledged to be increasingly necessary. An understanding of policy must be based on the existence of several levels of discussion, including analysis within single departments, interdepartmental analysis, discussions between ministers and deputy ministers, and discussion in Cabinet without the presence of officials. In addition, policy discussions reflect different concerns about long-run as opposed to short-run considerations.

While the concepts of policy, administration, and management are partly distinguishable in an abstract sense, this brief introduction to the relationships between them obviously counsels that we view such distinctions *in practice* with a great deal of caution. The means-ends chain in government is obviously not a simple one and hence so-called "policy", "administrative", and "managerial" roles and tasks easily and frequently blur into enormous grey zones of multiple and mixed activities.

RESTRUCTURING OF THE POLICY-MAKING MACHINERY

Most, if not all, of the issues of policy, administration, and management have been both reflected in, and influenced by, efforts over the past decade to restructure the federal policy-making machinery. This restructuring will be described and evaluated in detail in later chapters, but it is essential to have a broad understanding of these changes at the outset. The restructuring and reorganization has occurred both in the general area of central cabinet-policy machinery and in the more specific areas of economic management. In addition changes have been made through the creation of new institutions, external to the governmental system.

A major area of structural reform has been in the cabinet committee systems.[29] There are four co-ordinating committees and five committees dealing with functional areas of governmental policy and activity. The four co-ordinating committees are: Priorities and Planning; Treasury Board; Legislation and House Planning; and Federal Provincial Relations. The five functional committees are: External Policy and Defence; Economic Policy; Social Policy; Science, Culture and Information; and Government Operations. Supporting this system of committees are the four major central agencies of the federal government: the PCO, the PMO, the Treasury Board secretariat, and the Department of Finance.

The strategic co-ordinating committee is the Committee on Priorities and Planning chaired by the Prime Minister. Although its membership is secret, it most certainly contains the Minister of Finance, the President of the Treasury Board, and other chairmen of the standing cabinet committees. The committee develops the basic governmental priority and expenditure guidelines and hence is clearly the most influential committee of the Cabinet. It deals with the broadest dimensions of government policy. Because its functions go well beyond "economic" policy, its deliberations and decisions obviously severely constrain and influence economic-policy choices.

The Treasury Board also assumes an important co-ordinating function. A committee of six ministers headed by the board president, it has the responsibility to deal with the general management of the government, including overall expenditures, personnel policy, collective bargaining, language policy, and administrative policy. Previously a part of the Finance Department, the Treasury Board was given its own minister in 1966 thus establishing an implicit differentiation of the general functions of managing the economy (the Finance Department role) from the functions of managing the government.[30] The impact of this change has been enormous and thus will warrant detailed analysis in later chapters.

Cabinet-policy structure and processes must always strike an uneasy balance between the collective nature of cabinet decision-making and the concept of individual ministerial responsibility and delegation. We will focus on the intricacies of this balance. In addition to the two major co-ordinating committees we will relate economic management to the economic policy and social policy committees, two of the so-called functional committees of the Cabinet.

Central restructuring has also been influenced in recent years by arguments about the appropriate sources of economic-policy advice for the Prime Minister. The chief economic advisor is, of course, the minister and the Department of Finance. From time to time, however, efforts have been made to equip other central agencies such as the PMO and PCO with greater economic-policy capabilities, a practice invariably resisted by the Finance Department.

Moving "down" from these changes in central machinery there have been other changes in the more specific areas of economic management. Prior to the early 1960s the key economic departments had scarcely changed over the previous few decades. Since the early 1960s, however, in quite rapid succession, new departments of Industry (later merged with Trade and Commerce), Regional Economic Expansion, Consumer and Corporate Affairs, and Manpower and Immigration have been established, thus widening the range of ministerial and departmental participants in the processes of economic management. There is, therefore, a great deal of delegation of authority and responsibility in the economic-policy field. For example, debt-management and foreign exchange are the responsibility of the Minister of Finance and the Bank of Canada; policies to arrest regional disparities are delegated to the Department of Regional Economic Expansion; income maintenance is dealt with by the Department of Health and Welfare; and the Department of Manpower and Immigration deals with training and mobility with the Unemployment Insurance Commission providing unemployment insurance. Complementary to the above-mentioned arrangements is a system of interdepartmental consultation and co-ordination based on functional specialization. Thus policy-formation and decision-making are carried out both at the ministerial level and at the level of officials.

Partly in anticipation of these changes, and partly in response to them, the Finance Department has also had to change internally. Over the years it has divested itself of several routine financial-management functions (to departments like the Treasury Board, Taxation and National Revenue, and Supply and Services) and correspondingly had to broaden its internal policy and monitoring capabilities in such areas as manpower policy, regional policy, and resource policy. It has also created a long-term forecasting and planning branch.

The latter was created partly in response to other changes in the overall machinery of economic management, especially the establishment of the Economic Council. The council, created in 1963, became the principal focus for external medium- or longer-term economic advice. It was intended to be a more public organization and hence would make the process more open. From the beginning there were disagreements within the Cabinet and the bureaucracy concerning the priority which should be given to the strengthening of the Department of Finance as compared to the establishment of the Economic Council. Since then controversy has continued about the Council's role and reporting relationships. In the early 1970s, the Senate Committee on National Finance took the view that the Economic Council as an external body should make its recommendations to the PCO which in turn should take a co-ordinated view across departmental lines.[31] A number of senior officials in the PCO took the view, however, that the PCO is not expected to be a co-ordinating agency in regard to economic matters. The co-ordination of economic policy, it was felt, should be carried out within departments, primarily through the Department of Finance. At the other end of the spectrum the Council itself suggested in 1966 that its reports should also go to a Joint Committee of Parliament. The Council would report on the state of the economy, thus more publicly fulfilling its task of evaluating and reporting on the performance of the economy in relation to its potential.

We have been discussing economic-policy evaluation primarily within government. However, evaluation is also conducted in Parliament through budget debates and through various standing and select committees. In addition, there is the Auditor General, an officer of Parliament who reports to Parliament and to its Public Accounts Committee. Non-governmental bodies, such as the Conference Board of Canada and the C. D. Howe Institute have also begun to make important contributions to public debate and scrutiny. We will be returning to the broad issues raised by these external participants in economic-policy formulation.

SUMMARY

Economic management is the process through which the increasingly complex and competing goals, instruments, agencies, and research needs of economic policy are co-ordinated and controlled. It encompasses decisions about taxing and spending, debt management and the supply of money, the management of demand and supply, the delegation of economic policy functions, the acquisition and use of economic data and research, and the horizontal and vertical co-ordination of several government agencies. It involves the basic institutional relationships between governments and industry, labour, agriculture, and welfare in the determination and implementation of Canada's multiple and shifting economic priorities. The processes of federal economic management, moreover, cannot be understood without reference to the evolving concepts of public policy and public administration and of the efforts in recent years to restructure the general public-policy and administrative machinery in the Government of Canada.

NOTES

1. On the general comparative dimensions of economic management and planning see P. Bauchet, *Economic Planning: The French Experience* (London, 1962); R. Bicanie, *Problems of Planning: East and West* (The Hague, 1967); Neil Chamberlain, *Public and Private Planning* (Toronto, 1975); G. Denton, *et al.*, *Ecomomic Planning and Policies in Britain, France and Germany* (London, 1968); Jan Tinbergen, *Central Planning* (New Haven, 1964); and Ely Devons, *Planning and Economic Management* (Manchester, 1970).

2. Remarks made by Michael Pitfield, Institute of Public Administration of Canada, Ottawa, September 3, 1975.

3. On "indicative planning" and "corporatism" see Andrew Schonfield, *Modern Capitalism: The Changing Balance of Public and Private Power* (London, 1965); John K. Galbraith, *Economics and the Public Purpose* (Bergenfield, N. J., 1975); and K. J. Rea and J. T. McLeod, eds., *Business and Government in Canada*, second ed. (Toronto, 1976), pp. 334-45.

4. The relationship between economic-policy goals and the nature of the governing instruments available to politicians is assessed in Chapter 3. See

also Lawrence Pierce, *The Politics of Fiscal Policy Formation* (Pacific Palisades, Ca., 1971).

5. Bertram Bross, "The Managers of National Economic Change", in R. C. Martin, *Public Administration and Democracy* (Syracuse, 1965), pp. 101-28.

6. See Hugh Heclo and Aaron Wildavsky, *The Private Government of Public Money* (London, 1974), *passim*.

7. See A. H. Hanson and Malcolm Walles, *Governing Britain* (London, 1970), chapters 5, 6, and 9; Heclo and Wildavsky, *The Private Government of Public Money;* and Samuel Brittan, *The Treasury under the Tories* (London, 1964), and *Steering the Economy: The Role of the Treasury* (London, 1970).

8. Richard W. Phidd, "The Economic Council of Canada, 1963-74", *Canadian Public Administration*, Vol. XVIII, no. 3 (1975).

9. For an analysis of the Ministry of State for Science and Technology see Peter Aucoin and Richard French, *Knowledge, Power and Public Policy*, Science Council of Canada, Special Study No. 31 (Ottawa, 1974).

10. See Peter Self, *Administrative Theories and Politics* (Toronto, 1973), and J. E. Hodgetts, *The Canadian Public Service: A Physiology of Government* (Toronto, 1973).

11. See Self, *Administrative Theories and Politics*, especially chapters 3 and 7, and Desmond Keeling, *Management in Government* (London, 1972).

12. See Hodgetts, *The Canadian Public Service*, and J. E. Hodgetts, W. McCloskey, R. Whitaker, and V. Seymour Wilson, *The Biography of an Institution* (Montreal, 1972).

13. The above structural developments are described and assessed in G. Bruce Doern and Peter Aucoin, eds., *The Structures of Policy-Making in Canada* (Toronto, 1971), chapters 2, 3, 8, and 9.

14. On the main issues of the politics-administration dichotomy see Self, *Administrative Theories and Politics*, chapters 1 and 5; E. S. Redford, *Democracy in the Administrative State* (New York, 1969); Keith Henderson, *Emerging Synthesis in American Public Administration* (London, 1966), pp. 9-11; and Brian Smith, *Policy Making in British Government* (London, 1976), chapters 2 and 3. For a legal view see also R. C. Davis, *Discretionary Justice* (Baton Rouge, 1969).

15. Canada, *Royal Commission on Government Organization*, Vol. I (Ottawa, 1963).

16. See Victor Thompson, *Bureaucracy and Innovation* (Alabama, 1968).

17. Sir Geoffrey Vickers, *The Art of Judgement: A Study of Policy Making* (London, 1965), p. 98.

18. Sir Geoffrey Vickers, *Value Systems and Social Process* (London, 1968).

19. Theodore Lowi, "Four Systems of Policy, Politics and Choice", *Public Administration Review* (July/August 1972), pp. 293-310. See also G. Bruce Doern and V. Seymour Wilson, eds., *Issues in Canadian Public Policy* (Toronto, 1974).

20. Keeling, *Management in Government*, p. 35.

21. Ibid., p. 32.

22. Ibid., p. 92

23. Ibid., p. 18.

24. Quoted in ibid., pp. 19-20.

25. Quoted in ibid., p. 23.

26. See Committee on Government Productivity, *Interim Report Number Three* (Toronto, 1972).

27. See Hanson and Walles, *Governing Britain;* and Brittan, *The Treasury under the Tories* and *Steering the Economy.*

28. See, for example, D. Katz and R. L. Kahn, *The Social Psychology of Organization* (New York, 1966); R. A. Johnson, *et al., The Theory and Management of Systems* (New York, 1963); and Keeling, *Management in Government*, pp. 75-90.

29. See Chapter 3.

30. See A. W. Johnson, "The Treasury Board of Canada and the Machinery of Government in the 1970s", *Canadian Journal of Political Science,* Vol. VI, no. 9, pp. 346-66, and M. Hicks, "The Treasury Board of Canada and Its Clients", *Canadian Public Administration,* Vol. XVI, no. 2, pp. 182-205.

31. Standing Senate Committee on National Finance, *Growth, Employment and Price Stability* (Ottawa, 1972).

CHAPTER TWO

The Politics of Economic Policy

With the general relationships between economic management, public policy, and public administration as background, we can now proceed to a more detailed analysis of the politics of Canadian economic policy. Because politics involves *both* the selection and pursuit of values and goals and the need by political authorities to select and apply certain instruments of governing to secure social support and/or compliance, this chapter will examine both of these critical dimensions of politics as applied to economic policy.

The dimension of values and goals involves both an examination of the several sets of perceptions which exist regarding the role of the state in Canada, and an understanding of the increasingly complex trade-offs and conflicts which exist among an ever-lengthening list of economic-policy goals. The first part of the chapter will explore the role of the state and the political evolution of economic-policy goals. The second part will explore the efforts of bodies like the Economic Council of Canada to articulate goals and indicators of economic performance.

The other half of the reality of politics is to be found in the real problems of governing. Politicians in a democratic state are judged not only by the goals they pursue but also by the way they pursue them. Thus values and goals must be related to the equally critical choices faced by Canadian politicians, particularly governing politicians, regarding the character and range of governing instruments available to them. What forms of governing instruments are available through which political authorities can secure or warrant the necessary support and/or compliance for the goals and policies they pursue? The third part of the chapter will thus explore the use of the main governing instruments (exhortation, expenditures, and regulation) with emphasis being placed on the extent to which these "instruments" cannot be viewed as problems of mere technique. The consummate political difficulty in all economic policy-making is that, to a certain extent, the instruments of governing are *ends* in themselves. Our discussion of governing instruments will also be related to the broader processes through which complex societies have sought to order their basic needs for calculation, incentives, and control. Some of these processes, such as the functioning of the price system, and electoral processes, though related to and influenced by the question of governing instruments, are broader and important in other respects, even though they will not be fully explored in this book.

This chapter will thus present the central political basis for the analysis in Chapters 3, 4, and 5 where we will explore in greater detail the organization of the Cabinet and central economic-policy processes, the nature of economic-policy instruments, the location of these instruments in Cabinet portfolios and in bureaucratic agencies, and the consequent intra-Cabinet and interagency roles and dynamics that characterize the economic-policy process in the Government of Canada. The latter organizational dimension will include an analysis of the roles of economic-policy leaders.

THE ROLE OF THE STATE AND CANADIAN ECONOMIC POLICY

In comparison with other states Canada is usually grouped with those western states that possess strong traditions of liberal democratic government. Liberal democracy implies a belief in a maximum degree of individual freedom within a system of democratically elected government. In economic terms it implies an encouragement of, and/or an acceptance of, wide areas of private economic and entrepreneurial activity. In technological terms it implies a general belief in progress and in the application of scientific rationality to the development of goods and services in both the public and private sectors.[1] With respect to these very broad values Canada's economic policy is derived and conducted in a manner much like that of any other western democratic state.

Confined even to this level of generality, Canada's broad political and economic processes are subject to the same range of controversy and historic ideological conflict that has been encountered in other western states.[2] Thus, critics from the political left tend to view the role of the state as being basically the agent of the capitalist and entrepreneurial classes. Critics from the political right would tend to bemoan the already excessive (in their view) intervention of the state in areas of private activity. Spokesmen of the centre would tend to view the role of the state as a social referee acting in the broad public interest to distribute resources more equitably and to cushion the excesses of the marketplace.

While it is important to begin any analysis of the politics of Canadian economic policy by drawing primary attention to the existence of liberal democratic values (for they are undoubtedly critical influences), it would be quite misleading to give a total explanatory weight to these values. Canada's economic-policy processes and outcomes are far more complex than that and an understanding of them requires ultimately that the details and peculiarities of Canada's political and economic values be incorporated. While the identification of the peculiarities of the Canadian system of political and economic values is an important undertaking it is by no means an easy one.

The difficulty of the task is, perhaps, best illustrated by Presthus's analysis of the Canadian "political culture". Citing and reviewing several earlier analyses of Canadian society, Presthus outlines four elements of the Canadian political culture which, in part, reveal Canada's liberal traditions, but which also reflect the Tory and socialist streaks in our political and economic make-up. The four elements are corporatism, pragmatic state intervention, deference, and quasi-participation.[3]

"Corporatism" implies a conception of society in which "government delegates many of its functions to private groups which in turn provide guidance regarding the social and economic legislation required in the modern state."[4] "State intervention" implies a belief and a willingness to use the state to intervene in situations of social injustice or economic disequilibrium.[5] Reflected in such areas as the historic Canadian inclination to use state enterprise and Crown corporations, the belief in pragmatic state intervention is held to be much stronger in Canada than in the United States and is perhaps a reflection of both Tory and socialist collectivist streaks which have emerged in English and French Canada.[6] "Deference" implies a greater trust in formal authority and reflects a willingness to leave to such governing authorities a great degree of discretion and freedom in making public choices on behalf of the public. The cabinet-parliamentary form of government, which concentrates power in the Cabinet, and the general absence of a constitutionally enshrined bill of rights are but two examples frequently cited to illustrate the deferential nature of Canadian politics.[7] Related to the greater deferential nature of Canadian politics is the claimed quasi-participative character of our political processes. "Quasi-participation" is related to such questions as electoral participation and political-party identification where Canadian practice (especially in comparison with American practice) tends to reveal less-established traditions of participation. The more limited opportunities for participation are reflected in the generally closed, secretive decision-making processes encouraged by cabinet systems of government.[8]

The difficulty with the above characterizations is that, while evidence for each of them can undoubtedly be found or extracted from Canada's historical evolution, their meaning and relative influence at any single point in time is difficult to determine. The elements, moreover, are not fully or logically exclusive. All of them ultimately reflect attitudes toward the state and about the role of the state. Some interpretations of corporatism suggest that the state is an unrepentant agent of the powerful big capital and big labour interests. It is held, moreover, that Canada's brokerage politics cover up and cloud the underlying class conflicts that exist and that ought to receive greater political expression.[9] State intervention suggests the more aggressive use of the state to remedy injustices, be they marginal or major in nature. Deference and quasi-participation suggest a need to trust the state as a social referee, even though the risks of doing so are apparent and are understood. Thus, the four elements reflect a series of distinctions difficult to determine with precision.

Because each of the elements ultimately reflects different perspectives about the role of the state it is important to begin the analysis of the politics of Canadian economic policy by stressing these several views. They are still very central both to practitioners and to researchers who seriously wish to understand the processes and outcomes of Canadian economic policy.

The importance of these broad characterizations of the Canadian political economy was especially illustrated by the federal government's imposition of its income controls program in 1975 and by the subsequent debate on the claimed need for new tripartite (industry, labour, and government) institutions of economic management, especially those suggested by the Canadian Labour Congress's 1976 Manifesto.[10] While we will examine the tripartism debate in Chapters 12 and 14, it is important to stress at the outset how close to the surface the several views of the role of the state held by business, labour, and government are, and how quickly they emerge when the "normal" processes of economic management are breached, as they clearly were by the 1975 income-controls program.

The Canadian labour movement saw the controls program and the post-controls period (the period following the lifting of the controls in 1978) as being one in which they would have to guard against being co-opted into a form of "liberal corporatism" in which labour, through the CLC, would become effectively an arm of the state and of big business interests. They thus saw the use of ultimate regulatory instruments of economic management as requiring a restructuring of the role of the CLC and of the need for new "power sharing" institutions to manage the economy.[11] Such a transformation of power would alter the traditional role of the CLC as a loose, only moderately influential, confederation of member unions which had heretofore been content to exercise influence through collective bargaining at the plant level, and through indirect political expression as an interest group and through the New Democratic party.[12]

While the CLC saw the 1975-76 changes in the economic "rules of the game" as an occasion for avoiding a future form of corporatism, other analysts saw the events as being a more natural unfolding of Canada's historic preference for a form of corporatism.[13]

The basic belief by economic-policy makers during the past two decades in the general tenets of Keynesian macro-economic management is ultimately a variation of belief in the role of the state which must be understood in the context of the broader values discussed above. Although Keynesian theory contains specific tenets about how to use the levers of economic policy, it ultimately reflects the same ambivalence about the role of the state described above. Despite the fact that Keynesian approaches about using the state as an economic balance wheel imply an interventionist role, they are inherently silent on the question of *for whom* the intervention is conducted and on the questions of the *openness* of the processes to be used in a *federal* system in arriving at decisions.[14]

There can be no doubt about the fact that basic liberal-democratic traditions critically influence the conduct of economic policy in Canada. Such traditions, however, must be more specifically understood in the context of the values inherent in the somewhat general but nonetheless important characteristics reflected in such concepts as corporatism, state intervention, deference, and quasi-participation. All reflect different possible attitudes about the role of the state and hence about the way in which Keynesian economic management could be interpreted, criticized, and applied in Canada. This leads us inevitably to a more detailed look at the goals of economic policy in Canada.

THE GOALS OF CANADIAN ECONOMIC POLICY

The goals of Canadian economic policy have already been briefly referred to in Chapter 1. These goals are held to be: i) full employment; ii) price stability; iii) economic growth; iv) balance-of-payments equilibrium; v) equitable distribution of income; and vi) removal of regional economic disparities. A recent analysis of Canadian economic problems asserted that a general consensus seemed to exist about the first four of these objectives but treated the distributive and regional objectives as "secondary objectives", along with other objectives such as decent housing, access to medical care, reduced foreign investment, and maintenance of the environment.[15]

While the first four objectives undoubtedly represent the core of economic policy, particularly the short-term stabilization objectives, the political history of Canada, since the Second World War in particular, strongly suggests that the political process has been less able to treat the distributive and regional issues as secondary. Indeed it is precisely in the relationships among these four objectives and in the relationships between the so-called "primary" and "secondary" objectives that the politics of Canadian economic policy is to be most clearly understood.

The strength of regionalism in Canadian politics is especially well established and cannot be treated as merely a recent phenomenon made more visible by the presence of governmental departments such as Regional Economic Expansion. As Simeon and Elkins point out:

> Canadian politics is regional politics; regionalism is one of the pre-eminent facts of Canadian life, whether reflected in the principles of Cabinet-building, the acrimony of federal-provincial conference or the virtual elimination of class voting on at least a national scale.[16]

Several other observations about the objectives can be made. Some of the observations are elementary and are increasingly acknowledged. Others are less obvious and are rarely acknowledged.

First, it is important to stress that we are talking about the politics that surround the choice of *goals* and *objectives*. This is obviously not the same as talking about the real effects or *outcomes* of economic-policy choices. To argue that Canadian politicians and political processes have given greater priority in recent years to distributive and regional objectives is not to suggest that the result has been a significant *redistribution* of resources in favour of the disadvantaged classes and regions. Indeed there is mounting evidence to suggest that little net redistribution has been achieved,[17] and that even NDP provincial governments have weak records in respect of real income redistribution (see Appendix B).[18]

It is important, moreover, to stress that the overall goals of economic policy are not often openly ranked by governing politicians precisely because of their ingrained understanding that it is the trade-offs among the goals rather than the goals themselves that present the political difficulties. This is especially true in a federal system of government, a system which, almost by definition, legitimizes and encourages the pursuit of different priorities by the federal and provincial governments. As we will see, politicians have been particularly reluctant to be pinned down to achieving prescribed targets in the economic goal areas.[19] Economists have also increasingly acknowledged the difficulty, on economic grounds, of making several of the core trade-offs between the employment and price stability goals or between balance-of-payments equilibrium and economic growth.[20]

Second, while the removal of regional economic disparities and the redistribution of income have been goals for some time, they are goals whose more persistent appearance on the economic policy agenda in Canada is directly attributable to the relatively strong collectivist influences in Canada. These influences are reflected in and through strong provincial centres of political and governmental power, the role of "third" political parties, and the single-member constituency electoral process. The goal of removing regional disparities has been far more explicitly enunciated in Canada, for example, than it has been in the United States. Similarly, although to a lesser degree, general income redistribution *goals* have been articulated in the Canadian federal political arena primarily by the presence and persistence of socialist political expression centred in the NDP and its predecessor, the CCF.[21] Some observers also attribute the greater presence of distributive goals to the liberal social welfare philosophies of important senior public servants, especially in the late 1940s.[22]

Third, the differentiation of primary and secondary goals alerts us to the need to differentiate and understand the relationships between, and the balance of power between, the primary departments and agencies which attend to the primary objectives of economic policy (e.g., Finance, Bank of Canada, and Industry, Trade and Commerce) and the secondary departments who attend to the so-called secondary objectives (e.g., Regional Economic Expansion, Labour, and Manpower and Immigration).

Finally, while trade-offs in the above goal areas have been increasingly difficult, the prospects of even broader and more difficult trade-offs that strike more at the structural heart of the Canadian political economy are already apparent. Foreign investment policy, wage and price controls, competition policy, and environmental policy are already reflected organizationally and will add a further, perhaps more fundamental, dimension to both the goals of economic policy and to the structures and processes of economic policy-making. Thus the meaning and organizational reflection of economic policy has increasingly been broadened beyond its initial Keynesian stabilization parameters.

The evolution of these goals and their connection to structural and organizational change can be seen by dividing the quarter of a century since 1950 into five periods, 1950-56, 1957-61, 1962-65, 1966-72, and 1973-76. In the analysis for each period we will briefly summarize the general state of fiscal and economic policy, the economic-policy goals which received priority, and the degree and nature of structural and organizational change.[23]

1950 to 1956

The period was characterized by general economic prosperity and growth. Economic-policy priorities were geared to maintaining the level of growth. Unemployment was generally low. Anti-inflationary priorities were prominent in the early 1950s because of the heavy demands imposed by the Korean War. With respect to structural change the period was notable for the absence of it. The assumption in 1954 by the Bank of Canada of more of the responsibilities for managing the Canadian money and credit system was the only organizational change of any significance. The creation of the Royal Commission on Canada's Economic Prospects (the Gordon Commission) in 1956 was the only other structural event of note. Its commissioning, however, and its subsequent recommendations were largely a reflection of the complacency of the period. The period began with the urgency of the Korean War and ended with the acrimony of the Pipeline debate. In general, however, it was a period characterized by economic complacency, relative federal fiscal dominance over provincial governments (reflected in part through the tax rental agreements) with economic policy influence shared by the Finance department and the Department of Trade and Commerce, the latter headed by C. D. Howe. The making and management of economic policy was a far simpler, more closed, process than it has since become, involving fewer values, variables, and departments.

1957 to 1961

The 1957 to 1961 period was plagued by a general recession of economic activity. Unemployment hovered around seven per cent and economic growth was generally less than three per cent. Economic-policy priorities were thus generally geared to promote economic growth and reduce unemployment. Four of the five years were characterized by large deficit budgets. In 1961-62 economic priorities had to be altered to meet a foreign exchange crisis. While economic priorities were thus concentrated on the traditional areas of stabilization, the early years of the Diefenbaker government also witnessed the emergence of a more explicit concern for redistribution and for some so-called supply-management issues. This concern tended to emerge in an *ad hoc* fashion as the Diefenbaker government sought to respond to the constituencies which helped bring it to power. Thus increased pensions, the ARDA program, and more generous equalization payments to provinces emerged. At the same time, programs such as the Winter Works program, and the technical and vocational training programs were rushed into place to deal with economic management issues which were becoming increasingly apparent.

Structural change continued to be very limited, but not unimportant. The Coyne Affair raised the question of the degree of independence of the Bank of Canada, a question which still remains critical. In the early 1960s the question centred on making the Bank subject to greater control by the Finance Minister and the government. If there are any trends on this issue in the mid-1970s, they seem to lean in the direction of a concern that the bank's management of the supply of money is too much subject to the dictates of expenditure politics and not enough to the dictates of economic management. The National Productivity Council was created during this period and reflected institutionally a concern for the public sector-private sector dimensions of detailed economic management. In real terms it presented an effort to help plan industrial-sector productivity without calling it "planning".

Beyond these specific changes, the Diefenbaker period was notable for the number of major policy issues it launched via the mechanism of the royal commission. Many of these commissions and their subsequent recommendations later affected economic management in important ways. The Glassco Commission on Government Organization, the Borden Commission on Energy, the Carter Commission on Taxation, the McPherson Commission on Transportation, the Hall Commission on Health Services, and the Porter Commission on Banking and Finance, all raised a number of structural and value issues which re-emerged on the public policy agenda of the mid- and late 1960s.

The *ad hoc* populist politics of the Diefenbaker regime can be considered to have altered the basis on which economic management would have to be conducted even if the government was not particularly good at managing it. Thus, wider distributive variables were reinserted into economic-policy processes. Formal economic-policy processes were centred in the Finance Department, but the latter had become a more conservative department than it had been earlier under Clifford Clark. By 1962, the tax rental system ended and the abatement system began thus reflecting an emergent increase in fiscal power by provincial governments.

1962 to 1965

This period was characterized by general economic recovery and growth. Average growth rates exceeded 6 per cent and unemployment fell from 7.1 per cent in 1961 to 3.9 per cent in 1965. Prices were relatively stable. Economic-policy priorities were thus tied to the twin priorities of promoting and maintaining growth and full employment. Significant growth was, however, increasingly tied, as a necessary precondition for more explicit redistributive priorities. The redistributive objective was in evidence in fairly concrete ways such as through the Canada Pension Plan, medicare, and a further development of the Winter Works, municipal incentives, and vocational training programs. These policies reflected the early influence of Prime Minister Pearson, and Walter Gordon, as well as Pearson's principal advisor, Tom Kent. Thus during this period the relationship between social policy and economic policy became more explicit, resulting in an alliance of influence in the economic-policy system between Finance, the PMO, and the PCO.

With respect to structural change the period was characterized by an increased rate of change. The Economic Council of Canada, the Department of Industry, and the Department of Forestry and Rural Development were organizational responses to the questions of overall economic consensus, industrial growth, and regional economic issues, respectively. By 1965-66 the Treasury Board had been separated from the Finance Department thus differentiating the functions of the management of the government from the management of the economy.

Economic management during this period could not be isolated from the influence of the then-emerging issue of bilingualism and biculturalism which was itself a broad reflection of the cultural and economic inequality of French Canadians. The relationship of these forces to the development of federal-provincial opting-out arrangements was obvious and their relationship to the federal government's capacity to have a sufficient tax leverage to manage the economy became questions of increasing concern. By the mid-1960s it was quite clear that the making of economic policies, including fiscal policies, was no longer exclusively in federal hands. The values which would impinge on economic-policy deliberations were broadened to include greater concern for structural regulation in areas such as foreign investment. Walter Gordon's 1963 budget demonstrated the emergence of the foreign investment issue, but also demonstrated the rather frail level of support it had at that time.

1966 to 1972

Uneven growth, rising unemployment, and inflation characterized the 1966 to 1972 period. The need for economic policy priorities to strike increasingly finely-tuned balances between the goals of growth, price stability, and full employment was complicated even more by the fact that this period also involved the most explicit articulation of the objective of removing regional disparities. This was especially the case after the Trudeau government assumed power in 1968. Other redistributive and social policy initiatives were also pursued concurrently, involving an expanding medicare program, a tax reform process, special social employment programs such as the Local Initiatives (LIP) and Opportunities for Youth (OFY) programs, and changes in the unemployment insurance program.

Both program and organizational changes reflected the emergence of very explicit supply-oriented economic management priorities. The full range of economic values and goals thus became far more explicitly institutionalized during this period. Issues which heretofore had tended to be parts of other departments now became departments in their own right headed by ministers with obligations to defend and articulate these goals. Thus the departments of Manpower and Immigration, Consumer and Corporate Affairs, Industry, Trade and Commerce, and Regional Economic Expansion were created. In addition, policy ministries of Science and Technology, and Urban Affairs were established. Other structural events revealed the growing difficulties and the increasing range of policy objectives which were impinging on economic management. A Prices and Incomes Commission was utilized as a research and possible consensus vehicle in response to rising rates of inflation. An elaborate White

Paper process on tax reform sought, with mixed results, to elicit greater participation and consensus in a major question of economic management. The Watkin's Report of 1968 and the Gray Report of 1972 revealed the increasing strength of the foreign investment issue, and the Senate Report on Poverty reflected the inadequacy of redistribution policies.

All of these changes meant that economic-policy leadership within the Cabinet was increasingly pluralized and made more diffuse. The Priorities and Planning Committee of the Cabinet symbolized this interdependence bringing together the roles of the Prime Minister, Finance minister, and President of the Treasury Board as well as other ministers in a more explicit formal way both for purposes of economic policy and for overall governmental-management and priority-setting functions.

1973 to 1976

The period from 1973 to the time of writing in 1977 has been characterized by high inflation and unemployment coupled with little or no growth. Economic priorities have thus had to continue to pursue all of the traditional objectives while at the same time continuing to consolidate the other dimensions of economic policy which emerged in the 1966 to 1972 period. The most important dimension to emerge in the 1973 to 1975 period was the energy crisis which along with food and other renewable resource supplies, brought the broadest supply dimensions into the economic debates. Real economics was thus reintroduced in a forceful way in that resources of all kinds were becoming scarce and hence economic choices on all issues had to be made. The difficulty of concurrently pursuing all of the goals of economic policy and hence of politically managing the economy became more obvious.

During this period the pace and nature of aggregate organizational changes altered. Rather than seeing the development of newer departments, the period tended to reveal a focus on particular dimensions, primarily at the micro, intradepartmental level, or in particular sectors of the economy. Thus the departments of Industry, Trade and Commerce, Manpower and Immigration, Regional Economic Expansion, and Consumer and Corporate Affairs all sought to decentralize their operations and decision-making so as to better understand and respond to particular problems in different areas of the country or in particular industries. The Western Economic Opportunities Conference was held in 1973 to develop a better response to western alienation from central Canada. The establishment of the Foreign Investment Review Agency, the Energy Resources Allocation Board, and the Food Prices Review Board reflected the emergence of other particular dimensions of overall economic management. In addition, reviews of communications policy, immigration policy, transportation policy, and emerging policies on the status of women all revealed a growing tendency to incorporate the regulatory dimension in the policy responses. Thus, even in the short run, the manipulation of regulatory instruments as a complement to expenditure and taxation policies become increasingly possible. The 1974 federal election was largely fought on the issue of the regulation of wages and prices and thus, at least temporarily, foreclosed this ultimate form of regulation as an economic-policy option. The entrance of these wider instruments was, of course, itself an indication of the unusual degree of economic decline which characterized this period.

The search for both a new basis for, and institutions to achieve, a further, new economic consensus was revealed in the Economic Council's effort to establish a National Conference Secretariat, the establishment of a Royal Commission on Corporate Concentration, and the Canada Labour Council. Finance Minister John Turner's efforts to seek voluntary wage and price guidelines, from labour and industry, and the Trudeau government's informal suggestion that industry-wide collective-bargaining mechanisms be established were attempts to help overcome the disruptive effects of multiple labour dislocations in the same industry. The inability of government to manage the economy also helped foster the establishment in the private sector of bodies like the C. D. Howe Institute and the re-energized Conference Board of Canada to develop alternative or at least "other" views of economic and other policies.

It is in the light of the above evolution that the watershed events of late-1975 and 1976 should be seen. The announcement on October 15, 1976, of the Trudeau government's controls program and of the establishment of the Anti-Inflation Board, as well as the resultant controversy between the apparent Galbraithian views espoused by the

Prime Minister and the Keynesian and neo-classical views espoused by former Finance Minister John Turner and former Deputy Minister of Finance Simon Reisman, must be seen in the context both of what had been happening to economic values, and to economic policy organizations within the Government of Canada.

The Prime Minister, in his December 28 interview on CTV, asserted that the controls program

> is a massive intervention into the decision-making power of the economic groups and it's telling Canadians we haven't been able to make it work, the free market system. We've ended up with very high unemployment and very high inflation. We can't go back to what was before with the same habits, the same behaviours and the same institutions.[24]

The Prime Minister went on to suggest in Galbraithian tones the possible need for more permanent controls. He seemed to be adopting the Galbraithian view that the contemporary political economy is divided into two sectors, the planning sector and the market sector, the latter remaining sensitive to market and price decisions, but the former being a power unto itself with both big labour and large corporations being able to pass on price increases to the consumer. While apparently hinting strongly at permanent controls the Prime Minister seemed simultaneously to disavow "corporatism" and its variations. Corporatism implies more formal, perhaps even statutory processes whereby big labour, big government, and big business would negotiate in tripartite forums the division of the economic pie. In the Prime Minister's words:

> I was never a follower of syndicalism or corporatism or guild socialism. . . . I still believe that Parliament and direct representation is the best way for a government to get the feel of a country, particularly one which is as vast and diverse as Canada.
>
> I don't believe any corporation of managers and workers and the state together could get a better feel of what Canadians want than our present system. . . .[25]

Both the replies of John Turner and Simon Reisman stressed a more classic view of the continuing validity of market forces and of the need for economic policies to reflect the standard responses, namely controlling the supply of money and credit and reducing government expenditures.[26] Of the two replies, Reisman's reflected the changing realities of power and the growing dispersal of economic policy-making power within the federal government and hence should be quoted directly:

> The official explanation [by Trudeau] of the nature of our inflation placed much emphasis on the behaviour of big business and big unions. There was also much moralizing based on the notion that the greed of Canadians had aggravated the problem. Very little was said about big government, fiscal imbalance or excessive monetary expansion. All this is very close to Galbraith's analysis . . . .
>
> The design of the control system, its selective application to large enterprises and unions, the relatively long period envisaged for its application and the rejection of a temporary freeze were also reminiscent of Galbraith's method.[27]

While Reisman acknowledged that Canadian economic policy had not drifted over entirely to Galbraithian concepts, he clearly implied the growing influence of the PCO and PMO. Somewhat paradoxically he seriously underplayed the growing impact, if not influence, of other economic departments. He noted, almost as an afterthought:

> Some mention needs to be made of structural economic policies. I refer to such matters as competition policy, labour training and mobility, industrial relations, regional development and productivity. Important though these may be for the better performance of the economy over time they have little to do with the problem of inflation; and should not be confused with it. Removal of the control system should not be linked with efforts to improve these structural defects of our economy.[28]

The paradox is that some of these so-called structural issues were precisely the areas where new departments headed by their own ministers had been created and where some of the greatest areas of expenditure growth had occurred. Thus, traditional Keynesian fiscal strategies spearheaded by the Finance Department were no longer aimed at easily controllable subsidiary *programs*, but rather had to be aimed at whole *departments*, and ministers put in place to defend the ongoing medium- and long-term expenditures over which they had custody.

Since the end of the Second World War, therefore, one can observe an ever-widening array of economic priorities that must be politically ranked, but which are increasingly being pursued concurrently. Thus redistribution and more fundamental regulative goals have joined the other objectives of economic policy. Structurally, Canada has moved from a period when organizations charged with economic responsibilities remained largely without change until the mid-1960s, after which time a vast new array of departments was created both in response to new goals, and to help alleviate general economic conditions. Following the establishment of these newer units we have witnessed, beginning in the early 1970s, more specific concern for the micro dimension of economic management, both in terms of particular departmental constituencies and in terms of public sector-private sector consensus mechanisms. Finally, there has now surfaced an important debate about the relationships between economic theory, political processes, and the internal governmental processes of economic management.

The politics of economic policy, however, is not adequately understood merely by pointing out the conflict among an expanding list of goals. The experience with the Economic Council of Canada's effort to *articulate* performance goals and indicators during the last decade illustrates further both political and technical dilemmas. The second part of this chapter will briefly review this experience.

THE ARTICULATION OF GOALS

Central to the Economic Council's articulation of performance goals was the concept of potential output, i.e., its measure of the supply of goods and services which the economy could be capable of producing under conditions of relatively full and increasingly efficient utilization of resources. On this basis five performance goals were discussed in successive Council reports between 1963 and 1972. These goals related to employment levels, growth, price stability, distribution, and balance-of-payments equilibrium.

The Council was most specific on three of the five performance goals. It was very specific on the level of employment; it was quite specific on the level of economic growth which it considered feasible; and it was very specific on the level of price stability which could be achieved. However, prior to the publication of these figures, Canada had done worse on the full employment issue than the Council was

then suggesting. Between 1953 and 1964, for example, the average rate of unemployment in Canada was five per cent. It would appear, then, that there was an element of psychological motivation in the Council's *First Annual Review* when its targets were assessed against performances prior to its publication.

Regarding *employment levels*, the Council noted:

> Levels of employment and unemployment experience since the war have reflected these fluctuations and trends in economic conditions. The average rate of unemployment in Canada was 2.8 per cent in 1946-53. It rose by more than 50 per cent, to an average of 4.3 per cent in 1947-54, and then by more than 50 per cent, to an average of 6.7 per cent in 1958-62.[29]

The Council also observed that unemployment was concentrated in the Atlantic region and among the old and young members of the labour force.

The problem of establishing an unemployment target became a difficult and controversial issue. Within the Council it presented conflicts between the labour and management representatives. The Council showed awareness of the complexity of this target when it stated:

> In the light of careful studies, we have concluded that a 97 per cent rate of employment, or a 3 per cent rate of unemployment, of the labour force would constitute a realistic objective to be aimed at over the balance of the 1960s, and that economic policies should be actively directed towards the achievement of this target. We recognize that this target has important implications for other basic economic objectives—such as the maintenance of reasonable price stability and a viable balance-of-payments position.[30]

The Council tried to explain four features of the employment target. First, the 97 per cent employment potential was an average annual rate. Second, it pointed out that the figure represented a national average. Third, the Council suggested that the 3 per cent unemployment figure was intended to reflect a goal for a year of high activity within the short-term business cycle. Finally, the Council emphasized that the level of utilization of the labour force could be achieved on a sustained basis only if effective labour-market policies are developed to promote higher and more efficient use of manpower resources.

In its *Sixth Annual Review*, the Council attempted to elaborate on its employment target:

Originally, in the Council's *First Annual Review*, the definition was translated into a target of a 97 per cent employment rate (or 3 per cent unemployment rate) for 1970. By the *Fourth Review*, the Council reconsidered this time horizon and reset the target—again, not as one which we should aim to attain within a year or two, but in the medium-term future—that is, by the mid-1970s. We believe that this goal, having regard to the various aspects mentioned above, is still valid. This is not, of course, an ultimate goal, satisfactory for all time to come. We continue to hope that with sustained improvement in our economic performance it may ultimately be a realistic aim.[31]

Notwithstanding the commitment of governments to full employment, its quantification has been controversial. Accordingly, some critics have suggested that the Council should have recommended alternative objectives. Dr. André Raynauld made these observations on the unemployment goal before a parliamentary committee in 1972:

I wonder myself at the present time about the opportunity of keeping an objective which, to my knowledge, was not reached in many years in Canada. I do not feel capable, nor do I think that any economist could change the basis for setting a definite rate. To try and change this basis would imply the assessment of real economic possibilities capable of creating full employment. At the moment, I would be most reluctant, as would be other economists, I believe, to set a figure not reflecting this ideal, more or less arbitrarily, but based on real possibilities.

Another difficulty arising from what I have just said, is the period of time during which the rate would apply. Would it be a rate of 5 per cent for 1975; a rate for next year when the situation will be quite different? It is said that if we were to raise the rate of employment to any degree tomorrow, prices would also increase markedly. So it may be wise not to set an objective today, even at the rate of 4 per cent and pretend to apply this rate next year, for the transition of an unemployment rate of 5.8 per cent, as it is now, to a rate of 4 per cent in one year also presents insurmountable difficulties. For this rate to be made effective and constitute a real guide, we would be forced to select a much higher rate than what the population, I feel, is ready to accept. For 1972, one might give 5 per cent as a possible rate without excessive cost.

> If one said today: "We are aiming at 5 per cent unemployment", I think we would be asking for more difficulties than benefits. Therefore, I feel that if we do not set out objectives from the beginning, we will have to be satisfied with temporary or provisional objectives. There lies the solution, perhaps: to maintain a long-term objective as an ideal embodying the long-term and meanwhile accept a slightly higher unemployment rate which would only represent one step in the attainment of a long range objective.[32]

As indicated in Chapter 1, the Council was established to facilitate better *growth performance* in the Canadian economy. In its *First Annual Review*, the Council pointed to the fact that the goal of rapid and sustained economic growth, especially in terms of growth in productivity, does not appear to have been a consistent objective of general economic policy in Canada throughout the postwar period.

The Council showed in its *First Annual Review* that it regarded growth as a precondition to the attainment of several of the other targets. Thus, the Council projected for an advance in output per man-hour of 3 per cent per year over the period 1963 to 1970. It noted that output per man-hour was the best measure of economic growth and that 3 per cent was its target growth (later changed to 5 per cent for the *Fourth Review* and 5.5 per cent for the *Sixth Review*).

The 5.5 per cent figure was an ambitious one, because the Council noted that in 1963 the economy was operating at an actual level of about 6 per cent below potential. The Council assumed that potential productivity and potential output would be amelioriated. The following factors were isolated as key variables in the attainment of the target: accelerating industrial research and technology and its more widespread application; an increasingly educated and skilled labour force; improving managerial competence and know-how; rapidly growing population and markets in Canada and abroad; and the provision of increasing opportunities for larger scale and more efficient production of many commodities.

In its *Fourth Annual Review*, the Economic Council attempted to bring its 1964 analysis up to date. It noted that by 1966 the slack in the Canadian economy had been substantially taken up and, as a result, it was obvious that growth in Canada's potential output in the years ahead would depend primarily on the future increase in both the quantity and quality of the productive resources and the efficiency with which they were used. The Canadian economy had experienced a boom from March 1961 to June 1967. The Council noted that the potential growth rates for 1965-70 and 1970-75 were slightly below the very high actual growth rate achieved in 1960-65, when the substantial economic boom was being absorbed. But the rate of potential growth over the decade to 1975 was above the average annual rate of actual growth recorded in the decade of the 1950s.[33] The Council anticipated that in moving from actual output in 1966 to potential output in 1970, the overall growth in total demand would be five per cent per year.

The Council took the position in 1967 that the nature of the economic problems confronting Canada into the 1970s would be different from those experienced in the 1960s. By the late 1960s there was much less slack in the economy than earlier in the decade and the longer term underlying demand trends were strong. This posed new and, in some respects, more difficult problems for economic policies, both private and public.

Notwithstanding the favourable conditions which existed in the Canadian economy up to 1967, the Council pointed to a few defective areas on the demand side. Thus, it noted that a substantial volume of new housing was built during the period 1961-66, but the rate of growth was clearly not adequate to the nation's needs. By 1966, a severe housing shortage was developing. A major element in this situation was a shortage of mortgage funds, which severely curtailed the supply of new housing at a time of high and rising new family formation.

The Council also noted that governmental expenditure showed some inconsistencies. Accordingly, the considerable increase in government expenditure on goods and services in 1965 and 1966 was superimposed on the already strong expansion of demand taking place in other sectors of the economy, thus adding significantly to the excessive demand pressures which were building up during this period. In contrast to expenditures, the rise in government revenues slowed a little in 1966.

In its *Sixth Review*, the Council again dealt with Canadian productivity growth, the growth of output in relation to the resources used to produce it, as the most essential element of economic growth. The Council estimated the average growth rate, from actual output in 1967 to potential output in 1975, at about 5.5 per cent a year. Economic growth cannot be easily detached from the other goals. Insufficient growth restricts the society's capacity to make progress in pursuing redistributive policies and programs and to finance new programs.

On the goal of *price stability*, the Council was vague, but optimistic. The Council recognized that this was a very complex area and it concluded that:

> . . . keeping price movement within the average annual increases in consumer prices and in prices of all goods and services produced in Canada were 1.4 per cent and 2.0 per cent, respectively, so . . . will undoubtedly be a difficult task to achieve, especially under the high demand and high employment conditions which we have postulated.[34]

The Council explained the basis of its optimism by pointing to the following factors which it considered to be important:

i) the recent record of price stability under conditions of strengthening demand and the devaluation of the Canadian dollar;
ii) the higher productivity growth which we indicate as being possible for the years ahead;
iii) stronger consciousness for particular products among consumers and purchasers; and
iv) various policy measures to facilitate attainment of these objectives.

In its *Sixth Annual Review*, the Council suggested that a satisfactory price performance would involve reducing the rate of increase in the general price indices as soon as possible to less than two per cent per year. However, the Council added, this would be neither the sole nor the ultimate criterion in the sense that this would require some price declines and a market reduction in the range of price advances.

Maintaining price stability has obviously been a persistent problem, especially in recent years. Thus, following the report of the Economic Council on its reference on prices, productivity, and employment, the federal government established a Prices and Incomes Commission to conduct a more particular study of the problem of prices. The Commission, after experiencing difficulties in gaining the support of labour, advised that the government keep a wide option open to cope with this very complex problem.[35]

Quite predictably the Council did not quantify the goal of *equitable distribution* of rising income. Instead, it dealt with the problem of "balanced regional development". Thus, it stressed that ever since Confederation, the notion of "balanced regional development" had been an implicit, if not an explicit objective of national policy. In this regard, the Council operated under the stipulation of its Act, which requires it to study how national economic policies can best foster the balanced development of all areas of Canada. Accordingly, the Council directed its attention to regional divergencies in the participation of the labour force and to variations in income.

The Council was least emphatic on the politically sensitive area of income redistribution in that it felt that the public must ultimately decide what degree of income redistribution it is prepared to make and what form it should take.

It was not until the *Sixth Annual Review* that the Council attempted to put the question of income distribution in perspective. Thus, in regard to equitable distribution of rising incomes, the Council noted that it was the most complex of the basic goals, and accordingly defied any easily grasped quantitative measurement. In Canada, it involves at least the narrowing of regional income disparities and the elimination of poverty.

The performance of an economy is particularly dependent on international trade. It is very much so in the case of Canada and hence the goal of *balance-of-payments equilibrium* is especially important. In this regard, the Council reviewed Canada's postwar experiences with interest rates and the value of its dollar. The Council pointed to the 1960-62 exchange crisis and it advised that there was a special need for appropriate reconciliation between domestic policy and the international environment.

The Council had taken the position in its *First Annual Review* that

> . . . the strengthening of Canada's international competitive position over the medium-term future should also imply that, although the absolute size of the current account deficit and net capital inflow at potential output might be above the levels of the early mid-1960s, there should be basic, long-term declining trends in the ratio of the net capital inflow in relation to total investment.[36]

However, in its *Fourth Review*, the Council emphasized that the balance-of-payments objective has been not merely maintenance of a flow of total international receipts to cover the country's international payments, but also some strengthening of Canada's economic position. The Council has expressed the view, therefore, that there should be some improvements in the international competitive position of Canadian industry and the maintenance of reasonably good access to external sources of capital.

By the early 1970s the political and technical difficulties inherent in the above discussion of goals had persuaded the Council to alter its approach. In 1972 the Council adopted the concept of performance indicators.[37] The indicators are medium-term targets developed for three-year intervals, but adjusted annually to take into account changing circumstances and government policies. The indicators deal with more specific aspects of economic activity such as consumer spending, business capital spending, and transfer payments, as well as growth in gross national product, employment, and prices.

The above description of the Council's continuing efforts to articulate goals and indicators illustrated the dimensions of the problem in both political and technical terms. One obvious deficiency in the process was the government's failure to state its position on the goals articulated by the Economic Council. In political terms the lack of government support was a thoroughly predictable deficiency in the Canadian model of economic "planning" or economic-policy formulation. It demonstrated the realities of the Canadian political economy, the lack of commitment to a formal institutional framework, and the absence of any governmental commitment to the performance goals.

By the mid-1970s it was becoming increasingly obvious, for example, that not only were goals and indicators difficult in intra-governmental terms, but there were also no mechanisms by which they could be translated or meaningfully understood in specific sectors of industry. There were not even the rudimentary "neddies" (joint government, industry, and labour consultative bodies) such as were established in specific industrial sectors in the U.K. in the early 1960s, let alone the more elaborate French system of "indicative planning".[38] In this respect the Canadian experience has witnessed an interesting cycle of events. In the early 1960s the Progressive-Conservative government had planned to create a National Productivity Council which would hopefully generate further industry by industry-productivity consultations. These councils were spiritually inspired by the then-developing British experience with a National Economic Development Council (NEDC) and its off-shoot, "neddies". The plans for a Productivity Council were superceded by the Liberal government's creation, in 1963, of the Economic Council of Canada. Maurice Lamontagne, then Secretary of State in the Pearson government, was a principle influence in the Council's creation.[39] His model, in principle or form, but certainly not in substance, was the French system of indicative economic planning. The notion of industry-by-industry consultation, however, was quickly lost sight of. In the mid-1970s, however, both the Economic Council and governmental economic leaders are again acknowledging the need for special industrial consultative mechanisms.

The problem of securing economic consensus and commitment in the aggregate sense or in specific industries is obviously a difficult one, and is no doubt exacerbated by other factors such as the structure of particular industries, the differing legitimacy and efficacy of formal industrial associations, the fragmented structure of Canadian unions, and the differing perceptions of provincial authorities and governmental regulators. We will examine these issues more fully in Chapter 12.

ECONOMIC POLICY AND THE INSTRUMENTS OF GOVERNING

While the real outcomes of economic policy are ultimately determined by several socio-political processes we feel it is essential to take the analysis of Canadian economic policy one step further into the core of political behaviour. The core of political behaviour involves not just the pursuit of objectives and values and the securing of electoral success; it also requires the selection of the governing instruments available to politicians to secure support and/or compliance for the objectives and priorities of economic policy.

The role of governing instruments in the context of Canadian political analysis has been discussed in an earlier work by Doern and Wilson and is derived from Theodore Lowi's important reminder that we must ultimately relate all policy and politics to different degrees of application of the legitimate coercive powers of the state.[40] Lowi identifies four basic types of policy output—distributive, redistributive, regulative, and constituent.[41] Each type is differentiated by varied degrees of directness or indirectness in the application of legitimate coercion, and by the size of the unit (ranging from individuals to groups to classes) to which the legitimate coercion is applied.

While there are problems with the precision of Lowi's classification of policies there are some important elementary insights to be gained from it because it assists in the identification of the kinds of basic instruments of governing available to politicians. Certain types of governing response, such as creating a study, involve minimum coercion and might be even referred to as being symbolic in nature. The allocation or distribution of spending resources is an instrument of governing which involves more moderate coercion because the coercion is basically less noticeable. It is indirect in that it is displaced on to the taxation system at the time that taxes are collected. Direct regulation, on the other hand, is an instrument of governing which involves a more direct exercise of legitimate coercion in which rules of behaviour are enacted with the sanction and/or penalties of the state more directly applied.

Based on this classification of governing instruments, Doern and Wilson have suggested a hypothesis of political policy-making in Canada:

> This hypothesis would suggest that politicians (especially the collective Cabinet) have a strong tendency to respond to policy issues (any issue) by moving successively from the *least coercive* governing instruments to the *most coercive*. Thus, they tend to respond first in the least coercive fashion by creating a study, or by creating a new or reorganized unit of government, or merely by uttering a broad statement of intent. The next least coercive governing instrument would be to use a distributive spending approach in which the resources could be handed out to various constituencies in such a way that the least attention is given as to which taxpayers' pockets the resources are being drawn from. At the more coercive end of the continuum of governing instruments would be a larger redistributive program in which the resources would be more visibly extracted from the more advantaged classes and redistributed to the less advantaged classes. Also at the more coercive end of the governing continuum would be direct regulation in which which the sanctions or threat of sanctions would have to be directly applied. It is, of course, obvious that once a policy issue has matured and has been on the public agenda for many years, all or most of the basic instruments could be utilized.[42]

Several factors suggest the need to keep in mind both the classification of symbolic or constituent, expenditure and regulatory instruments, and the hypothesis of movement along a continuum of governing instruments.

First and foremost there is the relationship between the continuum and the way in which politicians are likely to view the means-ends chain of democratic political relations. Lawrence Pierce's excellent analysis of American fiscal-policy processes identifies the political character of economic-policy instruments as being voluntary, donative, or compulsory.[43] While these characterizations are obviously similar to the degrees of coercion inherent in the continuum of governing instruments described above, Pierce does not draw sufficient attention to the fact that the politician is far less likely than anyone else to view these instruments as being merely techniques of governing.

The politician often must perceive these basic governing instruments not as instruments or *means* but as *ends* in themselves. The performance of spending or regulatory functions may be viewed by some (such as economists and policy analysts) as being the *means* of achieving certain objectives or goals (so-called real policy), but to the politician there must be a greater awareness that these very same activities are the essence of his stock-in-trade, namely, the application of various *forms* and *degrees* of legitimate coercion, which in a democratic state are not merely means or techniques, but ends in themselves.

The analysis of economic policy-making in Canada must have some understanding of the importance of this basic governing dilemma. We will later relate the development of price- and wage-control strategies and objectives to the continuum of governing instruments. The preference for voluntary and distributive instruments and the avoidance of regulative and perhaps also redistributive instruments is a tendency which we will relate not only to the general problems of political governing but also as governing tendency especially characteristic of federal, liberal democratic states like Canada.

A second factor about the continuum is its relationship in the Canadian federal constitutional system to the governing choices available to federal politicians. To choose governing instruments is, in part, to choose constitutional powers. In the Canadian context this is important because on the whole there are fewer political obstacles in the way of the federal government when it chooses to spend its way to the solution of problems that lie in part or totally in provincial jurisdiction.

The use of the federal spending power is a reasonably well established avenue of federal involvement. On the other hand the use of direct regulation by federal politicians generally produces greater obstacles in that they must be sure that they can in fact make laws and thus regulate in the area concerned. Thus the preference for spending instruments may be reinforced by the requirements of governing in the federal system. This characteristic will be identified in Chapter 14 as a middle-level variable in the explanation of the growth of public expenditure in Canada.

We will also later suggest the existence of a "market" in governing instruments in which governing politicians trade. For reasons partly outlined above the preferred instrument of governing, in the past ten years, has been expenditure incentives. If the supply of financial incentives declines due to increasing political criticism of the growth of public spending then, we will argue, governing politicians will turn to other governing instruments such as exhortation and regulation. The choices are limited because the option of doing absolutely nothing is not usually available in the current political climate. Thus, in its 1976 Working Paper on the post-controls period, the federal liberal government asserted that it would seek to meet its economic policy objectives through "non-expenditure" methods. While the document, as an alternative, stressed the need for new consultative instruments, its key policy suggestions involved the implicit use of regulatory instruments in such fields as unemployment insurance, community employment, and public-sector collective bargaining.[44]

In relation to spending *versus* regulatory instruments, it is frequently the case that each instrument may be largely housed in different departments or agencies of the federal government. Spending instruments, for example, are largely (though not totally) located in the regular departments of government while many regulatory functions (though certainly not all) tend to be farmed out to so-called independent agencies, boards, and commissions.[45] The organizational location of various economic policy instruments will be analysed in Chapter 4. It is essential to note, however, that the importance of the organizational location of governing instruments for economic policy increases the more one defines economic policy in terms of the broad secondary objectives described earlier in this chapter as distinct from the primary objectives centred on the traditional parameters of stabilization policy.

The use of regulatory instruments also exacts costs in financial, political, and human terms. Virtually all government regulations directly effect and alter *private* spending. The difficulty in assessing the costs of regulation is that the private expenditure *consequences* (on individuals and corporations) do not normally appear in government budgets.[46] The budgetary process in government is a highly visible and central rhythm of activity in which values are at least partly converted into the common denominator of money. There is a central budgetary process and there is a Treasury Board. There is no such equivalent central rhythm to the regulatory process. Money is needed and is calculated to operate the regulatory machinery, but the expenditure *consequences* of regulation are rarely calculated in any direct financial sense, although they certainly are calculated in more general political terms.

For example, in response to increases in urban crime, governments could respond by acquiring more policemen and police patrol cars, an act which would appear directly in public budgets. On the other hand, governments could regulate a requirement that all homes be equipped with burglar alarms, an act which would affect private budgets but not appear in public budgets at all. While governments would typically not directly calculate the financial costs, they would certainly be aware in political terms of who was paying the price.

Even the above example, however, does not adequately reveal the nature of who wins and who loses in the use of regulatory instruments. It fails to reveal the *redistributive effects* of regulation. For less wealthy home-owners the cost of the burglar alarm would effectively be a regressive tax in comparison with a wealthy owner. This is a central issue in the regulation of wages and prices since the costs of regulation fall disproportionately on different economic classes.[47]

While the classification of policy outputs, the identification of a market in governing instruments, and the suggestion of linear movements over time along a continuum of governing instruments are useful concepts for analytical purposes, they cannot capture all of the related day-to-day, circular, less static, less linear realities of political and organizational behaviour.

This book focusses on the politics and management of economic policy and hence the twin dimensions of politics, values, and goals, and the instruments of governing are central to our analysis. This focus is essential if one wishes to analyse economic policy processes in the context of governing in a federal state and in the context of the central processes of cabinet government. It would be quite inaccurate, however, to equate all of the politics of economic policy to the above dimensions. Politics obviously occurs in the context of electing governments, as well as in the actual processes of governing. The outcomes of economic policy are obviously dependent upon complex incentives which operate in the marketplace and in the organizations of the non-governmental sector.

SUMMARY

This chapter has presented an analysis of the basic politics of Canadian economic policy with the focus on the role of the state, economic-policy goals, and the instruments of governing. The values and objectives of Canadian economic policy have much in common with other states with a liberal democratic tradition. They depart marginally, but importantly, in ways which ultimately reflect different perceptions about values and about the role of the Canadian state. The more persistent overt appearance of regional and other distributive goals on the economic-policy agenda are a reflection of these differences. The politics of Canadian economic policy are centrally tied to the need for making trade-offs in the usually conflicting goals of economic policy, whether the goals are construed in traditional terms or in the context of broader, so-called secondary goals. The understanding of the politics of Canadian economic policy cannot be based on a quantum jump from values and goals to administration and practice. We must follow a more torturous chain of cause and effect that requires an intellectual and a practical appreciation of how the politician in a federal state perceives and chooses the basic exhortative, spending, and regulatory instruments of governing, and of the complex and frequently confusing impact that these choices have on the broader socio-political processes. In short, it is essential that the politics of economic policy, and hence its management, be understood in terms of the problems of governing.

NOTES

1. See George Grant, *Empire and Technology* (Toronto, 1969), and G. Bruce Doern, *Science and Politics in Canada* (Montreal, 1972).

2. For a spectrum of interpretations, both Canadian and comparative, see George Grant, *Lament for a Nation* (Toronto, 1965); John Porter, *The Vertical Mosaic* (Toronto, 1965); Frank H. Underhill, *In Search of Canadian Liberalism* (Toronto, 1960); K. J. Rea and J. T. McLeod, eds., *Business and Government in Canada*, second ed. (Toronto, 1976), pp. 13-79, 334-45; Ralph Miliband, *The State in Capitalist Society* (London, 1969); Milton Friedman, *Capitalism and Freedom* (Chicago, 1962); and R. L. Heilbroner, *Between Capitalism and Socialism* (New York, 1970).

3. Robert Presthus, *Elite Accommodation in Canadian Politics* (Toronto, 1973). On the presence of Tory and socialist streaks see G. Horowitz, *Canadian Labour in Politics* (Toronto, 1968), and S. M. Lipset, *Agrarian Socialism* (New York, 1968).

4. Presthus, *Elite Accommodation*, p. 25.

5. Ibid., pp. 21-22.

6. See Rea and McLeod, eds., *Business and Government in Canada*, pp. 334-45 and Horowitz, *Canadian Labour in Politics*, Chapter 1. See also Harold Innis, *Essays in Canadian Economic History* (Toronto, 1956). For a case study of state intervention via private corporate means see Robert Chodos, *The CPR: A Century of Corporate Welfare* (Toronto, 1973).

7. Presthus, *Elite Accommodation*, pp. 28-30. For criticisms of the Presthus analysis see R. Whitaker, "Political Science Fiction", *Canadian Forum*, Vol. LIV (March 1974), pp. 11-12.

8. *To Know and Be Known*, Report of the Task Force on Information (Ottawa, 1969).

9. This was one of the central themes of Porter's analysis in *The Vertical Mosaic*, Chapter XII.

10. Canadian Labour Congress, *Labour's Manifesto for Canada* (Ottawa, 1976).

11. Ibid., pp. 10-11.

12. For analysis of the CLC and the labour movement see Horowitz, *Canadian Labour in Politics;* David Kwavnick, *Organized Labour and Pressure Politics* (Montreal, 1972); R. Miller and F. Isbister, *Canadian Labour in Transition* (Toronto, 1971); John Crispo, *International Unionism: A Study of Canadian-American Relations* (Toronto, 1967); and Robert Laxer, *Canada's Unions* (Toronto, 1976).

13. See J. T. McLeod "The Free Enterprise Dodo is No Phoenix", *Canadian Forum,* Vol. LVI, no. 663 (August 1976), pp. 6-9, and K. W. McNaught, "Plus ça change", *Canadian Forum,* Vol. LVI, no. 663 (August 1976), pp. 10-11.

14. See R. M. Burns, "The Operation of Economic and Fiscal Policy", in G. Bruce Doern and V. S. Wilson, eds., *Issues in Canadian Public Policy* (Toronto, 1974), Chapter 11.

15. L. J. Officer and L. B. Smith, eds., *Issues in Canadian Economics* (Toronto, 1974), p. 3.

16. Richard Simeon and David J. Elkins, "Regional Political Cultures", *Canadian Journal of Political Science,* Vol. VII, no. 3 (September 1974), p. 397. See also Donald V. Smiley, *Canada in Question: Federalism in the Seventies* (Toronto, 1972) and "Canada and the Quest for a National Policy", *Canadian Journal of Political Science,* Vol. VIII, no. 1 (March 1975), pp. 40-62.

17. See Porter, *The Vertical Mosaic, passim;* R. Manzer, *Canada: A Socio-Political Report* (Toronto, 1974), chapters 2 and 5; K. Bryden, *Old Age Pensions and Policy Making in Canada* (Montreal, 1974); Senate of Canada, *Poverty in Canada: A Report of the Special Senate Committee* (Ottawa, 1971); and Allan Maslove, *The Pattern of Taxation in Canada* (Ottawa, 1973). For comparative perspectives see Irving Kristol, "Taxes, Poverty and Equality", *The Public Interest,* no. 37 (Fall 1974), pp. 3-28; Hugh Heclo, *Modern Social Politics in Britain and Sweden* (New Haven, 1974); and J. F. Sleeman, *The Welfare State* (London, 1973).

18. See Douglas McCready and Conrad Winn, "Redistributive Policy", in C. Winn and J. McMenemy, eds., *Political Parties in Canada* (Toronto, 1976), pp. 206-27.

19. See R. W. Phidd, "The Role of Central Advisory Councils: The Economic Council of Canada", in G. Bruce Doern and Peter Aucoin, eds., *The Structures of Policy-Making in Canada* (Toronto, 1971), pp. 204-45.

20. See André Raynauld, "Unemployment-Inflation Trade-off on the Way Out?" *The Financial Post,* November 4, 1972, p. 33.

21. See Lipset, *Agrarian Socialism;* Allan C. Cairns, "The Electoral System and the Party System in Canada, 1921-1965", *Canadian Journal of Political Science,* Vol. I, no. 1 (March 1968), pp. 55-80; C. B. McPherson, *Democracy in Alberta* (Toronto, 1967); and M. Pinard, *The Rise of a Third Party: A Study in Crisis Politics* (Englewood Cliffs, N. J., 1971). On American regional policy see G. C. Cameron, *Regional Economic Development: The Federal Role* (Baltimore, 1970).

22. See Denis Smith, *Gentle Patriot* (Edmonton, 1973), pp. 21-26. See Porter, *The Vertical Mosaic,* Chapter XIV, and J. W. Pickersgill and D. F. Forster, *The Mackenzie King Record,* Vol. III (Toronto, 1970), Chapter 6.

23. The periods and the fiscal-policy data are usefully summarized in J. C. Strick, *Canadian Public Finance* (Toronto, 1973), pp. 138-55. To Strick's summary we have added the political and organizational summary. Sources used include *The National Finance,* published annually by the Canadian Tax Foundation, the *Canadian Annual Review,* and the Canada Year Book.

24. Quoted in *The Globe and Mail,* January 8, 1976, p. 7.

25. Ibid.

26. See excerpts from John Turner's speech, *The Globe and Mail,* March 16, 1976, p. 7.

27. See excerpts from Simon Reisman's speech, *The Globe and Mail,* April 2, 1976, p. 7.

28. Ibid.

29. Economic Council of Canada, *First Annual Review* (Ottawa, 1974), pp. 9-10.

30. Ibid., p. 38.

31. Economic Council of Canada, *Sixth Annual Review* (Ottawa, 1969), p. 7.

32. André Raynauld, Statement in House of Commons, *Minutes of Proceedings and Evidence of the Standing Committee on Finance, Trade and Economic Affairs* (Ottawa, 1972), 28th Parl.

33. Economic Council of Canada, *Fourth Annual Review* (Ottawa, 1967).

34. Economic Council of Canada, *First Annual Review,* p. 105.

35. Prices and Incomes Commission, *Summary Report: Inflation, Unemployment and Incomes Policy* (Ottawa, 1972).

36. Economic Council of Canada, *First Annual Review,* p. 23.

37. Economic Council of Canada, *Ninth Annual Review* (Ottawa, 1972).

38. See Sir Robert Shone, "The Machinery for Economic Planning: The National Economic Development Council", *Public Administration* (U.K.), Vol. XLIV (Spring 1966), pp. 18-22; and Andrew Shonfield, *Modern Capitalism: The Changing Balance of Public and Private Power* (London, 1965), pp. 71-175.

39. See Richard W. Phidd, "The Economic Council and Economic Policy Formulation in Canada". Unpublished PhD thesis, Queen's University, Kingston, 1972.

40. Doern and Wilson, eds., *Issues in Canadian Public Policy,* pp. 337-45.

41. Theodore Lowi, "Four Systems of Policy, Politics and Choice", *Public Administration Review* (July/August 1972), pp. 298-301.

42. Doern and Wilson, eds., *Issues in Canadian Public Policy*, p. 339.

43. Lawrence Pierce, *The Politics of Fiscal Policy Formation* (Pacific Palisades, Ca., 1971).

44. Government of Canada *The Way Ahead,* Working paper (Ottawa, 1976), pp. 23-27.

45. See G. Bruce Doern, Ian A. Hunter, O. Swartz, and V. Seymour Wilson, "The Structure and Behaviour of Canadian Regulatory Boards and Commissions: Multidisciplinary Perspectives", *Canadian Public Administration,* Vol. XVIII, no. 2 (Summer 1975), pp. 189-215.

46. See G. Bruce Doern, ed., *The Regulatory Process in Canada* (Toronto, 1978).

47. See C. D. Goodwin, ed., *Exhortation and Controls* (Washington, 1975).

PART TWO

The Central Processes of Economic-Policy Formulation and Management

The purpose of Part II is to examine in more detail the central processes of economic-policy formulation and management in the Government of Canada.

Chapter 3 will first place these processes in the context of cabinet government, including the collective and individual responsibilities of ministers, the cabinet committee system, the roles of central agencies, the priority-setting and budgetary process, and the different bases of political influence which characterize different Cabinet portfolios.

Chapter 4 will relate economic-policy processes to the dynamics of executive, bureaucratic behaviour. This requires specific understanding of the location among departments of the numerous instruments of economic management, the relationships between the Prime Minister and the Minister of Finance, between the Finance Minister and the President of the Treasury Board, and between the latter and the principal "spending" ministers.

Finally, Chapter 5 relates these more behavioural characteristics to the roles and career patterns of economic-policy leaders at the ministerial and deputy-ministerial levels.

CHAPTER THREE

Economic Policy and Cabinet Government

The making of Canadian economic policy occurs in a cabinet-parliamentary system of government and hence a major part of the politics and management of economic policy occurs in the executive-bureaucratic arena of the Canadian political system. The task of this chapter is to describe and evaluate the basic organization of economic policy-making in that arena which roughly encompasses the Cabinet itself and the upper levels of the federal bureaucracy.

It ought to be clear from our analysis in previous chapters that the organization of the Canadian government defies simple description. The Cabinet and its surrounding and supporting organizations are complex and hence an understanding of the politics and management of economic policy in the context of the organization and functioning of cabinet government requires a detailed and orderly assessment. Accordingly, this chapter will first relate economic-policy processes to the question of the cabinet role as a collective policy-making and decision-making body. With the importance of the collective features of the Cabinet in mind the analysis will then deal with the evolving cabinet committee system and with the central support organizations of the Cabinet, the PCO, the PMO, and the Treasury Board. In addition to the somewhat formal aspects of cabinet organization it is necessary to understand cabinet behaviour in terms of the different bases of influence which Cabinet portfolios generally provide for incumbent ministers. The chapter will therefore present a further classification of Cabinet portfolios to illustrate more completely the cabinet environment in which economic policy takes place. Finally, the chapter will focus more particularly on the central stages of economic policy and budgetary processes. This will involve the development of an understanding of both the revenue and expenditure budgetary processes.

With all of the above basic features of cabinet government and organization in mind we will be better able to assess in Chapter 4 the dynamics of cabinet and interagency bureaucratic processes as they affect the conduct of economic policy.

THE CABINET AS COLLECTIVITY

The Canadian Cabinet is first and foremost a collective decision-making body in which ministers are both collectively responsible to Parliament for general government policy and individually responsible for their own Cabinet portfolios and departmental programs.[1] While the position of the Prime Minister is obviously pre-eminent there are strong norms of collective responsibility and hence of the importance of some rough formal equality of all ministers in the Cabinet. In the Canadian context the imperatives of collectivity are reinforced not only by the growing complexity of government decision-making but also by the fact that the Canadian Cabinet is more than just a decision-making body.

The Canadian Cabinet is also a representative or legitimating institution notwithstanding the existence of Parliament, in that it is judged not only on what it does but on what it *appears* to do. Thus the Cabinet has had always not only to represent, but to appear to represent, the diverse regional and ethnic components of the Canadian population. Successive governments have not always been able to in fact achieve the optimum representation but most have been required to make a serious attempt. While it will be clear from our later analysis in this and succeeding chapters that the Prime Minister and some ministers and portfolios are obviously more influential than others, it is important to stress at the outset the continuing strength of collectivist norms in Canadian cabinet organization and behaviour. These norms are clearly more visibly tested precisely when, as in recent years, efforts are made to structure "inner" groups of decision-makers such as in the Cabinet Committee on Priorities and Planning, or "inner" groups of advisors such as in the PMO.[2]

The norms and traditions of cabinet collectivity, responsibility, and solidarity also influence policy-making, including economic policy-making, through the strong strictures regarding secrecy and confidentiality in intra Cabinet and intra bureaucratic decision-making processes.[3] Economic-policy processes have been influenced by arguments to break down the secrecy norms and to make the policy process more openly subject to external scrutiny.

The dispersal of influence and responsibility among ministers is also a function of the related constitutional practice in parliamentary systems of assigning responsibility for legislation and programs to individual ministers and departments to facilitate parliamentary accountability. The assignment of individual responsibility is also a function of the sheer complexity of government and of the need to delegate functions to ministers and departments on administrative and technical grounds. The constitutional principles and administrative necessities which generate individual ministerial authority and influence both reinforce the collective nature of the Cabinet in the broad sense of dispersing influence, and at the same time create one of the formal reasons for the need to view the Cabinet in ways that begin to break down the collectivist models.

In recent years many changes have been made to formal cabinet organization and policy processes. It is important to assess the changes made to the cabinet committee system and in the central support organizations of the Cabinet. Each of these areas of change has had different effects on the Cabinet as a collectivity.

THE CABINET COMMITTEE SYSTEM

The structure and dynamics of cabinet behaviour have been influenced in recent years by the development and evolution of the cabinet committee system as outlined in Figure 3:1. The existence of four co-ordinating committees, Priorities and Planning, Treasury Board, Legislation and House Planning, and Federal-Provincial Relations, and five standing subject-matter committees on Economic Policy, External Policy and Defence, Social Policy, Science, Culture and Information, and Government Operations has resulted in a more systematic management of cabinet deliberations.[4] Public policy proposals (economic or non-economic) must now run a gamut of evaluation and criticism which usually involves at least one subject-matter committee and usually more than one co-ordinating committee. This system stands in relative (though clearly not absolute) contrast to earlier periods when policy proposals could and frequently did reach the full

Figure 3:1 The Cabinet Committee System

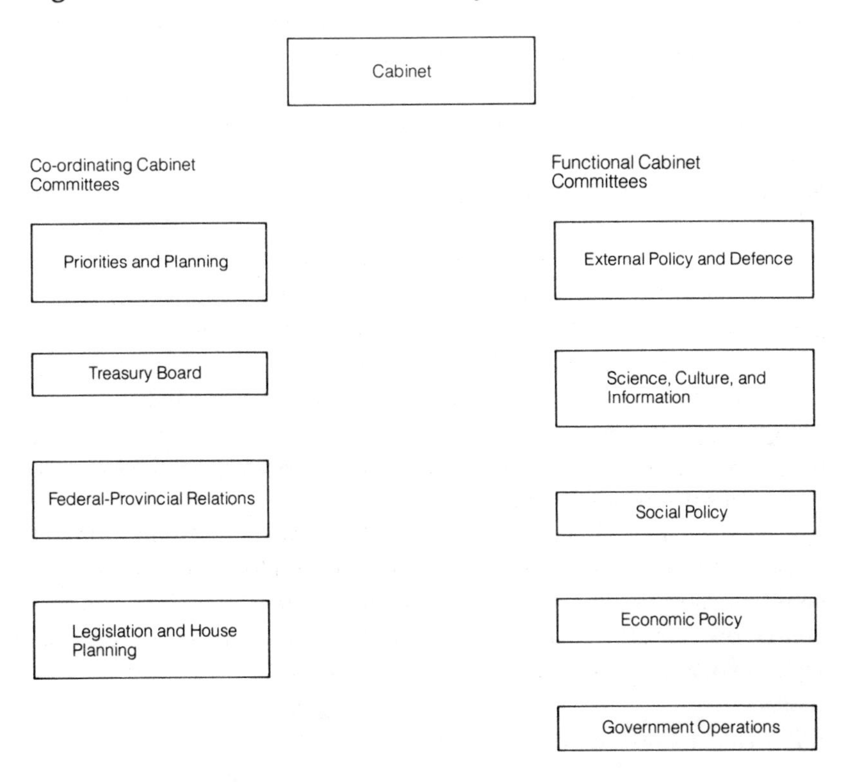

Cabinet without much prior assessment. Many of the committees now possess what amounts to *de facto* decision-making power in many areas albeit always subject to possible alteration or defeat when presented to the full Cabinet. Each of the cabinet committees will be briefly described but our focus in the economic-policy sphere will be primarily on the Priorities and Planning Committee, the Treasury Board, and the Economic Policy Committee, and secondarily on the Social Policy and Government Operations committees.

The Priorities and Planning Committee is chaired by the Prime Minister, and although its composition has not been officially revealed it includes the Minister of Finance, the President of the Treasury Board, and the chairmen of the functional cabinet committees. Its main functions have been described in the following terms:

(a) to consider the main areas of concern to ministers and develop the government's objectives;
(b) to establish the government's priorities by selecting the major objectives and policy thrusts;
(c) to ensure that Minister's main concerns and priorities are communicated within the government and outside;
(d) to ensure that planning issues are considered in the context of the current relevant political factors;
(e) to develop the framework and objective of each of the policy thrusts;
(f) to guide the allocation of resources, i.e. money, personnel, and time (ministerial, legislative, official, policy analysis), in accordance with the priorities;
(g) to ensure that Cabinet work is proceeding in accordance with the priorities, by monitoring the work programs of Cabinet Committees;
(h) to assess the degree to which the government's objectives and policy thrusts are being met.[5]

The committee is therefore central in the development and recommendation of the government's overall priorities to the full Cabinet. This priority-setting process is centrally linked to the economic policy and budgetary processes to be examined in more detail later in this chapter.

While the Priorities and Planning Committee does not ordinarily deal with the details of programs it is important to note that its functions are subject to change. For example, following the 1972 election, when the Trudeau government had to deal with a minority government situation, the Priorities and Planning Committee was required by the political realities of minority government to become more of a management committee of Cabinet. It also had to develop particularly close relationships with the Legislation and House Planning Committee in order to deal with the tenuous day-to-day exigencies of the minority House of Commons.

The Treasury Board, as noted in our earlier discussion, is the only statutory committee of the Cabinet.[6] It is headed by the President of the Treasury Board and consists of five other ministers including the Minister of Finance. The Treasury Board is the major management committee of the Cabinet as well as the expenditure committee. In its managerial role it has responsibilities regarding overall personnel policy, language policy, collective bargaining, and administrative policy. On the expenditure side the Treasury Board has a major co-ordinating role arising out of its preparation of annual expenditure plans, based on the priorities developed in the Priorities and Planning Committee. It is only in the past decade that the Treasury Board was separated from the Finance Department and was headed by its own minister. As pointed out earlier, this differentiation of role was suggested by the Glassco Commission to give greater emphasis to the general questions of governmental management.

The Federal-Provincial Relations Committee is also chaired by the Prime Minister and, as its name implies, it has responsibilities for insuring that federal policies are related to, and take into account, the implication of action by the provincial level of government.[7] Thus, constitutional issues and federal-provincial consultation are partly, though not exclusively, examined through this committee.

The Legislation and House Planning Committee is chaired by the President of the Privy Council who in recent years has been the governmental House Leader. The committee's role is to facilitate the legislative priorities of the government and to see that government bills reflect the specific policies of the government. The committee prepares, for Cabinet consideration and approval, the government legislative program for each parliamentary session.

In contrast to the horizontal, cross-governmental roles of the above four co-ordinating committees, the five functional committees tend to deal with the more vertical dimensions of government, dividing the total range of policies and programs into functional or broad subject-matter areas, albeit still involving horizontal relations with several departments in their functional area. The External Policy and Defence Committee is involved in the development and review of Canadian foreign and defence policies. The growing relationships between economic policy and foreign policy need little elaboration and thus the external policy and defence committee possesses an important latent role in economic-policy issues. The Science, Culture and Information Committee has policy-review and development responsibilities in a wide range of government activity. The areas covered include science and technology, culture and information, as well as environment, urban affairs, broadcasting and communications, publishing, official languages, education, fitness and amateur sports, and national parks. The above list of areas illustrates that the title of the committee is not entirely reflective of the policy domain for which it has responsibility.

The Social Policy Committee has responsibilities very closely related to economic-policy considerations, particularly on the supply side of economic policy and with regard to redistributive issues. The committee's role involves the development and review of policies dealing with health, the education of native Canadians, students' summer employment, vocational and occupational training, Indian policy, penal policies, status of women, regional equity, social security programs, and equality under the law.

The Government Operations Committee is responsible for policies regarding the renewable and non-renewable resource sectors as well as the infrastructure needed to support their development. Thus the committee deals with many specific programs having an economic character including energy policy, mining and transportation, public works, fisheries, agriculture, trade, and industrial development. It also deals with items not clearly falling within the policy area assigned to another committee.

Many of the areas under the Government Operations Committee were once part of the responsibility of the former Economic Policy and Programs Committee. Recently these have been divided between the Operations Committee and a separate Economic Policy Committee. The Economic Policy Committee is involved in periodic reviews of the current economic situation to insure that the short-term economic goals of the government and economic policies designed to attain these goals are compatible, and to insure that the longer-term economic-growth policies are examined in a co-ordinated way. Thus, the committee is involved in commenting and reporting on the main indicators of economic activity, taxation policy, the aggregate impact of expenditure allocation, and the structure and adaptability of Canadian industry. While its title would imply a lead role in economic policy, the committee does not function as an aggressive initiator of economic policy. It is quite clearly a support committee to its chairman, the Minister of Finance, and to the Cabinet Committee on Priorities and Planning.

The brief description of the cabinet committee functions illustrates all too clearly the difficulty of putting "economic" policy or any other policy into watertight compartments. Spillovers abound in the committee process. Three other observations about the committee process are warranted. First, ministers are members of more than one committee and thus the impression of policy integration occurring through multiple membership must be qualified by the time demands of committee work and the widely varying degrees of interest and preparation by individual ministers. Of even greater importance to the economic-policy process is the fact that so-called economic-policy issues in the Cabinet increasingly emerge from cabinet committees other than the Committee on Economic Policy, the Treasury Board, or the Committee on Priorities and Planning. Finally, it is important to stress that the committee process has resulted in a considerable amount of decentralization in that the committees have taken on *de facto* decision-making roles on some areas of decision-making which in early periods of Canadian cabinet government would have been decided by the full Cabinet.

The cabinet committee system is itself a reflection of the multiple and conflicting roles played by contemporary governments. The recent reorganizations are perhaps the most explicit reflection in Canada of an evolving concern both about the management of government and about the management of the economy. No understanding of economic-policy processes in the Government of Canada can be complete until the role of the committee system is taken into full account. It is also essential to have an awareness of the role of the central support organizations of the Cabinet, namely the PCO, the Treasury Board secretariat, and the PMO.

NB

THE CENTRAL SUPPORT ORGANIZATIONS OF THE CABINET

Coinciding roughly, though not entirely, with the emergence of the Trudeau government in 1968, have been extensive elaborations of the roles of the central support agencies of the Cabinet, the Privy Council Office (PCO), the Prime Minister's Office (PMO), and the Treasury Board and the Finance Department.[8] Since we will be discussing the Finance Department's role in great detail in Chapter 6 this section will focus on the PCO, PMO, and the Treasury Board. The development of each of these agencies has been influenced by a concern, which began to emerge in the mid-1960s, about the adequacy of the Prime Minister's and the Cabinet's central policy-support organization. This concern about central public-policy organization was a general one and was reflected in the development, during the 1960s, of a planning, programing, and budgeting system (PPB), the previously described cabinet committee system, the creation of major central advisory councils such as the Economic Council of Canada and the Science Council of Canada, the emergence of normative planning philosophies among Prime Minister Trudeau and his advisors, and the influence of the Glassco Commission recommendations.

The PCO, PMO, and the Treasury Board are important in three respects. First, they have considerable influence as organizations because of their custody over central cross-cutting activities of government. Second, they have been involved in various efforts to restructure economic-policy advice in that they have been suggested as possible locations for alternative centres of economic-policy advice either in competition with, or perhaps as a complement to, the Finance Department. Finally, the organizations afford to their bureaucratic heads, the Secretary to the Cabinet, the Principal Secretary to the Prime Minister, and the Secretary to the Treasury Board, great personal influence in the policy process generally and in the economic-policy process as well.

In a general sense the roles of the PCO, PMO, and Treasury Board have always existed. The roles of strategic governmental co-ordinator, partisan political advisor, and general manager, are present in any government in one form or another. In the 1960s these central roles in the Government of Canada underwent a transformation in that the roles became more organizationally differentiated, less personalized, more bureaucratic, and more active. The organizational differentiation occured with the separation of the Treasury Board from the Finance Department and with the clearer identification of a Prime Minister's Office. Roles previously played by key officials supported by very small organizational staffs became less personalized precisely because of the bureaucratization and growth of the support organizations around them. This bureaucratization was perhaps most visibly reflected by the development in the late 1960s of "planning" units or branches in each of the central organizations.

It was precisely because of the differentiation and bureaucratization that the key roles were given more time and capacity and hence could be carried out in a more active manner. This activeness has undoubtedly made it possible for more aggressive initiatives to emerge from the central agencies. Hence, with regard to the PCO and PMO in particular, we have witnessed far more concern about both the degree of influence, and the legitimacy of the influence of these agencies and their key personalities. They create and foster concern about super-groups of unelected advisors usurping the legitimate roles of the elected politicians.[9] This concern is normal and important but its real import can be easily exaggerated, especially in the long run when one considers the other interplay of forces reflected in the cabinet committees and in the regular departments of government.

The transformation from a fused, personalized, and passive relationship to a more differentiated, bureaucratized, and active one is clearly a relative change. The new pattern does not totally replace the old. Recent changes in fact reflect the constant contradictory demands of government policy organization. When differentiation occured, it raised, in a renewed way, the need for new elements of co-ordination and integration. When significant bureaucratization occured, it did not replace the personalized nature which characterized the way most policy information is exchanged between policy actors. Indeed it creates a new need to insure that the bureaucratized units do not take on roles, or interpretations of roles, which distort the complementarity of policy roles which the key actors in the PCO, PMO, Treasury Board (and Finance Department) must understand.[10] And finally, when activism becomes more possible, it is important to stress that it too will only be a relative change because no matter how differentiated and bureaucratized the main roles become, they will always be severely constrained by the greater volume of incoming demands of the even larger organizations which surround them.

The essence of the central roles is still complementary in nature. The provision of strategic political advice, including the values and priorities of the political system, are fed to the Prime Minister and Cabinet by the PMO and in part by the PCO (as well as, of course, by a host of other channels of political communication). The PCO, however, tends to be the main source of overall governmental and strategic organizational advice. It provides the basic staff support to the Cabinet and to all of the cabinet committees except the Treasury Board and it insures that adequate analysis and co-ordination of policies and policy proposals is carried out. The main source of advice regarding the broad economic and fiscal impact of government activity is the Department of Finance, and the main source of advice on the general, expenditure, administrative, and managerial implications of both new and existing programs (and of the relationships between the two) is the Treasury Board and its staff.

An analysis of these basic roles and their recent transformation alerts us to the importance and continuing presence of what might be called a "functional" inner cabinet. Certain cabinet roles are obviously inherently more important than others. The Canadian cabinet system as a collectivity does not constitutionally admit the existence of an inner cabinet for the reasons previously discussed, but the analysis of central organizational roles requires some considerable alteration of the formal constitutional characteristic. The analysis in the next section of this chapter will elaborate further on the varying bases of Cabinet portfolio influence.

The periodic and recurring discussions about the establishment of an economic policy advisory capability in the PCO, PMO, or Treasury Board, in competition with the Finance Department must be assessed in the light of the above features of central policy organization. Such discussions have usually reflected a concern about the perceived monopoly power of the Finance Department in matters of economic policy and about ways of counteracting it. Such concern is not new and has been reflected in various ways. Walter Gordon's use of "outside" advisors in his ill-fated budget of 1963, and the establishment of the Economic Council of Canada in the same year were illustrations of early concern.[11]

The question can also be raised less visibly by the transfer of key senior personnel. For example, the movement of Robert Bryce from the Finance Department to the PCO immediately gave to the PCO a highly personalized form of countervailing economic-policy capacity arising out of Bryce's previous experience in the Department of Finance. In recent years concern has surfaced about giving to the PCO and the PMO a greater economic advisory capability. In the late 1960s strong suggestions were made that the PCO ought to have greater staff resources in the economic-policy field to support the Economic Policy and Priorities and Planning committees. In 1975 the Prime Minister began to utilize a small group of non-governmental advisors operating through the PMO to augment his economic advice.[12]

The desire to have some alternative source of economic advice is understandable when viewed from the perspective of the PCO and the PMO and when viewed from the larger democratic perspective of avoiding the concentration of power. At the same time, however, the nature of government organization in general, and cabinet government in particular, suggests the limitations of dispersing formal economic advisory power too greatly. There must obviously be a focal point. Thus the Finance Department's instinctive opposition to such dispersal must not be seen entirely as an unbridled desire for power. Its opposition is, in part, also a reflection of a genuine concern about the need for an overall co-ordinative focus. The contradictory need both to disperse power and to concentrate it, if co-ordination is to be approximated, are thus amply illustrated both in the general organization of the Cabinet and in the arguments about competitive or complementary economic policy centres within the central support organization of the Cabinet.

THE BASES OF CABINET PORTFOLIO INFLUENCE

While the evolving system of cabinet committees and cabinet central support organizations are important formal arenas of cabinet and executive-bureaucratic behaviour, it is important to place the making of economic policy in the context of other less openly discernible characteristics of cabinet behaviour. These characteristics relate to the different bases of cabinet portfolio influence.

In an earlier work we have presented a classification of horizontal and vertical cabinet portfolios.[13] This classification of four clusters of cabinet portfolios is reproduced below.

Traditional Horizontal Co-ordinative Portfolios*

External Affairs	Finance	Fisheries
Justice	Treasury Board	Small Business
Prime Minister and President of the Privy Council		

New Horizontal Co-ordinative Portfolios

Urban Affairs
Science and Technology

*By "portfolio" is meant the formal designation of a cabinet minister. The list clearly does not include the large number of other units of government such as agencies, boards, and commissions, which report to or through each minister.

Administrative Co-ordinative Portfolios
- National Revenue
- Public Works
- Supply and Services

Vertical Constituency Portfolios
- Agriculture
- Communications
- Consumer and Corporate Affairs
- Energy, Mines and Resources
- Environment
- Indian Affairs and Northern Development
- Industry, Trade and Commerce
- Manpower and Immigration
- National Defence
- National Health and Welfare
- Post Office
- Regional Economic Expansion
- Secretary of State
- Solicitor General
- Transport
- Veterans Affairs

The classification is based on criteria related to the basic aggregate sources or categories of cabinet portfolio influence. These criteria include: the size of the portfolio's budget (and the related importance of the portfolio's constituency), the portfolio's degree of responsibility for co-ordination, and knowledge or research. It is intended to assist the development of an understanding of the Cabinet beyond the normal generalizations we make about cabinet behaviour. These generalizations as described earlier include: the acknowledged importance of the rough *formal* equality of all ministers in the Cabinet; the pre-eminent position of the Prime Minister; and the importance of regional and ethnic balance in Canadian cabinet-making. The classification is based on the reasonably simple fact that portfolios do possess differing combinations of assets or bases of influence which can be reduced, for analytical purposes, to include financial resources, hierarchical responsibility for co-ordination, and knowledge or research. The first two assets are probably more familiar but the latter warrants separate mention particularly in view of the creation in the early 1970s of Cabinet portfolios which are based largely on policy research criteria.

The classification is thus intended to provide further insight into the additional informal judgments and estimates of the real or potential influence of cabinet portfolios. In anticipation of the analysis in Chapters 4 and 5, however, it is important to utilize the classification, at this stage of our analysis, with the clear understanding that the bases of influence utilized do not exhaust all of the determinants of Cabinet portfolio influence or of individual influence of cabinet ministers.

It is recognized, of course, that reliance upon three or four aggregate variables cannot possibly do justice to the role of other more particular variables that can, and do, affect the more precise ranking of influence among particular portfolios and among particular ministers at different times. In certain circumstances variables such as the seniority or experience of particular ministers, the demonstrated competence or ability of a minister to exercise leadership and to manage his portfolio (especially when under intense parliamentary, intergovernmental, and media scrutiny and controversy), the personal relationship of a minister to the Prime Minister, and the extent to which the minister's policy field is high on the government's current political agenda, can have a major impact on the real or perceived influence of a portfolio and its incumbent minister.

Because of the importance of these other variables it is not possible to use the classification suggested above to determine, for example, whether at any given time the Minister of Regional Economic Expansion is more influential in the Cabinet than the Minister of Justice, or whether the Solicitor General is more influential than the Minister of Supply and Services. No classification could adequately capture those more precise relationships. The classification of portfolios presented here is based on broader characteristics of influence. It is clearly a more static classification and hence has obvious weaknesses with respect to detailed comparisons of individual portfolios. It is presented, however, as a classification which, by identifying several clusters of portfolios, can serve a useful analytical purpose. It is presented on the premise that it is both useful and important to step back and take a broad snapshot of the basic horizontal and vertical patterns of government illustrated by the Cabinet portfolios. As was the case in our previous discussion of cabinet committees it needs to be stressed that the designation of what is "vertical" and "horizontal" is an imprecise process. Generally, though, it is still important to identify portfolios in these relative categories.

The cluster identified as *traditional horizontal co-ordinative portfolios* includes the most politically influential portfolios, namely the Prime Minister, External Affairs, Finance, Justice, and the Treasury Board. These portfolios form the basis of a functional "inner" cabinet which is not an "inner" cabinet in a legal or constitutional sense but rather in a functional sense if one considers the political criteria noted above. With the exception of the Finance department these portfolios do not directly possess large operating budgets. They have inherent high policy influence because of the formal authority they possess and because they afford their occupants the highest number of strategic opportunities to intervene in almost any policy issue. They each deal respectively with the traditionally most basic horizontal or cross-cutting dimensions of government policy, namely overall political leadership and strategy, foreign policy and the foreign implications of domestic policy fields, aggregate economic and fiscal policy, the basic legal and judicial concepts and values of the state, and the overall management of government spending programs.

The cluster identified as *new horizontal co-ordinative portfolios* includes the ministries of state, such as the Ministry of State for Science and Technology and the Ministry of State for Urban Affairs.[14] The federal ministries of state have been created explicitly on policy-research criteria. They were generally not intended to have large expenditure programs as such, but rather were created to develop policy research and to claim a co-ordinative role on the basis of their research and policy-analysis functions. Hence, they represent the first explicit attempt to differentiate a research criterion as being almost the sole basis for potential influence of a Cabinet portfolio.[15] It should be stressed, however, that the above portfolios are not the only new aspirants as relatively new horizontal co-ordinative portfolios. At least three other recently created portfolios, Regional Economic Expansion, Environment, and Communications, were accorded co-ordinative responsibilities. They join a very old portfolio, the Secretary of State, in having functions which, it can be argued, represent newly discovered (relatively speaking) cross-cutting horizontal dimensions of government. They could be included in this cluster because their mixed research and program responsibilities represent recently differentiated cross-cutting activities of government. Hence, one of the important features of current cabinet structure is the impressive (and relatively sudden) increase in the sheer number of portfolios which claim and covet co-ordinative policy roles.

The cluster identified as *administrative co-ordinative portfolios* includes portfolios such as National Revenue, Public Works, and Supply and Services. These portfolios are usually perceived to be among the least influential of cabinet positions. They are more likely to be perceived as administrative, "nuts and bolts" departments needed to keep government operating. In recent years the functions which these portfolios carry out have been viewed more and more by some as "common service" agencies. This implies a non-policy function, although frequently the occupants of these portfolios will quite appropriately refuse to accept such a designation. The portfolios deal with budgets that are quite modest, but the mere fact that they deal with the means of government (e.g., buildings, real estate, supplies, tax and revenue collection) implies a latent and sometimes manifest co-ordinative role. These activities also are closely related to traditional but, nonetheless, important values such as probity and honesty in government.

The final cluster identified as *vertical constituency portfolios* includes well over half of the Cabinet portfolios. These include the portfolios with the largest budgets and represent the vertical dimension of government in that they tend to extend outward to deal with their respective constituencies. It is likely that within this cluster are the group of portfolios which, generally speaking, are second in order of general influence, ranking behind the traditional horizontal co-ordinative portfolios identified earlier. The largest part of the budgets of these portfolios represent existing ongoing programs, but within these programs there are often large amounts of discretionary spending. The occupants of these portfolios therefore possess a fairly strong constant base of influence. This base can be augmented or reduced when the policy field in their portfolio becomes the object of political review, criticism, or controversy. Occupants of these portfolios, however, likely have mathematically fewer opportunities to intervene in other policy fields or portfolios, at least in comparison with the traditional and perhaps even the new horizontal co-ordinating portfolios. They obviously possess some opportunities to intervene because of their cabinet committee memberships, but these will still be less frequent, generally speaking, than the traditional co-ordinative portfolios.

Certain elementary observations emerge after one has developed an understanding of Cabinet portfolios and their aggregate bases of influence. These observations will be made generally in the first instance and then related more specifically to the main "economic" portfolios. Having in mind the classification of the four clusters of Cabinet portfolios presented above, the practical meaning of cabinet policy *co-ordination* ought not be viewed in simplistic terms. Co-ordination is a concept which is dear to the heart of all management reformers. It is always viewed with approval, but it is rarely examined in terms of the logic of its meaning in a political and governmental setting. It is precisely in the governmental sector that simplistic managerial notions of what co-ordination involves can be not only naive but ludicrous. Co-ordination implies some agreement, over a fairly constant period of time, about both objectives and priorities.

The above analysis has suggested that there are logically several broad clusters of portfolios, three of which carry out functions which cross-cut government and hence imply co-ordinative roles. But each cluster, and each portfolio within each cluster, represents a bundle of competing political objectives, and ultimately of competing priorities — and these in total suggest two important realities about real co-ordination in a political setting. First, there is constant positional competition over who, or what portfolio, will be co-ordinating other portfolios. This competition has been intensified by the recent insertion of new co-ordinative portfolios. Finally, because of the constant competition over values and priorities which the portfolios represent, it remains true that many elements of government and of the constituencies served by various programs and portfolios, literally and naturally, do not wish to be fully co-ordinated, precisely because of their desire to have maximum political flexibility and freedom. It is to be stressed as well that questions of co-ordination can have a strictly technical dimension as well, generating both centrifugal and centripetal forces in interagency relations.

Very much related to the question of co-ordination is the question of the separation of policy from administration referred to in Chapter 1. While the four clusters of Cabinet portfolios clearly imply differentials in power and influence they also illustrate the different bases of influence on which certain portfolios inherently rely. Hence, they suggest very real limits on how differentiated these tiers of influence are or will be permitted to become. Attempts to separate the roles or overtly publicize their differences will likely serve only to reinforce the reality of their close relationship. In political terms the availability of several potential sources of influence for portfolios suggests that what in fact exists are two broad structures of policy which are continuously engaged in intense competition over on-going and new resources and, just as importantly, over on-going and new positions in the governing organizations.

None of the above observations on co-ordination should be taken to imply that no co-ordination exists. There are obviously centres of power and regular cycles of behaviour which contribute greatly to the co-ordination of economic policy. In this regard it is essential that our analysis of Canadian cabinet government processes must relate the making of economic policy to the basic stages in the annual economic policy-budgetary process, the central process around which the making of economic policy primarily, though not totally, occurs.

THE ANNUAL ECONOMIC POLICY-BUDGETARY PROCESS

It is important to stress that we are describing the supposedly normal sequence of events in rather formal terms. The dynamics and abnormalities of the process must await assessment in Chapter 4. The making of basic economic policy is tied to the regular priority-setting and budgetary process of the Government of Canada. The linkage between the economic budget and the expenditure determination process can be broken, of course, because economic circumstances may require the Finance Minister to present more than one economic budget in a year. Thus it is important to keep in mind the continuous process of short-term economic forecasting and evaluation which may, and frequently does, operate apart from the regular expenditure budget process. There are, therefore, two senses in which the "budget" may be viewed. The economic budget and the expenditure budget must in part answer to the requirements of the management of the economy and the management of the government respectively The two are increasingly interrelated but they are clearly *not* identical.

At the level of budgetary information it is also important to keep in mind the important fact that the federal government presents its budget on three different accounting bases, with each base serving a different purpose. The three budgets are the administrative budget, the consolidated cash budget, and the national accounts budget:

> The administrative budget is the budget presented to the House of Commons incorporating the departmental estimates of expenditure and estimates of tax proceeds. It is the least comprehensive of the three budgets and excludes the transactions of some major government funds, notably the Old Age Security Fund, the Unemployment Insurance Fund, government superannuation and pension funds, and various loans and advances made by the federal government. This budget serves administrative and control purposes. . . . It is commonly referred to as "the budget", and is the focus of the budget speech of the Minister of Finance.
>
> The consolidated cash budget is a measure of all government cash flows. It incorporates the administrative budget and all other government payments and receipts, including net borrowing and lending transactions. It is the most comprehensive of the three budgets and is useful for internal cash management purposes. . . .
>
> The national accounts budget serves economic analysis. It is more comprehensive than the administrative budget, but excludes certain transactions found in the consolidated cash budget. Transactions from the Old Age Security Fund and the Unemployment Insurance Fund, and from other government trust funds are included, but government borrowing and lending operations are excluded, as are transactions of a purely bookkeeping nature which have no impact on the economy. The national accounts budget concentrates on income-creating and resource-absorbing transactions and therefore includes only those operations that have a direct impact on the flow of incomes in the economy. Furthermore, it is based on the accrual method of accounting in which revenues are accounted when earned rather than received, and expenditures are recorded when liabilities are incurred rather than when actually paid, and therefore more appropriately measures the timing of the impact of government operations on the economy.[16]

Figure 3:2 portrays the basic stages of the annual economic policy-budgetary process and indicates the primary agencies involved in this process. For purposes of analysis the three stages are identified as forecasting, cabinet decision-making, and parliamentary scrutiny.[17] The last stage involving parliamentary scrutiny takes us beyond the strict limits of the executive-bureaucratic arena of Canadian govern-

FIGURE 3:2—THE FISCAL AND BUDGETARY POLICY-MAKING PROCESS

	Prime Minister (PMO, PCO)	*Priorities Planning Committee*	*Economic Policy Committee*	*Finance*	*Treasury Board*	*Bank of Canada*	*Industry, Trade and Commerce*	*Statistics Canada*	*Manpower and Immigration*	*Taxation and National Revenue*	*Parliament and Parliamentary Committees*	*Other Outside Agencies*
	Departments, Agencies and Units											
Policy Process Stages												
1. *Forecasting*												
forecasting sectoral activity and intentions				X		X	X	X	X	X		*e.g.:* CMHC, Conference Board of Canada, Economic Council, Institute of Quantitative Analysis
estimates of Gov't 'A' Budget spending					X							
development of fiscal framework options		X	X	X	X	X						
2. *Cabinet Decision-Making*												
approval of Fiscal Framework and 'B' Budget limits	X	X		X	X							
expenditures guidelines for A and B budgets		X										
tax changes	X			X								
approval of estimates					X							
3. *Parliamentary Scrutiny*												
Blue Book Estimates					X						All Committees	
Budget Speech and Debate				X							House of Commons	
Budget Resolutions				X							House Committee on Finance	
Budget Bills				X							House Committee on Finance	
Auditor General's Report											Public Accounts	

ment, the area with which this book is primarily concerned, but is presented to develop a full description of the cycle. In addition, it is important to point out that the anticipation of parliamentary reaction or opposition, even in times of majority government, is a normal part of the executive-bureaucratic political calculations of economic-policy measures. In terms of general timing the process begins roughly twelve months prior to the fiscal year for which the particular budget is applicable.

The *forecasting stage* involves forecasting and data-gathering by Statistics Canada, the departments of Finance, Taxation and National Revenue, Supply and Services, and Industry, Trade and Commerce regarding the current and likely activity in each of the major sectors of economic activity—for example, business inventories and investment, housing starts, growth in households, consumer spending and saving intentions, and expenditure projections of other levels of government. Estimates of government revenue from various tax and revenue sources are also developed. In consultation with the Treasury Board, the central expenditure and management committee of the Cabinet, estimates of the government's own likely expenditures for on-going programs (the so-called "A" Budget) are also developed. Working through the support of the Economic Policy Committee of the Cabinet (chaired by the Minister of Finance) the Department of Finance develops the so-called "fiscal framework" options. The framework sets out the *aggregate* relationship between revenue and expenditure and the way in which any deficit differential (the norm in recent years) might be funded (by borrowing and/or tax changes). The specifics of the taxes to be changed are not assessed at this stage although senior officials in the Finance Department, and the Minister of Finance in particular, may already have formulated detailed plans in this regard. In general, however, the forecasting stage is intended to set out the likely topography of the Canadian economy for the time period in question. The fiscal framework goes a long way toward settling the aggregate amount of leeway available for new spending (the so-called "B" Budget) and toward settling the basic stabilization assumptions and parameters of the government. Some manoeuvring room undoubtedly remains but not much.

The *Cabinet decision-making stage* involves the approval and final determination of the fiscal framework. While, as noted earlier, the

Economic Policy Committee of the Cabinet is a major working committee, it is the Cabinet Committee on Priorities and Planning that finally settles on the fiscal framework and on the priority guidelines that are to govern the allocation of expenditures among programs and departments, especially the allocation of so-called new money for the "B" Budget. It is on the basis of the guidelines, and on the basis of the total new money available as determined by the fiscal framework, that the Treasury Board negotiates and "haggles" with departments to determine the final detailed allocation of resources. These are ultimately presented as the estimates to Parliament.

This latter phase should not be interpreted as being wholly a "nuts and bolts" exercise because the guidelines that emanate from the Priorities and Planning Committee are usually sufficiently broad and vague as to generate considerable room for departmental and agency rivalry and for a considerable reinterpretation of *de facto* priorities even though still done within the rubric of the language contained in the guidelines. Thus the guideline may simply express and endorse a high priority for "regional economic development", leaving to the politics of the budgetary process the details of whether the money will go to the Department of Regional Expansion or the Department of Transport or other departments which could (and would) claim that their programs are related to the priority expressed in the guidelines. It is because of this manoeuvrability in the budgetary process and because of the extensive recent use of the expenditure instruments that the making of "economic" policy in Canada must increasingly contemplate the role of the Treasury Board and the major "spending" departments.

While the economic and budgetary processes are the most normal and visible rhythms of behaviour in governments, not all of the priority-setting process or the processes of economic management can be understood or subsumed under the budgetary processes. For example, let us assume that the Cabinet, through its priority-setting exercises (which, in the Trudeau years, have included full Cabinet "think" sessions in the rustic splendor of Meach Lake) determines that the governments priorities are (hypothetically) as follows; i) the reduction of inflation; ii) the promotion of national unity through language policy; iii) the reduction of regional disparities; iv) the re-equipment of the armed forces; and v) improving competition in the economy.

The political realities of governing are such that not all of these priorities have equal expenditure or general economic consequences. For example the first priority might be achieved by regulatory means by creating an Anti-Inflation Board. While the use of the regulatory instrument would have enormous *private* expenditure impact, it would not have an impact on the government's expenditure budgets, other than perhaps the increased cost of running the board. The second priority might be achieved by increasing the spending, through provincial governments, on language programs in primary and secondary schools. The third might be promoted by altering the regulation of transportation freight rates. The fourth priority would require an expenditure, say, of one billion dollars. The fifth priority could be recognized by creating a royal commission on corporate concentration, a kind of symbolic but fairly inexpensive governing response.

In the above hypothetical scenario of priorities, the second and fourth items have the largest *government* expenditure impact. The first and third would have minimum impact on government budgets but would have *regulatory* impact on *private* budgets and behaviour and certainly on the national and regional economies. The final priority might only be symbolic but could affect the climate of economic management because business might read it as a sign of uncertainty and of changing government views.

Each of the above priorities, moreover, has different needs for legislation. Some may require no legislation; others may require extensive legislative changes. Thus the overall governmental priority, economic, and expenditure budget processes become entangled with different legislative and regulatory processes, as the goals and instruments of governing are chosen, altered, and balanced.

It should be stressed, moreover, that the above-noted hypothetical priorities do not reveal the considerable variation that has occurred under the overall priority-setting processes instituted since 1968. These processes have reflected the changing political and economic circumstances in which the federal government has found itself. For example, in 1968-69 and 1969-70 the priority-setting exercise was characterized by the development of a short list of general but tough priorities including language policies and the removal of regional disparities. Most other programs were held constant in budgetary terms. The priorities reflected the initial flowering of the Trudeau "rational" priority-setting process, and were aided by the newness and hence the power of the 1968 Trudeau mandate. The toughness and shortness of the priority list were also aided by the 1969 fight against inflation which included an effort to curtail government expenditure growth. The 1968-69 effort included, among other things, the development of an "x" budget of so-called expendable programs, and resulted in the cancellation of programs such as the Winter Works scheme (albeit soon to be resurrected in a new form a few years later when unemployment was perceived as the main problem).

By 1970, however, both the general political environment and the pressure of ministers and bureaucratic departments made the priority exercise less formally "rational" in the abstract sense of that word, but quite politically rational. Thus the October Crisis of 1970 converted the priority-setting exercise into a vague search for programs that would aid "national unity". In addition the pressure from ministers and departments that had been "ranked" low for two or three years in a row increased greatly. They increasingly demanded fairer treatment and equity in the budgetary and priority-setting process. These internal arguments and the need to maintain bureaucratic and ministerial peace and tranquility were aided by, and reflected in, the declining political strength of the Trudeau government in 1971 and 1972 and by growing unemployment. By the 1972 election, the priority-setting process generated a veritable "wish-list" of priorities.

Between 1972 and the election of 1974, during a time of minority government, the priority-setting process, all efforts to the contrary notwithstanding, was virtually indistinguishable from the processes of parliamentary survival. Thus, during this time the Priorities and Planning Committee and the Legislation and House Planning Committee of the Cabinet had to work even more closely than usual.

As with most experiments in human organization, people charged with responsibility for the priority-setting process tried to learn from their early experience. Thus, following the return to a majority Trudeau government in 1974, efforts were made to enhance both the legitimacy of the priority-setting process among ministers and their officials, and the follow-up and implementation of the process. Hence the 1975 priority exercise included more elaborate ministerial meetings as well as the submission from departments of their plans regarding how they would contribute to and implement the priorities. An effort was also made in the mid-1970s to make the priority list more explicit and detailed.

But alas, political and economic circumstances would not stand still. The imposition of the October 1975 anti-inflation program relegated most of the 1975 priority exercise to the dustbin. By 1976 a further apparatus, the committee of ten deputy ministers known as DM 10 had been added to help ministers generate priorities and options for the post-income controls program.

Thus again it is essential to stress that, while considerable effort has been expended to rationalize, in a formal way, the priority-setting process, and that the economic-policy and budgetary process is tied to these more rationalized processes, the political pressures imposed by the economy as well as the internal dynamics of the Cabinet and bureaucracy exert their own "rationality". Hence the concept of an A and B Budget reflects the political conflict between new and ongoing programs and values, and the concepts of a fiscal framework, the economic budget, the priority guidelines, and the expenditure budget reflect the growing tension between the management of the economy and the management of the government.

The Cabinet-level decision-making phase of the economic and expenditure budget process which annually attracts the most attention is the final determination and approval of tax changes to implement and give effect to the fiscal policy. It is at this stage that the principle actors become reduced to the Minister of Finance, the Prime Minister, and senior officials in the Department of Finance. Maximum secrecy is imposed at this stage, primarily to insure that individuals or groups cannot unfairly profit from advance knowledge of the details of tax changes. Needless to say the determination of precise tax changes, despite its lateness in the basic stages of the economic-policy process, still confers on this small coterie of policy-makers enormous power to affect millions of individual Canadians.

Ordinarily the *parliamentary scrutiny phase* would be treated as a fairly routine and predictable part of the economic-policy process. It involves the presentation of the Blue Book containing the expenditure estimates which are then considered and scrutinized and approved by the various parliamentary committees. It involves the presentation of the Budget Papers and the Budget Speech by the Minister of Finance, the former containing the review of economic conditions and a preliminary review of the government's accounts for the fiscal year then ending, and the latter outlining the specific proposals the minister has in mind. At the close of his address the minister tables the formal resolutions for changes in existing tax rates and customs duties, which, in accordance with parliamentary procedure, must precede the introduction of any money bills. The Budget Speech is delivered in support of a motion that the House go into committee and the debate, lasting up to six sitting days, ensues. With the passage of the motion the way is clear for the consideration of the Budget Resolutions, and, when they have been approved by the Committee, a report to this effect is made to the House of Commons and the tax bills are introduced. The final feature of the parliamentary scrutiny stage is the audit, after the fiscal year is over, of the government's accounts by Parliament's agent, the Auditor General, whose invariably critical reports and comments are gleefully assessed by the media, the opposition, and the Public Accounts Committee of Parliament.[18]

The foregoing process still applies but is less "automatic" in times of minority government in Canada. The withdrawal of Walter Gordon's budget in 1963, the near-defeat of Mitchell Sharp's 1968 tax bill, and the defeat in 1974 of John Turner's budget reflect the obvious influence that opposition political parties can have when majority governments do not prevail. Even majority governments do not enjoy an invariably easy time over economic policy as the Diefenbaker government's difficulties in 1959 with the Coyne Affair amply demonstrated.

Two final observations about the economic-policy process seem warranted. First, in general there have been few outside advisors. The Economic Council exists as an advisory body but its role, while important as a source of public information and advice, has not been central in the annual short-term economic-policy and budgetary process as described above. The Council's public role is, nonetheless, important but will be more fully examined in later chapters.

The second observation is that the process described above deals with the regular cycle of economic-policy events. Needless to say, there are other occasions when economic-policy issues are assessed in the course of the introduction and consideration of other policy questions, not immediately or primarily perceived as economic policy. It has also not been uncommon for ministers of Finance to bring down more than one budget in a year should economic circumstances warrant.

SUMMARY

The purpose of this chapter has been to place the making of economic policy in the context of the general characteristics of Canadian cabinet government. Both the collective characteristics of cabinet government and developments in the cabinet committee system and central policy organizations have been assessed. Economic policy-making must also be seen in the context of other informal bases of Cabinet portfolio influence and in relation to the central annual priority-setting and economic policy-budgetary processes. Much of the above has been of necessity presented in a formal way. An understanding of these characteristics and structures of cabinet government are essential, however, before one can fully understand the dynamics of economic-policy processes, an analysis of which is the chief task of Chapter 4.

NOTES

1. For both Canadian and comparative dimensions of Cabinet government see R. M. Dawson, *The Government of Canada,* fourth ed., revised by Norman Ward (Toronto, 1971); R. J. Van Loon and M. Whittington, *The Canadian Political System,* second ed. (Toronto, 1975); Thomas Hockin, ed., *Apex of Power* (Toronto, 1971); Anthony King, ed., *The British Prime Minister* (London, 1969); and Bruce Headey, *British Cabinet Ministers* (London, 1973).

2. See Peter C. Newman, "Reflections on a Fall from Grace", *Maclean's* (January 1973), pp. 22-23, 64, 66-67.

3. See *To Know and Be Known,* Report of the Task Force on Information (Ottawa, 1969).

4. The descriptions of the Cabinet committee systems are based on published sources as well as on the authors' interviews, and the reading of

unpublished documents provided by the Privy Council officials. See also Gordon Robertson, "The Changing Role of the Privy Council Office", *Canadian Public Administration*, Vol. XIV, no. 4, pp. 487-508; Marc Lalonde, "The Changing Role of the Prime Minister's Office", *Canadian Public Administration*, Vol. XIV, no. 4, pp. 509-37; A. W. Johnson, "The Treasury Board of Canada and the Machinery of Government in the 1970s", *Canadian Journal of Political Science*, Vol. IV, no. 3, pp. 346-66; M. Hicks, "The Treasury Board of Canada and Its Clients", *Canadian Public Administration*, Vol. XVI, no. 2, pp. 182-205; and J. E. Hodgetts, *The Canadian Public Service, 1867-1967: A Physiology of Government* (Toronto, 1973).

5. Unpublished Privy Council document.

6. On the Treasury Board see Johnson, "The Treasury Board of Canada and the Machinery of Government", and Hicks, "The Treasury Board of Canada and Its Clients".

7. The appointment of Gordon Robertson in 1975 to head the federal-provincial relations secretariat of the PCO was accompanied by a legislative change which established the secretariat on a statutory basis. The effect of the change is not possible to determine at the time of writing.

8. For analysis of these changes in relation to prime-ministerial policy philosophies see G. Bruce Doern and Peter Aucoin, eds., *The Structures of Policy-Making in Canada* (Toronto, 1971), Chapter 2.

9. Newman, "Reflections on a Fall from Grace". For comparative views on Britain see V. Herman and James Alt, *Cabinet Studies* (London, 1975).

10. See Thomas D'Aquino, "The Prime Minister's Office: Catalyst or Cabal?" *Canadian Public Administration*, Vol. XVII, no. 1, pp. 55-84.

11. On Walter Gordon's use of three "outsiders" to help prepare his 1963 budget see Denis Smith, *Gentle Patriot* (Edmonton, 1973), pp. 138-40.

12. Interviews. See also *The Financial Post*, January 25, 1975, pp. 1, 7.

13. See G. Bruce Doern and V. S. Wilson, eds., *Issues in Canadian Public Policy* (Toronto, 1974), Chapter 12. On a comparative level see Thomas E. Cronin, "Everybody Believes in Democracy Until He gets to the White House . . . : An Examination of White House Departmental Relations", *Papers on the Institutionalized Presidency* (Washington, 1970), pp. 603-17, and Peter Self, *Administrative Theories and Politics* (Toronto, 1973), pp. 121-46.

14. At time of writing, two further ministries of state, one for Fisheries, and one for Small Business, were created.

15. On ministers of state see Peter Aucoin and Richard French, *Knowledge, Power and Public Policy* (Ottawa, 1974); David Cameron, "Urban Policy", in Doern and Wilson, eds., *Issues in Canadian Public Policy*, Chapter 9; and Richard Paton, "The Ministry of State for Urban Affairs: The Institutional Basis of Federal Urban Policy-Making". Unpublished MA research paper, Carleton University, Institute of Canadian Studies.

16. J. C. Strick, *Canadian Public Finance* (Toronto, 1973), pp. 132-33.

17. See Donald Gow, *The Progress of Budgetary Reform in the Government of Canada* (Ottawa, 1973); Johnson, "The Treasury Board of Canada and the Machinery of Government"; and Hicks, "The Treasury Board of Canada and Its Clients".

18. See Douglas G. Hartle, "The Role of the Auditor General of Canada", *Canadian Tax Journal*, Vol. XXIII, no. 3 (May/June 1975), pp. 193-204.

CHAPTER FOUR

Economic Policy and the Dynamics of Executive-Bureaucratic Processes

Economic policy ultimately is developed in an executive-bureaucratic arena whose processes bear witness to the importance of legal mandates, organizational roles and obligations, the rationalities and pathologies of bureaucratic behaviour, and the values, goals, and influence of individual personalities. This chapter will analyse the dynamics of economic-policy processes in the Government of Canada. Such an analysis requires a detailed appreciation of the basic *instruments* of economic policy and their organizational location. An understanding of the current assignment of economic-policy instruments will help us, in turn, understand the institutional perceptions which the major economic portfolios tend to carry with them in economic-policy discussions. The chapter will then focus more closely on the key relationships between the Prime Minister and the Finance minister, between the Finance minister and the President of the Treasury Board, and between the latter and the principal "spending" ministers. These behavioural dynamics will then be related to patterns of bureaucratic behaviour at which stage we will critically assess and build upon recent analysis of economic-policy organization through the use of bureaucratic theory. This will help prepare the way for the analysis in Chapter 5 which will relate these bureaucratic characteristics to the important leadership roles played by recent ministers of Finance, deputy ministers of Finance, and other central economic-policy leaders in the economic-policy process.

THE INSTRUMENTS OF ECONOMIC POLICY AND ORGANIZATIONAL LOCATION

In Chapters 1 and 2 we have presented the general evolution of economic-policy values, goals, instruments, and organizations in a largely chronological fashion. Our task now is to present a more detailed portrait of the nature of economic-policy instruments and their organizational location in the Government of Canada.

Figure 4:1 presents nine categories of basic instruments of economic policy and then relates them to the federal departments and agencies having a *primary* responsibility and/or involvement in the use of these instruments.[1] Needless to say, in some instances other secondary departments and agencies are also involved. Since our task is to present a basic classification we are confining the allocation to those departments known to have primary relationships to the instrument in question. The relationships are derived from the departments' legal mandate and observed behaviour and activities.

As Figure 4:1 illustrates, the traditional instruments of economic policy (stabilization policy), the regulation of government receipts, the regulation of the supply of money and credit, the regulation of foreign exchange rates, and the management of government borrowing and lending are basically located in the Department of Finance with the Bank of Canada playing an important role in the last three of the above instruments.

The instruments of government spending, moral suasion, the acquisition, forecasting, and publication of economic data and information, and structural regulation tend, on the whole, to be located in an ever-broadening range of economic portfolios.

Government expenditures are the basis on which all departments can (and do) claim a role in economic policy. The more important departments, however, are the Treasury Board, Industry, Trade and Commerce, Regional Economic Expansion, National Health and Welfare, Consumer and Corporate Affairs, Manpower and Immigration, Energy, Mines and Resources, and Transport, and Labour. All possess budgets, the allocation of which can influence economic policy both generally and in particular sectors.

Moral suasion as an instrument of economic policy has historically been most associated with monetary policy. As an instrument at the voluntary end of the continuum of governing instruments, however, it serves as a suitable heading under which one can place other consultative and advisory processes such as are reflected in the Economic Council of Canada and in experiments with the Prices and Incomes Commission, and voluntary price and wage guidelines.

FIGURE 4:1—ECONOMIC POLICY INSTRUMENTS AND ORGANIZATIONAL LOCATION

	Finance	*Bank of Canada*	*Treasury Board*	*Industry, Trade and Commerce*	*Statistics Canada*	*Taxation and National Revenue*	*Economic Council of Canada*	*National Health and Welfare*	*Regional Economic Expansion*	*Consumer and Corporate Affairs*	*Manpower and Immigration*	*Labour*	*Other Agencies*
	Departments and Agencies (Primary Location)												
Instrument of Economic Policy													
1. *Regulation of Government Receipts*													
Personal Income Tax	X												
Corporate Income Tax	X			X									
Sales Tax	X					X							
Customs Duties	X					X							
Social Security Contributions	X							X					
Intergovernmental Tax Agreements	X												
Property Taxes	X					X							
Inheritance and Gift Taxes	X												
Transfers from rest of the world	X												
2. *Regulation of Supply of Money* and Conditions of Credit (Interest Rates)	X	X											
3. *Regulation of Foreign Exchange Rate*	X	X											
4. *Management of Government Borrowing* (Debt Management)	X	X											

Department and Agencies (Primary Location) *Instrument of Economic Policy*	*Finance*	*Bank of Canada*	*Treasury Board*	*Industry, Trade and Commerce*	*Statistics Canada*	*Taxation and National Revenue*	*Economic Council of Canada*	*National Health and Welfare*	*Regional Economic Expansion*	*Consumer and Corporate Affairs*	*Manpower and Immigration*	*Labour*	*Other Agencies*
5. *Management of Government Lending*	X	X	X	X									*e.g.* : CMHC, Export Development Corp., Farm Credit Corp., Federal Business Development Bank.
6. *Government Expenditures* Government Investment	X		X										Public Works, Crown Corporations
Subsidies and Capital Transfers to Business	X			X					X				Agriculture, Transport, Energy
Transfers to Households	X							X			X		Unemployment Insurance Comm.
Intergovernmental Transfers	X												
Purchase of Goods and Services			X										Supply and Services, All Departments
Wages and Salaries			X										All Departments
Transfers to rest of the world	X			X									CIDA, External Affairs

	Finance	*Bank of Canada*	*Treasury Board*	*Industry, Trade and Commerce*	*Statistics Canada*	*Taxation and National Revenu*	*Economic Counc of Canada*	*National Health and Welfare*	*Regional Econor Expansion*	*Consumer and Corporate Affair*	*Manpower and Immigration*	*Labour*	*Other Agencies*
7. *Moral Suasion* formal and informal consultation with banking and credit industry	X	X		X									
wage and price guidelines	X		X							X			Food Prices Review Board, Prices and Incomes Commission
economic consultative bodies				X			X				X		All Departments
Instrument of Economic Policy *Department and Agencies (Primary Location)*													
8. *Acquisition forecasting and Publication of Economic Data and Information*	X	X	X	X	X	X	X						*e.g.:* Conference Board, Institute of Quantitative Analysis
9. *Structural Regulation*													
regulation of competition	X			X						X			*e.g.:* Marketing Boards, CTC, CRTC, NEB
regulation of foreign investment	X			X						X			FIRA
regulation of labour relations	X			X			X						CLRB, PSSRB
regulation of technology exchange and transfers	X			X						X			Ministry of Science and Technology
regulation of banking	X	X		X						X			
other regulation (transportation, communications, energy, agriculture)													*e.g.:* CTC, CRTC, NEB
regulation of incomes	X		X										Anti-Inflation Board

The acquisition, forecasting, and publication of economic data and information is not likely to be found as an instrument that normally warrants separate mention. We suggest that it warrants a separate identification, however, because of the increasing degree to which separate agencies such as Statistics Canada, the Food Prices Review Board, and the Economic Council of Canada (not to mention international agencies such as the OECD) have been created and differentiated precisely to generate information and the timing of whose information is frequently (indeed usually) not in the direct control of central policy-makers.

In many respects, the instrument of structural regulation represents the instrument which has been historically the least available for use in the short run because it deals more closely with the very core and ideology of economic organization in a liberal democratic state.[2] The general regulation of incomes, competition, foreign investment, labour relations, banking, and technology exchanges and transfers (not to mention more specific regulation of transport, communication, and energy) represent increasingly important instruments whose imposition, on even the short-run economic agenda, is increasingly suggested in Canada. It is precisely because these instruments lie on the more coercive and compulsory end of the continuum of governing instruments that their use has generated the greatest uncertainty and concern in the total economic-policy system in Canada. And the more one contemplates the possible use of these instruments the more one takes the making of economic policy out of the domain of the Department of Finance.

The inventory of economic-policy instruments and their organizational location presented in Figure 4:1 again alerts us to both the wide range of instruments available, and to the ever-widening range of portfolios that covet (and sometimes have the power to challenge) the obvious dominance of the Department of Finance in its traditional custody of the instruments of stabilization policy.

The list of economic-policy instruments begins with those traditionally assigned to stabilization policy—fiscal and monetary—and then proceeds to a consideration of broader instruments, including moral suasion, consultation, information acquisition and publication, and, ultimately, structural regulation. The list reflects a reality of economic policy-making processes already given repeated emphasis, namely the presence of ever-widening goals, organizations, and instruments.

The mere presentation of a full inventory or full range of instruments does not, of course, define the real range of choices available at a particular time or on a particular issue. Each instrument inherently presents different risks, uncertainties, and time lags between its selection for use and its ultimate impact on the marketplace and on the behaviour of governments, individuals, and interest groups.

As Pierce has pointed out, the policy-maker's task is to select from the wide variety of instruments "the one instrument (or combination of instruments) which is most likely to achieve the economic goals of the government [assuming that the goals can be decided upon], and which is also likely to be (politically) acceptable". Furthermore, it must be stressed that:

> For each of these general instruments there is a wide range of variations that policy-makers can choose from. In selecting an instrument, however, the range of alternatives is limited by the specific problem, the organizational constraints on the generation of alternative policy actions, and the policy-maker's limited capability for considering more than a few instruments at a time.[3]

The differences of opinion about economic-policy objectives and instruments that emerge between and among departments, ministers, and individuals within the executive-bureaucratic arena are thus a product of many legitimate factors, including the values to be given priority, the groups or sectors to be rewarded or sacrificed, and the uncertainty of the impact of instruments to be utilized. In this sense the economic-policy processes and dynamics are an accurate reflection of the broader Canadian political economy.

It is also essential to bear in mind the simple fact that in political terms, economic-policy *instruments* are not merely instrumental techniques. To exhort by moral suasion or the creation of consultative/informational bodies, to spend, and to regulate is to select different instruments of governing. We have strongly emphasized in Chapter 2 the governing politician's need to view this continuum of governing instruments as an end in itself, since politicians are partly judged on how they govern as well as on what goals and priorities they pursue. If there is validity in our hypothesis of political policy-making, namely that governing politicians will prefer to move from the least coercive to the most coercive instruments, then there is likely to be a general preference for using minimally coercive instruments such as moral suasion or spending rather than direct regulation. Pierce's characterization of the politics of economic-policy instruments as being voluntary, donative, and compulsory reinforces this point:

> . . . a change in income tax rates leads to a compulsory increase or reduction in an individual or a corporation's disposable income. If an individual accepts a transfer payment, or a corporation's subsidy, it likewise experiences an increase or reduction in disposable income, even though it is not forced to accept the government's donation. When the government changes the level of its purchases of goods and services or changes the amount of government debt held by the private sector, individuals or corporations can freely choose whether they want to do business with the government or whether they want to buy or sell government securities. . . .
>
> The voluntary aspect of monetary policy, debt management policy, and the government's purchase of goods and services explains, at least in part, their more frequent use for stabilization purposes than changes in taxes or the use of transfer payments.[4]

None of the above is intended to suggest that the immediate use of direct regulation never occurs. The history of government regulation of the economy is filled with instances where industries or sectors have succeeded in securing direct regulatory protection from the state to protect them from having to compete in the marketplace.[5] As a general tendency, however, political authorities tend to want to try out other governing instruments first. As specific or general policy issues evolve over a few years, it is, of course, likely that several instruments will have been used. Hence, using the carrot and the stick (in that order) is a concept well understood by political authorities.

A final important factor about the use of economic instruments is that there is far more agreement (or there was at least until recently) about what instruments to use in the narrower domain of stabilization policy, the home base of Keynesian guidelines, than there is in the wider parameters of economic policy. Pierce's summary of the basic norms of fiscal policy covers the general and central tenets:

> During periods of high unemployment, when there is insufficient aggregate demand, the government wants to increase disposable income (and, in turn, the level of aggregate demand) so that more people are put to work to meet the

demand. It can do this by reducing taxes on individuals and corporations, by increasing its purchases of goods and services in the economy, and by increasing government transfer payments.

During periods of inflation, when there is more demand than goods and services to meet the demand, the government wants to decrease disposable income to bring aggregate demand in line with the economy's productive capacity. It can do this by increasing taxes, reducing government purchases of goods and services, and reducing transfer payments.

During periods of full employment and price stability, the government wants to ensure that the growth of demand and the growth of productive capacity are such that full employment and price stability are maintained. This can be done by adjusting the tax structure so that an optimal amount of corporate income is diverted into investment for increases in productive capacity. The amount of investment necessary will depend primarily on the rate of growth of the labor force and the rate of growth of productivity.[6]

While the basic tenets still command much support, it is clear, particularly in a federal state such as Canada, that the central thrust of Keynesian guidelines are encountering rough water. Conflicting taxation policies of federal and provincial governments and the introduction of so-called "secondary" objectives such as income redistribution and the removal of regional economic disparities greatly complicate the Keynesian norms of short-term stabilization and greatly complicate the medium- and long-term economic policy agenda as well.[7]

ECONOMIC-POLICY MANDATES AND CABINET ROLES AND OBLIGATIONS

The making of economic policy is greatly influenced by the frequently and necessarily conflicting mandates, roles, and obligations of the major economic-policy portfolios. Thus, the achievement of economic-policy co-ordination in the confines of cabinet government is at best a transitory and elusive goal. Economic-policy co-ordination is achieved to a degree but it is clear that the political meaning of co-ordination can only be contemplated when one acknowledges that such co-ordination involves in part the temporary victory of one or two economic objectives over other values and objectives, the use of one or more instruments over other instruments, and the relative triumph of one department over another and of one or more ministers over others. Economic-policy co-ordination issues can be illustrated both by some general observations about roles and through the use of cases or examples. The roles normally impose strong and overriding obligations on the incumbent minister and are thus a major determinant of the way he or she behaves in cabinet deliberations. Each of the major economic portfolios reflect strong institutional obligations.

Because of its responsibilities for tax policy, debt-management, balance of payments, and (with the Bank of Canada) monetary policy, the Department of Finance is sometimes held to have a relatively greater institutional concern for price levels and inflation than it has for unemployment. In part this may be true simply because its array of instruments on the "demand" side of the economy is more complete than on the so-called supply side. On the supply side for example, the Department of Labour and the Department of Manpower and Immigration (and to a certain extent, the Department of Consumer and Corporate Affairs) are the chief custodians of important goals and instruments related to the quality and quantity, not to mention the "human" side, of the economic equation.

In recent years the role conflict has been illustrated by the Winter Works programs of the 1950s and 1960s and the Opportunities for Youth (OFY) and Local Initiatives (LIP) programs of the early 1970s. The analysis by Burns and Close indicates the extent to which the Finance Department of the late 1950s opposed the development of the Winter Works program.[8] The program provided for a federal sharing with provincial and municipal governments of the cost of hiring unemployed labour during the winter construction season to complete needed local public works. The program was directed at evening out the cycle of seasonal unemployment with which Canada was afflicted. The Department of Labour was the chief advocate of the program and its perception of the goals and instruments of the program came in conflict with those of the Finance Department. The latter opposed the program, preferring instead to utilize what it viewed to be the normal self-adjusting mechanisms of regular fiscal policy to attack the problem. The Winter Works program was approved, nonetheless, and was in operation for a decade prior to its cancellation in 1968. The cancellation occured after a Finance Department and Treasury Board assessment determined that it was not meeting its intended objectives.

Within three years of its cancellation, however, in response first to increasing unemployment among young people and then to increasing unemployment generally, the OFY and LIP programs were established.[9] These programs granted funds directly to unemployed persons to work on socially useful projects which they had developed themselves. On this occasion the program advocates were lodged primarily in the Department of Manpower and Immigration and the Secretary of State departments. These advocates viewed the programs not only in quantitative terms but also in *qualitative* terms in that the programs would generate both participation and more meaningful employment. Again the Finance Department lent opposition to the concept arguing that it failed to attack the underlying causes of unemployment. It was also joined, though somewhat less strenuously, by the Treasury Board. The latter's criticism, evolved in part from its role, in that its institutional responsibilities for well-developed, well-managed, orderly program-development caused it to question the development of a "crash" employment program. In the final analyses the LIP and OFY programs were launched although their rate of increase in funding has levelled off.

In both of the above instances, the perceptions of the programs were greatly affected by roles. They may also have been affected by the personalities and values of incumbent ministers in the several portfolios. At this point, however, it is important to draw attention to the portfolio role as a distinctive variable, separate from the values of incumbents be they conservative, liberal, or radical in their personal views. In both instances the Labour, and then the Manpower and Immigration, departments relied upon the spending instruments, and in both instances the Finance Department asserted the need to rely upon the more traditional array of stabilization instruments. The Treasury Board demonstrated in the latter case its institutional aversion to the use of quick-spending programs that had not been subject to the test of managerial analysis. In both cases, the spenders prevailed in the short run while the fiscal and managerial role-players had the satisfaction of seeing some of their criticisms prove to be valid in the longer run.

With respect to other major economic portfolios, similar tendencies can and frequently do prevail. As Chapters 8 and 9 will show, the Department of Industry, Trade and Commerce's efforts to develop a so-called national "industrial strategy" brings it into conflict with the Department of Regional Economic Expansion. The DREE mandate is

directed towards the elimination of regional economic disparities. Its redistributive goals bring it into partial, although not total, conflict with the Industry, Trade and Commerce concern for aggregate national industrial development. The co-ordination dilemma arises because the Canadian political system has insisted that both of these goals be pursued *concurrently*.

The debates on unemployment insurance and on a guaranteed annual income also reflect differences in perception between the Finance Department and the departments of Manpower and Immigration and National Health and Welfare respectively. The generous degrees of support for the unemployed that have accompanied the 1971 policy changes were viewed by Manpower and Immigration Minister Bryce Mackasey in terms of their redistributive and social welfare value whereas the Finance officials were concerned relatively more about total cost and about the possible impediments the program would create in the placement of the unemployed in the available job openings. Similarly the Department of National Health and Welfare's apparent advocacy of a guaranteed annual income scheme is motivated by redistributive goals. The opposition by the Finance Department rests on its concern over the aggregate cost of the scheme and of the disincentives to work which the program might encourage.[10]

The examples of policy conflict cited above all involve conflicts over the traditional economic policy objectives and redistributive or so-called secondary objectives. To point out that such conflicts between redistribution and traditional objectives exist and are increasingly present in the Cabinet is not to say that a significant amount of real redistribution occurs. Degrees of redistribution pressure and values, moreover, would likely differ greatly among particular governments or political parties in power. It might be expected, for example, that a federal NDP government would likely stress redistributive issues and portfolios much more than a Liberal or Conservative government. An analysis of provincial NDP governments has suggested, however, that their redistributive efforts have not been marked by greater success.[11]

Differences in governmental ideology, in bases of electoral support, and in interest-group and provincial pressure obviously are important factors.[12] The point which we wish to stress, however, is the extent to which interagency role-conflict is built into cabinet processes, especially with the recent institutionalization of economic values in new departments headed by their own ministers. Conflict occurs, moreover, not because cabinets and bureaucracies are filled with men and women incapable or unwilling to co-operate and co-ordinate (although some characteristics of this kind clearly exist). Rather a considerably greater part of the explanation of interagency tension arises from the simple fact that each agency has been accorded, legally and through practice, primary custody over certain goals and instruments. Each of these goals, when viewed separately, is deemed to be desirable. The presence of these organizational tendencies cannot lightly be ignored by those who wish to reform either the structure and outputs of government in general or the structures, processes, and outputs of economic policy in particular.

We thus have some further initial clues to the additional bases on which the power and role of the Department of Finance is based. Even though one is able to show the emergence of an ever-increasing number of departments which claim and covet economic-policy roles, and even though one can cite programs which show these agencies prevailing in their views, the fact remains that the Finance Department still possesses by far the greatest and most inclusive array of aggregate instruments and information. Paradoxically, in some respects, the more that new departments are added or old agencies reshuffled, the more significant the Finance Department's potential advantage over any *single* department becomes. Moreover, the sheer number and breadth of the instruments available to the Finance Department helps explain its cautious posture toward many issues. It is precisely this custody over several objectives and instruments whose interrelationships are uncertain and unpredictable that goes a long way toward explaining the conservatism of Finance portfolios.

THE CENTRAL DYNAMICS

Economic-policy processes ultimately rest on day-to-day, month-to-month relationships between and among individual cabinet ministers, particularly those who head the major spending departments, and between the Minister of Finance, the president of the Treasury Board, and the Prime Minister. We will first explore the general relationships between spending ministers and the Finance and

Treasury Board ministers in the general expenditure process, and then explore the narrower but crucial dynamics between the Prime Minister and the President of the Treasury Board and the Minister of Finance.

Though ministerial influence is affected by the broader sources of aggregate influence (such as we outlined in Chapter 3), a minister is ultimately judged by what he gets done. His reputation as a fighter for his department and for his own ideas, his skills as an expenditure combatant, and the degree to which he is informed and prepared in defending his proposals in Cabinet ultimately determine his real standing in the Cabinet. While there are many Cabinet- and minister-watchers in the media and in the bureaucracy it is ultimately the judgment of his or her cabinet colleagues that determines the current value of a minister's most precious political currency—his reputation. Political credit most easily accrues from spending in that it is the most visible instrument and indicator of political action. This is not to suggest that spending for the sake of spending is the basic drive. Obviously spending in the pursuit of certain public-policy objectives is central but the important value of spending as a governing instrument is that it is an essential grease for the cabinet wheel.

One should not equate the above point with the notion that reputations as strong ministers are built by an indiscriminate use of mutual back-scratching. The budgetary process is sufficiently structured and the norms of cabinet behaviour are sufficiently well ingrained that the successful minister must ultimately demonstrate some temperate qualities as well. The size of the Canadian Cabinet alone makes formal alliance-building a difficult process. Similarly the minister must be constantly conscious of the fact that he can only infrequently appeal to the court of final ministerial appeal, the Prime Minister, or to the full Cabinet. Frequent appeals in these forums would be indicative of one's inability to carry the day in other arenas such as before the Treasury Board or before other cabinet committees.

The dynamics of the expenditure and fiscal-policy process must also be understood in terms of the relationship between the President of the Treasury Board and the Minister of Finance, and the Prime Minister. Both ministers, but especially the former, are dependent on the fairly constant backing of the Prime Minister. Constant appeals over the heads of both to the Prime Minister would be intolerable for all three ministers. On a reciprocal basis the Prime Minister needs the support of strong Finance and Treasury Board ministers to manage the overall governmental processes.

Thus, there is a strong political need to leave considerable leeway in the budgetary process for negotiation and trade-offs to occur between the President of the Treasury Board and the departmental ministers. The breadth of the priorities expressed in the expenditure guidelines developed by the Priorities and Planning Committee of the Cabinet leaves considerable room for interpretation and accommodation. The fact that the budgetary process occurs over several months and weeks also facilitates the development of political accommodations among ministers.

The relationship between the Minister of Finance and the Prime Minister is obviously one of the most critical in cabinet government. Heclo and Wildavsky's comment about the British Chancellor of the Exchequer applies with equal force to the Canadian Minister of Finance:

> The lot of the Chancellor is rarely a happy one. His every move in the economic sphere is watched by critical eyes. He is second-guessed on all sides: within the Treasury, by his ministerial colleagues, by financial interests, and by a myriad of reporters specially designated for the task. A look through the major book on . . . postwar economic management . . . suggests that in retrospect Chancellors rarely do the right thing, and if they do, it is often for the wrong reasons. They inflate when they should deflate, cut when they should expand, act when they should do nothing. The outsider begins to wonder if the British economy is that precarious or if perhaps these men are being called on to make adjustments too delicate for the kind of knowledge at their disposal. Be that as it may, the public preoccupation with the Chancellor as manager of the economy suggests an important truth: "The big role of the Chancellor", as a former occupant of that position put it, "is not expenditure but as minister of the economy."[13]

The difficulty of the Finance minister's position must be particularly acknowledged by the Prime Minister. In recent years the special character of this relationship has been formalized by the holding of weekly meetings on the state of the economy. The Prime Minister and Finance Minister must ultimately agree also in the critical annual determination and shape of the fiscal framework. Once arrived at, the basic ballpark figures on revenue and on the aggregate sum available for new expenditure—figures largely determined by Finance—can be only marginally juggled. While relying on the latent and sometimes manifest support of the Prime Minister, the Minister of Finance's major weapon is taxation. The outer parameters of the politics of the budgetary and fiscal-policy process are set by the argument, frequently advanced by Finance portfolios, that either spending must be held down or taxes will have to be increased. This, of course, has always been an important political club. In recent decades the Keynesian clout has been added to this traditional and potent weapon, namely, if expenditure plans are too great and taxes not increased, the economy may be destabilized.

Ministers who otherwise may be inclined to challenge fiscal policy even in the face of the above weapons are likely to be ultimately dissuaded by the fact that they often possess inadequate information to make a successful challenge. This is not to suggest that they do not offer advice, as politicians, to the Minister of Finance at budget time, but they are fully aware that they cannot challenge in the core areas of stabilization policy. The specific information gap is reinforced by the broader practice in cabinet government which sees ministers being briefed by their staffs, more to "defend" their own portfolios rather than to be aggressive critics of other portfolios.[14]

The information advantage of the Finance portfolio occurs despite the fact that economic-policy forecasting is far less sophisticated than most forecasters would have us believe. As Heclo and Wildavsky point out, "the ability of forecasters to predict demands for goods, services, exports, investment and other crucial variables has not been exactly overpowering."[15] This is no reflection on the ability of economic forecasters, but rather reflects the inherent human inability to both predict and manipulate complex human and social behaviour.

Obviously ministers are in part captured and constrained by the nature of their portfolios and by other political constraints. But within these constraints there is considerable room for individual competence, drive, and ability to be the basis of political power. Once again, Heclo and Wildavsky capture the central question in cabinet dynamics:

> Ministers will always be concerned with standing and reputation, and spending ministers will always find ways to make their interests manifest in the expenditure process. There will always be fighters, moderators, and weak-

lings. The problem is not that ministers are narrow—they are paid to defend departmental interest—or that a broader view no one possesses is ignored. Rather, the vital question is: How can these proclivities be structured so that ministers have strong incentives to behave in more productive ways—ways actually leading to better policies with better consequences for the people they are designed to help?[16]

To prepare the way for an examination of some of the prospects for restructuring it is necessary to take the analysis of economic-policy processes further into the realm of bureaucratic theory and behaviour.

BUREAUCRATIC BEHAVIOUR AND ECONOMIC-POLICY PROCESSES

In recent years there have been several published analyses of particular federal government agencies and departments which have incorporated various aspects of bureaucratic and organizational theory as insights in explaining agency behaviour and in demonstrating the close links between public policy and administration. These analyses have utilized a wide variety of theoretical models and have dealt with organizations whose mandates relate closely to economic management,[17] and with those that are only tangentially related.[18] We will examine two of the former, namely the work of Albert Breton on the behaviour of "Exchequers", and Acheson and Chant on the Bank of Canada. It has in particular not been a tradition of Canadian academic economists to incorporate theories of bureaucracy in their explanations of economic behaviour and thus these recent efforts are long overdue and deserve attention and comment. An assessment of this work will permit us to relate the Cabinet and interagency dynamics to the basic bureaucratic processes of single agencies.

Albert Breton's work has attempted, albeit very briefly, to explain one aspect of the behaviour of Exchequers (the name he gives to fiscal authorities) through the use of bureaucratic theory.[19] The particular aspect of the behaviour of Exchequers which he seeks to explain is their pronounced tendency to generate revenue far *in excess* of forecasted revenue, a tendency in evidence in the case of the Canadian Department of Finance. Breton advances the hypothesis that:

> the underestimation of revenues by Exchequers is the most efficient way of minimizing the risk of confrontation with other departments of government, while at the same time providing the Exchequer with an instrument—a form of

internal patronage—whereby it can maintain some control and exercise some power over these departments.[20]

He argues that the *overestimation* of revenues would mean difficult expenditure cuts and hence difficult confrontations with other departments. The alternative of borrowing from the central bank to offset any shortfall is held by Breton to be unlikely because Exchequers are held to have a strong preference for inflation "as long as the public does not develop 'correct' expectations about the rate of price increases". Breton goes on to suggest:

Exchequers are large net borrowers, and the greater the rate of inflation and the more biased the public's expectations about this rate of inflation, the less the real cost of carrying the outstanding debt becomes. Only if the public held "correct" expectations about the rate of inflation, would Exchequers develop neutral or negative preference about inflation.[21]

Thus the Exchequer's functions dealing with debt management give him an incentive to avoid borrowing unreasonable amounts from the central bank. Consequently, Breton suggests that underestimation of revenue is functional both to reduce the risks of borrowing and, in addition, to provide "patronage" resources (the excess funds) which can facilitate influence over operating departments:

The distribution of patronage is almost totally inseparable from the exercise of power, so much so that efforts to eliminate patronage—usually proposed and favoured by those who have no power—only succeed in transforming the form that patronage takes. In the case of the relationship between Exchequers and other departments of government, patronage can take many forms. For example, part of the excess funds can be made available to all departments, but only after some departments have been told of their existence and, as a consequence, have been able to prepare the formulation of programs to absorb these funds. Or patronage can take the form of proposals for expenditure, originating in the Exchequer, that clearly favour one department over another. It is interesting to note in this connection that Exchequers, even when they recommend that taxes be cut to deal with the excess funds resulting from their underestimation of revenues, rarely go the full way and recommend that the tax-reduction eliminate the excess completely; indeed, they usually come up with a package of tax cuts and expenditure increases, the latter not usually tailored in a way that would lead an outsider to deny with certainty the existence of internal patronage.[22]

Because of these behavioural tendencies Breton goes on to suggest three areas of reform. First, the reduction of the incidence of under-estimation requires reducing the "monopoly position of Exchequers", a reduction which could be achieved, Breton suggests, by creating alternative sources of forecasting. A second reform proposal is to remove from the control of the Finance Department "everything that has to do" with debt management, thus removing one of the incentives to underestimate. The third reform is to require the Treasury Board to formulate "alternative budgets for alternative states of the world", namely for possible over- as well as underestimation of revenues. In Breton's view this would "eliminate internal patronage, since it would remove the disposition of excess funds from the discretion of the Exchequer".

Breton's hypothesis and reform proposals illustrate both the value and some of the pitfalls of this kind of analysis. Our analysis would certainly support the general view that the behaviour of Exchequers must, in part, be explained by the tendencies of bureaucracies to expand their realm of influence and power and that such expansion is a function of their ability to accumulate internal political instruments. Two of these instruments are implicitly or explicitly a part of Breton's hypothesis. The explicit instrument is "loose cash" or the spending instruments which Breton chooses to call patronage. The implicit variable is "uncertainty". Persons or organizations who are subject to the uncertain exercises of choice by other persons or organizations are inherently in an inferior power position. Thus the Finance Department, because of its command over debt-management instruments (not to mention the other array of instruments cited in Chapter 3), is in a position to generate uncertainty for other departments.

When the criterion of diffusion of power is applied there is clearly a great deal of sense in Breton's first and second proposals. But what about the criterion of developing *more* co-ordination of overall economic policy? The need for better co-ordination might suggest a greater rather than a reduced concentration of functions and instruments in the Finance Department. Breton's specific analysis of revenue under-estimation probably seriously undervalues the fact that economic managers are simply not very good forecasters, the faith of economists to the contrary, notwithstanding.

With respect to the validity of the second part of Breton's hypothesis regarding the Exchequer's manipulation of patronage, there is at least one structural error. In the Canadian context, the Finance Department cannot directly, at its sole discretion, reallocate excess revenue to operating departments. This is a "patronage" function which must operate through the Treasury Board. Hence one element of the Exchequer "monopoly" which Breton seems to ascribe to the Finance Department is not wholly in its domain.

A second and more extensive analysis which has utilized bureaucratic theory is to be found in the Acheson and Chant assessment of the Bank of Canada.[23] Their analysis seeks to determine the degree to which a theory of bureaucracy emphasizing the goals of self-preservation and prestige can provide an explanation of the behaviour of the Bank of Canada. The analysis is particularly directed at the possible influence of these goals on the Bank's "modes of operation" for conducting monetary policy. By "prestige" Acheson and Chant refer to the "position of the bureau in the social hierarchy of government bureaus".[24] By self-preservation, they rely on the observations of Anthony Downs and others about the high priority which all organizations place on their own survival.[25]

Given these functions, Acheson and Chant go on to indicate the likely ways in which the maximization of these functions will likely be pursued, and to describe the constraints within which the effort will be made:

> These constraints include the degrees of freedom allowed under the legislation which created the bureau, the existence and aggressiveness of other bureaus, and the state of knowledge about "social engineering". Within the set of options available to it the bureau will choose a "best" point but it will also be concerned with the long-run problem of expanding these options. Since prestige and self-preservation are not necessarily independent of each other, many of the bureau's decisions involve a trade-off between them.
>
> A typical bureau has a number of strategies for influencing its status in the community. It can, to some extent, decide on the goals it will be held responsible for, as well as the range of tools that it will maintain in order to perform its functions. It can decide to encourage or discourage the sharing of responsi-

bility for an objective with other agencies. If it can choose, and has chosen, to make available a number of alternative ways of achieving its objectives, it has to decide on the best way to proceed in a given situation. Since prestige involves the judgment of others, the bureau will attempt to influence the way the public views it, through its publications and its other contacts with the community. This proffered image may not match the reality.[26]

Acheson and Chant suggest that, in choosing among the instruments of monetary policy, the Bank of Canada has demonstrated an increased tendency to prefer covert rather than open methods of operation. The use of covert methods, coupled with a "skilfully created mythology" can increase the bank's immunity to critical investigations.[27] Covert or less-visible instruments can be used as can a "judicious combination of a number of different instruments". Thus moral suasion might be preferred because it "need not leave any direct evidence for outside observers."[28] In contrast the use of open-market operations, changes in the bank rate, or changes in legal reserve requirements are more visible and formal instruments. Formal moral suasion involves securing commitments from the commercial banks or other financial institutions to "refrain from activities judged to be in conflict with the policies of the central bank.[29] More informal moral suasion consists of numerous casual discussions. These more casual devices are backed up by the Bank's implicit powers to determine such things as money-market lenders' eligibility for day-to-day loans.

Thus the use of moral suasion has many advantages. As Acheson and Chant point out:

Through traditional methods of control, central banks are quite limited in their powers to determine the allocation of credit by financial institutions, even those under its direct control. With use of moral suasion, central banks are able to discourage financial institutions from particular types of lending and even influence the behaviour of institutions over which it does not have any direct authority. To the extent a central bank desires this wider range of authority, use of moral suasion has distinct advantages relative to other more direct methods. By relying on moral suasion, the powers of the central bank remain ill defined and in some cases may become apparent after the fact, if at all. If the central bank were to seek direct instruments explicitly incorporated within the legal framework within which it operates, the prospect is raised of public discussion of the merits of the extension of central bank powers into this sphere and even of explicit prohibition of certain actions by the central bank.

The evidence derived from examination of the Bank of Canada's actions is not inconsistent with an appreciation by the Bank of the advantages of moral suasion for extending its powers. In a number of instances the Bank appears to have had a preference for adoption of new techniques by this means rather than through the amendment of its legislative powers.[30]

The bank's preference for moral suasion is related by Acheson and Chant to basic policies and attitudes towards competition in the Canadian banking industry:

A virtual requirement for effective use of moral suasion over a prolonged period is the existence of only a small number of financial institutions to be influenced by the central bank. With large numbers of financial institutions the low cost of noncompliance for any single financial institution will reduce the impact of moral suasion.[31]

Thus the bank would be expected to either encourage or "at least not actively discourage, concentration of any part of the financial sector that is vulnerable to the use of moral suasion."[32]

The preference for covert methods is also related by Acheson and Chant to the Bank of Canada's (and the Finance Department's) approach to balance-of-payments policy and to the Bank's ability to transfer government deposits between itself and the chartered banks. While the latter is a slightly more visible practice, its increasing use, rather than the equally effective use of regular open-market operations, is attributed to bureaucratic traits as well. It is more difficult to observe than open-market operations and it contributes to the multiplicity of instruments available to the Bank of Canada.

Of the goals usually posited as suitable for central banks, price stability, full employment, economic growth, removal of regional disparities, viable balance of payment, minimization of interest costs on government debt, and development of an efficient and flexible financial system, only one, minimization of government interest expense, is *not* shared by the Bank with other agencies of government.[33] The goal of developing an efficient and flexible financial system is not overtly claimed by any agency, in Acheson and Chant's view, because of the intricate intergovernmental dimensions of the problem. Thus when assessing preference among the latter goals, it is suggested by Acheson and Chant that the interest-minimization goal will be given priority attention because it is more visible, as it is closely identified with the Bank, and responsibility for it cannot be deflected to other agencies.

Thus the minimization of interest charges brings the Bank into a central concern for a part of debt management. With respect to its divided responsibilities over other goal areas, they note that the Bank of Canada has not exercised moral suasion with respect to the goal of regional development. With respect to the trade-off between unemployment and price stability the Bank has sought to deflect criticism by steadfastly denying the relevance of a trade-off between the two goals, and by stressing the complex lags and interdependencies inherent in the use of the instruments available.

On the whole, therefore, Acheson and Chant find better explanations of the Bank of Canada's behaviour through reference to general bureaucratic tendencies related to prestige and self-preservation. They conclude that:

> Bureaus have a predictable but contrary desire not to leave a clear record of their actions and instead prefer to have the power to select a favorable account of their actions. The availability of covert instruments permits the Bank of Canada to extend its activities into sensitive areas without having the explicit power to do so and permits it to choose whether to accept responsibility for the outcomes. The Bank can further obscure its actions by using a number of technically redundant instruments or by making the process of interaction between monetary policy and the economy more superficially confusing than they need to be.[34]

Because of the Bank's inherent capacity to manipulate multiple goals and instruments the main thrust of Acheson and Chant's reform proposals is to define and assign goals and instruments more precisely. Thus, they would prefer that there be a general prohibition of moral suasion and that a presumption exist that the Bank does not have the power to act in a particular area and that explicit permission of the government should be sought before action is initiated. More specifically they suggest that government deposits "be kept either exclusively at private financial intermediaries or exclusively at the Bank of Canada so that switching of such deposits would no longer be possible."[35] Similarly they suggest that responsibility for debt management be delegated to a bureau other than the one responsible for monetary policy, and that all statistical material gathered by the Bank as well as the right to make decisions about publications be transfered to Statistics Canada.

As with Breton's much briefer analysis, there is much merit in the Acheson and Chant analysis in that basic bureaucratic processes are identified and related to the command over goals and instruments. They lead to reform proposals which broadly make sense in terms of diffusing the bureaucratic power of a single organization and of promoting a more precise allocation of accountability. Both Breton, and Acheson and Chant, want to constrain power by bureaucratizing it, that is, by establishing reliable, predictable, non-discretionary relationships among departmental goals and instruments. As with all proposals for the bureaucratic reorganization of *single* organizations, however, they fail to adequately address the question of *total* system effects.

If goals and instruments are disaggregated and assigned to independent units (as much as possible) who or what authority or authorities will assess the spillovers? In political terms, who or what organization will command sufficient instruments to *mobilize* power, rather than constrain power? The timely mobilization of power is often as necessary a characteristic of effective government and economic management as is the capacity to constrain and diffuse power.

The Breton and Acheson and Chant analyses could be applied to all the other major departments in the economic-policy process. The tendency to seek out discretionary spending resources (patronage) as bases of interagency bargaining, the tendency to prefer "soft" goals and indicators which cannot be proven to reflect unfavourably on the department concerned, and the tendency to maximize prestige are characteristics of most public bureaucracies. At some point however the total system effects must be assessed and taken into account. In terms of overall cabinet government and in terms of economic-policy processes there is also evidence which will support those who feel that economic-policy power might need to be more significantly concentrated rather than dispersed. We will return to this important dilemma of economic-policy organization.

SUMMARY

The analysis in this chapter has suggested the need to view economic-policy processes in terms of the organizational location and allocation of economic-policy instruments, and the dynamics of both intra-Cabinet, and intra-bureaucratic behaviour. It is important, moreover, to view these dynamics not only in terms of the jurisdictional sparring and bureaucratic pathologies which we are frequently prepared to assign to public bureaucracies and politicians but also in terms of the inherent and inevitable conflicts over values, goals, and instruments which form the causal basis for much of the behaviour. The analysis of *single* bureaus and organizations, be they Exchequers, central banks, or any other organizations, clearly shows that they have a strong and endemic capacity to pursue goals of self-preservation and prestige, and a strong tendency to select the instruments which will assist in the maximization of these goals, thus modifying their intended purpose. A bureaucratic analysis of *single* organizations can, however, be misleading since it fails to relate the organization's behaviour to the concurrent behaviour of other bodies and to the shifting economic and governing priorities constantly in evidence within the Cabinet.

NOTES

1. Figure 4:1 is similar to, but a significant adaptation of, a table developed by Lawrence Pierce. See his *Politics of Fiscal Policy Formation* (Pacific Palisades, Ca., 1971), p. 26.

2. For an overview of the regulatory dimension see G. Bruce Doern and V. S. Wilson, eds., *Issues in Canadian Public Policy* (Toronto, 1974), Chapter 1.

3. Pierce, *Politics of Fiscal Policy Formation*, p. 25.

4. Ibid., p. 28.

5. See M. Trebilcock, "Must the Consumer Always Lose?" Paper presented to the Institute of Public Administration of Canada, Ottawa, September 1975. See also G. Bruce Doern, ed., *The Regulatory Process in Canada* (Toronto, 1978).

6. Pierce, *Politics of Fiscal Policy Formation*, p. 29.

7. See C. L. Barber, *Theory of Fiscal Policy as Applied to a Province* (Toronto, 1976); and R. M. Burns, "The Operation of Fiscal and Economic Policy", in Doern and Wilson, eds., *Issues in Canadian Public Policy*, pp. 286-309; and André Raynauld, *The Canadian Economic System* (Toronto, 1967).

8. R. M. Burns and L. Close, *The Winter Works Program—A Case Study in Government Expenditure Decision-Making* (Toronto, 1971).

9. See Robert Best, "Youth Policy", in Doern and Wilson, eds., *Issues in Canadian Public Policy*, pp. 137-65.

10. See Michael J. Prince, "A Redistributive Policy Output and Its Impact on the Canadian Executive: The New Unemployment Insurance Act of 1971". Unpublished research essay, School of Public Administration, Carleton University, 1975. For an analysis of social security policies see Simon McInnes, PhD thesis (in progress), Department of Political Science, Carleton University, Ottawa.

11. D. McCready and Conrad Winn, "Redistributive Policy", in C. Winn and J. McMenemy, eds., *Political Parties in Canada* (Toronto, 1976), pp. 206-27.

12. For two other excellent analyses of redistributive and labour-market policy processes see Kenneth Bryden, *Old Age Pensions and Policy-Making in Canada* (Montreal, 1974), and J. S. Dupré, *et al.*, *Federalism and Policy Development: The Case of Adult Occupational Training in Ontario* (Toronto, 1973).

13. Hugh Heclo and Aaron Wildavsky, *The Private Government of Public Money* (London, 1974), p. 160.

14. Ibid., p. 151.

15. Ibid., p. 173. See also Burns, "The Operation of Fiscal and Economic Policy", pp. 286-309.

16. Heclo and Wildavsky, *The Private Government of Public Money*, pp. 196-97.

17. See Albert Breton, "Modelling the Behaviour of Exchequers", in L. J. Officer and L. B. Smith, eds., *Issues in Canadian Economics* (Toronto, 1974), pp. 110-13; Albert Breton, *The Economic Theory of Representative Government* (Chicago, 1974); Keith Acheson and John Chant, "The Bank of Canada: A Study in Bureaucracy". Manuscript, Queen's University, Kingston, 1971;

R. W. Phidd, "The Economic Council of Canada, 1963-1974", *Canadian Public Administration,* Vol. XVIII, no. 3; and J. C. H. Jones, "The Bureaucracy and Public Policy; Canadian Merger Policy and the Combines Branch", *Canadian Public Administration,* Vol. XVIII, no. 3, pp. 269-96.

18. J. E. Hodgetts, W. McCloskey, R. Whitaker, and V. S. Wilson, *The Biography of an Institution* (Montreal, 1972); John W. Langford, *Transport in Transition* (Montreal, 1976); and G. Bruce Doern, *Science and Politics in Canada* (Montreal, 1972).

19. Breton, "Modelling the Behaviour of Exchequers", p. 110.

20. Ibid., pp. 111-12.

21. Ibid., p. 112.

22. Ibid., pp. 112-13.

23. Acheson and Chant, "The Bank of Canada". For other views on the Bank of Canada see George S. Watts, "The Bank of Canada from 1948 to 1952; The Pivotal Years", *The Bank of Canada Review* (November 1974), pp. 1-16, and "The Origins and Background of Central Banking in Canada", *The Bank of Canada Review* (May 1972), pp. 14-25; and E. P. Neufeld, ed., *Money and Banking in Canada* (Toronto, 1964).

24. Acheson and Chant, "The Bank of Canada", p. 1. The pages cited refer to the originally unpublished paper. The paper was later published as "Bureaucratic Theory and the Choice of Central Bank Goals: The Case of the Bank of Canada", *Journal of Money, Credit and Banking* (December 1973).

25. Ibid., pp. 1-2.

26. Ibid., pp. 3-4.

27. Ibid., p. 8.

28. Ibid.

29. Ibid., p. 10.

30. Ibid., pp. 15-16.

31. Ibid., p. 20.

32. Ibid.

33. Ibid., p. 34.

34. Ibid., p. 58.

35. Ibid., p. 59.

CHAPTER FIVE

Economic-Policy Leaders in the Government of Canada

An analysis of the politics and management of Canadian economic policy cannot ignore the important influence of economic-policy leaders at both the ministerial and deputy-ministerial levels of the Government of Canada. As politicians and as organizational leaders these leaders have influence and power, and covet such influence and power, not only as means to pursue desired ends and policy goals, but also as ends in themselves. Such mixed motives and drives are endemic to all political and organizational leadership roles.[1] In the case of deputy ministers these motives are constrained (but not eliminated) by the important norms governing the role of public servants. Thus, most deputies (following the British civil service tradition) will formally attribute policy roles to their ministers and will seem to place their own roles and influence in subordinate positions.

The purpose of this chapter is to analyse more precisely the economic-policy leaders in the Government of Canada. Any analysis of economic-policy leaders must be based on an understanding of the extent to which such leaders are constrained by the forces around them, both in the broadest sense of the pervading values and characteristics of the Canadian political economy, and in the narrower executive-bureaucratic arena of Canadian cabinet government.

In addition to the constraints which we have analysed in earlier chapters there are other reasons for being cautious about the kind of analysis presented in this chapter. These reasons deal largely with the continuing dilemma in determining cause-and-effect relationships between aggregate or individual background characteristics of leaders (e.g., class, ethnicity, and occupation), the actual behaviour of leaders, and the policy outputs and consequences of the system being analysed.[2] Despite important methodological and analytical difficulties it is important to develop some understanding of the characteristics and behaviour of economic-policy leaders by examining aggregate background characteristics and the roles of specific individuals.[3]

We wish to stress that we are examining economic-policy leaders in the Government of Canada rather than Canadian economic "elites" generally. An analysis of economic "elites" in the broader sense is beyond the bounds of this book. For such a broader task the economic leaders of provincial governments, labour unions, and corporations would have to be included.[4] Thus the observations made and conclusions reached here are tentative. The findings are tentative in a further sense because even our analysis of economic-policy leaders in the Canadian government is confined at the aggregate level to the ministers and deputy ministers of Finance, Industry, Trade and Commerce, Regional Economic Expansion, Manpower and Immigration, and Consumer and Corporate Affairs, and to the presidents and secretaries of the Treasury Board and the governors of the Bank of Canada. While these leadership positions are the most central to economic policy-making they obviously are not the only potential positions of economic-policy leadership. As stressed in Chapter 3, the Clerk of the Privy Council and the Secretary to the Cabinet, the Principal Secretary to the Prime Minister and, of course, the Prime Minister have an important influence both directly and indirectly through their strategic positions. The above-mentioned officials also have had influence through their roles in advising on policy and on making senior appointments. In recent years ministers of National Health and Welfare, and Energy, Mines and Resources have also been increasingly involved in economic controversy within the Cabinet, as both social security issues and the supply and price of energy resources have crowded the economic-policy agenda.

Because we are dealing with two kinds of economic-policy leaders, elected ministers and non-elected senior public servants, we are interested in two related sets of information at the aggregate level. It is important to know something about the occupational/professional, ethnic, and regional/electoral backgrounds of ministers as well as their previous Cabinet portfolio experience. It is also important to know something about what Vickers has called their "appreciative systems" about economic management.[5] Each of the above components deals with important characteristics of cabinet government and of individual political perceptions. For deputy ministers it is similarly important to know something about their occupational/professional, ethnic, and regional backgrounds, as well as their career and departmental experiences and their "appreciative systems" about economic-policy processes and objectives, including their views about the organization and management of economic policy. Recent Canadian political history has testified to the importance of "representativeness" in the senior bureaucracy and thus the above components are especially important.[6] It is also essential to know something about the relationships between ministers and deputy ministers. At the aggregate level this would require information about the relative turnover among ministers and deputy ministers as well as the relationships between laymen and experts.

Not all of the above information is readily or uniformly available nor can it be easily portrayed in brief narrative form. Keeping in mind the important constraints and caveats attached to the information, we shall proceed in three stages. Thus, the remaining parts of this chapter will deal first with the aggregate characteristics of ministers and deputy ministers, and then with the more specific characteristics of selected recent ministers and deputy ministers of Finance. Finally we will make several general observations about other features of the career patterns of economic-policy leaders, especially at the bureaucratic level.

AGGREGATE CHARACTERISTICS OF ECONOMIC POLICY LEADERS

Appendix C lists the ministers and deputy ministers of Finance, and Industry, Trade and Commerce (until 1969 the Department of Trade and Commerce) between the Second World War and 1975; the ministers and deputy ministers of Regional Economic Expansion, Manpower and Immigration, and Consumer and Corporate Affairs since the creation of these departments in the 1960s; the presidents and secretaries of the Treasury Board since 1966; and the governors of the Bank of Canada. Biographical information and data on these economic-policy leaders reveal the following characteristics and patterns.

With respect to ethnic origins it is clear that economic portfolios have been predominantly held at both the ministerial and deputy-ministerial levels by English Canadians. While the appointment, by

Prime Minister Trudeau, of Jean-Luc Pépin to the Industry, Trade and Commerce portfolio in 1968, and Jean Chrétien to the Finance portfolio in 1977 have been important breakthroughs for French Canadians, it is very clear that they remain seriously underrepresented in terms of economic Cabinet portfolios. No French Canadians have been appointed to head the most senior economic portfolios at the deputy-minister level although the appointment of André Raynauld as Chairman of the Economic Council is perhaps an indication of a change in this situation. The continuing absence of French Canadians, however, is a reflection of the Canadian political economy in historical terms.

The above imbalance is but a further reflection of the concentration of economic policy power in ministers whose electoral political base is overwhelmingly lodged in Ontario. This is especially the case with ministers of Finance. Of the nine ministers of Finance between the Second World War and 1976, six have had their political base in Ontario, one in English-speaking Montreal, and two in Nova Scotia (one of the latter holding office for less than one year). None of the Finance ministers have had an elected political base in western Canada. Ministers of Industry, Trade and Commerce have been slightly more widely distributed but are dominated by ministers with Ontario or English-speaking Quebec electoral bases. It is not, of course, impossible that such ministers could and would take a broader based perspective on economic-policy issues, but the above aggregate political indicators would certainly reflect the historical development of the Canadian economy with its base in English-speaking central Canada. It also suggests that other regional and redistributive values might have emerged had the economic portfolios been differently allocated.

Interestingly enough, the appointment of T. K. Shoyama as Deputy Minister of Finance in 1975 and the earlier appointment of A. W. Johnson to the Treasury Board and then to the Department of National Health and Welfare may represent a situation in which the senior levels of the bureaucracy may have become more "representative" of political regions than the Cabinet has. Both Johnson and Shoyama were previously senior officials in the Saskatchewan government of T. C. Douglas and were thus presumed to bring important so-called "western" (and some say, socialist) perspectives to the councils of federal-policy processes. That claim is doubtful but the point remains that the informal representative characteristics of senior public servants should not be ignored.

The pattern of electoral, regional, and ethnic distribution is less concentrated when one examines the other economic Cabinet portfolios. Of the eight ministers who have occupied the portfolios of Regional Economic Expansion, Manpower and Immigration, and Consumer and Corporate Affairs three have had their base in French-speaking Quebec, one in English-speaking Quebec, two in Ontario, one in British Columbia, and one in Newfoundland. This somewhat wider pattern of distribution is important both in the aggregate and in individual cases. Donald Jamieson's occupancy of the DREE portfolio gave DREE a minister whose political base is in Newfoundland, clearly a "have not" province. Jean Marchand's association with the early development of both the Manpower and Immigration and the Regional Development portfolios brought the perspective of both a Quebec-based politician and a former labour leader. Bryce Mackasey's involvement with Manpower and Immigration and with the major revision to the unemployment insurance program also reflected this wider political base within the Liberal party. It is not impossible that these newer portfolios could provide a base from which future Finance and Industry ministers will come, thus setting up a pattern of experience and exposure which could in the long run change perceptions about economic values and issues. The mere existence of the newer economic portfolios broadens the base of representation and the possibility of acquiring broader cabinet experience in economic management.

With respect to occupational background and career patterns, some interesting points emerge, especially when comparing ministers to deputy ministers. Six of the Finance ministers were lawyers, two were accountants, and one was a career civil servant with an economics background. Lawyers are also the dominant occupational background for presidents of the Treasury Board and ministers of Consumer and Corporate Affairs. The businessman is the most representative occupation for Minister of Industry, Trade and Commerce, with lawyers and engineers being the next most common occupation. Ministers of Manpower and Immigration and Regional Economic Expansion have been drawn from a wider range of occupations including law, communications, and labour.

Generally most Finance ministers have had only one previous Cabinet portfolio with the most prevalent one being National Revenue. Only fifty per cent of the ministers of Industry, Trade and Commerce have had previous portfolios, and these have included a very diverse range of mandates including Public Works, Transport, Energy, and Defence Production. The Treasury Board presidents have held previous portfolios in National Revenue, Industry, and Indian Affairs and Northern Development. Few if any incumbents of the central economic-policy portfolios have assumed their positions after previously having experience in the so-called "supply" portfolios such as Labour, Manpower and Immigration, Consumer and Corporate Affairs, or National Health and Welfare.

At the deputy-ministerial level almost all of the deputies have had their occupational/professional background in the areas of economics and finance. Degrees in economics and commerce are typical and predominant. In addition, deputy ministers of Finance in particular have had extensive experience at senior levels in other economic portfolios and often in the PCO. They have been, in effect, career economic managers. These characteristics can be interpreted in different ways. When compared with ministers it is clear that senior public servants possess not only more occupational expertise but also more experience in several economic-policy portfolios. Among senior decision-makers they are, therefore, the only people with extensive experience in dealing with the multiple facets of economic policy. In terms of day-to-day considerations, this is an essential characteristic. In a very real sense these senior public servants view their role as being the "guardians" of the overall economic-management process as they are more actively and permanently involved in it than any other group. They are virtually the only group to have viewed economic issues in a catholic way. Their basic conservatism arises out of their experience which constantly reinforces the complex interrelationship of economic variables. In terms of the legitimacy of political power this guardian role raises some troublesome questions.

These questions are especially troublesome when one examines the historical pattern of ministerial turnover, especially among Finance ministers. There is an obviously important relationship between the permanence of civil service expertise and the transient nature of political leaders. Since the Second World War there have been ten ministers of Industry, Trade and Commerce, and eight deputies. Since 1966, there have been three presidents of the Treasury Board and four secretaries. A similar approximate "one-to-one" rate of turnover has characterized the other portfolios. These latter aggregate turnovers seem reasonable in that the deputy does not have the advantage of relative permanence in the portfolio. In the Finance portfolio, however, there have been nine ministers and five deputy ministers since the Second World War. The prospects for an excessive amount of bureaucratic influence are present in the aggregate Finance minister turnover pattern since greater permanence can secure leverage for the deputy. This factor has been of concern to the Trudeau government in particular and has undoubtedly contributed to recent efforts to increase the rate of deputy-minister turnover, especially between and among the major Cabinet portfolios, including the economic portfolios.

The general notion of the expert public servant and the generalist minister in the economic-policy field must be qualified by one further, especially critical, variable. While deputy ministers in these portfolios have had much more extensive professional experience in economic matters than ministers, it is important to note that they are also in one sense "ex-economists" or "ex-finance experts". They ought to be viewed more accurately as *political economists and economic-policy managers*. They are leaders who command large organizations and whose career experience has required them to deal with many of the separate and interrelated dimensions of economic policy in an organizational and managerial context.

While aggregate characteristics of economic-policy leaders are important, the leadership dimension must also be understood in the more specific personalized level of individual ministers and deputies. We will thus briefly explore the roles and perceptions of *selected* individual ministers and deputy ministers of Finance who have significantly influenced the conduct of Canadian economic policy in recent years, particularly with respect to the machinery of economic management. Accordingly we will present more capsule assessments of individuals focussing on their "appreciative systems" about economic-policy organization and their relationship with the Prime Minister on economic-policy issues.

MINISTERS OF FINANCE

Of the six ministers of Finance between 1957 and 1975 three, Donald Fleming, Walter Gordon, and John Turner are especially illustrative both in terms of their overall influence and their views of the evolving processes of economic management and organization. George Nowlan (who was minister for less than one year), Edgar Benson, and Mitchell Sharp will be referred to in other respects but the need to keep the total analysis within manageable limits means that the focus will clearly be on Fleming, Gordon, and Turner. While we will focus on ministers in this section, it is important that the roles of corresponding deputy ministers not be lost sight of, particularly since it is the combination of ministerial and deputy-ministerial roles that greatly affects the conduct of, and approaches taken in, economic management in each period. Thus, the relationships between Donald Fleming and Kenneth Taylor, Walter Gordon and Robert Bryce, and John Turner and Simon Reisman must be explored.

All ministers of Finance are influential members of Cabinet, both because of the portfolio and because of their own senior position in the political party. To the extent that individual Finance ministers can have even greater influence on economic policy this influence is likely to be a product of at least three factors. In basic political terms his role will be influenced by the future leadership prospects which the minister has, and which others see for him. Is he or she viewed as a likely future leader of the party? If the minister is, then this cannot help but affect perceptions and choices. A minister with strong leadership possibilities, for example, might be more inclined to follow expansionary and/or profligate spending policies with a view to building up future support both among his cabinet colleagues and in the country as a whole. A Finance minister who is viewed as on the downward part of his leadership curve might be able to afford to be more tight-fisted and tough. Even these generalizations must be qualified, however, since economic and budgetary processes go through cycles where "spending" and then "controlling" values are in the ascendency. Hence, a Prime Minister may pick a person to be his minister precisely on the basis of the need for tough controls or more generous spending, as the occasion dictates. Mitchell Sharp and Edgar Benson were both more cautious and conservative Finance ministers but they also assumed their roles after a period in the mid-1960s of quite heady budgetary expansion under Walter Gordon. Thus the images and behaviour of the previous minister influence the style and behaviour of his or her successor. The variable of leadership

aspirations, on its own, is difficult to pin down precisely because, in economic-policy terms, all other things are usually not equal.

A second and closely related factor influencing the ministerial role will be his relationship with the Prime Minister. As stressed in Chapter 4, the Prime Minister and Finance minister must, by virtue of their roles, develop a special, mutually supportive, relationship. However, while the relationship is usually special, there is obviously room for wide variations between particular incumbents of these offices. Prime Ministers take varying degrees of personal or political or intellectual interest in economic policy and related aggregate expenditure decisions. No Prime Minister of Canada could be said to have had a professional background in economics or economic management. Their strictly personal relationship with the Finance minister can vary greatly as can their differences on particular issues along the left-right continuum of political philosophy and ideology.

Finally, a third factor influencing the ministerial role is the minister's own "appreciative system" about economic policy and economic-policy organization. Because Canada has been governed only by the Liberal and Progressive-Conservative parties, it is fair to say that all of the Finance ministers (and their deputies) have held views that generally accept the legitimacy of the capitalist mixed-economy model. Within this liberal democratic view of the role of the state, however, there is obviously room for differences of view about the important specifics of economic policy. For example, views about Keynesian assumptions and prescriptions have varied among ministers as have their intellectual interests in economic organization and management.

The above three factors obviously do not exhaust all the potential influences on individual ministers of Finance, as previous chapters have made clear. These factors are, however, important and can be related more specifically to recent occupants of the Finance portfolio.

Although the basic tenets of Keynesian economics had by then been in intellectual circulation both in and out of government for many years, the role of Donald Fleming, as the Progressive-Conservative Finance minister during most of the Diefenbaker years, was most characterized by Fleming's philosophical opposition to Keynesian concepts. Fleming believed in the concept of a balanced budget and hence saw little value in the use of the budget as a counter-cylical economic tool.[7] Politically he has been described as the "epitome of the right-wing Tory".[8] Despite his support for balanced budgets his stewardship was characterized by the unexpected size of his deficits. As Peter Newman has accurately described it:

> . . . Fleming spent the Diefenbaker years vainly attempting to set limits on the politically motivated spending plans of his cabinet colleagues. Probably the main reason he failed was that in trying to block higher spending requests he and his officials seldom offered alternative methods for stimulating the economy. Faced by the two main factions in cabinet—the ministers advocating higher welfare benefits and those urging the adoption of industrial and development incentives to stimulate private capital investment—Fleming came down against both sides since their ideas ran counter to his hallowed objective of balancing the budget.[9]

Also contributing to the above pattern of behaviour was the fact that Prime Minister John Diefenbaker was both philosophically to the left of Fleming in the general ideological spectrum of the Conservative party and also not generally interested in the *overall* management of government or the economy.[10] Moreover, Fleming had been a two-time loser in the Conservative party leadership race and hence, although respected for his prodigious work and commitment, was viewed as a cabinet minister whose career had peaked, even in the early years of the Diefenbaker government.

Fleming's performance must be related to his initial reliance on the conservative views of James Coyne, the Governor of the Bank of Canada, and to the subsequent manner in which he handled the dismissal of Coyne when the latter refused to adhere to government policy. Despite the Coyne Affair, Fleming's early reliance on Coyne is illustrative of the extent to which individual Finance ministers can, in part at least, lean toward certain advisors whose views are known to coincide more with their own. In the case of Fleming this selectivity occurred despite the fact that the Finance Department, headed by Kenneth Taylor, was, at that time, viewed increasingly as a more conservative institution than it had been in earlier years.

It would be quite inaccurate, in absolute terms, to view Taylor as the bureaucratic equivalent of Donald Fleming. Taylor understood Keynesian concepts. On the other hand, Taylor, relative to his predecessor, Clifford Clark, and his successor, Robert Bryce, was viewed as a much less creative idea-man and policy-advisor.[11] As a consequence, the older historic image of Finance as the "keeper of the till", an image no doubt reinforced by the views of his minister, but in different ways, was reasserted. Hence, in relative terms the Fleming–Taylor relationship was symbiotic although each man's view of economic management had different roots. Departments are obviously partly judged by the behaviour of their leaders but such strictly leadership-oriented interpretations can be partly misleading. For example, during this period the Finance Department had other senior officials who were tendering other forms of advice. Although Fleming's stewardship as Canada's chief economic-policy manager has not generally been viewed as successful, his relative performance as a controller of expenditure growth probably looks more favourable to Conservative critics in retrospect when compared to most of his Liberal successors. It is to be remembered, however, that Fleming was minister at a time when the formal instruments of control, lodged in the Treasury Board, were relatively more under the Finance minister's control than they are now. Most of his successors had to deal with expenditures in a more arm's-length mode of operation after 1966, when the Treasury Board was made a separate department headed by its own minister.[12]

The contrast between Walter Gordon, the first minister of Finance in the Pearson government, and Donald Fleming is significant in almost every respect. Gordon was the chief idea-man and, some say, "conscience" of the Liberal party.[13] As a former advisor to the Finance Department he had been strongly influenced in his younger days by the liberal reformist ideas of Clifford Clark, the deputy minister of Finance who had significantly influenced the post-Second World War development of social programs.[14] As idea-man for the Liberal party he had urged the creation of, and subsequently chaired during the mid-1950s, a Royal Commission on Canada's Economic Prospects. He did this both as a device to discredit, and then to reform, the more conservative economic policies of a Liberal Party dominated by C. D. Howe.[15] He had become especially concerned about the degree of American ownership and control of the Canadian economy. He had been Prime Minister Pearson's campaign manager and enjoyed a close personal and political relationship with him. Although he had no apparent party-leadership aspiration of his own, he obviously assumed the Finance portfolio with the full support of Pearson and hence had a great deal of political influence. Hence, in comparison with most Finance ministers he brought to his portfolio a breadth of experience and knowledge of the Canadian political economy.

Two other factors are important in assessing Gordon's role. First he came to office with general views about the need to reorganize and energize the Finance Department. Second, he came to office under the operating assumption that great increases in public-sector expenditures would be necessary to achieve the Liberal social welfare programs. He also tended to assume that such resources would be accumulated without great increases in taxation because of the projected growth in the Canadian GNP through the mid-1960s.[16]

Regarding the Finance Department, as Denis Smith's biography of Gordon points out, Gordon,

> . . . knew that it was no longer the energetic and purposeful institution that it had been under Clifford Clark. Gordon believed that the Department would need a new Deputy Minister to restore its vitality, and he had chosen his man. R. B. Bryce, whom Gordon had known and admired since his wartime service in Ottawa, held the senior position among Ottawa civil servants as clerk of the Privy Council and secretary to the Cabinet.[17]

Again, the relationship between the minister and deputy minister of Finance assumes considerable importance. As an economist Bryce was associated personally with Keynesian concepts. He was an energetic, respected public servant known more as an idea-man than as a manager. In some quarters he was portrayed as a one-man gang developing policy ideas "on the back of an envelope". He was clearly more in the Clifford Clark model, and his presence invigorated the Finance portfolio.[18] Superficially at least, the Gordon–Bryce era seemed to bring together like-minded men. Both seemed inclined to want to relate the making of economic policy to a wider range of goals and values. On this score, however, Gordon was the stronger, more committed individual. This was due to his interventionist political philosophy but was also a reflection of the fact that Bryce's custody of the Finance Department occured at a time when some of his attention to policy was diverted by the reorganizations and restructuring of central government following the suggestions of the Glassco Commission.

Walter Gordon clearly did not fit the typical mold of the Finance-minister role. Contrary to most incumbents in the position he was by nature an activist who frequently took a pro-spending position, both to facilitate redistributive and distributive goals and to generate political support. The contrast between Gordon and both his predecessor, Donald Fleming, and his successor, Mitchell Sharp, was especially noticeable in this respect. His abortive efforts in the 1963 budget to use the wider regulative instruments to begin the process of regulating foreign investment was also illustrative of his more radical position. Thus, Gordon, and to a certain extent John Turner (although for quite different reasons), illustrate some of the strengths and weaknesses involved when the Finance-portfolio role is lodged in a minister whose political approach is more activist. The activist incumbent and the largely control-oriented, more conservative role of Finance portfolios result in interesting conflicts and outcomes. It is difficult to generalize from the Gordon case. On the one hand, the Pearson government produced many important social welfare programs, but on the other hand, Gordon found himself in conflict with the Prime Minister and with the conservative Liberal cabinet majority when he pushed the foreign investment issue too far and too fast.

John Turner's occupancy of the Finance portfolio is more difficult to judge for the obvious reason that it is, at time of writing, only recent history. Nonetheless, his role deserves some tentative assessment of the economic-policy leadership variables discussed earlier. More than any recent minister, Turner was assessed not only according to the normal criteria of evaluation, but also because he had been viewed to be so obviously a strong contender to succeed Pierre Trudeau as a leader of the Liberal party. He was, therefore, a very activist political Finance minister although more conservative than Walter Gordon. His relationships with Prime Minister Trudeau appear to have been less warm and personal precisely because they are both aggressive, relatively young political personalities.

Of perhaps equal importance is the fact that Turner's occupancy of the Finance portfolio had occured at precisely the time when the management of the economy (or perhaps its unmanageability) and the management of economic conflict were most graphically illustrated. The relationships between price stability and full employment, energy supplies and balance of payments, foreign investment review and regional development, unemployment insurance and work incentives, and price regulation and food supplies have thrown conventional Keynesian concepts into disarray. The relationships between the management of the economy and the management of the government are obvious and more difficult. From the point of view of Prime Minister Trudeau, who has had a strong intellectual interest in government structure, these increasingly obvious relationships may be among the reasons for his experimentation with complementary economic policy advisors located in the PMO. Similarly within the Finance Department, the growing reality of these relationships has forced the department to adapt by creating strengthened longer-range-policy capability, and by strengthening such sectors as its own energy-policy capability.

It could be argued that Turner's leadership ambitions would not make him into a very aggressive controller of expenditures since, on the whole, greater political credit is likely to flow from expenditure initiatives. The growth of government expenditures is influenced by such variables but leadership ambitions and the presumed inability to control spending cannot alone explain the greater growth of spending in the early 1970s. It must be stressed that the Finance minister is institutionally less able to control expenditures because of the separate existence of the Treasury Board and also because of the control over priorities by the Planning and Priorities Committee of the Cabinet headed by the Prime Minister. The minister is also required to deal with the situations he inherits from his predecessors. Turner's predecessor, Edgar Benson, was criticized for being too tight-fisted and for deliberately and inhumanely creating unemployment.

In retrospect, therefore, the evolution of both economic-policy organization and the political perceptions of recent incumbents of the Finance portfolios seem to have resulted in a diminished will and capacity to control expenditures. This may not prevent a future period when greater control will be secured. However, although Mitchell Sharp and Edgar Benson, Turner's predecessors, were more control-oriented Finance ministers, the trend in the early 1970s has been towards less and less control. This may be good or bad depending upon one's point of view. In terms of economic-policy organization it reinforces the growing paradox of the Finance minister and Finance Department roles. The Finance portfolio is expected to manage the economy but it is increasingly less capable of controlling public expenditure.

The paradox may receive further illustration when one relates these developments to the evolution of leadership at the deputy-minister level in the Department of Finance. Until the appointment of T. K. Shoyama in 1975, Turner's deputy minister had been Simon Reisman. Turner and Reisman had a great deal of respect and admiration for one another, perhaps arising out of their respective reputations of being tough, skilful, hard-nosed individuals, who relished intra-Cabinet and interagency negotiations. Reisman, more than any other recent deputy minister, has acquired the reputation of being a tough, powerful civil servant.[19] To a significant extent this is true and Reisman deserves credit for several changes in the Finance Department's personnel and structure and, contrary to his public reputation, for expanding the sources from which economic advice is sought within the government. In another sense, however, the all-powerful image is grossly misleading. The diffusion of expenditure roles among departments and the emergence of cabinet committee systems has altered the Finance mandarin's role, both in general terms, and in the management of economic policy.

DEPUTY MINISTERS OF FINANCE

It will be clear from the above analysis that ministerial leadership roles and influence are difficult things about which to generalize, but that the minister's personal characteristics and preferences do affect the conduct of economic policy. Similarly it is clear that the roles of deputy ministers of Finance matter, as do their relationships with their ministers. Several other points need to be raised, however, about the roles of deputy ministers of Finance and about the career patterns of other bureaucratic economic-policy leaders.

Each of the five deputy ministers of Finance since the Second World War have brought to the Finance portfolio different strengths and weaknesses. We have stressed earlier that all of them must be viewed as ex-economists or, more positively, as economic managers or political economists. Together, along with their colleagues and other "graduates" of the Finance Department, they have shaped over the years the Finance mystique. They know government well and their career exposure to several, if not all, of the facets of economic management make them an indispensible and valuable commodity and source of co-ordination and leadership. They are also quite capable of becoming isolated from important economic values and have been known to resent too much external criticism by either parliamentary opposition, other parts of the Cabinet and bureaucracy, or appointed critics such as the Economic Council of Canada.

Although all of the deputy ministers of Finance fall into the broad category of economic managers it is possible to categorize them into two types of economic-policy leaders—the organization man, and the idea man. Clifford Clark and Robert Bryce, as we have already noted, fit most readily into the idea-man category, while Kenneth Taylor and Simon Reisman, relatively speaking, fit more into the organization-man category, albeit for quite different reasons. T. K. Shoyama's role is more difficult to categorize since, at the time of writing, he has just assumed his duties.

Clifford Clark's role as economic-policy leader cannot be underestimated. He was clearly a catalyst and source of many social welfare measures and possessed a leadership quality that attracted and inspired others.[20] It is to be remembered, of course, that Clark's period in office (1932 to 1952) coincided with a simpler era of government than today's, and with a much smaller public service where, in a very real sense, individual influence could be more readily achieved and could be noticed by others. Despite these differences, however, Clark's influence both relatively and absolutely was enormous.

Kenneth Taylor's role was bound to pale into insignificance in comparison with his predecessor, Clark. Leaders who succeed so-called "charismatic" leaders are usually obliged to act as a consolidator and to serve as a routinizer of past achievements. This institutional tendency was reinforced by Taylor's own background as a reliable, competent manager. The 1950s were a period of consolidation for the Department of Finance. This period of normalcy was also a reflection of the broader political normalcy generated by the prosperity and growth of the 1950s and by the comfortable period of federal Liberal government rule. Moreover, a great deal of economic-policy influence in the early 1950s was centred in the Department of Trade and Commerce headed by C. D. Howe.

Walter Gordon's choice, Robert Bryce, was regarded as an intellectual public servant. It is difficult to attribute the same obvious creativity to Bryce, however, that one can with Clifford Clark. This is because of the more obvious early influence of his minister, Walter Gordon, and even of other early Pearson officials such as Tom Kent. Moreover, Bryce's previous experience over many years in international finance, and as Secretary to the Treasury Board and later Clerk of the Privy Council meant that he brought to the Finance portfolio a broader governmental experience, an experience which usually counsels one against the prospects of radical or major change.

Simon Reisman had come to the Finance portfolio in 1970 after previously being the Secretary of the Treasury Board, Deputy Minister of the Department of Industry (where he had won a well-deserved reputation as the man who negotiated the auto pact), and an Assistant Deputy Minister of Finance. His principal experience had, however, been in international finance. The area of each deputy minister's substantive expertise is not unimportant because in addition to his general experience and personal qualities, he may be appointed because of the need to give emphasis to certain aspects of economic policy. It is important to view the appointment of T. K. Shoyama as Deputy Minister of Finance in this light because his principal expertise and experience has been in intergovernmental finance and policy. He becomes the first Deputy Minister of Finance to have spent a significant part of his career in the provincial-government sector. Shoyama had also been a major catalyst in the 1973 Western Economic Opportunities Conference where the federal Liberals hoped to begin the process of redressing both the historic and the recent pattern of western grievances.

Shoyama's appointment is perhaps a reflection of a general tendency in recent years to open, at least slightly, the career patterns of bureaucratic economic-policy leaders, by drawing on wider sources of recruitment. The Finance Department's deputy ministers and the Bank of Canada's governors have, however, been selected on the basis of a strong adherence to career experience within and around the Finance Department and Bank of Canada realms. All of the governors of the Bank of Canada have been appointed by promotion from within the Bank.

There is a strong and important sense of the guardian role created by these career patterns. To manage the economy one needs experience and thus there is an important element of truth to be understood in the guardian role suggested by the Finance Department and Bank of Canada leadership and recruitment patterns.

In other respects, however, some interesting patterns are emerging. The successive chairmen of the Economic Council of Canada over the past decade — John Deutsch, Arthur Smith, and André Raynauld — illustrate a pattern of recruitment in which extensive previous governmental experience is relatively less important.[21] Deutsch knew government circles extremely well and his interpretation of the Economic Council's role reflected his experience. Arthur Smith was clearly more of an outsider, having spent several years with the predecessor of the organization, the Conference Board of Canada, which he subsequently headed. Smith's experience with the Economic Council and the more aggressive role he gave to the Council has prepared him well for his duties with the Conference Board, where he has significantly built up the professional resources of the Board to act as a public, competing source of information including information on short-term economic forecasting. André Raynauld is clearly more of an outsider as well, although he has previously acted as an advisor to the Finance Department. Generally his career has been more in academic circles and he brings to the Council a more rigorous view of its research role. The beginnings of a two-way flow of personnel between the Council and the government has also begun with the secondment of George Post, a former Assistant Secretary to the Cabinet Committee on Economic Policy, to the Economic Council.

Recruitment patterns need not be confined to the top level of the Economic Council or other organizations. T. K. Shoyama, Sylvia Ostry, and Otto Thür have all come into senior positions from the Economic Council staff, with Ostry appointed to Statistics Canada and then Consumer and Corporate Affairs in a deputy-ministerial capacity, and Thür appointed to Finance as an Assistant Deputy Minister for long-range planning. Similarly John Young moved from an academic post and from his chairmanship of the Prices and Incomes Commission to an Assistant-Deputy-Minister position in the Finance Department. These appointments illustrate, perhaps, that it may be necessary to view the value of commissions and councils less in terms of their substantive policy advice, and more in terms of the career avenues they facilitate.

The pattern of appointments to the several economic policy agencies is also a reflection of the importance of the process of making senior appointments. This process is largely centred in the PCO and the PMO. Thus the Secretary to the Cabinet and the Prime Minister's principal policy secretary influence economic-policy processes by the kinds of recommendations they make to the Prime Minister regarding the people to be appointed to head the major economic portfolios and agencies.

It is perhaps in this broader light that the appointment of Michael Pitfield in 1974 as Clerk of the Privy Council and Secretary to the Cabinet should be viewed. His appointment disturbed the normal pattern of recruitment. His predecessors in this position, Gordon Robertson and Robert Bryce, were products of the more normal, self-contained career path. Pitfield's previous experience had been more limited, and was more political or quasi-political in the PCO, coupled with a period as Deputy Minister of Consumer and Corporate Affairs.

The Secretary to the Cabinet, of course, occupies a powerful role in government-policy processes generally including the management of the economy. The fact that he is secretary to the Cabinet Committee on Priorities and Planning, the strategic economic policy committee of the Cabinet, means that his potential influence becomes even more institutionalized and reinforced.

In historical terms, therefore, there is some evidence that the overall bureaucratic economic-policy leadership patterns are becoming relatively more open and fluid than they have been in the past. This increase in openness is perhaps augmented by the shortening length of incumbency in these positions. Clifford Clark was deputy for twenty years but his successors, Taylor, Bryce, and Reisman, occupied the post for eleven, six, and five years respectively. These shortened periods of incumbency will likely continue; however, it is doubtful that they can be shortened too much further, lest the process degenerate into a meaningless game of deputy-ministerial musical chairs.

SUMMARY

The portrait of economic-policy leaders in the Government of Canada presented in this chapter must be interpreted with caution. It is not a total portrait of the Government of Canada and certainly must be related to leadership values in other sections of the Canadian political economy. The aggregate characteristics of ministers and deputy ministers reveal both disturbing and encouraging elements. While tendencies toward greater openness in recruitment can be observed, the system is still largely a closed one. In one respect it is closed because of the need to have economic-policy advice tendered by people who have knowledge and experience. Because there are inherently only a few general leadership roles in government there are only a few individuals who will command influence based on such roles and experience. The influence of individual ministers and deputy ministers is real and important, and it varies greatly. It cannot be assessed, however, without regard to the minister's relationship to his deputy, to the organizational realities they both face, and ultimately to the broader causal forces and values which receive political expression in the Canadian political economy.

NOTES

1. See Phillip Selznick. *Leadership in Administration* (New York, 1957), and Charles Perrow, *Organizational Analysis* (Belmont, Ca., 1970), pp. 5-14.

2. On the methodological issues of elite analysis see L. Dexter, *Elite and Specialized Interviewing* (Evanston, Ill., 1970); E. Black, "The Fractured Mosaic —John Porter Revisited". Paper presented to the Canadian Political Science Association, 1974; Robert D. Putnam, *The Beliefs of Politicians: Ideology, Conflict and Democracy in Britain and Italy* (New Haven, 1973); and Lewis J. Edinger and Donald D. Searing, "Social Background in Elite Analysis", *American Political Science Review*, Vol. LXI (1967), pp. 428-45.

3. Aggregate data in this chapter were compiled from individual resumes, the *Canadian Parliamentary Guide*, and the *Canadian Who's Who*. Assessments are derived primarily from confidential interviews with some ministers and senior officials. Supplementary sources are cited in the accompanying notes.

4. In this connection see the important work of John Porter, *The Vertical Mosaic* (Toronto, 1965) and Wallace Clement, *The Canadian Corporate Elite* (Toronto, 1975.)

5. Sir Geoffrey Vickers, *Value Systems and Social Process* (London, 1968).

6. See V. Seymour Wilson and W. A. Mullins, "Representative Bureaucracy: Its Relevance to Canadian Public Policy". Paper presented at Carleton University, Ottawa, 1976. See also J. E. Hodgetts, *et al.*, *The Biography of an Institution* (Montreal, 1972).

7. Interviews.

8. Peter C. Newman, *Renegade in Power: The Diefenbaker Years* (Toronto, 1963), p. 125. See also H. Scott Gordon, "A Twenty-Year Perspective: Some Reflecting on the Keynesian Revolution in Canada", in Canadian Trade Committee, *Canadian Economy Policy Since the War* (Montreal, 1966), pp. 28-46.

9. Newman, *Renegade in Power*, p. 125.

10. For a comparative assessment of the Diefenbaker, Pearson, and Trudeau approaches to governmental organization and public policy see G. Bruce Doern and Peter Aucoin, eds., *The Structures of Policy-Making in Canada* (Toronto, 1971), Chapter 2, and Thomas Hockin, ed., *Apex of Power* (Toronto, 1971).

11. Interviews.

12. See M. Hicks, "The Treasury Board of Canada and Its Clients", *Canadian Public Administration*, Vol. XVI, no. 2 (September 1973), pp. 182-205.

13. Denis Smith, *Gentle Patriot* (Edmonton, 1973).

14. Ibid., p. 21.

15. Ibid., pp. 32-34.

16. Interviews.

17. Smith, *Gentle Patriot*, p. 137. See also Peter C. Newman, *The Distemper of our Times* (Toronto, 1968), pp. 13-14, and *Mike, The Memoirs of the Rt. Hon. Lester B. Pearson*, Vol. III (Toronto, 1975), chapters 4 and 8.

18. Interviews.

19. Interviews. Reisman's views have also been reported in several press interviews. See Clair Balfour, "Simon Reisman: He Knows What's Best for Us", *Financial Times of Canada*, November 25, 1974, p. 2; Stephen Duncan, "Job Assumptions Changed", *The Financial Post*, December 14, 1974, p. 13; Ian

Porter, "Is a Mandarin Caught in the Middle?" *The Globe and Mail,* November 9, 1972, p. 7 and "It's Really a Whole New Ball Game", *The Financial Post,* April 21, 1973, p. 4. See also his speech excerpted in *The Globe and Mail,* April 2, 1976, p. 7.

20. See Porter, *The Vertical Mosaic,* pp. 425-527; Smith, *Gentle Patriot,* p. 21; and J. W. Pickersgill and D. F. Forster, *The Mackenzie King Record,* Vol. III (Toronto, 1970), especially Chapter 6.

21. See Richard W. Phidd, "The Role of Central Advisory Councils: The Economic Council of Canada", in Doern and Aucoin, eds., *The Structures of Policy-Making in Canada,* Chapter 8.

PART THREE

The Operation of Economic-Policy Formulation

The purpose of Part III of the book is to describe in greater detail the primary *roles of the major economic management departments. The complete role of all departments is not described. Each chapter examines the evolution of the departments' respective policy mandates and relates that evolving mandate to departmental structure and organization.*

Part III will demonstrate in greater detail that the Finance Department is a department unlike all the others in the degree to which it plays a central co-ordinative role. At the same time, however, the growing interrelationships between Finance and the other economic portfolios, and among the several economic departments will emerge more obviously.

Part III does not attempt to evaluate all of the policy dimensions under the custody of the departments examined. It does describe these dimensions and, in so doing, brings out the increasingly acknowledged importance of the micro dimensions of Canadian economic management. Such a micro managerial, organizational, and administrative perspective is absolutely essential if an intellectually complete understanding of the politics and management of Canadian economic policy is to be developed.

Viewing economic policy through the organization and mandates of departments is of course not the only legitimate way to examine the Canadian political economy. But they are an important reflection of economic policy processes, values, and changing priorities. Through departments one can see more clearly the interdepartmental, federal-provincial, public-private, technical and distributive variables in the politics and management of Canadian economic policy.

CHAPTER SIX

The Evolution of Economic-Policy Organization in Canada

This chapter presents a brief analysis of the general historical evolution of economic-policy organization in Canada in order to provide important background information for the analysis in subsequent chapters. The analysis will illustrate the close linkage between the nature of economic research and techniques, the objectives of economic policy, and the constant need to accommodate new organizations designed to ameliorate the evolving economic conditions. The chapter will focus on the evolution of economic-policy machinery since the latter stages of the Second World War. The review is not intended to be a detailed account of administrative history; rather it will describe the broad developments in economic-policy organizations and events.

The chapter will first discuss the early postwar developments by relating the broad organizational changes, in such departments as Labour, Trade and Commerce (now Industry, Trade and Commerce), and the Dominion Bureau of Statistics (now Statistics Canada), to the search for better techniques and economic intelligence. Particular attention will then be paid to the evolution of the Department of Finance since its role is obviously central in economic-policy making. The role of the Bank of Canada will be briefly described as will the influence of the Glassco Commission recommendations in the early 1960s. Finally the emergence of new centres of economic-policy influence such as the Economic Council of Canada, the Department of Manpower and Immigration, the Department of Consumer and Corporate Affairs, the Department of Regional Economic Expansion, and Statistics Canada will be described along with external centres of economic analysis. Other major changes in the organization and functioning of the Cabinet were explored in Chapter 3, since these were changes developed in response to more general concerns about the policy-making process rather than concerns about economic policy as such.

THE EARLY YEARS: TECHNIQUES FOR IMPROVING ECONOMIC POLICIES

Economic-policy formulation may be looked at from two interrelated dimensions, both linked to the politics of economic management discussed in Part I. These are the need to develop techniques and new structures to conduct research and to formulate particular aspects of economic management.[1] These two dimensions may be further explained in an evolutionary and historical manner. First, analytical techniques and new economic information have been developed. There is, therefore, a close relationship between the development of economic knowledge and the formulation of economic policy. Second, broad objectives have been developed which have been influenced by the political climate prevailing at the time of their formulation. Third, the broadening of techniques and the increased complexities of societal goals have required greater emphasis on economic management in that various organizations involved in economic-policy making have had to be co-ordinated to achieve these goals.

In relative contrast to recent years the early postwar years concentrated more on the development of techniques to improve economic-policy analysis rather than on major governmental reorganization and the creation of new departments. Canadian techniques for forecasting were developed fairly recently. They have their origin in the 1945 White Paper on Employment and Income, published one month before the end of the war in Europe. The major theme of that paper was the adoption of "high and stable levels of employment and income, and higher standards of living, to be a primary aim of government policy in the postwar period". The objectives were rooted in part in the experience of the depression of the 1930s, but were also profoundly influenced by the emergence of Keynesian economics and by the 1942 publication in the U.K. of the famous Beveridge Report on social insurance.[2] The Keynesian and the Beveridge revolutions influenced the strengthening in the mid-1940s of the departments of Finance and National Health and Welfare which, as we shall observe later, have performed major roles in Canadian economic management.

The evolution of analytical techniques was closely related to the Department of Reconstruction and Supply, which was established in 1945 as part of a program of reconstruction. After the conclusion of hostilities in the Pacific, the wartime functions of the Department of

Munitions and Supply declined rapidly and the department became concerned primarily with problems of reconversion.

Economic research was given considerable priority in the Department of Reconstruction and Supply. Even before the publication of the White Paper, the government had, in November 1944, established an Economic Research Branch in the department. To maintain continuity, the senior personnel of the branch were drawn from the research secretariats of the Reconstruction Committee and the Economic Advisory Committee, two important groups which were utilized during the war.

The most important work of the Branch was to make national forecasts of employment and income as a basis for policy decisions, through an analysis of imports and exports, investment and consumer expenditure, inventory holdings, possible bottlenecks in supply, the progress of reconversion and expansion, labour management relations, and related matters.

This overall appraisal was supplemented by special reviews of the outlook for the development of major economic regions and industries and by numerous other economic studies. The branch also prepared a forecast of building-material requirements for housing targets of varying dimensions and began an inventory of federal, provincial, and municipal public projects in terms of type, location, estimated cost, and state of planning.

Recent reviews of policies regarding economic forecasting confirm the influence of the White Paper on Employment and Income and the Department of Reconstruction and Supply, and emphasize the extent to which the government acted to establish a more comprehensive system of economic reporting. The initial task was to improve and extend the statistical tools available for charting the course of current and prospective economic developments and to establish a framework for measuring the level and outcome of the nation's economic performance. No attempt was made, however, to integrate all the separate approaches to short-term analysis into a single administrative body, structure, or even committee.[3]

In accordance with the goal of improving short-term analytical techniques in 1945, a Central Research and Development Staff was established at the Dominion Bureau of Statistics, charged with the task of co-ordinating the Bureau's work in the field of economic statistics and of developing a set of national income accounts for Canada. A quarterly labour force survey was begun at about the same time. In addition, steps were taken to establish a survey of capital-investment intentions of business and government. These measures had the effect of strengthening the work of the Economic Research Branch of the then Department of Reconstruction and Supply, which was assigned responsibility for preparing on a regular basis short-term forecasts of the level of economic activity.

Considerable thought was given to developing a co-ordinated approach to economic policies. It was pointed out that:

> Departmental policies have to be aimed at more than Departmental responsibilities; they have to be considered also in relation to their effectiveness on the general level of economic activity, which by itself has become one of the Government's principal concerns. In time, the problems associated with this new Government responsibility may call for new administrative techniques, but meanwhile, it is desirable to develop a wider understanding and recognition of the broad national objectives against which individual departmental policies have to be considered and developed.[4]

Interdepartmental co-ordination was reflected in co-operation and consultation between the Economic Branch of the Department of Trade and Commerce, the Financial Affairs and Economic Analysis Division of the Department of Finance, the Economic and Research Branch of the Department of Labour, and the Research Department of the Bank of Canada. While the departments adhered to certain particular approaches, they tended to develop a general outlook common to all four groups.[5]

It is clear that emphasis was placed on techniques. It was emphasized that forecasting could minimize the nature of remedial measures.

> Its aim is to foresee broad movements sufficiently in advance to give the Government time to prepare compensatory or remedial action. Thus, it was noted that the importance of timing cannot be too strongly emphasized. The earlier action is taken, the less action will be required and the more effective it will be.[6]

A fair degree of co-ordination of techniques took place between the Department of Trade and Commerce, the Department of Finance, the Economic Research Branch of the Department of Labour, and the

Research Department of the Bank of Canada. Forecasts on capital expenditures were based, to a large extent, upon surveys of investment intentions carried out by the Dominion Bureau of Statistics in collaboration with the Economic Research Branch of the Department of Trade and Commerce. The Central Mortgage and Housing Corporation, which administered the National Housing Act, prepared forecasts of housing expenditures. Forecasts of government spending were based on an analysis of budgetary estimates compiled by the Federal Department of Finance, together with the available information on the spending plans of the provincial and municipal authorities. Regular short-term forecasts of employment and unemployment were made by the Department of Labour in connection with its responsibilities for the analysis of developments in the labour market.

It is worth noting at this stage that the Canadian Department of Labour was viewed by many to be a department that lacked adequate analytical capacities. In the postwar period, the department was asked to handle a survey of the labour market. The requested survey involved the assembling of information to facilitate the matching of skills against the requirement of the whole economy. The department possessed neither the orientation nor the manpower to conduct the survey. Consequently, the task was given to the Dominion Bureau of Statistics. The Economic Council, almost twenty years later, also strongly criticized the work of the Department of Labour.[7]

It is particularly important to note that the national accounts reference framework, to which all of the above projections were anchored, was prepared at the Dominion Bureau of Statistics. The DBS played an important role in the development of the above techniques and a significant number of Canada's research economists commenced their careers at the Bureau. Thus, the Bureau provided a form of apprenticeship in regard to the acquisition of statistical experience.

Forecasts of government expenditure were based on capital-investment intentions and on an analysis of the regular budgetary estimates of the various levels of government. Continuing reviews of government estimates and analysis of budgetary revenues and financial transactions for the public accounts were carried out by the Securities Department of the Bank of Canada, the Department of Finance, and the Taxation Division and the Cash Management Division of the Staff of the Controller of the Treasury. A detailed forecast of federal government transactions on the national accounts basis were kept in the Research Department of the Bank of Canada and they were reconciled frequently with the budgetary presentation. Considerable progress was made also in the Research Department of the Bank of Canada in the development of an integrated set of accounts for the federal sector. Eventually the Bank of Canada became much more analytically capable than the Department of Trade and Commerce and the Department of Finance.

In the area of capital investment intentions, work had been initiated by the Department of Reconstruction and Supply in 1945.[8] The first trial survey, which was done in 1945, was published in 1946. The survey, which covered about 12,000 businesses in 1946 and about 20,000 in 1948, was the responsibility of the Department of Reconstruction and Supply and the Department of Trade and Commerce; the DBS did the actual mailing and the machine tabulations of the returns. After 1950 the DBS accepted prime responsibility for the survey, including sampling, collecting, and processing data. However, the Department of Trade and Commerce continued to be responsible for analytical material and the publication of the reports.

In the area of balance-of-payments forecasts, responsibility was shared jointly by the Department of Trade and Commerce, the Bank of Canada, the Department of Finance, and the DBS. The forecast was prepared by a working committee of representatives from the four government agencies.

Work on the construction of econometric models was initiated in the Department of Reconstruction and Supply in 1947.[9] Further work on the use of models was carried out as an integral part of short-term forecasting work in the Economics Branch of the Department of Trade and Commerce. The original model consisted of eleven equations. However, by 1962 the model contained over sixty equations. It was taken over by the Department of Finance in 1964.[10] This tends to reinforce a continued strengthening of the analytical capabilities of the Department of Finance. Forecasts on employment and unemployment were done to a considerable extent in the Department of Labour. Reports were prepared twice a year and were circulated on a confidential basis between the departments.

Our historical review, to this point, demonstrates two things: first, that the Department of Reconstruction and Supply had provided the nucleus for the analytical inputs which went into the co-ordination of economic policies after the war; second, while analytical methods and techniques were developed extensively throughout various departments, there seemed to have been very little co-ordination through a single formal organization. The co-ordination was done primarily as a part of the budgetary process. Techniques were developed to a far greater degree than structural reform. The strengthening of the cabinet committee system and the development of planning secretariats in the PCO and the Treasury Board were as we have seen in Chapter 3 later developments of the Pearson and Trudeau administrations. The strengthening of the Dominion Bureau of Statistics, now renamed Statistics Canada, further reflected improvements in the gathering of economic intelligence for various users.

The above description illustrates the fact that the approach to forecasting in Canada has been eclectic in nature, with the final product being a fusion of several approaches so that no single school or method predominates. As R. B. Crozier noted, in the early 1960s, short-term forecasting in Canada did not form a part of a general economic "plan" aimed at the achievement of certain "target" objectives, but simply served as background information in connection with the formation of government programs.[11] The overall approach to forecasting in Canada is interdepartmental and forecasts draw heavily upon materials and expert knowledge from various departments and agencies of the government.[12]

Very little emphasis, however, was placed on structure since most of the co-ordination took place on an interpersonal basis. The Department of Reconstruction and Supply ceased to exist in 1949; its functions were transferred to the Department of Trade and Commerce. Despite this change, emphasis was still placed on analytical techniques, rather than on broad co-ordination of economic policies. The Department of Trade and Commerce became, for a while, a focal point of economic analysis in Canada with the Department of Finance providing a central guiding role.

In all western countries during the 1960s organizational procedures have been established to reduce the burden of comprehensive analysis. These procedures achieve their objectives by imposing organizational constraints on the decision-making process through the specification of goals such as full employment, price-level stability, an adequate rate of economic growth, and balance-of-payments equilibrium.[13] In Canada these developments may be initially analysed through the historical evolution of the Department of Finance.

THE DEPARTMENT OF FINANCE: ITS ADAPTATION TO AN ECONOMIC MANAGEMENT DEPARTMENT

The Department's Early History

A review of the role of the Department of Finance in Canada demonstrates that it has evolved from a primarily accounting and financial-control agency toward a broad economic-management department. It has in recent years developed a stronger emphasis on fiscal policy and on strategies and ancillary problems associated with an expansionary economy.

The Department of Finance is one of the oldest government agencies and it has always been intricately linked to the Treasury Board. The Board has existed since Confederation as the financial committee of the Privy Council (Cabinet) dealing with estimates, expenditures, revenues, accounting, and related matters. In 1869 the Department of Finance Act placed the Board on a statutory basis consisting of the Minister of Finance as chairman and five members of the Privy Council served by a secretariat within the Department of Finance.

Article 2 of the Department of Finance Act made provision for the supervision, control, and direction of all matters relating to the financial affairs and public accounts, revenue, and expenditure of the Dominion. The Department of Finance's role was more or less adapted from that of the British Treasury.

Article 4 of the Department of Finance Act made provision for the Treasury Board which remained in the department until 1966.[14] It is worth mentioning that some pertinent objections to the establishment of the Board were made on the grounds that its creation had the potential for removing the Minister of Finance from direct accountability to Parliament for financial matters.[15] These objections were somewhat negated by the fact that the Minister of Finance until 1966 chaired the Board. However, the 1966 changes reintroduced this controversy.

Thus, from the beginning there has been a close relationship between the Department of Finance and the Treasury Board. This relationship has been modified on several occasions as the financial and economic management roles of government became increasingly more complex. These modifications include: the Department of Finance Act of 1869 under which the Auditor General and the Deputy Inspector General were ranked equally; the Audit Act of 1878 which created the independent office of the Auditor General; the Consolidation of the Revenue and the Audit acts in 1886; the revised Consolidated Revenue and Audit Act of 1931 which removed control of issue from the Auditor General, leaving him responsibility for legislature post-audit only; the 1951 Financial Administration Act which consolidated the Audit and Revenue Act of 1931; and finally, the 1969 Financial Administration Act, the successor to the Consolidated Revenue and Audit Act, which abolished the Office of the Comptroller of the Treasury (who had been given the duty of making all payments out of the Consolidated Revenue Fund) transferring his pre-audit functions to departments and vesting his issue or payment functions in the Receiver General for Canada.[16]

Since the 1930s the Department of Finance has always performed a central role in the co-ordination of economic policies partially because of its responsibility for preparing the budget and partially because of its extraordinary co-ordinating in financing the war. Prior to the budget, a common view was generally established through informal interdepartmental consultation. At other times, short-term forecasts relating either to the general outlook or to more particular sectors of the economy (e.g., the balance of payments, unemployment, and government cash requirements) were made either through interdepartmental working parties or by the individual departments and agencies primarily concerned. In this way, the short-term forecasts, which provided background information in connection with the formulation of government economic policy, were subject to continuous review and change, rather than to periodic adjustment at specified intervals.

The department's staff remained small after the First World War and was organized under two deputy ministers, the Deputy Inspector General and the Deputy Receiver General. In 1923 the department was divided into five branches still primarily of an accounting and administrative nature. The 1931 Consolidated Revenue and Audit Act provided a complete overhaul of the controls imposed by Parliament over the expenditures of the government. It provided for control and responsibility for accounting to be centralized in a Comptroller of the Treasury, and to be audited by the Auditor General, and it provided for publicity in regard to expenditure. By 1935 the Department had developed a Tax Investigation Branch and had taken over responsibility for the Royal Mint. In 1938 a Housing Branch was created and certain new initiatives began to emerge with the creation of the Bank of Canada in 1935 and the broadening of its role in 1938. The list of the branches within the Department of Finance in 1939 presented in Figure 6:1, shows its early accounting role in the management of the Government of Canada.

FIGURE 6:1
Department of Finance, 1939

Departmental Administration
Deputy Minister and Secretary of the Treasury Board—W. C. Clark
  Assistant Deputy Minister—W. C. Ronson
    Clerk of Estimates—W. Smellie
    Treasury Board Staff
  Solicitor of the Treasury—D. M. Johnson
  Financial Investigator—R. B. Bryce
  Taxation Investigator—A. K. Eaton

Accounts Branch
Chief Dominion Bookkeeper—J. G. McFarlane
  Accounts
  Cheque Adjustment Branch
  Securities Deposits

Bank Inspection
  Inspector General of Banks—G. S. Tomkins

Bankruptcy Act Administration
Superintendent of Bankruptcy
  Legal Examiners
  Accountant—Examiner

Commissioner of Tariff's Office
Commissioner of Tariff—H. B. McKinnon
  Tariff Investigators

Housing Branch

Royal Canadian Mint
Master
 Assay
 Coining
 Engraving
 Refining

Old Age Pensions

Superannuation and Retirement

Commission for Payment of Interest on Public Debt

Tariff Board
Chairman
 Members
 Staff

Office of the Comptroller of the Treasury
Comptroller of the Treasury—B. J. McIntyre
 Central Accounting Office
 Central Pay Office
 Chief Treasury Office

While the Department of Finance had central responsibilities, it did not undertake, until quite recently, a significant portion of the research which preceded the preparation of the budget. Instead, it relied on the Bank of Canada and the Department of Trade and Commerce. The Department was nonetheless extremely influential as a policy agency. This was due, in part, to the fact that it included a prominent Canadian economist, Dr. Clifford Clark, who was the dominant figure in economic management during the inter- and postwar years. The period between 1939 and 1950 demonstrated an excellent policy-co-ordination role with greater research and investigatory roles being assumed under the direction of R. B. Bryce (Financial Investigator) and A. K. Eaton (Taxation Investigator) within the Treasury Board.

The economics orientation of the department further emerged in 1946 when R. B. Bryce became head of a new "Economic Division" with a strong Keynesian orientation.[17] Dr. Eaton became an Assistant Deputy Minister and head of the Taxation Division and J. J. Deutsch (who was later to become the first Chairman of the Economic Council) became head of International Economic Relations. A Secretariat on Dominion Provincial Relations was created in 1947.

Kenneth Taylor became Deputy Minister of Finance in 1952 but no major changes occured in the department under his leadership with the department continuing to carry out what was by then a more mixed accounting and fiscal policy role. Much of the postwar debate over the machinery for formulating economic policy has touched primarily on the role of departments of Finance.

The Department of Finance from the 1930s to the Early 1960s

John Porter asserts that the Department of Finance was dominated from 1932 to 1952 by W. C. Clark, an economics professor from Queen's University, who assumed the prominent role of Deputy Minister of Finance at the beginning of that period. As described by Professor Porter, "Dr. Clark's Boys" included those who were to become such prominent Canadian economic-policy makers: Graham Towers, R. B. Bryce, K. W. Taylor, W. A. Mackintosh, Louis Rasminsky, Mitchell Sharp, and Harvey Perry.[18] The relationship between the Liberal party and the bureaucracy may be demonstrated if the then young economists such as Jack Davis, who was at the Department of Trade and Commerce, is added to that of Mitchell Sharp and Jack Pickersgill.

From November 1944 to C. D. Howe's defeat in June 1957, economic-policy formulation was shared by the Department of Finance, the Department of Reconstruction (which later became the Department of Reconstruction and Supply), and the Department of Trade and Commerce, with some adjustments in 1948, when C. D. Howe became Minister of Trade and Commerce. Under C. D. Howe, a large Canadian economic-research unit and advisory group was built up which functioned as a unit until 1950. After the outbreak of the Korean War, the large economic-research branch at Trade and Commerce, which had acquired some of the most competent analysts from the Department of Reconstruction and Supply in 1949, was divided among several research units. The economists were widely distributed among different departments and Crown corporations, namely, the

Department of National Defence, the Defence Research Board, the Department of Transport, the Bank of Canada, and the Dominion Bureau of Statistics, leaving a much smaller nucleus remaining in the Department of Trade and Commerce.

Economic-policy formulation continued to be shared between the departments of Finance, Trade and Commerce, and the Bank of Canada, with the Department of Trade and Commerce (with a considerably reduced economic-research staff) providing a central service function to the government as a whole. The analytical inputs included the preparation of regular and quarterly forecasts on a national, industrial, and regional basis. The work was supplemented by regular conferences of business and government economists held twice a year on a confidential basis, chaired by three men over its entire existence, namely, Stewart Bates, Mitchell Sharp, and O. J. Firestone, the latter in the capacity of Economic Advisor to the Department of Trade and Commerce.

The Department of Finance, which performed a major co-ordinating role during the war through its influence over the budget was adversely affected when C. D. Howe, the most dominant economic and political figure in the Cabinet, was asked by Prime Minister Mackenzie King to become the first Minister of the Department of Reconstruction. C. D. Howe refused to assume responsibility for the new department for five months until some of the top policy advisors at the Department of Finance and the PCO were transferred to the new department.[19] Prominent policy advisors involved were: Dr. W. A. Mackintosh, M. C. Urquhart, Dr. O. J. Firestone, Dr. Claude M. Isbister, and Mitchell Sharp.

The Department of Finance, however, began to recoup its losses by the early 1950s. As noted earlier, Kenneth W. Taylor, a graduate of McMaster University, who had worked in the postwar machinery, became Deputy Minister of Finance in 1952. Dr. J. J. Deutsch became an assistant deputy minister, but he soon took over the duties in the Treasury Board from R. B. Bryce. Claude Isbister and A. F. W. Plumptre were other assistant deputy ministers. The Economic Policy Division was under J. F. Parkinson in 1954.

In the late 1950s major analytical inputs came from the Department of Trade and Commerce. Generally speaking, between 1957 and 1962, economic-policy formulation gradually shifted once more toward the

Department of Finance. The department was assisted during this period primarily by the Bank of Canada, which expanded its economic research staff and became the largest and strongest research establishment, surpassing by a considerable margin the research unit of the Department of Trade and Commerce, which had shrunk in size from fifty economists at its peak to ten at the time of the break-up mentioned earlier.[20] In the late 1950s, an economic policy "crisis" developed which emanated from a major analytical disagreement between the Bank of Canada and the Department of Trade and Commerce. The Bank of Canada had forecast an upturn in the economy, while the Department of Trade and Commerce had forecast a downturn. This occurrence precipitated a major controversy between the Conservative and Liberal parties concerning the role of the bureaucracy.

A number of senior public servants have expressed the view that in the early 1960s co-ordination of policies was carried out more at the PCO than at Finance. The focal point was R. B. Bryce, who was then in the PCO. The PCO was supported by groups of deputy ministers which varied according to the issues being dealt with. However, the number of departments had grown considerably and there was need to co-ordinate a broader number of policy instruments, thus introducing new controversies concerning the role of the Department of Finance.[21]

The Department of Finance acquired a few very influential people in the early and mid-1960s, although it did not expand significantly either in size or in formal organizational structure. The department has always served as a major training post for high-level public servants and, accordingly, it has thus also suffered from a high degree of personnel turnover. However, it was further strengthened in the mid-1960s.

A new Liberal government was elected in 1963 and Walter Gordon was appointed Minister of Finance. As stressed in Chapter 5 his appointment was important for two reasons. First, he had previously been head of the Royal Commission on Canada's Economic Prospects; and second, he had been associated with views relating to the need to change the governmental machinery.[22]

The personnel changes which occured in the mid-1960s included Simon Reisman, who had worked on the Gordon Commission on Canada's long-term economic prospects and who, during this period, was appointed Deputy Minister of the Department of Industry. He was previously Assistant Deputy Minister in charge of domestic programs and of international economic services in the Department of Finance. In 1964-65, Dr. A. W. Johnson, who had previously been with the Government of Saskatchewan, took over responsibilities for taxation policy and federal-provincial relations. Later, A. B. Hockin, with training and interest in international and government financial activities, took over responsibility for that area. J. F. Grandy was in charge of tariffs, international economic relations, and resources development. J. R. Brown became responsible for taxation policy.

The organizational charts for the department in 1964 and 1974 are shown in Figure 6:2 and 6:3, respectively. They demonstrate a trend toward horizontal expansion. In addition, they reflect the particular interests of certain influential individuals rather than the organizational structure which the formulation of economic policy in its broadest sense might otherwise necessitate. Most senior members of the department performed co-ordinating roles and thus officials in Ottawa have expressed the view that the Department of Finance in Canada has evolved so that it is now, in many ways, analogous to European departments of Economic Affairs. The Glassco Commission's rather limited comments on economic organization further substantiated this view.

When Robert Bryce was transferred from the PCO in 1963 to become the new deputy minister of the Department of Finance under Walter L. Gordon as minister, the department acquired the services of a competent scholar. Bryce had been a bright young Keynesian disciple who, as indicated earlier, had served in a research capacity in the department. However, his appointment as Deputy Minister of Finance in 1963 was considered in some quarters to have had some negative consequences in that he displayed a tendency to rely more on his technical competence than on organizational development. The department nevertheless expanded under his leadership. The activities strengthened during his tenure lend weight to the point made earlier that emphasis was placed on personalities, rather than on the development of organizational structure.

The former Liberal Minister of Finance, Walter Gordon, noted that when he took over in 1963, the Department of Finance was poorly organized, but he was too involved with more immediate problems to

Figure 6:2 Department of Finance Organization Chart (1964)

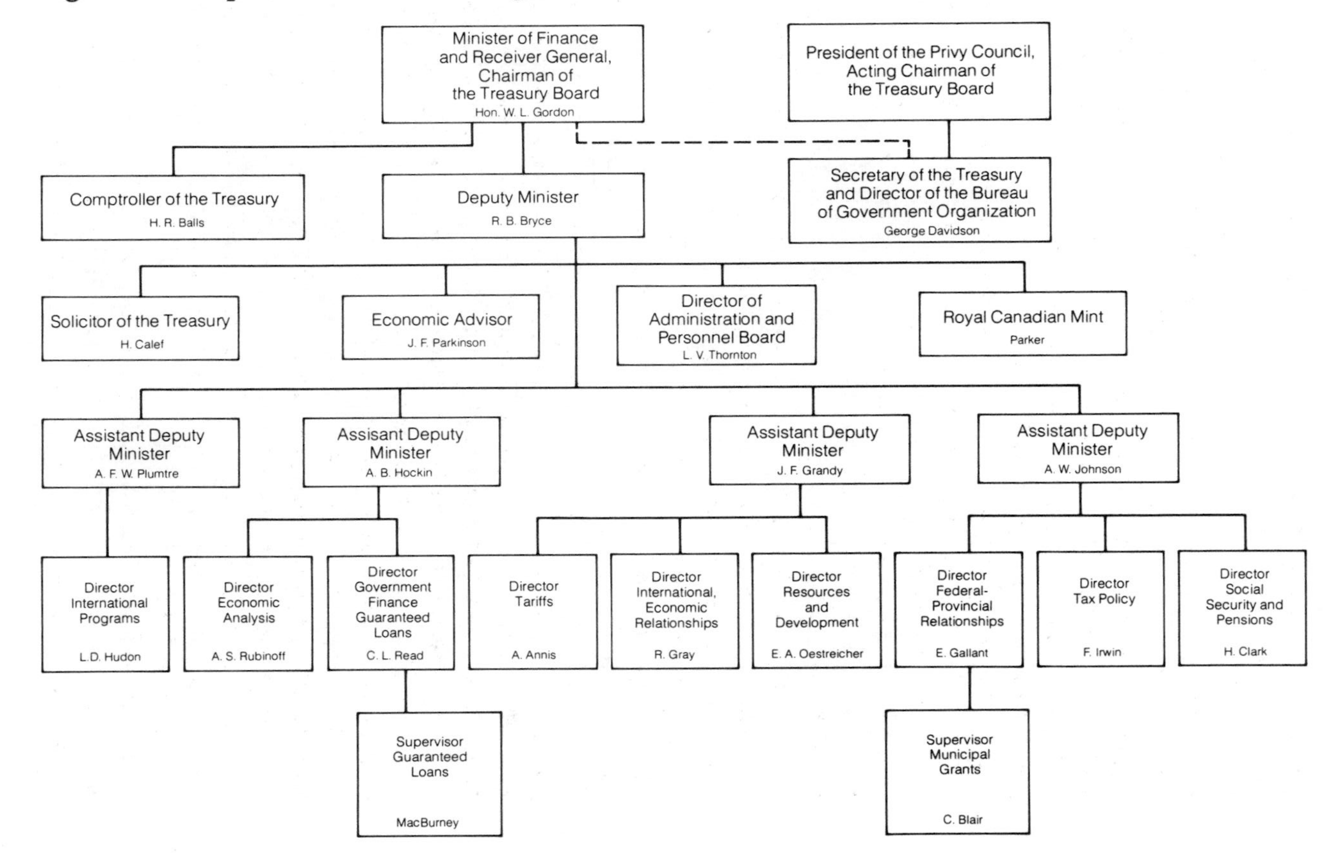

Figure 6:3 Department of Finance, General Organization (March 1974)

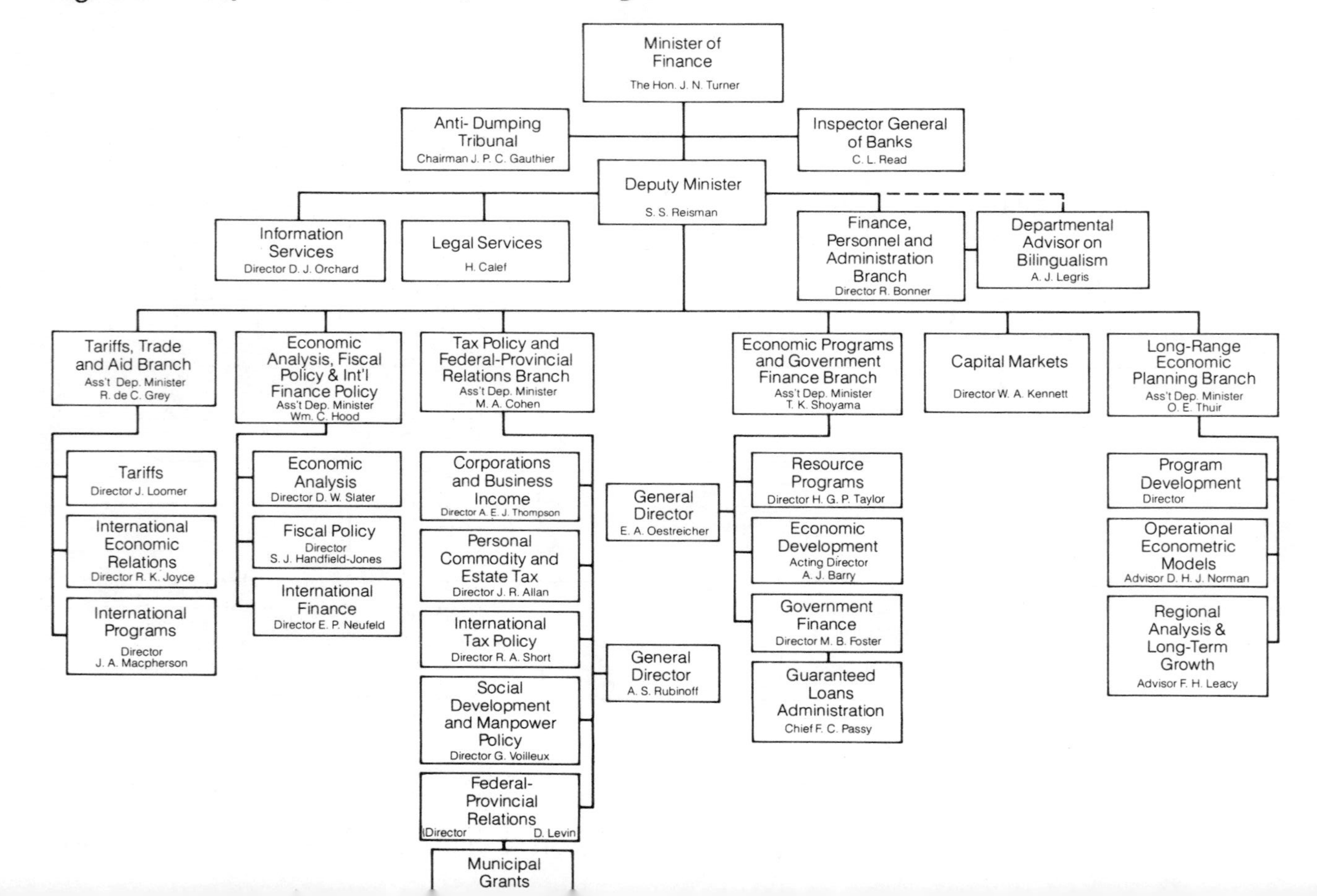

do anything about the organization of the department. Kenneth Taylor was then deputy minister, with Simon Reisman, Claude Isbister, and Wynne Plumptre as assistant deputy ministers. Gordon also expressed the view that the department could better perform its multiple roles if it was served by a senior and a junior minister. Thus he was in favour of adopting the approach followed at times in the British Treasury which inolved dividing the department's responsibilities between two ministers rather than transferring some of its responsibilities elsewhere.[23]

Notwithstanding the above criticisms, in 1964 the Department of Finance took over the econometric model which had been developed initially in the Department of Reconstruction and Supply, but was later transferred to the Department of Trade and Commerce. While the Department of Finance attempted to strengthen its analytical capabilities, it was at a disadvantage with respect to the already strong technical personnel located in the Bank of Canada. The Bank later developed one of the most sophisticated econometric models in Ottawa, although it dealt with more particularistic aspects of policy than the broader concerns which the Department of Finance is expected to incorporate.

The Bank of Canada expanded its staff and analytical capabilities to a significant extent under Louis Rasminsky's governorship. In this regard the influence of Gerald K. Bouey, who subsequently became the Bank's fourth governor, should be mentioned. The effect of these developments was much more observable in the late 1960s when the Bank of Canada became involved in the building of an econometric model and, consequently, acquired a number of competent econometricians.

The model at the Department of Finance was designed to forecast the gross national product, employment rates, and price levels. It facilitated the estimation of government revenues and government balances, and concentrated more on the effects on the economy of fiscal policy as compared to the model used by the Bank of Canada, which placed more emphasis on monetary aspects. Assisted by Statistics Canada, the Department of Finance can now better assess the effects of variables, such as government, export, and investment spending.

Later developments between the early 1960s and early 1970s showed a tendency for the Department of Finance to transfer a number of relatively autonomous functions to new organizations, both prior to and subsequent to the Glassco Commission Report on the Organization of the Government of Canada. These transfers include the Central Mortgage and Housing Corporation in the early 1940s, and the Royal Mint and Pensions and Social Insurance in the late 1960s. The creation of the Treasury Board as a separate agency from the Department of Finance occurred in 1966. Despite these transfers, the staff of the Department of Finance increased considerably between 1956 and 1970, as the department sought to increase its analytical capabilities. In 1956 there were about 95 officers; by 1962 this number had risen to about 115; and by the mid-1970s the number approached 200. More importantly the department had acquired a new group of prominent economists.

The Department of Finance in the Early 1970s: Economic Expansion

In June 1970, when Simon Reisman replaced Robert Bryce as Deputy Minister of Finance, he immediately established an International Economic Analysis and Fiscal Policy Branch under William C. Hood, who had been the Assistant Director of Research of the Gordon Commission on Canada's long-term economic prospects and had also been associated with the University of Toronto and the Bank of Canada. There were five major branches: Tax Policy, Federal Provincial Relations and Economic Programs, Tariff Trade and Aid, Economic Analysis, Fiscal Policy and International Finance, and Financial Operations. These branches demonstrate the increasingly strong economic-affairs orientation of the department.

The 1970s saw "an economic growth" emphasis in the Department of Finance. This has been reflected in the various budgets presented, but it has also been reflected in the various reorganizations which have taken place. There is now a Tax Policy Branch which has been upgraded from a mere advisory group. Greater emphasis is now being placed on developing some awareness of long-term dimensions of economic policy. Accordingly, in 1974, a Long Range Economic Planning Branch was created under Otto Thür, a former Vice-Chairman of the Economic Council. Simon Reisman, the Deputy Minister, expressed interest in strengthening the capability of the department in the area of capital markets and thus W. A. Kennett, the Branch Director, at the time of writing, reports directly to the Deputy Minister.

In summary, it may be stated that the Department of Finance, which was very powerful before C. D. Howe carried off some of its most competent economists to the Department of Reconstruction, had become, in the early 1950s, primarily a steering group related to the preparation of the budget. H. E. English later concluded:

> No significant changes took place in the structure of economic policy-making between 1950 and 1956. Even more striking is the fact that from 1945 to 1955 Canadians were not challenged to examine the foundations of their economic policy. Even the Royal Commission on Canada's Economic Prospects, conducting its investigation in a mid-1950's boom, found little need for a comprehensive revision of the institutions charged with policy formulation.[24]

With the increasing complexity of contemporary economic management, a number of structural and institutional changes have taken place since 1963. On the so-called "supply-management" side new departments of Employment and Immigration and Consumer and Corporate Affairs have been established. On the "demand-management" side, the Bank of Canada has improved its analytical techniques and the Department of Finance has also strengthened its analytical capabilities. The Department of Industry, Trade and Commerce has been combined and energized and, in addition, has been establishing a number of liaison committees with industry. In order to improve the position of depressed areas, the Department of Regional Economic Expansion, although adversely affected in the initial years by inadequate economic intelligence, was created to stimulate the level of economic development in depressed areas of the economy. These developments created a new challenge for the Department of Finance to establish an efficient administrative framework to co-ordinate overall economic management.

THE BANK OF CANADA

The Bank of Canada was established in 1935, relatively late in comparison with the development of central banks in other countries.[25] It originally opened for business as a privately owned body with capital of $5 million, divided into $50 shares. The intention was to disseminate shares as widely as possible. The Bank was established by a Conservative government and every effort was made to keep the Bank independent of the intervention of party politics, but, as we shall see later, this commitment to independence was eventually modified under its third governor, Louis Rasminsky, in response to the conflicts over policy which arose between his predecessor, James Coyne, and the Diefenbaker government.

The management of the Bank was vested in a Board of Governors, consisting of a governor and deputy governor, the deputy minister of Finance without power to vote, and seven directors. The directors were elected for overlapping terms by the shareholders, two representing primary industries, two representing other sectors. The first governors were appointed by the government, but thereafter they were to be appointed by the directors, with the government's approval. The governor, guided by the executive committee of the board, which met weekly, exercised control over the Bank's operation. The executive committee consisted of the two governors, one director, and the deputy minister of Finance. The Bank immediately took over the note-issuing activities of the Department of Finance.

The Conservative government which established the Bank of Canada was defeated shortly afterwards and a Liberal government took office with the objective of nationalizing the Bank. However, it did so in an incremental fashion. The Bank of Canada Act was amended in 1936, but it merely provided for the ownership of the majority of the stock by the government. Thus, the government owned capital stock classified as "class B", while the existing shares in private ownership became known as "class A". The number of directors were increased to provide for further government appointments. However, provision was retained that the governor should be appointed by the board and not by the government.

In making the appointment to the position of governor, the Conservative government attempted to satisfy a multiplicity of interests. Graham F. Towers, an economist and a banker who was known to have been in favour of sponsoring a central bank and a "soft" monetary policy, was appointed to the post.

In 1938 the Liberal government in Ottawa further nationalized the Bank. On this occasion the private shareholders were bought out. The number of directors was stabilized at eleven and all were required to be appointed by the government "from diversified occupations" and each to have a single vote. Thus, the major change was related to the capitalization. No major changes occurred in the Bank of Canada Act until 1954 but a few important policy shifts occurred between 1948 and 1952.

The Bank of Canada until 1952 did not perform any major role in monetary policy during what has been described as its pivotal years (1948-52). It was aided in its approach to policy-making by a relatively autonomous agency, the Foreign Exchange Control Board. However during the Korean War the Bank, for the first time in its history, followed a policy of monetary restraint, albeit somewhat cautiously and in conjunction with moral suasion. This period was important in other respects also because considerable emphasis was placed on promoting broader financial markets and on improving the Bank's analytical tools. The Bank, during this period, was significantly affected by W. C. Clark, who had been especially influential in establishing the Bank, Graham Towers, the first governor, and Donald Gordon. Following Dr. Clark's departure from the Department of Finance, the Bank became for many years perhaps the strongest analytical unit in Ottawa.

The revision of the Bank of Canada Act in 1954 contained two major features which broadened the scope of the Bank's lending role: first, it established a mortgage-lending scheme and made provision for loans against petroleum resources "in, under or upon the ground"; and second, it significantly modified the technique by which the central bank limited the level of the chartered bank cash reserves and, hence, the total volume of credit and currency in the economy.

The role of the central bank is an issue of major importance in economic management. There are two separate but interrelated aspects of the Bank's role: first, there is the question of its independence from political parties and from politics in general; and second, there is the question of broad representation to insure that the Bank is not dominated by the views of the commercial banks.[26] With the broadening of the aims of economic policy, it is highly important that monetary policy be related to other instruments of public policy. The 1954 changes marked the beginning of an "arms-length" but important relationship between the Bank of Canada and important sectors of the economic policy-making machinery. Thus, the Bank, which soon after its establishment had become involved in war, finance, and postwar readjustment, was activated in 1954 and became, for the first time, "the Bank for the Canadian financial system".

The role of the Governor of the Bank of Canada provides an example of the political role of experts. This problem was demonstrated by the conflict between Governor James Coyne and the Conservative government in 1961. Pursuant to the Coyne Affair, and upon his acceptance of the post of Governor of the Bank of Canada, Mr. Louis Rasminsky outlined two main principles which he thought the Bank should follow in relation to the government. "In the ordinary course of events," he noted, "the Bank has the responsibility for monetary policy." However, he added, "if the Government disapproves of the monetary policy being followed by the Bank, it has the right and the responsibility to direct the Bank as to the policy which the Bank is to carry out."[27] He suggested the need for amendments along these lines.

The relationship between the central bank and the government has evolved toward a middle-of-the-road approach between making the Bank either completely independent of or dependent on the government. Thus, the endorsement of a strategy similar to that suggested above by Louis Rasminsky has been adopted and strengthened by law. If there is disagreement between the government and Bank which cannot be resolved, the government may, after further consultation has taken place, issue a directive to the Bank as to the monetary policy that it is to follow. Any such directive must be in writing, in specific terms, and it must be applicable for a specified period. What is especially important is the stipulation that the directive must be made public.

The policy adopted by Mr. Rasminsky remains in force. Following his resignation in 1973, G. K. Bouey, previously Assistant Governor, was appointed Governor of the Bank of Canada. There have been no major confrontations between the Bank of Canada and the Department of Finance. However, between 1973 and 1976 Bouey had been advocating the need to place equal emphasis on controlling both employment and inflation simultaneously rather than shifting emphasis from one priority to another, the approach taken during the Rasminsky years. The Bank of Canada's role is obviously essential and we will be examining its behaviour again in Chapter 7.

THE ROYAL COMMISSION ON THE ORGANIZATION OF THE GOVERNMENT OF CANADA (THE GLASSCO COMMISSION)

As noted in Chapter 1, the Glassco Commission, which studied the organization of the Government of Canada, did not deal with economic policy. The Commission concerned itself with the overall management of government, and with government departments as separate policy spheres. Consequently, while it suggested ways in which the establishment of central priorities and the assessment of efficiency may be achieved through the Treasury Board, it did not provide guidelines about the management of economic policies, or about the relationships between the management of the government and the management of the economy.

The Commission did refer to the use of economists in government, but its effect upon economic policy-making was confined to certain changes in the Department of Finance. It should be emphasized that economic-policy formulation was added to the Glassco study at a very late stage, when H. Scott Gordon was asked to write a section of the report on statistical information. The Glassco Commission, when it reported in 1962, made only implicit statements about the role of the Department of Finance. It noted that a Department of Finance may become, imperceptibly, preoccupied with economic planning. Elsewhere it noted that the Department of Finance, in its concern with economic policy, has a central interest in all policy. Clearly this illustrated the impossibility of prescribing any functional basis for the allocation of ministerial tasks that will provide automatically for the interrelationships among federal activities. Later, the Commission characterized the Finance portfolio as a staff agency almost devoid of any operating responsibilities.[28]

The Commission recommended that the Treasury Board be separated from the Department of Finance. The former would become the department responsible for management in the public service and the expenditure budget and the latter, to the extent that economic policy was a central component of all policies, would be a central coordinating department in the economic-policy sphere. In short the Glassco Commission Report took the position that the main responsibility for economic policy was vested in the Department of Finance. Thus in the early 1960s, particularly after 1963 when R. B. Bryce came to Finance, the department, together with the Bank of Canada, was considered to be the focal point of government economic policy-making. By the mid-1960s several senior officials considered the Finance Department to be Canada's Department of Economic Affairs.

NEW CENTRES OF ECONOMIC-POLICY FORMULATION: THE ECONOMIC COUNCIL AND EMERGING ECONOMIC PORTFOLIOS

Two important developments in the 1960s and 1970s in the machinery of economic-policy formulation in Canada have been the establishment of the Economic Council of Canada and the creation of new departments with separate political heads intended to incorporate new dimensions of economic management in the cabinet structure. The Economic Council was preceded by the creation of a National Productivity Council with the objective of improving economic productivity. The Productivity Council involved trade unions and business as part of a new effort at political and economic consensus.[29] The development aknowledged the fact that economic management required the co-operation of the private sector. The Productivity Council reported to both the Department of Labour and the Department of Trade and Commerce. The development of other economic portfolios reflects the broadening of the economic objectives pursued by the Government of Canada. The postwar emphasis on maintaining full employment has meant that efforts had to be taken to retrain the labour force so that it could adapt to technological changes. This was most clearly reflected in the creation of the Department of Manpower and Immigration. Later a Department of Consumer and Corporate Affairs was established to deal with the problems of the consumer in the marketplace and to insure that competition served the interest of the consumer. The Department of Regional Economic Expansion was established to improve the input of the regional dimension in economic-policy formulation, and Statistics Canada was reorganized to further improve economic intelligence. Each of these new centres will be briefly introduced here and will be examined later at greater length.

The Economic Council of Canada

The Economic Council was established in 1963 as a mixed, externally located, advisory body to the federal government. It consists of twenty-eight members: a chairman and two directors who are trained economists, and twenty-five other members appointed from representative sectors of the economy and the society in general. The Council is primarily concerned with medium-term economic growth but given the fact that the goals established by the 1945 White Paper on Employment and Income were not previously institutionalized, the Economic Council Act embodied these and others and accordingly incorporated some challenging objectives consistent with the mood of the early 1960s. The Council's act also incorporated a time dimension in that it placed greater emphasis on the attainment of medium-term objectives which its creators felt was not given adequate emphasis within the governmental machinery. The Economic Council was established to perform the following functions, among others:

To advise and recommend to the Minister how Canada can achieve the highest possible level of employment and efficient production, in order that the country may enjoy a high and consistent rate of economic growth and that all Canadians share in rising living standards and, in particular, it shall be the duty of the Council:

(a) to regularly assess on a systematic and comprehensive basis the medium-term and long-term prospects of the economy and to compare such prospects with the potentialities of growth of the economy;
(b) to recommend what government policies, in the opinion of the Council, would best help to realize the potentialities of the growth of the economy;
(c) to consider means of strengthening and improving Canada's international financial and trade position;
(d) to study means of increasing Canadian participation in the ownership, control and management of industries in Canada; to study how growth, technological change and automation and international economic changes may effect employment and income in Canada as a whole, in particular areas of Canada and in particular sectors of the economy. . . .[30]

In its *First Annual Review*, the Council appraised Canada's postwar economic position and pointed to some unique demographic trends. Before assessing these postwar economic trends, the Council, as we have seen in Chapter 2, attempted to articulate the performance goals for Canada.[31] It suggested certain targets which could be achieved by Canadians between 1964 and 1970. In so doing, it attempted to indicate a feasible and desirable long-term strategy of economic development.

It should be noted at this point that the emergence of the Economic Council introduced at least two important institutional perspectives in Canadian economic-policy formulation. First, an extraordinary attempt was made to institutionalize the 1945 White Paper on Employment and Income. This was most clearly articulated by the Council's first chairman, Dr. J. J. Deutsch. The Council established a high rate of employment which it set at 97 per cent. Second, the Council placed strong emphasis on the attainment of a high rate of economic growth which it linked to the concept of economic potential. Its strong institutional commitment to growth led to confrontation with the Bank of Canada which had a stronger commitment to the maintenance of price stability. Thus the Governor of the Bank of Canada issued strong warnings that the growth target could set off an inflationary spiral. The implications of the attempt to specify goals and indicators was reviewed in Chapter 2.

There is a definite link between economic research and the formulation of economic policy and this has become more pronounced since the establishment of the Economic Council. The formulation of economic policy involves the articulation of societal values and the means which will be utilized to achieve the attainment of the objectives stipulated. The Economic Council of Canada arrived at its potential output target by making projections of the population, the labour force, and the length of the work week of the working population to 1970. Two policy issues were isolated from the Council's stipulated potential targets for immediate attention.

First, the Council emphasized that the dominant challenge in Canada's medium-term economic horizon was that of providing very rapidly expanding employment opportunities in increasingly productive, and therefore more remunerative, activities. It asserted that Canada was then crossing the threshold of a period of unprecedented growth of its labour force. A net increase of 1,500,000 jobs from 1963 to 1970 was required. Accordingly, the Council recommended expansionary policies to generate adequate levels of demand, both locally and nationally. Second, the Council concluded that Canada's labour market policies were in adequate.[32]

The Council concluded as well, and in even more general terms, that there would undoubtedly also be advancing levels of minimum educational requirements for many occupations and jobs. Hence it felt it was vitally important that general education and training should be given a very high priority in the economic system. The emphasis on economic growth and the simultaneous attainment of a multiplicity of goals represented what was regarded during the 1960s as "The New Economics". The new economics was further reflected in the establishment of three new departments, Manpower and Immigration in 1966, Consumer and Corporate Affairs in 1967, and the Department of Regional Economic Expansion in 1969.

A number of new initiatives were taken in economic-policy formulation in 1963 when a Department of Industry was established to promote expansion in manufacturing. The then new department was to be the promotional arm of the Economic Council of Canada, an advisory body which had no operational responsibilities. The legislation passed in the early 1960s had important implications for government-industry relations. Economic management during this period was intended not only to mobilize the private sector but also to regulate it.

Economic management is obviously concerned with synchronizing the goals of both the public and private sectors, and hence has an implicit regulatory aspect. While the term "indicative planning" is frequently used in Canada, it was not until the mid-1970s that the government seriously began to establish government-industry consultative mechanisms which somewhat approximated the more formal indicative-planning machinery in France. This was partly reflected in the 1973 National Conference on the Economy sponsored by the then newly formed National Conference Secretariat of the Economic Council and by the subsequent creation by the Department of Industry, Trade and Commerce of consultative councils for particular industrial sectors. It should be noted, however, that these Canadian mechanisms are unlike the French model of indicative planning which involved, in addition to the machinery, more direct forms of government leadership through civil service participation, public ownership, and financial instruments.[33]

The Department of Manpower and Immigration

The Economic Council of Canada's analysis of labour-market policies contributed directly to the establishment of the Department of Manpower and Immigration in 1966. In 1965 it had noted that there was need for improvements in three facets of supply-management policies, including more effective administration to co-ordinate the activities of the National Employment Service and the Unemployment Insurance Commission, expansion of programs for training and retraining, and the development of a new and more specialized form of labour-market information. All three facets were important components of a package to complement demand-management policies then being emphasized by the Bank of Canada and the Department of Finance.[34]

The Liberal government, which had already taken initiatives in the area of social policy through the Special Planning Secretariat in the PMO, established the Department of Manpower and Immigration in 1966. The fundamental purpose of this department was to further the growth of Canada through effective allocation and development of manpower resources in response to changing needs of the national economy. The department, since its inception, has used two main channels to insure that the supply of qualified manpower is adequate to meet the demands of the labour market: first, counselling, placement, and, where necessary, training and relocation of workers; and second, the introduction of new manpower through immigration.

It should be evident that the Department of Manpower and Immigration introduced a more explicit supply-management component to the economic-policy-formulation process. The establishment of the department initially left the Department of Labour to operate in the more specialized area of industrial relations, employment standards, and research. The Department of Labour has encouraged and assisted in the establishment of labour-management committees through its Labour-Management Consultation Branch, and analysis of economic and social trends affecting the labour force through its Economics and Research Branch.

The Department of Consumer and Corporate Affairs

The growth of the economy has led to greater government intervention to insure greater fairness in the marketplace. In response to a reference from the Government of Canada, the Economic Council recommended that the Registrar General Department be strengthened to become a forum for consumer policies. In 1967 a Department of Consumer and Corporate Affairs was established with functions relating to: consumer affairs; corporations and corporate securities; combines, mergers, monopolies, and restraint of trade; bankruptcy and insolvency; patents, copyrights, and trademarks; standards of identity and performance in relation to consumer goods; and legal metrology.

The structure and function of this department shows that it was created to perform an important mediating role between the business sector and the consumer. It operates on the principle that effective competition is beneficial to the corporate sector and the consumer. The early work of the department has been primarily of a legal nature; however its goal and objectives make provision for an important supply-management role. The Department of Consumer and Corporate Affairs has had an input in all of the budgets presented to Parliament in recent years.

The 1969 Government Reorganization Act

The 1969 Government Reorganization Act further altered the economic policy-making machinery by the creation of the Department of Industry, Trade and Commerce, representing a combination of the departments of Industry, and Trade and Commerce. In addition it established a Department of Regional Economic Expansion. The Department of Industry, Trade and Commerce now has an expanded mandate to further the growth, productivity, employment opportunities, and prosperity of the Canadian economy through the efficient development of Canada's manufacturing and processing industries and the expansion of trade and tourism.

Although the Department of Regional Economic Expansion has growth and promotional objectives it has a more restricted mandate. It is responsible for matters relating to economic expansion and social adjustment in areas requiring special measures to improve opportunities for productive employment and access to those opportunities. The department was also granted authority to prepare and implement, in co-operation with provincial governments and other federal agencies, development plans and programs designed to meet the special needs of areas where the growth of employment and income lags behind other parts of Canada.

Statistics Canada

The increasingly important relationship between information and economic-policy analysis has been further demonstrated in recent developments concerning the reorganization of Statistics Canada. Several studies of the decision-making structure and process have pointed to the importance of statistical and other forms of information and have recommended improvements in the system. The Glassco Commission, the Economic Council of Canada, and the Science Council, among others, have all emphasized the need for new and improved statistical information.

Dr. Sylvia Ostry, a former Director of the Economic Council and former chief statistician, stated in May 1973 before the Trade, Finance and Economic Affairs Committee that she had been asked at the time of her appointment to undertake a general review of the role and responsibilities of Statistics Canada.[35] The review was completed at the end of 1972 and reached a number of major conclusions.

The report stressed the dilemma which Statistics Canada faces in its relations with users and suppliers. On the one hand, as the principal producer of statistics within the national system, it is the agency which feels the main brunt of the continually increasing demand for statistical information for use in the analytical and decision-making processes of government, business, and other users. On the other hand, however, Statistics Canada faces a growing and serious resistance on the part of its survey respondents to supplying the basic data on which its output depends. The report pointed out that Statistics Canada had to respond to the challenge of user-demands in a number of ways, including the need for improved planning procedures for the formulation of the extensions and refinements of its own statistical data base; more effective channels of communication with users, particularly federal government users, through which their emerging needs can be identified as far in advance as possible; and a capacity for fast and flexible response to urgent statistical demands relating to current social issues, for which the customary lead time is not feasible. Emphasis was placed, furthermore, on the fact that Statistics Canada is part of a total statistical system which includes other federal and provincial agencies. Hence the report focussed on the need for greater collaboration with the provinces and other federal government departments in exploiting administrative files for statistical purposes.[36]

Statistics Canada has also sought in recent years to strengthen the main indicators of economic activity, notably the quarterly income and expenditure accounts, on the important grounds that the information needs of those who influence the development of a strong economy through fiscal, monetary, investment, and trade policy, are an "overwhelming statistical priority". It has also sought to improve the development of social statistics so as to better assess the growing share of resources allocated to health care, education, and justice, the latter constituting an area of statistical neglect.[37]

Statistics Canada has also greatly expanded its organizational structure to cope with increased demands for statistics for policy-formulation and for policy-monitoring. These demands originate from the provinces, which also require increased information in the decision-making processes, from municipalities, the academic community, the business sector, and from the public at large who want information about the society and the economy in which they live.

Reorganization of Statistics Canada became necessary to upgrade the most senior levels of the organization to create a group of executives whose major function is policy-oriented. It was also necessary to create a new level of management to act primarily in terms of co-ordinating the greatly expanded operational activity of the organization. An example of the changing horizontal relationships between Statistics Canada and departmental users is to be found in the relationships with DREE. DREE is concerned with many aspects of information in related areas in given provinces. There is a joint federal-provincial relationship in this regard. Statistics Canada also co-operates with DREE, among others, in the attempt to build the CANDIDE model which will help the government to project economic activity and to analyse policy. Both structures have been concerned with getting more and improved regional information in the model. There has been an interdepartmental working group to facilitate this process.

Both the early sections of this chapter as well as the above review show the central role of new techniques and the importance and availability of statistical data in contemporary economic management.

THE 1975-76 EVENTS: THE SEARCH FOR NEW ORGANIZATIONAL ORDER

By the mid-1970s concurrent and persistent high rates of inflation and unemployment, the rapid growth in governmental expenditure, and growing concern about the economic performance of both big business and small business had resulted in another flurry of organizational change and experimentation. These events are too recent to be properly assessed here but a brief mention of them will take the evolution of economic-policy organization fully into the mid-1970s. These events include the creation of the Anti-Inflation Board (AIB), the establishment of "DM 10", the appointment of the Royal Commission on Corporate Concentration, the creation of a Ministry of State for Small Business, and the appointment of the Royal Commission on Financial Management and Accountability.

The creation of the AIB was announced on October 15, 1975, as part of the Trudeau government's incomes policy. It was established to administer the government's wage and price regulations, and hence was the ultimate successor to earlier efforts in the late 1960s and early 1970s at securing voluntary wage and price restraints including the Prices and Incomes Commission and the Food Prices Review Board. Following the imposition of the income-controls program and the public speculation about the "post-control" society, the Prime Minister, early in 1976, created "DM 10", a group of ten deputy ministers from the main economic portfolios whose task was to develop alternative policies for the post-1978 controls period. This would include alternatives respecting government spending, regulation, industrial relations, employment, competition, and a number of related areas of economic management.

The creation earlier in 1975 of the Royal Commission on Corporate Concentration headed by Robert Bryce, and the appointment of a Minister of State for Small Business late in 1976 were prompted by criticism of policies toward big business and small business respectively. Both were created despite earlier extensive work on competition policy by the Economic Council of Canada and the Department of Consumer and Corporate Affairs. Concern about the co-ordination of manpower and broader employment problems also resulted late in 1976 in the restructuring of the Manpower and Immigration Department into the Commission and Department of Employment and Immigration; the new title also indicating a closer relationship between the department and the Unemployment Insurance Commission.

The establishment of the Royal Commission on Financial Management and Accountability in November 1976, symbolically at least, seemed to bring the issues of economic management and public spending full circle. The issues which prompted its creation were the prolific growth in government spending and the need to restore what critics (including the Auditor General) felt was a greater semblance of a financial control, including a return to the old-fashioned concepts of honesty, probity, and accountability in public management. Thus, in contrast to the early 1960s when Glassco had warned against excessive tight-fisted central control of financial management, the events of the mid-1970s seemed to stress the need for new mechanisms of control.

EXTERNAL CENTRES OF ECONOMIC ANALYSIS

The changes in Statistics Canada were really a part of a broader concern in the early 1970s about the adequacy of economic-policy analysis. An important additional dimension of this concern was the extent to which economic analysis was dominated by the federal bureaucracy centred in the Finance Department. There were, it was felt, no competing sources of expertise particularly for short-run economic analysis.[38] The emergence in the 1960s of sophisticated fiscal-policy expertise in several provincial governments, especially Ontario, was one source of alternative expertise but this source did not, of course, operate fully in an open public fashion. The Economic Council meanwhile was concerned more with medium-term analysis. The relative monopoly of expertise in Canada was compared unfavourably with the presence in other states of competing non-governmental sources of analysis which were more readily and openly available.

In response to this concern a number of non-governmental public centres of economic and policy research emerged in the 1970s. These centres included the Conference Board in Canada headed until 1976 by Arthur Smith, a former chairman of the Economic Council of Canada; the Institute for Quantitative Analysis at the University of Toronto; the C. D. Howe Institute; and the Institute for Research on Public Policy. The Conference Board and Institute for Quantitative Analysis prepare and present quarterly economic-analysis reports and hence are centrally concerned with economic and fiscal policy. The C. D. Howe Institute and the Institute for Research on Public Policy are more broadly concerned with public policy issues of which economic policy is only one dimension. In terms of expertise and analytical sparring, the presence of these external centres of analysis suggests the emergence of a somewhat more competitive or pluralist presentation and discussion of data and information.

SUMMARY

Contemporary debates about Canadian economic policy and economic policy organization must be placed in the context of the historical evolution of governmental economic-policy machinery. This chapter has sketched the broad outlines of that evolution, seeking to stress, albeit in a very descriptive form, the close relationship between economic research, economic goals, and governmental organization for economic policy. The early postwar concentration of economic analysis in the Department of Finance, the Department of Trade and Commerce, the Bank of Canada, the Department of Labour, and the Dominion Bureau of Statistics has been altered to include organizations such as theTreasury Board, the Economic Council of Canada, the Department of Manpower and Immigration, the Department of Regional Economic Expansion, the Department of Consumer and Corporate Affairs, and Statistics Canada. Part III will present a more detailed examination of these organizations and their evolving policy mandates.

NOTES

1. Andrew Shonfield, *Modern Capitalism: The Changing Balance of Public and Private Power* (London, 1965).

2. These aspects of the immediate postwar period were summarized by R. W. Phidd, "The Economic Council and Economic Policy Formulation in Canada". Unpublished PhD thesis, Queen's University, Kingston, 1972, Chapter 2, pp. 70-95. See also R. G. S. Brown, *The Management of Welfare* (London, 1975).

3. See R. B. Crozier's treatment of these developments in C. W. McMahon, *Techniques of Economic Forecasting: Short-Term Economic Forecasting used by the*

Government of Canada, France, The Netherlands, Sweden, the United Kingdom, and the United States (Paris, 1956), pp. 37-62.

4. Ibid., p. 39.

5. Ibid., p. 38.

6. Ibid., p. 40.

7. Economic Council of Canada, *First Annual Review* (Ottawa, 1964), and *Second Annual Review* (Ottawa, 1965).

8. McMahon, *Techniques of Economic Forecasting*, pp. 50-51.

9. Ibid., p. 52.

10. See First Session, 28th Parl., 1968-69. The Senate of Canada, *Proceedings of the Special Committee on Science Policy*, no. 34 (March 5, 1969), especially pp. 4634-38.

11. McMahon, *Techniques of Economic Forecasting*, pp. 60-62.

12. Department of Trade and Commerce, *History of Reconstruction in Canada* (unpublished).

13. Lawrence Pierce, *The Politics of Fiscal Policy Formation* (Pacific Palisades, Ca., 1971), and R. Lee, *et al.*, *Public Budgeting Systems* (Baltimore, 1973), pp. 53-80.

14. A. A. Sterns, *History of the Department of Finance.* Mimeo (Ottawa, 1965).

15. H. R. Balls, "Planning, Programming and Budgeting in Canada", *British Journal of Public Administration*, Vol. LVII, no. 18 (Autumn 1970), p. 296.

16. Sterns, *History of the Department of Finance.*

17. J. K. Galbraith identified Bryce as one of Keynes's best young disciples. See J. K. Galbraith, *Money* (London, 1976), p. 239.

18. John Porter, *The Vertical Mosaic* (Toronto, 1965), pp. 427-28.

19. Interviews.

20. On the strengthening of the analytical techniques of the Bank of Canada see C. S. Watts, "The Bank of Canada from 1948 to 1952: The Pivotal Years", *Bank of Canada Review* (November 1974), pp. 1-16.

21. House of Commons, *Debates*, First Session, 26th Parl., 12 Elizabeth II, Vol. I (1963), pp. 791-801; Vol. II, pp. 2205-89, 2095-2118; and Vol. III, pp. 2205-30, 2307-26.

22. For a further analysis of Walter Gordon, see Chapter 5.

23. Interviews.

24. T. N. Brewis and H. E. English, *et al.*, *Canadian Economic Policy* (Toronto, 1965), p. 358.

25. E. P. Neufeld, ed., *Money and Banking in Canada* (Toronto, 1964), pp. 324-46; our review of the evolution of the bank is based on the excellent articles by G. S. Watts: "The Origins and Background of Central Banking in Canada", *Bank of Canada Review* (May 1972), pp. 14-25; "The Legislative Birth of the Bank of Canada, *Bank of Canada Review* (Novemer 1972), pp. 7-20; "The Bank of Canada During the War Years", *Bank of Canada Review* (April 1973), pp. 3-16; "The Bank of Canada During the Postwar Adjustments", *Bank of Canada Review* (November 1973), pp. 4-17; and "The Bank of Canada from 1948 to 1952". For comparative purposes see Galbraith, *Money*.

26. See the discussion of Acheson and chant's analysis (Chapter 4). See also Economic Council of Canada, *Regulation and Efficiency: A Study of Deposit Institutions* (Ottawa, 1970).

27. L. Rasminsky, Governor of the Bank of Canada, Press Release, July 31, 1961, in Neufeld, ed., *Money and Banking in Canada*, pp. 347-48; L. Rasminsky, *The Role of the Central Banker Today*. Lecture delivered in Italy, November 9, 1956 (Washington, 1957), pp. 27-28.

28. Canada, *Report of the Royal Commission on Government Organization*, Vol. I (Ottawa, 1963).

29. R. W. Phidd, "The Role of Central Advisory Councils: The Economic Council of Canada", in G. Bruce Doern and Peter Aucoin, eds., *The Structures of Policy-Making in Canada* (Toronto, 1971), Chapter 8.

30. Economic Council of Canada Act assented to August 1963.

31. Economic Council of Canada, *First Annual Review*. We have discussed these goals in Chapter 2.

32. Ecomomic Council of Canada, *Second Annual Review*.

33. See Shonfield, *Modern Capitalism*, chapters 1-5.

34. Economic Council of Canada, *Second Annual Review.*

35. Remarks by Dr. S. Ostry, House of Commons, *Minutes of Proceedings and Evidence of the Standing Committee on Finance, Trade and Economic Affairs,* no. 18 (Ottawa, 1974).

36. Ibid., *passim.*

37. See Economic Council of Canada, *Eighth Annual Review* (Ottawa, 1971).

38. See Standing Senate Committee on National Finance, *Growth, Employment and Price Stability* (Ottawa, 1972) and E. S. Ritchie, *An Institute for Research on Public Policy* (Ottawa, 1971). See also E. B. Sheldon and N. E. Freeman, "Notes on Social Indicators", *Policy Sciences,* Vol. I, no. 1, pp. 97-113.

CHAPTER SEVEN

The Role of the Department of Finance

This chapter examines in detail the role of the Department of Finance in economic management by examining the concept of demand management, and the fiscal and monetary policies which affect revenue and expenditure decisions in the economy.[1] It further demonstrates how the role of the department has changed operationally in response to the various demands both within and outside of government. Second, the chapter reviews the legislative basis demonstrating that the Finance role is only partially explained by its statutory responsibilities. The other functional and residual responsibilities of the department are also examined.[2] By its detailed examination of the structure of economic management the chapter introduces in the Canadian context a frequently debated issue in the United Kingdom concerning the role of the Treasury in economic and governmental management and the relative merits of a Department of Economic Affairs.[3] In fact, as we have stated earlier, some Canadian practitioners consider the Department of Finance to be a Department of Economic Affairs.[4]

Third, and closely related to the above, the role of the Canadian Department of Finance is discussed from the perspective in which it has been perceived by ministers and former officials such as the Hon. Edgar Benson, Robert Bryce, and Simon Reisman. The analysis shows that, in the past, the department's role was perceived by strategic actors to encompass policy advice, policy initiation, and policy evaluation. The performance of these roles has required close working relationships with the PCO and the Treasury Board.

Fourth, the structure of the department is described in great detail to illustrate, from an organizational perspective, the meaning of demand management. Briefly stated, the structural review shows that the department is primarily concerned with the following aspects of economic management: (i) economic analysis, fiscal policy, and international finance; (ii) tax policy and federal-provincial relations; (iii) tariffs, trade, and aid; (iv) economic programs, government finance, and capital markets; and (v) long-range economic planning. However, several of the responsibilities of the Minister of Finance also impinge on a number of relatively autonomous agencies. In order to illustrate these dimensions the role of the Bank of Canada in relation to the Department of Finance is analysed further. Finally, the chapter examines the rationale used by the department and the Bank of Canada in formulating economic advice. This rationale will be contrasted in a later chapter with reforms suggested by the Senate Committee on National Finance. The debate which followed the Senate Committee report on *Growth Employment and Price Stability* brought to the public forum several controversial issues which influence the management of economic policy in Canada.[5] In order to further illustrate the dynamics of economic management, we discuss, in the concluding pages of this chapter, the changes being made, at the time of writing, to cope with the fiscal crisis by restructuring the mechanism by which revenue and expenditure decisions are made. The chapter emphasizes a managerial approach to economic-policy formulation by analysing the political and organizational dimensions of the process.

ECONOMIC MANAGEMENT AND DEMAND MANAGEMENT

From the perspective of this chapter "managerial economics" or "economic administration" encompasses economic theory, decision theory, and realistic appraisals of the ways in which organizations behave. Economic administrators must cope with the ways in which organizations behave and with how administrative structures become adapted to the pressures imposed on them.[6] As this chapter progresses it will become increasingly apparent that while demand management constitutes a central component of economic management it is heavily influenced by secondary and tertiary considerations which significantly influence policy outcomes. As such, the organizational allocation of demand- and supply-management instruments defy simple formulae for delegating responsibilities. In order to effectively formulate economic policy a wide range of resources, human and other, must be managed. Since societal goals are constantly changing, the instruments used for achieving these goals must be constantly reappraised. Accordingly, as we have seen, there have been several efforts at reorganizing the economic policy-making machinery.[7] It is clear that the reorganization of economic portfolios must be considered as an important dimension of any meaningful attempt to understand economic management.

As indicated earlier, recent attempts to improve economic management have revealed at least three major structural changes in governmental decision-making: first, there has been the reorganization of existing government departments especially Finance ministries which have traditionally dealt with demand-management. The reorganization of Finance ministries has attempted to create special divisions concerned with medium- and long-term growth policy. In addition, the reorganization has sought to give these new decision-making centres adequate influence *vis-à-vis* those units concerned with short-term policies. The second method, which may well follow an unsatisfactory experience with the first, has been to set up new departments with separate political heads. This development has involved a stronger supply-management emphasis than was utilized in the past. The new initiatives were aimed both at reconciling economic growth with other political objectives and at insuring that the more narrowly defined objectives of economic policy were passed to the cabinet level rather than being determined within a single department which was primarily concerned with short-term financial problems. The third development with which this chapter will be partially concerned has led to the formation of new multipartite institutions or consensus-mobilization institutions such as the Economic Council. These institutions were established to associate business and trade unions more closely with government in the management of economy. The foregoing developments are illustrative of the breadth of the concept of economic management of which demand-management, although perhaps the most important, is merely one component.[8]

Economic management is significantly influenced by limitations in economic knowledge.[9] Those concerned with managing the economy, more so than others, know that despite the exaggerated emphasis placed at times on "economic intelligence", economic policy is formulated under conditions in which ignorance is real, uncertainty is the order of the day, and experience advocates the necessity to consider a wide range of policy options and time horizons. Economic managers are aware of the fact that economic and non-economic considerations must be woven together. They have discovered also that "there is no such thing as economic policy in isolation from other aspects of policy, there is only policy". While a central agency such as the Department of Finance may exercise a *primary role* in economic management it cannot do so in isolation from other agencies. In recent years it has been increasingly recognized that the Department of Finance must develop various strategies for influencing the behaviour of several governmental and non-governmental agencies. We shall observe later that strategic actors in the Department of Finance have defined its role along these lines. The manner in which these officials have perceived their roles demonstrates that economic management has broadened beyond traditional stabilization techniques and includes the use of budgetary measures to achieve a multiplicity of objectives described earlier in Chapters 2 and 3.

A brief historical review demonstrates that economic management in the 1930s was concerned basically with "currency management". In the 1940s, following the war, economic management became associated with budgetary measures for stabilizing the economy. Economic management was carried out in terms of the management of demand. The emphasis was on the regulation of demand and on the elimination of cyclical fluctuations in growth, unemployment, and prices.[10] However, almost concurrent with the Keynesian revolution was the political endorsement of what is now called "the welfare state".[11] The commitment to the redistribution of income has since represented one of the most significant challenges to economic management. During the 1960s an important shift occurred in the approach of economic theory toward the goal of maintaining at least four objectives of economic policy simultaneously. Prior to this change economic policy was regarded as being mainly corrective, responsible for leaning against the prevailing winds of business cycles.[12] Consequently, the first major debate between the Economic Council of Canada and the Department of Finance was on the efficacy of short-term *versus* long-term stabilization strategies and the feasibility of simultaneously achieving various economic objectives. As stressed in previous chapters, the four basic objectives of economic policy as they have evolved in the postwar period are: (i) equilibrium in the international balance of payments; (ii) the attainment of full employment; (iii) the maintenance of stable economic growth; and (iv) the maintenance of price stability. All of these objectives are of major significance for the domestic economy. Full employment and economic growth are integrally related. Price stability affects a nation's performance internationally. In the 1960s concern with these objectives led to the endorsement of the concept of "economic potential".[13] Economic policy was to be used to propel the economy into achieving its potential growth. Accordingly various measures to achieve tradeoffs in the pursuit of these goals were unsuccessfully adopted during the 1960s.

More specifically, there was an unsuccessful attempt to formulate anti-poverty policies. Thus the initial postwar effort to improve the welfare of citizens was expanded in the 1960s to endorse "a war on poverty". In Canada, these efforts were endorsed by the Special Planning Secretariat in the PCO and even later by the *Working Paper on Social Security*.[14] By the 1970s, therefore, economic management had gained an even broader application since it represented the means for achieving the objectives of the welfare state which further extended the scope of public expenditures on health, education, family allowances, and housing. However, while the 1960s placed emphasis on human resources and more generally on labour supply problems, the 1970s saw a new emphasis on increasing the supply of natural resources to meet new energy demands and to cope with increases in the price of energy. This development brought the Department of Energy, Mines and Resources in closer relationship with the Department of Finance. The Department of Finance now works closely with the departments of National Health and Welfare and Energy, Mines and Resources in an attempt to supplement its more traditional links with agencies such as Industry, Trade and Commerce, and Labour.

Since the 1930s the Department of Finance has responded to various demands for a wider form of management by delegating some of its responsibilities to various semi-autonomous and autonomous agencies such as the Central Mortgage and Housing Corporation, the Royal Canadian Mint, Pension and Social Insurance, and the Industrial Development Bank. The department, through its representation on various Crown corporations, still exercises strong control over these agencies since they are all closely involved with the government's capital and expenditure policies.[15] Despite these changes the type of economic management practised does not normally involve mandatory controls even though a higher degree of government involvement may take place through the use of Crown corporations and through various regulatory devices. The government relies, as indicated in earlier chapters, on moral suasion, co-operation and on incentives of various kinds such as those operating through the Department of Industry, Trade and Commerce.

Given these periodic changes in the structure of policy-making the type and nature of the authority delegated to various agencies must be constantly reviewed. Therefore, in the mid-1970s, it is debatable as to whether or not some of the responsibilities delegated to agencies such as the Central Mortgage and Housing Corporation and the National Energy Board are in need of further governmental direction given the current crisis in the energy and housing sectors of the economy.[16] At the time of writing various efforts were being made to improve co-ordination between the new Crown corporations operating in the energy field and between the Central Mortgage and Housing Corporation and the Department of Finance.

Periodically it has become necessary for the government to endorse stronger regulatory powers and even to resort to mandatory controls.[17] The instruments available to the Minister of Finance include the fiscal tools implemented through the budget, monetary policy delegated to the Bank of Canada, and administrative controls recently assigned to the Anti-Inflation Board. The use of these instruments are all highly debated issues. There are both technical and political dimensions to this debate. In the first instance economists have not and cannot agree on the basic question of how the budget should be presented.[18] The interested reader has only to examine the debates concerning which format of the budget is most useful for policy-making: the cash, the national income, or the administrative budget.[19] The presentation of the budget can influence how policy is perceived. There is an ancillary problem which relates to the measurement of the impact of budget changes on the economy.[20] If controls are introduced at what point does the minister decide when they should be removed? At this point economic management is highly influenced by divergent views on how the economic environment should be interpreted.[21] The Minister of Finance together with his technical advisors has a formidable task. It has been suggested that no one minister can effectively handle international financial discussions, wage and price policy, regional policy, and government spending and taxing.[22] Needless to say, these are the very strategies which have been adopted and the discussion of the issues have necessitated "a political economy approach" to the formulation of economic policy. The issues also demonstrate the importance of improving public knowledge of the complexities of economic management.

These varied and interrelated aspects of economic management must be delegated to chosen ministers, departments, and agencies and subsequently co-ordinated if the diverse objectives of economic policy are to be achieved. Recently, a number of analysts concerned with the formulation of economic policy have raised important questions concerning the respective roles which are performed by officials in the Department of Finance and the Department of National Revenue in the policy-formulation process. They have pointed to the close relationships between tax policy and tax administration but our review of the complexities involved in economic management demonstrates that there are several aspects to be accommodated in any effort to improve the present system.

There are also legal and administrative problems which affect policy-formulation. In the Canadian system of policy-making each minister has authority and responsibility for his department. However, an almost insoluble problem of economic management occurs because of the fact that the diverse areas of economic policy are highly interrelated. These intricate interrelationships defy simple ministerial or agency delegation. Further controversy arises from the fact that several analysts have proposed reforms based only on the technical issues. As such they mistakenly relegated the political and managerial issues to secondary or tertiary importance.

There is no doubt that the Department of Finance has followed conservative methods and techniques in formulating economic policy. However, the system which has evolved itself makes difficult, or indeed often, inhibits further reform of the system. Accordingly, in order to change the system of economic policy-making, the roles performed by several agencies would have to be simultaneously altered. To this end, there has been a continuing debate in Ottawa concerning whether or not the role of the Department of Finance in policy co-ordination should be strengthened by adopting a more formal planning approach[23] or reduced by further delegating some of its responsibilities.[24] The debate impinges on what should be the appropriate roles of the Department of Finance, the Bank of Canada, the Department of Industry, Trade and Commerce, the PCO, the Treasury Board, and even the Economic Council of Canada, to name a few of the agencies concerned.[25] New policy conflicts emerge because there are a number of new departments concerned with more functionally oriented sectors of economic policy such as the departments of Manpower and Immigration, Consumer and Corporate Affairs, and Regional Economic Expansion which are the subject of later chapters. These changes present new challenges for improved co-ordination. Consequently, the reform of the structure must be seen as a complex activity. To this end, we have chosen in this and in the ensuing chapters to review the roles performed by the Department of Finance, the Bank of Canada, and the Department of Industry, Trade and Commerce and their tangential agencies. Although these agencies are legally and administratively segregated, there is a history of close informal relationships between them. All of these agencies participate in the process of economic policy-making and economic management and each has developed "its appropriate ideology" for participating in the process of economic management.[26]

Efforts to interpret and sometimes to even revise agency ideology or philosophy have led to simplistic conclusions as to the nature of economic management. In Chapter 4 we pointed to the criticism of Breton that Finance departments or "Exchequers" characterize the economic environment to be one of low-level economic activity and as a result these officials underestimate revenues.[27] Breton further argues that in the Canadian governmental system the Department of Finance is in a monopoly position in that no competing organization can effectively challenge its revenue forecasts. He asserts that the persistent and systematic underestimation of revenues constitutes the most efficient way of minimizing the risk of confrontation with other departments of government and which, at the same time, provides the Department of Finance with an instrument — a form of internal patronage—whereby it can maintain control and exercise power over these departments.

From these assertions have emerged suggested organizational reforms of which three should be mentioned. First, the monopoly of the department over forecasting should be discontinued by creating alternative sources. Second, the management of the national debt and the administration of the government's finances should not be part of the department. Third, budgetary practices should be reformed so that the Treasury Board would be required to formulate alternative budgets for potential states of the economy and society.[28] We have earlier stressed that proponents of these reforms have not presented any arguments concerning whether or not these role differentiations would adversely affect policy co-ordination.

note → Briefly stated, we adopt the position that improvements in policy-making require technical, organizational, and political changes. While economic management encompasses more than that which is reflected in the Department of Finance, the department, nevertheless, is the focal point of economic management in Canada. In addition to the current organization of the department it should be noted that several traditional functions have been delegated to autonomous agencies with indirect linkages to and/or control by the Minister of Finance. The Bank of Canada and the Treasury Board are important examples but we must also take cognizance of the functions performed by the Department of National Revenue and agencies such as the Anti-Dumping Tribunal since they enter into the process of economic management. The remainder of this chapter shows the operational complexities of economic management in Canada as reflected in the contemporary roles of the Department of Finance.

THE STATUTORY AND INFORMAL ROLES: BEYOND DEMAND MANAGEMENT

In Chapter 6 we dealt briefly with the historical evolution of the Department of Finance. Since this chapter deals with the contemporary setting, it is worth a reminder that the Department of Finance Act was passed initially in 1869.[29] Article 2 of the Act made provision for the supervision, control, and direction of all matters relating to the financial affairs—public accounts and revenue and expenditure of the Dominion. Article 4 made provision for a Treasury Board, a committee of Cabinet consisting of six ministers. Until 1966 the Board was presided over by the Minister of Finance at which time the ministerial position of President of the Treasury Board was created. Both the

Department of Finance and the Treasury Board now function under the Financial Administration Act.

It should also be remembered that support functions such as those performed by the Department of National Revenue and the Central Accounting and Financial Services, now under the Minister of Supply and Services, were transferred from the Department of Finance in order that it could more effectively carry out the analytical and policy roles necessary for economic management.[30]

The role of the Department of Finance is dealt with only briefly by the Financial Administration Act which points to very broad functions in contrast to the very specific references made to the Treasury Board in the same statute. The Act simply states that:

> There shall be a department of the Government of Canada called the Department of Finance over which the Minister of Finance appointed by commission under the Great Seal shall preside (R.S., c. 116, s. 8; 1968-69, c. 27, s. 19).
>
> The Minister has the management and direction of the Department of Finance, the management of the Consolidated Revenue Fund and the supervision, control and direction of all matters relating to the financial affairs of Canada not by law assigned to the Treasury Board or to any other Minister (1966-67, c. 74, s. 4).
>
> The Governor in Council may appoint an officer, called the Deputy Minister of Finance, to be the deputy head of the Department of Finance and to hold office during pleasure (R.S., c. 116, s. 10; 1968-69, c. 27, ss. 4, 19).[31]

Economic management is even more complex in Canada as compared to unitary states because of the federal structure. The Department of Finance has performed and continues to perform a major role in federal-provincial relations because of the predominance of finance matters notwithstanding the fact that several "line departments" such as Energy, Mines and Resources, Health and Welfare, and Regional Economic Expansion perform major operational activities and have developed their own intergovernmental machinery for interfacing with the provinces. There have often been suggestions that the Bank of Canada should also develop mechanisms for more responsive reactions to regional interests. The Department of Finance, for reasons mentioned above, has strong inputs into the PCO which performs a major role in policy co-ordination both at the federal level and in the federal-provincial realms.

What then constitute the central formal roles of the Department of Finance? The majority of the staff of the Department of Finance concentrates on its main objective which has been stated as follows:

> To assist the government in deciding upon and implementing financial and other economic policies and measures that will best accomplish its major economic and other objectives. To effectively achieve the above objectives the department performs the following functions:
>
> —analyses and appraises the economic situation and prospects in Canada and in other countries of interest to Canada;
>
> —advises on fiscal and other economic policies and measures including those originating in the department;
>
> —recommends measures to meet the requirements of the government within appropriate fiscal policies, by action in expenditure, lending, taxation, borrowing, and cash management;
>
> —advises on matters concerning the balance of payments, exchange reserves, international monetary and financial arrangements, coinage, and related matters;
>
> —participates in international negotiations and other meetings related to trade, finance, taxation, economic development, and other subjects and makes contributions to international financial institutions;
>
> —advises on policies relating to federal-provincial fiscal and economic relations; carries on discussions with provincial authorities and pays grants to provincial governments and grants in lieu of taxes to municipalities;
>
> —administers statutes relating to guaranteed loans, the capital budgets, and financing of Crown corporations and agencies.[32]

A more meaningful understanding of the role of the department can be obtained by drawing a distinction between its primary and secondary roles and responsibilities since the above-mentioned listings represent a formalistic description of responsibilities. The department performs its primary roles in economic management through the management of demand which consists, essentially, of "fiscal, monetary, and debt-management policies".[33] However, this primary responsibility cannot be understood without taking cognizance of the fact that the Department of Finance is intricately involved in the appraisal of the spending decisions of other agencies. In a later section of this chapter these aspects of the department's role will be illustrated through comments by various ministers and deputy ministers. However, even in the realm of fiscal and monetary policies for which the minister has direct responsibilities there are complexities.[34] Since 1967 the Minister of Finance has retained undisputed responsibility for monetary policy but there are economists who come close to arguing that politicians should not be trusted with the determination of the money supply. However, if the economy is to be managed then the Minister of Finance must perform a pivotal role in relationships between the department and the Bank of Canada.

In an even more politically sensitive way, the Department of Finance is involved in issues which, from a strictly statutory interpretation, would be considered to be of secondary concern to the minister. Thus it deals with the provinces in the formulation of resources (energy) policy, manpower policy, and more generally with social policy.[35] However, it should be emphasized that when the Department of Finance is involved with these policy issues it is mainly responding to initiatives which emanate elsewhere. In short, the Minister of Finance maintains responsibility for two separate, but interrelated, variants in determining the fiscal stance in Canada; namely, decisions affecting levels of taxes and those affecting levels of expenditures. These primary components of economic management must be carefully examined before the secondary considerations such as the redistribution of income between groups and between regions can be accommodated. It should be equally asserted that it is the necessity to incorporate these broader considerations which present major challenges for contemporary economic management. The central challenge to the Department of Finance, therefore, is to incorporate within the narrower confines of demand management the broader societal concerns which influence tax, social, and manpower policies. In these decisions economic analysis is really a tool to improve rational decision-making. The views which come from Finance must be balanced against those emanating from the Treasury Board and the PCO.

The prevailing view of the role of the Department of Finance was summed up by the Hon. Donald S. Macdonald in his budget speech of May 25, 1976. After reviewing the state of the domestic and international environments the minister outlined four closely related elements in the government's anti-inflation program — fiscal and monetary policy, government expenditure policy, structural policies, and prices and incomes policies. While some observers would argue that the minister is primarily responsible for fiscal and monetary policies, he also performs an important role in co-ordinating the other components mentioned above. The role which the minister performs in the Cabinet was further demonstrated when in concluding his budget Donald Macdonald asserted: "Mr. Speaker, I have provided the House with a full account of the approach of the *government* to economic policy."[36]

Another dimension of the role of the minister and the department in economic management arises out of the need to mediate between the various groups in society. The department continuously discusses tax issues with various sectors of the economy before formulating tax policies. Sometimes special efforts at consultation have been attempted. For example between 1973 and 1975 the Hon. John Turner met with representatives from labour and business in a futile endeavour to gain voluntary support in the fight against inflation. The government subsequently introduced wage and price controls on October 14, 1975, after the initiatives had failed. Yet, the extent to which the Minister of Finance must adopt policies which gain the support of various groups in the society at large was again referred to in the budget speech of May 1976 in which the Hon. Donald S. Macdonald asserted:

> We see ourselves as partners and not sole proprietors in this enterprise. It is well to remember that in our economy that there is not only a recognized role for governments and their enterprises but also a massive and crucial role for private firms, labour unions, and a great diversity of other private institutions and associations. If government alone is held responsible for the performance of the economic system, then government will be driven increasingly into the

> regulation of the private sector, at the cost of both efficiency and of economic freedom. In general we all look to the private sector to deliver the right goods and services to the right place at the right time and at the right price. Productivity growth results primarily from the actions of the private sector not the policies of the government. The private sector can expect government to provide a framework of law and economic policy in which it can best function. But government can expect the private sector to operate efficiently, competitively and with due regard to the interest of society within that framework.
>
> Indeed, all Canadians have their roles to play in the achievement of our common economic goals.[37]

The foregoing clearly demonstrates that in Canada the management of economic policy is primarily delegated to the Minister of Finance. This role, however, requires enormous and continuous support from other agencies of the government. In recent years, the various budgets have demonstrated strong influence from the departments of Agriculture, Consumer and Corporate Affairs, Energy, Mines and Resources, and Manpower and Immigration both in their preparation and in their execution. This point was further symbolized by Michael Pitfield's statement in September 1975 that "Finance has been maintained as the department responsible for stabilization policy and a *court of last review* for economic policy, while at the same time there have been created a number of new economic departments . . ." (our emphasis).[38]

Within the department a collegial relationship is maintained so that it can develop the necessary interface at one level with the other central agencies, namely, the Treasury Board and the PCO and at another level with line departments such as National Health and Welfare, Manpower and Immigration, and Energy, Mines and Resources, to give a few examples. This relationship has been further supported by the cabinet committee in which a collegial relationship is sought. The importance of economic affairs requires that the Department of Finance operate as a central agency together with the Treasury Board and the PCO.

The almost inseparable relationship between the Treasury Board and the Department of Finance has developed because both agencies conduct program analysis, albeit of a different nature. The Treasury conducts program analysis through its appraisal of departmental estimates. However, the Department of Finance also constantly does so when it examines the financial implications of transportation, regional development, energy, and social policies. The policy decisions often involve long-term capital considerations. The department retains close relationships with Crown corporations since in many instances it guarantees their loans, and with the PCO partly through the new Federal-Provincial Relations Office.

THE ROLE AS PERCEIVED BY SENIOR OFFICIALS: THE DEPARTMENT AS INTERNAL OPPOSITION

Our analysis in Chapter 5 of economic policy leaders and the brief historical portrait of the Finance Department in Chapter 6 have already given an indication of how successive ministers and deputy ministers have both viewed the Finance role and influenced its evolution. These included the perceptions of such ministers as Donald Fleming, Walter Gordon, and John Turner as well as deputy ministers such as W. C. Clark, R. B. Bryce, and Simon Reisman. A further sample of views will help reinforce this earlier analysis especially in a more direct operational sense.

These statements show that operationally, the Department of Finance performs three important roles in economic management. First, it reacts to and considers proposals put forward by other departments and agencies; second, it participates in the deliberation of the cabinet committees; and third, it participates in the annual budget process. The last-mentioned role is extremely complex and involves several subsidiary processes which will be further explained in the remaining portions of this chapter.

Thus in the late 1960s R. B. Bryce, then deputy minister, and other officials attempted to define its role.[39] Bryce argued that "much of the work of the Department of Finance is of the nature of a critical appraisal of the proposals of others". The government considers, from week to week, various proposals put forward by individual ministers, departments, or agencies, or groups of them in consultation. These proposals must be analysed, appraised, tested against a general framework of policy, reconciled with federal constitutional powers, and responsibilities, and finally fitted into a budget and financial program. The main groups that engage in this critical appraisal are the staff of the Treasury Board, the staff of the PCO (Cabinet Office), and the Department of Finance. He noted that "the delineation of responsibilities for this work of analysis, appraisal, and criticism is nowhere laid down clearly and precisely, particularly since the Treasury Board staff has been split off from the rest of the Department of Finance."[40] Broadly speaking, it may be said that the Finance department concentrates on economic matters and the government's budget. Officials have thus perceived the main role of the Department of Finance as one of analysing and appraising the economic proposals that are brought forward by others and helping the government to decide whether these should be accepted, modified, deferred, or rejected. In this work the Department of Finance uses all the information and critical judgment it can muster and engages in continuous discussions with those departments putting forward the proposals and with the other departments examining them. Senior officials usually stress, moreover, that this work is all too frequently done under considerable pressure of time and urgency.

The Finance department must bring to bear not only particular economic considerations for which it has to rely on people with special knowledge and techniques, but also an integrative role that takes into account a wide variety of technical, economic, social, legal, and political considerations. Whether proposals emanate from the department or elsewhere they must be judged in relation to current government priorities, policies, and programs. As Bryce noted: "Merely because an idea is a good one or its purpose is desirable is not sufficient to warrant the government implementing it. Relative values, and the cost of the program in relation to the cost of other programs, all have to be judged, as well as whether or not the matter is something which properly falls within the responsibilities of the federal government rather than a province, or, for that matter, within the private sector."[41] He further commented: "The government does not lack for central control agencies or authorities; the problem is to have them work effectively and have them work sensibly." Hence, in Bryce's view, "the great bulk of the work of Finance is to try and participate in the work of the cabinet committees directly. The advice the department gives to the minister and the advice it gives to the cabinet committees and the Treasury Board is for consideration in the decisions of the Cabinet and the Board."[42]

As indicated earlier the central work on priorities is done by a group of cabinet committees, whose deliberations are secret. The most important of the committees is that on Priorities and Planning, which as its name implies endeavours to determine and reconcile governmental priorities. In the central work of appraising or helping the ministers to appraise relative priorities the Department of Finance takes a major part along with the Treasury Board Secretariat and the PCO.

With regard to the evolution of priorities, Bryce stressed: "The highest priority I suppose, if you look back in the last dozen years in Canada, has been given to expenditures for the old and the sick and the poor."[43] "High policy" is formulated essentially "in the various cabinet committees and the Treasury Board looks at overall programs annually, in setting program objectives in dealing with estimates and in dealing with specific programs like regional development, industrial incentives and things like that, that are going to have a major impact on the financial picture." The former deputy minister concluded: "In fact, I feel myself that no particular new machinery is needed; we want to make the existing machinery work better."[44]

In clarifying the difference between the roles of the Department of Finance and the Treasury Board, Bryce further observed: "It is the proper function of the Treasury Board to see whether something should be done in this department or that department, or if there is duplication or if there is poor management." On the other hand, "if some department is bringing forward a proposal for some kind of economic measure, let us say, for example, trying to get industry to locate in the areas of economic disparity . . . we feel we should exercise and we do exercise, a responsibility there to examine such a proposal and try to judge its economic impact and whether it is the most sensible way of achieving that objective." This comment by Bryce is most important because it was made in 1969 during the embryonic stage of a new regional development strategy. Bryce went on to conclude: "Once the government has decided on it and approved it, scrutiny of how effectively it is being managed really falls on the Treasury Board."[45]

The Department of Finance, however, ultimately influences economic policy through its role in the budgetary process. Bryce outlined its influence in relation to three aspects of the budgetary process. The first is a general economic appraisal which the Department of Finance does repeatedly during the year of the situation "as far ahead as we can see it". It is relevant to look a considerable distance ahead when making decisions, particularly on expenditure programs that will run for years. It is part of the general task of the Department of Finance "that all senior and key officers are kept aware of the state of the economy, and of the prospects for the economy. They are all expected to read the reviews and studies of the Economic Council and other things." Accordingly, the Department tries to have a prospectus of the general economic situation and a periodic detailed forecast of the short term.

The second aspect is the spending decisions of the government which take place almost throughout the year and are brought together around April by the Treasury Board and the Cabinet Committee on Priorities and Planning to assess where the government is going, not just in the next fiscal year commencing the following April but in the several years following. In these reviews by the Treasury Board, by officials meeting in groups, by the Cabinet Committee on Priorities and Planning, and ultimately by the Cabinet itself, an endeavour is made to relate expenditures to the revenue appraisal of the Finance department and to its economic forecast.

Thirdly, the Department of Finance looks at the plans for tax changes. During the late 1960s while the post-Carter Commission tax review was being conducted in the Department of Finance, there was also a major review of priorities being conducted in the PCO. At that time Bryce observed:

Currently we have two reviews going. We have the major one for the reform of the income tax, which is looking a long way ahead and has regard basically to the structure of the tax system. Then, in addition, we are now asking whether changes in the weight of tax or in some of the details of the taxes are needed, given the prospects for expenditure for this year and next year and our appraisal of the economic situation. This is going on as well. This is part of the budgeting process that takes place very largely within the Department of Finance, with the Minister of Finance, and discussants whom he feels are more directly concerned. When the Minister of Finance has his Budget proposals ready he takes them to the Prime Minister and then to the Cabinet to get them settled. This constitutes a brief outline of the budgetary process.[46]

However, the budget process involves a great many more people and a great deal more detail on the expenditure side than it does on the revenue side. The deputy minister noted that "in the economic background we consult with other departments that are informed and normally engaged in work on these things, notably the Department of Trade and Commerce, the Department of Industry and the Bank of Canada so that our view as to what is going to happen is checked against others who do forecasting work."

In reply to questions concerning the respective roles of the Department of Finance and the PCO in the area of federal-provincial relations Bryce remarked: "Broadly speaking, in Finance we deal with the fiscal relations and certain other more general economic relations with the provinces. The Privy Council Office deals with the whole range of relations, including the constitutional ones. . . . A number of men who have worked in the Department of Finance have gone over there to assist them in as much as the department has had considerable experience in this general field. However, there is a sharing of responsibility in that we deal with essentially fiscal and general economic issues with the provinces, normally those that concern the provincial treasuries rather than, let us say, the Attorney-General Department or the Health Department or things of that sort."[47] Again, it is clear that the Department of Finance has to develop close working relationships with the PCO. To quote Bryce again:

> We are both shorthanded, there is not a duplication of work and the two groups are closely in touch with one another. Naturally, in recent years there has been an increasing amount of work in relation to the provinces, both because of the more active and continuing discussions with the provinces on fiscal matters. It seems to go on interminably nowadays, so there is a functional sharing along the broad lines I have described plus a close contact, which means that we do not overlap with what each other is doing.[48]

When the new regional development policy was in its embryonic stages Bryce commented on the review process in the following manner. In response to a question concerning the kind of liaison which was expected to take place between the Department of Finance and the then new Department of Regional Economic Expansion he remarked: "The Department of Finance has had quite extensive discussions with the Department since it began to crystallize in 1968."[49] He went on to point out:

> We have had very considerable discussions in the past three months about its broad budget for the next few years and the terms of the legislation that will replace the ADA legislation, inducements for industry to locate here or there. All this has been part of the central governmental process in budgeting. However the problem is even more demanding since there is now a new department assembling a lot of programs, changing them and giving a new emphasis and direction to it. In accordance with the above, it has been the view of the Department of Finance that "there is, or should be more concerted planning if we are going into a greater effort on this regional development, particularly in those areas where substantial progress has been made.[50]

From another perspective Bryce noted that two new additions to the policy-making machinery of importance were the Economic Council and the Science Council. In his words "both of these bodies are giving the government advice publicly so that the public is quite able to see what advice the government is getting from these distinguished groups on this matter. This makes it possible to have a much better public debate about the issues than heretofore."

It is important to reiterate, however, that although the Economic Council has earned good reputation in terms of its contribution to public information and, consequently, to the improvement of public understanding and debate on significant aspects of economic policy, it continues to experience difficulty in integrating its external advice into the traditional decision-making process.

In the area of economic analysis apart from informal consultations between economists in the various departments, Statistics Canada, the Department of Trade and Commerce, and the Bank of Canada, etc., the Department of Finance has, as we have seen earlier, developed during the 1960s its own staff of econometricians who continually reviewed the old equations which in the past were used in forecasting. They constantly tested them against subsequent experience, altered, and added to them so that they did not get out of date. It tried to utilize the equations in other areas where the department thought they had been deficient and where more detailed information was required. This work was carried out by the Department of Finance itself. During the 1960s also the department maintained an advisory group of consultants and econometricians drawn from the various universities in Canada chosen as individuals for their technical competence who examined the department's model periodically and made suggestions as to how the equations could be improved.

A. B. Hockin, when he was Assistant Deputy Minister of Finance, supported the view that Canada needed to avoid an over-centralized system in regard to research on economic policy-making:

> . . . in the forecasting area when we took over the model from the Department of Trade and Commerce as it was then, I had a number of sessions with the responsible officers in the Department of Trade and Commerce at which we discussed the pros and cons of moving the model in this way, but throughout.
>
> The basic approach we followed was that we did not want, whichever way the decision was taken, either agency to reduce its own input into the forecasting field. We were unhappy at the idea of reducing the number of people who were working in the forecasting field, so that the government would not have

> to rely on one small group who were doing the forecasting for all divisions in this area. . . . it is unlike some of the efforts in research in the physical sciences where you cannot be just that sure of your results and you do not want the government to be in the position of having to rely on the judgment of just one or two individuals.[51]

Accordingly, Dr. Hockin concluded, "in these areas we have tended to say, let us compare our results, let us work together, but let us go on doing so separately so that we will have something to check against."

The foregoing statement depicted the department in the mid-1960s. With the building of a number of econometric models at the Bank of Canada (RDX1 and RDX2), the Institute of Quantitative Studies at the University of Toronto (TRACE), the Economic Council (CANDIDE), and within various governmental departments the Finance department continued to draw on the resources available elsewhere rather than to develop an elaborate and separate econometric model.[52] In a sense the philosophy has remained the same with very little emphasis placed, in recent years, on developing an exclusive model within Finance. The department's data has been improved as reflected in the annually published *Economic Review*.

Major efforts were made during the late 1960s and the early 1970s to improve the analytical capabilities of the Finance department. This was due, in part, to the difficulties the ministers faced in fighting both inflation and unemployment. Between 1968 and 1971 the Hon. Edgar Benson attempted to fight inflation but shortly before he left office in 1971 made a dramatic reversal and attempted to fight unemployment. The Hon. John N. Turner, his successor, started his reign as Finance minister with an expansionary policy but soon found that he had to fight inflation also. During the Turner and Reisman management at Finance a Long-Range Economic Planning Branch was established.

In June 1971 the then Deputy Minister of Finance, Simon Reisman, in response to a series of questions on the use of monetary and fiscal policy to "manage the economy" described the process:

> There is a standard procedure in the hands of the Priorities and Planning Committee of the Cabinet, which is chaired by the Prime Minister. There is a role in that process for the agencies which have responsibilities for giving advice and providing information and data. I know that the Minister of Finance is called upon. To be precise, let us assume that we are now discussing the

expenditure plan of the Government for the period from April 1972 to March 31, 1973. The process for making decisions with respect to that expenditure plan commenced at the beginning of 1971 and a number of meetings were scheduled with the Priorities and Planning Committee. . . .

One of the first papers required in the process is by the Minister of Finance on the general economic outlook, medium and long term. The paper he submitted on this occasion was entitled "Some Emerging Economic Issues", in which he attempted to take an overview of the shape and direction of the economy, looking ahead a decade and more. . . .

The committee had a detailed discussion of the paper, with officials invited to attend and respond to questions. The second paper, which is presented during the following week or two, focuses in a little more. This again is by the Minister of Finance to the Priorities and Planning Committee of the Cabinet. In the paper he delivers a picture of the economy as it is today and seems to be developing over a two-year period, in considerable detail. The minister usually chooses to be accompanied by some of his officials, who respond to enquiries, questions and requests for further information.

On the basis of that consideration the Minister of Finance recommends to his colleagues the fiscal settlement for the period in question. If we are talking about February 1971, now, and about a period that begins April 1, 1972, then we are talking about a period that commences 14 months and runs through to 26 months from the time he offers that fiscal recommendation. This is forward planning, and forward planning of a kind that must inevitably become subject to adjustments and corrections as the process goes on, as time goes by, and as you learn more about the economy and its direction.[53]

With respect to the more long-term aspects of policy formulation Reisman remarked:

I can tell you that in a variety of departments of Government they do try to engage in longer term thinking. I was a deputy with the Department of Industry for a while. It is now the Department of Industry, Trade and Commerce. They have been working away at developing a long-term industrial strategy.

Each of the departments of Government has some personnel who are charged with the task of looking further ahead, trying to anticipate some of the longer term problems. This is true in my department. My predecessor said he found that his efforts in this regard were always frustrated by the emergence of a whole series of problems from day to day. I also find that is happening, but we are making a real effort to have people who do look at the long-term.

More important than what happens in individual departments is, I think, the apparatus of the Government decision-making process. The introduction into the Cabinet system of the Planning Committee of Cabinet over which the Prime Minister presides, and it is the body at the decision-making level which tries to pull in a good deal of the longer-term thinking and analysis, and tries to mesh that into some kind of coherent total policy.[54]

By the late 1960s and early 1970s there were at least two thrusts to the suggested reforms of the economic-policy-formulation process. Some reformers felt that the Department of Finance should be strengthened analytically but that it should continue to be the central advisory and co-ordinating agency on economic policy. Others advocated a further strengthening of the economic-intelligence process externally. It was further argued that this new source of information and analysis should be plugged into both the PCO and the PMO. This conflict led to heated debate and appears to have played a role in the resignation of both John Turner as minister and Simon Reisman as deputy minister.[55]

FINANCE, THE TREASURY BOARD, AND THE PUBLIC BUDGETARY SYSTEM

The Department of Finance is one of the primary actors in the public budgeting system of Canada. The budgeting system is a system for making choices about ends and means. It is a form of decision-making. The Department of Finance is part of a system of information handling. Accordingly, it is important to know from whom, and to whom, the Department of Finance gets and presents information of a financial and economic nature.

Economic information or "organizational intelligence" is gathered and compiled within agencies, such as the Department of Supply and Services, Statistics Canada, the Bank of Canada, the Department of Industry, Trade and Commerce, and the International Economic Analysis and Fiscal Policy Branch within the Department of Finance.[56] Information enters the Department of Finance from diverse sources and they are included in the "Fiscal Framework", a document which the Minister of Finance submits to the Cabinet Committee on Priorities and Planning. This information is largely on the input side of the budgetary process and deals generally with the state of the economy.

TABLE 7:1
National and Public Expenditure Indicators, 1955 and 1975

	1955	*1975*	*Change*
		($ Million)	
Gross national expenditure	28,528	154,752	126,224
Expenditures of all governments	7,178	63,215	56,037
		(Per cent)	
Government share of GNE	25.2	40.8	15.6
Before intergovernmental transfers:			
Federal	15.6	22.5	6.9
Provincial and local	9.6	18.3	8.7
After intergovernmental transfers:			
Federal	15.0	17.6	2.6
Provincial and local	10.2	23.2	13.0

Source: Based on data from the Department of Finance, Economic Review, April 1976. E.C.C. *Thirteenth Annual Review*, p. 60.

On the output side, the Treasury Board is concerned with the expenditure of the government. Thus, one must again operationally distinguish economic management as reflected in the economic budget from management of the public service and the public sector as reflected through the government expenditure budget.

Tables 7:1 and 7:2 portray very starkly the aggregate nature of governmental expenditure in relation to other governmental levels and in terms of its internal breakdown (see also Appendix D and E). Thus, drawing on figures reproduced in Table 7:1, the Economic Council noted in 1976:

A generation ago, government expenditures accounted for 25 percent of all national expenditures but, by 1975, this share had risen to 41 percent. . . . Canada's gross national expenditure in current dollars last year was almost five times its level in 1955; but, during the two intervening decades, federal expenditures had multiplied slightly over six times, local expenditures ten times, and provincial expenditures close to twenty times, their 1955 levels. Whereas, in 1955, federal expenditures accounted for close to 60 percent of all government expenditures, by 1975 the federal share had dropped to 43 percent. Over the twenty-year period, local and provincial expenditures—after intergovernmental transfers—accounted for five-sixths of the increased share of government expenditures, federal expenditures, for only one-sixth.[57]

TABLE 7:2
Gross General Expenditure by Function
For Selected Fiscal Years Ending March 31, 1967 to 1976
(%)

	1966-67	*1971-72*	*1972-73*	*1973-74*	*1974-75*	*1975-76*
Defence	15.8	10.3	9.1	8.7	7.3	7.1
Welfare	27.7	29.7	32.8	33.4	32.5	34.0
Health	5.4	8.8	8.6	8.0	7.3	7.6
Debt charges	8.5	7.8	7.2	7.1	7.4	6.5
General purpose transfers to other governments	5.7	8.5	7.8	7.8	8.7	7.7
Development of regions	.4	.8	.7	.6	.6	.5
Transportation and communications	10.2	6.6	6.6	7.3	7.1	7.2
Natural resources, agriculture and environment	5.7	4.6	5.1	6.3	8.4	8.7
Other—People						
Education	3.9	4.7	4.1	3.8	3.0	3.3
Recreation and culture	.9	.9	1.0	1.0	.9	.8
Labour, employment and immigration	.7	1.6	2.3	1.4	1.5	1.5
Housing	.1	.4	.5	.6	.5	.8
	5.6	7.6	7.9	6.8	5.9	6.5
Other—Business and Property						
Protection	1.9	1.9	1.9	2.0	1.9	2.0
Payments to own enterprises	1.8	1.5	1.4	1.5	1.5	1.5
Trade and industry and tourism	1.7	2.0	1.8	1.4	1.4	1.5
Research	1.3	1.8	1.2	1.3	1.3	1.4
	6.8	7.1	6.4	6.5	6.1	6.4
Miscellaneous						
Foreign affairs and international assistance	2.6	1.7	1.8	1.8	1.7	2.0
General government	5.6	6.4	6.0	5.7	7.0	5.8
Other	—	—	—	—	—	—
	8.2	8.1	7.8	7.5	8.7	7.8
Total Gross General Expenditure	100.00	100.0	100.0	100.0	100.0	100.0

Similarly, but over a shorter time period, Table 7:2 shows the increasing proportion of federal expenditures that have been allocated to welfare, health, resource, and employment areas of economic management.

In June 1971, the Hon. E. J. Benson, then Minister of Finance, summed up the then prevailing view in Ottawa concerning the role of the Department of Finance:

I think people—and its partially the Government's fault—think there really is much less coordination than there really is. Coordination must take place at the Cabinet level in the Government and indeed it does through a wide system of Cabinet committees which have been set up. . . . The Governor of the Bank of Canada is not really a line adviser. The Department of Finance is not really a department; it is a policy department. The Treasury Board, which has many line functions, was deliberately moved from the Department of Finance, as was the Comptroller of the Treasury. The result of this has been the elimination of mechanical functions in the Department of Finance. Therefore, the Department can devote its time to policy. Although the policy advice is generally good, now and again we should change a deputy minister, which we have done once, as well as the minister. If the advice is wrong and we do not like it, the thing to do is to fire the minister and the deputy minister, rather than appoint an official to second-guess the economic decisions. Those decisions can be coordinated, with any kind of throughput desired, with the cabinet committee.[58]

The foregoing viewpoint depicted the department up to the Report of the Senate Committee on *Growth Employment and Price Stability* which was critical of the then existing arrangements.[59] No major changes occurred in the Department of Finance until the resignation of Simon Reisman as Deputy Minister and John Turner as Minister of Finance in 1974 and 1975 respectively. However, the development of measures for improving the process by which revenue and expenditure decisions are made have, in recent years, absorbed a significant portion of the time of decision-makers and analysts in Ottawa.

The resignation of Simon Reisman as Deputy Minister of Finance led to the appointment of Thomas K. Shoyama as Deputy Minister and William C. Hood as Associate Deputy Minister of Finance. Hood, an experienced economist, had previously been responsible for economic analysis and fiscal policy. These changes further reflect the increased complexities in economic policy-making. This is most strikingly demonstrated by comparing the situation in the mid-1970s with the organizational chart for 1963 shown in Chapter 6. The changes reveal that by the late 1970s the responsibilities of the deputy minister of Finance had grown to the point where two deputy ministers (A deputy and an associate) were required, each reflecting different leadership qualities and different professional skills. A number of new initiatives were also taken to improve the co-ordination of economic policy.

The Department of Finance and the Treasury Board perform important economic, financial, and general management roles in the formulation of the government's expenditure decisions through the preparation of the fiscal framework and through their control of expenditures. The formulation of the fiscal framework involves the preparation of a single paper, or more accurately a pair of papers, by the Department of Finance and the Treasury Board. These papers must be reconciled at the macro-economic policy-making level so that they are consistent with the annual *Economic Review*. The revenue and the expenditure decisions are made within a system of structural relationships which operate in the following manner.

The long-term planning decisions (which are always plagued by short-term expediencies) are discussed by Cabinet well in advance of the annual expenditure cycle. For example, the fiscal framework for 1974-75 was discussed by Cabinet in April 1973, and the fiscal framework for 1975-76 was discussed in April 1974.[60] The decision on the size of the government's reserves is a Privy Council decision but, as has been explained earlier, the Department of Finance, because of its control over "economic intelligence", has had a major input into the formulation of priorities since all decisions will ultimately involve the spending of money. In order to understand this process, we should look retrospectively on how the expenditure budget has been developed.

In March 1974, the Treasury Board received the spending proposals for the fiscal year 1975-76 from each government department. The proposals contained both A-budget estimates and B-budget estimates. The A Budget contained estimates of the amount of money needed to finance the existing level of activity in each program. Expenditure forecasts are also made for three years ahead. The B Budget contained the proposals for new activities and for expansion of existing activities. The Treasury Board's Secretariat (which is divided into functional groups such as economic development and natural resources, manpower policy, and social policy, among others) examined the expenditures within a functional framework before the proposals were submitted to Treasury Board at the end of May 1974. The Treasury Board's Secretariat wrote letters to each of the departments advising them of what amount of spending would be recommended to the Board and later to Cabinet.

During April 1974 the Cabinet had conducted a "planning exercise" having discussed the fiscal framework for 1975-76. The fiscal framework was based on a forecast of revenue and of A-Budget spending prepared by the Department of Finance and the staff of the Treasury Board. Upon the basis of this fiscal forecast the Cabinet established guidelines or a framework for the Treasury Board to use in examining the A- and B-Budget proposals which were described above. The significance of the A and B Budgets is that they distinguish between resources required to continue existing programs and those being requested for the enrichment of existing programs or the initiation of new ones. The Program Review which should be distinguished from the Program Forecast involves interaction between the Treasury Board and the various departments between March and June. The nature and scope of delegated responsibility cannot be overemphasized because of its importance in influencing governmental decision-making.

During the month of June each cabinet minister had the right to appeal to the Treasury Board for reconsideration of particular proposals. At this point there is another reconciliation of short-term and long-term decisions given the fact that the Cabinet must review the economic circumstances against the setting within which it had made its earlier expenditure decisions. By July 1974 the Treasury Board was able to formulate a more detailed set of proposals taking into account changes in prices and costs.

In November 1974, the main estimates were reviewed in a manner similar to the Program Review. The Treasury Board then reviewed the Main Estimates Submissions and made recommendations to Cabinet. Cabinet approval of the Main Estimates was given in mid-December. The Main Estimates was presented to Parliament in February 1975 in the Blue Book, a document of over 1,000 pages. The Main Estimates were subsequently referred to Parliamentary Committees before March 1, 1975.[61]

It is important to note that "major policy decisions" should be distinguished from the normal managerial and administrative decision-making process. At the beginning of a particular fiscal year the Treasury Board must make decisions of a "non-policy" nature. These ongoing decisions should be distinguished from "the new policy" decisions made by the Cabinet and cabinet committees from time to time. One of the most significant decisions of this type was the 1973-74 bill amending the family allowance system. This was not treated as part of the B-Budget exercise. The proposals for the new family allowance went directly to the Cabinet from the Department of Health and Welfare. It was sent to the Treasury Board only for administrative approval and to provide for adequate support services. The foregoing illustrates that major spending decisions are made from time to time directly by Cabinet. In short, spending decisions are made to a significant degree at two points in the system. First, there are the decisions made at the departmental level which are subjected to the normal Treasury Board scrutiny. Second, there are those made at the Cabinet level where spending guidelines are determined and where major new programs first enter the approval stage.

The Department of Finance enters the picture from the point of view of its concern with the government's revenue-expenditure situation and quite frequently takes a negative position on requests for new spending. The Treasury Board is concerned more with the efficiency in achieving the desired objectives after the policy has been adopted. While it is important to distinguish the role of the Department of Finance from the Treasury Board they are closely related for historical and other reasons. There are obvious linkages because the Treasury Board constantly monitors expenditures through its quarterly expenditure reviews in which it revises the forecast of statutory expenditure items. Unplanned expenditures must be charged against the reserves. Two budgets were presented in May and November 1974 which demonstrated the complexities of the economic-management process.[62] However, the most significant adjustments which have been made in revenue and expenditure decisions in recent years began with the June 1975 budget subsequent to which the whole process was examined. In this regard, the budget speeches given by the ministers of Finance and the secretary of the Treasury Board between 1975 and 1976 should be carefully reviewed.[63]

In the budget of June 1975, for example, it was discovered that the expenditure decisions which had been made in 1974 had begun to place serious pressures on the reserves.[64] The fiscal framework was revised and on this occasion a moratorium enforced after an X-Budget exercise was carried out. The X-Budget process involved a request to departments to indicate the areas where they could reduce spending from the original requests in their A- and B-Budget submissions. These examples suggest that the failure to cut government spending is not for want of a procedure but is due to inherent difficulties in the nature of the political process itself.

It is worth stressing that in recent years greater emphasis has been placed on formulating a more long-term approach to making revenue and expenditure decisions. Thus, attempts have been made to separate tax-policy decisions from those affecting expenditures despite their interrelatedness. To the extent that government expenditures significantly affect the economy greater efforts are being taken to further rationalize governmental expenditures especially in terms of their long-term implications. The role of Crown corporations in government expenditure policies were also being evaluated in terms of their impact on these policies.

Prior to the new considerations mentioned above, the Cabinet Committee on Priorities and Planning, which is really the Executive Committee of Cabinet, made the significant decisions concerning the expenditure targets and the size of the government "reserves". Under that approach, emphasis was placed more on determining the size of the surplus or the deficit in the economic budget.[65] In the new approach, which is still evolving, the expenditure decisions are, relatively speaking, made separately from the revenue exercise. Consequently, it is the expenditure planning process which is now longer term. In this regard the impact of agencies such as the Economic Council in the formulation of expenditure policy has been partly reflected. Short-term fiscal decisions on the revenue side are used to a greater degree in stabilizing the economy. Periodically a certain number of short-term expenditure decisions are taken. The budgetary initiatives adopted in 1975 to stimulate housing and job creation were illustrative of these changes. Accordingly, a number of direct measures were announced in the June 1975 budget to meet specific needs. The rationale behind these stabilization measures is that they can be turned off on relatively short notice if the situation warrants a change in policy.

The foregoing demonstrates that the Department of Finance must be understood in the context of a central agency closely related to the PCO and the Treasury Board. It also forms a staff-line relationship with the major economic policy-making departments. Summarily, the Department of Finance assesses the fiscal capacity of the economy. Within the governmental sector, information is fed from various departments to the Treasury Board, particularly its Program Branch, which deals with the estimates review and the program view. The Treasury Board must compare and integrate the various expenditure programs of the departments. From the perspective of the planning, programing, and budgeting process there is definitely a "public budgeting system" framework which is diagrammatically portrayed in Figure 7:1.

From a political-science perspective there are demands which in Figure 7:1 we assume to be backed by the public willingness to support them. The politics of the budgetary process involves issues such as *subsidization, fairness, equity, distribution of income*, and, especially in recent years, *regulation* and its consequences on private spending. From this perspective, the budgetary process involves the maintenance or the changing of values in the society. The various proposals for *tax reform* and the new *social security* policy review must be regarded in this context. A major component of the politics of inflation relates to the difficulties the government encounters in placing restraints on the economy without antagonizing too many of the interest groups which can put pressure on it. The framework presented here fits the analogy used by some analysts who evaluate contemporary *fiscal policy* from the perspective of the public household. Inasmuch as the demands from the various groups in society always add up to more than the real resources available major initiatives must be taken to *manage* the public budgeting system. At this point, therefore, we must distinguish financial management from economic management. By way of illustration one should look at a few distinct but interrelated systems of co-ordination and management.

First, there is the Prime Minister operating through the PCO and more specifically, through the Cabinet Committee on Priorities and Planning which he chairs. Second, there is the Cabinet Committee on Economic Policy which is chaired by the Minister of Finance. This committee serves as a major source of advice to the Priorities and

Figure 7:1 Budgeting as a Resource Allocation System

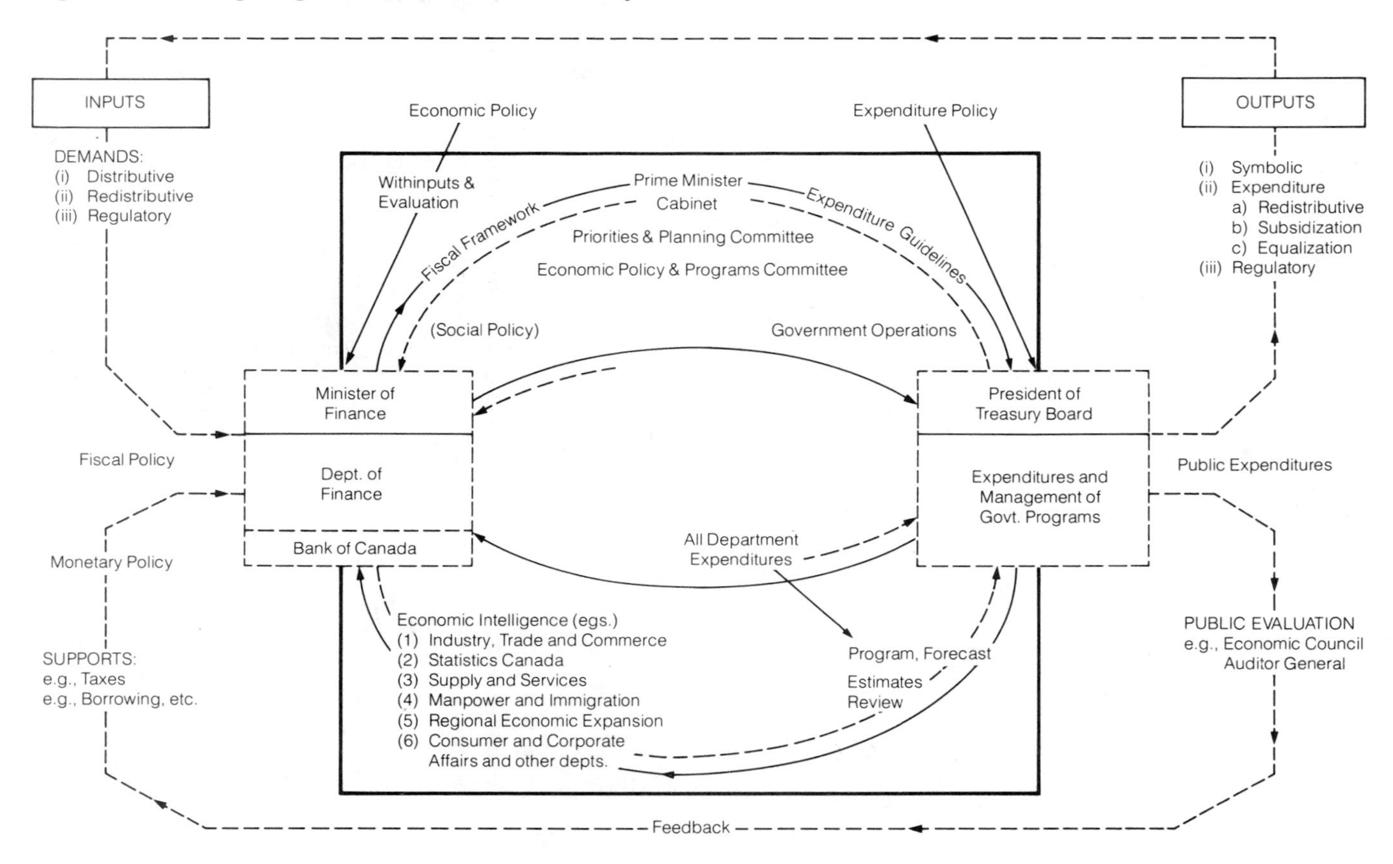

Planning Committee. Third, there is the Treasury Board which is the Cabinet Committee on the Expenditure Budget and the Cabinet Committee on Management. The Board is chaired by the President of the Treasury Board. Fourth, budgeting must be regarded as part of the planning process. It is intended as a mechanism for setting goals and objectives, for identifying weaknesses or inadequacies in organizations, and for controlling or integrating the diverse activities which are carried out by numerous sub-units within large organizations, both public and private. For example, the budget presented in November 1974 in response to the oil crisis was most illustrative of the private- and public-sector aspects of public budgeting.[66] Fifth, budgeting involves questions of accountability and responsibility. In the Canadian setting these aspects may be traced through the evolution of the Financial Administration Act, the Revenue and Audit Act, the Public Accounts Committee, and through the role of the Auditor General, particularly his report to Parliament.[67]

In accordance with the above, budgeting may also be viewed as part of the evaluation process in government. There are at least three aspects of this evaluation process.[68] First, there is the realm of goals or priority setting which involves the PMO, the PCO, and indirectly the Economic and Science councils. Second, there is the internal evaluation process conducted by the Treasury Board as part of the ongoing process of the budget cycle or review of the expenditure budget. Third, there is the review by Parliament and the Auditor General. The Minister of Finance performs an important role in this regard when he gives his budget speech which involves a "ways and means motion" to the House of Commons sitting as a plenary committee.[69] The Department of Finance thus performs very broad and inclusive roles in what we have described as the management of economic policy. It is a major advisory department performing functions similar to the British Treasury. The rest of this chapter examines the structure and functions of the Department of Finance in order to elucidate the operational roles performed by it.

STRUCTURE AND ORGANIZATION IN THE MID1970s

The organization of the Department of Finance should be interpreted with caution for at least two reasons. First, the department has been a training centre for top-level public officials and it has suffered from a high degree of staff turnover. Second, the department has always been organized around personalities and accordingly there is not always a logical relationship between the sub-objectives of the department and the structure of the various divisions. In addition the department has functioned as a loose co-ordinating agency despite recent efforts to formalize its structure. The department can be aptly described as "a pool of economic talent divided into a number of loose but closely interrelated compartments [to facilitate] the flow of data as flexibly as possible [and] to facilitate communication between the subdivisions. This pool of economic, legal, and other talents is placed at the disposal of the Minister of Finance who performs an important role in the Cabinet."[70] The role of the Deputy Minister is to bring this loosely organized pool of economic intelligence and advice existing in the department into a coherent package for the Minister of Finance and subsequently for the Cabinet, the apex of the managerial system.

The Minister of Finance in his capacity as head of the department performs at least two distinct but closely interrelated roles. First, he performs a role as an initiator of policy in that he has primary responsibility for the preparation and presentation of the budget. He is the minister primarily responsible for fiscal policy issues and decision-making. Second, the Minister of Finance reacts to policy initiatives from other departments since he has an important responsibility for financial management. In this second role the Minister of Finance performs a broad economic management role, i.e., he assesses the impact of more particularistic aspects of departmental policies on the overall economy of the country. He makes major decisions relating to the politics and economics of taxing and spending. It should be stressed, however, that most of the detailed information gathering process and work on the implementation of policy is carried out by numerous other agencies and accordingly the Department of Finance's responsibilities in these matters are primarily of an advisory and co-ordinating nature. The department does carry out special task-force studies in important areas of policy formulation as the situation demands.[71] Invariably parallel work would be conducted by line departments or within provincial governments.

In the mid-1970s the Department of Finance is still regarded as the central agency of the federal government primarily responsible for advice on the economic and financial affairs of Canada and concerned with all aspects of improved performance of the Canadian economy. It is concerned with the harmony of various government actions affecting the economy, the external factors that bear on the nation's domestic performance, and the consistency of economic actions by other levels of government. The department has primary responsibility for the preparation of the federal budget; a document which reviews the government's accounts for the past year and makes proposals for the year ahead, relating the government's expenditure program to the revenues from existing sources and charting taxation changes as necessary. Most recently the budget speech, which is sometimes presented several times a year, "has been broadened to provide an authoritative review of past, present and future economic factors that will affect the outlook of business and the nation's finances".[72]

For purposes of comparison, it is worth pointing out that in the mid-1970s the Department of Finance was organized into five branches with a sixth reporting to the deputy minister. These were: Tariffs, Trade, and Aid; Economic Analysis, Fiscal Policy, and International Finance; Tax Policy and Federal-Provincial Relations; Economic Programs and Government Finance; Long-Range Economic Planning; and Capital Markets. Comparison between the 1974 and the 1976 organizational charts (Charts 7:1 and 7:2) reflect the personalities and styles of two different ministers and two deputy ministers of Finance. The 1976 chart shows two branches reporting through the associate deputy minister, a newly created post. Consequently, below the minister and deputy minister there were five ADM's for the following areas: Tax Policy and Federal Provincial Relations; Economic Programs and Government Finance; Long-Range Economic Planning; International Trade and Finance; and Fiscal Policy and Economic Analysis (see 1976 Organization Chart, p. 232).

A review of the role performed by the above-mentioned branches facilitates comprehension of the role of the department in economic management. As the chapter progresses it will become increasingly apparent that the department's role transcends economic intelligence and includes a strong managerial and co-ordinating role which is emphasized throughout this book.

Chart 7:1 Department of Finance, General Organization (1974)

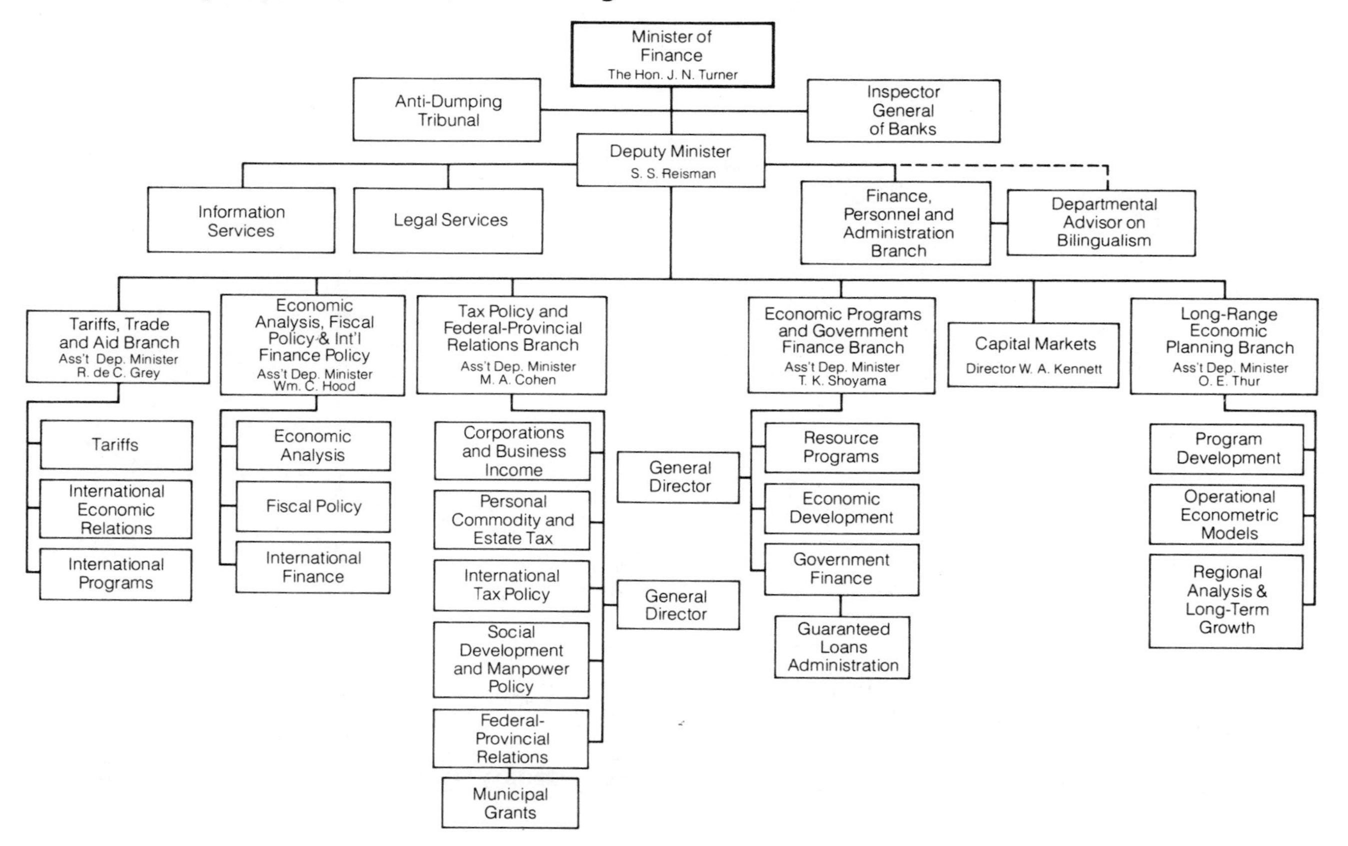

Chart 7:2 Department of Finance, General Organization (1976)

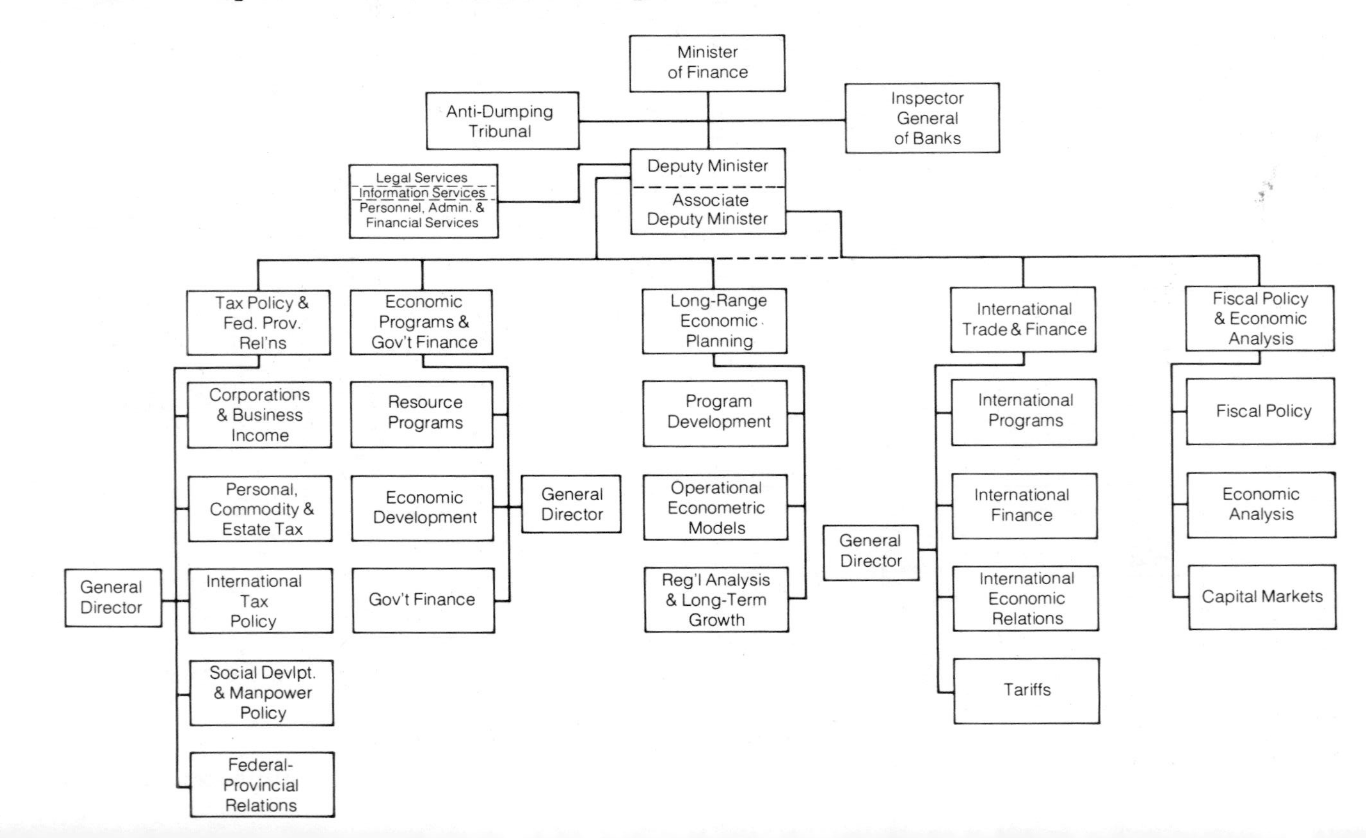

The Economic Analysis, Fiscal Policy and International Finance Branch

The Economic Analysis, Fiscal Policy and International Finance Branch provides the necessary technical inputs to advise the Minister of Finance on the broad area of economic-policy formulation. This Branch has experienced the most rapid expansion in recent years particularly with respect to technical personnel. Its staff includes prominent economists such as Dr. Wm. C. Hood and Dr. E. P. Neufeld. The Branch provides "the economic intelligence" base for fiscal and financial management at the federal level. The International Finance Division provides the necessary interface between the domestic and the international economy. Accordingly, it works closely with the Tariffs, Trade and Aid Branch. The Economic Analysis, Fiscal Policy and International Finance Branch carries out its work through three divisions: Economic Analysis; Fiscal Policy; and International Finance. Four sections of the Economic Analysis Division are concerned with general economic conditions, regional and sectoral analysis, economic forecasting, econometric research, and development and data services. The Economic Analysis Division is the central economic intelligence service in the Department. It provides continuing assessment of the general economic situation and is responsible for the economic forecasts used in preparing budgets and in the development of overall fiscal, financial, and economic policy. Given the pool of economic intelligence at its disposal it evaluates specific proposals and events often related to particular sectors or regions of the economy.

The Fiscal Policy Division has three units concerned with short-term stabilization: a monetary analysis unit; a short-term stabilization unit; and a simulation and model-building unit. The Short-term Stabilization Unit analyses and assesses the use of revenue and expenditure programs for short-term stabilization purposes. The Monetary Analysis Unit reviews monetary developments in the economy and analyses the monetary implications of fiscal changes. The Simulation and Model-Building Unit conducts the underlying econometric research work in model-building and carries out simulation analysis as an initial step in identifying and analysing the various policy measures.

The Fiscal Analysis and Forecasting Division has responsibility for forecasting and analysing the revenues and expenditures and accordingly the financial requirements of the Government of Canada. This division has close relationships with parallel divisions in the Federal-Provincial Relations Branch in that it monitors and analyses the fiscal position and fiscal developments of the provinces. It is responsible for the development of fiscal data necessary for meetings of ministers of Finance and provincial Treasurers.[73]

The Division is concerned with macro-economic analysis as compared to the micro concerns of the Tax Policy Branch. It interfaces with a number of important agencies. The Division works closely with the Planning and Program Branches of the Treasury Board in ascertaining the effects of direct employment by the government on the economy. It receives data from the Department of Supply and Services which is the keeper of the government accounts. The Department of National Revenue deals with the actual collection of taxes. The Division works closely with their provincial peers in developing an optimal fiscal strategy for the whole country.

The division performs an important role in the development of overall budget policy. In conjunction with the Treasury Board it has an early input into cabinet discussions particularly with matters relating to the state of the economy. The division receives broad guidelines from the Cabinet, i.e., the rationale for shifting the economy from the forecast path on the basis of which it attempts to develop an effective framework for policy.[74] Political discussion would be concerned with what strategy should be used with respect to sales and income taxes which are major allocative decisions. Such discussions would be initiated with papers from the PMO. This would be followed by proposals from the Minister of Finance assessing the total level of government outlays. The foregoing stages are followed by the Program Review which is subsequently followed by the Estimates Review.[75]

Fiscal-policy formulation involves complex political and economic considerations and accordingly it illustrates several difficulties encountered in economic management. There are several problems associated with *expectations* and *lags* which militate against effective forecasts.[76]

The Fiscal Analysis and Forecasting Division includes a public-sector forecasting unit which is further subdivided into three groups: a revenue and expenditure forecasting section, an intergovernmental and regional analysis section, and an econometrics section.[77]

The International Finance Division advises on foreign exchange policy, deals with matters relating to international monetary affairs, and administers Canada's relations with the International Monetary Fund, the Group of Ten, and the Committee of Twenty of the International Monetary Fund. It is particularly concerned with the Canadian balance of payments and with financial arrangements between Canada and the United States.

With the development of major trading blocs around the world and given the difficult international monetary situation, the Division follows these developments closely. It participates in the work of the Organization for Economic Co-operation and Development (OECD) and related agencies concerned with regional and international economic performance.[78]

The complexities of modern economic analysis and management are reflected in the evolution of these broad-ranged machineries in the international sphere. The Minister of Finance has been performing a major role in his attempt to establish more effective multilateral agencies in order to reduce volatility in international economic relations. By way of illustration there has been a major controversy in Ottawa recently as to whether or not the inflationary spiral can be controlled domestically in Canada in contrast to approaches requiring primarily international solutions. If the latter approach is adopted then measures must be taken to improve international organizations.

The Tax Policy and Federal-Provincial Relations Branch

The Tax Policy and Federal-Provincial Relations Branch has responsibility for formulating changes in tax policy, for example, the White Paper proposals for Tax Reform. Since the White Paper proposals constituted the most significant reform in recent years the degree of public participation which occurred in the discussions of the proposals illustrates the work of the Tax Policy Branch. It should be noted that most of the officials in the Tax Policy side of the recently reorganized Branch are lawyers and accountants and as such the Branch operates in the micro areas of tax policy; ascertaining how various tax proposals affect individuals and groups in the society as compared to the economics orientation of the Economic Analysis, Fiscal Policy and International Finance Branch. The Branch is expected to be responsive to public reactions to tax policy since the formulation of tax policy necessitates adherence to principles of equity and redistribution. The Department of National Revenue has responsibility for the collection of taxes which is an administrative function. It should be noted also that in earlier organization charts for the Department there was a Senior Tax Advisor's Office.[79] The Tax Advisor's Office was reorganized into what until recently were two divisions of the Tax Policy Branch, namely: a Corporations and Business Incomes Division; and a Personal and Commodity Tax Division. To achieve its objectives these divisions perform a number of roles: initiate, analyse, and evaluate proposals for tax changes and tax reform; hear and study representations concerning taxes from taxpayers, members of parliament, associations, and other departments; develop tax proposals in detail and assist in the preparation of resolutions prior to announcing them and in the drafting of legislation to put them into effect; deal with international tax treaties, the taxation of international organizations and their employees, and tax problems arising from the movement of individuals and goods across international borders; and assist on work in federal-provincial tax problems, review tax developments in other countries, assist with regulations, handle correspondence, and provide information related to taxation as required.[80] The foregoing illustrates that there are several quasi-administrative activities involved in tax policy.

The foregoing also demonstrates that a high degree of legal and administrative considerations go into fiscal policy as an aspect of economic management. Thus, although major technical inputs and research on fiscal policy perform an important role in the development of tax policy, there are a significant number of political considerations which go into the process. The Branch therefore becomes a focal point for responses from individuals and groups affected by tax changes. It is important to note that tax policy must be translated into legislative terms and this process frequently imposes pragmatic considerations on the policy formulated. Accordingly, the Tax Policy Branch interfaces with the Department of Justice in translating the economics-oriented aspects of fiscal policy into legislative terms.

Although its significance should not be exaggerated since such changes are usually responsive to personnel moves, the Tax Policy Branch was reorganized in 1974 to include federal-provincial relations which was a special branch prior to the change.[81] Given the federal system of government in Canada a significant amount of interface takes place between the federal government and the provinces. What used to be called the Federal-Provincial Relations Branch could have been regarded as the fiscal division since it dealt with tax-sharing, shared cost, and equalization programs.[82] Another aspect of its work dealt with financing in actual dollars and cents, in the realm of fiscal relations.

A 1974 departmental reorganization integrated the closely related work on taxation and federal-provincial fiscal relations within one branch. This reorganization was intended to provide increased concentration by senior management on resource and economic-management programs the effects of which appeared in the November 1974 budget.[83] The Branch now includes the Federal-Provincial Relations Division which works closely with two other divisions, Municipal Grants, and Social Development and Manpower Policy.

The Federal-Provincial Relations Division undertakes technical analysis and provides advice on the development of fiscal federalism in Canada. Areas include arrangements with the provinces regarding the joint occupancy of tax fields, conditional and unconditional fiscal transfers to the provinces and to municipalities, shared-cost programs, and opting-out provisions, and mechanisms for intergovernmental co-operation in fiscal and economic matters.

The Social Development and Manpower Policy Division conducts and co-ordinates major studies of the short- and long-term economic and financial effects of policies and programs in various areas of specialization, and assesses their policy initiatives. The work of this division impinges on the development and utilization of manpower policies (partly a provincial responsibility), the broad field of social policy, demographic change, and the social and economic environment in urban centres and in rural communities. Through this division the Department of Finance is involved in the realm of social policy.[84] In recent decades Canada has experienced a significant structural shift from a rural economy to a strongly urban one. Accordingly, the Department of Finance must interface with the Ministry of State for Urban Affairs, the Department of Agriculture, and the Department of Health and Welfare.[85] By way of illustration, it should be noted that selective aspects of the social policy review at the time of writing were being conducted in the Long-Range Economic Planning Branch but this work will most likely be transferred to the Social Development and Manpower Policy Division since it will involve significant contributions by this Division eventually.[86] The Division has a general responsibility for studying and advising on the implications of emerging social problems and alternative responses to them, typified by such issues as the problem of youth and the native Canadian people. If several of the problems associated with inflation are considered to disproportionately affect such groups then tax policy should incorporate sociological dimensions directed at groups seriously affected in this way.

The Economic Programs and Government Finance Branch

The Economic Programs and Government Finance Branch emerged as a separate group in 1974. Prior to this reorganization its role could be more clearly understood in relation to the earlier Federal-Provincial Relations and Economic Programs Branch which was reorganized in 1974. The 1974 reorganization placed four divisions under an assistant deputy minister. These were: the Resource Programs, Economic Development, Government Finance, and Guaranteed Loans Administration.[87] The reorganization seemed to emphasize an investment and developmental orientation which may be viewed as a distinct aspect of economic management. It is worth emphasizing that since 1969 an economic-development or an economic-expansion orientation has been emerging in federal economic policies.[88] Many of these dimensions of the department's activities were discussed above under Tax Policy and Federal-Provincial Relations and Economic Programs.

Since 1969 the Department of Finance has been developing a more aggressive approach to investment decisions through the establishment of the Canadian Development Corporation, through the then pending amendment to the Industrial Development Bank Act and through its orientation toward influencing financial institutions presented in the 1974 budget.[89] The foregoing measures were illustrative of these trends. The Department of Finance has been developing its own initiatives as distinct from the Bank of Canada. Following a 1974 reorganization the Guaranteed Loans Administration Division was placed under a Government Finance Division (under M. B. Foster*).

*John Young was appointed ADM responsible for this branch in 1975. However, he left the department in 1976.

The Government Finance Division advises on the allocation and the use of non-budgetary funds. A major concern is the financing of Crown corporations, including lending agencies. Capital expenditure programs and the financial requirements of Crown corporations and other government investments are reviewed from the perspective of terms, conditions, timing, amount, and the need to guarantee such loans. The investment of the Canada Pension Plan funds and advances to the Unemployment Insurance Commission are also major concerns of the Branch.

A policy section of the Government Finance Division handles recommendations by the Department of Regional Economic Expansion for the extension of government guarantees of bank loans to businesses in designated areas. Responsibility for the administration of the government's guaranteed lending programs for students, farmers, fishermen, and small businesses lie with the Government Finance Division. The Economic Programs and Government Finance Branch depicts a stronger economic development role on the part of the federal government and points to a somewhat different approach to federal-provincial relations. The Branch, as reorganized in 1974, had four major divisions: resource programs, economic development, government finance, and guaranteed loans.

The Economic Development Division is concerned with secondary industry, general industrial developments, consumer and corporate affairs, transportation, communications and energy, science policy and research, regional and area developments, and tourism. As such the division interfaces with related departments such as Industry, Trade and Commerce, Consumer and Corporate Affairs, and Regional Economic Expansion and with corresponding divisions in the provinces. The economic and financial implications of new or changing programs are examined to insure that they conform to overall government economic policy. The division interfaces with the Department of Industry, Trade and Commerce given its concern with general policy problems of the future such as industrial innovation, effective rates of tariff protection, and the role of the service sector in the economy. The division interfaces with the Department of Consumer and Corporate Affairs with respect to policies concerning patents and copyrights.

The Economic Development Division conducts studies so that it can brief the Minister of Finance with respect to the spending programs of the government.[90] Nuclear energy and hydro-electric power, as they affect economic policies, are reviewed in terms of their contribution to economic development. Since the department is concerned with broad economic-development policies it reviews different and frequently alternative approaches to energy policies for nuclear, as compared with hydro-electric, power of the various provinces, albeit through the department of Energy, Mines and Resources and through autonomous Crown corporations. In this respect the Department of Finance is concerned with the economic expansion of the country. In reviewing a policy proposal for new energy development from a province, the division would review the power needs of the province, the resource needs of related provinces, the national needs, including requirements for capital, balance-of-payments, and manpower needs, and the use of financial resources in general. In order to arrive at reasonable decisions the Economic Development Division participates in many interdepartmental committees including those on topics such as forestry and steel development. The Economic Development Division together with the Government Finance, Loans, Investment and Guarantees Division is involved in the development planning process since it assesses alternative ways of promoting economic development.[91] Accordingly these divisions interface with appropriate divisions in the Ministry of State for Science and Technology, the Ministry of Transport, and the departments of Regional Economic Expansion, Communications, Agriculture, and Energy, Mines and Resources.

The Resource Program Division is concerned with the encouragement and the development of natural resources policies and programs which accord with the government's overall economic, financial, environmental, and social policies. The Division interfaces with departments such as Energy, Mines and Resources. Much of the Division's work arises out of proposals made by the resource departments and agencies. The officers in this division carry out their work through participation in interdepartmental committees and working groups, which are given responsibility for the development of various facets of federal resource policy.[92] The Division considers both narrow and broad aspects of policy, encompassing resources, agricultural, and environmental dimensions including fisheries and forestry. In these respects as well as in others, the role of the Department of Finance is to reject or amend the proposals coming from various departments even after they get to Cabinet. Once the policy is approved it is reviewed and controlled by the appropriate divisions in the Treasury Board. By way of illustration, the division was intricately involved in the discussions on the MacKenzie Valley Pipeline. It is worth pointing out that resources policy usually spills over into External Affairs and the division would receive copies of telecommunications from External Affairs in its attempt to assess how existing developments or problems in the international environment may affect resource policy. Similarly proposals from the Department of Agriculture would come to the Department of Finance. The department is to a large degree concerned with whether or not these proposals coming from the various departments will impose severe financial burdens on the government. It is in this respect that the Department of Finance is considered to be primarily negative in its orientation, given the fact that there are more programs than the government can afford.

The Tariffs, Trade and Aid Branch

The Tariffs, Trade and Aid Branch encompasses the following divisions: Tariffs, International Relations, and International Programs. The Tariffs Division receives, investigates, and reports on representation and proposals regarding Canadian customs, tariff, and related matters. References to the Tariff Board are prepared in the Division which reviews the Board's reports and the representations on these reports. The International Economic Relations Division participates in the development of international trade and economic policies other than those associated with Canada's international programs. It helps negotiate bilateral and multilateral agreements with other countries engaged in trade and commercial policy and works with such international organizations as GATT, OECD, etc.[93] The division also evaluates short- and long-term trends in international trade and assesses the impact on Canada of likely changes in the world-trading environment.

The work of the Branch was well illustrated in the 1973 budget which introduced a wide range of reductions in tariffs on agricultural products.[94] The work was carried out through an interdepartmental liaison group including the departments of Industry, Trade and Commerce and Agriculture. A list of potential items was drawn up after the idea was initiated with the Deputy Minister of Finance and the Assistant Deputy Minister in charge of the Branch. In the early stages of policy development the proposals were discussed with the relevant departments. However, when the proposals reached an advanced stage they were discussed for example with the Minister of Agriculture but not with officials below. It should be noted that Rod Grey, the ADM with responsibility for this Branch, had a strong role in Canada–U.S. trade negotiations particularly in the Kennedy Round and in the Canada Auto Pact. However, the point being made here is that the 1973 tariff reduction was most illustrative of the work of the Tariff Division.

The International Programs Division carries out responsibilities with international organizations and has involvement with developing countries mainly through provision of aid and long-term export credits. It engages in program analysis of the United Nations and Commonwealth Organizations, the World Bank, International Development Association, the Asian Development Bank, and the Caribbean Development Bank.

The Long-Range Economic Planning Branch

This branch was created in 1973 and is responsible for the co-ordination, planning, and development of medium-term and long-term economic policies and measures. It should be stressed that the absence of a long-range planning branch in the federal government was a major concern of the Senate Committee on National Finance. It should also be noted that when the Economic Council of Canada was created in 1963 it was to be concerned primarily with questions of long-term growth and it made a number of recommendations to this end in its *Third Annual Review*.[95] In accordance with the foregoing the Long-Range Economic Planning Branch analyses and evaluates various policies which have a significant impact on the structure of the economy. A principal activity is to direct the utilization, refinement, and development of techniques and sources of information relating to economic models (including those of population growth and its inter-relationships with industrial demand), analyses of outputs and inputs, the net impact of tax transfer programs, and inter-regional flows for funds, energy, goods, and population.[96] Shortly after its establishment the Branch was immediately involved with food and energy in an attempt to put more emphasis on supply-management policies. In some respects this new Branch may be considered as a modest attempt to up-date the work of the Gordon Commission on Canada's long-term economic prospects. Accordingly its work on the demographic and industrial structure and its input-output analyses are most illustrative of its long-term orientation. However, the Branch has already become engrossed in more immediate concerns; for example, in 1974 it was involved in the preparation of a position paper on the review on social security. The work of the Branch illustrates the complexity and difficulty of the various attempts to segregate long-range planning units. Earlier in this chapter reference was made to various attempts to create autonomous long-range planning units in departments of Finance and to the difficulties of integrating such units into the policy-formulation process. Elsewhere we have pointed to administrative difficulties in separating long-term policy from short-term policy.[97] These problems still plague effective governmental management. With the appointment of T. K. Shoyama as Deputy Minister of Finance, the ADMs for Long-Range Economic Planning, Economic Programs and Government Finance, and Tax Policy and Federal-Provincial Relations branches have since reported to the deputy minister directly. With the appointment of William C. Hood as Associate Deputy Minister, the ADM's for International Trade and Finance, and Fiscal Policy and Economic Analysis now report to the associate deputy minister—as shown in the organization chart for 1976 (Chart 7:2). These changes reflect the specialized expertise and experience of the two officials.[98]

The Capital Markets Branch (Division)

The Capital Markets Branch is concerned with the management of the public debt and the ways in which the government's cash requirements can be met through borrowing. It advises on policy related to capital markets, chartered banks, and other financial institutions. The division provides advice on general policies related to the structure and management of the public debt as well as the size, nature, terms, and conditions of government treasury bill, marketable bond, and Canada Savings Bond issues. This new branch is concerned with commercial policies in the realm of capital markets, financial institutions, and their regulation. Through its work general guidelines are made available to all financial institutions.

In 1973 the Department's organization chart showed a Financial Operations Division with two subsidiary divisions. As depicted then the Financial Operations Division conducted its work through officers in two subsidiary divisions: the Capital Markets Division and the Government Finance, Loans, Investments and Guarantees Division. The first division continually assesses conditions, trends, and special developments in the capital markets, particularly the bond markets, short-term money market, mortgage market, and equity markets in Canada and abroad. The Government Finance Division advises on the allocation and use of non-budgetary funds by evaluation of the financing of government programs and Crown corporations including lending agencies. Capital expenditure programs and financing requirements of Crown corporations are reviewed in the light of terms, conditions, timing, amount, and guarantee. It advises on the financial provisions of new Acts and is responsible for legislation in respect of Crown corporations, including the CNR Financing and Guarantee Act.

The 1974 organization chart provided for the establishment of a separate Capital Markets Branch under W. A. Kennett. Since the Economic Council of Canada was also conducting studies in these areas which resulted in major recommendations the Branch can be expected to become an important instrument in the future management of the economy. However, as Chart 7:2 demonstrates it was subsequently placed under the Fiscal Policy and Economic Analysis Branch. The 1977 revision of the Bank Act was also pending at the time of writing.[99]

Other Responsibilities of the Minister of Finance

The Department of Finance has certain related responsibilities with a number of autonomous agencies including: the Inspector General of Banks; the Anti-Dumping Tribunal; the Auditor General; the Tariff Board; the Canada Deposit Insurance Corporation; the Industrial Development Bank prior to its reorganization as the Federal Business Development Bank; and the Department of Insurance.

The Inspector General of Banks is required by Parliament to conduct examinations and inquiries into the affairs and business of chartered banks and the bank incorporated under the Quebec Savings Bank Act to satisfy himself that the provisions of the respective acts are being observed and that the banks are in a sound financial position. He reports to Parliament through the Minister of Finance;

The Anti-Dumping Tribunal is a court which determines whether the dumping of goods causes material injury to Canadian industry, or retards the establishment of Canadian production;

The Auditor General audits the accounts of the Government of Canada and of certain international and other agencies, and reports annually to the House of Commons the results of his examination;

The Tariff Board makes inquiries into and reports upon any matter in relation to goods that, if brought into Canada, are subject to or exempt from customs duties or excise taxes. Under the Customs, Tariff and Excise Tax Acts the Board acts as a court to hear appeals on rulings in these areas;

The Canada Deposit Insurance Corporation provides insurance against loss of deposits, up to $20,000 for each separate account, to banks, trust companies, or mortgage loan companies that are members of the Corporation;

The Industrial Development Bank until 1974 assisted in the development of industrial enterprises appearing to have good prospects of successful operation and needing additional term financing. These firms because of their relatively small size, lack of established earnings record, geographical location, or other reasons, may not be able to obtain necessary funds from other sources on reasonable terms and conditions; and

The Department of Insurance administers the statutes of Canada applicable to insurance, trust loan, and investment companies incorporated by or pursuant to an Act of the Parliament of Canada. Its activities extend to the following: British and foreign insurance companies operating in Canada; money-lenders, and small loan companies incorporated by or pursuant to an Act of the Parliament of Canada; co-operative credit societies to which certificates have been granted under the Co-operatives Credit Associations Act; pension plans with the legislative authority of the Parliament of Canada; and life insurance policies under the Civil Service Insurance Act.

THE DEPARTMENT, THE BANK OF CANADA, AND MONETARY POLICY

The relationships between the department and the Bank of Canada deserve special attention in economic management. In addition their roles are being critically examined as this book goes to press.

Some economists would argue that monetary policy is so important that it should be managed by a separate agency. Others would argue that the level of money supply can be set at a fixed position and subsequently de-emphasized as a stabilization tool. In effect, it would reduce the role of an agency directly concerned with the implementation of monetary policy.

Monetary policy must be closely synchronized with fiscal policy and with economic policy in general. For reasons explained in Chapter 6 the Bank of Canada was given autonomy so that it would be free from day-to-day political interference. Following the Coyne Affair, the Bank of Canada was brought under closer political scrutiny but the principle of autonomy was not removed. The Bank is also closely associated with a subordinate agency, the Industrial Development Bank, described briefly in the preceding section.

The structure of the Bank of Canada raises an important aspect of public administration given the fact that monetary policy conducted primarily through the banking system can, in some respects, be implemented with greater ease particularly in comparison with fiscal policy. There may be definite advantages therefore in retaining it as a Crown corporation. Departments are subject to greater parliamentary scrutiny and attempts to get legislative approval would slow down the process of policy changes. Accordingly, debates over the management of economic policy must constantly wrestle with the structure and role of the central bank.

The Bank of Canada is responsible for monetary policy which it manages primarily through the cash reserves held by the chartered banks. Under the Bank Act the chartered banks are required to maintain minimum cash reserves in the form of deposit with, or notes of, the Bank of Canada against their Candian-dollar deposit liabilities. The Bank acts as the fiscal agent for the government without charge carrying out a number of related activities such as operating the government's deposit account, handles debt-management and foreign exchange transactions for the government, and acts as an adviser. It has the sole right to issue notes intended for circulation in Canada.

Monetary policy is handled by a relatively autonomous agency, hence the Bank of Canada is under the supervision of a board of directors, composed of the governor, deputy governor, and twelve directors. The latter are appointed for terms of three years by the

Minister of Finance with the approval of the Governor-in-Council. The Deputy Minister of Finance is a member of the Board but he does not have the right to vote. The governor and the deputy governor are appointed for terms of seven years by the directors with the approval of the Governor-in-Council.[100] There are at least four reasons presented for the relatively autonomous position of the Bank. First, dealings with the financial market should not be subjected to day-to-day political considerations. Second, the Bank was to be part of a broad financial system, both national and international, and should be respected as a market-oriented institution. Third, there was a prevailing view that banks dealing with other central banks are best handled independently. Fourth, as an independent agency the Bank could best remind the government of the importance of price stability. In this respect even governments should not be trusted with the expansion of the money supply.

The Bank is controlled by a Board of Governors which operationally functions as an Executive Committee. The Bank Act provides for the Governor of the Bank to be the Chief Executive Officer of the Committee. Appointments to the Board of Governors have been regional with one from each province and two from Ontario and Quebec.

The Bank of Canada operated through nine departments which in the mid-1970s included: Research, Securities, Banking and Financial Analysis, International, the Secretary's, Personnel Administration, Administrative Operations, the Chief Accountant's, and Audit.

The foregoing considerations have influenced the structure of the Bank of Canada and its relationship to political authority and decision-making. We can now direct our attention to the Bank's role in the management of economic policy in Canada. A number of points should be emphasized in this regard.

First, the Bank of Canada performed an influential but largely complementary role to the Department of Finance during the period between the early 1960s and 1970s.[101] As indicated elsewhere, the Bank improved its technical competence as well as its political relationship to the government under the leadership of Louis Rasminsky. Shortly before his retirement as Governor, Mr. Rasminsky confirmed the institution's commitment to the goals of economic policy before the Senate Committee investigating problems of Growth, Employment and Price Stability. The Bank of Canada had committed itself earlier to these goals in its testimony to the Royal Commission on Banking and Finance which reported in 1964.[102]

Second, the Bank has denied on several occasions the accusation that it had "a single-minded dedication to the goal of price stability and little concern with the great human misfortune of unemployment". Mr. Rasminsky remarked in 1971: "This is not true. We are greatly concerned. . . . If there is in fact any difference in this respect between us and some others, it is a difference of time perspective. We take the view that this country is going to be here for some time, and that our chances of achieving sustained growth and a sustained increase in employment will be considerably greater if we can manage to achieve a reasonable degree of stability in the value of money at the same time."[103] The Bank of Canada, nevertheless, has an ideological orientation and a natural organizational bias in favour of emphasizing the preservation of price stability.

Third, the Bank is primarily concerned with monetary policy which exerts its influence on the total level of spending by the way it can affect credit conditions, that is, the cost and availability of money. Monetary policy is thus less selective than fiscal policy in that the latter can be more readily directed at specific sectors or particular objectives. This fact imposes limitations on the use of monetary policy which consequently must be synchronized with other instruments.

Fourth, monetary policy is subject to other constraints such as the level of interest rates in the United States and to the difficulties in interpreting *lags* which may undermine the effectiveness of the instruments used. The Bank must calculate the proper time to intervene and must attempt also to assess the duration of the intervention adopted.[104] Here again we are confronted with the limitations of technical knowledge and major emphasis must be placed on managerial judgments.

Finally, fiscal policy must be integrated with monetary and debt-management policies. This is especially necessary due to the fact that the government's fiscal position determines how much borrowing it has to do and how much new public debt it has to issue from time to time. The management of the public debt therefore has an important influence on the liquidity of the banking system. As expressed by Mr. Rasminsky:

The approach we follow in the Bank of Canada, is that demand management should be responsive to the trend of activity and the trend of inflation in the country and that fiscal and monetary policy should normally try to steer the economy towards sustained high levels of production and employment, but that, if at some stage the economy shows or threatens to show signs of appreciable inflation, *financial policy* should try to moderate the rate of growth of demand for a time to cool off the economy in order to give prices and costs a chance to stabilize. The cooling off should be gradual.[105]

There has been considerable debate over the desirability or the adequacy of such intervention and there was for a while in the Economic Council of Canada the view that interventions of the type mentioned by the former Governor of the Bank were themselves destabilizing. It should be emphasized that the approach outlined by the former Governor of the Bank of Canada was followed between 1968 and 1972. Periodically, the government has shifted its emphasis from the unemployment goal to the price-level goal.[106] Both the Department of Finance and the Bank of Canada have emphasized the importance of demand-management policies notwithstanding the fact they have periodically given support to supply-management policies. However we can arrive at a pragmatic conclusion that these agencies exist to take precisely such actions. It must be recognized also that the absence of effective competition in the economy increases the necessity for these interventions in that the growth of powerful organizations in the economy militates against perfect competition.[107] We will deal with these aspects later when we examine the role of the Department of Consumer and Corporate Affairs.

The Bank of Canada, through its management of monetary policy and the Department of Finance through its manipulation of fiscal policy, usually reflected in the budget, have always been ready targets for criticism. They are usually charged with mismanaging the economy particularly in regard to the timing of their interventions in the economy. These criticisms, moreover, are deeply rooted in conflicting attitudes about the scope and effectiveness of governmental intervention.

The position of both the Department of Finance and the Bank of Canada was well expressed by the Governor of the Bank of Canada when he concluded in 1969:

Unless we are prepared to accept widespread direct government intervention there is really no choice, but to place major reliance on monetary and fiscal policies if we seriously wish to control inflation and avoid major damage to the economy. Naturally, it would be better if inflation could be dealt with by increasing the supply of goods and services rather than by restricting demand . . . supply policies designed to increase the efficiency and mobility of our resources (such, for example, as retraining and the development of labour skills) are indeed of fundamental importance to the long-run performance of the economy, and much emphasis has properly been placed on them by governments. But such policies cannot, unfortunately, be expected to make an important contribution to the present urgent problem of controlling inflation.[108]

In 1971 The Bank of Canada was even more direct in its confrontation.

In respect of economic policy, the Standing Committee on National Finance in its report on "Growth Employment and Price Stability" emphasized that because there are long lags between policy action and the response of the economy policy cannot be set simply in response to the immediate situation. . . .

The task of monetary policy is to contribute as much as it can to the forward-looking management of aggregate demand in the economy. It may be *that demand* management *will be found to need assistance from supplementary policies, such as price-incomes policies;* but whether or not this proves to be the case, good demand management will always be a necessary condition for the achievement of our economic objectives.[109]

The Economic Council of Canada especially between 1966 and 1969 had argued that the short-run policies adopted by the Government of Canada were inherently destabilizing. Consequently, the Council advocated a policy position in which long-term growth could occur with a steady rate of, or low rate of, both inflation and unemployment.[110] Such an environment would require a constant and predictable rate of growth in the money supply and a fiscal policy which does not impose a fiscal drag on the economy and which would prevent full-employment levels from being reached. Thus, there are technical problems in achieving a well-co-ordinated fiscal and monetary policy stance.[111]

The fourth Governor of the Bank of Canada, Gerald Bouey, stated in 1973 that there were some errors in the policy approach adopted by the government between 1969 and 1972 which supported the arguments made by the Economic Council of Canada.[112] The Governor attributed these errors to changes in political demands. In his words:

Looking back on the experience of Canada and other countries over a longer period, it is difficult to avoid the impression that from time to time there have been more substantial and persisting departures from reasonably steady monetary growth than would appear in retrospect to have been desirable. Since the lags associated with monetary policy are rather long, the full effects of such departures do not become apparent until well after the event. This helps to explain how they come about. It is not very difficult to understand, for example, that so long as an economy is operating much below satisfactory levels there is a natural tendency to err on the high side so far as rates of monetary growth are concerned. Moreover, in a world where economic forecasting is necessarily imperfect, the temptation is strong in such circumstances to respond to troublesome short-run developments by adding somewhat further to the rate of monetary expansion. I believe that the high rates of monetary expansion around the world during the two years leading up to the surge in economic activity in the latter part of 1972 and early 1973 illustrate this basic problem.

In the light of these considerations, I have a certain amount of sympathy with the case that is often made for more stable monetary growth over time, even though I am aware that there are various difficulties involved in such an approach. The Bank of Canada certainly has no intention of basing its operations on any mechanistic formula, but in framing its judgments about the appropriate policy to be followed, it has been giving considerable weight to underlying rates of monetary growth.[113]

The Governor of the Bank of Canada subsequently adopted policies which were endorsed by the Minister of Finance to restrict the money supply. The policy was announced in stages. The objective is to gradually restrict the growth of the money supply from fifteen to ten per cent.[114] The strategy has been to do so without throwing the economy into a deflationary position. Attempts have been made also to synchronize various policy instruments as part of the government's new initiatives to combat inflation and to manage the economy.

TOWARD A NEW APPROACH TO MANAGING THE ECONOMY

The foregoing discussion has again demonstrated that economic management is a complex human activity. This recognition has been reflected in the type of budget speeches presented to Parliament in recent years by the ministers of Finance in which the target goal has shifted from single directed attacks on inflation, unemployment, recession, and energy to a combined assault on all of these problems simultaneously. Since October 1975, the big levers of monetary and fiscal policy have been supplemented by wage and price controls. The manner in which the income policy was adopted demonstrated the reluctance of the Government of Canada to adopt such policies.

a combined assault

Various sectors of Canadian society have demanded the reduction of governmental expenditures and the Trudeau government has responded with a few initiatives which, in turn, have been criticized for being inadequate. The problem clearly stems from the fact that there are both political and administrative difficulties which inhibit the sudden reduction in governmental expenditures. These difficulties were explained by the President of the Treasury Board between 1975 and 1976.[115] The 1976 budget which was introduced under wage and price control conditions was somewhat all-encompassing in its attack on inflation in that it enumerated four components of a comprehensive strategy: fiscal and monetary policy; government expenditure policy; structural policies; and prices and incomes policies.

The structure within which these policies are formulated was outlined earlier when we discussed the budgetary system. Within this system the Cabinet Committee on Priorities and Planning which is really the Executive Committee of Cabinet makes the significant decisions concerning the expenditure targets and "the size of the government's reserves". At the time of writing, a gradual change was being adopted in the system for making revenue and expenditure decisions. While in the past, major emphasis was placed on determining the size of the *surplus* or the *deficit* in the economic budget, the recent demands for reductions in governmental expenditures have led to the adoption of an approach in which expenditure decisions are made in a relatively more separate way from revenue decisions.[116] The new approach attempts to develop a more long-term approach to expenditure planning. Greater emphasis is being placed on long-term investment strategies especially in the energy and transportation fields. In contrast to the long-term approach to formulating expenditure decisions, an attempt is being made to make more short-term decisions on the revenue side to help stabilize the economy.

The new approach also makes provision for a limited number of short-term expenditure decisions in order to redress specific problems as was done in the adoption of the direct employment measures and the housing assistance measures in the June 1975 budget.[117] The rationale in adopting those expenditure measures was that they could be turned off at relatively short notice depending on how the economy is characterized in the future. The budget measures also reflected a new employment strategy which will be examined in Chapter 9.

These recent measures again demonstrate that the Department of Finance must be understood in the context of a central agency which must operate closely with the PCO and the Treasury Board. It also performs a staff-line relationship with the major economic policy-making departments. While specific decision-making responsibilities can be delegated to selected agencies there is a continuing, indeed growing, need to co-ordinate a multiplicity of conflicting objectives, instruments, and agencies in the economic-management process. In the 1977 budget, for example, the Minister of Finance endorsed "the stragey of gradualism" recommended by the Governor of the Bank of Canada and which was considered to be "the new monetary policy" being followed since 1975. In addition, the reluctance of the Minister of Finance to further increase government expenditures on job creation revealed the commitment of the federal government to curtail public expenditures and to facilitate expansion within the private sector of the economy.

NOTES

1. On the concept of economic management see A. Cairncross, ed., *The Managed Economy* (Oxford, 1970) and *Essays in Economic Management* (London, 1971); M. D. Reagan, *The Managed Economy* (London, 1963). The latter emphasized the problem of executive co-ordination. See also Lawrence Pierce, *The Politics of Fiscal Policy Formation* (Pacific Palisades, Ca., 1971); Robert Eyestone, *Political Economy: Politics and Policy Analysis* (Chicago, 1972); and the Standing Senate Committee on National Finance, *Growth, Employment and Price Stability* (Ottawa, 1972), pp. 77-87.

2. A. A. Sterns, *History of the Department of Finance.* Mimeo (Ottawa, 1965). This point was made most explicitly in the department's submission to the Special Senate Committee on Science Policy in 1969: "The department has no

general statutory definition of its duties, and wields little direct authority over anything except a few special programs which it carries out, such as grants to provinces and municipalities and some guaranteed loan programs", Standing Senate Committee on National Finance, *Growth, Employment and Price Stability,* pp. 77-87.

3. See, for example, J. A. Cross, *British Public Administration* (London, 1970), Chapter 4.

4. Interviews.

5. See Standing Senate Committee on National Finance, *Growth, Employment and Price Stability.*

6. Cairncross, ed., *The Managed Economy* and *Essays in Economic Management.*

7. See Chapter 6.

8. T. E. H. Reid, ed., *Economic Planning in a Democratic Society* (Toronto, 1963). Perhaps the most significant use of the concept of economic management has been presented in Standing Senate Committee on National Finance, *Growth, Employment and Price Stability.* See especially Chapter 9, "Management for Decision Making", pp. 77-87.

9. R. Heilbroner, ed., *Economic Means and Social Ends* (Englewood Cliffs, N.J., 1969).

10. See Cairncross, ed., *The Managed Economy* and *Essays in Economic Management,* and Eyestone, *Political Economy.* For an earlier treatment of economic management from the perspective of the executive branch see Reagan, *The Managed Economy.*

11. See J. F. Sleeman, *The Welfare State: Its Aims, Benefits and Costs* (London, 1973); H. L. Wilensky, *The Welfare State and Equality: Structural and Ideological Roots of Public Expenditure* (Berkeley, 1975). In Canada reference should be made to the *White Paper on Employment and Income with Special Reference to the Initial Period of Reconstruction* (Ottawa, 1946). See also S. F. Kalinski, ed., *Economic Policy Since the War* (Montreal, 1965), and A. Armitage, *Social Welfare in Canada* (Toronto, 1975).

12. Economic Council of Canada, *Conference on Stabilization Policies* (Ottawa, 1965). See also D. A. White, *Business Cycles in Canada* (Ottawa, 1967).

13. A. Okun, *The Battle Against Unemployment* (Washington, 1970).

14. The most recent position has been outlined in Hon. M. Lalonde, *Working Paper on Social Security in Canada* (Ottawa, 1973).

15. Department of Finance, "Economic Programs and Government Finance", in *This is Your Department of Finance* (Ottawa, 1974). See also Hon. D. S. Macdonald, "Pricing of Government Services". Budget Speech, May 25, 1976; Treasury Board of Canada, *How Your Tax Dollar is Spent, 1975-76* (Ottawa, 1975); and R. M. Bird, *Charging for Public Services: A New Look at an Old Idea* (Toronto, 1976).

16. The role of Crown corporations in Canadian governmental management was seriously being debated at the time of writing. The establishment of Petro-Canada marked a new development. See Hon. J. N. Turner, Budget Speech, June 23, 1975, *The National Finances, 1975-76*, pp. 234-49, especially p. 247.

17. The Hon. D. Macdonald, "Prices and Incomes Policies". Budget Speech, May 25, 1976, pp. 11-14. On the introduction of the program, see the following: House of Commons of Canada, Bill C-73, passed December 3, 1975; *Anti-Inflation Regulations: A Summary;* and *Explanations and Statement in House of Commons by Finance Minister D. S. Macdonald,* December 18, 1975.

18. R. M. Will, *The Budget as an Economic Document,* Studies of the Royal Commission on Taxation, no. 1. (Ottawa, 1964).

19. Ibid., and J. C. Strick, *Canadian Public Finance* (Toronto, 1973).

20. Economic Council of Canada, Conference on Stabilization Policies.

21. See *The Globe and Mail,* October 8, 1976. Report on Conference on Controls.

22. S. Brittan, *Steering the Economy: The Role of the Treasury* (London, 1970).

23. Standing Senate Committee on National Finance, *Growth, Employment and Price Stability*.

24. A. Breton, "Modelling the Behaviour of Exchequers", in L. J. Officer and L. B. Smith, eds., *Issues in Canadian Economics* (Toronto, 1974), pp. 107-14.

25. Standing Senate Committee on National Finance, *Growth, Employment and Price Stability,* pp. 77-87.

26. Peter Self, *Administrative Theories and Politics* (Toronto, 1973), Chapter 3.

27. Breton, "Modelling the Behaviour of Exchequers".

28. Ibid., p. 113.

29. Sterns, *History of the Department of Finance;* H. R. Balls, "Planning, Programming and Budgeting in Canada", *Public Administration*. vol. LVII (Autumn 1970), p. 296.

30. Department of Finance, *Who We Are . . . What We Do* (Ottawa, 1972). On the responsibilities of Finance *vis-à-vis* the Treasury Board, see the Financial Administration Act (RSC 1970, c. F-10).

31. See the Financial Administration Act.

32. Department of Finance, *Who We Are . . . What We Do,* p. 4. The responsibilities were also outlined in a brief to the Special Senate Committee on Science Policy, pp. 4644-45.

33. Maurice Archer, *Introductory Macroeconomics: A Canadian Analysis* (Toronto, 1973), chapters 8-14. See also J. A. Sawyer, *Macroeconomics: Theory and Policy in the Canadian Economy* (Toronto, 1975), chapters 4, 6, and 15.

34. Archer, *Introductory Macroeconomics*, chapters 4, 6, and 15; R. Shearer and D. E. Bond, *The Economics of the Canadian Financial System: Theory, Practice and Institutions* (Scarborough, 1972).

35. Sawyer, *Macroeconomics;* Y. L. Bach, *Making of Monetary and Fiscal Policies* (Washington, 1971); M. Friedman and W. W. Heller, *Monetary vs. Fiscal Policy: A Dialogue* (New York, 1969).

36. Hon. D. S. Macdonald, Minister of Finance, Budget Speech, May 25, 1976.

37. Ibid., p. 34.

38. M. Pitfield, "The Shape of Government in the 1980s: Techniques and Instruments for Policy Formation at the Federal Level", *Canadian Public Administration,* Vol. XIX, no. 1 (1976), p. 14. See in general pp. 8-14.

39. First Session, 28th Parl, 1968-69. The Senate of Canada, *Proceedings of the Special Committee on Science Policy*, Hon. M. Lamontagne, Chairman, no. 34 (March 5, 1969), pp. 3644-52, especially p. 3647. The phrase "internal opposition" was also used by Bryce in his statement to the House of Commons, *Committee on Finance, Trade and Economic Affairs* (April 24, 1969), p. 2138.

40. *Proceedings of the Special Committee on Science Policy*, p. 4647.

41. Ibid.

42. Ibid., p. 4628.

43. Ibid., p. 4630.

44. Ibid., p. 4628.

45. Ibid., p. 4632.

46. Ibid.

47. Ibid.

48. Ibid.

49. Ibid.

50. Ibid.

51. Ibid., p. 4635.

52. Ibid.

53. See S. S. Reisman, Deputy Minister of Finance, Senate of Canada, Standing Senate Committee on National Finance, *Growth, Employment and Price Stability*, no. 22 (June 29, 1971), p. 29.

54. Ibid., p. 42.

55. Interviews. See also Chapter 5.

56. Interviews. See also House of Commons, *Committee on Finance, Trade and Economic Affairs* (April 1969), pp. 2122-74.

57. Economic Council of Canada, *Thirteenth Annual Review* (Ottawa, 1976), p. 60.

58. *Proceedings of the Standing Senate Committee on National Finance*, no. 22 (June 29, 1971), Hon. E. J. Benson, Minister of Finance, p. 6.

59. Standing Senate Committee on National Finance, *Growth, Employment and Price Stability* pp. 77-87, especially pp. 86-87.

60. Interviews.

61. See J. Maxwell, *Policy Review and Outlook, 1975: Restructuring the Incentive*

System (Ottawa, 1975), Chapter 3; Treasury Board of Canada, *How Your Tax Dollar is Spent, 1974-75.*

62. Hon. J. N. Turner, Budget Speech, May 6, 1974. This budget introduced tax measures on petroleum and mining corporations. However, the measures were adjusted in the subsequent budget. See J. N. Turner, Budget Speech, November 18, 1974, in which the resource taxation proposals were moderated by increasing the special abatement for petroleum profits and restoring the 100 per cent write-off for exploration expenditures. The federal-provincial consultations were also very involved.

63. Hon. J. N. Turner, Budget Speech and Notices of Ways and Means Motions, June 23, 1975, in which the targets of policy were inflation, recession, and energy. On the control of government expenditure an attack encompassing five aspects was launched.

64. Ibid., and later speeches by Hon. D. S. Macdonald and J. Chrétien further explained the strategy adopted.

65. This approach is not unique to Canada, see "Budget Controllability and Planning", Chapter 7 in B. M. Blechman, E. M. Gramlich, *et al., Setting National Priorities: The 1976 Budget* (Washington, 1975). The Canadian approach was derived from confidential interviews. Below we refer to the budgetary process in terms of the public household. On this conceptualization see D. Bell, *The Cultural Contradictions of Capitalism* (New York, 1976), especially pp. 220-82.

66. Hon. J. N. Turner, Budget Speech, May 6, 1974. Note the revenue-raising measures adopted in the budget; petroleum and financial institutions were taxed. The political process was reflected in the subsequent reversal of the measures in the Budget Speech of November 18, 1974.

67. See, for example, Balls, "Planning, Programming and Budgeting in Canada".

68. There has been an evolving literature which links budgeting to the evaluation process. See, for example, C. Schultze, *The Politics and Economics of Public Spending* (Washington, 1968); Y. Dror, *Public Policy Making Re-examined* (San Francisco, 1968); C. O. Jones, *An Introduction to the Study of Public Policy* (Belmont, Ca., 1970); J. Anderson, *Public Policymaking* (New York, 1975); and Standing Senate Committee on National Finance, *Growth, Employment and Price Stability*, pp. 83-87.

69. See, for example, the budgets by Hon. J. N. Turner between 1974 and 1975 in Budget Speech and Notices of Ways and Means Motions, June 23, 1975.

70. Interviews.

71. See, for example, the Task Force on the Mackenzie Valley Pipeline. Most recently the Department of Finance established a Task force on "Tax Policy in Relation to Social Policy". See *The Financial Post,* November 6, 1976, "Your Tax Return is up for Grabs Again".

72. See Department of Finance, *Who We Are . . . What We Do.*

73. Ibid.

74. Ibid.

75. Ibid.

76. For early discussions of this issue, see Economic Council of Canada, *Conference on Stabilization Policies,* University of Western Ontario, London, August 30 to September 1, 1965 (Ottawa, 1966).

77. Department of Finance, *Who We Are . . . What We Do.*

78. Ibid.

79. Department of Finance. For comparison, see Chapter 6 in which organizational charts were shown for 1964 and 1974.

80. The importance and significance of the Tax Policy Branch is most clearly reflected in the publications of the Canadian Tax Foundation. It was intricately involved in the work of the Carter Commission on Tax Reform. See also Audrey Doerr, "The Role of White Papers in the Policy Process". Unpublished PhD thesis, Carleton University, Ottawa, 1975.

81. Interviews.

82. Given the federal character of the Canadian political system, the work done by this divison is most important (see Chapter 12). For analysis of such relationships see D. Smiley, *Canada in Question: Federalism in the Seventies* (Toronto, 1976). In subsequent sections of this chapter we make reference to revenue and expenditure decisions between 1974 and 1976. However, for earlier discussions of budget speeches and budget policy, refer to the following: S. K. Kalinski, *Canadian Economic Policy Since the War* (Montreal, 1965),

especially the contribution by H. S. Gordon; J. H. Crispo, ed., *Wages, Prices, Profits and Economic Policy* (Toronto, 1968), Note Hon. M. Sharp's statement about his budget measures, pp. 101-11; and W. I. Gillespie, "The Federal Budget as Plan, 1968-1972", *Canadian Tax Journal*, Vol. XXI (January/February 1973), pp. 64-84; and Strick, *Canadian Public Finance*, especially pp. 94-166.

83. See Hon. J. N. Turner, Budget Speech, November 18, 1974.

84. Interviews. However, the Department subsequently established a Task Force to look into tax policy in relation to social programs. See *The Financial Post*, November 6, 1976.

85. The Social Policy Review has presented a major challenge to policymakers in recent years. Here the Department of Finance has been involved in close working relationships with the Department of National Health and Welfare.

86. Interviews.

87. Department of Finance, *This is Your Department of Finance.*

88. This emphasis began with the appointment of Simon Reisman as Deputy Minister.

89. These aspects impinge on the role of Crown corporations in Economic Development. The establishment of the Federal Business Development Bank followed the Western Economic Opportunities Conference.

90. This aspect of governmental activity is frequently ignored in discussions of public planning and management. See *The National Finances, 1975-76* (Toronto, 1976), Chapter I.

91. Department of Finance, *This is Your Department of Finance.*

92. Interviews.

93. Interviews.

94. See Hon. J. N. Turner, Budget Speech, February 19, 1973, especially pp. 11-22.

95. See Economic Council of Canada, *Third Annual Review* (Ottawa, 1966).

96. Department of Finance, *Who We Are . . . What We Do*, p. 10. See also House of Commons Standing Committee on Finance, Trade and Economic Affairs, *Estimates, 1973-74, Department of Finance.* See also 29th Parl.,

Miscellaneous Estimates, no. 51, November 23, 1973, especially pp. 9-10.

97. R. W. Phidd, "The Economic Council of Canada: Its Establishment, Structure and Role in the Canadian Policy-Making System, 1963-1974", *Canadian Public Administration*, Vol. XVIII, no. 3 (Fall 1975).

98. The structure of the Department of Finance was reorganized again in late 1976. Consequently, reference should be made to the current structure.

99. See Hon. D. S. Macdonald, *White Paper on the Revision of Canadian Banking Legislation* (Ottawa, 1976). See also Economic Council of Canada, *Efficiency and Regulation: A Study of Deposit Institutions* (Ottawa, 1976).

100. See Bank of Canada Act.

101. See R. Shearer, *et al.*, *The Economics of the Canadian Financial System* (Scarborough, 1972).

102. Government of Canada, *Royal Commission on Banking and Finance* (Ottawa, 1964).

103. Standing Senate Committee on National Finance, *Growth, Employment and Price Stability*, no. 21 (June 17, 1971), L. Rasminsky, Governor of the Bank of Canada, p. 5.

104. Ibid.

105. Ibid., p. 9.

106. Ibid.

107. Ibid., p. 27. See, for example, Economic Council of Canada, *Interim Report on Competition Policy* (Ottawa, 1969), and *Efficiency and Regulation*.

108. *Annual Report of the Governor of the Bank of Canada to the Minister of Finance for the Year, 1969* (Ottawa, 1970).

109. *Annual Report of the Governor of the Bank of Canada to the Minister of Finance for the Year, 1971* (Ottawa, 1971), pp. 10-11.

110. Economic Council of Canada, *Sixth Annual Review* (Ottawa, 1969).

111. Bach, *Making of Monetary and Fiscal Policies*.

112. Bank of Canada, *Annual Report, 1973* (Ottawa, 1974).

113. Ibid., p. 7.

114. Bank of Canada, *Annual Report, 1974* (Ottawa, 1975). For a critical analysis of Canadian monetary policy see T. J. Courchene, *Money, Inflation and the Bank of Canada: An Analysis of Canadian Monetary Policy from 1970 to Early 1975* (Montreal, 1976), especially Chapter 12. This is a very controversial debate and the Governor of the Bank of Canada became increasingly more explicit in the approach he has followed. See Bank of Canada, *Annual Report, 1975* (Ottawa, 1976), especially pp. 7-13.

115. See speeches by Hon. J. Chrétien, President of the Treasury Board between 1974 and 1975. On earlier approaches to budget policy see the following: Kaliski, *Canadian Economic Policy Since the War;* Strick, *Canadian Public Finance;* and Hon. D. S. Macdonald, Budget Speech, May 25, 1976. For other views on recent economic policy see D. Wolfe, "The State of Recent Economic Policy in Canada, 1968-1975". Paper presented to the Canadian Political Science Association in Quebec City, May 31, 1976; and John Helliwell, "Managing the Economy". Paper given at the Liberal Party Conference, March 1977.

116. Interviews. See also *The Financial Post,* November 6, 1976, "Your Tax Return is up for Grabs Again".

117. Confidential interviews. See Budget Speech, June 23, 1975. On the use of monetary and fiscal policy see Cairncross, ed., *Essays in Economic Management,* Chapter 6.

CHAPTER EIGHT

The Role of the Department of Industry, Trade and Commerce

While the Department of Finance through the use of fiscal and general economic management policies influences all actors in the system and while the Bank of Canada through monetary policy attempts to influence broad spending decisions in the economy, the Department of Industry, Trade and Commerce (IT&C) deals with several operational aspects of government-industry relations. In the Canadian mixed economy the public sector attempts to influence the private sector through consultation, moral suasion, incentives, and regulation. In a broad sociological sense it can be said that the government provides both positive rewards, and negative sanctions to industry, activities which lend support to analyses which show the close relationships between the state, the processes of legitimation and capitalism.[1] The conscious utilization of various instruments to bring about desired objectives has been defined by Shonfield, among others, as a form of planning, which blurs the distinction between the public and the private sectors. Recent analysts of contemporary political economy have described this relationship between government and industry as a system of interpenetration.[2]

This chapter and Chapter 9 focus on two government departments which use selective instruments to influence demand-management policies, particularly spending decisions dealing with investment. The Department of Industry, Trade and Commerce continuously assesses the domestic and international environment through various monitoring devices at home and abroad and, through the use of incentive grants, entrepreneurial training, and various trade promotional activities, attempts to foster efficiency and effectiveness in Canadian industry. To achieve these objectives the department attempts to establish effective liaison with industry and with other governments.

The Department of Regional Economic Expansion (DREE) attempts to stimulate economic expansion in the slow-growth regions. Prior to the establishment of this department in 1969 governmental efforts to assist selected regions were dispersed and fragmented.[3] The approach adopted by DREE has been largely spatial. However, while the approach initiated in 1969 emphasized "special" and "designated" areas in a limited number of provinces, a decentralized strategy adopted by the department in 1974 culminated in the signing of General Development Agreements with all Canadian provinces. Both departments demonstrate that the Canadian economy is, to a large degree, managed through governmental intervention. Thus, economic management must be distinguished from pure economic analysis.

The conflicts between international political and economic objectives and regional political and economic objectives within Canada are well illustrated by the roles and behaviour of these two departments. Economists speak of comparative advantage, i.e., specialization within areas of production efficiency. National growth is fostered by specialization. If each region is producing efficiently then it improves Canada's competitive position abroad.[4] In this regard IT&C is concerned with Canada's international competitive position. To this end, decision-makers within the department must be concerned with some of DREE's policies. A point of contention therefore is whether the primary objective of regional development policies is aimed at maximizing the growth of the whole country while at the same time reducing regional disparities. The objectives of these two departments can only be jointly optimized by following such a strategy. However, political leaders from the depressed areas are concerned with maximizing regional participation and as such would be opposed to an optimal economic growth strategy.[5] They are concerned therefore with the decentralization of industrial activity.

Our review of the role of these two departments in economic management at the federal level brings out two important political dimensions which affect government-industry relations. First, the federal government supports the private sector because several of the societal objectives are achieved through the assistance provided and because other countries support their private sectors. Several studies of the evolution of modern capitalism including the United States have supported this approach to government-industrial relations.[6] Governmental supports to industry minimize or socialize the risks which the private sector undertakes. To this end, the provision of grants, tax incentives, and general governmental assistance for research and development facilitates the maintenance of a desirable level of investment and an adequate production of goods and services. These programs have also been severely criticized as being not much more than corporate welfare programs.

The criteria on which support is given to larger industries are different from those on which assistance is provided to the smaller industries. The latter are sometimes criticized by economists in that such small firms do not benefit from economies of scale.[7] General assistance and specific subsidies to small industries including small farmers are illustrative of government policies of this kind. Sometimes the value system of the society endorses support to big businesses while at the same time it objects to assistance to individual citizens on grounds that it destroys individual initiative. The assistance provided by the Unemployment Insurance Commission can be regarded as an illustration of this conflict.[8]

Economic policies maintain or change group relationships in society. Accordingly, it is important to examine the policies formulated by governments and their economic advisors to ascertain the extent to which they alter group relationships in the political system. In the final analysis, political behaviour and political choice are determined by political resources. Leaders act to further their perceived goals and preferences. Analysis requires disaggregation of the system into sectors with sometimes conflicting interests. Before resources can be distributed they must be produced. Yet the ultimate objective of private production is to satisfy wants. This chapter examines selective aspects of economic-policy formulation in IT&C primarily concerned with influencing, sustaining, or altering private-sector production and investment decisions.

Our review of the structure and policy orientation of IT&C illustrates the subtle distinctions which must be made between economic stabilization, economic management, and mere economic administration.[9] Thus a significant portion of the activities of this department are promotional rather than economic-research oriented. The Canadian government must provide supports to industry because other governments do so and failure to do so would reduce the nation's competitive position. This role helps explain the large percentage of personnel with business administration and industrial backgrounds employed by the department.

THE MANAGEMENT OF GOVERNMENT-INDUSTRY RELATIONS

An important aspect of economic management particularly in the Canadian mixed economy is concerned with government-industry relations.[10] In many respects the concept of economic planning centres on methods to gain private co-operation and support for the broad goals established by government. Without using the term "economic planning" the then Minister of Industry, Trade and Commerce, Alastair Gillespie, pointed, in January 1975, to the importance of consultation and co-operation between business and government in what he termed "the Responsible Enterprise System" which required co-operation between "businessmen, labour, farmers, and consumers".[11]

In the words of the Minister of Industry, Trade and Commerce:

> Governments acting in the public interest, have legislated to increase the accountability of the business enterprise to each of its separate publics. . . . I would include disclosure provisions, labour law, consumer legislation, environmental protection, and measures to increase the accountability of non-Canadian multi-national corporations operating in Canada as important elements of this accountability.[12]

It is important to note that the minister then added: "this government has no desire to intervene unnecessarily in the business process. . . . our policy is to stimulate and promote business growth." The Department of Industry, Trade and Commerce operates on the principle that "the key to success in international markets is the closest possible working arrangement between government and industry."[13] To assist Canadian industry the department has representatives located in other countries.

While Chapter 7 showed that there is an established *ad hoc* stabilization or contra-cyclical approach to economic policy-making anchored in the Department of Finance, there is also a second managerial role performed by the government which is concerned with synchronizing the objectives of the private sector with those of the government. This role commences when more specific objectives and targets are posed for the economy as a whole, in the long-run as well as in the short-run, and when governmental actions and programs are designed to influence the decisions of the private sector in ways which interact with public sector activity to achieve the objectives.[14]

In many respects we are talking about something analogous to "indicative planning". In this role government acts as the top co-ordinator of the economic system as a whole. The government needs the co-operation of the private sector in order to achieve the growth and the full employment objectives which have been sought in the postwar years. Thus the partnership is related to the evolutionary nature of the role of the state from Adam Smith's *laissez-faire* system to the positive state in the post-Keynesian period, although rampant *laissez-faire* views or practices have not been as prevalent in Canada as they have been elsewhere.

While the Department of Finance designs policies to influence both governmental and private spending decisions, IT&C together with other departments must attempt to influence the private sector through various incentives as well as through major promotional activities to foster greater trade.[15] Similarly, DREE, to be dealt with in Chapter 9, has been formulating policies to promote growth in the depressed sectors of the economy.

In this chapter we are concerned with managerial relationships, investment policy, and incentives strategies as viewed through an analysis of IT&C. However, it should be stressed that the Government of Canada provides many other services to business, defined in a broad sense. These are housed in a large number of departments and agencies of which the following are illustrative:[16] the *Department of Agriculture* provides meat-inspection services, administers through its Production and Marketing Branch programs designed to help producers obtain a fair return for management and, through its Economics Branch, identifies economic problems and opportunities and projects trends and prospects in agriculture; (ii) the *Department of Consumer and Corporate Affairs* gives advice on the Weights and Measures Act, the Electricity Inspection Act, and the Precious Metal Marketing Act. More significantly it advises on all problems and regulations concerning consumers and consumer goods and administers and advises on the Patents and Copyright Act and the Canada Corporations Act; (iii) the *Department of Energy, Mines and Resources* provides advice and assistance to companies on offshore mineral development and provides in-depth studies and analyses to the mineral industry in particular; (iv) the *Department of the Environment* provides technical advice to the fish-processing and handling industries, marketing and management services to the fishing industry, scientific and charting services to marine transportation; (v) the *Department of Finance,* as indicated earlier, through its detailed studies of the economic situation in Canada and abroad, provides advice on exports; (vi) the *Department of Labour* provides conciliation services in industrial disputes and advisory and consultative services on employment and safety; (vii) the *Department of Manpower and Immigration* through its 460 Canada Manpower Centres advises employers on the state of the labour market and assists in the finding of suitable personnel. Moreover, it counsels employers on manpower needs and on methods for obtaining suitable employees; (viii) the *Department of Health and Welfare* through its Health Protection Branch is responsible for enforcement of the Food and Drugs Act, the Narcotic Control Act, and the Proprietary or Patent Medicine Act; (ix) the *National Research Council's* scientists and technicians help and advise on technical or scientific problems which relate to any phase of industry or business about which they have knowledge or experience; (x) *Statistics Canada* has a large information dissemination program and consequently provides statistical data on almost all aspects of Canada's social and economic life, which can be extremely beneficial to business and industry; (xi) the *Department of Regional Economic Expansion* provides services to business and industry encompassing industrial-site location, land costs, transportation rates, and federal, provincial, and municipal taxes; and (xii) the *Ministry of Transport* guides and advises all businesses and industries on the standards, licensing, and rules and regulations related to all forms of land, sea, and air transport.[17]

IT&C attempts to stimulate demand both domestically and internationally and, accordingly, is concerned with influencing innovation and various promotional activities to foster trade. It performs both micro- and macro-economic management roles in that, while it is concerned with broad growth policies nationally and internationally, it operates through specific incentives to selected industries.[18] The department thus performs a complementary role to the Department of Consumer and Corporate Affairs. These two departments are concerned with the national aspects of growth policy and the health of the marketplace while DREE is concerned with more regional aspects of economic policies. However, the activities of both departments are closely related to those of IT&C since price performance will determine to a considerable degree the magnitude of trade. Stated differently, price stability will affect Canada's competitive position. Accordingly, we must review briefly the evolution and nature of the machinery designed to promote industrial innovation, production, and trade.

THE EVOLUTION OF THE DEPARTMENT

In Chapter 6 we described the postwar machinery which formulated economic policy. More specifically, we reviewed the role of the then Department of Trade and Commerce stressing that it was preceded by a powerful Department of Reconstruction and Supply under a highly influential minister, C. D. Howe. We noted also that in 1961 a National Productivity Council was formed with representation from, and which reported to, the departments of Trade and Commerce and Labour. This was followed by the Economic Council Act in 1963. In the same year a Department of Industry was established to perform the following functions:

a) . . . to acquire a detailed knowledge of manufacturing industries in Canada;
b) promote the establishment of growth, efficiency, and improvement of manufacturing industries in Canada; and
c) develop and carry out such programs and projects as may be appropriate:
   (i) to assist the adaptation of manufacturing industries to changing conditions in domestic and export markets and to changes in the techniques of production,
   (ii) to identify and assist those manufacturing industries that require special measures to develop an unrealized potential or to cope with exceptional problems of adjustment, and
   (iii) to promote the development and use of modern industrial technology in Canada and improve the effectiveness of the participation by the Government of Canada in industrial research.[19]

The Minister of Industry was also granted powers to exercise and perform all the duties, powers, and functions vested in or required to be exercised and performed by the Minister of Defence Production. As will be demonstrated later IT&C now administers the Defence Industry

Productivity Program (DIP) through which many opportunities exist for Canadian companies to participate in the Canada–United States Defence Production Sharing Program and in programs for the export of defence equipment and components to members of NATO and other friendly foreign countries. The creation of the Department of Industry also provided some new initiatives in the realm of regional development in that provision was made for the creation of an Area Development Agency with responsibility for a designated area, locality, or district to be determined by the Governor-in-Council.[20]

Since economic management is always involved with relationships between economic analysis, production, and resource allocation, it is essential to review, albeit briefly, some of the corresponding developments which took place in the area of economic techniques. It was indicated in Chapter 6 that the old Department of Trade and Commerce had inherited the econometric model developed in the Department of Reconstruction and Supply. The model was developed for short-term forecasting needs. It was utilized primarily for formulating monetary and fiscal policies and as such the strong analytic group in the former Trade and Commerce department provided significant advice to the Department of Finance in the preparation of the budget. The Department of Trade and Commerce at that time possessed one of the most efficient groups of economists in Ottawa. In fact, it was a report prepared in the Department of Trade and Commerce concerning conflicting forecasts of the economy which led to the controversy noted in Chapter 6 between the Conservatives and the Liberals in the late 1950s.[21]

In the early 1960s, when R. B. Bryce went to Finance, it was recognized that the model was more oriented toward the big levers of stabilization than toward industrial policy. Hence, the model was transferred to the Department of Finance.[22] The use of economists in the Department of Trade and Commerce then began to be oriented toward micro rather than macro considerations, i.e., toward efficiency studies in industrial sectors. This process was accelerated by the amalgamation of the departments of Trade and Commerce and Industry in 1969.[23]

The recently established Planning and Evaluation Branch of IT&C, to be dealt with below, has begun the building of models to handle the vast data necessary to compare rates of growth in industrial sectors and to simulate the impact of these sectors on the economy. These changes in the location and use of techniques in economic management are important in that they ultimately affect the behaviour of ministers in the Cabinet.

Given the fact that, at the time of writing, less emphasis is being placed on maximum economic growth, economic analysis has shifted toward the efficient utilization of resources *within industrial sectors.*[24] The technical skills of economists are required to improve the effective allocation of scarce resources. It is in this respect that it can be said that in IT&C emphasis has shifted to micro-economic analysis. Technical analysis is required to rationalize the various subsidies and grants provided. The management of the economy involves continuous interface between the Planning Branches in the departments of Industry, Trade and Commerce, Finance, Manpower and Immigration, Consumer and Corporate Affairs, Regional Economic Expansion, and Environment[25] in an endeavour to establish the appropriate trade-offs between the more particularistic objectives which each department is attempting to maximize. These are major allocative and distributive decisions which require both interdepartmental co-operation at each level of government, intergovernmental co-operation, and public sector-private sector co-operation.

It should be noted that the Department of Industry was not the product of advanced planning, having been established shortly after the 1963 federal election. Thus, the urgency imposed by the government on the creation of the Department of Industry meant that the task of planning and organizing the new department had to be borne by a small group of officers from the two departments who were active in the field of industrial development, the Department of Trade and Commerce, and the Department of Defence Production.[26] In the Department of Defence Production industrial development was performed under the department's responsibility to develop and maintain an adequate defence production base in Canada in relation to the procurement of major defence items. The Department of Trade and Commerce placed more emphasis on economic analysis and the in-depth study of particular industries or products.[27] Given the fact that it was a marriage of two different types of department, the then newly created Department of Industry had two deputy ministers reporting to the Minister of Industry. The initial strategy stressed that "the successful application of the concept of a Department of Industry whose role it was to know industry, understand its problems and promote solutions, required that qualified people be attracted primarily from industry and from the ranks of specialists in the fields of production, marketing, and research''.[28] Consequently, the creation of the department constituted an important attempt in the early 1960s to improve government-industry co-operation.

The 1969 Government Reorganization Act merged the Department of Industry with the Department of Trade and Commerce.[29] It should be stressed that while the Economic Council absorbed some of the activities of the National Productivity Council it was specifically prohibited from engaging in promotional activities. These activities were envisaged for the then new Department of Industry. They are now the responsibility of the Department of Industry, Trade and Commerce.[30] Thus, IT&C has a potential for operationalizing selective aspects of the work of the Economic Council of Canada.[31] In fact, this was stated as one of the main reasons for creating the Department of Industry in 1963. Yet, it has only been since 1972 that the Department of Industry, Trade and Commerce has been emerging as an active department concerned with the development of an industrial strategy.

The Department of Industry, Trade and Commerce was established when the new planning, programing, and budgeting system was being implemented. Accordingly, between 1969 and 1972 the department's structure was influenced by that system.[32] Thus, during the fiscal year 1969-70 the expanded Department of Industry, Trade and Commerce introduced the planning, programing, and budgeting system (PPBS) into all elements of its programs and activities. To facilitate the implementation of PPBS the department established, in that year, a Program Planning and Analysis Branch to develop uniform systems of planning and to provide guidance to personnel in the application of the system. As we shall observe below the approach was not successful.

The legislative bases of the department's activities are related to three principal areas: manufacturing and processing industries in Canada; tourism; and trade and commerce generally. Accordingly, the PPBS approach adopted in 1969 identified four major programs: Industry and Trade Development; Tourism; Grains; and World Exhibition.[33] It will be observed below that the department has expanded its activities considerably and the decentralized strategy adopted in 1974 attempts to regionalize the broad objectives stated in the Act establishing the department.

The Department of Industry, Trade and Commerce then has a major potential for influencing economic policies, particularly in the private sector. Its role is related closely to DREE's, however, particularly under the General Development Agreements enunciated in 1974. These agreements require that all levels of government must co-operate to identify strategic development initiatives. This co-ordinated approach is intended to give additional assurance that all private-sector elements are encouraged to act in a concerted way within the community and with federal and provincial governments. The strategy was based on the rationale that the best way for DREE to plan, formulate, implement, and administer the development efforts required a substantial decentralization of its activities and decision-making to regional and provincial offices.[34] This aspect of DREE's policies will be dealt with in the next chapter. It is worth mentioning here that the Department of Industry, Trade and Commerce is in the process of implementing a further decentralized strategy. Here the attempted industrial strategy becomes linked with the employment strategy which will be discussed in Chapter 10.[35]

STRUCTURE AND ORGANIZATION IN THE MID-1970S

The role of the Department of Industry, Trade and Commerce is exceedingly broad. The department provides a major operational input to the Department of Finance and to the Cabinet Committee on Economic Policy. The objectives of the department were stated in 1974-75 as follows:

> To achieve efficient and sustained growth in the production and trade of Canadian goods and services and to assist Canadian industries to adjust to changes in the domestic and external economic environment.

The sub-objectives were:

> —to improve the performance and the international competitive position of Canadian industries;
> —to increase the total effective market for goods and services produced by the Canadian economy;

—to assist all sectors of Canadian society in an orderly conversion to the International System (SI) of metric units in a manner consistent with the main objective of the program.[36]

The department deals with broad and powerful constituencies. The Export Development Corporation, the Machinery and Equipment Advisory Board, the Textile and Clothing Board, the Foreign Investment Review Agency, and the Federal Business Development Bank, among others, significantly influence the activities of this department.[37] There are a number of other important advisory bodies and boards reporting to the Minister of Industry, Trade and Commerce.

The department's policies are formulated on the basis that Canada's future prosperity and the achievement of its economic objectives will continue to depend on its ability to trade and to meet the challenge of international competition. To this end, the department assists in designing policies to improve industrial efficiency and overall performance in all facets of production and marketing. The department has developed trade programs, industrial programs, and a wide range of services and assistance ranging from research, design, and development through to production and marketing. The industrial thrust of the department is directed at establishing programs or strategies that are tailored to the needs of individual industry sectors.

The department has been reorganizing its regional offices across the country to give greater regional autonomy in the administration of a number of programs. In this respect it can be considered to be strengthening its role in federal-provincial relations.[38] However, as we will see later, the approaches to decentralization by DREE and IT&C have been somewhat different. IT&C has established ten regional offices (the office in Fredericton also serves Prince Edward Island). IT&C deals with the provincial departments of industry but there are constraints on the degree of openness displayed by the federal department. The federal regional offices are primarily concerned with the promotion of the services provided by the department in the respective regions. The department is primarily concerned with industrial development and trade and provincial objectives often conflict with those of the federal government. This fact imposes constraints on the prospects for developing joint federal-provincial offices in the regions in that such a step could confuse businessmen in ascertaining the level of government with which they are discussing industrial support. It should be pointed out nevertheless that the main task of the regional director is to establish good rapport with the provinces.

The regional offices have provided the focal point of another major thrust of the emerging industrial strategy; namely, support to small businesses.[39] The majority of Canadian industries are small and they, more so than the larger firms, need governmental support. One source has noted that over eighty per cent of the Canadian business community on the industrial side can be considered as small.[40] From this perspective, IT&C has always had to be somewhat decentralized. It offers services in the various regions in an endeavour to aid small businesses in their preparation of applications for assistance and support. In a vast country like Canada, government must provide services to assist small businesses. To this end, the federal government developed the Counselling Assistance to Small Enterprises (the CASE program). Also, since 1945 financial assistance has been provided through the Industrial Development Bank mentioned in Chapter 7. In 1975 the activities of this bank were expanded and transferred to IT&C, where, as the new Federal Business Development Bank, it has taken over the CASE program. As such it is concerned with managerial activities in addition to its banking activities.[41]

The Regional Offices Branch has the more specific objective of providing in each province the expansion of trade and tourism in the areas of IT&C responsibility through the efficient development of manufacturing and processing industries. It attempts to promote and foster growth, productivity, employment opportunities, and prosperity of the regional economies. More specifically, through the formulation and implementation of appropriate plans, policies, programs, and assistance the Regional Offices Branch endeavours to:

a) promote the establishment, growth, and productivity of efficient and competitive manufacturing and processing industries in the regional areas and contribute to the sound development of Canadian industry generally;
b) assist manufacturing and processing industries in the regions to adjust to changing conditions in domestic and international markets and to realize their full potential;
c) promote and assist product and process development and improved productivity through the greater use of research, advanced technology, mod-

ern management, and better design, and to encourage the development and application of sound industrial standards in the regions and in trade generally;

d) maintain compatible federal-provincial and interdepartmental relations to provide the best service possible to industry, trade, and tourism;

e) maintain a detailed knowledge of manufacturing, processing, and distribution industries in the regional areas and of trends and developments in Canada and abroad relating to Canadian regional industrial development, trade, and tourism;

f) assist the access of Canadian goods into external markets through the provision of information on trade and tariff restrictions to regional firms and provincial governments, and the reporting of regional information related to trade negotiations and the promotion of trade relations with other countries; and

g) analyse the implications for regional industry, trade, and tourism of relevant government policies and ensure that the resultant information is available and taken into account during the formulation and review of such policies.[42]

In the national context, IT&C is concerned, among other things, with the following five activities which were identified under program budgeting adopted in the fiscal year 1969-70: product innovation; production efficiency; review of the international and domestic environment; the promotion of market development; and the promotion of tourism. It should be noted that while IT&C isolated these *functional* categories, it no longer tries to divide work exclusively within this framework because there were some administrative difficulties with the implementation of the PPBS in the department.[43] IT&C experienced difficulties in utilizing program budgeting because of the diversity of interests to which it had to respond.

During the early 1970s the department tried to integrate a number of programs which hitherto had been administered separately. First, there was the new manufacturing thrust which came from the newly created Department of Industry. As indicated above, in the 1969 reorganization a section was carried over from Defence Production. Second, there was the old Department of Trade and Commerce which contained an effective economic research unit. However, the department had a trade promotion section which was both located in, and oriented toward, the international environment. Third, there was the research and development activity which was partially related to defence activity but which had begun to be broadened with the emergence of the National Productivity Council and the Science Council.[44] In addition, the Ministry of State for Science and Technology (MOSST), since its creation in 1971, has performed a major advisory role in the area of innovation. MOSST, however, looks at the broader picture primarily from a research perspective. Its role is primarily advisory and liaison, particularly as it affects scientific inputs into programs.[45] It has tried to develop basic advice on Canada's science policies. Prior to the establishment of MOSST, the Department of Industry, Trade and Commerce (along with NRC) was the major departmental spokesman for science and technology in the civilian area. There have clearly been some major disagreements as to the best method of assisting industry, such as whether greater emphasis should be placed on research and development as compared to the development of entrepreneurial talent. A number of ministers of Industry, Trade and Commerce have attempted to integrate these highly diversified activities.

By way of illustration, the department's objectives in regard to innovation are to encourage companies to develop new and unique products that will help to expand domestic and export markets through the Defence Industry Productivity Program (DIP); the Industrial Design Assistance Program (IDAP); the Industrial Research and Development Incentive Act (IRDIA); and the Program for the Advancement of Industrial Technology (PAIT). These programs range from IDAP, an industrial design program which provides operational and administrative costs of up to fifty per cent non-repayable, through to tax-free cash grants or credits against federal income tax (IRDIA) and to shared-cost programs on a fifty per cent basis, as for example with PAIT.[46]

With respect to productivity, the department grants subsidies for feasibility studies on selected projects involving a significant departure from a company's normal productivity improvement practices and also involving only existing available technology (PEP). The assistance through the PEP program thus supports projects in which there exists a marked but unproven potential for significant productivity gains requiring a feasibility study before a decision can be made concerning implementation. The department also provides forms of financing from the General Adjustment Assistance Program (GAAP) which is designed to assist the Canadian manufacturing industry to improve its position in meeting international trade competition. There is also special assistance to the pharmaceutical industry through PIDA. In the managerial area the department provides assistance through CASE, which provides an opportunity for the owners and managers of small businesses engaged in manufacturing or tourism to benefit, at nominal cost, from a service provided by retired business executives. A recent study by Gordon Sharwood suggested the scrapping of many of the rather dated programs and the development of a more dynamic and flexible approach to assist industry.[47] However, the various incentive programs which existed during the 1960s and early 1970s are listed in Appendix F.

In order to explain the difficulties faced by the department in adopting a more active role in economic management it is important to examine the five functional areas which were identified under program budgeting but which were later de-emphasized in organizational terms.

Product Innovation

As indicated above the department is concerned with product innovation which involves keeping pace with technological advances essential to long-term economic growth and to insure a continuing flow of new and improved products, processing, and services. To this end, the department formulates and administers incentives programs designed to stimulate technological innovation; establishes and supports research institutes and centres; and provides industry with specialized advice and information on scientific developments and techniques. The department chairs the secretariat of the federal government's Interdepartmental Committee on Innovation whose function is to evaluate and recommend government policies and programs intended to further industrial research and development.[48]

Production Efficiency

The department is responsible for production efficiency which is achieved through a comprehensive program designed to help Canadian enterprises to operate more efficiently and to successfully withstand foreign competition. To achieve this goal the department performs the following tasks: analyses supply and demand patterns in domestic and world markets; assesses the effectiveness of production methods at home and abroad; provides specialized advice and information to industry; and operates incentive programs designed to help Canadian firms improve their efficiency. The industry-sector branches of the department, together with industry, carry out and sponsor a continuous program of research and analysis to determine opportunities in different industry sectors and to gauge their competitive potential regionally and internationally. In this regard two critical aspects of the department's program converge: responsibility for research in areas such as the clothing industry or the electrical requirements of the proposed Mackenzie Valley pipeline, and incentive programs such as the General Adjustment Assistance Program (GAAP) designed to help finance the restructuring of industries and the Counselling Assistance to Small Enterprises Services (CASE) which provides a much needed counselling service to small businesses in the manufacturing and tourism sectors, mainly by employing the talents of retired business managers.

The strategies adopted to improve production efficiency have shifted on occasions and as noted earlier there are differences within the bureaucracy concerning the relative emphasis which should be placed on research and development incentives as compared to the promotion and development of stronger Canadian managerial talents. Supporters of the latter have pointed to the role of managerial talents in the efficiency of industries in countries such as Japan.

At the macro level of policy development, there is the recently expanded Minister's Advisory Council consisting of approximately forty representatives of trade, industrial, and regional interests with which the minister periodically discusses important issues concerning government-industry relations. The role of this council is to examine and review the policies, programs, and services of the department; evaluate the extent of knowledge and use of the department's industrial and trade programs and services in the Canadian business community; and recommend means of stimulating and maintaining interest in the department's activities on the part of management in industry, business, trade, education, and the professions.[49]

Government-industry relations are concerned ultimately with the promotion of international trade. Three components of the department's activities are directed at the international environment: the International and Domestic Economic Division, Market Development, and Tourism.[50] During the 1969-70 program-budgeting exercise the "International Trade" side of the department was categorized under the following three functional areas: International-Domestic Environment, Market Development, and Tourism. Although we will briefly review these additional functional areas it will be demonstrated below that they were not directly helpful in formulating the department's policies.

International-Domestic Environment (International and Domestic Economy)

While the Department of Finance can set the general direction of economic policy, IT&C must evaluate the domestic implications of the broad policies on such areas as import policy, taxation policy, and competition policy in an endeavour to assess their effects on the direction and rate of industrial development. Internationally the department must assess the effects of trade barriers, both tariff and non-tariff, on accessibility to foreign markets for Canadian products.

It is the responsibility of IT&C to draw attention to the impact of the foregoing policies on trade and industry and to recommend actions and policies that are beneficial to Canadian interests. In the international realm the department reviews the international trade environment with major trading blocs such as the United States and the European Economic Community, regional integration with Latin America, and problems affecting the Third World in general through the Canadian International Development Agency (CIDA) and through the Export Development Corporation. In the early 1970s the department was actively involved with policy reviews in areas such as taxation, labour legislation, competition policy, tariffs, packaging and labelling regulations, and environmental protection measures.[51] In these areas the department participates in a large number of interdepartmental committees.

Market Development

Through this activity the department performs an important role in fostering improved foreign trade. To this end, domestically oriented companies are assisted to enter the export market through the market development service which analyses international trade trends and surveys new opportunities for export, grants day-to-day assistance to exporters through the department's offices in Canada and abroad, grants support through trade fairs, trade missions, and export publicity, and through the provision of indirect market support through the Program for Export Market Development.[52] The promotional orientation of the department has been reflected in the fact that ministers of IT&C have led trade missions to many countries.

The 1975 organizational structure of the Department of Industry, Trade and Commerce shown in Figure 8:1 is indicative of its policy-making role. As the chart shows, below the Minister and Deputy Minister, there were two Sr. Assistant Deputy Ministers, one for Industry and one for International Trade. The Sr. ADM for Industry had responsibility for two main divisions: Industrial Development and Industrial Policies. The ADM for Industry Development had responsibility for what can be described as promotion inasmuch as he dealt with particular industrial sectors.[53] The ADM for Industrial Policies dealt with problems which could be considered as horizontal policy responsibilities in that they cut across departmental boundaries or given industrial sectors. Accordingly, under the ADM for Industrial Policies were groups such as the following: Office of Science and Technology, Office of Industrial Policy, Office of Design and Productivity Analysis. There were also four officers reporting directly to the Sr. ADM for Industry: a senior policy advisor, a small business co-ordinator, a program offices director, and the General Director of the Regional Offices Branch. The department also contained an ADM for Tourism and an ADM for Planning, Research and Evaluation. The position of Sr. ADM for International Trade was subdivided organizationally into two, an ADM for Export Development and an ADM for International Trade Relations. The Planning, Research and Evaluation Group under its ADM served the two major components of the department.

As indicated in our historical analysis there is an export promotion side of the department which was carried over from the "old" Trade and Commerce department, an important aspect of its responsibilities being the status of non-tariff barriers which, as we shall observe later, has become a critical area in the rapidly changing international

Figure 8:1 Organization of the Department of Industry, Trade and Commerce (1975)

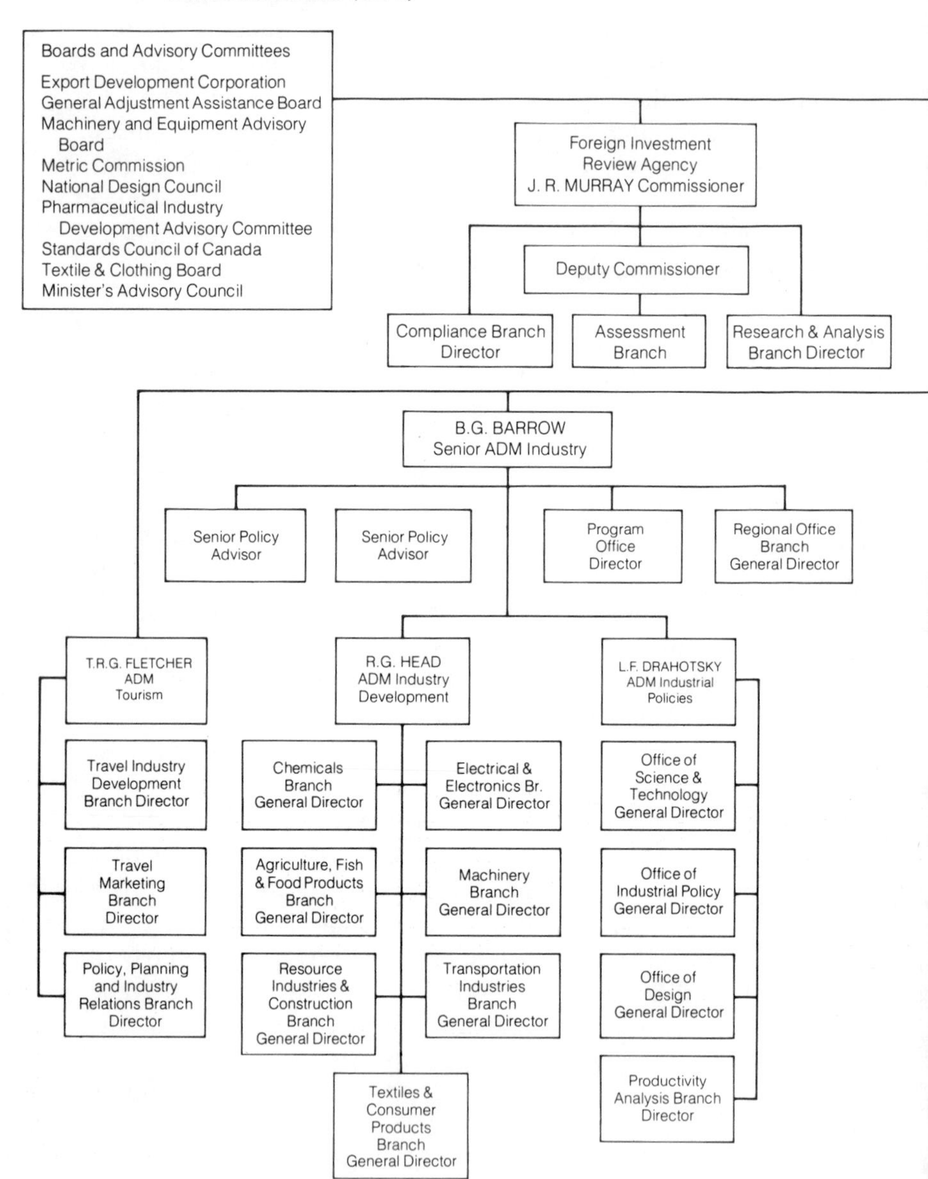

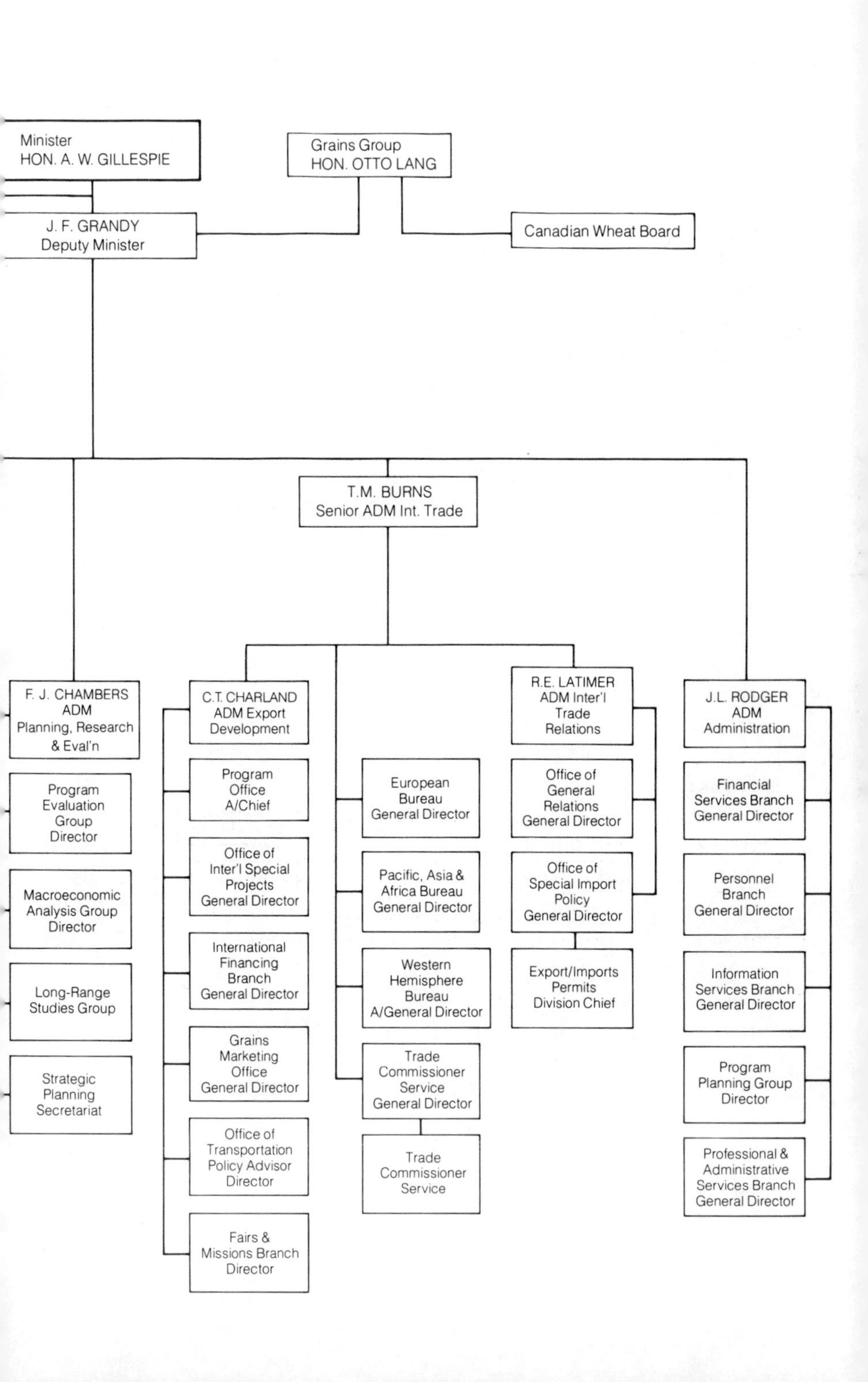

Minister
HON. A. W. GILLESPIE
Grains Group
HON. OTTO LANG
J. F. GRANDY
Deputy Minister
Canadian Wheat Board
T.M. BURNS
Senior ADM Int. Trade
F. J. CHAMBERS
ADM
Planning, Research & Eval'n
C.T. CHARLAND
ADM Export Development
R.E. LATIMER
ADM Inter'l Trade Relations
J.L. RODGER
ADM
Administration
Program Evaluation Group Director
Macroeconomic Analysis Group Director
Long-Range Studies Group
Strategic Planning Secretariat
Program Office A/Chief
Office of Inter'l Special Projects General Director
International Financing Branch General Director
Grains Marketing Office General Director
Office of Transportation Policy Advisor Director
Fairs & Missions Branch Director
European Bureau General Director
Pacific, Asia & Africa Bureau General Director
Western Hemisphere Bureau A/General Director
Trade Commissioner Service General Director
Trade Commissioner Service
Office of General Relations General Director
Office of Special Import Policy General Director
Export/Imports Permits Division Chief
Financial Services Branch General Director
Personnel Branch General Director
Information Services Branch General Director
Program Planning Group Director
Professional & Administrative Services Branch General Director

economic environment. In this respect, the role of the department should be distinguished from that of Consumer and Corporate Affairs which is more interested in competitiveness from the perspective of the users of the products, while IT&C is concerned with the industrial viewpoint, albeit from the perspective of their relationship to the attainment of national objectives. IT&C's role is becoming more important in view of the recent emphasis placed on efficiency and the expansion of production in the supply of goods — in contrast to the expansion of the social services *per se*.[54] The efficiency and expansion emphasis was stressed in the *Working Paper on Social Security in Canada* in which economic growth was posited as the major objective.

On the industry-development side emphasis is placed on encouraging and promoting greater investment both nationally and regionally. Here the department is concerned with promoting the interest of diverse industrial firms. Support for scientific innovation in particular industries is provided both from a functional as well as a sectoral perspective. Here IT&C does nationally and internationally what DREE is doing regionally. IT&C is also confronted with another dilemma — the role of foreign investment in Canada as part of an industrial strategy.[55] The creation of, and the role granted to the Foreign Investment Review Agency is most illustrative of such developments and will be examined later.

On the international-trade side there were two major groups: an Export Development Group and an International Trade Relations Group. These two groups could conveniently be categorized into two distinct organizational activities, the former being promotional while the latter could be said to be more policy-oriented. There was also a geographical, regional orientation as depicted by the European, Pacific Asia and Africa, and the Western Hemisphere bureaus which work closely with the Department of External Affairs.[56] These groups have been actively involved in Canada's recent attempts to diversify her trading relations. Indeed, the Hon. Donald Jamieson, during his short stay as Minister of Industry, Trade and Commerce between 1975 and 1976, was preoccupied with trade promotion given the then-existing problems with Canada's balance of trade and payments. With his subsequent appointment as Minister of External Affairs he was still actively involved with international trade matters. The Hon. Jean Chrétien who succeeded him had begun in late 1976 to enunciate an even more active approach to industrial and international trade policies.

From the perspective of the department as a whole, it is especially important to distinguish the horizontal and vertical roles of the two ADMs who serve on the industry side of the department. Both ADMs are concerned with policy development but the ADM for Industrial Policies has primary responsibility for horizontal relationships with industry. For example, while the ADM for Industrial Policies is concerned with horizontal relationships, such as the impact of tax, trade, competition, and science policies on industrial development, the Industry Group is concerned with particular industries or sectors of the economy. It should be noted, however, that in the past the department had not operated on the principle of developing leading industrial sectors to which it maintains major commitment.[57] Instead, it has attempted to shift the emphasis from specific industrial sectors as circumstances demand. There are some indications, however, that the review of the incentives programs carried out by the department in the mid-1970s helped produce some policy changes under Jean Chrétien.[58]

The Industry Group is responsible for the creation, development and maintenance of policies and programs which encourage and assist in the achievement of efficient and sustained growth. The group is further divided into two sub-groups, namely Industry Development and Industrial Policies. The Industry Development Group is responsible for assisting industries to innovate, develop, and produce goods and services to satisfy domestic demand and to compete successfully in international markets. Its components include chemicals, agriculture, fish and food, resource, and industries and machinery, among others. The Industrial Policies Group is responsible for the formulation of departmental policies as they impinge on a wide number of sectors related to industrial development, innovation and technology, fiscal policy, capital markets, competition policy, environmental quality, transportation, and labour and management. The corresponding organizational components for these functional activities are: the Office of Science and Technology; the Office of Industrial Policy Advisor; the Office of Design; and the Productivity Analysis Branch. It should be apparent that these sub-structures provide the basis for further interdepartmental relationships with several departments such as Finance,

Regional Economic Expansion, Energy, Mines and Resources, Agriculture, Transport, Consumer and Corporate Affairs, and the Ministry of State for Science and Technology.

The "economics" input to the department was provided by a group under an ADM for Planning, Research and Evaluation. The branch included among others, a Strategic Planning Secretariat, a Program Evaluation Group, a Macro-Economic Analysis Group, a Program Planning Group, and an International Trade Analysis Division. The Planning, Research and Evaluation Group attempts to balance and co-ordinate demands into a comprehensive and integrated plan for industry and trade that will insure maximum contribution to national objectives. The group must identify changing priorities and their implications for the allocation of departmental resources. In recent years, an attempt has been made to integrate long-term national, industrial, and trade strategies by drawing on the resources of other groups in the department, other government agencies, and various private institutions.[59]

The Planning, Research and Evaluation Group is divided into four divisions: Program Evaluation; Macro-Economic Analysis; Long-Range Studies; and the Strategic Planning Secretariat. The department is primarily a promotional agency and what used to be the Office of Economics provides economic intelligence as a means to facilitate the industrial and trade promotion process. An Office of Science and Technology provides the operational component necessary for industrial innovation.

Some reorganization has taken place recently due to the emphasis placed on formulating an industrial strategy and the creation of the Ministry of State for Science and Technology. Consequently, the 1975 organization chart of the department showed what used to be the Office of Economics as a unit transformed into a strategic-planning role. Immediately below the deputy minister there was, also, an important "intelligence and policy advisory group". However, by 1976 the department was again reorganized with a Bureau of Co-ordination reporting to the deputy minister. By then, there were seven assistant deputy ministers. In 1974, the then newly formed Planning Secretariat provided the broad integrative approach for achievement of the department's objectives. The Strategic Planning Group is concerned with long-term objectives and with a continuous evaluation of the labour force and the patterns of demand. One group works on the CANDIDE econometric model assessing its implications from the perspective of the department's objectives. Here the influence of the Economic Council of Canada can be seen in that the building of the CANDIDE model created an environment which led to IT&C developing its own model. Yet there are important differences in that IT&C has had to disaggregate its model considerably to make it operationally useful for industrial planning. The department has also extended the time frame of its model to facilitate new policy-making requirements.

The survey of investment intentions carried out originally in conjunction with the Economic Council has been absorbed into the department's Strategic Planning Branch. Investment intentions are an important aspect of business decision-making processes and require careful scrutiny. It should be noted also that when the Economic Council of Canada commenced this activity the review process involved a shorter time path but has been gradually extended. In order to influence demand management it is important to know the magnitude of investment intentions not only in a theoretical sense but in an applied way. Thus, the Economic Council of Canada in its *Eleventh Annual Review* published in November 1974 was very concerned that the budget presented to Parliament in November 1974 did not provide adequate scope for expanding investment opportunities.[60] As studies of French "indicative planning" have demonstrated, major efforts must be taken by government either directly or indirectly to maintain an adequate level of investment to keep the economy close to potential.[61]

At a more policy-oriented level, there are, as noted earlier, several representative groups through which consultation occurs. These consultative mechanisms are both essential and indicative of the complexities of the government-industry interface. The organization chart for 1976 (Figure 8:2) provides, as do all organizational portraits, a simplified but nonetheless useful snapshot of the various elements which influence government-industry relationships.

By 1976 the department had begun to strengthen its planning role, a fact reflected in the 1976 chart. By the mid-1970s the Hon. Alastair Gillespie had identified three critical problem areas faced by the government which required business co-operation: the need to develop measures to avoid the pervasive effects of inflation; the need to in-

Figure 8:2 Organization of the Department of Industry, Trade & Commerce (1976)

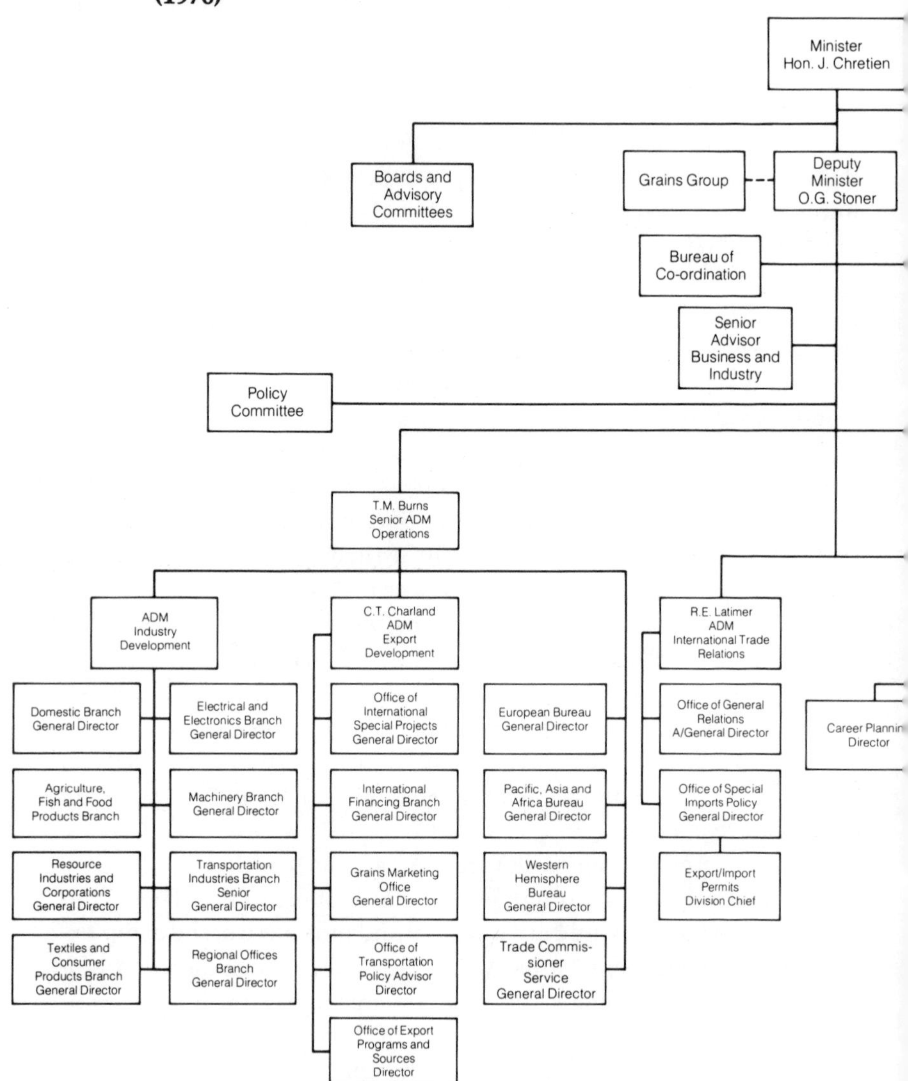

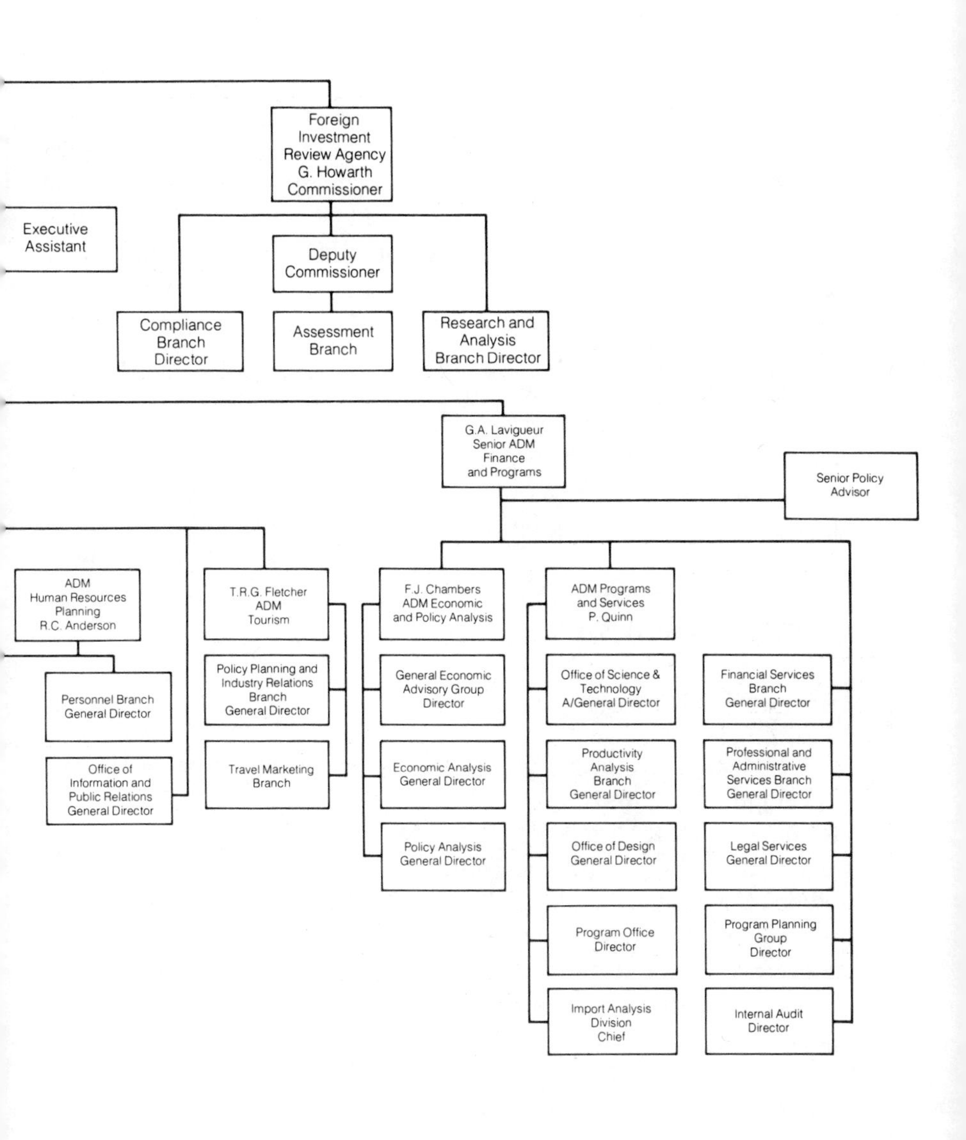
Foreign Investment Review Agency G. Howarth Commissioner
Executive Assistant
Deputy Commissioner
Compliance Branch Director
Assessment Branch
Research and Analysis Branch Director
G.A. Lavigueur Senior ADM Finance and Programs
Senior Policy Advisor
ADM Human Resources Planning R.C. Anderson
T.R.G. Fletcher ADM Tourism
F.J. Chambers ADM Economic and Policy Analysis
ADM Programs and Services P. Quinn
Personnel Branch General Director
Office of Information and Public Relations General Director
Policy Planning and Industry Relations Branch General Director
Travel Marketing Branch
General Economic Advisory Group Director
Economic Analysis General Director
Policy Analysis General Director
Office of Science & Technology A/General Director
Productivity Analysis Branch General Director
Office of Design General Director
Program Office Director
Import Analysis Division Chief
Financial Services Branch General Director
Professional and Administrative Services Branch General Director
Legal Services General Director
Program Planning Group Director
Internal Audit Director

crease industrial productivity and to insure its fair distribution; and the need to avoid the pitfalls of protectionism.[62] The publication in October 1976 of the working paper *The Way Ahead* provided further evidence of the search for a new and detailed consensus.[63]

Figure 8:2 describes the structure of the Department of Industry, Trade and Commerce in 1976. By then, the Hon. Jean Chrétien was minister and O. G. Stoner, his deputy minister. A number of boards and advisory committees described earlier reported directly to the minister, including the Foreign Investment Review Agency.

The titles of the two Senior Assistant Deputy Ministers were changed from Industry and International Trade to "Operations" and "Finance and Programs" respectively. There were now seven ADMS including: under "Operations", the ADM for Industry Development, Export Development, International Trade Relations, Human Resources Planning, and Tourism, the last two reporting directly to the DM; and under "Finance and Programs", the ADM for Economic and Policy Analysis and Programs and Services. A further major change took place in 1976 with the elevation of the status of small businesses.[64] To this end, a Minister of State for Small Businesses was established. The ADM for Programs and Services was designated to perform an important role in this regard.

THE INSTRUMENTS OF INTERVENTION

The Minister of Industry, Trade and Commerce is responsible for the development of trade policy. Most recently this has involved the formulation of policy affecting trade relations with the European Common Market, with the United States and with Japan, among others. On the domestic side, the Minister of IT&C is concerned with the promotion and upgrading of resources. In the broader sphere he is concerned with trade and tariff policy in general and in more specific areas with particular industries, for example, with the promotion and development of the textile industry. Generally speaking, the Minister of IT&C has the specific objective of influencing the size and structure of the industrial sector through tariffs, subsidization, research and development, and export policy in general. He is concerned with overall performance of Canadian industry from the perspective of efficiency.

Some senior public servants have argued that the old Department of

Trade and Commerce had a better image in Canadian industry. The old department had a more definite role.[65] The role of the minister was considered then to be one of promoting exports abroad. The later-established Department of Industry had a more ambitious objective, which was much less popular in the business community in general, of attempting to change the structure of Canadian industry, particularly manufacturing. Thus, it can be argued that the image of the department from the perspective of the aggregate private sector deteriorated with the amalgamation of the two departments in 1969. It is worth pointing out that the creation of a Department of Industry in 1963 was a political decision made because it was felt by some that the manufacturing sector of the economy did not have a spokeman in Cabinet.[66] This development had the adverse effect of narrowing the constituency orientation of government-industry relations. The attempt to formulate industrial strategies as espoused in 1974 demonstrated a trend toward formulating strategies for a wider range of industrial sectors,[67] for example, shipbuilding and the chemical industries. The foregoing demonstrates that in the mid-1970s there is no umbrella approach to government-industry relationships analogous to the immediate post-war period when C. D. Howe provided an extraordinary degree of ministerial leadership.

The role of the Minister of IT&C is further affected by the absence of regulatory instruments, the latter being more generally delegated to the departments of Energy, Mines and Resources and Consumer and Corporate Affairs, as well as numerous other specific regulatory agencies. IT&C works on the basis of persuasion and incentives rather than on strong governmental sanctions to enforce compliance as has been done in France.[68] In Canada, government-industry relations are scattered throughout the government in various departments. The question may be posed therefore: to what extent does such a trend affect the prospects for more effective economic planning? There is no strong tendency in the department to regulate business. Even the establishment of FIRA does not reveal a strong regulatory orientation, yet it has been the object of major criticisms in the press. It is worth emphasizing, therefore, that whereas formal machinery existed between the wars for providing communication and consultation between government and industry this general process has not existed in recent years. Significant industrial sectors of course continue to make their annual submissions to Cabinet as one means of maintaining a dialogue with government. Some consultation occurs through the Advisory Council to the Minister of IT&C whose members participate as individual businessmen. This body meets twice a year to discuss important issues with the minister. A 1976 study, however, expressed general dissatisfaction with consultative processes.[69]

Jean-Luc Pépin made a major attempt in June 1972 to formulate a comprehensive industrial strategy. In his June 5 speech he outlined what he considered to be the major components of "a government strategy for industry" which would be largely "indicative" with contributions by several departments such as Finance, Energy, Mines and Resources, Science and Technology, and Transport. The minister identified a number of sector strategies including the following industries: automotive, tourism, textiles, electronics, footwear, food products, book publishing, and grains.[70]

As explained elsewhere the "industrial strategy" espoused by Alastair Gillespie has placed more emphasis on improving the machinery for consultation with the various industrial sectors. For example, attempts have been made to improve the consultation process with the shipbuilding, textile, clothing, electrical, and footwear industries.[71] The Industrial Development Division of the department has been broadened from concentration on only nine sectors. The incentives grants are being revised in order to facilitate the development of a more flexible system of grants to industry. The new approach will allow the department to extend assistance to a wider range of industries than was previously the case.

The need for close co-operation with other departments such as Finance and External Affairs is obvious. For example, the significance of oil and gas negotiations between 1973 and 1975 required extensive interdepartmental co-operation. The Department of Finance conducted broad analytical work relating to the effects of oil and gas-price changes on the economy. This work was closely integrated with the departments of External Affairs and Energy, Mines and Resources. Another example of joint negotiations and policy development was reflected in the negotiations relating to the Kennedy Round Tariff negotiations and the Tokyo Round discussions in 1976-77. The Kennedy Round negotiations were actually headed by an official from IT&C. At the time of writing, the Tokyo Round negotiations were being led by

Rod Grey who had previously been an Assistant Deputy Minister in the Department of Finance. When a policy position is developed the actual memorandum may be signed jointly by the ministers of Finance and Industry, Trade and Commerce.

The Minister of IT&C is expected to give a sympathetic ear to the problems and demands of the business community. While he is not the only spokesman for business in the Cabinet he must take its views seriously since he must recommend policies to promote trade and efficient industry within the context of an efficient economy. Some observers have remarked that IT&C has experienced a greater degree of internal role conflict than Consumer and Corporate Affairs because some of the former's policies were designed to support greater competition while others were designed to protect Canadian industry from competition; sometimes by tariff barriers and at other times through incentive grants. However, in general, with the exception of his role in the Foreign Investment Review Agency, the Minister of IT&C does not perform a regulatory role, and hence he becomes a major promoter of industrial development.

If the role of the Minister of IT&C is placed in the context of government-industry relations, then there is clearly a need for a broad umbrella function which would impinge on several departments such as Energy, Mines and Resources, Transport, and the Ministry of State for Science and Technology in that there are several different types of industrial policies to be co-ordinated. Such discussions impinge on the planning of industrial development.[72] In this regard, the most recent attempt to formulate policies on Foreign Investment and Industrial Strategies are illustrative of the scope of government-industry relations.

The establishment of a Planning, Research and Evaluation Branch in IT&C was partially deliberate and partially opportunistic. During the 1972-73 fiscal year it was generally felt at the federal level that ministers and deputy ministers should have planning and policy-oriented groups "on close call" and that these Planning and Evaluation Groups should be located close to deputy ministers and should be plugged in at a fairly high level in the departmental policy-making process. In the case of IT&C the Planning and Evaluation Branch incorporated what was left of the Office of Economics which had been developed by Victor Macklin.

In keeping with the recognition that it is very difficult to plan globally, the emerging planning process in IT&C is attempting to formulate sector strategies. It is now acknowledged that the process requires far more detailed knowledge of given industries than general models could provide. Consequently, the planning group is increasingly attempting to weigh the benefits of putting resources into one particular industrial sector as compared to another. The department is attempting to assemble vast data on an input-output basis to facilitate efficiency improvements within particular industrial sectors.

It should be apparent from the foregoing that CANDIDE is not a satisfactory model for the Department of Industry, Trade and Commerce. CANDIDE is far too aggregative to serve the department's needs. Thus, at the time of writing, IT&C is developing a more elaborate model to handle more specific data within a longer time frame. Given the orientation of the department, any meaningful model must handle both the specific sectors of the economy and the international trade side. A useful model should be able to generate important information on policies affecting Canada's major foreign markets in a rapidly changing international environment. The model will operate within a longer time frame than either CANDIDE, the TRACE, or RDX2 models now in use within the federal government. The new model being developed by IT&C starts with a given industrial structure. It does not use historical data to the extent utilized by the other models. The new approach would allow IT&C to assess the implications of the policy thrusts of the other major departments such as Manpower and Immigration and Regional Economic Expansion. In short, IT&C is attempting to develop a wide-ranging but extremely flexible model to facilitate policy-making in a highly changing and volatile environment. The model must cope with both micro and macro problems of industrial development.

PROBLEMS OF INTERDEPARTMENTAL CO-ORDINATION

Between 1972 and 1976 the Department of Industry, Trade and Commerce participated in a large number of interdepartmental committees and task forces. These included an Interdepartmental Task Force on Energy to insure that Canada has enough energy to meet its needs; a review of government aid policies with CIDA; a review of foreign investment and multinational enterprises; a comparative review of major industrial policy developments; a study of the service sector; and a review of the department's industrial support programs (PAIT, IRDIA, DIP, etc.) to increase their efficiency and effectiveness. It also conducted policy assessments of direct concern to Canadian industry including taxation, labour legislation, energy policy, minerals policy, regional development, competition policy, tariffs, and environmental protection measures.[73]

Because IT&C is concerned with both domestic and international demand structure in the broadest sense, it must work closely with DREE whenever incentive grants are being provided to a particular industry. Since the reorganization of DREE in 1973-74, IT&C has played a major role in the work of the Regional Development Incentives Board[74] which advises the Minister of Regional Economic Expansion on whether or not a large incentives grant (one exceeding $1.5 million) should be offered to an industry and, if so, the amount and conditions of the grant. For appropriate cases, consultations are also held with other departments such as Agriculture and Environment. Membership on the Board consists of the Deputy Minister, the ADM for Planning and Co-ordination(DREE), and ADM from Finance, IT&C, Manpower and Immigration, Environment, and if appropriate, an ADM from such departments as Agriculture, and Energy, Mines and Resources.

There are conflicting objectives of the various departments in the regions. DREE has a major concern in creating jobs in the depressed areas but IT&C is concerned with the competitive position of these industries and accordingly with their long-term survival. DREE adopted a more co-ordinated approach with the provinces in 1974. There has always been some fear that DREE could be pulled into supporting short-term projects as was the case with the Atlantic Development Board. To avoid such a development, DREE, following its policy review, has improved its technical capabilities in the regions and is better able to conduct more cost-benefit analysis of the incentive grants program.

There is another dimension to the decentralization and co-ordination process, namely the dispersal of power and authority within and among different industries.[75] The decentralization of industrial organization can facilitate the achievement of greater flexibility in the structure of decision-making between various industries and within given industrial sectors. Efficiency in particular industries can be partly achieved through in-depth studies of specific industrial sectors. Efficient utilization of capital requires that it moves in the most efficient industrial sectors. It is worth recalling that the National Productivity Council had initiated efficiency studies within specific industrial sectors. Effectiveness requires that the movement of capital serve broad economic and social goals. Both aspects of a more decentralized approach to industrial location were referred to by the Hon. Alastair Gillespie when he concluded: "We need to develop many more Canadian entrepreneurs and support them with private and public venture funds. . . .we require much greater entrepreneurial and business thrust in the less developed parts of Canada."[76]

PROBLEMS IN GOVERNMENT-INDUSTRY RELATIONS

This chapter, more than any so far, demonstrates the unwieldy nature of economic management. We have looked at attempts to foster government-industry relations in order to provide jobs and to export goods and services. We turn now to an appraisal of some problems in government-industry relations. In addition to the problem, already stressed, of the general nature and scope of incentives to industry, there are four other areas which illustrate the complexities of government-industry relations in Canada. First, there is the problem of co-ordinating activities which are scattered throughout a diversified range of government departments. More specifically, there is the problem of integrating regional development with national growth. We will discuss later the efforts directed at formulating an industrial strategy. These are all closely related activities which are difficult to separate. Second, there is the issue of decentralization of industry which is indirectly related to the concentration of industries and to the provision of employment opportunities across the country. This aspect of economic management is affected by an important dimension of the Canadian political process, namely, federal-provincial relations. Third, there is the problem of small businesses. To what extent should government support small businesses? What relationship should exist between small businesses and large multinational exporting firms? Finally, there is the relationship which should exist between the Department of Industry, Trade and Commerce and selected policy groups such as the Ministry of State for Science and Technology. We will briefly summarize these issues before we conclude this chapter with a discussion of foreign ownership and the effort to develop industrial strategy, as illustrative cases in economic management.

First, since 1972 IT&C has been concerned with the formulation of a comprehensive industrial strategy for Canada which will be discussed later in this chapter. Initially, a comprehensive approach was outlined. However, due to the myriad policy spillovers the latest approach has attempted to identify a number of strategies. These strategies involve separate interfaces with a large number of departments. The Department of Industry, Trade and Commerce has been involved in consultation with Energy, Mines and Resources since the so-called "oil crisis" in 1973 especially since, in the short run, increases in the price of oil had placed Ontario in a disadvantageous position. The Department of Energy, Mines and Resources has a more clearly defined clientele than Industry, Trade and Commerce. IT&C also performs major promotional activities for the Department of Agriculture given the importance of farm products to some provinces.

Second, economic expansion and development involve important trade-offs between national growth and adequate participation from people in the depressed areas of the country. Consequently, the department has responded to demands for greater responsiveness to regional interests by decentralizing responsibilities to regional offices as in the case of the PAIT program. The department works closely with DREE which now has regional offices somewhat similar to the one adopted by IT&C. The two departments reflect a high degree of decentralization to the regions. DREE has established regional offices which are managed by assistant deputy ministers and IT&C has established a Regional Offices Branch under the Sr. ADM for Industry.

Between 1973 and 1974 IT&C, in order to improve its services to business and bring about better co-ordination with provincial governments on industrial, trade, and tourism matters, reorganized, strengthened, and expanded its regional offices.[77] An important aspect of this decentralization program was the decision to administer a number of industrial incentives and development programs on a regional basis. The department's efforts in this area were directed primarily at increasing the responsiveness to, and communication with, provincial government organizations and at expanding regional industrial development and export promotion services to medium- and small-sized businesses regardless of a company's location. From the perspective of an industrial strategy decentralization involves the formulation of a variety of policies to support and influence a variety of industries; for example, oil, gas, forestry (sulphur, potash, and forest products), and machinery.The western provinces had a role in the strengthening of regional offices which had the objective of establishing some balance between the capital-intensive oil and gas industries and the manufacturing industries.[78] An important aspect of the programs carried out by the regional offices is the recognition that the regions serve different types of industries in the respective provinces. In some provinces the forestry industry is most important while in others fisheries is the crucial aspect of the development program. There are, therefore, interdepartmental and federal-provincial committees for the forestry and fishing industries, among others.

The foregoing illustrates the reluctance of the provincial governments to support the broad development strategy which was adopted by DREE in 1969. The provinces have opposed a centralized approach to regional development. It can be said therefore, that the demand for decentralization in 1973 came partly from the provinces and their concern over the fishing, mining, and wood industrial sectors to give a few examples. The view was expressed that to get a proper feel for the development effort the responsible officials should be in the regions. The development of manufacturing industries has been a major demand in recent years by the western provinces.[79] In cases where there has been demand for improved regional development, strong emphasis has been placed on promoting small fabricating industries even in relatively rich Alberta. At the same time, major increases in oil prices which would be beneficial to Alberta and Saskatchewan can increase the cost of industries in central Canada and consequently, increase unemployment in these provinces. As a result there are major political difficulties associated with designing a development strategy and with the dispersal of industry in a federal state.

Third, the Department of Industry, Trade and Commerce, through its regional offices, attempts to aid small businesses which constitute over eighty per cent (in terms of number of businessmen) of the Canadian business community. In this regard, the department has always been decentralized given the fact that its clientele are located in the regions. It offers services in various regions in an endeavour to aid small businesses in their preparation of applications for assistance and support. The department has been delegating some of its activities to autonomous agencies. Accordingly, the recently established Federal Business Development Bank has assumed some of the regional activities of the department.[80] The counselling assistance program to small business, for example, has been transferred to the Federal Business Development Bank. It is worth emphasizing here also that many of the activities relating to small businesses have been linked to the goal of regional development. In fact, the establishment of DREE has been linked to demands made by officers of the Industrial Development Associations first created by the Area Development Agency which operated through the Department of Industry. At the March 1975 federal-provincial meeting of Ministers of Industry the primary goal endorsed by the ministers was "to achieve a greater balance of the distribution of people across Canada and within regions by extending the benefits of economic growth to all regions of Canada . . .".[81] Accordingly, social and political considerations impose severe constraints on economic criteria which may favour the location of industries in already developed areas. This fact reinforces again the necessity for links between DREE, IT&C, and the various economic policy-making departments mentioned above.

Finally, IT&C has also been redefining its role in relation to more specialized agencies such as the Minister of State for Science and Technology which now shares certain responsibilities for industrial innovation. R&D plays an important role in industrial development. IT&C has also been concerned with investment policy for a long time but there have been certain shifts in its development recently. As indicated earlier, IT&C initiated a system by which it conducted a quick survey of preliminary investment intentions. Shortly after the Economic Council was established it developed a five-year investment survey on the rationale that IT&C was concerned primarily with the short-term aspects of investment policy. Currently the work on investment intentions is carried out by the Planning, Research and Evaluation Branch of IT&C whose activities include economic advice to the department and some economic research into the longer-term objectives of the government.

Two critical areas which illustrate the complexities of planning and policy-making in IT&C are the "foreign ownership policy reviews" and the quest for "an industrial strategy" for Canada. Both areas were embarked on with broad general statements of the federal government's objectives but they were subsequently modified through various pressures from given industrial sectors and by varied demands from provinces with different problems to solve. Our review of these two policy reforms suggests that there can usually only be a consensus when policy objectives are stated in the broadest possible terms. However, when an attempt is made to operationalize the general framework the policy-making process is slowed down considerably. Thus, the two policy-making initiatives illustrate the move from a comprehensive framework to a more incremental approach when the policy was implemented. They are also illustrative of the planning process in Canada.

FOREIGN OWNERSHIP AND INDUSTRIAL STRATEGY: TWO CASES IN ECONOMIC POLICY-MAKING

Foreign ownership is a very political issue in that there are disagreements between political parties as well as between the federal government and the provinces.[82] The Province of New Brunswick, for example, has been less concerned with foreign ownership than with Canadian companies with headquarters in Toronto or Montreal. Foreign ownership therefore poses major questions of choice in economic-policy formulation.

Foreign investment has always been a significant component of total investment in Canada. It is clear that the evolution of past national policies has had a major influence on the nature of foreign investment in Canada. Major studies on foreign investment were done by the Gordon Commission in 1957 and by a task force and a parliamentary committee in the late 1960s and early 1970s. Other forces influencing foreign investment policies were discussions concerning natural resources development and attempts to protect Canadian secondary industry.[83] Most recently, attempts have been made by the government to build up Canadian-owned businesses *vis-à-vis* the foreign-control sector. These efforts have been reflected in the attempts to strengthen the role of the Industrial Development Bank, the subsequent establishment of a Federal Business Development Bank in 1975, and the establishment of the Canadian Development Corporation,[84] both designed, albeit in different ways, to provide financial support for Canadian ventures. The passage of the Foreign Investment Review Act and the establishment of the Foreign Investment Review Agency have intensified previous measures to restrict or, more accurately, to screen foreign investment.

In the analysis of the foreign investment issue political rhetoric should be distinguished from actual policies. For several political and economic reasons foreign investment still constitutes a major component of domestic investment.[85] Ontario, the most highly industrialized province, has adopted an ambivalent position toward foreign investment, placing major emphasis on Canadianization of management rather than on the restriction of foreign investment.[86] In general, the less-developed provinces have opted in favour of more foreign investment.

The various measures adopted in Canada with respect to Canadian investment show once more that there is a strong endorsement of the free-market system and that there has been strong support for an open economy. The commitment to private property and to a free competitive system is deeply rooted in Canada. The government of Canada has limited its role to overall regulation and support.

Foreign investment is a very pervasive issue affecting several closely related aspects of economic-policy formulation, including federal-provincial relations, the development of an industrial strategy, policies in specific sectors of the economy such as resources policy, manufacturing, and research and development. More specifically, it affects the nature and scope of Canadian capital markets and the nation's competitive position in the international environment.

The positions taken in recent years by Quebec, New Brunswick, Alberta, and Ontario on foreign investment illustrate provincial differences which prevent the endorsement of a national approach to foreign investment in a federal state. The quest for an industrial strategy also commenced with a grandiose design but recent demands by the western provinces to reverse the industrial structure in Canada make the endorsement of a comprehensive strategy even more difficult. The latest approach to formulating "the industrial strategy" seems to be restricted to endorsing strategies for industrial sectors.

The evolution of Canadian national policy on foreign investment illustrates the complex nature of the economic policy-making process. Furthermore, it demonstrates the tendency toward incrementalism rather than comprehensiveness in policy-making.

When couched in general terms, it has been demonstrated elsewhere that Canadians, for some time, have been in favour of reducing foreign investment. However, when the actual cost of such a decision is discussed, or when the trade-offs between the benefits *versus* the costs are presented the situation is rather different. It has been shown also that attitudes differ between elites and the population at large.[87] There are also strong regional variations in attitudes which have been reflected in federal-provincial negotiations. In short, it can be said that variations in the position of the provinces have served as a deterrent to any comprehensive policy. The Hon. Alastair Gillespie when he was Minister of IT&C experienced difficulty in gaining support of the provinces to develop a national investment policy.

Even more striking is the fact that the various departments at the federal level have adopted different approaches to the issue. For example, the Economic Council of Canada, since its establishment, has been a supporter of maintaining levels of foreign investment.[88] This position was directly related to the high priority given to economic growth and to the maintenance of high levels of employment. Within the Liberal party there have been differences between former influential ministers, such as Walter Gordon and Mitchell Sharp.[89] Consequently, while there has been a lot of discussion of foreign investment, the actual development of policies and programs have been rather slow. In short, the formulation of a strategy on foreign investment has been influenced on the one hand by public opinion and on the other by a variety of uniquely Canadian factors such as diversity of interests, government-business relationships, federal-provincial relations, and elite-mass relationships.

Let's look at how these issues have moved through the political process. The evaluation of the foreign investment issue tends to confirm the hypothesis of movement along a continuum of governing instruments, identified in Chapter 2, in that the federal response has been to launch several studies which suggested strong action on foreign investment. These include the 1957 Gordon Royal Commission on Canada's Economic Prospects, the 1968 Task Force on Foreign Investment under Professor Melville Watkins, and the Gray Report. They also include in the overall process a Report by a Select Committee of the Ontario legislature; and a study on multinational corporations by the Science Council of Canada.[90] Only reluctantly was the creation of a "screening" agency (FIRA) adopted in the early 1970s.

The economic policy issues which, in one way or another, all impinged on the role of IT&C encompassed such areas as research and development, capital markets, management-entrepreneurship considerations, and international competitiveness. If the issues are viewed more from the direction of production and marketing then they are influenced by policy considerations in areas such as product specialization, rationalization of industry, the formulation of tariff policy, and ultimately by international trade arrangements such as the Kennedy and the Tokyo Round negotiations. In a more practical way, the Canada–U.S. Auto Pact, the STOL Project, the Michelin Plant in the Maritimes, and assistance to the Petrochemical Industry all affect Canada's employment, balance-of-payment, capital-market, and industrial policies.[91]

Given the limited size of the Canadian market and given the vastness of the United States' economy some kind of product specialization has been considered to be most attractive to some influential policy-makers. In fact, it was such considerations which led to the Automotive Agreement. In addition, the rationalization of selected Canadian industries through merger could make Canadian firms more internationally competitive. Accordingly, at the time of writing, a number of electrical companies were in the process of merging. The then new Minister of Industry, Trade and Commerce, Jean Chrétien, had begun to talk in terms of supporting selective industries in Canada to enhance the nation's competitive position abroad.

If the above-mentioned issues are taken into account then we should not be surprised to discover that rather than reducing foreign investment by regulation, the Canadian government established a "screening" agency such as FIRA which is really a negotiating body rather than a regulatory agency in the traditional sense.[92] Similarly, it is not surprising that opinions have differed among groups across the country on the role and significance of this agency. The government's position has been stated in the recent Annual Report of FIRA. The agency determines "significant benefit" by taking into account such factors as employment, exports, use of Canadian goods and services, technology, and Canadian participation.

More specifically, the factors taken into account are:

a) the effect on the level and nature of economic activity in Canada, including the effect on employment, on resource processing, on the utilization of

Canadian parts, components and services, and on exports;

b) the degree and significance of participation by Canadians in the business enterprise and in the industry sector to which the enterprise belongs;
c) the effect on productivity, industrial efficiency, technological development, innovation, and product variety;
d) the effect on competition within any industry or industries in Canada;
e) compatibility with national industrial and economic policies, taking into consideration industrial and economic policy objectives enunciated by a province likely to be significantly affected by the proposed investment.[93]

Foreign investment has increased in recent years. Moreover, both public and private organizations have forecast a requirement of investment in excess of domestic savings.[94] Given this paradox the government has repeatedly stated that the purpose of the Act is not to block investment nor to discourage it as such, but rather to insure that the foreign investment constitutes "a significant benefit to Canada".

The search for an industrial strategy under two ministers in the department, namely Jean-Luc Pépin and Alastair Gillespie, shows how difficult it often is to define public policy-making problems. The review shows further that the strategy must be broadly set and that allowances must be made for adjustments particularly at the implementation stage. The Hon. Jean-Luc Pépin had initially defined the industrial strategy by identifying every conceivable policy instrument as being related to the attainment of an optimal industrial strategy. He noted, for example, that an industrial strategy for Canada included issues ranging from "women's lib" (e.g., its effects on rates of participation in the labour force) and control of foreign investments to bilingualism and competition policy. Applied to industry "the term means the proper planning by government (federal) for the optimum coordination of policies and decisions, on the use of all productive resources, in order to achieve defined (and accepted) social and economic goals. The strategy must embrace all sectors of economic activity from resources to services, but must emphasize manufacturing and processing."[95]

As we have noted earlier, the Hon. Alastair Gillespie abandoned the earlier approach and adopted a series of "sector strategies" on an integrated basis. The new approach reflects incrementalism rather than comprehensiveness. The department has taken the position, at the time of writing, that it should look closely at major industrial sectors (for example, machinery and transportation) and constantly review them in accordance with the changing economic situation. The department was seriously concerned that if Canadian production "costs" were not significantly reduced the country's competitive position would be eroded.

In short, economic management in IT&C has been moving in the direction of micro considerations or a more detailed assessment of the efficiency of particular industrial sectors. The government's strategy then is to concentrate its incentives and other forms of support to industry in leading sectors. The government will aid sensitive industries which are placed in a disadvantageous position due to rising costs. The long-term goal is to rationalize the competitive position of Canadian industries.

What are some of the factors which have influenced the rejection of a comprehensive industrial strategy? Historically, Canada's industrial strategy had two components. First, it was based on the development of natural resources supported by an appropriate tax and communications network. Second, the policy was geared to the development of manufacturing behind a tariff wall to serve the domestic market. The 1972 policy review enunciated by Jean-Luc Pépin did not appear different from the general aims of economic policy. In addition to economic growth, the strategy included equitable distribution of income both personal and regional, equilibrium in the balance of payments, sovereignty over natural resources, environmental protection, and improvements in the quality of life. On a more pragmatic level two issues were most significant: the creation of jobs for a growing and increasingly more diversified population; and the achievement of a high level of sophistication of Canadian industry. Both national and regional industrial strategy suggests the slowing down of the resources sector and the need to accelerate manufacturing given the fact that the latter produces more jobs.

Greater restrictions will be placed on the export of Canadian resources as compared to the previous resources policy. However, rather than an absolute reduction in exports more emphasis has been placed in recent years on insuring that the income derived from these nonrenewable resources are effectively utilized. In response to the sudden increase in oil prices in 1973 the federal government introduced tax measures to capture the excess profits and later introduced a two-price system as a form of subsidy.[96] At the provincial level the government of Alberta has been most aggressive in insuring that long-term benefits accrue to the province from its resources. Since 1973 the issue of resources taxation has been a central part of budget policy and concomitantly of federal-provincial discussions. The decision to raise the price of oil to a level closer to the world-market price and the decision to grant concessions to the mining industry to encourage exploration were heatedly debated during the mid-1970s.[97] Vigorous measures have been adopted since 1972 to expand manufacturing in order to reduce the rising level of unemployment.

The establishment of the Canada Development Corporation, the establishment of the Federal Business Development Bank, and the invigoration of the Export Development Corporation were all aimed at facilitating some type of industrial strategy. The relationship which should exist between large corporations and small businesses became more apparent in 1976 when a Ministry of State for Small Business was established. The establishment of the Ministry of State for Science and Technology, the strengthening of the division in the Department of Finance dealing with capital markets, and the most recent attempts to create greater product specialization are also illustrative. The transfer of Jean Chrétien from the Treasury Board to become Minister of Industry, Trade and Commerce further illustrates the emphasis being placed on formulating a set of industrial strategies. The announcement by Mr. Chrétien that the federal government will discriminate in its support of selected industries seems to demonstrate a greater readiness to take risks and to plan a more aggressive industrial policy. Apart from the developments in the areas of research and development, capital markets, and entrepreneurship, efforts were also being made to diversify Canada's trade relationships.

A number of steps have been taken to broaden Canada's trade relationships. The United States is Canada's greatest trading partner. The prevailing view is that this will continue into the future. However, with the development of trading blocs Canada has been attempting to strengthen its trade links with the European Common Market, with Latin America, and with Japan. Notwithstanding these moves there are strong pressures supporting a Continental Trading Bloc with the United States. The foregoing demonstrates that foreign ownership, industrial strategies, and trade policies are highly complex and interrelated areas of economic-policy formulation.

Both the foreign investment and the industrial strategy reviews which took place between 1972 and 1976 required extensive inter-departmental co-ordination of policy-making. Jean-Luc Pépin as Minister of Industry, Trade and Commerce was the central cabinet figure behind the industrial strategy review. However, while the centre of co-ordination was a relatively small unit in the Department of Industry, Trade and Commerce, the discussions evolved into a much broader approach. Consequently, by 1976 the revised approach to the work encompassed contributors from departments such as External Affairs, Finance, Labour, and related agencies. Both policy areas demonstrate therefore the role of IT&C, the interrelatedness of economic policy, the persistence of intergovernmental and public-private sector conflict, and the necessity to develop effective mechanisms for economic planning.

NOTES

1. See M. Weber, *The Theory of Social and Economic Organization* (Toronto, 1964). See also N. Birnbaum, "Conflicting Interpretations of the Rise of Capitalism: Marx and Weber", *The British Journal of Sociology*, Vol. IV (June 1953).

2. B. L. Smith, ed., *The New Political Economy: The Public Use of the Private Sector* (New York, 1975), p. 8.

3. See T. N. Brewis, *Regional Economic Policies in Canada* (Toronto, 1969), and R. W. Phidd, "Regional Development Policy", in G. Bruce Doern and V. S. Wilson, eds., *Issues in Canadian Public Policy* (Toronto, 1974).

4. See, for example, A. G. Green, "Regional Economic Disparities", in L. H. Officer and L. B. Smith, eds., *Issues in Canadian Economics* (Toronto, 1974), pp. 354-70.

5. See Economic Council of Canada, *First Annual Review* (Ottawa, 1964). See also the regional economic objectives agreed to by federal and provincial Ministers of Industry, 1975.

6. See, for example, D. Waldo, *The Administrative State: A Study of the Political Theory of American Public Administration* (New York, 1948); A. Shonfield, *Modern Capitalism: The Changing Balance of Public and Private Power* (London, 1969), pp. 298-357; and Smith, *The New Political Economy*.

7. The current discussions concerning the role of small businesses in Canada are worth examining. Note the establishment of the Federal Business Development Bank. See also G. Sinclair, "We Lack Innovative Industry But Don't Really Know Why", *The Financial Post*, January 15, 1977.

8. See Economic Council of Canada, *People and Jobs: A Study of the Canadian Labour Market* (Ottawa, 1976).

9. A. Cairncross, ed., *Essays in Economic Management* (London, 1971), chapters 1 to 3.

10. See Hon. J. L. Pépin, Minister of Industry, Trade and Commerce, "On Industrial Strategy". Speech to the Annual General Meeting of the Canadian Manufacturers' Association in Edmonton, June 5, 1972.

11. Hon. A. Gillespie, Minister of Industry, Trade and Commerce, Speech to the Canadian Manufacturers' Association, January 30, 1975.

12. Ibid.

13. Ibid.

14. See the most useful analysis of this issue by N. W. Chamberlain, *Private and Public Planning* (New York, 1965).

15. The policy instruments used by this department should be compared with those used by the Bank of Canada, the Department of Finance, Regional Economic Expansion, Consumer and Corporate Affairs, and Manpower and Immigration. On the broader issue of the role of incentives in the modern Canadian economy see J. Maxwell, *Policy Review and Outlook, 1975: Restructuring the Incentive System* (Montreal, 1975).

16. Information Canada, *Federal Services for Business: A Guide to Grants, Loans, and Sources of Counsel Available from the Federal Government* (Ottawa, 1974), especially pp. 43-51.

17. Ibid., pp. 50-51.

18. This is a most important aspect of planning which is generally not

emphasized. It represents a critical aspect of an industrial strategy. In February 1977, for example, it was announced that the federal government plans to pool six major assistance programs under a new concept, "Enterprise Development Program". The macro-micro aspects of the policy are reflected in the creation of a National Board to be supported by the regional Boards. Department of Industry, Trade and Commerce, *Annual Report, 1976-77* (Ottawa, 1977).

19. J. M. DesRoches, "The Creation of New Administrative Structures: The Federal Department of Industry", *Canadian Public Administration,* Vol. VIII (September 1965), pp. 285-91.

20. Brewis, *Regional Economic Policies in Canada,* pp. 138-40.

21. Interviews.

22. 28th Parl., 1968-69. The Senate of Canada, *Proceedings of the Special Committee on Science Policy,* no. 34 (March 5, 1969), Department of Finance, pp. 3644-52. See also appendix statement by R. B. Bryce, then Deputy Minister of Finance.

23. Interviews between 1969 and 1975 with several officials in the Department of Industry, Trade and Commerce.

24. Interviews.

25. See Chapter 12 in which we discuss various aspects of "conflict and consensus management". See also Phidd, "Regional Development Policies".

26. DesRoches, "The Creation of New Administrative Structures", pp. 285-91.

27. Ibid.

28. Ibid., p. 286.

29. Government of Canada, Government Organization Act, 1969. See also DesRoches, "The Creation of New Administrative Structures".

30. See R. W. Phidd, "The Role of Central Advisory Councils: The Economic Council of Canada", in G. Bruce Doern and Peter Aucoin, eds., *The Structures of Policy-Making in Canada* (Toronto, 1971), p. 211.

31. With the Economic Council's abandonment of the National Conference Secretariat, the Department of Industry, Trade and Commerce has been moving in the direction of a stronger industrial and regional planning role.

Note the announcement in February 1977 of the formation of a National Board and Regional Boards under the Enterprise Development Program. See "Government to Pool 6 Aid Plans to Spur Industrial Activity", *The Globe and Mail*, February 9, 1977, p. B1.

32. Hon. J. L. Pépin, *Annual Report of the Department of Industry, Trade and Commerce* (Ottawa, 1971), p. 10.

33. Ibid.

34. See Department of Regional Economic Expansion, *The New Approach* (Ottawa, 1976), pp. 14-16.

35. Here again the close relationships between the various economic-policy instruments should be noted. See, for example, Government of Canada, *The Way Ahead: A Framework for Discussion* (Ottawa, 1976), pp. 23-31.

36. Department of Industry, Trade and Commerce, *Annual Report, 1974-75* (Ottawa, 1975).

37. These various advisory bodies reflect the micro-macro linkages which must be established in economic planning.

38. The gradual emergence of a more centralized strategy has been reflected in various departmental policies since 1972. The Annual Meeting of Federal and Provincial Ministers of Industry should be noted.

39. See Western Economic Opportunities Conference, *Industrial and Trade Development*. Background paper, Conference on Western Economic Opportunities in Calgary, July 24-26, 1973, pp. 10-16, 23-24.

40. Interviews.

41. See Federal Business Development Bank Act.

42. Department of Industry, Trade and Commerce, *Regional Offices Branch*. Document (Ottawa, 1974), pp. 1-9.

43. Interviews. However, for details on the actual approach adopted see *Annual Report of the Department of Industry, Trade and Commerce*, April 1, 1969 to March 31, 1970.

44. For the development of these aspects see the following: Economic Council of Canada Advisory Committee on Industrial Research and Technology, *A*

General Incentive Programme to Encourage Research and Development in Canadian Industry (Ottawa, 1965); R. W. Phidd, "The National Productivity Council" and "The National Productivity Council, 1961-63", in "The Economic Council and Economic Policy Formulation in Canada". Unpublished PhD thesis, Queen's University, Kingston, 1972; and A. H. Wilson, *Background to Invention*. Science Council of Canada Special Study No. 11 (Ottawa, 1970) and *Governments and Innovation* (Ottawa, 1973), especially pp. 53-77.

45. For an excellent analysis of MOSST see Peter Aucoin and R. French, *Knowledge and Power* (Ottawa, 1975). See also G. Bruce Doern, *Science and Politics in Canada* (Montreal, 1972).

46. The various incentives programs were under revision at the time of writing. Thus the sources cited below reflected the program up to 1976. In early 1977 IT&C announced the integration of the programs under the Enterprise Development Programme: 1977. On the position prior to this see R. A. Mathews, *Industrial Viability in a Free Trade Economy: A Program of Adjustment Policies for Canada* (Toronto, 1971) and Wilson, *Governments and Innovation*.

47. This study influenced the changes referred to in note 46 above.

48. Wilson, *Governments and Innovation* and Mathews, *Industrial Viability in a Free Trade Economy*.

49. *Annual Report of the Department of Industry, Trade and Commerce,* April 1, 1969 to March 31, 1970, p. 13.

50. Ibid.

51. Department of Industry, Trade and Commerce, *Annual Report, 1973-74*.

52. Ibid.

53. For a more detailed analysis of the earlier promotional role of the National Productivity Council see Phidd, "The Economic Council and Economic Policy Formulation in Canada", pp. 119-22, 140-52.

54. The recent concern for our productivity improvements have led to a stronger emphasis on production as compared with social welfare measures which have been reoriented to support the work ethic.

55. On the search for an industrial strategy see Pépin, "On Industrial Strategy".

56. Interviews.

57. This approach has been emerging more explicitly with the appointment of J. Chrétien as Minister of Industry, Trade and Commerce late in 1976.

58. See note 46 above.

59. Pépin, "On Industrial Strategy".

60. See Economic Council of Canada, *Eleventh Annual Review* (Ottawa, 1974), Chapter 8, pp. 177-200. See also *Twelfth Annual Review* (Ottawa, 1975), especially p. 113. The emphasis on productivity should be noted. On the role of the Council in regard to planning and industrial policy see R. W. Phidd, "The Economic Council Annual Review: Whither Economic Planning in Canada?" *Canadian Public Policy*, Vol. II (1976), pp. 262-69.

61. S. S. Cohen, *Modern Capitalist Planning: The French Model* (Cambridge, 1969). See also V. Lutz, *Central Planning for the Market Economy* (London, 1969).

62. Gillespie, Speech to the Canadian Manufacturers' Association.

63. Government of Canada, *The Way Ahead*, pp. 16-23.

64. This was manifested in the creation of the position of Minister of State for Small Business. See Chapter 3 for an analysis of ministries of state.

65. Interviews.

66. DesRoches, "The Creation of New Administrative Structures".

67. Gillespie, Speech to the Canadian Manufacturers' Association.

68. Cohen, *Modern Capitalist Planning*. However, indications early in 1977 seem to reflect a change in Canadian policy. The early speeches by Hon. J. Chrétien as Minister of Industry, Trade and Commerce seem to point to a stronger planning role and strategy. On the relationship between planning and regulation see L. Mizard, "Planning as the Regulatory Reproduction of the Status Quo", in J. Hayward and M. Watson, eds., *Planning Politics and Public Policy: The British, French and Italian Experience* (London, 1975), pp. 433-44.

69. See *How to Improve Business-Government Relations in Canada: A Report to the Minister of Industry, Trade and Commerce* (Ottawa, 1976).

70. Pépin, "On Industrial Strategy", p. 12.

71. Gillespie, Speech to the Canadian Manufacturers' Association.

72. Again, it should be emphasized that a number of separate but inter-related changes in the mid-1970s seem to be moving toward a more comprehensive strategy.

73. Industry, Trade and Commerce, *Annual Report, 1974-75.*

74. Regional Economic Expansion, *The New Approach.*

75. For an excellent analysis of this issue see Robert A. Solo, *The Political Authority and the Market System* (Cincinnati, 1974).

76. Gillespie, Speech to the Canadian Manufacturers' Association.

77. Industry, Trade and Commerce, *Annual Report, 1974-75.*

78. Western Economic Opportunities Conference, *Industrial and Trade Development,* pp. 7, 17-31; *Mineral Resource Development,* pp. 7-35; and *Capital Financing and Financial Institutions,* pp. 7-50.

79. Western Economic Opportunities Conference, *Regional Development Opportunities,* pp. 18, 20-22.

80. See Federal Business Development Bank, *Annual Report, 1976.*

81. News Release, Federal-Provincial Trade Ministers Meeting, March 10-11, 1975. The ministers subsequently released a statement on Industrial Development Goals.

82. J. Fayerweather, *Foreign Investment in Canada: Prospects for National Policy* (Toronto, 1974).

83. For studies on foreign investment see *Foreign Ownership and the Structure of Canadian Industry,* Report of the Task Force on the Structure of Canadian Industry (Ottawa, 1968); *Foreign Direct Investment in Canada* (Ottawa, 1972); *Report of the Commons Standing Committee on External Affairs and National Defence* (Wahn Report), (Ottawa, 1970); and D. Godfrey and M. Watkins, eds., *Gordon to Watkins to You* (Toronto, 1970).

84. See W. Gordon, *Storm Signals: New Economic Policies for Canada* (Toronto, 1975), Chapter 6.

85. For an early review of foreign investment see T. E. H. Reid, ed., *Economic*

Planning in a Democratic Society (Toronto, 1963), pp. 56-64. See also Foreign Investment Review Act and Industry, Trade and Commerce, *Annual Report, 1974-75.*

86. Government of Ontario, *Report of the Interdepartmental Task Force on Foreign Investment* (Toronto, 1971).

87. See, for example, Fayerweather, *Foreign Investment in Canada.*

88. See Gordon, *Storm Signals,* especially p. 93.

89. Ibid.

90. Fayerweather, *Foreign Investment in Canada.*

91. Ibid.

92. On the relationships between FIRA and other types of regulatory boards see G. Bruce Doern, ed., *The Regulatory Process in Canada* (Toronto, 1978), chapters 1 and 2. See Hon. D. Jamieson, "Foreign Investment Review Act", *Annual Report, 1974-75.*

93. Jamieson, "Foreign Investment Review Act".

94. See Economic Council of Canada, *Twelfth Annual Review.*

95. Pépin, "On Industrial Strategy".

97. See J. Maxwell, *Policy Review and Outlook, 1975: Restructuring the Incentive System* (Montreal, 1975) and *Policy Review and Outlook, 1976: Challenges to Complacency* (Montreal, 1976).

CHAPTER NINE

The Role of the Department of Regional Economic Expansion

The establishment, structure, and functioning of the federal Department of Regional Economic Expansion (DREE) demonstrates several difficulties encountered by policy-makers in defining economic policy areas and in implementing relevant programs. Contemporary studies of public-policy formulation show that these difficulties permeate several governmental agencies.[1]

This chapter will demonstrate the difficulties in defining the parameters of regional development policy because of the varied perceptions of groups within provinces which are affected by the policies and programs adopted by various governments. Central to an analysis of regional policies is the recognition that regional institutions emerge to satisfy a myriad of needs, including material resources, the integration of local and autonomous demands with the broader institutional requirements, and the need for an adequate organizational structure staffed with competent personnel capable of performing the functions assigned.

Early Canadian regional programs were basically *ad hoc* approaches to cope with demands in a specific location or from given groups, albeit with different problems. For example, the Prairie Farm Rehabilitation Program and the Maritime Marshland Rehabilitation Scheme dealt with problems associated with drought and floods, and hence were directed at a given geographical region. The Agricultural Rural Development Act, which had a narrower base when passed in 1961, has been broadened to include fisheries and tourism. On the whole an attempt has been made over the years to extend earlier programs in at least three respects: first, there has been an attempt to expand the original rural base of the programs; second, there has been a tendency to emphasize both their economic and social aspects;

and third, there has been a trend toward extending the programs throughout the country rather than restricting them to given regions. The inclusion of Northern Ontario within the most industrialized province as part of a northern development strategy illustrates this trend. Consequently, the term "region" has been used in the past as that area defined as a region for the purpose of the particular problem under consideration.

The shifts in values which have preceded legislative changes have also produced changes in the location of the programs among a number of related departments such as Agriculture, Forestry, and Rural Development and Industry. The early 1960s saw an emphasis on infra-structure projects (roads, sewage, schools), particularly in the Atlantic provinces. Subsequent strategies directed at reducing regional disparities emphasized both economic growth and social development simultaneously. The policies pursued between 1969 and 1973 placed greater emphasis on the urban-centred region in contrast to the previous rural emphasis reflected in the work of the Canadian Council on Rural Development, originally an advisory body to the Department of Forestry and Rural Development.

These changes have blurred the distinction between economic and social policies. Thus the diversity of interests which must be captured in formulating regional policies impose new strains on the various governmental structures operating in the regions and they constitute a major component of the demand for more horizontal co-ordinating mechanisms to handle problems which cut across departmental lines.

The diversity of programs adopted are clearly reflected in the following governmental reforms: the Prairie Farm Rehabilitation Administration (PFRA); the Agricultural and Rural Development Agency (ARDA); the Fund for Rural Economic Development (FRED); the Area Development Agency (ADA), and the related Area Development Incentives Act; the Atlantic Development Board (ADB) which provided the nucleus for special areas; the 1969 Government Reorganization Act which made provision for the Department of Regional Economic Expansion (DREE) and the Regional Development Incentives Act; and finally the General Development Agreements, a conceptual framework within which subsidiary ten-year agreements are made. These different programs reveal the heterogeneity rather than homogeneity of Canada's regions and the necessity for a decentralized development planning strategy.[2]

The changes being made since 1970 show that, despite the creation of the Department of Regional Economic Expansion, a number of difficulties have been encountered and greater emphasis is being placed on more horizontal linkages between a number of departments and between urban and rural policies and programs. The increased complexity and interrelatedness of these programs have created new demands and responses for better policy-planning, co-ordination, and implementation strategies between various departments at the federal level and between the federal government and various provincial governments with different administrative capabilities and with varied problems to solve. The changes have also necessitated collaboration between the public and private sectors.[3]

The evolution of regional development policy demonstrates that there are intricate conflicts and contradictions in the program pursued. First, there is the conflict between growth objectives, as represented in the policies pursued under ADA, and distributional objectives on an area-basis as well as on a personal income basis, as shown, for example, in ARDA. Second, there is the conflict between a centralized, as compared to a decentralized, response which is compounded by the fact that the seeming unity of the federal government is unlikely to be reflected in regional development administration because of strong sectoral pressures working in the opposite direction. Yet there is the general belief that the initiative in regional development must rest in federal hands because that is where the available funds are to be found. Third, there are conflicts related to isolating the planning of regional development policies from its implementation, a major dilemma which may undermine the achievement of the objectives sought.

In recent years both the federal and provincial governments have attached importance to management of the economy which in turn has led to increased concern with regional development. Thus more persistent attention has been given to the possibilities for integrating the work of the Department of Finance, the Bank of Canada, the Federal Business Development Bank, the Treasury Board (the Management Committee of Cabinet), the Ministry of Transport (transportation policy), Industry, Trade and Commerce (industrial strategies), the Department of the Environment, and the Department of Agriculture with the relatively new Department of Regional Economic Expansion. The recognition of the need to improve consultation and co-ordination between a number of departments and agencies operating in various regions has led to demands for the decentralization of the governmental machinery and of strategic decision-makers.[4] However, decentralization may take the form of either regionalization of central agencies (deconcentration) or of co-operation among the provinces themselves, as demonstrated recently by the Prairie provinces, two of which, generally speaking, have governments with similar ideological orientations. The foregoing considerations exemplify the inherent political and administrative problems which led the former Minister of Regional Economic Expansion, the Hon. Donald Jamieson, to advocate a "multi-dimensional approach" to regional development. In order to improve the mechanism for co-ordination a Regional Development Incentives Board (RDIB) was established under RDIA to give advice on large incentives loans.

This chapter reviews inherent difficulties in formulating a comprehensive regional development policy. In fact there are always spill-over problems which inhibit neat compartmentalization of a policy field. For example, welfare programs may be more effective in arresting regional disparities than policies deliberately contrived for that purpose. The recognition of these problems will influence the political and managerial strategies adopted by the various governments. Given these difficulties the chapter adopts a selective approach. First, it examines the evolution of a number of regional development programs adopted during the past decade and accordingly shows how changes in values were reflected in various governmental reorganizations. Second, it reviews the development and structure of DREE in the planning and implementation of a public policy field. Third, it evaluates current and prospective problems in the agency's operation. Finally, the chapter concludes with a brief commentary on structural problems in decentralizing a department which is expected to formulate a coherent regional policy from a multiplicity of disparate programs.

ECONOMIC MANAGEMENT AND REGIONAL POLICY

The Conservative government under John Diefenbaker, with strong rural support, played an important role in the initial stages of regional development policies when it passed the Agricultural Rehabilitation Development Act (ARDA) in 1961. The Act had four basic provisions:

(1) To authorize the Minister of Agriculture to enter into agreements with the provinces concerning projects dealing with alternative land use, development of income and employment opportunities in rural agricultural areas, and land and water conservation;
(2) To make payments to the provinces with regard to such agreements;
(3) To undertake research in connection with the kind of project envisaged; and
(4) To establish advisory committees in respect of the first three provisions.

The orientation of the legislation was, clearly enough, resource-based. As the minister responsible phrased it: "If any person tries to divorce this (ARDA) from the over-all agricultural policy of the government, that person does a great injustice to what we are attempting to do here."[5]

The ARDA legislation extended the operation of strategies initiated earlier under the Prairie Farm Rehabilitation Act (PFRA), which established policies for improvements in land use and the development of agricultural soil and water resources. It is worth emphasizing that the PFRA program was launched in the drought years at a time when repeated crop failures and widespread farm abandonment gave rise to fears that large areas of western Canada would be lost to agriculture.[6] ARDA was an integral part of an overall agricultural development policy of the federal government.

The conflicting orientation of ARDA and related forestry and rural development programs was demonstrated in 1966 when responsibility for ARDA was transferred from the Department of Agriculture to the then new department of Forestry and Rural Development. Two analysts have observed that the transfer of ARDA to Forestry and Rural Development could only detract from its close relationship to other on-going programs of agricultural development in the areas of price stabilization, credit, crop insurance, and so forth. These analysts observed simultaneously that ARDA was nevertheless placed in a position to encourage a unique approach to regional development.[7]

The program was based on federal-provincial financial contributions, and some provinces were placed at a disadvantage in utilizing the allocated resources. Consequently, by the time the first agreement expired in 1965 only two-thirds of the $50 million set aside under the legislation had actually been committed, and only Quebec, Manitoba, and Saskatchewan had exhausted their allotment.

A second conflict in regional development strategies in the

mid-1960s followed from the fact that primary responsibility for the initiation and implementation of projects remained with the provinces. At this point it should be mentioned that we are now confronted with the complex task of isolating planning and administrative problems in a federal state.[8] The main functions of the federal government were limited to cost-sharing, policy co-ordination, and the provision of technical and specialist services, and, where required, to supplement the comparatively less substantial staff resources of the provinces.[9] In this regard an analysis of DREE becomes in fact a case study of development planning.[10]

The creation of the Atlantic Development Board (ADB) represented the first comprehensive, albeit essentially spatial, strategy to arrest regional disparities in Canada. The Board, established in 1962 by the Conservatives but expanded in 1963 by the Liberals, was the product of recommendations by the Atlantic Provinces Economic Council (formed in 1954) and the Royal Commission on Canada's Economic Prospects, a federal body which reported in 1957.

The Board was established to deal with policy issues which were of provincial or joint federal-provincial jurisdiction. The Board (ADB) required close co-operation with provincial authorities in all phases of its work. The ADB performed at least three important functions: first, it was given the responsibility for preparing, in consultation with the Economic Council of Canada, an integrated overall co-ordinated plan for the promotion of the economic growth of the Atlantic region; second, it co-ordinated measures of an interdepartmental nature initiated by departments which dealt with the Atlantic region; third, it became a convenient vehicle for administering various special assistance programs to the region.[11] In all three respects the Board was confronted with a conflict between proceeding with development projects on an *ad hoc* basis as compared to the preparation of an overall co-ordinated plan for the region.[12]

In 1966 a Fund for Rural Economic Development (FRED) was established to deal with rural economic development programs in special rural development areas. The initial $50 million was increased in 1967 to $300 million. Consequently, the Department of Forestry and Rural Development, DREE'S predecessor, was administering in 1967, one year after its establishment, two programs which had two distinct aspects:

(1) The individual ARDA project approach, not necessarily integrated with other developmental projects, which in practice had tended toward improvement of the physical resource base; and

(2) The new FRED comprehensive plan which was a package of essentially related projects of economic development and social development.

In December 1960 the first federal program designed specifically to assist the manufacturing industry, the "Area Development Program", was launched. The 1963 establishment of an Area Development Agency closely allied to the Department of Industry represented another step toward a more comprehensive regional development policy. The 1963 Act which established the Department of Industry simultaneously made provision for the establishment under the direction of the minister of an area development agency. It made provision also for the appointment of a commissioner for area development. The Area Development Agency had a number of important objectives related to regional development; first, it was specifically directed at areas with high and chronic unemployment; second, it was intended to facilitate or speed up economic development or industrial adjustment; third, it was to be a co-ordinating mechanism at the federal level which would include an input from the Minister of Industry; fourth, by creating a co-ordinating mechanism at the federal level it would act as a catalyst to facilitate new investment by both the federal and provincial governments with the specific objective of creating new employment; and fifth, the agency was to encourage research and prepare programs and projects which would improve economic development in designated areas.[13] Consequently, the major thrust of the Area Development Agency and the Area Development Incentives Act of 1965 was one of arresting chronic unemployment. The extraordinarily high level of unemployment in particular regions introduced another contradiction in developing a comprehensive policy in that attempts to reduce unemployment in depressed areas have the potential for reducing aggregate economic growth.

Thus far, our brief review of regional development policies has described the numerous *ad hoc* approaches. These ranged from attacks on floods and droughts, and social development in given rural areas, to investment strategies designed to achieve growth and to arrest unemployment and even an indirect endorsement of economic planning depicted by the Acts which established the Economic Council, and the Atlantic Development Board.

Regional planning, if it is to be successful, must be part of a comprehensive system of planning. Accordingly, the early 1960s saw the emergence of "two planning agencies", the Economic Council of Canada and the Atlantic Development Board.[14] The Economic Council pointed to the need for better federal-provincial liaison in regional policies. It emphasized, among others, two aspects of Canada's regional policies: first, improved administrative co-ordination; and second, that stronger emphasis be placed on a growth-oriented approach which would provide for greater spill-over effects from the more prosperous areas to the more depressed ones. The second point illustrates the concern of economists that without adequate economic growth income distribution would be regressive for the country as a whole.

The two points converge in the Council's recommendation that the federal government develop an integrated approach to regional development because "a favourable national environment may not in itself ensure balanced regional participation". In order to achieve optimal national growth and redistribution of income to the lower regions it was necessary to develop a co-ordinated administrative machinery. The Atlantic Development Board was specifically instructed by its Act to formulate in consultation with the Economic Council a comprehensive, long-term plan aimed at the expansion of employment and the increase of productivity needed to raise relative levels of growth in the entire Atlantic region.

In 1966 the Council advocated the development of a deliberate and consistent focus on the regional problem within the federal administration. Hence, it took the position that:

> The objective of regionally balanced growth, as we have defined it, raises the larger issue of attempting to assess the total potential impact of numerous separate programs upon a particular region and bringing them together in the most consistent, efficient manner. The question might be illustrated, for example, simply by asking whether and how such activities as the rural adjustment and relocation program of the Department of Forestry and Rural Development, the manpower training and mobility measures of the Department of Manpower and Immigration, the area industrial grants and incentives of the

Department of Industry, the transportation subsidies of the Department of Transport and the capital grants of the Atlantic Development Board, are all brought together, along with other federal activities in a consistent, mutually reinforcing way in helping to raise the levels of productivity and income in the Atlantic Provinces.[15]

The Council's recommendations implied that there should be a highly centralized machinery at the federal level complemented by deconcentration within the regions. "This suggests the need for collation and analysis of activities in a *horizontal* or area perspective, as well as from a *vertical or functional* point of view." The Council concluded that:

. . . such collation and appraisal of federal programs belongs *not in any one operating department, but within the central machinery of government.* In the present organizational framework, one obvious possibility for assuming this responsibility is the *Treasury Board.* The Board has, as one of its main duties, the detailed study of all operational proposals from departments. Hence it would be in an excellent position to extend this examination to appraise the overall regional impact of all federal operations, draw attention to conflict or clarifying the functions and responsibilities of different agencies, help in avoiding duplication or effort and expenditures, identify gaps which might well be filled by existing policies and generally assure adequate interdepartmental communication [emphasis added].[16]

Beyond the need for co-ordination of federal policies and programs in Ottawa the Council felt it was necessary to provide an improved administrative framework to assure the consistent, yet appropriately flexible, implementation of programs in the field. While most federal departments had branch organizations, the Council argued, they were not necessarily related to effective regional administration or decentralization.

In the economic sphere it was further argued that there should be a coherent set of policies with particular emphasis on stabilization, transportation, tariff, development expenditure, education and training, and manpower components. Several governmental expenditures were considered to be regressive by the Council:

Most of the expenditures in the lowest-income regions, the Atlantic Provinces, were in transportation and various residual or undefined programs. The transportation expenditure programs in the Atlantic Provinces have not been those relating to our requirements for accelerating regional growth. At least it is not apparent that they have been part of any co-ordinated and conscious design in the appropriate directions.[17]

Paradoxically, the Council considered the large manpower expenditures conducted "in all regions *except* the Atlantic Provinces . . ." to rate high in respect to the requirements for accelerated regional growth. If these arguments are correct, then manpower policies should be a prerequisite to mobility programs, which in turn should be considered as a major component of the strategy to arrest regional disparities. It should be noted, however, that some sociologists and economists support the creation of controlled job opportunities within the region rather than the movement of people to jobs.

In contrast to the economics-oriented emphasis of the Economic Council, the Liberal party introduced a more politically oriented strategy. In 1968 this strategy became associated with Pierre Elliott Trudeau's assertion that arresting regional disparities would facilitate national unity. In the words of the Prime Minister: "If the underdevelopment of the Atlantic Provinces is not corrected . . . then the unity of the country is almost as surely destroyed as it would be by the French-English confrontation."[18] The politically oriented approach suggested the extension of the expenditure patterns, initiated in the Atlantic Provinces, over the country as a whole. In fact this strategy was adopted between 1969 and 1972. The 1974 General Development Agreements can be considered to be even more politically motivated since it adopted a universalistic approach with DREE now operating in all provinces. Accordingly it suggests that a decentralized approach to regional development can also facilitate national unity.[19] However, before looking at the evolution of DREE itself it is worth mentioning a few alternative paths which could have been followed in co-ordinating regional policies.

First, there was the alternative of continuing or expanding the activities of various Crown corporations or boards designed to expedite development in the depressed areas, such as the Atlantic Development Board and the Industrial Development Bank.[20] Such a strategy would provide a greater degree of flexibility as compared to the departmental form of organization. In fact, even after the creation of DREE development policies are being carried out through the Newfoundland

and Labrador Development Corporation, the New Brunswick Multiplex Corporation, the Cape Breton Development Corporation, and the Halifax–Dartmouth Area Development Corporation.[21] A major defect in the Crown corporation strategy is that it is less amenable to political and parliamentary evaluation and as such becomes a target for opposition parties.

Second, the co-ordination of economic development could have been carried out through a group established in the Treasury Board as recommended by the Economic Council. Major inputs could come from the departments of Finance, Industry, Trade and Commerce, and Transport, among others, in establishing an overall investment strategy to meet the varied needs of all the depressed areas. In fact, the Industry and Natural Resources Division of the Treasury Board and the Economic Development Division in the Department of Finance are still active participants in the regional field despite the existence of DREE. The advantages of a "Board" as against a departmental strategy is that it facilitates interdepartmental co-ordination, which is an integral component of a comprehensive regional policy. Furthermore, in cases where the provinces have established central planning machineries they can interface with a more prestigious body at the federal level which has close relationships with the Department of Finance, the primary actor in the formulation of economic policy.

Third, there could be deconcentration of a number of federal departments; for example, Transport, Energy, Mines and Resources, Industry, Trade and Commerce, and Agriculture.[22] While the departments would be staffed federally, they would be more regionally located, thus making them more responsive to the demands of the provincial governments. An effective strategy for regional development must incorporate the views of various provincial governments and even the municipalities. Such an approach would insure that development strategies reflected the convergence of the views of the three levels of government.

Fourth, the role of the Atlantic Development Board could have been broadened so that, in conjunction with the Economic Council, the Department of Industry, Trade and Commerce, and the Industrial Development Bank, a national development strategy or plan might have been worked out prior to the escalation in expenditures which followed the establishment of DREE. This approach, while highly flexible, would lead to a proliferation of boards and commissions.

It can be seen that the various alternatives suggested are complementary, and this should be borne in mind when we attempt later to evaluate the effectiveness of DREE. Policies directed at a particular region may have to be reformulated from a problem-solving perspective, hence the emphasis placed in this chapter on development administration.

THE EVOLUTION OF THE DEPARTMENT

The establishment of DREE in the Government Organization Act of 1969 was thus the culmination of a series of *ad hoc* measures to arrest regional disparities in Canada. The creation of the department must still be seen, however, as only an initial phase in a long-term attempt to arrest regional disparities. In many respects, DREE is not a regular line department in that it is expected to perform a co-ordinating role, somewhat along the lines suggested by the Economic Council of Canada in its early reviews. One could compare part of DREE's mandate with the abortive British attempt to co-ordinate long-term growth policies through the Department of Economic Affairs. The creation of the department reflected a direct attempt to institutionalize a new ministerial position in the hope that the growth objective would be reconciled with other political objectives and that this reconciliation would, henceforth, take place at the cabinet level. DREE was established "to carry out, in co-operation with the provinces, a vigorous and co-ordinated effort to reduce regional economic disparities in Canada." The disparities have been persistent and large for many decades, despite considerable national growth.

The Department of Regional Economic Expansion Act stipulates that the Governor-in-Council, after consultation with the government of any province, may by order designate as a special area, for the period set out in the order, any area in that province that is determined to require, by reason of exceptional inadequacy of opportunities for productive employment of the people of that area or the region of which that area is a part, special measures to facilitate economic and social adjustment. Section 25 emphasized the need for development planning:

(1) In exercising his powers and carrying out his duties and functions under section 23, the Minister shall
   (a) in co-operation with other departments, branches and agencies of the Government of Canada, formulate plans for the economic expansion and social adjustment of special areas; and
   (b) with the approval of the Governor-in-Council, provide for co-ordination of the implementation of those plans by departments, branches and agencies of the Government of Canada and carry out such parts of those plans as cannot suitably be undertaken by such other departments, branches and agencies.

(2) In formulating and carrying out plans under subsection (1) the Minister shall make provision for appropriate co-operation with the provinces in which special areas are located and for the participation of persons, voluntary groups, agencies, and bodies in those special areas.[23]

At this point it should be mentioned that the discretionary powers cited above were severely criticized by opposition political parties. The Act provides, however, that DREE must co-operate with the provinces in formulating plans of economic expansion and social adjustment.

The Act specifies the need for interdepartmental co-ordination. Thus, although the Department of Manpower and Immigration was established three years before DREE, its functions and duties are intricately bound to the latter. DREE provides incentives under the Regional Development Incentives Act, but the Department of Manpower and Immigration must provide the necessary training programs or mobility grants so that the new industries can become operative.

Following a 1972-73 policy evaluation the department adopted a more elaborate incentives consultation process. Under the reorganization each regional Assistant Deputy Minister is principally responsible for the incentives program in his region. The decentralized provincial offices evaluate all incentive applications and have authority to offer incentives for smaller projects (up to $500,000 in approved capital costs). The regional offices review the large-scale and more significant medium-sized projects. The regional ADMs have authority to approve medium-sized cases (up to $1,500,000 in approved capital cost or 100 jobs).[24]

The Incentives Branch in Ottawa, in addition to providing planning and staff support, assists with the evaluation of large-scale projects and reviews the policy implications of cases submitted to the Regional Development Incentives Board. The minister, on the advice of the Board, makes final decisions with respect to incentives for highly sensitive and large-scale projects.[25]

The Minister of Regional Economic Expansion is empowered under Section 5 to "co-operate with the provinces and other federal agencies for the economic expansion and social adjustment of Special Areas". In 1974 the Regional Development Incentives Board, provided for in the legislation, was restructured as to membership and given responsibility to consider and advise the Minister of Regional Economic Expansion on whether or not a large incentive grant should be offered, and if so what amount and under what conditions. All applications involving approved capital costs above $1.5 million are to be considered by the Board before decision by the minister. In addition to its role as advisor on large incentive applications, the Board also advises the minister respecting guidelines for decisions on smaller cases and particularly on sensitive issues, as well as considering loan guarantees proposals. For appropriate cases, consultations have been held with other departments, such as Agriculture and Environment. Membership on the Board consists of the Deputy Minister and the ADM for Planning and Co-ordination of DREE, an ADM from Finance, Industry, Trade and Commerce, Manpower and Immigration, Environment, and if appropriate, an ADM from such departments as Agriculture and Energy, Mines and Resources.[26]

Between 1969 and 1973 DREE's strategy consisted of three major and closely interrelated activities: industrial incentives, infrastructure assistance, and social adjustment and rural development. The objective of the first was to create continuing productive employment by making investment in viable industry more attractive in the relatively slow-growth regions of the country. The second assisted in providing additional social capital for water systems, roads, housing, etc., which were necessary prerequisites for economic and social adjustments in the depressed areas. The third facilitated the access of people in rural areas to productive employment opportunities through social adjustment, as well as to improve their incomes through more efficient utilization of rural resources.[27] However by 1974 DREE had developed a broader approach through a fourth instrument or strategy; the General Development Agreements.[28] While existing DREE programs were still being pursued the "developmental opportunities" concept had increasingly become the central element of regional development policy. Under this concept, DREE concentrated more of its resources in co-operation with provincial governments, and in close consultation with interested federal departments and agencies, on the identification and development of opportunities of strategic importance to the regional and provincial economies. The approach adopted in 1974 was universal in contrast to the earlier selective approach in that the concept would be used in every province but would be limited in application to opportunities affecting geographic areas where economic activity was lagging. The relevant areas would change with changing circumstances but, at the time of writing they included all the Atlantic Provinces, Quebec, Manitoba, Saskatchewan, the northern and some eastern parts of Ontario, parts of Alberta outside Edmonton and Calgary, and parts of British Columbia outside the lower mainland and Victoria.

In short the strategies adopted between 1969 and 1973 and in 1974 demonstrated that DREE was given a broad mandate to bring together a number of predecessor programs and to develop a much more comprehensive attack on regional economic disparities. The shifts from a rural development strategy to an urban development one and most recently to "the general development agreements" show that the approach to regional development has become multi-disciplinary and multi-dimensional. The latest approach calls for the identification and pursuit of major developmental opportunities by means of a co-ordinated application of public policies and programs, both federal and provincial, in co-operation with elements of the private sector where appropriate. The foregoing illustrates, once again, the pervasive nature of economic policy and the mixed composition of the Canadian economy. It also points to the heterogeneity of the Canadian political system.

The objectives of DREE have thus been stated as follows: "To facilitate economic expansion and social adjustment in areas of Canada requiring special measures to improve opportunities for productive employment and the access of people to opportunities." The sub-objectives are:

—To perform the basic economic planning for the department's program and to manage the department's operations so as to facilitate economic expansion and social adjustment in conjunction with related programs and capabilities of other federal departments and agencies and provincial governments;

—To induce and assist industrial development in slow-growth regions of Canada; and

—To assist in providing incremental social capital investment to facilitate the access of people to productive employment opportunities by assisting the provinces on social adjustment measures and by improvements in the productivity and efficiency of resource utilization.

Since 1969 the department has evolved into a planning agency with regional sub-structures. When the department was formed, it was primarily a co-ordinating mechanism encompassing planning, programing, implementation, and incentives components each under an Assistant Deputy Minister. However, a major reorganization carried out in late 1973 considerably decentralized the personnel in the department leaving only two Assistant Deputy Ministers in Ottawa. It is important to review briefly how the change was brought about.

Structure and Organization in the Mid-1970s

Until late 1973, the department was organized into planning, regional, functional, and co-ordinating responsibilities in order to achieve the objectives stated above. Thus, below the Deputy Minister there were six ADMS with the following responsibilities: Planning, Eastern Region, Central Region, Western Region, Incentives, and Co-ordination and Liaison. There was also a Director General for Technical Services and Special Projects Division, a derivation from ADB, and a Director of Evaluation and Administration. Other aspects of the department's activities were performed by a Director of Personnel and a Director of Public Information. Two advisory bodies, the Atlantic Development Council and the Canadian Council on Rural Development reported directly to the minister. The Canadian Council on Rural Development attempted in the early stages to emphasize the rural dimensions of regional development, but later it advocated the need to design a national development strategy and the need for improved public participation and evaluation of the department's policies. Between 1969 and 1973 the major vehicle for arresting regional disparities was the Regional Development Incentives Act of June 1969, which was amended in December 1970. Under this Act, the federal government, in consultation with the provincial governments, had "designated" certain broad areas for development to all provinces. There was also a provision for "special area programs" to facilitate the development process in slow-growth regions.[29] The Incentives Program was carried over from the Department of Industry, Trade and Commerce and the Director General for Technical Services and Special Projects Division dealt with problems which were formerly the responsibility of the Atlantic Development Board. Figure 9:1 is useful as a point of comparison with the approach adopted by the department after 1973. It shows the provincial location of special, designated, and incentive regions. Prior to the 1973-74 changes, for example, British Columbia did not receive incentives grants. Federal assistance to the provinces was selective rather than universal. By 1974 the department had adopted the strategy of general development agreements which meant that it had identified developmental opportunities wherever they existed.

Before the 1974 changes several of the department's programs were directed at human and social development and accordingly, there was a special branch under the ADM for Planning, which dealt with problems such as:

a) The federal-provincial ARDA and FRED agreements which provided for upgrading the skills and for improving the mobility of the rural population.
b) The special area agreements which included projects for the creation of a manpower corps which provided experimental training for people whose opportunity of obtaining access to employment was otherwise limited.
c) The Canada Newstart Program which incorporated experiments with new methods in preparing unemployed and underemployed people in particularly disadvantaged areas to take advantage of new or improved job opportunities.

The endorsement of the new General Development Agreements in the 1973-74 fiscal year made provision for a broad economic and social development strategy with extensive consultation between the federal government and the provinces. It presented, nevertheless, a planning problem given the fact that major economic-growth, transportation, employment, and resource-development strategies were formulated in departments such as Finance, Industry, Trade and Commerce,

FIGURE 9:1—REGIONAL DEVELOPMENT BY PROVINCE AND AREAS—1973

Province	*Incentive Area A*	*Incentive Area B*	*Incentive Area C*	*Special Areas*
Newfoundland	Entire Province	—	—	Hawkes Bay; Corner Brook; Stephenville; Gander; Come By Chance; St. John's; Burin
Prince Edward Island	Entire Province	—	—	
Nova Scotia	Entire Province	—	—	Halifax; Port Hawkesbury
New Brunswick	Entire Province	—	—	Saint John; Moncton
Quebec		Southern Quebec	Montreal; Hull; Hawkesbury	Sept-Iles; Lake St. John; Quebec City; Trois Rivières; Ste. Scolastique
Ontario		Southern Ontario		Pembroke; Renfrew
Manitoba		Southern Manitoba		The Pas
Saskatchewan		Southern Saskatchewan; Swift Current; Moose Jaw; Weyburn; Estevan		Meadow Lake; Saskatoon; Regina
Alberta		Southeastern Alberta; eg. Kimberley; Lethbridge; Medicine Hat		Lesser Slave Lake
British Columbia	—	—	—	—

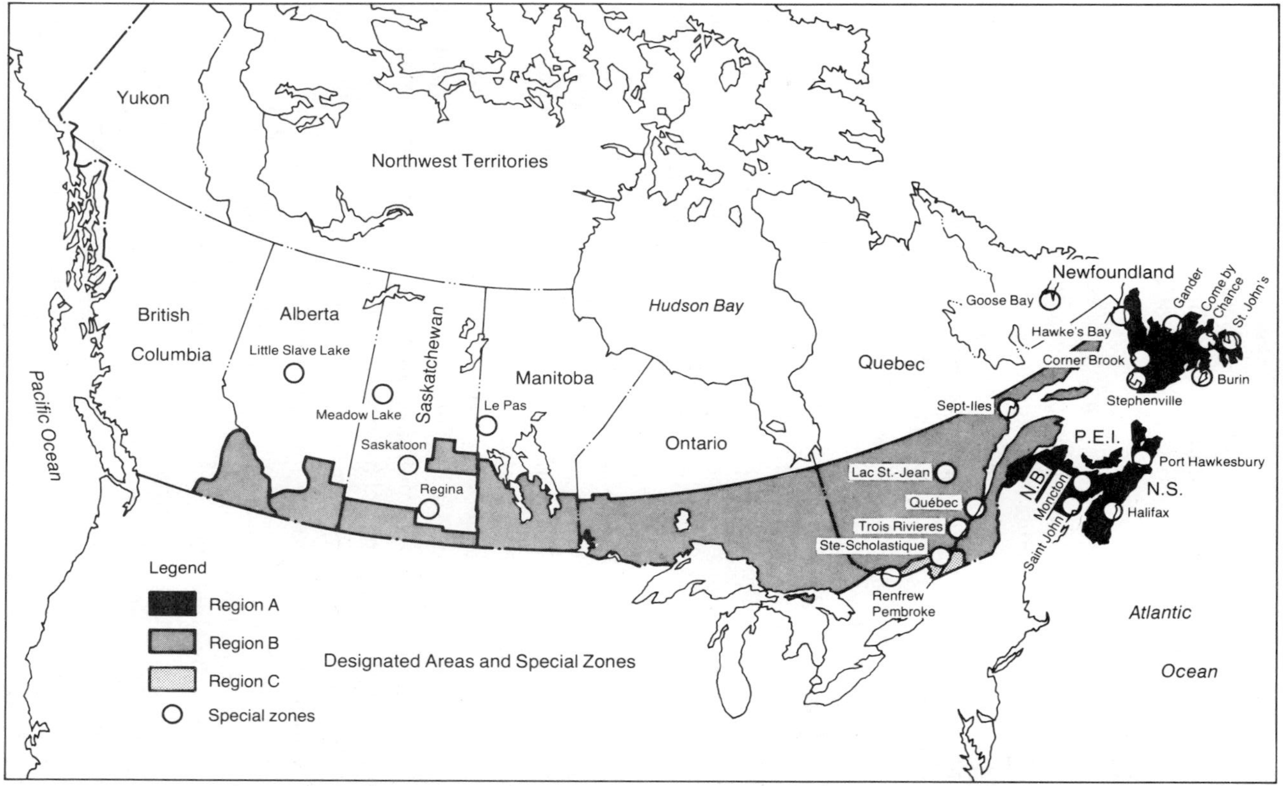
Yukon
Northwest Territories
British
Columbia
Alberta
Saskatchewan
Manitoba
Ontario
Quebec
Hudson Bay
Newfoundland
Pacific Ocean
Atlantic
Ocean
Little Slave Lake
Meadow Lake
Saskatoon
Regina
Le Pas
Goose Bay
Hawke's Bay
Corner Brook
Gander
Come by
Chance
St. John's
Burin
Stephenville
Sept-Iles
P.E.I.
Port Hawkesbury
N.B.
Moncton
N.S.
Halifax
Saint John
Lac St.-Jean
Québec
Trois Rivieres
Ste-Scholastique
Renfrew
Pembroke
Legend
Region A
Region B
Region C
Special zones
Designated Areas and Special Zones

1972, DREE

Transport, and Energy, Mines and Resources with which DREE must engage in extensive consultations. Thus again the necessity for interdepartmental co-operation and co-ordination is paramount. Indeed, it is perhaps the most important aspect of development, planning, and administration.[30]

Planning is clearly a necessary aspect of economic management. It requires the establishment of long-term objectives, especially those dealing with investment; the adoption of strategies to achieve those objectives; and the establishment of procedures for effective budgetary allocations and managerial procedures with built-in review or evaluation mechanisms. The structures involved in this process are the Privy Council Office, Finance, the Economic Council, the Treasury Board, the economic development departments of the provinces, and since 1969, DREE. Accordingly, the department's early planning endeavoured, in concert with provincial governments, to identify the strategies needed to reduce the magnitude of regional disparities and to develop the policies, plans, and programs which would most effectively ameliorate these problems. The DREE planning process thus sought to identify the key economic and social causes of disparities in a particular region from which it defined the main goals. It also developed the basic priorities and strategy by which the goals would be achieved and developed, and assessed alternative policies, plans, and programs needed to achieve the goals.

The Planning Division was divided in the early years into three branches, an Economic Analysis Branch, a Social and Human Analysis Branch, and a Plan Formulation Branch. The Economic Analysis Branch analysed and tested hypotheses about economic expansion. It analysed and developed micro-economic models respecting the natural resources, primary manufacturing, construction, trade, and service sectors. The Social and Human Analysis Branch assisted in developing plans, programs, and projects to help the disadvantaged people in the slow-growth areas to respond promptly and effectively to the opportunities for improving earnings, for new employment, and for access to gainful employment opportunities. The Plan Formulation Branch prior to the 1974 changes was organized into three regional groups: the Atlantic Region, the Central Region, and the Western Region. In addition, four sectoral planning groups on Natural Resources, Human Resources, Private Capital, and Social Capital provided special expertise for the development of plans with the provinces and within the respective areas of concentration.

The planning process turned out to be far more complex than was anticipated. Both interdepartmental and federal-provincial conflicts emerged and seriously affected the formulation of a consensus.

In order to cope with a number of problems the department established in 1972 a Co-ordination and Liaison Division which dealt with problems of co-ordination both as they affected the various programs commenced in 1969, and as they affected work with other departments at the federal level, as well as with the provincial departments. Accordingly, the Co-ordination and Liaison Division worked closely with the Planning Division, which also worked with the provinces through Joint Planning Committees, created to facilitate consultation.

The Co-ordination and Liaison Division collated information about development projects, including the reconciliation of cost-benefit ratios. The provinces were thus in a better position to relate with a federal group which looked at all development programs in a comprehensive manner. In addition to an overall (vertical) co-ordinating relationship with the Privy Council Office, the Department of Finance and the Treasury Board, the Division also worked more closely with the related departments of Manpower and Immigration, Transport, Public Works, Industry, Trade and Commerce, Agriculture, and Consumer and Corporate Affairs. Many of these departments had been evolving an elaborate system of regional offices, thus promoting greater deconcentration of their activities.

By the establishment of DREE, the federal government embarked on a more comprehensive strategy of regional development. However, the comprehensive strategy was questioned at the Western Economic Opportunities Conference held in Edmonton in July 1973. This, among other factors, led to a more decentralized approach to facilitate more provincial inputs.[31] This was well symbolized in the 1974 organizational structure of the department shown in Figure 9:2.

The organizational structure was complemented by ten provincial offices under the direction of ten Director Generals. The 1974 structure reflected the new approach which operates under the general development agreements.[32] It is important to review the political and administrative considerations which led to the adoption of the new comprehensive and decentralized approach.

Figure 9:2 Organization of the Department of Regional Economic Expansion (1974)

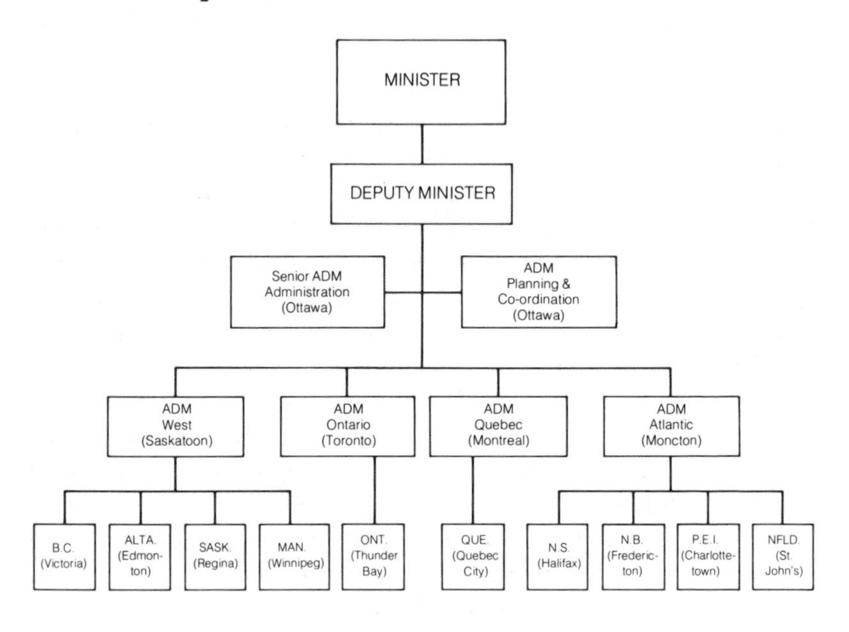

THE PROCESSES OF POLICY CHANGE: TOWARDS DECENTRALIZATION

Following the 1972 federal election, which returned a minority government and showed continuing Liberal party weakness in the west and the Maritimes, the Trudeau government promised an overall reappraisal of its regional development policies. DREE was placed under the guidance of the Hon. D. C. Jamieson whose political base was in Newfoundland. He replaced Jean Marchand, the department's first minister. An attempt was made to integrate and strengthen several aspects of Canada's economic development programs. The new approach involved branches in the Treasury Board, the Department of Finance, and IT&C. The orientation of the Trudeau government in 1973 was toward decentralized national development planning as opposed to centralized planning and administration. Consequently, while DREE's policies were under review, measures were being adopted for "decentralizing" the Department of Industry, Trade and Commerce, although in many respects deconcentration was preferred given the national orientation of IT&C. This was part of an attempt to relate national growth areas with depressed areas and for integrating the work of other departments such as Transport, Energy, Mines and Resources, among others, with DREE. These steps were taken after intensive consultation with the provinces,[33] especially after adamant demands came from the western and the Atlantic provinces.[34]

During 1973, for example, negotiations were carried out on programs in Quebec such as "ARDA 3", a project which was designated by the various departments in the Quebec government concerned (agriculture, forests, mines, and tourism). The project covered the Saguenay–Lac-Saint-Jean regions and the Abitibi–Temiscamingue regions where DREE had earlier decided to concentrate ARDA funds for several years. While these developments were taking place in Quebec, the minister of DREE noted that "a large area of Ontario reveals economic performance which has been more like that of Manitoba or New Brunswick than like that of the rest of Ontario".[35] In addition to the integration of Quebec and Ontario into a central region, the new policies identified Northern Ontario as a particular intraprovincial region with specific developmental problems. The adoption of this policy reduced the possibilities of the department being criticized for "dumping money into the province of Quebec".

Two fundamentally different dimensions of the concept of regions emerged out of the later policy review. First the earlier attempt to integrate Ontario and Quebec into a central region which would reduce cultural considerations was subsequently abandoned. The 1974 structure of the department depicted four regions: the western region, the Ontario region, the Quebec region, and the Atlantic region. Second, the identification of Northern Ontario and the western northlands were illustrative of analytic regions in that they pointed to the existence of areas within the broader regions. The subsequent establishment of ten provincial offices demonstrated once more the realities of Canadian federal-provincial relations.[36] Here the strength of provincial forces which were further augmented by the highly regionalized voting patterns of the 1972 federal election. Any realistic regional development policies, therefore, must incorporate provincial perspectives. The regional strategy adopted in 1974 shifted more of the initiative to the provinces and hence may have impinged on the attainment of a coherent national development policy frequently advocated by economists and by politicians with centralist preferences.[37] It should be noted, however, that the national and international environments often demand new central economic leadership initiatives and hence forces may work in the opposite direction.

The policy changes were thus the result of three separate but interrelated developments, the 1972 federal elections which showed Liberal weakness in the west and the Maritimes, the 1972-73 policy evaluation conducted within the department, and the post-election pressures which were later reflected in the Western Economic Opportunities Conference held in July 1973.[38] These political forces demonstrated the need for a more multi-dimensional approach to regional-development planning and policy-making.

The 1972-73 internal policy evaluation of the performance of DREE was carried out using staff drawn from different parts of the department and from other federal agencies as well as a variety of outside consultants, including the head of the policy review group.

The evaluation of the incentives grant program revealed that by December 31, 1972, 6,036 applications had resulted in a net total of 1,957 accepted offers of incentive grant assistance. Projects associated with these offers were expected to generate a total of $1,616 million in fixed capital investment, create 81,750 direct new jobs and result in incentive payments totalling $324 million. After allowing for "adjustment" the number of jobs created would fall to approximately 64,400: 11,300 in the Atlantic Region, 39,300 in Quebec, and the remainder in Ontario and the West.[39] A number of policy and organizational changes were recommended as a result of the evaluation.

First, it was suggested that the effectiveness of the program might be further improved by greater decentralization, assigning to the regions a large part of the decision-making about relatively small projects, which accounted for a large proportion of all cases. However, the work of the departmental evaluation should be further linked to the subsequent work of the Western Economic Opportunities Conference in which strong initiatives came from Finance and IT&C. While the DREE document dealt with decentralization generally the IT&C input identified primary, secondary, and tertiary aspects of industrial and trade development policies. Thus, strong emphasis was placed on the need to develop small business to supplement the strong resource base of the western provinces. Oil, gas, sulphur, potash, and forestry products were isolated for detailed consideration.[40] Consequently, proposals were outlined to strengthen the Industrial Development Bank (to create a Federal Business Development Bank), to strengthen the Loan Development Corporation, and to decentralize several components of the manufacturing thrusts of IT&C.[41] The decentralization of industrial activities, therefore, was a focal point of the Western Economic Opportunities Conference.

Second, in response to criticisms that the incentives program had been applied in such a way as to relocate existing jobs, new regulations adopted in 1974 prohibit any application of this kind insofar as designated regions are concerned.

Third, it was concluded that the regional development incentives programs had produced beneficial results at reasonable cost. Since this was not apparent to external critics, the department in late 1973 began issuing monthly reports on the award of the incentive grants in order to improve parliamentary evaluation of its programs.

Fourth, the study concluded that on the whole the slow-growth areas of the country had experienced the effects of the DREE programs and the effects were essentially good for the whole country. Significant improvements had occurred in the following areas: land utilization under ARDA; the provision of irrigation and other forms of water supply under PFRA; improvements resulting from the emphasis on mechanisms of social adjustment in some of the badly disadvantaged areas covered by FRED programs; the provision of support for roads, sewer, and water supplies to service industrial land and other forms of essential infra-structure in selected urban centres; and the availability of financial incentives to encourage job-creating investment.[42]

The twelve-volume federal study tabled in the House of Commons on June 29, 1973, recommended, in brief, the following development strategy to build stronger regional economies: the improvement of transportation facilities in the Atlantic provinces; expansion of the manufacturing of steel in Quebec; and the development of agricultural processing in the western provinces.[43] It suggested also that special efforts should be made to bolster the manufacturing, communications, and transportation industries in Montreal, a vitally important area in the Quebec economy. The report concluded that the prospects for Alberta and British Columbia were good for the 1970s. In contrast, the report projected a poor outlook for Saskatchewan and Manitoba.[44] Consequently, it recommended that these provinces place greatest emphasis on agricultural processing and small resource-based industries, processing a variety of agricultural products, minerals, oil, gas, and wood. The review further suggested that greater emphasis be placed on rural development and on secondary centres rather than on major cities. By implication the study suggested that greater stress should be placed on training and on mobility programs.

The study recommended that in the Atlantic provinces transportation should be developed to link the regional economy to potential markets. The "Atlantic Region" can be regarded as a "massive pier forming a point of entry to the North American market from Europe". The adoption of such a strategy would involve the development and expansion of rail, air, and port facilities. Quebec required increased investment in steel which would facilitate growth in the durable goods industries based on steel production. On the Quebec economy, the study concluded that a healthy steel industry could inject new life into a whole host of manufacturing industries ranging from agricultural implements to electrical products. The economy of Northern Ontario could be improved by placing greater emphasis on tourism and service industries. Elsewhere the report suggested that Northern Ontario had more severe problems of disparity than was the case in many of the depressed provinces.

These 1973 recommendations again indicated that the federal and provincial governments had moved toward the adoption of a "multi-dimensional approach" to regional development. It has been recognized that single-factor programs cannot be expected, by themselves, to maximize the potential of these regions. The Minister of Regional Economic Expansion thus commented in 1973:

> I have become increasingly impressed by the range of opportunities for economic development that exist in most parts of this country and by the large number of public policies and programs that bear or could be brought to bear upon a concentrated effort to realize some of these opportunities. This is what has led me to speak publicly in recent weeks about the possibilities inherent in a "multi-dimensional approach"—an approach that could call for the identification and pursuit of major developmental opportunities by means of the co-ordinated application of public policies and programs, federal and provincial co-operation where appropriate with elements of the private sector. I intended to explore this concept with the provincial governments and I am

prepared to consider its use of a basis for new federal-provincial initiatives in the field of regional development.[45]

The approach outlined by the minister in 1973 suggested the need for greater understanding and utilization of the concept of development planning and development administration. In order to achieve this more ambitious objective it was necessary to designate a national development strategy for Canada. However, in a manner similar to the search for an industrial strategy the new approach to regional development turned out to be a variety of strategies.

How should this national development strategy be designed? As pointed out elsewhere, regional development strategies can be designed either from above or from below. DREE was criticized, in the past, on grounds that despite pronouncements that national growth was the prime concern in the formulation of its policies the proposals to reduce regional inequality started with specific local problems.[46] An alternative approach would place the major emphasis on maximizing the growth of the whole country while at the same time reducing regional disparities. "The new approach" adopted in 1973-74 will still have to cope ultimately with these issues.

The first stage in the development of such a strategy would involve significant co-ordination among such departments and agencies as Finance, the Bank of Canada, Industry, Trade and Commerce, and the Industrial Development Bank, working closely with DREE in determining an aggregate investment strategy.

The second step would involve the designation of federal-provincial regions to reflect the new policy objectives. The 1973 policy statement by the minister suggested that the following regions, among others, be identified for analytical purposes and be managed to realize their greatest potential: the Atlantic Region; Quebec and Ontario; the Western Region; and the Western Northlands.[47] This was accompanied by the appointment of four new Assistant Deputy Ministers who since November 1, 1973, have operated from new regional headquarters in Moncton, Montreal, Toronto, and Saskatoon. This reorganization was in keeping with the regions defined in the department's policy evaluation carried out in 1973, and with the goal of giving more decision-making authority to regionally based senior officials.

However, the comparative analysis of regions showed that socioeconomic criteria transcended political boundaries, which nevertheless had to be regarded as given. While the analytic regions proved useful, the policy outcome reflected *provincial priorities.*[48] Thus, by placing greater emphasis on the concepts of developmental planning and development administration within the provinces it was increasingly realized that many developmental problems were both political and structural and could not be dealt with by pure economic analysis. For example, it was suggested that "the rationalization of the mineral resources sector may have to be curtailed or slowed down because of its greater responsiveness to capital than to labour." Accordingly, there may be greater realization on a more long-term basis and greater new benefits from investment in processing and manufacturing facilities and on related expansion in service activities than on physical resources development. Again, close relationships between DREE and the departments of Energy, Mines and Resources (physical resources), Manpower and Immigration (employment), and Industry, Trade and Commerce (industrial strategy) are essential. Alberta and Saskatchewan have clearly been making strong demands that the revenue which accrues from their non-renewable resources should provide benefits to their people.[49] In 1973 the federal government had suggested a stronger role for manufacturing in an attempt to establish greater balance in the industrial structure of western Canada.[50]

The research findings meant that quite different strategies had to be designed for the various regions identified above. The use of transportation policy as a means for bringing about greater complementarity between the regions seems to be a natural by-product. The western provinces may adopt the strategy of greater concentration on resource exploration, development, and related processing as the principal engines of growth. There has been marked concentration of growth in the major urban centres of Alberta and British Columbia. In contrast, across the Western Northlands there is a dichotomy between high income and high mobility in the resource centres and extreme poverty and relative immobility in the remote communities, the partial remedy of which requires co-operation from the Department of Manpower and Immigration. Although influenced by these considerations the General Development Agreements seem to be reflecting stronger provincial priorities.

The urban-rural dimensions in regional policy were reflected in the increased recognition of the need for concerted managerial strategies between the Ministry of State for Urban Affairs on the one hand and the departments of Agriculture, Forestry and Fisheries, and Energy, Mines and Resources, on the other. Consequently, development, planning, and administration must aspire to the achievement of *balance*. There were, moreover, further difficulties which had to be resolved in order to co-ordinate policies in the respective departments. One such difficulty involves the relative balance which should be placed on economic and social policies. There are important questions concerning the relationship between economic and social policies which are in constant tension in the processes of economic management. Certainly the location of industries in the less-developed areas of Canada has overriding political and social rather than just economic implications. The primary role of DREE, therefore, has been a subject of major controversy.[51] Should industries be located mainly in the highly developed areas? Should urbanization be highly concentrated? Recently, the federal system has been operating as a centrifugal force supporting dispersal—hence the emphasis on decentralization. However, as students of public management are well aware there are perennial problems in establishing an appropriate balance between centralization and decentralization. Given the presence of "regionalism" in Canada, it is most difficult to obtain a balanced perspective on this subject.

Since 1973, DREE has had to stress once more the importance of social policies. This need was reflected in the multi-dimensional approach analysed above as well as in the public statements of influential ministers such as the Hon. Marc Lalonde, Minister of Health and Welfare, who concluded in a 1973 statement:

> Regional and sectoral economic policies cannot be expected to overcome every economic disadvantage of every industry or every region nor can they be expected to preserve every present industry and promise new industries to every community and every area . . . . it remains that there is extended unemployment, even when the economy as a whole is manifestly buoyant. Again special measures are called for to supplement general economic policies, if we are to get all Canadians to work.[52]

From the perspective of social policies, therefore, there was a necessity to co-ordinate policies with the departments of Health and Welfare and Finance.[53]

It is important to note also that the Hon. Bryce Mackasey, in his capacity as Minister of Manpower and Immigration, had also emphasized in May 1972 the importance of improved co-ordination of a number of policies and programs administered by a number of closely related departments. Thus, he asserted:

> I do not think that manpower should be welfare in disguise. Programs should not be just handed out because the person is unemployed, it should have meaning; it should be correlated to DREE; it should be correlated to Trade and Industry; it should be part of an industrial policy for the country; and it should be better co-ordinated with the Unemployment Insurance Commission.[54]

In April 1973, the Hon. D. C. Jamieson stated that the Department of Regional Economic Expansion had now formulated a conceptual plan. He went on to add:

> We want to see just exactly how the provinces feel that our plan would work with them. The basic premise is that we would move in each of the regions someone who would have quite a high status within the public service, perhaps at the ADM level, something of that order—Assistant Deputy Ministry level. In each of the regions we would then also have, if you like, a sub-region again with officials and representatives present, widely distributed geographically throughout these regions certainly with a minimum of one such office per province within the region. But in the case of northern Ontario, probably with something located specifically in northern Ontario.[55]

Regional development policy has subsequently reflected a broad strategy encompassing three interrelated components: government-industry relations, interdepartmental co-ordination, and federal-provincial co-operation.[56] Central to all aspects is the issue of public investment which requires inputs from the departments of Finance and Industry, Trade and Commerce. The shifts in emphasis which took place between 1969 and 1976 can be further illustrated through a review of regional-development expenditures.

REGIONAL DEVELOPMENT EXPENDITURE POLITICS AND THE GENERAL DEVELOPMENT AGREEMENTS

Between 1969 and 1973 the Department of Regional Economic Expan-

TABLE 9:1
Federal Assistance for Regional Development
1966-67 to 1970-71*

Year	*Infrastructure Development*		*Incentives to Industry*		*Social Adjustment and Rural Development*		*Total*	
	$M	%	$M	%	$M	%	$M	%
1966-67	38.1	66.9	1.2	2.0	17.7	31.1	57.0	100.0
1967-68	37.9	43.8	15.4	17.8	33.2	38.4	86.5	100.0
1968-69	37.8	40.3	14.6	15.6	41.3	44.1	93.7	100.0
1969-70	30.5	22.0	54.5	39.3	53.6	38.7	138.6	100.0
1970-71	104.1	38.4	107.7	39.7	59.2	21.9	271.0	100.0

Source: DREE, *Regional Development Programs,* April 1973.

*The first federal programs specifically designed to tackle the socio-economic problem of the disadvantaged regions of Canada were introduced in the 1961-63 period. Major expenditures under them did not commence until 1966-67. The figures in this table represent direct expenditures (exclusive of loans) only. From 1969-70 onward, the figures represent expenditures on new programs as well as continuing expenditures on earlier programs absorbed into the Department of Regional Economic Expansion.

sion experienced a rapid increase in its expenditures from $240 million in the first year to over $500 million in its fourth year of operation.[57] In some respects this significant increase in expenditure was inconsistent with "rational planning", in that intensive assessment of the potentials of regions had not been carried out prior to embarking on a large number of projects. Alternatively, the government could have embarked on a selective number of comprehensive development projects, but this could have led to a discriminatory policy adversely affecting the most depressed provinces.

The expenditure policy of DREE was a reflection of strong political pressures. A conglomerate of *ad hoc* unintegrated expenditure schemes of economic- and social-development projects were created, with a more co-ordinated and comprehensive planning phase developing only later. The early expenditure was considered as a form of short-term "political appeasement" while a more comprehensive policy was being formulated.

As Table 9:1 indicates, between 1966-67 and 1970-71 general federal spending for regional development (including pre-DREE spending) had given ever increasing relative emphasis to incentives to industry, in

TABLE 9:2*

DREE Expenditures ($ millions)

Programme	*1969-70*	*Loans*	*1970-71*	*Loans*	*1971-72*	*Loans*	*1972-73*	*Loans*	*1973-74 (Est.)*	*Loans*
1. Developmental Planning and Administration	12.1	—	15.4	—	18.8	—	26.2	—	35.2	—
2. Industrial Incentives	56.2	—	62.0	—	105.5	—	129.8	16.0	163.7	6.0
3. Infrastructure Assistance	39.8	39.8	107.1	68.6	96.1	33.2	96.0	50.9	108.5	69.9
4. Social Adjustment and Rural Economic Development	71.2	0.4	76.0	1.7	88.2	3.0	125.9	7.2	117.5	12.2

*Adapted from: DREE, *Regional Development Programs,* Ottawa, April 1973.

TABLE 9:3*
DREE Expenditures: 1969-1976
($ million)

	1969-74	*1974-75*[a]	*1975-76*[b]
Industrial and commercial development	421.3	—	—
Industrial incentives	—	73.3	92.4
Development opportunity incentives	—	90.7	186.1
Infrastructure assistance	454.3	—	—
Social adjustment and rural economic development	447.1	—	—
Other programs	—	186.0	152.8
Departmental planning and administration	89.1	29.7	37.1
Total	1411.8	379.7	468.4

*Adapted from *The National Finances 1975-76* (Toronto: Canadian Tax Foundation, 1976, p. 136)

comparison with infrastructure-development, and social-adjustment and rural-development expenditures. In 1966-67 industry incentives accounted for 2 per cent of federal assistance but by 1970-71 the percentage had grown to 39.7 per cent. The percentage of expenditures on infrastructure development had declined from 66.9 per cent to 38.4 per cent and the percentage of social adjustment expenditure had declined from 31.1 per cent to 21.9 per cent during the same period.

By 1973, as Table 9:2 shows, the expenditures by DREE itself continued to reflect the relative priority being given to industrial incentives. Table 9:3, however, shows, in addition to a levelling-off of total DREE expenditures, a somewhat reduced priority being given to industrial incentives, thus reflecting the 1974 changes. The table also reflects new program categories for compiling the data.

The regional distribution of expenditures in comparison with percentage of total Canadian population is shown in Table 9:4. It illustrates that, in aggregate terms, the Maritime provinces with 9.54 per cent of the population received 45.8 per cent of the expenditures. The western provinces, with 26.61 per cent of the population received 17.9 per cent of the funds. Quebec received 26.5 per cent of the funds although its population is 27.76 per cent of the total. Predictably, Ontario with 35.85 per cent of the population received only 4.9 per cent of the resources.

TABLE 9:4*
Cumulative Expenditures
Five-Year Period 1969/70 to 1972/73
Distribution by Province
All Programs

	BUDGETARY		LOANS		TOTAL		% OF
Province	*Expenditures ($ million)*	*% of Canada Total*	*Expenditures ($ million)*	*% of Canada Total*	*Expenditure ($ million)*	*% of Canada Total*	*Population in Canada*
Newfoundland	113.8	10.1	77.8	35.2	191.6	14.2	2.44
Prince Edward Island	55.4	4.9	10.9	5.0	66.3	4.9	0.52
Nova Scotia	126.6	11.2	39.8	14.0	166.2	14.3	3.64
New Brunswick	161.3	14.3	159.4	72.2	192.2	14.3	2.94
EAST	457.1	40.5	53.1	24.0	616.5	45.8	9.54
Quebec	303.9	27.0	—	—	357.0	26.5	27.76
Ontario	66.1	5.9	53.1	24.0	66.1	4.9	35.85
CENTRE	370.0	32.8	—	—	423.1	31.4	63.61
Manitoba	68.7	6.1	4.6	2.1	73.3	5.4	4.54
Saskatchewan	67.7	6.1	1.5	0.7	69.2	5.1	4.20
Alberta	68.6	6.1	2.2	1.0	70.8	5.3	7.59
British Columbia	28.3	2.5	—	—	28.3	2.1	10.29
WEST	233.3	20.8	8.3	3.8	241.6	17.9	26.61
NON-ALLOCATED	65.8	5.9	—	—	65.8	4.9	—
TOTAL	1126.2	100.0	220.8	100.0	1347.0	100.0	99.76

*Adapted from: DREE, *Regional Development Programs*, Ottawa, April 1973.

The criticisms made against the department's expenditures have varied. The New Democratic party has criticized the incentives grants as a corporate rip-off. David Springate, in a Harvard PHD thesis, concluded that, of eighteen companies studied which received incentives grants totalling $34 million, only seven based their decision on the special incentives.[58] The Conservative party, while critical of the incentives grants, has directed its attack primarily at the failure of the Liberal government to grant the provinces greater autonomy. It has also been argued that the minister had too much discretionary power and in this regard the Hon. Jean Marchand, the first minister of DREE, was regarded by some as a patronage "bagman".

It should be pointed out, however, that there is a real dilemma in mixed economies in determining how much and through what processes public funds should be spent to encourage new employment opportunities. While the utilization of cost-benefit analysis can improve the ratio between jobs created and the costs incurred, the decision to expend public funds in this manner is a highly political and discretionary one whether the discretion is exercised by elected politicians or by appointed public servants. It is thus one of the perennial issues in regional policy, and is intensified in a federal system because of strong local pressures to encourage expenditures on short-term projects, a dilemma experienced in the past by the Atlantic Development Board. Nevertheless, the federal Conservative party has been advocating greater autonomy to the provinces and perhaps would like to see greater expenditures in the Atlantic provinces rather than in Quebec.

DREE is still plagued with inadequate statistical information and of course has been further constrained by the economy's poor performance. Thus, as the third chairman of the Economic Council of Canada, André Raynauld, remarked:

> As an example of large-scale government programs which could easily be put in jeopardy by prolonged high unemployment would be, paradoxically some part of DREE's activity. The scenario on this matter could be: an increasing number of "mistakes" of abortive investments; a mounting outcry from the public against waste and disillusion among implicated workers and local officials, then, more rules, less flexibility; DREE could either fall back on the relatively sterile approach of static project evaluation rules or be eliminated altogether.[59]

For André Raynauld the earlier DREE experience reflected also a failure by economists to do good research and to provide effective policy alternatives.[60]

The Western Economic Opportunities Conference held in Calgary in July 1973 was, perhaps, the most symbolic reflection of the limitations of pursuing regional policy through an excessive dependence on the expenditure instruments. The federal government background papers on Industrial and Trade Development, Capital Financing and Financial Institutions, Mineral Resource Development, Agriculture, Transportation, and Regional Development Opportunities[61] reflected concern not only for comprehensiveness and decentralization but also contemplated the use of regulatory devices as well. The conference also more readily acknowledged the significant variations in the structure as well as the performance of the western provinces. For example, British Columbia and Alberta were performing well above the national average.[62] Both the heavy resource and agricultural bases of these provinces demanded new initiatives to diversify the economic structure of western Canada.[63] These factors as we have stressed significantly influenced the demands for decentralization of both IT&C and DREE. Thus the strengthening of the Federal Business Development Bank, the Export Development Corporation, and the subsequent establishment of the Ministry of State for Small Business were all consequential to policies outlined at the Western Economic Opportunities Conference which advocated further diversification of the economies of the western provinces. When the unique characteristics of the western provinces were placed against the Maritimes and Quebec, we observe a diversity of developmental opportunities, and hence developmental politics.

Thus in the mid-1970s DREE focusses on three main areas: Developmental Opportunity Initiatives, Industrial Incentives, and Other Programs.[64]

Developmental Opportunity Initiatives

The identification and pursuit of major developmental opportunities in the various provinces of Canada "have been consolidated in comprehensive and individual form in the new General Development Agreements (GDAS) signed by the department and individual provincial governments." The GDA provides the framework for encouraging co-ordinated federal-provincial action to realize the potential for economic and social growth in a particular province. The emphasis placed on the social aspects is clearly important since it is consistent with the multi-dimensional approach necessitated by Canadian regional politics. Social policies are far more redistributive than economic policies, notwithstanding the fact that the former are dependent upon the latter, and DREE performs an important role at the cabinet-ministerial level in establishing some balance between the more traditional approach to economic policy and the new approach which incorporates social policy.[65]

The agreement with the provinces declares a ten-year period of close, co-ordinated partnership between the federal government and the province. "It defines objectives, a broad strategy to achieve them, the extent of activity, and the types of co-operation and support that will be required." It is important to note that "the GDA does not provide for a commitment of resources. This is done by means of specific subsidiary agreements, which outline the relevant details of individual programs and projects." Consequently, rather than a generalized system greater emphasis is now placed on *sector strategies* which fit the specific needs of the provinces.[66] Here again, we detect a more micro-oriented approach to industrial development.

By way of illustration a careful examination of the human resources, governmental institutions, and resources in Kent County in eastern New Brunswick led to strong criticisms of the then-existing regional economic development strategy. Thus it was asserted that "there is a feeling in some places that agriculture should be written off in our area and all production moved to the areas with the so-called comparative advantage. We don't feel this is good enough in terms of people."[67]

In response to such criticisms there is now an Agricultural Development Subsidiary Agreement under the General Development Agreement with New Brunswick, with an estimated cost of $7.5 million over three years (of which the federal contribution is 80 per cent), the termination date being March 31, 1977. The agreement provides financial assistance to develop the following: commodity areas such as blueberries, greenhouse apples, vegetables, sheep, beef, dairy, feed-grain and protein production, and export seed potatoes; farmers (through farm management training), commodity groups, farm-labour supply, professional and technical staff, and information and demonstration services; and planning for future agricultural development (through an Agricultural Resources Study group).[68]

The shift toward smaller community development strategies without the abandonment of the growth centres suggests a more diversified regional development policy. The criticisms voiced against governmental programs in Kent County were similar to those made against the Newfoundland Resettlement Schemes. Consequently, between 1973 and 1975 separate GDAS were concluded with all provinces of Canada—with the exception of Prince Edward Island, with which a fifteen-year Comprehensive Development Plan, signed in 1969, still operates. The approach thus provides for both GDAS and sub-agreements between the federal government and the provinces on a province-by-province basis.

Industrial Incentives

The Regional Development Incentives Act (RDIA) makes provision for incentives to support the establishment, modernization, or expansion of manufacturing and processing industries and certain types of commercial facilities. It was indicated in an earlier section of this chapter that incentives may take the form of grants or loan guarantees to increase or maintain employment opportunities in certain regions of Canada, as identified by the Governor-in-Council. DREE's Act made provision for consultation with the provinces subsequent to which grants or loan guarantees can be made available to firms willing to locate, expand, or modernize in areas specified by the Governor-in-Council.

The departmental policy review described above produced some changes in the RDIA program; accordingly, specific province-wide areas of Canada were identified for assistance in Newfoundland, Prince Edward Island, Nova Scotia, New Brunswick, Manitoba, Saskatchewan, Quebec (excluding the Montreal–Hull corridor), and the northern part of Ontario. Incentives can be provided also through specific sub-agreements to the GDA, to resource-based industries in rural areas of Alberta and British Columbia.

Other Programs

Notwithstanding the new approach, a number of Acts affecting the fishing, forestry, and farming industries are still active. These include:

the Agricultural and Rural Development Act (ARDA), the Prairie Farm Rehabilitation Act (PFRA), and the Fund For Rural Economic Development (FRED). ARDA operates under cost-sharing agreements with the provincial governments and seeks to improve the income and employment opportunities of people in rural areas. The program is in operation in all provinces except P.E.I. where comparable activities are carried out under a comprehensive development plan. Since 1935 PFRA has been concerned with water conservation on individual farms and land-use adjustment in the western provinces. Recently, the adjustment program of PFRA has been broadened. FRED provides a broad mixture of programs encompassing infrastructure development, improved resource utilization, recreational development, and basic education and counselling. It should be added that the Special Areas Program which provides infrastructure assistance under federal-provincial agreements is also still in place, thus enabling the department to provide financial assistance for projects such as roads, water, and sewer systems, industrial parks, and schools throughout the system.

There are examples which demonstrate that regional economic and social policies have, once again, begun to emphasize rural development which had been an important consideration between 1966 and 1969. In 1969 the emphasis shifted to a more urbanized approach. However, by 1976, the emphasis had shifted again to accommodate primary industries including agriculture.[69] Thus the Small Farm Development Program which was established in 1969 as a subordinate agricultural program has been strengthened in recent years. While it is felt that the momentum which began in 1969 with the expansion of the urban centres in the Atlantic provinces, referred to in the introductory sections of this chapter, should be continued, there has been a revived emphasis on the development of primary industries including agriculture. This shift in policy followed both the Western Economic Opportunities Conference and the Report of the Standing Senate Committee on Agriculture which examined the agricultural potential of eastern New Brunswick.[70]

The latter enquiry concluded that major emphasis should be placed on community development as distinct from the growth pole concept. This trend of rural development is consistent with the new decentralized strategy being adopted by both the federal and the provincial governments.[71] Here we detect a more sociologically oriented approach to regional development based on the criterion that it is sociologically and politically advantageous to create job opportunities in lagging areas rather than moving people to the massive urban centres in which urban povery has become a major problem.[72] Thus the management of regional economic development policy is a complex activity. It would appear that neither a pure market system with its bias in favour of moving people to jobs nor an exclusive public sector strategy designed to create jobs in the lagging areas regardless of cost can solve the dilemmas in regional development policies which we have outlined. In fact, the most recent evaluation of the cost of creating new job opportunities demonstrates that the job-creation aspects of the program have been performing less efficiently than expected.[73] Since both development and underdevelopment are manifestations of chronic economic and social processes it is correct to assume, especially in a federal state, that regional development policies will continue forever.[74] Public policies although significantly influenced by economic considerations are not formulated exclusively on economic values. The Department of Regional Economic Expansion was established therefore to formulate policies with multiple goals and objectives; hence the difficulties encountered with the evaluation of regional economic development policies.

CENTRALIZATION AND DECENTRALIZATION

This chapter has reviewed the Canadian evolution of what one analyst has referred to as "the regional movement". More specifically, it has discussed the complexities inherent in any attempt to formulate a comprehensive regional policy. The concepts of planning and regional development administration were summarily introduced.

We have identified a trend from *ad hoc* "programs to policy" and from particular regions to interprovincial ones. DREE has made significant achievements in formulating a national development strategy. There is also a trend toward identifying horizontal characteristics (i.e., ones which cut across departmental lines), but we should recognize that regional analysis requires more careful examination of the unique characteristics of regions so that particular strategies can be identified within an overall framework. In many respects this has been the major achievement of DREE. However, DREE has begun to experience the complexities of the planning process in a federal state in that the 1973-74 reorganization saw the emphasis shift once again toward provincial initiatives. Perhaps the arrangements now require a new designation of responsibilities between the federal government and the provinces. The planning process therefore involves complex mixes between centralization and decentralization which must be reviewed continuously.

Regional planning and administration have imposed new strains on the cabinet system of government, on federal-provincial relationships, and on the regular approaches to politics and public administration. To what extent should Crown corporations be used to arrest regional disparities? Which departments should be integrated in the region to improve the implementation of policies? At what points should authority and responsibility lie? In this respect the popular and sometimes over-utilized concept of decentralization should be critically reviewed. Are we talking of centralization in a new form, of deconcentration, or of devolution? Here the relationship between federal, provincial, and municipal government administrations identifies conflicting issues which cannot be easily reconciled. Greater discretionary powers can be given to the provinces and the municipalities, but it should be recognized that such a step may adversely affect the development of a comprehensive approach to regional planning and policy formulation. Furthermore, increased decentralization can lead to fragmentation especially in a political system with weak national institutions. In this respect, economic-planning institutions must be carefully designed to reflect centripetal and centrifugal forces.

Thus, the regional movement may provide a new intersystem linkage between federal, provincial, and municipal levels of government. Even the urban issue may be approached within the "growth pole concept". We have also seen strong movements in recent years emphasizing the importance of rural development, at a time when there is a problem in the management of food supplies. Accordingly, agricultural development may once again become a central component of regional development policies. The creation of a Ministry of State for Small Business and the reorientation of Canada's Department of Agriculture provide examples of a somewhat new emphasis.

Whatever approach is adopted, adequate allowances must be made for "policy spillover" as demonstrated in recent attempts to formulate coherent strategies in policy fields encompassing the regional, manpower, industrial, and social spheres. These difficulties point to the need for flexibility in whatever approach is adopted.

Understanding regional policies impinges on the separate and often non-communicating disciplines of economics, sociology, geography, and politics. The regional concept depicts a problem-oriented approach to formulating and implementing relevant policies and programs. A critical problem is that of isolating those issues which should be dealt with by the central government having greater revenue capabilities as against those issues which should be the responsibility of the regions. Regional administration becomes increasingly more complex in a federal state such as Canada.

If the new slogan is decentralization, then it deserves a critical review. Such a review should have as one of its central objectives a proper explanation of the concept of decentralization — its political, economic, sociological, and managerial components — to make manifest certain dimensions which are otherwise latent in a concept generally used without clarification.

Between 1969 and 1973 the Department of Regional Economic Expansion demonstrated a Canadian response to a complex problem. DREE responded to the more fragmented approach to regional policies depicted by FRED, ADA, and ADB. However, its programs had to be reviewed, evaluated, and constrained by the Treasury Board and the PCO. The new demands for further co-ordination among DREE, Manpower and Immigration, Industry, Trade and Commerce, and Health and Welfare demonstrate, in part, the limits of departmental co-ordination. There is a need for the integration of programs in the field to synchronize centralizing forces with those tending toward greater regionalization. This was demonstrated in the new administrative arrangements which became operative late in 1973.

The new approach launched in 1973, which emphasized decentralization, has presented new problems; for example, the intensification of increased regional demands which could lead to fragmentation. Thus the critical problem for the 1980s will involve the establishment of an appropriate mix between a centralized and a decentralized regional development strategy; an issue which has plagued economic-policy formulation in all federal systems.

Regional politics is inherent both in federalism and especially in Canadian political processes. The creation of DREE places in the federal cabinet a political minister whose task is explicitly to help reduce regional economic and social disparities. In the first instance DREE was a kind of holding company of disparate programs. To a certain extent, it still is. Its own analysis and experience, coupled with the territorial pressure of other federal departments, and the pressure of provincial and opposition political criticism, has resulted, however, in a gradual process of policy and organizational change thus reflecting again the judicious mixture of politics, economics, and administration inherent in the economic-management process.

NOTES

1. On approaches to the study of public policy-making see C. O. Jones, *An Introduction to the Study of Public Policy* (Belmont, Ca., 1970), pp. 1-16 and T. Dye, *Understanding Public Policy* (Englewood Cliffs, N. J., 1972), pp. 87-183.

2. T. N. Brewis and G. Paquet, "Regional Development and Planning in Canada: An Exploratory Essay", *Canadian Public Administration*, Vol. XI, no. 2, p. 123 and T. N. Brewis, *Regional Economic Policies in Canada* (Toronto, 1969), pp. 43-53. For a brief recent discussion see A. Donner and F. Lazar, "Cost of Decentralizing Canada Could be High", *The Globe and Mail Report on Business*, January 29, 1977.

3. Department of Regional Economic Expansion, *The New Approach* (Ottawa, 1976), p. 15. See also Atlantic Development Council, *Regional Development Incentives Program: Atlantic Region* (Ottawa, n.d.), especially Chapter 3, pp. 71-91. This emphasis on the private sector is also reflected in Government of Canada, *The Way Ahead* (Ottawa, 1976). For recent discussions of regional co-operation see Dr. G. J. Gartner, "A Review of Cooperation Among the Western Provinces", Annual Conference of Institute of Public Administration of Canada (IPAC) in Halifax, September 8-10, 1976; E. A. Lomas, "The Council of Maritime Premiers: A Report and an Evaluation after Five Years", IPAC Meeting in Halifax, September 7-10, 1976; and A. Careleas, "Whither Canadian Federalism: The Challenge of Regional Diversity and Maturity". IPAC Meeting in Halifax, September 7-10, 1976.

4. Canadian Council on Rural Development, *Toward a Development Strategy for Canada* (Ottawa, 1972), pp. 7-28. House of Commons, *Minutes of Proceedings and Evidence of Standing Committee on Regional Development Respecting: Estimates, 1972-73, Department of Regional Economic Expansion* (March 28, 1972), pp. 57, 58, and Atlantic Development Council, *Regional Development Incentives Program: The Atlantic Region.*

5. H. Buckley and E. Tihanyi, *Canadian Policies for Rural Adjustment: A Case Study of the Economic Impact of ARDA, PFRA, and MMRA* (Ottawa, 1967). See also Canadian Council on Rural Development, *Rural Canada 1970: Prospects and Problems* (Ottawa, 1970), p. 34.

6. Buckley and Tihanyi, *Canadian Policies for Rural Adjustment,* p. 11. The MMRA program originated in the same period which saw the major irrigation projects launched in Alberta under PFRA—its rationale was characterized by overly optimistic assumptions concerning prospective increases in the productivity of agricultural lands.

7. Ibid., p. 104.

8. Ibid., p. 96. See also Canadian Council on Rural Development, *Rural Canada 1970,* p. 35.

9. See A. Waterston, *Development Planning: Lessons of Experience* (Baltimore, 1965), Chapter 8. The emergence of a development planning approach has been most significant in recent years. It points also to the difference between stabilization of economic management and the management of economic development. The increased use of boards for planning and co-ordination should be noted.

10. Cited in C. S. MacKaay, "Canadian Regionalism: The Atlantic Development Board, A Case Study". MA thesis, McGill University, Montreal, 1969.

11. Ibid., and Atlantic Development Board, *Annual Report, 1968-69* (Ottawa, 1969), pp. 16-23.

12. Atlantic Development Board, *Annual Report, 1968-69,* pp. 19-23. It should be emphasized that the recent decentralization of regional development planning reintroduces the same problems.

13. Brewis, *Regional Economic Policies in Canada,* pp. 138-40.

14. R. W. Phidd, "The Economic Council and Economic Policy Formulation

in Canada". PhD thesis, Queen's University, Kingston, 1972, Chapter 1. The recent organizations in Finance, DREE, IT&C, EM&R, M&I and the increased use of boards are all illustrative of the managerial aspects of economic planning outlined in that chapter.

15. Economic Council of Canada, *Third Annual Review* (Ottawa, 1966), p. 265.

16. Ibid.

17. Economic Council of Canada, *Fifth Annual Review* (Ottawa, 1968), pp. 144-80, especially p. 153.

18. P. E. Trudeau, *Federalism and the French Canadians* (Toronto, 1968). See also T. N. Brewis, "Regional Economic Disparities and Policies", in L. H. Officer and L. B. Smith, eds., *Canadian Economic Problems and Policies* (Toronto, 1970), p. 335. It should be noted, however, that others have identified regional policies with postwar developments. See S. F. Kaliski, *Canadian Economic Policy Since the War* (Montreal, 1966), especially pp. 9-22.

19. Department of Regional Economic Expansion, *The New Approach* (Ottawa, 1976). This is undoubtedly the most significant issue facing Canadian federalism and economic development strategy.

20. A study of the Atlantic Development Board shows, however, that it was constrained by the Treasury Board and that there were difficulties in complementing its work with other boards and departments. See MacKaay, "Canadian Regionalism", pp. 35-36, 43-49, especially p. 43. The 1973 Policy Review seemed to have repeated this process. However, the reorganization of the IDB to create the Federal Business Development Bank is most significant. Note also the use of RDIB and other "boards" in Industry, Trade and Commerce.

21. Department of Regional Economic Expansion, *Regional Development Programmes* (Ottawa, 1973). House of Commons, *Minutes of Proceedings and Evidence of the Standing Committee on Regional Development Respecting: Estimates, 1973-74, Department of Regional Economic Expansion.*

22. On the concept of deconcentration, see the following: H. Maddick, *Democracy, Decentralization and Development* (London, 1963); R. W. Phidd, "Development Administration: Its Meaning and Its Application in the Developing Countries". MA research essay, Carleton University, Ottawa, 1966, pp. 35-42; H. F. Alderfer, *Public Administration in Newer Nations* (New York, 1967), pp. 53-72.

23. Department of Regional Economic Expansion, *Annual Report, 1970-71* (Ottawa, 1972).

24. Regional Economic Expansion, *The New Aproach*, p. 28.

25. Ibid.

26. Ibid.

27. Department of Regional Economic Expansion, *Annual Report, 1971-72* (Ottawa, 1973), pp. 3-6.

28. Regional Economic Expansion, *The New Approach*, pp. 19-22. For criticisms of the previous approach see the following: Atlantic Development Council, *Regional Development Incentives Program: The Atlantic Region;* D. J. V. Springate, *Regional Development Incentive Grants and Private Investment in Canada, A Case Study of the Effect of Regional Development Incentives on the Investment Decisions of Manufacturing Firms* (Cambridge, 1972) and *Regional Incentives and Private Investment* (Montreal, 1973).

29. See J. P. Francis and N. A. Pallai, *Regional Development and Regional Policy: Some Issues and Recent Canadian Experience* (Ottawa, 1972), especially pp. 53-78. The special areas program can be compared with the Regional Development Incentives Programmes and subsequently the General Development Agreements. The maps and tables presented in this chapter should be compared as a reflection of the changes in policy. It should be noted that the concept of region also changed significantly.

30. Waterston, *Development Planning*. See G. Hallett, *et al.*, *Regional Policy for Ever?* (London, 1973).

31. The background papers prepared by the federal government reflect the concerns of the conference: Western Economic Opportunities Conference, July 24-26, 1973, *Regional Development Opportunities, Capital Financing and Financial Institutions, Mineral Resource Development,* and *Industrial and Trade Development*. Following the conference the DREE reorganization was implemented. Later, the Federal Business Development Bank was established and IT&C was significantly reorganized with the establishment of the Ministry of State for Small Business.

32. Regional Economic Expansion, *The New Approach*.

33. Hon. D. C. Jamieson, House of Commons, *Minutes of Proceedings of*

Evidence of the Standing Committee on Regional Development Respecting: Estimates, 1973-74, Department of Regional Economic Expansion.

34. See Western Economic Opportunities Conference, *Regional Development Opportunities,* and *Industrial and Trade Development*, and Atlantic Development Council, *Regional Development Incentives Program: The Atlantic Region*.

35. Jamieson, *Estimates, 1973-74*.

36. Regional Economic Expansion, *The New Approach*, pp. 34-37.

37. A. Green, "Regional Economic Disparities", in L. H. Officer and L. B. Smith, eds., *Issues in Canadian Economics* (Toronto, 1974), pp. 354-70.

38. On the significance of economic policies in the 1972 elections see W. A. Wilson, *The Trudeau Question: Election 1972* (Don Mills, 1973).

39. Jamieson, *Regional Development*, no. 2 (April 10, 1973), p. 7.

40. The central governmental official behind the Western Economic Opportunities Conference was T. K. Shoyama who was then an Assistant Deputy Minister in the Department of Finance but who later became Deputy Minister of Energy, Mines and Resources and ultimately of Finance. One of the background documents dealt with *Capital Financing and Financial Institutions*. Policy changes were expected in this area in 1977. For a comparative approach to decentralization see International Institute of Administrative Sciences, "The Administrative Side of Regionalization within States". Mexico City, July 22-26, 1974.

41. See Western Economic Opportunities Conference, *Industrial and Trade Development*, pp. 6-35.

42. Jamieson, *Regional Development*.

43. Department of Regional Economic Expansion, Hon. D. C. Jamieson, 12 vols. (released April 1973). For more up-to-date analysis consult the following: *Climate for Development: The Atlantic Region* (Ottawa, 1976); *Climate for Development: The Western Region* (Ottawa, 1976); *Climate for Development: Ontario Region* (Ottawa, 1976); *Climate for Development: Quebec Region* (Ottawa, 1976); and *Climate for Regional Development* (Ottawa, 1976).

44. Jamieson, 12 vols. (1973).

45. Jamieson, *Regional Development*, pp. 11-12.

46. Green, "Regional Economic Disparities".

47. Jamieson, *Regional Development*, p. 12. See note 45 above.

48. It is clear that considerable conflict occurred over the attempt to formulate economic regions as distinct from political regions. The issue of Maritime union is one example of this conflict.

49. See, for example, J. N. Turner, Budget Speech, 1974 and the subsequent approach adopted by Saskatchewan and Alberta.

50. Western Economic Opportunities Conference, *Industrial and Trade Development*, pp. 22-25.

51. In order to create jobs in these regions a concerted approach must be adopted by IT&C, M&I, DREE, Agriculture, and other departments. The establishment of the Department and Commission of Employment and Immigration points in this direction. See Chapter 10.

52. Hon. M. Lalonde, Minister of National Health and Welfare, *Working Paper on Social Security in Canada* (Ottawa, 1972), p. 7.

53. In fact, in late 1976 a Special Task Force was established in Finance to look at this problem.

54. Hon. B. Mackasey, *Minutes of Proceedings and Evidence of Standing Committee on Labour, Manpower and Immigration Estimates, 1972-73*, p. 6.

55. Jamieson, *Regional Development*, p. 18.

56. This is reflected in the reorganization of Industry, Trade and Commerce, Regional Economic Expansion, Finance, and the Department and Commission of Employment and Immigration.

57. Department of Regional Economic Expansion, *Regional Development Programmes* (Ottawa, 1973).

58. Springate, *Regional Development Incentive Grants and Private Investment in Canada*.

59. A. Raynauld, "What if Unemployment is Unavoidable?" Notes for a speech to the Institute of Public Administration, Ottawa, February 9, 1972, and notes for a talk to the Ottawa Political Economy Association, February 7, 1972.

60. Raynauld, Notes for a talk to the Ottawa Political Economy Association.

61. Government of Canada, Western Economic Opportunities Conference, *Industrial and Trade Development, Capital Financing and Financial Institutions, Mineral Resource Development, Agriculture, Transportation*, and *Regional Development Opportunities*.

62. Western Economic Opportunities Conference, *Regional Development Opportunities*, p. 7.

63. Western Economic Opportunities Conference, *Industrial and Trade Development*, p. 7.

64. Regional Economic Expansion, *The New Approach*, pp. 14-30.

65. See the policies and programs administered by Finance, Manpower and Immigration, National Health and Welfare, and Regional Economic Expansion. For a most useful analysis of the broader approach to regional development see N. M. Swan, "Evaluating Regional Development Policies". Paper presented to the Atlantic Provinces Economic Council, Halifax, October 25, 1976.

66. Regional Economic Expansion, *The New Approach*.

67. See Standing Senate Committee on Agriculture, *Kent County Can be Saved. An Agricultural Inquiry into the Agricultural Potential of Eastern New Brunswick*. Report (Ottawa, 1976), p. 27.

68. Ibid., pp. 61-65, especially p. 65.

69. Ibid., p. 64. Statement by J. D. Love, Deputy Minister, Department of Regional Economic Expansion.

70. Ibid. See also Government of Canada, Western Economic Opportunities Conference, *Agriculture*.

71. The Federal Government established a Task Force on Decentralization.

72. For a sociological study critical of regional planning see R. Mathews, *There's No Better Place Than Here: Social Change in Three Newfoundland Communities* (Toronto, 1976).

73. Department of Regional Economic Expansion, Statement before the Regional Development Committee, House of Commons, November 30, 1976, p. 19.

74. Institute of Economic Affairs, *Regional Policy for Ever?*

CHAPTER TEN

The Role of the Commission and Department of Employment and Immigration

There are a number of departments in the federal government which are concerned with the management of the supply of resources in its broadest sense. This chapter focuses primarily on the Department of Manpower and Immigration (M&I) created in 1966 and renamed the Commission and Department of Employment and Immigration in 1976.* The department was established to improve the management of manpower policies specifically as well as the management of supply more generally. There are many other departments which influence supply management policies. These include Transport, Energy Mines and Resources, Agriculture, and Health and Welfare.[1] For example, the Department of Energy, Mines and Resources is at the centre of the stage as this book goes to press. Supply management encompasses the managing of both natural and human resources. It thus involves primary and secondary industries and renewable and non-renewable resource sectors of natural and physical resources management. However, an adequate examination of all these departments would take us far beyond our immediate concerns.

Whether we are dealing with the supply of energy, the supply of agricultural products, or the supply of human manpower we must also be concerned simultaneously with the demand side since broad economic strategies are designed to bring about some kind of overall equilibrium of the system as a whole. Psychological and technological changes can also influence the scope and nature of supply-management policies. Because political actions have direct impact on the behaviour of participants in the political system, we are concerned, not only with structure and government organization, but also with

*Since the re-naming of the department in 1976 is so recent in relation to the publication of this book, we will refer almost exclusively to its previous title, the Department of Manpower and Immigration (M&I).

the *effects* of the policies formulated by government departments on various groups in the Canadian political system. For example, the Unemployment Insurance Commission (UIC), which reports to the Minister of Manpower and Immigration, has been criticized for adversely affecting the work ethic.[2] The validity of this critism, however, undoubtedly varies greatly among different groups in the population.

ECONOMIC MANAGEMENT AND THE ELUSIVENESS OF SUPPLY MANAGEMENT

It is important to stress that since the early 1960s Canadian "supply management policies" were couched primarily in terms of human resources and, to a certain extent, coincided with the establishment of the Department of Manpower and Immigration in 1966.[3] The then new approach was related to the emphasis on "growth economics". Most recently, the debate has shifted to energy supplies, that is, to concern over the most efficient utilization of limited physical resources, especially non-renewable resources. The continued existence in the late 1970s of problems such as inflation, energy, and unemployment has simultaneously brought forward demands for stronger job-creation efforts.

However, manpower policies are only one aspect of broad human resource policies and, as such, the Department of Health and Welfare is concerned in an ancillary way with the supply of labour and with consumer demand since adequate maintenance of the entire labour force and their families is a primary objective of governmental policies.[4] These concerns reflect much broader considerations than labour supply by encompassing such issues as income-support and income-maintenance programs of which the recent revision of the social security system is most illustrative.

Since the supply of goods and services is partially dependent on the presence of competition in the marketplace the role of the Department of Consumer and Corporate Affairs is an important feature of supply management in that it is concerned with maintaining the adequacy of the market. However, as Chapter 11 will show, various societal groups have responded differently to recent proposals for an effective competition policy, thus demonstrating once again that different groups in the political system respond to policy changes in terms of how they perceive their particular interests to be affected.

Both of the above departments are concerned with important aspects of some of the major goals or objectives of economic policy and these objectives are further associated with the preservation of certain ideological commitments inherent in the Canadian "state". If the market is to function efficiently and effectively, then there should be adequate information and there should be mobility of resources, both human and physical. Governmental *intervention* is usually predicated on the belief that the market-allocative mechanism should be complemented. Many groups, of course, have challenged such governmental intervention on grounds that attempts to alleviate bottlenecks in the market system merely leads to still more intervention.

By providing for such things as training, assisted mobility, improved labour-market information, vocational counselling, and placement services, the government has attempted to promote a better matching of supply to changing labour demand, thereby reducing the bottlenecks, structural unemployment, and other market pressures and strains that impede and distort the process of economic growth.[5] While there is always *autonomous* mobility (that is, movement undertaken at the initiative and expense of the worker or his employer) there has been, since 1967, *assisted* mobility. Governmental assistance is predicated on the belief that there are barriers to movement caused by inadequate information or the cost of moving. In this regard, the programs endorsed by the federal government have been designed to assist market forces. Hence governments provide subsidies to workers in a manner similar to the subsidies provided to "ailing industries" but for quite different ideological reasons. The Minister of Manpower and Immigration has been under attack for the allocation of resources in these areas. These criticisms range from a concern that the programs are disguised welfare to the view, as mentioned above, that the work ethic is being effectively curtailed.

Manpower policies reflect partly the work of the Economic Council. Moreover, because of the emphasis placed on demand-management policies prior to the establishment of the Department of Manpower and Immigration, "manpower policy is conceived of in Canada largely as a policy affecting the supply side of the labour market." In Sweden manpower policy is far more comprehensive in scope in that it controls many "expenditure programs" affecting the level and location of employment and thus operates more on the demand side of the market too. In Canada, there have been many recommendations to broaden the scope of manpower policies. Many of these demands are now being translated into new programs within the department.

From the perspective adopted in this chapter it will be demonstrated that while the creation of new departments concerned primarily with supply management policies was based on the belief that such concepts were useful and that the creation of departments specifically designed to emphasize supply dimensions in policy would lead to improved functional organization, to date the performance of these departments has demonstrated that no clear-cut distinction can be made between demand- and supply-management policies. Moreover, the instruments used by these agencies must be co-ordinated at the Cabinet Level. These developments have created new strains on the political system and have led to demands for more effective co-ordination particularly in the economic policy-making sphere.[6] The recent suggestions that the Department of Manpower and Immigration, for example, emphasize demand-management policies (Job Creation Programs) further shows the managerial component of economic policy-making and the dynamic nature of economic management.

The argument has been made also that certain benefits flow from "economies of scale" so that large firms produce goods and services more efficiently than small firms and accordingly there have been demands for greater concentration of industry. Yet the Canadian state is committed to the maintenance of competition. To this end, the Government of Canada requested that the Economic Council of Canada explore the role of competition policy and in 1975 established a Royal Commission to look further into the state of corporate concentration in Canada.

The Economic Council of Canada outlined at least three components of competition policy: the attainment of the most efficient possible performance from economy; the raising of total output in accordance with consumer demands; and the recognition of the importance of research, invention, and innovation. The Council advocated "the improvement of economic efficiency and the avoidance of economic waste, with a view to enhancing the well-being of Canadians." An examination of the responsibilities and policies pursued by the departments of Manpower and Immigration and Consumer and Corporate Affairs therefore demonstrates several aspects of the conflicting goals inherent in the formulation of economic policies. The rationale for governmental intervention in the manpower and consumer-policy fields and concomitantly for the establishment of these departments has been directed at achieving a number of conflicting goals, including growth, stabilization, and equity.

It has been argued for example that "manpower policy"[7] is a misnomer and that policies directed at matching worker to job are doomed to failure since broader objectives encompassing educational and cultural goals are also included among the so-called "economic objectives". Similarly, Canadian consumer policies have been criticized on grounds that they incorporate two conflicting and irreconcilable groups: namely, "consumer interests" and "corporate interests".

Thus both manpower and consumer policies can be considered as being both redistributive and distributive policies since they deal with mobility of resources. Manpower policies ultimately redistribute resources at least on a regional basis since there has always been transfer of income from some provinces to others through the use of training and mobility programs.[8] Competition policies serve similar objectives. Both policies also demonstrate "the federal character" of the Canadian political system. Our appraisal of these departments illustrates, once again, the goal conflict and hence the political dimensions of the management of economic policies in a federal state.

Late in 1976 the Minister of Manpower and Immigration submitted proposals for a Commission and Department of Employment and Immigration which were accompanied by a number of new policy emphases. First, it emphasized "the dignity and personal satisfaction provided by real and worthwhile jobs, and an earned income higher than unemployment benefits". Second, it stressed that the new strategy had to be consistent with the restraint of expenditures and the moderation in the increase of the money-supply policy stated by the Department of Finance. Third, the statement clearly enunciated an employment strategy by stressing three interrelated components: job creation based on a decentralized community priority system; youth employment and employability measures to ease the transition from school to work; and a group of selective, preventive measures to reduce the loss of work and hasten a return to employment.[9]

THE EVOLUTION OF MANPOWER POLICIES

The evolution of Canadian manpower policies can be best understood by examining the following policy and organizational reforms: the postwar changes which occurred in the Department of Labour; the early recommendations of the Economic Council for the development of an effective labour-market policy; the subsequent establishment of the Department of Manpower and Immigration; and recent emphasis in the 1976 "new employment strategy" on the demand side of manpower policies, a focus which can be contrasted with the earlier emphasis on supply-management considerations.

Former officials in the Department of Labour have argued that important initiatives were taken by the department during the late 1950s and the early 1960s to formulate an active manpower policy in Canada.[10] However these efforts were constrained by the diffuse responsibilities of the Department of Labour which were primarily concerned with industrial relations. Consequently, many efforts were undertaken to achieve co-ordination by functional specialization of the tasks performed by the Department of Labour. In fact, a group of consultants had made some recommendations for the reorganization of the department well before the recommendations of the Economic Council of Canada were voiced.[11] The recommendations pointed to alternative ways of managing labour-market policies.

An "interest group" approach to policy-making would consider the Department of Labour to be concerned with the interest of the workers while Industry, Trade and Commerce would be seen as serving the interests of industry. However, the recent evolution of the policy-making machinery would make such an interpretation somewhat simplistic in that there have been significant policy spill-overs between the departments of Manpower and Immigration, IT&C, Labour, Regional Economic Expansion, Health and Welfare, and Secretary of State, not to mention the diverse and changing clientele which they serve.

Former senior officials in the Department of Labour have stressed several items of legislation as the central benchmarks of its evolution, including the Wartime Labour Relations Regulations adopted in 1944, the Industrial Relations and Disputes Investigation Act of 1948, the Technical and Vocational Training Act of 1961, and the Manpower Mobility Program of 1965.[12] Following the establishment of the Department of Manpower and Immigration new measures were adopted to facilitate the development of a more comprehensive labour-market policy. These measures were reflected in the Government Reorganization Act of 1966, the Adult Occupational Training Act of 1967, the revisions of the Adult Occupational Training Act in 1970 and 1972, the revision of the Unemployment Insurance Act in 1971, and the establishment of a permanent Job Creation Branch within the Manpower Division in 1973. At the time of writing, steps were being taken to integrate the Unemployment Insurance Centres with the Canada Manpower Centres as a further effort toward a more comprehensive approach.

In 1965 Mr. George Haythorne, then Deputy Minister of Labour, outlined a new policy orientation for the department which included increased emphasis on employment policy, manpower-development policy, labour-market policy, and industrial-relations policy.[13] These responsibilities were subsequently divided between two departments, the Department of Labour and the Department of Manpower and Immigration. The importance of identifying the various thrusts is that we can more readily appreciate the diverse policy areas which are in need of co-ordination. In fact, it will be demonstrated that the increased tendency to define responsibilities in functional areas has led to new initiatives for policy co-ordination.

The early recommendations of the Economic Council of Canada provided the main rationale for a separate Department of Manpower and Immigration. This left the Department of Labour to be concerned primarily with industrial-relations policy. But this has led to demands for co-ordination which are different from those which existed prior to the changes. Statements made by the Minister and Deputy Minister of Labour in 1976, in the midst of the debate on tripartism, stressed the need for a stronger and more aggressive Department of Labour. This indicates that the functional separation recommended by the Economic Council has not lived up to the expectations which precipitated the change. The minister indicated that "government-labour-management co-operation" should aim at reducing confrontation between the groups involved in the conciliation process.

Moreover, the constitutional division of responsibilities suggests the need for improved federal-provincial and labour-management consultation. In fact, the evolution of an active manpower policy in Canada was adopted amidst charges that the federal government had outmanoeuvred the provinces at the 1966 Federal-Provincial Relations Conference.[14] Thereafter, the Department of Manpower and Immigration emerged as a buyer of provincial services. Given the necessity for improved labour-management relations the situation now demands both federal-provincial and labour-management consultation. Above all, the view has been expressed recently that the Department of Labour should become once again more active in economic-policy planning.[15]

In order to appreciate the changes which have taken place in the structure of manpower policy formulation at the federal level since 1966 it is useful to compare the role of the provincial departments of Labour, where both functions are generally performed by one department. In fact, some reservations were expressed during the early stages of the creation of the Federal Department of Manpower and Immigration that it would thwart efforts at federal-provincial co-operation between the departments of Labour at the two levels of government. Developments since 1975 point to distinct spheres of federal-provincial co-operation and co-ordination taking place within the departments of Labour, and Manpower and Immigration, through the Canada Manpower Centres. Both departments are experiencing greater decentralization, more involved federal-provincial consultations and stronger efforts at improved government-industry relationships. In short, the demands which gradually grew in the mid-1960s for more effective *employment policies* have led to a need for improved consultations and co-ordination at the interdepartmental, federal-provincial, and government-industry levels. These changes should be borne in mind as we review developments since 1966.

J. D. Love who later became Deputy Minister of Labour observed that:

> In Canada, the big breakthrough came in 1961 with the Report of the Special Senate Committee on Manpower and Employment, which sounded a strong warning that failure to make optimum use of existing manpower resources and to adjust to changing manpower requirements would place severe restrictions on national growth and development. The theme was picked up and given more concrete expression by the Economic Council of Canada, whose first

Chairman, Dr. John Deutsch, had been a key witness before the Senate Committee. And in 1966, with the creation of a new Department of Manpower and Immigration, it was embedded in Government Policy.[16]

The Economic Council of Canada advocated the importance of improved co-ordination of research and policy formulation. The Council took the position that the Canadian Employment Service should be upgraded and accorded the task of promoting occupational, industrial, and geographic mobility of the labour force to meet the requirements of a changing industrial economy. It pointed to the importance of establishing proper policies to regulate the demand and supply aspects of Canadian manpower policies. Accordingly, the Council asserted:

> The objective of a labour-market policy as we conceive it, is to bring about the matching of the supply and the demand for labour in specific localities and occupation in a way that manpower resources can be most productively utilized. It has as its purpose both the achievement of high employment and the utilization of the labour force at its maximum productive potential. Workers who are employed at less than their productive potential, whether it's because of problems associated with lack of occupational, industrial, or geographical mobility, earn less than they are potentially capable of earning.[17]

The significance of the above definition for the management of economic policies is that "if labour market policy is regarded as an integral part of the general fiscal, monetary, and other policies for the purpose of promoting national economic objectives, then it follows that the employment service must have a key economic role."[18]

The Economic Council of Canada, given its concern with aggregate economic management, went on to identify several ways to improve labour-market policy. These included the establishment of an effective administration; the expansion of programs for training and retraining; more adequate labour market information; and effective programs and assistance to promote mobility. Having identified these measures the Council noted that the National Employment Service (NES) was handicapped by several deficiencies, including its status as a subordinate agency of the Unemployment Insurance Commission, its position outside of a department of government which has the responsibility for formulating over-all manpower policy, and the general failure to appreciate the important role which a public employment service should play in implementing an integrated manpower policy.[19]

The search for an adequate organizational structure to formulate labour-market policies was actively pursued between 1964 and 1966. This was reflected in the following observation of the Economic Council in 1965:

Since our *First Annual Review* was published, steps have been taken to separate the National Employment Service (NES) from the Unemployment Insurance Commission and have it transferred to the Federal Department of Labour. This is a necessary beginning towards achieving appropriate co-ordination of manpower policy. However, the way in which the NES is transferred to the Department is of crucial importance. Simply relocating the NES as a branch of the Department will not suffice.

It is imperative that the NES, together with relevant labour-market functions, be set up in such a way that manpower policy will achieve the highest possible stature. It will not be possible for manpower policy to achieve such stature as long as the Employment Service is treated as a subsidiary operation related merely to the payment of unemployment insurance. Nothing will have been achieved by this transfer if the NES becomes little more than another branch of the Department of Labour.[20]

In order to appreciate the complexities involved in governmental reorganization it is worth pointing out that officials from the Department of Manpower and Immigration expressed the view before the Senate Committee on National Finance, in March 1975, that the separation of the National Employment Service from the Unemployment Insurance Commission went too far and the 1976 changes which will be discussed later verified this statement.[21]

The Economic Council of Canada went on to recommend two alternative approaches for managing labour-market policy. Prior to doing so it identified the functions which should be performed by any agency assigned these responsibilities. Thus, the Council asserted:

What is needed is a manpower agency which would be more than a placement service, important as this service is. It should be a key operational agency for implementing manpower policies, and the sole co-ordinating agency of all policies and programs related to the labour market.[22]

The Council, under John Deutsch's leadership, substantiated its awareness of the problem by pointing to two alternative approaches. The first alternative for achieving the above objectives was a reorganized Department of Labour. However, the Council noted that:

> this would require a very major change in the function and character of the Department. Under such an arrangement, the head of this agency would need to have under him all the relevant manpower functions at present being carried out in a number of branches of the Department of Labour, such as technical and vocational training, the manpower consultative service, research, etc.[23]

The second alternative would be the establishment of a new ministry of manpower services. Such a ministry could be the sole co-ordinator of all manpower policies and programs, including not only those now in the Department of Labour, but also those in the Department of Citizenship and Immigration.[24]

It is interesting to note that the Council, in its *First Annual Review*, seemed to have been emphasizing "a co-ordinating role in labour market policy" by the National Employment Service within a reorganized Department of Labour. However, in its *Second Annual Review*, in a very short paragraph, it suggested a second alternative, namely, the combination of Manpower and Immigration, which the government later endorsed. The Government of Canada subsequently established a Department of Manpower and Immigration which meant that serious efforts were also to be given, in the future, to the synchronization of immigration policy with labour-market policy. The implications of this change have only recently begun to emerge as an important component of the debate regarding co-ordination of economic policy. This change illustrates that the conflicting pull of differentiation and integration constitutes an important reality in the management of economic policies.

The establishment of the new department attempted to integrate two separate policy areas: manpower policy and immigration policy. The primary concern of manpower policy is to facilitate the economic growth of Canada by endeavouring to insure that the supply of manpower matches the demand, qualitatively, quantitatively, and geographically. The prime objective of immigration policies and programs is to encourage and facilitate the movement to Canada of those who have skills and talents in strong general or specific demand in this country. Other objectives provide for the reunion of families and the alleviation of the international refugee problem. The attainment of these two policy objectives is achieved through research conducted by a strong Research, Planning and Evaluation component of the department. However, during periods of high unemployment and rising prices with wages constituting a significant component, both job creation and efforts to contain wages take on increased importance. The Department of Labour, therefore, must also perform an important role in labour-management conciliation.

Summarily, the approach to manpower policies which emerged in the mid-1970s followed initiatives taken in the early 1960s. This view has been corroborated by the Economic Council of Canada which asserted in 1971:

We have dated the initiation of an active, comprehensive and integrated federal manpower policy in Canada with the establishment in 1966 of the Department of Manpower and Immigration, which brought together in a single ministry the various manpower programs formerly operated by the Department of Labour, the Immigration Services of the Department of Citizenship and Immigration, and most of the former National Employment Service. But interest in selective manpower programs emerged at the beginning of the 1960s.[25]

Before embarking on a more detailed analysis of the role of the Department of Manpower and Immigration it is worth mentioning that the separation of this department from Labour still left a number of important problems unresolved. Given the presence of a high degree of labour unrest in the economy, "collective bargaining" has presented new problems. Thus, in the mid-1970s there were cogent arguments that a better reconciliatory system should be developed to reduce confrontations between labour and management. To this end, the Department of Labour has been attempting to promote good industrial relations through the formation of labour-management consultative committees. These committees have aimed at providing a variety of support services to the existing committees but they are also endeavouring to generate new dialogue between unions and management in all sectors of the economy.

It should be emphasized, therefore, that the splitting of the Department of Labour may have created a major problem for the economic management system, in that it de-emphasized the role of the Department of Labour relative to the Department of Manpower and Immigration. This situation was worsened by the subsequent severity of the inflation crisis. Consequently, industrial relations which was left in the Department of Labour became extremely critical between 1969 and 1975. Thus, the reorganization of economic management activities into functional areas still leaves new problems of co-ordination to be dealt with.

By way of further illustration the Hon. John A. Munro, then Minister of Labour, stated in May 1975 that his department was faced with two distinctly different, yet complementary, industrial relations tasks: the provision of direct aid to the parties in disputes through such measures as conciliation, mediation, and the services of specific industry specialists; and the ongoing provision of assistance aimed at improving union-management relationships by means of special programs and advisory services. To this end, the Department established a Labour-Management-Government Council which aimed at conducting studies, discussions, and resolution of specific industrial relations problems. The Department further announced its intentions to display a greater degree of involvement in economic policy-planning and decision-making.[26] It can be stated then that the Department of Labour is now seeking a national profile to reflect its deep involvement and concern in key areas of industrial relations and employment standards. It was felt that improvement in industrial relations, which may even include worker-management participation, can improve the quality of worker-management relationships. Thus, changes in labour-management relations can lead to further improvements in labour-industry relations. These issues will be discussed at greater length in Chapter 12 where we evaluate the mechanisms of conflict and consensus in economic management.

The Department of Manpower and Immigration was established in 1966 to achieve five basic goals: (i) to help the individual select and obtain productive and personally satisfactory employment through efficient counselling; (ii) to increase the level of skill of the labour force through adult occupational training; (iii) to facilitate the adjustment of the labour-market demand and supply by helping workers relocate to the nearest areas where suitable; (iv) to help members of the labour force and employers to adapt to technological and other changes; and (v) to help reduce fluctuations in employment and shorten the period of unemployment.[27] It should be apparent that these are highly selective measures geared to bridging the gap between micro- and macro-policy instruments. The policies are directed at people adversely affected by the market system.

Before the department was established it was noted that there were at least four inadequately utilized programs on the federal statute books which affected several groups in society: pre-employment training for people out of school, training in co-operation with industry, training of the unemployed, and training of the disabled. The following explanations were given for the inadequate utilization of the existing legislation:

—There is a lack of adequate knowledge among the general public, particularly with regard to what courses are available, the qualifications for taking the courses, the duration of the courses, and the conditions under which they may be taken.
—Workers, especially unemployed workers, are not being informed and counselled adequately about the need for retraining. Various surveys indicate that workers generally do not understand the need for training, even when they know that training facilities are available.
—Frequently, the curicula, timetables, and facilities are not suitable for meeting the needs of the adults.
—There is a scarcity of qualified vocational teachers, and the number of teachers being trained is declining, rather than increasing.
—Provincial and local education authorities do not have adequate information regarding developing future manpower needs.
—Because many authorities are involved, the responsibility for the initiation of programs is often not clear. Consequently, programs that are needed do not get implemented. Effective steps must be taken to overcome these deficiencies and short-comings.[28]

The Economic Council placed major emphasis on the need to improve data on job vacancies and on the need to facilitate mobility of labour by providing financial assistance. These ingredients were subsequently reflected in the organization of the Department of Manpower and Immigration and in the endorsement of new programs.

THE EVOLUTION OF THE DEPARTMENT

We will examine the evolution of the department by differentiating the 1966-to-1972 period from the subsequent changes made in the

1973-to-1976 period. In 1966 the federal Department of Manpower and Immigration absorbed the National Employment Service (NES), the Canadian Immigration Service (CIS), and the Economics and Research Branch from the Department of Labour. As one observer commented in 1967:

> Compared to either the old Labour Department or the old Citizenship and Immigration Department, the new Department will be larger, more complex, and more decentralized, with extensive field services and staffs. It will have representatives throughout the world and will perform a myriad of tasks, from family counselling to recruiting immigrants and even to running a school for its own staff. The Department will, undoubtedly, grow as new programs are developed and the picture presented above may be significantly altered in the process.[29]

In 1966, at the time of the reorganization, the department's staff numbered 7,997 but it was expected to grow to 9,000. Of the total, the NES constituted 5,049 and the CIS 2,304.[30] The Program Development Service (PDS) constituted a most important aim of the new organization in that it conducted research on training and manpower information and engaged in planning. The department, given its clientele orientation, operated in a decentralized manner. However, in the early years an attempt was made to control the regional offices given the novelty of the program. As will be observed below, both provincial pressures and the structure of the unemployed led to a more significantly decentralized approach as reflected by the community employment program. In short, the department's staff grew considerably over the years but it became progressively more decentralized.

In the early years of operation the Department of Manpower and Immigration was organized into three principal divisions: the Immigration Division; the Canada Manpower Division (previously NES); and the Program Development Service which had been the Economics and Research Branch in the Department of Labour.

In 1969, the Canada Manpower Division was headed by a Director General who served in the capacity of an Assistant Deputy Minister with five regional directors reporting to him. The Administrative and Support Branch, under an Assistant Director General, was responsible for six other branches, some absorbed from the Department of Labour and some from the Immigration Branch and a new Technical Services Branch.

The Department of Manpower and Immigration, given its functional responsibilities, established a highly decentralized structure particularly in a geographic sense. This has been most clearly reflected in the work of the Operations Division which until 1973 dealt with the clientele of the department. It has been repeatedly asserted in this study that administration constitutes an important component of policy formulation. This was recognized in 1968 when the department integrated the manpower and the immigration field operations. Consequently, in each of its five regions manpower and immigration operations were placed under a single Director reporting to a Director General in Ottawa. The department had to mount a major staff-training program since such a highly decentralized administration experienced difficulties in maintaining consistency. Yet the Director General in Ottawa was given responsibility for insuring consistency and coherence in, and improvement of, the department's policies and programs. This led to a more centralized form of administration up to the time of the 1973 policy review than was anticipated. Thus, the operations of the department once again illustrate the conflicts between centralization and decentralization. It will become increasingly more apparent that the activities of the department are integrated at the level of the regional offices. This has been achieved through the following measures: first, the strengthening of the over 450 Canada Manpower Centres; second, the establishment of Job Information Centres following the 1972 Policy Review; third, the integration of the Canada Manpower Centres and the Unemployment Insurance Centres; fourth, the adoption of a stronger community orientation for the purpose of program development under the Regional Director General; and fifth, the endorsement of a new organizational concept which provides for a greater decentralization of authority and responsibility to the working levels of management.

By 1971-72 the new department had crystalized into a structure encompassing four Assistant Deputy Ministers: the ADM for Manpower Policy, the ADM for Operations, the ADM for Research Planning and Evaluation; and the ADM for Immigration Policy. This structure provided the research and policy inputs to the Deputy Minister who in turn provided the necessary support to the Minister of Manpower and Immigration.

The Assistant Deputy Minister of Manpower was concerned with the general control of programs. He dealt with all aspects of program management in Canada. These programs included training, manpower problems, and manpower mobility. An overall perspective was attained through the Research Branch which looked at what was happening in the economy to the goods and services in the long-term against which the department attempted to develop appropriate occupational skills. The department was organized to cope with the *human factors* in an environment in which there is a rapid acceleration in the transformation of the Canadian economy from a rural to an urban one.

Between 1971 and 1972 the activities of the department were carried out through the following sectors: Operations Canada which dealt with manpower services and immigration services; the Manpower Branch which encompassed the Canada Manpower Training Program, the Canada Manpower Mobility Program, the Canada Manpower Adjustment Program, and the Agricultural Manpower Program — all further broken down into more specialized activities; and the Immigration Branch which attempted to achieve its objectives through the stimulation of economic, cultural, and social development by the recruitment of immigrants with the skills required by the Canadian economy and by the examination, apprehension, detention, or deportation of those persons whose presence in Canada might endanger national security, public health, or general welfare of the people.[31]

More specifically, in 1971-72 the Department of Manpower and Immigration included the following branches:

The Program Development Service, under an Assistant Deputy Minister encompassed research planning and evaluation activities and conducted studies to assist in the development and improvement of departmental programs. Through four branches — Research, Manpower Information and Analysis, Planning and Evaluation, and Training Research and Analysis — it provided essential labour-market information for Canada Manpower Centres, other government departments, and private industry. It assessed the effectiveness of Manpower and Immigration Programs and measured the social and economic impact of the department's policies within its sphere of influence.

The Planning and Evaluation Branch reflected a then novel development in Ottawa. This was later emphasized by the Economic Council of Canada when "it revisited manpower policies" in 1971. The Program Development Service (PDS) dealt primarily with research which in 1971 was carried out as a district activity from operations. The intention at the time was to make the research more objective. As such, it would not be plagued by past decisions. The primary role of the Program Development Service when it was established was to gauge the impact of the department's program to the needs of the economy. The Service provided information and feedback on the needs of the economy so that the department could perform its role in attempting to match the demand for jobs with the supply side of the economy.

The Operations Branch encompassed the regional structure which consisted of five Regional Directors with responsibility for 360 Manpower Centres and 80 Immigration Centres. It was the responsibility of the ADM for Operations to translate the policies and programs of the department into services to the public. Economic-policy formulation becomes significantly administrative at this level and impinges heavily on human-resources management.[32]

Thus, by 1971 the department's organization chart showed four major branches: Planning and Evaluation; Research; Training Research and Analysis; and Manpower Analysis and Information.

The Economic Council of Canada which had performed an important support role in the creation of the department conducted an evaluation of the department's policies in 1971 which aided certain new policy developments.[33] By 1974 the department had been further reorganized encompassing Strategic Planning and Research; Manpower; Immigration; and Administration branches. This progressive reorganization culminated in the presentation before Parliament in October 1976 of a bill to establish the new Commission and Department of Employment and Immigration.[34] The new approach was also a product of external research by a Special Joint Committee of Parliament. The 1976 reorganization brought the Unemployment Insurance Commission and the Department of Manpower and Immigration into a closer organizational form to develop a more comprehensive employment strategy. As we shall observe below, this new strategy began with the 1972 policy review.

The Minister of Manpower and Immigration has been responsible to Parliament for the controversial Unemployment Insurance Commission, a corporate body of three commissioners who are appointed by the Governor-in-Council. The Commission was established in 1941 under the Unemployment Insurance Commission Act which was revised in 1955, 1971, 1972, and 1975. The sweeping changes which were made in 1972 broadened the scope of the coverage and range of benefits to include any interruption of earnings by reason of illness and pregnancy as well as unemployment.[35]

Under periods of high unemployment the Unemployment Commission is subject to major strain on its resources and, given the existence of structural unemployment, the system is sometimes considered to be subjected to major abuse. The former Minister of Manpower and Immigration, Robert Andras, subsequently announced increased rates as one measure aimed at balancing the supply and demand for funds paid to, and made upon, the Commission. Following the 1971 amendments to the Unemployment Insurance Act, made under Bryce Mackasey's leadership, the Commission was subjected to especially extreme criticisms. It was against these criticisms that the Hon. Robert Andras, then Minister of Manpower and Immigration, announced in 1973 that action was to be taken to insure that there was "some balance between service and control". As will be discussed below, in recent years three ministers with somewhat different approaches to the role of the Department and the Commission have been subjected to severe criticisms. However, as our discussion in this and other chapters has demonstrated this controversy represents only one aspect of a complex set of problems involved in the management of economic policies.

The immigration side of the Department's role was not the central focus of the initial changes made in the late 1960s. Although the 1966 creation of the Department of Manpower and Immigration brought manpower policy and immigration policy closer together, it was not until 1976 that a more explicit integration was emphasized. It should be stressed that immigration, at various times, had been administered through various departments such as Agriculture (1867-1892), Department of the Interior (1892-1917), Immigration and Colonization (1917-1936), Mines and Resources (1936-1949), and Citizenship and Immigration (1949-1966) reflecting the particular orientation at a given period of time. The 1966 change reflected an initial attempt to integrate immigration, training, and mobility programs.[36]

A brief historical review demonstrates that since 1869, immigration into Canada has been controlled with varying degrees of intensity.[37] The approach became restrictive under the 1910 Immigration Act which, in principle, lasted until the early 1950s. Until the Conservatives came to power in 1957 three principles governed Canada's immigration policy. First, that immigration would augment the natural rate of increase in the Canadian population. Second, the volume of arrivals would be related to the "absorptive capacity" of the economy. Third, the national and racial balance of immigration would be regulated so as not to disturb the existing character of the Canadian population. These biases, if not enshrined in the 1910 Immigration Act and its 1919 Amendment, had evolved through various orders-in-council over the ensuing decades.[38]

The regulations governing admission between 1946 and 1957 moved out in a prescribed pattern of concentric circles. At the core, the "most preferred" nationals, regardless of trade or skill, were admitted with their relatives. Nationals in the next ring were selected on the basis of trades or skills needed in Canada; the widest interpretation was given to nationals from Belgium, Luxembourg, Norway, Denmark, Sweden, and Switzerland. The list of acceptable occupants, as one moved outward, narrowed to agriculturalists, and to those workers with prior approval from the minister. In terms of ethnic background, the core group which, in fact, meant the most-preferred nations included nationals from Western Europe while the least preferred meant Asiatics.[39] Nationals from Northern and Eastern Europe represented an intermediate group.

In 1957 changes gradually introduced a more antidiscriminatory principle with special admissions being given to Dutch farm workers and to Hungarian refugees as the situation warranted. However, the key to the 1957 changes was the emphasis placed on "the inflow of highly trained immigrants plus the abandonment of ethnic discrimination". As we shall see later, these two events were tightly interrelated. Consequently, Professor Allan Green notes "that changes in the state of the economy were decisive while political influences were marginal".[40] Ellen Fairclough was Minister of Immigration and Citizenship between 1958 and 1962, but although the Regulations were amended in March 1959, high unemployment and a hostile Department of Labour combined to give immigration a low order of priority in the Conservative Cabinet. Thus, during the period 1958-62 a number of amendments were made to the Regulations, culminating in the enactment of the Immigration Regulations Part I (OIC P.C. 1972-86 dated January 18, 1962) and the Immigration Regulations Part II established by Ministerial authority on February 1, 1962. A revised Act was considered during that time (and continuously since then to the current Bill C-24) but was never actually "rewritten".

By the early 1970s the so-called "sponsorship clause" had begun to conflict with the highly-trained-migrant provision and much of the controversy over immigration policy between 1969 and 1976 focussed on this issue. The new approach outlined in 1976 will place far greater emphasis on the employment prospects of immigrants. There were some problems also with the Immigration Appeal Board since until 1972 visitors to Canada were allowed to have their status changed while they were visitors to Canada. The new system prohibits this.

The department has indicated that between 1945 and 1974, Canada admitted more than 4,084,150 immigrants.[41] This figure constituted a significant proportion of Canada's population which in 1974 numbered 22 million. Consequently, immigrants constituted a major component of Canada's labour force. As stated in 1974, "Canada's immigration policy emphasizes the careful selection of immigrants who are likely to adapt successfully to life in Canada and contribute to this country's prosperity. The primary goal of this policy is to facilitate the admission of those immigrants whose talents, skills and knowledge will be an asset to our economic, social, and cultural fabric."[42]

The policy also provides for admission of relatives of Canadian residents, refugees on humanitarian grounds, and non-immigrants whose temporary entry is required on a short-term basis. During the 1974 federal election, significant emphasis was placed on immigration policy given the high level of unemployment. Subsequently, immigration policy was studied by experts, a green paper issued, and a Senate Committee investigated the issues. Consequently, in late 1976, an immigration bill was placed before Parliament.

It included, among other things, "a policy of maintaining levels of immigration" and a strategy to steer immigrants away from areas not considered to be in the best interest of national employment policy.[43] The minister will be better able, therefore, to adapt the flow of immigrants to the changing national and regional employment situation. Together with the new employment strategy, these initiatives culminated in the new approach to manpower and labour-market policy initiated in 1966.

THE PROCESSES OF POLICY CHANGE: THE EVALUATION OF LABOUR-MARKET POLICIES

The 1976 initiatives were partly influenced by the evaluation of manpower policies conducted by the Economic Council in 1971 as well as by internal criticism and evaluation. With regard to the department the Council noted:

> During its five years of operation, which included a period of austerity in government expenditure, the scope and range of programs have continued to grow, and federal resources allocated to this area have more than doubled. While some programs predate the establishment of the Department of Manpower and Immigration, manpower policy since 1966 has become one of the most important federal policy areas in this country.[44]

The Economic Council's evaluation of the department appraised in detail the Canadian Manpower policy in general, the Canada Manpower Training Program, and Canadian Manpower policy with special reference to mobility. It should be pointed out that the Council did not evaluate either the immigration program or the federal-provincial problems in manpower-policy formulation. These aspects were covered in a later 1976 study, *People and Jobs*.[45]

Canadian Manpower Policy: Training

The Economic Council reviewed the objectives of Canadian manpower policies and concluded that the program was designed "to serve the growth objective". More explicitly, the Council concluded:

> The above evidence shows that the Canadian government's strategy in the field of manpower policy is primarily a growth strategy, with the objectives of equity and stabilization clearly being secondary. This strong emphasis on growth and efficiency provides a sharp contrast with the manpower strategy of other countries, notably the United States.[46]

The foregoing emphasizes the importance of treating the Department of Manpower and Immigration as being primarily concerned with economic policy rather than with welfare. It is clear, however, that the department has broadened its programs considerably and has thus also become involved in social policy.

The federal government has been active in the manpower training area since the passage of the Adult Occupational Training Act of 1967 notwithstanding the prior existence of the Technical and Vocational Training Assistance Act of 1960 which had made provision for the training of the following groups: youths still in technical and vocational high schools; youths and adults requiring post-secondary training to qualify as technicians; and adults, employed or unemployed, requiring training to find jobs or to improve their employment prospects.[47]

The Adult Occupational Training Act of 1967 differed from the 1960 Act in that it was not a shared-cost program and it included only transitional arrangements. Furthermore, the program was confined exclusively to adults and permitted the payment of living allowances. A buyer and seller relationship developed between the federal government and the provinces.

The federal-provincial negotiations which preceded the 1967 Adult Occupational Training Act produced a fairly normal amount of intergovernmental conflict.[48] They had resulted in the emergence of the counselling, training, and placement components of the more comprehensive manpower policy advocated in 1966 by the late Prime Minister, Lester B. Pearson.

One of the most striking findings of the Council's review of the training program was the preponderance of governmental involvement *vis-à-vis* the private sector. Thus, the Council concluded:

> In striking contrast to several other countries, less than 5 per cent of total Canadian federal adult occupational training expenditures (excluding apprenticeship) is directed to training-in-industry. In the United States, about 80 per cent of federal training expenditures involve training and "work experience" in industry. . . . The heavy—in fact, almost exclusive—emphasis on institutional training in Canada is difficult to understand when experts generally agree that, for many occupations and for many individuals, training-in-industry appears to be preferable.[49]

It strongly suggested that greater emphasis should be placed on training in industry as opposed to institutional training, so as to achieve at least a more balanced mixture of the two methods. In the words of the Council:

> The very heavy preponderance of institutional, as opposed to industry training remains a unique (in international terms) feature of the Canadian

system despite considerable evidence that a different mixture would likely be more efficient.[50]

It also stressed a need to focus on training for skill development as compared to general training. Such development would require the projection of manpower needs by occupation and area. Concurrently, the projection of supply would have to identify training institutions and other sources. Finally, the Council urged improved federal-provincial co-ordination of manpower training programs.[51]

The Council's review demonstrated that there were major redistributive effects from expenditures on manpower-training programs. This was illustrated by the following table:[52]

TABLE 10:1
Net Fiscal Transfers Under Canada Manpower-Training Program, 1969-70

Region and Province	*Net Fiscal Transfers Fiscal Year 1969-70*
	($ million)
Atlantic Region	22.7
Newfoundland	7.8
Prince Edward Island	2.4
Nova Scotia	9.6
New Brunswick	2.9
Quebec	33.0
Ontario	−38.6
Prairie Region	− 4.1
Manitoba	− 1.6
Saskatchewan	− 2.0
Alberta	− 0.5
British Columbia	−13.0

NOTE: Excludes Yukon and Northwest Territories.
SOURCE: Based on data from Department of National Revenue, Dominion Bureau of Statistics, and Department of Manpower and Immigration; and estimates by Economic Council of Canada.

The Canada Manpower Program is closely integrated with the Mobility Program which operates to relocate workers to match the demand for their skills. The integration of these programs has increasingly become part of a comprehensive employment strategy being developed by the federal government in consultation with the provinces and with the private sector. Summarily it can be stated that manpower training has progressed since its expansion in 1967. By the adoption of the Adult Occupational Training Act in 1967 the department was able for the first time to pay 100 per cent of the training allowance costs up to a 52-week maximum for adults referred to training by Canada manpower counsellors. The Act was amended in 1972 to meet the expanded training demand brought about by the rapid entry of young people and women into the labour force. These people required training to bridge the gap between the traditional education system and the needs of the marketplace.

The department purchases and/or supports training through two avenues: first, institutional (public and private schools, community colleges, and vocational centres); and, second, industrial (contracts with employers and employer associations). The responsibility for designing and conducting institutional training rests with the provinces and the various training institutions. Federal-provincial co-operation is further reflected in the Joint Federal-Provincial Manpower Needs Committees through which the department seeks to identify the skill-needs of the provinces, determines how institutional training funds should be allocated, sets priorities for industrial training, and recommends future levels of funding for the Canada Manpower Training Program.

The Canada Manpower Industrial Training Program replaced three Industrial training programs formerly offered by the department: Training-in-Industry, Training-on-the-Job for Skill Shortages, and Training-on-the-Job for the Disadvantaged. By 1974-75 the department was spending about $401 million for the enrollment of 292,000 adults.[53]

Manpower Policy: Mobility

Economic management involved more than the mere training of workers to deal with demand. It is concerned also with labour mobility which contributes to improvement in the income of employed persons and, more generally, to better economic performance. The demand for and supply of the labour force must be dealt with at the regional level where the spatial relocation of human resources and the constraints of manpower bottlenecks can be more quickly seen. This in turn facilitates the attainment of economic growth.

Labour mobility is one means of adjusting the labour market to demand and supply factors which would create bottlenecks in the structure of the market if these programs were not provided. Thus, while there may be autonomous mobility, i.e., movement undertaken at the initiative and expense of the worker or his employer, there is also assisted mobility.

Economic motives perform an important role in labour mobility. However, for reasons explained earlier in this chapter, there are many barriers to labour mobility. Apart from mere motivation, other factors such as the actual cost of the move, the capital loss incurred in selling a house, and lack of adequate information influence the degree of mobility. These factors plus the reluctance of some private employers to finance the transfer of recruits has led the federal government to subsidize the movement of individuals and families on efficiency grounds particularly if such subsidies are directed to workers who are least likely or least able to move of their own accord.

In 1971 the Economic Council discovered that movement within all regions was far greater than movement between regions.[54] The Council also noted that the comparison between the intra-regional and inter-regional movement revealed some interesting facts. Quebec had a low ratio of inter-regional to intra-regional migration. The richer provinces, Ontario and British Columbia, tended to have low ratios because there was frequently less to be gained, in income terms, by moving to another region than by moving within the province. Close to two-thirds of out-migrants from the Atlantic region and from Quebec go to Ontario. Alberta received nearly two-fifths of the flow of workers from Manitoba and Saskatchewan while British Columbia received close to one-third of this outflow.

Data provided by the Economic Council in 1971 showed total expenditures under the manpower mobility program to have risen from $3.1 million in the fiscal year 1967-68 to $7.2 million in 1970-71. Close to sixty per cent of the expenditure was devoted to relocation grants and close to forty per cent for trainee travel grants.[55] As indicated earlier the subsidy program was initiated in April 1967 after an earlier program, which was more heavily oriented to loans than grants, had proven unsuccessful.

The Council's study of the training and mobility programs clearly indicated that these programs could only complement other economic policies. The general level of economic activity has had a major effect on the success or failure of the programs followed by the department. Thus, recent increases in the level of unemployment have had a particular impact on the programs. While it appears that, at any given time, the mobility rates of the unemployed are higher than those of the employed, an increase in the general level of unemployment tends to: depress the mobility rates of both the employed and unemployed; reduce the average distance of the move; and lead to a significant amount of "reverse" movement in the form of return migration to lagging areas.[56] The state of the economy has imposed more pressures on the programs developed by the department. During periods of high unemployment, individuals and families are, on average, less able to bear the costs of movement, and they face greater uncertainty regarding prospects in unfamiliar areas.

Notwithstanding the existence of the training and the mobility programs the department has been attempting to integrate various other programs into a comprehensive package. Accordingly, the Federal Transfer Program and the Unemployment Insurance Plan perform an important supporting role to the training and mobility programs. In fact, at the time of writing, the minister indicated that he was in favour of providing an incentive-training allowance to people receiving unemployment benefits. When these measures are assessed in conjunction with the social-security policy review one gets the impression that a more comprehensive system is gradually emerging.

The department has noted recently that evaluation of manpower training poses difficult problems. Officials have argued nevertheless that there have been strong economic and income redistribution effects resulting from the training and mobility programs. These programs point also to strong human and social benefits from the increased spending power of persons working at their potential who before training were unemployed and underemployed.

Through a new organizational concept, the Canada Manpower Centre, the department has implemented a decentralized system to give its staff a better capacity to deal with local problems. The new Manpower Needs committees have evolved into the principal instrument for federal-provincial consultation and co-operation on all manpower problems, policies, and programs.

The provision of tax exemptions for mobility expenses provides an example of the synchronization of programs between the Department of Finance and the Department of Manpower and Immigration. It further provides an illustration of the close relationships between demand- and supply-management policies. The development shows that demand- and supply-management policies must be synchronized for effective goal attainment. The new approach described above was a result of initiatives adopted during the 1972-73 fiscal year.

In 1972 the department itself carried out a thorough review of Canada's manpower policies, programs, and services. Accordingly, discussions were held with the provinces, the private sector, worker-clients, and other complementary agencies. The policy review further contributed to the reorientation of the program toward a more decentralized approach by which the programs were adjusted to suit the way manpower programs and services are delivered to the public. It also led to improvements in co-operation with other agencies concerned with labour-market policies and to improvements in co-operation with the private sector.

More generally, the major conclusions of the internal policy review were as follows:

i) manpower activities must reflect better balance between general economic objectives and needs of individual workers and employers;
ii) manpower services to individuals are to be applied in a continuous and flexible manner in close co-operation with other human resource agencies;
iii) improved co-ordination and co-operation between federal and provincial human resource agencies is essential to the achievement of the objectives of both levels of government, and for effective service to Canadians;
iv) employers and unions should be fully involved in the planning and implementation of manpower activities; and
v) improved labour-market data are required for effective manpower planning.[57]

The above policy evaluation demonstrated an emerging synthesis of views about the relationships between labour-market policies and economic management. First, it was clearly recognized that manpower policies should be synchronized with other instruments of economic policy. Secondly, manpower policies, like the big levers, must be subjected to periodic adjustments consistent with the prevailing state of the economy. As such, it is merely another instrument to complement the other tools utilized in the management of the economy.

Thirdly, human-resource management, like regional development and social security policies, required effective co-operation between the federal government and the provinces. Fourth, it was clearly realized that the private sector, more specifically employers and unions, should be intricately involved in the planning process. This recognition suggests that the Department of Labour and the Department of Manpower and Immigration should be closely integrated within the general policy-development process. Fifth, notwithstanding the improvements which had taken place in the collection of labour-market data, there was a need for further improvements, particularly a need for data of a disaggregative nature. We have seen, so far, that there has been a general shift toward data of a disaggregative nature. Planning has been taking place at a more disaggregative level than previously advocated since it now includes target groups such as young Canadian women and the native peoples.

During the period under review major changes thus occurred in the following five areas: Employment Service, Manpower Delivery System, Federal-Provincial Co-operation, the Canada Manpower Training Program, and Canada Manpower Services to Employers.[58]

In accordance with the more "people-oriented" approach the department operated a network of centres linked by a telecommunication system to serve cities, towns, and rural areas across the country. To make the "Manpower Delivery System" more effective, "Job Information Centres" were established to allow clients to decide for themselves the jobs they consider themselves capable of filling. These centres provide a wide range of services from general educational assistance to specialized counselling.

During this period federal-provincial co-operation was improved by the expansion of the terms of reference of the intergovernmental Manpower Needs Committees which were provided with full-time secretariats. These committees serve at least two important functions. First, they provide a consultative mechanism for a more concentrated approach to manpower programs in all provinces. Second, the committees provide an opportunity for the provinces to perform a role in the forecast of financial requirements and in the allocation of funds under the Canada Manpower Training Program. Here we observe a more decentralized approach to some aspects of policy formulation.

During 1972 the Canada Manpower Training Program continued to perform an important role in the assistance of the elimination of unemployment by the following activities: the provision of skill courses for workers requiring additional training before they can enter a trade or occupation; accelerated basic education upgrading courses for adults who lack the educational background required to enter an occupational skill course; language training in either of the two official languages for Canadians unable to obtain suitable employment because of insufficient knowledge of English or French; and apprentice training covering the classroom portion of courses provided in apprenticeship programs operated by the provinces.

As indicated above, during 1972-73 greater efforts were made to insure that employers were aware of the department's services and how they can work to help solve specific manpower problems in an industry or business. Departmental services available to employers include, labour market information to assist in manpower planning, recruitment of workers locally from other parts of Canada, or from outside the country, the training or retraining of workers, and assistance in adapting to technological or industrial change.

A major policy change occurred in August 1972 when the department, after consultation with the provinces, introduced a series of special programs. Thus a Special Programs Branch was created to provide leadership in the co-ordinated application of all manpower services to serve and assist "the difficult-to-place" and disadvantaged workers to become employable and to find employment. Two such programs introduced were the Outreach and the Local Employment Assistance Program (LEAP) which will be described below.[59]

THE DEPARTMENT IN THE MID-1970S: THE DEVELOPMENT OF AN EMPLOYMENT STRATEGY

The Department of Manpower and Immigration is concerned with the development and utilization of human resources. It deals with much more than a mere economic problem and it is subject to intense political scrutiny and criticism. The most recent departmental changes demonstrate the close relationship between economic and social policy, and show a strong trend toward the development of a more comprehensive employment strategy. By the mid-1970s the programs and services administered by the department were directed toward the following objectives:

—The effective meeting of Canada's labour needs by the rapid matching of jobs and workers through recruitment, counselling, development of job orders, and referral of workers to employers and employers to workers;
—The sponsoring of educational upgrading and training for Canadians to develop satisfying and productive careers while meeting the manpower requirements of employers and the economy;
—The provision of financial assistance to the unemployed and under-employed, enabling them to move with their families to areas where there are jobs or their skills are in demand;
—The production of employment through job-creation programs for the disadvantaged and those experiencing seasonal unemployment;
—The co-ordination of employment and labour-related programs and services in co-operation with other federal departments and agencies;
—The development of mechanisms for occupational forecasting and manpower planning and the facilitation of manpower adjustments precipitated by technological and other changes;
—The collection, collation, and distribution of labour-market information, and the detailed analysis and interpretation of the impact of departmental programs; and
—In immigration, the establishment of an equitable system of selecting and admitting immigrants based on (1) non-discrimination, (2) humanitarian concerns, and (3) meeting the needs of Canada's labour market.[60]

A comparison of the 1971-72 and the 1974-75 organizational arrangements reflects some of the changes in policy. As mentioned earlier, in 1971-72 the organization chart for the department showed four major divisions each under an assistant deputy minister. These included the ADM for the Planning and Evaluation Branch; the ADM for Manpower Analysis and Information; the ADM for Training Research and Analysis; and the ADM for Operations. By the 1974-75 fiscal year the Department of Manpower and Immigration, as Chart 10:1 shows, had evolved into a structure in which there were five major divisions each headed by an Assistant Deputy Minister. These included ADMs for Manpower, Immigration, Strategic Planning and Research, Administration, and Special Projects.[61]

The ADM for Manpower dealt with training, employer services, client services, special programs, community programs, job creation, and general co-ordination of the various components of what has been evolving as a comprehensive manpower policy.

Five Regional Directors General dealt with the various components of manpower policy within the five designated regions — Pacific, Prairie, Ontario, Atlantic, and Quebec. Below the five Directors General there were two Assistant Directors General; one for Manpower and one for Immigration. The entry points for immigrants and the points of service under the labour-market areas provide direct contact to the people served by the department. Thus below the regional offices there were over 460 Canada Manpower Centres which reported through the Regional Directors General to whom increased authority has been delegated in recent years.

The federal and provincial policies and programs are co-ordinated at the regional level through Regional Directors General. It should be noted, however, that there are multi-province regions. The Prairie region consists of Manitoba, Saskatchewan, and Alberta and the Pacific region consists of British Columbia and the Northwest Territories. The Atlantic region consists of the four Atlantic provinces. The foregoing reflects the increased decentralization of authority which has taken place through the strengthening of the Regional, Provincial, and Canada Manpower Centre offices. As will be explained below the decentralization has been somewhat different from the initiatives taken by the Department of Regional Economic Expansion.

By the early 1970s the ADM for Immigration was responsible for Facilitation and Enforcement, Priorities and Co-ordination, Recruitment and Selection, Settlement (Branch), and Foreign Service. As indicated earlier since 1966 immigration policy has been closely related to manpower policy with the exception of the Special Settlement Program which dealt specifically with refugees.

The ADM for Strategic Planning and Research provided the technical support for departmental policy-making. His Branch carried out research similar to that described earlier under the old Program Development Service. The Strategic Planning Branch consisted of four components: Economic Analysis and Forecasting, Strategic Planning and Evaluation, Research Projects, and Occupational and Career Analysis and Development.

Chart 10:1 Department of Manpower & Immigration (1975)

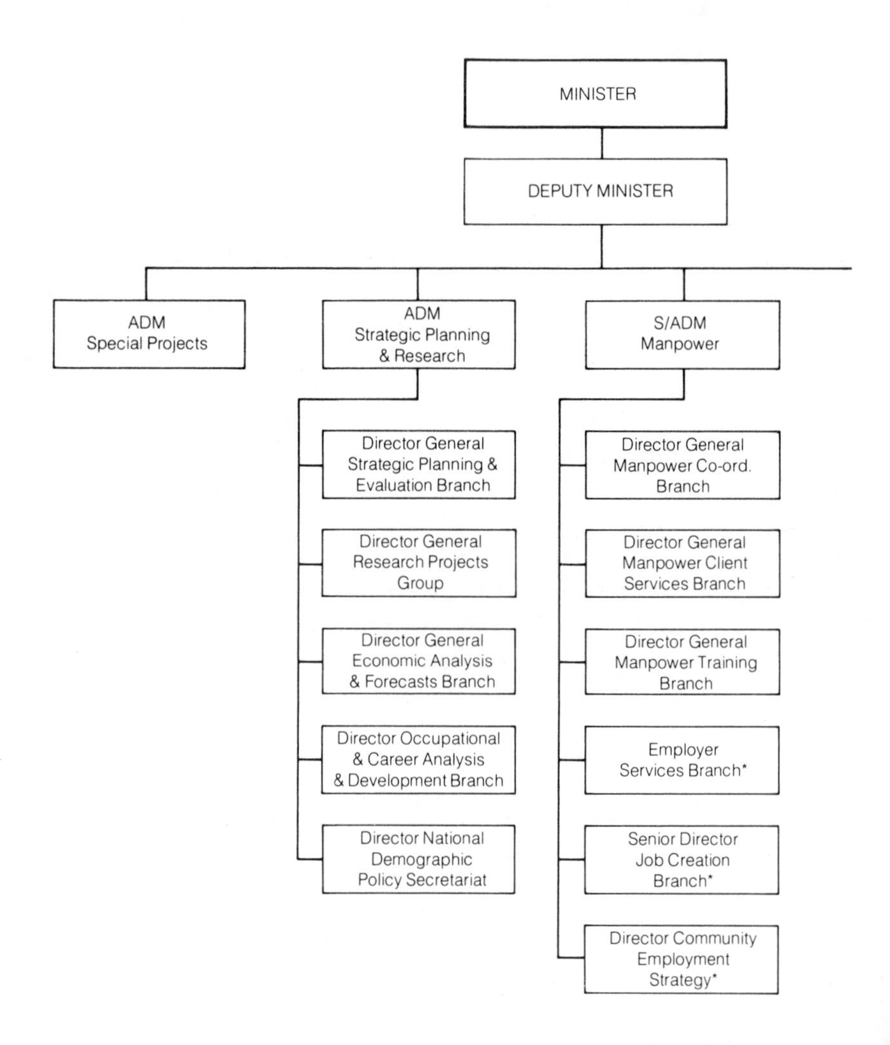

The Department of Manpower and Immigration, given the nature of its activities, has for several reasons always been decentralized, at least in an areal or geographic sense. In the first instance it was established shortly after the report of the Royal Commission on the Organization of the Government of Canada (the Glassco Commission had recommended that common services be centralized in each department). The

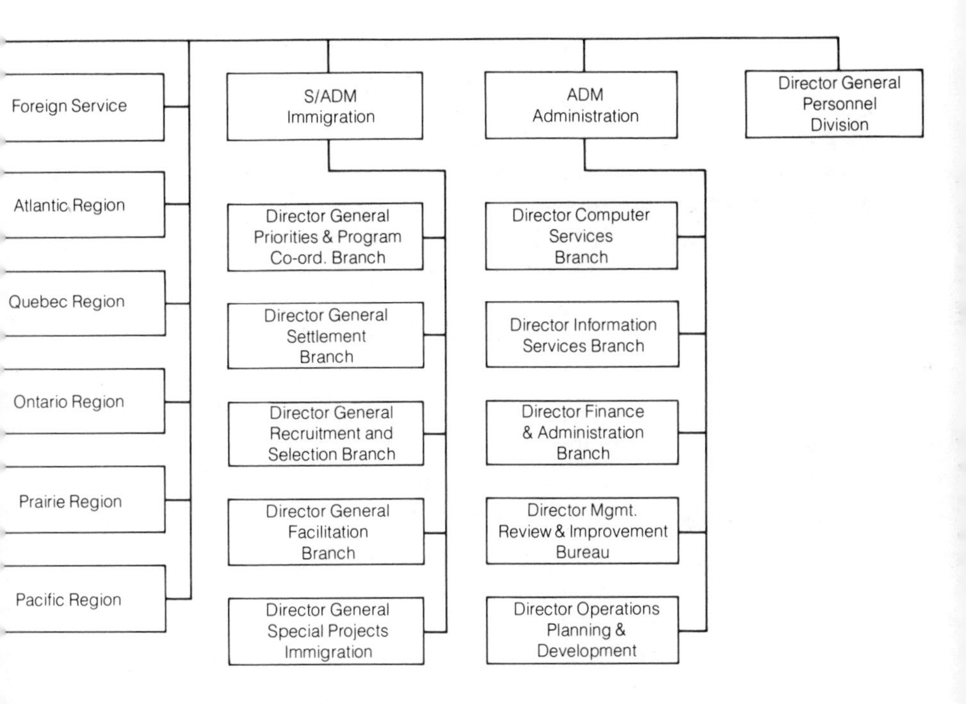

loyer Service, Job Creation, and Community Strategy form the Employment Development Group.

Department of Manpower and Immigration initially reflected this suggestion. However, in 1972 a policy decision was made to strengthen and reinforce the decentralized orientation mentioned earlier. Given the magnitude of the unemployment problem, the department made a major effort to eliminate "central operations control". This was most clearly reflected in the disbanding of "Operations Canada", and the integrated field offices, which had been created earlier.[62] While "Operations Canada" had been a geographically decentralized structure, control was exercised primarily in Ottawa through the ADM for Operations. With the adoption of the new approach in 1974 the responsibilities of the ADM for Operations were transferred to regional managers who now report directly to the Deputy Minister of the Department in Ottawa. The regional managers draw on the ADMs in the department for specialized services but they also report directly to the Deputy Minister on policy matters.

In Chapter 9 we outlined the evolution of the decentralization of the Department of Regional Economic Expansion. Here we can distinguish the two reorganizations as two similar but rather different approaches to economic management. Many senior officials in the Department of Manpower and Immigration have argued that DREE was highly amenable to decentralization in contrast to other departments. Manpower and Immigration while highly decentralized in an administrative sense attempts to formulate a national employment strategy.[64] However, since jobs must satisfy local needs the department gradually developed "a community approach to job creation". The new approach was also related to changing attitudes to work. The variety of technical skills incorporated in the department was partially responsible for the new approach adopted. Thus, the significant expansion of the Canada Manpower Centres, the creation of Job Information Centres, and the experimental exchange of staff between the Canada Manpower Centres and the Unemployment Insurance Commission Centres, prior to the reorganization in 1976-77, demonstrate the orientation of the decentralized strategy adopted by the department. However, as the policy paper stated, the decentralization in this instance merely reflected areal aspects of a national employment strategy.

In short, the new approach being followed in the department sought to:

(i) eliminate, to the extent possible, central operations and control and the transfer of these responsibilities to regional managers;

(ii) redefine the role of the staff at headquarters in Ottawa so that they would be concerned with policy and program development rather than with administration;

(iii) reinforce the executive-level staff in the field by expanding the staff almost 100 per cent;

(iv) redefine the position and role of the managers in the field (in effect their job was upgraded); and

(v) shift the department from a hierarchical structure to a more horizontal one.[63]

The orientation of the department has changed in other respects also. When the department was formed in 1966 training was most important and special steps were taken to avoid overlap and confrontation between the federal and provincial levels of government. Mobility was also emphasized. Gradually the department began to develop a more comprehensive strategy as reflected initially by the Job Creation Branch and, ultimately, in the enunciation of the 1976 new employment strategy.[64] The federal government in the initial stages tried to distinguish its role from the provinces by asserting that it was concerned with national stabilization policy and, accordingly, had an important role to perform in the area of manpower policies. The provinces, nevertheless, were primarily responsible for the administrative aspects. By 1972, the provinces were more willing to discuss employment with the federal government, given the extraordinarily high levels of unemployment which existed.[65] Previously, people had to be out of school for three years before they could take training under the federal program. The time period was subsequently shortened.

In another sphere, the federal and provincial governments co-operated by placing greater emphasis on the social dimensions of employment policy. Since stabilization policies, the so-called big levers, had not been able to reduce the rate of unemployment, greater emphasis had been placed on Local Initiatives Programs (LIP) which had both a social and an economic orientation in that they were intended to generate both participation by the unemployed and communities, and jobs. Despite criticisms against them, these measures provide needed employment. The foregoing has led to greater emphasis on the community planning of programs.[66] The Department of Manpower and Immigration, like the Department of Regional Economic Expansion, has placed more emphasis on planning from the bottom up. The Canada Manpower Centres, through community officers, have been attempting to initiate a work-orientation within communities. It is worth pointing out that given community participation in these programs, it was expected that people would be less critical of governmental spending. Moreover, the incorporation of the business sector would enhance the work ethic, and would reduce the prospects for criticisms to be levelled at the government for too much spending.

The department thus sought a better relationship between people adversely affected by the economy and the officials of the Canada Manpower Centres. It has also sought to improve relationships with employers by encouraging them to give greater assistance to those adversely affected by the market and by giving greater emphasis to training in industry. The broader implications of these strategies must be constantly assessed in relation to the Department of Finance whose custody over fiscal policy and transfer payments facilitate the new program orientation. In addition, there has been some recognition that manpower policies are closely related to industrial relations and that there is a clear need to co-ordinate policies with the Department of Labour. It has been recognized also that work dissatisfaction can lead to industrial unrest which in turn can adversely affect the whole economy.

The provision of services directed at employment (the Job Creation Program) constitutes significant change in the department's policies and programs.[67] This shift in emphasis is a direct consequence of high unemployment in the economy.

The main components of job creation are, the Opportunities for Youth Program (OFY), the Local Initiatives Program (LIP) both launched in 1971 and the Local Employment Assistance Program (LEAP) created in the autumn of 1972. Unlike the other programs, LEAP finances projects that will contribute to the ongoing self-sufficiency of project participants by providing resources such as occupational training, life and communications skills, counselling, and placement. A distinctive feature of OFY is that the projects must have close co-operation between the government and the private sector. One in three projects, regardless of the type of activity, establishes contact with federal or provincial government departments, social service agencies, municipal governments, citizens' groups or clubs, commercial enterprises, merchants, or the media. The program is based on a close working relationship between government and the community.

The Opportunities for Youth Program has proved to be a reasonably effective means of providing employment for students during the summer months, particularly in areas of limited job availability.[68]

The LIP and OFY programs stand in relative contrast to a much earlier job-creation program, the Winter Works program.[69] Begun in the late 1950s and cancelled in 1968, this program operated almost exclusively through federal, provincial, and municipal civil servants with little or no community or worker participation. LIP and OFY were also a direct reflection of the work of the Company of Young Canadians (CYC) in the mid-1960s.[70]

The LIP and OFY programs (as well as features of the manpower training programs) should also be seen in the context of our discussion in Chapter 9 of "expenditure" politics. They represented the direct use of federal spending powers, which, because of the highly distributive nature of the expenditures, helped the federal government in some instances to skirt provincial governments. As LIP and OFY evolved, more federal-provincial co-ordination occurred but in contrast to the big conditional-grant-expenditure politics of the 1950s and early 1960s, the nature of political negotiation was much more bilateral between particular provinces and the federal government rather than multilateral.

In 1974, OFY funds of $26,335,000 supported 3,846 projects and created 27,525 jobs. The 1975-76 estimate provided for $49 million and was expected to create 27,000 jobs. In 1973-74 LIP funds of $69,353,000 supported 3,425 projects and created 30,643 jobs. By 1975, $136.4 million was estimated for the 1975-76 budget. Expenditure on LEAP grew from $5,450,438 in1973-74 to a budgeted $13.6 million in 1975-76.[71]

Briefly, the LIP program assists unemployed Canadians in the creation of community-based projects. The program provides funds to local governments, private, non-profit organizations, and businesses and entrepreneurs who engage in non-profit activities, or devise programs or new services which create new jobs. Community consultation is achieved through Constituent Advisory Groups in most areas of Canada. The Local Employment Assistance Program (LEAP) assists persons who are regarded as being in the disadvantaged group of the unemployed in that they likely would remain unemployed regardless of normal labour-market activity. LEAP projects are designed to give participants an opportunity to be involved in the development, management, and evaluation of work experience. Projects are of three years' duration. The Opportunities for Youth Program (OFY), begun under the auspices of the Secretary of State Department, provides funds to create jobs for young people based on similar principles to those which apply to LIP.[72]

Because changes in the structure of the economy affect the type and nature of the labour-market policies followed, the department, as indicated earlier, must examine both macro and micro components of labour-market policies. Accordingly, it must look more closely at the structure, location, and clientele to which it delivers programs. It must adopt appropriate measures to ameliorate the conditions of the rather diverse clientele which it now serves. Hence, in addition to programs directed at young people, the department has devised programs directed at a more highly specialized clientele including women entering the labour force, inmates and ex-mates of correctional institutions, and native Canadians. In addition, an Agricultural Manpower Program supplements the normal labour force in areas of high demand by recruiting and moving workers within Canada as well as from other countries. Two other programs directed at particular groups are the Public Service Recruitment Program through which the department provides recruitment and referral services in the administrative supporrt and operational categories to federal departments and agencies, and the Civilian Employment Assistance Program conducted jointly with National Defence which offers services to people about to retire from the Canadian Armed Forces.

In the early 1970s the Department of Manpower and Immigration assumed greater responsibility for social policy.[73] For example the department participated actively in the joint federal-provincial Social Security Review which commenced in April 1973 and in which the Minister of Manpower and Immigration "assumed full responsibility for the employment aspects".[74] He is a member of the Committee of Ministers of Welfare which has provided overall direction to the review.

The department has developed and expanded an Industrial Training program.[75] By 1973-74 this industry-based or employer-centred training had begun to play an increasingly important part in the department's manpower training strategy, following the recommendations of the Economic Council of Canada noted above. This also facilitated and required public sector-private sector co-operation in manpower training.[76] As a result, during 1973-74, consultations were held with the provinces and with representatives of industry for the purpose of more clearly stating the objectives of government support for employer-centred training. The objectives agreed upon included, equalizing employment opportunities for people with special needs, alleviating skill shortages, preventing layoffs due to technological change, and supporting industrial development strategies. The need for improvements in consultation between the public and private sectors and between the federal and provincial governments were further reflected in two public documents issued in late 1976: *The Way Ahead* and *Employment Strategy*.[77] Whereas in the past it was felt that only the unemployed needed counselling, it is now recognized that employers also need counselling if they are to carry out their employment responsibilities.

A final illustration of the recent attempts to integrate the department's various programs into a more comprehensive system is reflected in the closer partnership which developed between the Manpower Division and the Unemployment Insurance Commission. Special programs were designed to get people off welfare and unemployment insurance and into jobs. In 1974-75, the Minister of Manpower and Immigration outlined measures to insure that the Unemployment Insurance Act functioned effectively and offered a better balance between service and control. The program was severely criticized following the 1971 amendments which, as we have noted earlier, broadened the scope of the Unemployment Insurance Act. In 1974 the Unemployment Insurance Commission reversed an earlier decision made in 1967 which had centralized its operations.[78] Accordingly, in 1974 a number of new offices were opened and the "benefit-control" staff was upgraded and expanded to bring their operations closer to the public in need of its services. The Directed Interview Program was geared to exposing the unemployment insurance claimant as quickly as possible to the Canada Manpower Centres in order to transfer them off unemployment insurance and into meaningful employment as quickly as possible.

Summarily this portion of the chapter has identified several components of the subsidies, grants, and assistance provided to improve the state of our human resources. We have identified a trend toward supporting individuals to gain jobs and in cases where this is not possible to provide training and mobility allowances. In cases where such programs do not operate, we have the work of the Unemployment Insurance Commission. Recently we have seen steps taken to integrate the separate components of human-resources development. The creation of the Commission and Department of Employment and Immigration culminated a most important phase of the integration process outlined in this chapter. The new policies being developed in the Department of Health and Welfare and the Department of Finance will further integrate tax policy and social policy.

Between 1973 and 1976 the department moved toward a more integrated approach to manpower policies in two ways. It undertook initiatives, first, to bring the Department of Manpower and Immigration and the Unemployment Insurance Commission closer together, and second, to introduce changes into the unemployment insurance program. In explaining the changes the Hon. B. Cullen noted:

> a central factor is that conditions in the Canadian society, economy, and labour market of the late 1970s are significantly different than they were in the late 1960s. During the last decade there has also been an important evolution in our manpower programs and in unemployment insurance. Manpower services generally, and in particular the counselling, placement, training and mobility programs, as well as the newer job creation programs have greatly strengthened and matured. At the same time, the unemployment insurance program has been extended to cover almost the entire labour force and has come to play a much more significant role in the operation of the Canadian labour market and the Canadian economy.[79]

In short, these developments warranted the integration of the department and the Commission.

The integration was expected to lead to the following results:

—a rationalization of the present network of local offices of the Unemployment Insurance Commission and the Department of Manpower and Immigration;
—the conversion of most service points into one-stop centres where the complete range of services of the two organizations would be available to the public;
—the faster and more systematic exposure of clientele to employment services;

—a simplification of the documentation required of clients and a streamlining of the procedures to be followed by them in using the services provided under the employment and insurance program.[80]

In addition, the recently integrated approach sought to bring the immigration policy objectives more closely in line with the labour-market objectives. Consequently, the 1976-77 proposals made provision for both a commission and a small support department (see Chart 10:2). Thus the new Canadian Employment and Immigration Commission will be responsible for the administration of labour-market programs and the policies underlying those programs. These will include the payment of benefits under the Unemployment Insurance program, immigration, recruitment, selection, settlement, enforcement, control, placement, counselling, training, and the administrative support functions for both the Commission and the Department.

The small support Department of Employment and Immigration will be responsible for strategic policy development, program evaluation, labour-market research, and information services. It will help to insure the closest possible linkages between labour-market policies and programs and the government's overall economic and social strategies.

Consistent with the trends we have identified in other policy areas the new initiatives will require close co-operation and consultation between government, labour, and business. Thus the well-established policy of tripartite consultation and co-operation will be continued through the representation of workers and employers in the new commission. In this regard the activities will even be strengthened since the new commission's authority will extend not only to the unemployment insurance program, but also to labour-market programs generally as well as immigration matters. Accordingly Bill C-27 makes provision for the establishment of a new Canada Employment and Immigration Advisory Council.

The second major purpose of Bill C-27 was to bring about appropriate changes in the program. Consequently, it introduced the following changes to the Unemployment Insurance Program:

1. An increase in the number of weeks required to qualify for UI benefits (the so-called "entrance requirement") from 8 weeks to 12.

2. A change in the benefit structure which is the framework used to

Chart 10:2 Canada Employment and Immigration Commission Department of Employment and Immigration

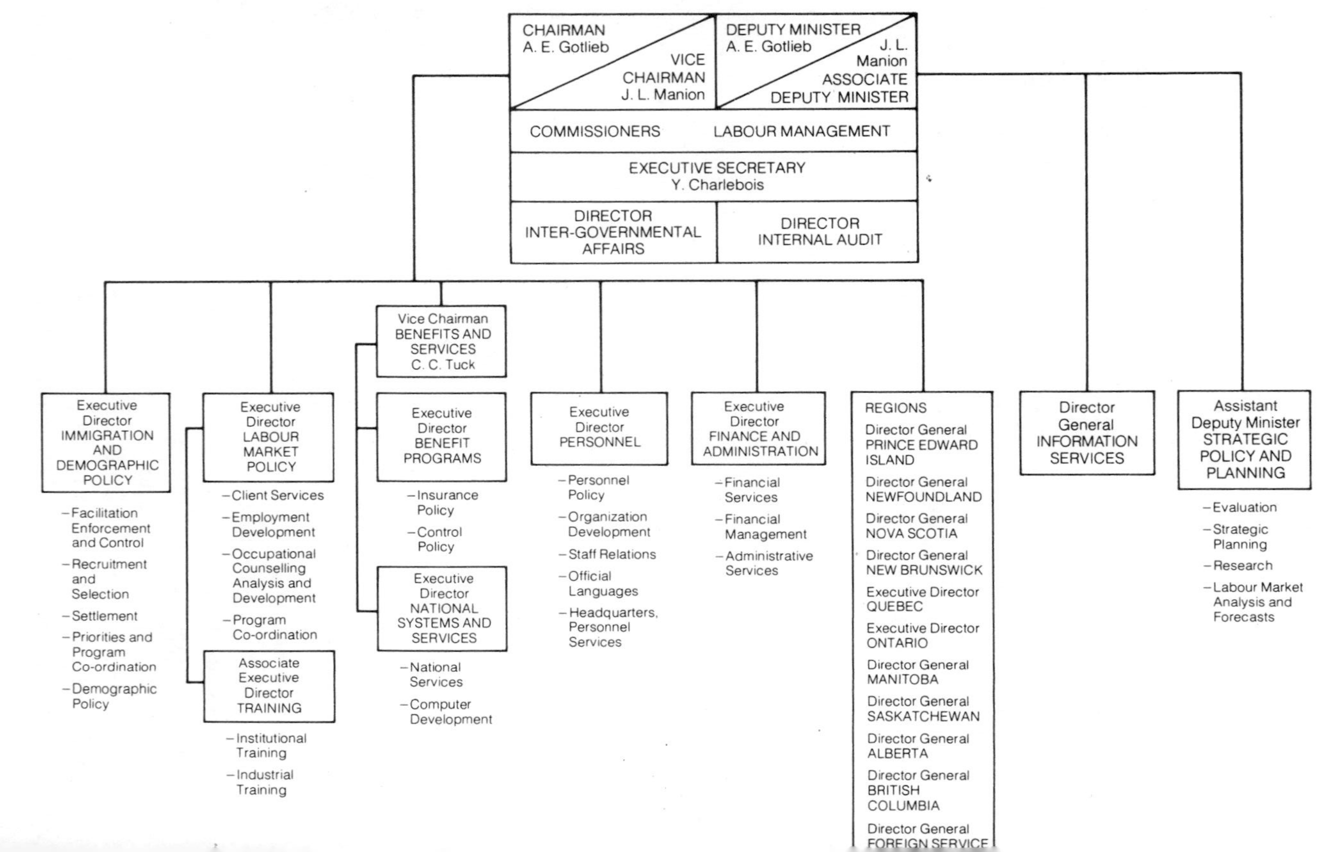

determine the duration of a claimant's entitlement to benefit.

3. The authorization of more productive or developmental uses of unemployment insurance funds, including the use of such funds as income maintenance for claimants participating in approved training courses, job-creation projects, and work-sharing programs.[81]

In short, the new employment strategy was accompanied by a new administrative framework which integrated manpower policy, unemployment-insurance policy, and immigration policy into a comprehensive employment policy which consisted of the components outlined below.

The 1976 employment strategy provides a most useful basis on which to summarize the evolution of the Department of Manpower and Immigration. Most significantly, from a structural point of view, the 1976 bill integrated the Unemployment Insurance Commission with the department to form the Commission and Department of Employment and Immigration. However, from the perspective of the management of economic policy it outlined the following measures: a Comprehensive Job-Creation Program; a Youth Employment and Employability Program; and Preventive Measures to avoid unemployment.[82]

The Comprehensive Job-Creation Program was developed on the premise that there were unacceptable levels of unemployment. Consequently, a special $350 million in expenditures were set aside for special employment measures between 1976-77 and 1977-78[83] Projects were to be reviewed and recommended by ministerial advisory boards in each constituency. Priorities were to be determined by joint federal-provincial mechanisms. Secondly, investments were to be made within a Canada Works Program which would be adjusted on a year-by-year basis. The Canada Works Program would operate only when private investments were lacking. Thirdly, mechanisms were established for a Summer Job Corps in which $10 million were to be invested to support employment opportunities within the area of federal governmental priorities.

Youth Employment and Employability programs constituted the second major component of the new strategy. Given the extraordinarily high level of unemployment among students, the strategy made provision for increased counselling and job-creation mechanisms for secondary and post-secondary students. This system would operate through counselling material called "Careers Canada" and "Careers Provinces" within the Canada Manpower Centres and school systems.

Preventative Measures encompassed "the development of new, and the strengthening of established, preventive measures". To supplement the expenditures in training conducted within provincial institutions the new strategy made provision for the further expansion of industrial training. This was expected to increase the productivity and lower the cost of the training program. The new approach, it was hoped, would facilitate the employment of young workers, women returning to new careers in the labour force, native people, and other Canadians who need assistance to enter the labour force.

A Work-Sharing Occupational Training Program was initiated to encourage employers to keep workers gainfully employed when market forces were unfavourable. Rather than pay unemployment insurance, the government would subsidize the employers.[84] In addition, unemployed people would be encouraged to use their idle time to take training and prepare themselves for the new jobs which would emerge subsequently. Finally, the new job-creation projects would encourage unemployed Canadians receiving unemployment insurance to participate in community service projects.[85]

In short the new approach re-emphasizes the work ethic, but also reflects other internal and external problems, with which the department has had to deal, and criticism to which it has had to respond. Thus, the recent renaming and reorganization is not mere window-dressing. The evolution of the Commission and Department of Employment and Immigration demonstrates also how a department and a government have attempted to adapt their policies and practices to reflect both what they believe to be current community beliefs and values, and what they see are the current needs of economic and social management.

NOTES

1. This represents a much broader approach to supply-management policies than that which appeared in earlier discussion by the Economic Council of

Canada. See Andrew Shonfield, *Modern Capitalism: The Changing Balance between Public and Private Power* (London, 1965), especially p. 351.

2. These criticisms were made in response to the 1971 amendments. Since then recommendations have been made to tighten up the administrative procedures to get people back to work. See Economic Council of Canada, *People and Jobs* (Ottawa, 1976), pp. 38-41. Other studies have presented mixed conclusions. Shonfield has argued that the management of supply was the critical issue in growth economies. In the discussion of the post-controls period the management of energy and food supplies has been presented as the critical issue. See also B. A. Frischke, *Inflation: Its Your Bag* (Toronto, 1976).

3. Economic Council of Canada, *Second Annual Review* (Ottawa, 1975) and *Eighth Annual Review* (Ottawa, 1971).

4. See K. Bryden, *Old Age Pensions and Policy Making in Canada* (Montreal, 1974). See also Simon McInnes, PhD Thesis (in progress), Carleton University, Department of Political Science. This thesis examines the policy processes in the income-security field, particularly the effort in the early 1970s to change the family allowance plan. The Finance and Health and Welfare departmental conflicts are an important factor. On the search for a more comprehensive "income security" system see Andrew Armitage, *Social Welfare in Canada: Ideals and Realities* (Toronto, 1975), especially Chapter 6. For comparative analysis of social policy see Hugh Heclo, *Modern Social Politics in Britain and Sweden: From Relief to Income Maintenance* (New Haven, 1974) and Harold L. Wilensky, *The Welfare State and Equality: Structural and Ideological Roots of Public Expenditure* (Berkeley, Ca., 1975). On governmental intervention see Karl Polanyi, *The Great Transformation: The Political and Economic Origins of Our Time* (Boston, 1965).

5. Economic Council of Canada, *Eighth Annual Review*.

6. See Hon. Bud Cullen, Minister of Manpower and Immigration, *Employment Strategy* (Ottawa, 1976). See also Barbara Goldman, *New Directions for Manpower Policy* (Montreal, 1976).

7. See G. G. Somers and W. D. Woods, eds., *Cost-Benefit Analysis of Manpower Policies* (Kingston, 1969), especially pp. 230-48.

8. Economic Council of Canada, *Eighth Annual Review*.

9. Cullen, *Employment Strategy*.

10. Interviews. See also Alan G. Green, *Immigration and the Postwar Canadian Economy* (Toronto, 1976), Chapter 2. This chapter is mainly concerned with manpower and labour market policies. For more in-depth focus on immigration policy see Freda Hawkins, *Canada and Immigration* (Montreal, 1972).

11. G. P. A. McDonald, "Labour, Manpower and Government Reorganization", *Canadian Public Administration*, Vol. x, no. 4 (December 1967), pp. 471-98.

12. See, for example, speeches by George Haythorne, "Our New Task and Responsibilities", Charlottetown, May 22, 1965; "The Role of the Department of Labour", Ottawa, September 3, 1965; and "Technology and Labour", Kingston, November 1, 1965.

13. Ibid.

14. See Stefan Dupré, David M. Cameron, *et al.*, *Federalism and Policy Development: The Case of Adult Occupational Training in Ontario* (Toronto, 1973), and G. Bruce Doern, "Vocational Training and Manpower Policy", *Canadian Public Administration*, Vol. xii (1969), p. 65.

15. See Hon. John Munro, Minister of Labour, Notes for an Address to a joint Union-Management-Government Conference, Brantford, January 23, 1975, especially pp. 5, 9-10. This speech was important in other respects too because by March 1975 the Minister of Consumer and Corporate Affairs, Minister of Labour, President of the Treasury Board, and the Minister of Finance had once again met in a series of meetings to establish a consensus on anti-inflation policies. See Chapter 12 for further analysis of this aspect of economic management. On the importance of establishing a new system of responsibility and accountability between employers and employees see the Government of Canada, *The Way Ahead: A Framework for Discussion* (Ottawa, 1976), pp. 26-28. With respect to attempts to improve the collective bargaining procedures and to bringing labour-management and government together in the public interest see Hon. J. Muncro, "A Better Work Environment for Canadians". Speech, March 14, 1977. With respect to the serious efforts being made to improve labour-management relations through examination of European developments see U.K. Department of Trade, *Report to the Committee of Inquiry on Industrial Democracy* (London, 1977) and Eric Batstone and P. L. Davies, *Industrial Democracy: European Experience* (London, 1976).

16. J. D. Love, Assistant Secretary (Personnel), Treasury Board Speech, International Conference of Public Personnel Association, Victoria (1967). On immigration policy see the excellent appraisal by Freda Hawkins, *Canada and Immigration*.

17. Economic Council of Canada, *First Annual Review* (Ottawa, 1964), p. 170.

18. Ibid., p. 173.

19. Ibid. p. 174.

20. Economic Council of Canada, *Second Annual Review*, pp. 179-80. For further details on the role of the Economic Council in manpower policies and the early organization of the department see R. W. Phidd, "The Economic Council and Economic Policy Formulation in Canada". Unpublished PhD thesis, Queen's University, Kingston, 1972, pp. 341-89.

21. For a comprehensive review see Standing Senate Committee on National Finance, *Canada Manpower* (Ottawa, 1976). For more specific analysis see also Department of Manpower and Immigration, *The Canada Manpower Centre* (Ottawa, 1975), Summary highlights. On the whole the department has operated much more on the demand side than was originally anticipated.

22. Economic Council of Canada, *Second Annual Review*, p. 180.

23. Ibid., pp. 180-81.

24. Ibid., p. 181.

25. Economic Council of Canada, *Eighth Annual Review*, p. 95.

26. Munro, Notes for an Address to joint Union-Management-Government Conference (1975), p. 5, 9-10. See also his speech in May 1975. The minister subsequently gave a number of speeches on economic justice and trends in industrial relations in which emphasis was placed on tripartism, broadening the collective-bargaining process, and improving industrial relations in general. See, for example, his address to the International Conference on Trends in Industrial and Labour Relations in Montreal, May 25, 1976. On developments in occupational health see G. Bruce Doern, "The Political Economy of Regulating Occupational Health: The Ham and Beaudry Reports", *Canadian Public Administration*, Vol. xx, no. 1 (Spring 1977), pp. 6-30.

27. Department of Manpower and Immigration, *Annual Report, 1969-1970*

(Ottawa, 1971). The 1970 Annual Report added a (vi) category: to provide topical information on the labour market, and more specifically on occupational demand and supply. By 1976 the Manpower objectives had broadened considerably. See, for example, *Report of the Standing Senate Committee of National Finance on Canada Manpower* (Ottawa, 1976), especially pp. 8-9 where it is stated that it now encompasses "the basic social and economic needs of Canadians".

28. Economic Council of Canada, *Second Annual Review*, pp. 183-84.

29. Macdonald, "Labour, Manpower and Government Reorganization", p. 476.

30. Ibid., p. 477.

31. Department of Manpower and Immigration, *Annual Report, 1971-1972*.

32. Ibid.

33. Economic Council of Canada, *Eighth Annual Review*.

34. Hon. Bud Cullen, Notes for an Address to the House of Commons on Second Reading of Bill C-27, December 9, 1976.

35. See the proposals which led to the adoption of the 1971 scheme. Hon. Bryce Mackasey, Minister of Labour, *Unemployment Insurance in the 70s* (Ottawa, 1970). On the effects of the new amendments see Hon. Robert Andras, Minister of Manpower and Immigration, Statement before the Labour, Manpower and Immigration Committee, 1973. For an analysis of the 1971 reforms see Michael Prince, "A Redistributive Policy Output and Its Impact on the Canadian Executive: The New Unemployment Insurance Act of 1971". Research paper, School of Public Administration, Carleton University, Ottawa, 1975.

36. Economic Council of Canada, *Eighth Annual Review*, chapters 5 and 6.

37. Hawkins, *Canada and Immigration*.

38. Green, *Immigration and the Postwar Canadian Economy*.

39. Ibid.

40. Ibid., p. 35.

41. Department of Manpower and Immigration, *Annual Report, 1975*.

42. Ibid.

43. Department of Manpower and Immigration, *The Immigration Bill: Explanatory Notes* (Ottawa, 1976).

44. Economic Council of Canada, *Eighth Annual Review*, p. 87.

45. Economic Council of Canada, *People and Jobs*.

46. Economic Council of Canada, *Eighth Annual Review*, p. 98.

47. Ibid., p. 100.

48. See, for example, Dupré, Cameron, *et al.*, *Federalism and Policy Development*.

49. Economic Council of Canada, *Eighth Annual Review*, p. 104.

50. Ibid., p. 115.

51. Ibid., chapters 6, 7, and 8. This approach to manpower and employment policies became more evident during the ensuing five years. See, for example, the following: Department of Manpower and Immigration, *Annual Report, 1975-76; Report of the Standing Senate Committee on National Finance on Canada Manpower*; and testimony by the Department to the Senate Committee on National Finance.

52. Economic Council of Canada, *Eighth Annual Review*, p. 97.

53. Department of Manpower and Immigration, *Annual Report, 1974-75,* p. 5.

54. Economic Council of Canada, *Eighth Annual Review*, p. 139.

55. Ibid., p. 147.

56. Ibid., p. 160.

57. Department of Manpower and Immigration, *Annual Report, 1972-73* (Ottawa, 1973). During this fiscal year the department added a seventh policy objective: "The provision of incentives for job-creation to alleviate winter unemployment." Here again we detect a gradual broadening of the strategy (p. IX).

58. Ibid., pp. 1, 1-9. Between 1972 and 1975 the Department made a number of submissions to Committee of the House of Commons and to the Senate. See the following: *Canada Manpower Programmes; The Employment Service; The*

Canada Manpower Centre; Job Creation; Manpower Training; and a comprehensive report as later published by the Senate, *Canada Manpower*.

59. Manpower and Immigration, *Annual Report, 1972-73*, pp. 8-9.

60. Department of Manpower and Immigration, *Annual Report, 1973-74* (Ottawa, 1974), pp. IX-X.

61. Ibid.

62. Interviews.

63. Interviews.

64. Cullen, *Employment Strategy*.

65. Interviews.

66. This was more explicitly reflected in Cullen, *Employment Strategy*.

67. Manpower and Immigration, *Job Creation*.

68. For a critical analysis of the OFY program see Robert Best, "Youth Policy", in G. Bruce Doern and V. S. Wilson, eds., *Issues in Canadian Public Policy* (Toronto, 1974), pp. 137-65.

69. See R. M. Burns and L. Close, *The Municipal Winter Works Incentive Program: A Study of Government Expenditure Decision Making* (Toronto, 1971).

70. Ibid., and Margaret Daly, *The Revolution Game* (Toronto, 1970).

71. *The National Finances, 1975-76* (Toronto, 1976), pp. 182, 217.

72. Best, "Youth Policy".

73. Manpower and Immigration, *Annual Report, 1973-74*.

74. Ibid., p. 7.

75. Manpower and Immigration, *Annual Report, 1974-75*.

76. Ibid.

77. This aspect of the new employment strategy should be emphasized in that it reflects a significant change. See Cullen, *Employment Strategy* and Government of Canada, *The Way Ahead*.

78. Interviews.

79. Cullen, Notes for an Address to the House of Commons on Second Reading of Bill C-27, p. 2.

80. Ibid., pp. 3-4.

81. Ibid., pp. 6-7.

82. Cullen, *Employment Strategy*.

83. Ibid., p. 7.

84. Ibid., pp. 16-21.

85. Ibid. This reflects the reprivatization strategy referred to above. The most recent attempts to integrate the UIC with the department, the strengthening of federal-provincial relations consultation through the Joint Federal-Provincial Manpower Needs Committee, the strengthening of the Industrial Training component, and the Canada Manpower Consultative Service all reflect a stronger privatization employment strategy. See Department of Manpower and Immigration, *Annual Report, 1975-76* (Ottawa, 1977).

CHAPTER ELEVEN

The Role of the Department of Consumer and Corporate Affairs

The market system implies competition between individuals and between organizations and the free movement of resources utilized by individuals and organizations in response to price changes.[1] However, modern industrialized societies have become complex reflecting a multiplicity of large organizations which produce goods and services but which do not necessarily function in a manner consistent with market behaviour.[2] In fact, governmental intervention has been utilized as a device to smooth out the imperfections and excesses of the marketplace. Karl Polanyi, among others, has argued that there is a paradox in governmental intervention which can lead to still further intervention.[3] Thus, in Canada a government Department of Consumer and Corporate Affairs has been established to regulate the marketplace in order to maintain competition. It was also established to formulate new economic law and in a very real sense is a kind of department of justice for the marketplace.

Governmental intervention poses a problem in that the government is both a participant in the economy as well as a type of neutral judge or umpire to insure that the "public interest" is protected.[4] Consequently, we are again concerned in this chapter with the changing role of the state in economic management especially the legal framework for this process.

The Department of Consumer and Corporate Affairs was set up to deal with economic law and to have special responsibility for the marketplace. As we shall observe below the department's principal objective is the fostering of an effective, efficient, and workable market system for the benefit of all Canadians. The department is concerned with insuring that all citizens are treated justly and fairly in the marketplace whether they are consumers, investors, or managers.[5]

Inherent in its philosophy is the belief that the competitive market system provides the basis for an efficient economy which can be structured to operate for the good of all members of the society. Competition is not seen as an end in itself but as the most important single means of achieving economic and industrial efficiency.

ECONOMIC MANAGEMENT AND COMPETITION POLICY

The ambivalence of the state in economic life is demonstrated by the fact that this contemporary economic philosophy further asserts that "it does not follow that to be most effective for these purposes the market can or should be totally self-regulating. Indeed experience has clearly demonstrated that government must play a vital role in our economic system to ensure that the public interest is properly reflected in its operation."[6]

The ambivalence can be further illustrated from the perspective of planning. Governmental intervention can be used to support selected industries considered crucial to the interests of the system as a whole.[7] To this end, the government has established Crown corporations and has supported industries through incentives grants. Yet the Department of Consumer and Corporate Affairs (C&CA) is "concerned with the total market system, and more especially with safeguarding the competitive aspect of that system. We see the marketplace as a semi-automatic device, a device that is better and more efficient than the alternative of a controlled or planned economy. The department's role is to propose appropriate policies and legislation to govern the basic structural aspects of the market and to insure that conduct and performance in the marketplace result in fair and just treatment of all Canadians."[8]

What is clearly missing in the above discussion is the absence of analysis of the role of organizations in society and in the economy. Economic theory has generally failed to deal adequately with this dimension because it has tended to deal with organizations by aggregating individual interests or preferences.[9] An economic management approach to competition policy must incorporate the pressures exerted by groups to maximize their preferred interests. What is even more significant is the necessity to recognize that such pressures may be supported by the state since the state also has specific interests; for example, Canada must compete with other nations for foreign markets and as a result may alter its internal competition policy to facilitate its trade objectives. Thus, as we saw in Chapter 8, the Minister of Industry, Trade and Commerce has been advocating mergers to improve Canada's productive and competitive capacities.

The difficulties experienced by the federal government in securing passage of the Competition Act further illustrate the power of organizations in the contemporary economic system.[10] Furthermore, given the size, structure, and history of the Canadian economic system, an effective competition policy would necessitate fundamental changes which are certain to be opposed by selective sectors and regions of the economy and society.

The Department of Consumer and Corporate Affairs is concerned with selected aspects of the major goals or objectives of economic policy. These objectives are to be achieved with the preservation of certain ideological commitments which exist within the Canadian "state". In fact, this department's activities reveal the conflicting ideologies which influence and determine the role of the state in the Canadian political and economic systems. If the market is to function efficiently and effectively then there should be adequate information and mobility of resources both human and other. Paradoxically, governmental intervention is predicated on the belief that the market allocative mechanism should be complemented, despite the fact that attempts to alleviate bottlenecks in the market system often lead to increased intervention.[11] In recent years, governmental intervention has been based, in part, on the assertion that the concentration of industries has removed the traditional commitment to competition.[12] Such developments have led to doubts that the market functions as an effective allocative mechanism. In fact, the presence of a Minister of Consumer and Corporate Affairs in the Cabinet justifies this disbelief. To complicate matters the argument has been presented also that certain benefits flow from "economies of scale" in that large firms produce goods and services more efficiently than small firms and they may even compete more effectively abroad.[13] Accordingly, there have been demands for greater concentration in Canadian industry. To this end, the Government of Canada requested the Economic Council of Canada to examine the role of competition policy with respect to the attainment of the general economic policy goals of growth, employment, and price stability. Later the Government of Canada established a Royal Commission to look further into the state of corporate concentration in Canada.

The Economic Council of Canada outlined at least three components of competition policy: the attainment of the most efficient possible performance from the economy; the raising of total output in accordance with consumer demands; and the recognition of the importance of research, invention, and innovation. The Council advocated the improvement of economic efficiency and the avoidance of economic waste, with a view to enhancing the well-being of Canadians.[14] The Economic Council further argued that the primary role of the Department of Consumer and Corporate Affairs is to maximize the growth objective through improved efficiency in the marketplace. The arguments used in this case were that consumer policies were designed to achieve complex objectives such as growth, stabilization, and equity simultaneously through efficient utilization of resources. It is in these respects that the Consumer and Corporate Affairs department can be said to be concerned with supply management.

It is important to stress, however, that Canadian consumer policies have been criticized on grounds that they incorporate two conflicting and irreconcilable groups: namely consumer interests and corporate interests. The department has attempted to avoid these conflicts in its early years by placing major emphasis on revising the Competition Act which, ultimately, it was hoped, would have the effect of insuring that the market functions more efficiently. However, the experience of the passage of the various competition bills demonstrate the power and influence of selected economic groups in the system.[15] Furthermore, they reflect the conflicting values and interests within the Cabinet itself. Subsequent to the publication of the reports of the Economic Council, designed to modernize Canadian competition policy, several bills were introduced in Parliament and even Phase I of the Competition Act, passed in December 1975, was a modified version of the original bill.

This chapter examines an important organizational component which must be incorporated into a more comprehensive economic-management system in Canada. In addition to its overall concern for the market, the department performs a micro-oriented role in economic-policy making because of its concern with efficiency in particular industries. Thus, in general, it provides an example of the effort to complement the main levers of economic policy utilized by the Department of Finance and the Bank of Canada.

THE EVOLUTION OF CORPORATE AND CONSUMER POLICY

The promotion and regulation of supply was a major objective in the establishment in 1966 of the Registrar General department which later in 1967 became Consumer and Corporate Affairs. As a former minister noted:

> The present Act, by regrouping under the authority of a single minister, all the legislation concerning the economy . . . will allow for a constant supervision of the consumer's interest and the application of the present Act will allow us to co-ordinate them all with a single economic policy.[16]

Thus the establishment of the Registrar General department and its subsequent incorporation into a Department of Consumer and Corporate Affairs marked an important phase in the development of a more comprehensive economic-management system. The presence of the department more visibly reflects the inter-relationship between law, economics, and society, and how they relate to the concept of economic management. In Part I reference was made to the institutional framework within which economic management must operate. The legal framework of the marketplace constitutes an important ingredient underlying the compliance which supports the system, and which demonstrates the function of legitimation in the economic system without which the system would fall apart. That the Department of Consumer and Corporate Affairs is not the only department operating in the marketplace is obvious from our analysis in the immediately preceding chapters. It was, however, to take an overview of the health of the market and hence spent most of its early years reforming and updating legislation affecting the marketplace.[17]

The department was expected to perform at least three critical roles in the planning and management of economic policies in Canada. First, it was expected to perform a co-ordinating and enabling function in the marketplace. In effect, the department endeavours to establish the general rules of the game for those in the private sector so that business may be carried out in an orderly fashion. Second, the department was established to insure that there is reasonable balance of power between the various participants in the marketplace. A major problem in this regard has been the growth of corporate power in relation to the individual citizen. Third, the department was established to insure that there was adequate output (to the extent output influences price reduction) within the market system. In this regard, the departmental objectives encompass effective functioning of the market to achieve the best allocation of both human and natural resources. In short, the department was established to bring together three interrelated and interdependent components of the economic system, namely "the law, the economy, and the public interest".[18]

In order to appreciate the intricate interrelationships between law, economics, and society we will briefly review the evolution of consumer and corporate policies and the orientation of the Department of Consumer and Corporate Affairs. The review demonstrates how an important component of economic management has developed and how the Minister of Consumer and Corporate Affairs has become an important, albeit emerging, actor in cabinet decision-making. It shows also the role the minister is attempting to perform in the Canadian economy in general where he has become involved in the process of reconciling the conflicts between different groups in the system. Consequently, at least five Ministers of Consumer and Corporate Affairs have been subjected to pressures from influential groups since the establishment of the department in the mid-1960s. In brief the conflict stems from the fact that influential representatives of the private sector would prefer to see several of the objectives of the department espoused in implicit rather than in explicit terms, hence their objection to the reform of the Competition Act.[19]

From an economic-policy making perspective it is worth pointing out that three research organizations influenced the creation of the department, namely, the Royal Commission on the Organization of the Government of Canada, the Porter Commission on Banking and Finance, and the Economic Council of Canada.[20] In addition to these external agencies it should be pointed out that the work of the Restrictive Trade Practices Commission was also influential in formulating policies in the early 1960s. Anti-combines administration between 1952 and 1960 has been analysed and evaluated by Professors Rosenbluth and Thorburn and a review of their work demonstrates the central influence of political considerations in the formulation of consumer and competition policies.[21] The slow progress which has been made in the areas of consumer and competition policies since the establishment of the department further demonstrates the imbalance in the power position of various groups in the economy and society.

The Royal Commission on the Organization of the Government of Canada (the Glassco Commission) stated that ". . . the function of The Secretary of State is best described by his other designation—Registrar General."[22] The Glassco Commission went on to suggest that:

> . . . a better distribution of burdens could be achieved by transferring to the Secretary of State certain responsibilities now borne by other ministers. . . . Some of these are concerned with the regulation of various business practices: for example, the Department of Insurance . . . and the Standards Branch. . . . Others that might be considered for transfer include . . . the Superintendent of Bankruptcy. . . . The dangers of excessive fragmentation . . . involve essentially a problem of co-ordination. . . . One area where there are co-ordination problems relates to federal policies affecting the pace and direction of industrial growth involving especially . . . the Restrictive Trade Practices Commission and the Secretary of State.[23]

The Commission also pointed to a number of "programs initiated outside the normal departmental framework. . . . Among them are to be found, . . . the Patent Office . . . and the Superintendent of Bankruptcy. This variation in outward form and title may be harmless — although meaningless — but, in no way, does it detract from their essential likeness as departmental organizations in the generic sense of the term." In short, the Glassco Commission, although concerned primarily with administrative and managerial issues, found it necessary to recommend changes in economic management.[24]

Later, in 1964, the Royal Commission on Banking and Finance (Porter) recommended a reorganization of departmental responsibilities in the area of "financial matters" for the protection of both the consumer and the investor.[25] The recognition of the need to modernize legislation affecting both consumers and investors was most important but it was not until late 1975 that Stage I of the Competition Act was passed and late in 1976 that a Borrowers and Depositors Protection Act was introduced in Parliament.[26] In early 1977 Stage II of the Competition Act (Bill C-42) was tabled in Parliament the key elements of which are mentioned later in this chapter. It was felt in the early 1960s, therefore, that there was a need to elevate the status of consumer and corporate policy as part of a long-term reform of Canadian economic management.

In June 1966 the federal government established the Registrar General department (along with many other changes). The late Hon. Lester B. Pearson remarked that "... legislation in these areas [of business law] must not merely record commercial rights but protect the national interest and the rights of individuals and act as an instrument in the promotion of social and economic goals."[27]

Differences in the ideological positions of political parties were evident. The New Democratic party emphasized the consumer rather than the corporate interest. Accordingly, the Hon. T. C. Douglas asserted that "... if the government is not going to set up a department of consumer affairs, then certainly the kind of department the Prime Minister proposed today could be the nucleus around which a department of consumer affairs could be built."[28]

Prime Minister Pearson went on to observe that "no member of the House conscious of the interplay between law and economics will fail to understand the significance of this new department and the role it can play in areas such as patents, combines, bankruptcy, and corporations ... where there is a common link of commercial interest. ... Legislation dealing with them will, therefore, have a strong economic foundation. ... " The Prime Minister further remarked: "one of the matters which will have to be considered early is to what extent the Registrar General can further assist and protect the Canadian consumer [and] can develop consumer protection programs and co-ordinate what is being done now in a number of departments. It is the government's intention to ask the Economic Council to look at the field of consumer affairs, along with some other functions."[29]

The New Democratic party introduced amendments with the objective of establishing a Department of Consumer Affairs which would include responsibilities regarding price and consumer protection.[30] The Liberal government, with Mr. Favreau as its spokesman, asserted that "the wording of the proposed legislation, as well as the powers suggested for the Registrar General were designed to protect the interests of the consumers."[31] The spirit of the legislation as proposed by the Liberal government emphasized an indirect, rather than a direct, role with respect to consumer protection, a view that the business community has also emphasized, both then and since.

The Registrar General Department, in Mr. Favreau's words, "groups together a number of agencies whose primary responsibilities can be described as reflecting public policy toward business organization. . . . All of these agencies have been engaged in the administration of the ground rules established by Parliament for the conduct of those engaged in business under our free enterprise economy. . . ." Mr. Favreau further asserted that "the various bodies of law tended to develop independently of each other, to be the object of separate disciplines, and to be administered by different government departments. . . . It is essential that the legislation which provides the ground rules within which corporations must operate is designed and co-ordinated in such a way as to encourage maximum efficiency and responsiveness to the needs of the public at large."[32]

In the minister's view there were a number of important reasons for grouping these agencies in the new department:

> Each agency shares the same ultimate goals of encouraging the corporate sector of the economy to work more smoothly and efficiently while remaining consistent with the public interest. Each agency is linked in a direct and special way with at least one of the others. . . . There is a danger that, in isolation, the legislation may be administered and revised with a purely technical bias rather than in terms of its fundamental social and economic purposes.
>
> In other words, I believe it will be readily understood that the new department of the Registrar General will, on the whole, be entrusted with co-ordinating, in the interests of the depositors as well as the consumers and any other party interested in either of those fields, such federal legislation as concerns the application of the major economic policies of the government. . . .
>
> In this sense, it can be understood that this department, although one of its functions will be to safeguard the rights and interest of the consumers, will have broader duties which will also comprise the application of the statutes to other areas.[33]

The necessity for a stronger consumer orientation in the department was emphasized by the work of a joint parliamentary committee. The Special Joint Committee on Consumer Credit, appointed March 15, 1966, and chaired by Senator David Croll and Ron Basford, MP, had earlier carried out a lengthy examination of "problems of consumer credit, . . . trends in the cost of living, and factors which may have contributed to changes in the cost of living." The final report of the Committee was issued in February 1967. The Committee recommended that the scope of the Combines Investigation Act should be enlarged to apply to service industries particularly in the sales and finance industries.[34] It further recommended the implementation of Part X of the Bankruptcy Act which dealt with the orderly payment of debts. Consequently, the newly established department integrated a number of disparate programs which were badly in need of a sense of direction.

The Department of the Registrar General was established by the Government Reorganization Act, proclaimed June 6, 1966. The duties of the Registrar General, as outlined in the Act, dealt generally with matters relating to combines, mergers, monopolies, and restraint of trade; patents, copyrights, and trademarks; bankruptcy and insolvency; and corporate affairs. As indicated in his speech supporting the establishment of the Registrar General Department, Prime Minister Lester B. Pearson submitted a reference to the Economic Council of Canada in an attempt to elucidate further the role which the new department should perform in economic management. The first of the subsequent reports placed major emphasis on consumer policies.

In July 1967 the Economic Council of Canada submitted its interim Report on Consumer Affairs and the Department of the Registrar General which placed major emphasis on consumer rather than corporate affairs. The Council subsequently issued a further report on competition policy. Whereas the earlier report had dealt with the optimal organization of the department, the second report attempted to provide a rationale for competition policy.

The Economic Council of Canada, in its First Interim Report, reviewed the existing legislation and the administrative functions in the consumer field. The Council acknowledged the existence of numerous *ad hoc* developments in the area of consumer affairs and, as such, was very cautious in recommending improved co-ordination. It surveyed the then existing distribution of federal government activities under the following headings: Protection against Fraud and Deception; Protection of Health and Safety; Establishing Product Standards and Grades; and Providing Consumer Information.[35] Two main impressions were derived from the survey.

First the various programs were developed as *ad hoc* reactions to periodic crises or pressures in particular problem areas. As a result, consumer protection programs were generally carried out in departments whose primary concern was with other matters and, in some cases, these programs were not always given adequate attention.

Second, adequate attention had not been given to the development of effective means for insuring efficient co-ordination of the administration of these programs. The Council's recommendations emphasized the importance of promoting greater functional co-ordination among departments and the necessity for improved emphasis on information gathering and research. The Council's work further demonstrated that economic-policy formulation like any other area required management. However, there are alternative ways of managing and administering economic policy. To this end, the Council recommended the establishment of six measures to improve policy co-ordination.[36]

First, it suggested the establishment of an Interdepartmental Committee on Consumer Affairs under the chairmanship of the Deputy Registrar General. The composition of the committee was indicative of the inherent problems in economic management, in that it had to consist of the Deputy Ministers of the departments of Trade and Commerce, Health and Welfare, Industry, Agriculture, Fisheries, Unemployment Insurance, Finance, Justice, and other departments having a continuing interest in consumer matters. The report recommended that the Registrar General's Department be made responsible for co-ordinating all consumer information programs of the federal government. In this regard, the basic purpose of the department should be to assist consumers in making more informed spending decisions so that the productive resources of the economy may be used to the best advantage. The Council further stressed that greater emphasis be placed on federal-provincial co-ordination given the fact that there were constitutional problems which plagued the development of sound administrative practices in the consumer field. It also noted that adequate emphasis should be placed on the role of the private sector in improving consumer policies. Hence, more adequate support should be given to the private sector. Finally, it recommended that a Canadian Consumer Advisory Council should be established, and that the Standards Branch of the Department of Trade and Commerce be transferred to the Department of the Registrar General.[37] The foregoing recommendations provide a relatively good indication of the structure which became the Department of Consumer and Corporate Affairs. However, before presenting a more in-depth analysis of the role of the department in economic management we should briefly review the Economic Council's conceptualization of an effective competition policy.

The Council asserted that "the main objective of competition policy should be that of obtaining the most efficient possible performance from the economy."[38] The economy should be using the resources available to it in ways that most contribute to raising total output in accordance with consumer demands. In the words of the Council, "we are advocating the adoption of a single objective for competition policy: the improvement of economic efficiency and the avoidance of economic waste, with a view to enhancing the well being of Canadians."[39] It should be noted, nevertheless, that the Council was evading a central issue in the politics of economic-policy making, namely the redistributive aspects of competition policy. The Council took the position "that a competition policy which assigned equal importance to maximizing economic efficiency and diffusing economic power would be likely, on occasion, to run into conflict of goals." To avoid such conflicts it asserted:

(1) That a competition policy concentrating on efficiency objectives is likely to be applied more consistently and effectively; and
(2) That there existed more comprehensive and faster working instruments, particularly the tax system and the structure of transfer payments, for accomplishing the deliberate redistribution of income and the diffusion of economic power, to whatever extent these are thought desirable.[40]

Having identified the major conceptual components of competition policy, the Council recommended several measures to insure its implementation. These included first, the retention of certain broad prohibitions of regulatory powers but also would involve a number of legal changes which would transfer responsibilities from a criminal law basis to a civil law one. The Council also suggested the establishment of a Competitive Practices Tribunal which would handle many competition problems on the new civil law basis. Finally however, the Council stressed the need to retain several practices on a criminal law basis.

These would include collusive arrangements between competitors to fix prices (including bid-rigging on tenders); collusive arrangements between competitors to allocate markets; collusive arrangements between competitors to prevent the entry into markets of new competitors or the expansion of existing competitors; resale price maintenance; and misleading advertising.[41]

The foregoing demonstrates that two basic components were brought together to form the new department; first, a number of regulatory components designed to protect the consumer but which were scattered throughout a number of agencies, and second, machinery to reform competition laws which had existed as the basis of the operation of the Restrictive Trade Practices Commission and the Director of Investigation and Research. We shall observe later that a Bureau of Corporate Affairs emerged to modernize corporate law. Another component, the Bureau of Intellectual Property, performs a complementary role to the other bureaus in the department.

THE EVOLUTION OF THE DEPARTMENT

The Act establishing the Department of Consumer and Corporate Affairs was passed by Canada's 27th Parliament and assented to on December 21, 1967. That action absorbed the Department of the Registrar General. Subsequently, the Department of Consumer and Corporate Affairs was augmented by the transfer of certain units from the departments of National Health and Welfare, Trade and Commerce, Agriculture, and Fisheries.

Briefly stated the department attempts to achieve both consumer protection and the orderly conduct of business and competition policy. Accordingly, the department is organized to serve the Canadian consumer, to promote competition, and to serve Canadian business.

In 1971 the Department was organized as follows. Below the Minister and Deputy Minister there were three major components in the department: Office of the Director of Investigation and Research (Combines Investigation Act); Assistant Deputy Minister (Consumer Affairs); and Assistant Deputy Minister (Corporate Affairs). The above components represented the basic elements initially brought into the department but between 1971 and the mid-1970s there were a number of more specialized elements created. Consequently, as Figure 11:1 shows, bureaus were established in the following areas: Consumer Affairs; Corporate Affairs; Intellectual Property; and Competition Policy. There were corresponding research groups for each area.

As demonstrated in Figure 11:1 the Department of Consumer and Corporate Affairs was established to strengthen policy initiatives in areas such as competition policy, and the reform of the Business Corporations Act, and to re-examine the nature and status of intellectual and industrial property. However, the most far-reaching component of its task dealt with competition policy of which the other elements are complementary components.

The essence of the paradox of using a bureaucratic structure to bring about greater competition was revealed when the Economic Council concluded:

> In the first place, we have taken the view that the general set of competition policy should be one that aims at the achievement of efficient resource use in the Canadian economy. Second, we believe that some form of social control should be exerted over all commercial activities, and that over the greater part of the Canadian economy, efficient resource use will be more readily brought about through policies that maximize the opportunities for the free play of competitive market forces.[42]

In the more specific area related to extending the application of the Combines Investigation Act to the "service industries" the Council was even more explicit:

> Such proof positive could in most cases only be obtained by setting up the formal machinery for investigation and analysis that already exists for the goods industry. But, there is, we believe sufficient information available to support the contention that markets for some services are not functioning satisfactorily and to justify the setting up of formal machinery.[43]

Because of its earlier work, and its internal influence, the Restrictive Trade Practices Commission and the Office of the Director of Investigation and Research provided the nucleus for the Bureau on Competition Policy. Hence, the centrepiece of the bureau and of the department was an economic administrative structure with quasi-judicial powers. Again the interrelatedness of law and economics should be noted because the court system helps to legitimize the enforcement of the economic rules.

Figure 11:1 Organization of the Department of Consumer and Corporate Affairs

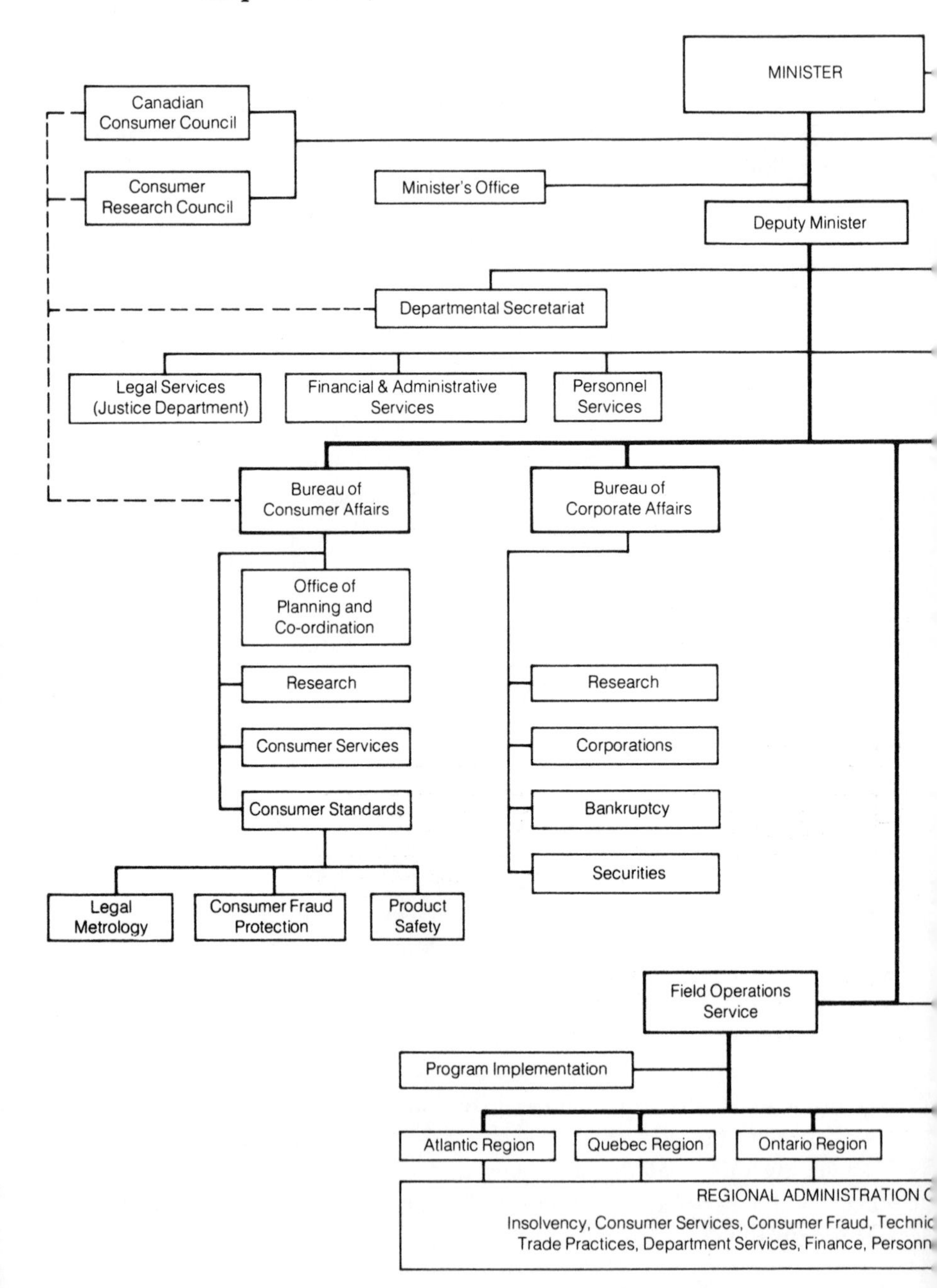

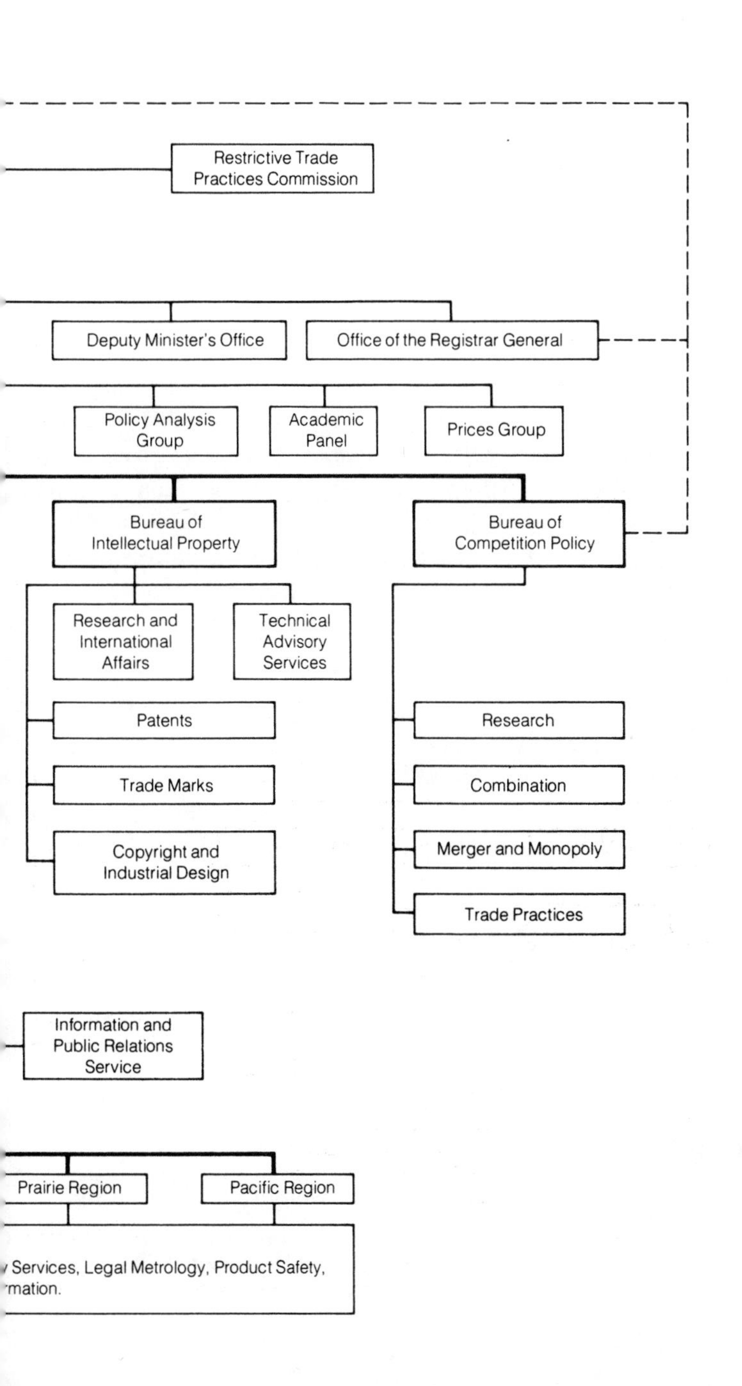
Restrictive Trade
Practices Commission
Deputy Minister's Office
Office of the Registrar General
Policy Analysis
Group
Academic
Panel
Prices Group
Bureau of
Intellectual Property
Bureau of
Competition Policy
Research and
International
Affairs
Technical
Advisory
Services
Patents
Trade Marks
Copyright and
Industrial Design
Research
Combination
Merger and Monopoly
Trade Practices
Information and
Public Relations
Service
Prairie Region
Pacific Region
Services, Legal Metrology, Product Safety,
mation.

Bill C-227 of November 1973 represented the first stage of implementation of the Speech from the Throne, delivered on January 4, 1973, in which it was stated that:

> The government will introduce legislation establishing a competition policy to preserve and strengthen the market system upon which our economy is based. The new policy will be in harmony with industrial policies in general and foreign investment policy in particular.[44]

The government had taken the position that the consumer interests can be met by reforming competition policy. As the Hon. Herb Gray observed in 1973:

> In its examination of food costs I was pleased to see that the committee did not overlook the importance of competition as a policy instrument that can have a key role to play in maintaining cost-effective markets for food in Canada . . . but I think there are other aspects of the proposed bill that are also of concern to the consumer and have a bearing on the issue of food costs. As the interim report notes, factors such as concentration in the food wholesaling, processing, packaging and retailing activities of the food industry and overcapacity in food distribution are areas where further examination is required by the committee.[45]

As an aside, it should be noted that while the Economic Council's recommendations were the subject of extensive public discussions, the Council was not as successful in affecting immediate changes in this area as it had been in the area of manpower policies. While the reform of competition policy appeared obvious to the researchers, the proposals were attacked by powerful economic groups.[46] Consequently, on July 18, 1973, the Ministry of Consumer and Corporate Affairs announced that the bill would be brought forward in stages rather than as a comprehensive bill.[47] The shift from a comprehensive to an incremental approach to policy-making is most important and will become more apparent as our analysis proceeds.[48]

THE COMPETITION ACT: REGULATION AND LAISSEZ FAIRE

On November 6, 1973, the Minister of Consumer and Corporate Affairs introduced Bill C-227 in the House of Commons to amend the Combines Investigation Act. The bill was reintroduced on March 11,

1974, as Bill C-7. This bill was subsequently reintroduced as Bill C-2 and was enacted into law and proclaimed in force on January 1, 1976, except for the application of section 32 affecting the services sector which was proclaimed effective July 1, 1976.[49] The bill represented the first stage of a new competition policy for Canada. Its principal features included: additional measures to deal with undesirable trade and advertising practices; the creation of a new civil function for the Restrictive Trade Practices Commission that would enable it to issue orders to modify or ease certain trade practices brought before it; and provisions to bring services in general under the Act. The provisions of the existing Act have remained in force and a number of cases have been handled under it affecting areas such as price fixing, resale price maintenance, price discrimination, merger, and monopoly.

Bill C-227, in accordance with the findings of both the Combines Branch and, consistent with the recommendations of the Economic Council of Canada, proposed a number of amendments to the Combines Investigation Act while retaining the basic machinery of that Act. The consumer protection measures proposed were also endorsed by the Committee on Food Price Trends.[50] As indicated earlier, the bill had provisions to bring services under the Combines Investigation Act. To this end, the Restrictive Trade Practices Commission was to be authorized "to review and make corrective orders in the case of certain situations generally agreed to which need careful supervision and yet not in all cases requiring prohibition."[51] Thus the bill provided the beginning of a civil jurisdiction in the field of competition policy.

The essential objective of the Competition Act was to bring a far wider range of market activities under its jurisdiction. The exceptions included *bona fide* collective-bargaining activities by employees. Similarly, services such as telephones and other forms of communication, electric power, and the professions would continue to be immune from the legislation to the extent that their activities were regulated or expressly authorized by law.[52] Furthermore, the bill broadened activities to include services in general and the financial sector in particular, bid-rigging, prohibition of foreign regulations considered contrary to the Canadian public interest, and the abuse of intellectual property.[53]

Stage II of the bill was to deal with policy areas relating to industrial structure, specialization agreements, and revisions to the institutions and processes under the Act that were considered necessary and desirable. The changes would provide an opportunity to consider faster and more flexible techniques for dealing with undesirable trade practices with a view to securing more effective protection of the consumer in the marketplace within areas of federal jurisdiction.

Hence, Stage II was aimed at determining whether and how to adapt the legislation so that certain restrictive agreements and acquisitions might be subjected to an "efficiency test". Under the existing law, agreements and mergers that lessen competition unduly are prohibited with criminal sanction. Consistent with the recommendations of the Economic Council that a given merger although destructive of competition may nevertheless be in the public interest if it promoted efficiency, the Tribunal would investigate such cases. The Tribunal would examine each case to determine in the first instance the merger's effect on competition and in the second its effect on efficiency.[54]

The second phase was intended to consider business practices in wide use which, while otherwise unexceptionable, may in some circumstances be used to the detriment of competition. The bill covered such areas as interlocking directorates, "delivered pricing", and quantity discounts. The bill proposed the establishment of an enlarged Tribunal endowed with wide powers to decide certain competition issues and to make such orders and regulations as would make its decisions effective.[55] These changes would be implemented in Stage II of the bill.

Stage II of the bill would deal with the reform of the Restrictive Trade Practices Commission to make it more effective in dealing with the contemporary business environment. The bill aims ultimately "to facilitate trade and commerce, both domestic and export." In short, the second phase of the bill would deal with the twin elements of competition policy encompassing both *laissez faire* and regulation. Accordingly, "the law will not only be designed to promote competition among competitors for the broad purpose of promoting efficiency and improving the allocation of resources but also to control unfair competitive trade practices as a matter of consumer protection in a market place characterized by high technology and massive organization of production and distribution." A subtle relationship exists, therefore, between the structure of organization, management, and competition policy in general. Accordingly, a relationship can be established between decentralization and the market mechanism for allocating resources.[56]

The central features of Stage II of the Competition Act are most important in that they deal with the relationship between competition policy and regulation. The proposals assert that "over the long-run the performance of a mixed economic system, predominantly founded on the private ownership, control, and direction of the means of production and distribution can satisfy more people than any other known system. It can only do this, however, if a market economy is fostered and allowed to work; one that is flexible and promotes industrial transformation, adaptation and dynamic change in response to broad market signals."[57]

Stage II of the Competition Act, therefore, endeavours "to encourage the adoption of real cost economies in production and distribution and to discourage restraints that result from mere market power rather than from superior economic performance. These objectives in turn will most likely be achieved to the highest attainable degree if persons who make the effective decisions are kept subject to effective incentives and pressures.[58] In a market economy these incentives and pressures come "from rivalry or threatened rivalry between firms each employing dynamic variables independantly so as to enhance its position with respect to profits, sales or market share."[59]

Consequently, strong emphasis is placed on freedom of entry and accountability. First, the dynamic forces that can operate to alter the size and relative position of firms — forces such as ability to enter an industry, innovation and change in technology, organizational methods and product lines, advertising, and so on — should be kept free. Second, there should be a system of direct accountability on the part of those who have the power to make strategic management decisions for the effectiveness with which they exercise that power.[60] Here the new approach touches on a fundamental aspect of the planning process; that is, the relative power of decision-makers in the economic system. Economic management must address itself, therefore, to the dilemmas of accountability in the modern economy.

From the perspective of selected research studies the new emphasis will not be based so much on *regulation* but on facilitating "dynamic change". "It is fundamentally important to minimize detailed regulation and control by government (or government appointed regulators) of the essential features of effective markets such as prices, profits, output levels, and entry."[61] Thus, in the modern Canadian economy, "in addition to laws of general application to keep the economy flexible we need government policies that facilitate change, not only by sharing the cost but by investing the necessary expenditures more productively—in programs such as retraining, relocation, and strictly short-term investments or income guarantees." Here we detect obvious linkages with policies being developed in the departments of Employment and Immigration, Industry, Trade and Commerce, Health and Welfare, and Finance. In the modern Canadian economy planned changes require that "industrial and labour groups should direct more attention... to assisting in the development of such policies."[62] The new approach envisages the responsibility of government "to prevent dominant market power from being used primarily so as to obstruct change or to preclude entry or expansion by possible rivals."[63]

Within the context of Stage II of the Competition Act "competition law is the very antithesis of what is commonly referred to as 'government regulation'."[64] Competition law is one of the basic tools of general application available to keep an economy open and flexible enough to adapt and transform itself. The new Competition Act, therefore, stands in contradiction to some of the policies being formulated by regulatory agencies such as the Foreign Investment Review Agency.[65] The proposed system makes provision for a "National Markets Board" to facilitate market analysis and identification of the assessment of economies of scale balanced by experienced judgments. The National Markets Board would operate on the principle of "thou shalt not" orders instead of "thou shalt" orders.[66] The Board would have an experienced judge as its head and strong measures would be adopted to insure that legal principles are retained in its operational procedures.

The foregoing demonstrates that competition law impinges on two critical issues affecting the role of government in the economy; the issue of regulation and the operation of the free-market system. The resolution of these conflicts is a never-ending dilemma for contemporary economic management. In March 1977, as promised, Stage II of Bill C-42, "An Act to amend the Combines Investigation Act and to amend the Bank Act and other Acts in relation thereto or in consequence thereof", was tabled in Parliament. The bill's full title describes its role in economic management: "An Act to provide for the general regulation of trade and commerce by promoting competition and integrity of the marketplace, and to establish a Competition Board and the Office of Competition Policy Advocate". Consequently, the twelve-member Competition Board replaces the Restrictive Trade Practices Commission. The bill provides that the Director of Investigation and Research assume the new title of Competition Policy Advocate. The Advocate is expected to serve as a spokesman on behalf of the maintenance of competition within the government and before federal regulatory agencies. Another challenge for the Department of Consumer and Corporate Affairs relates to the reform of corporation law. The proposals for a new Business Corporations Law also touches on selected aspects of the issues mentioned above. Accordingly, it is further argued that both economic and legal thinking have proven incapable of handling the modern corporation. Since "the corporation remains the chief vehicle of economic advance it has been argued that there is tremendous room for reform in this area." Thus, a recent publication by the department asserts:

> We believe that there are few places where administrative discretion is needed in a corporations act; there is certainly too much of it under the present Canada Corporations Act. Thus, whenever possible, we have set out the consequences which will follow the taking of certain steps, without requiring review or discretion by the Registrar. The Registrar's function, for the most part, is to ensure that the law has been observed where an adjudication on conflicting rights is required, the adjudication should be made by a court, not a government official. The Draft Act therefore provides liberally for simple and speedy applications to court by interested or affected parties, and it gives the courts wide discretion to make appropriate remedial orders.[67]

THE DEPARTMENT IN THE MID-1970S

By the mid-1970s the Department of Consumer and Corporate Affairs had integrated the several disparate programs which a wide variety of research agencies had suggested be brought together. Accordingly, there were four bureaus which reflected the core responsibilities of the department: the Bureau of Consumer Affairs; the Bureau of Corporate Affairs; the Bureau of Intellectual Property; and the Bureau of Competition Policy. The Canadian Consumer Council and the Consumer Research Council are also part of the department.

The Bureau of Consumer Affairs consisting primarily of the Consumer Services Branch, the Consumer Research Branch, and the Consumer Standards Directorate develops programs for consumer protection and information and, in addition, insures that consumers' views are represented in all government activities which affect the marketplace. The Consumer Research Branch conducts research into such far-ranging consumer problem areas such as consumer credit and informative labelling, drug prices, and accident data collection. This research is designed to facilitate the development of new information programs and legislation.

The Bureau of Competition Policy, headed by the Director of Investigation and Research, has primary responsibility for administering the Combines Investigation Act. The Director of Investigation and Research is given wide powers to conduct inquiries when there is reason to believe there has been a violation of the act with respect to combinations that are in restraint of trade, and mergers and monopolies that are detrimental to the public.

The Director of Investigation and Research also investigates unfair trade practices involving price discrimination, disproportionate promotional allowances, misleading representation of prices, false and misleading advertising, and resale price maintenance. The Director reports directly to the Attorney General of Canada who decides whether charges should be laid or, in exceptional cases, sent to the Restrictive Trade Practices Commission for consideration and public report.[68] The Director reports directly to the Deputy Minister of the department for the general interest and promotion of the department's responsibilities for the development of improved competition policy. Given its importance an organization chart for the Bureau of Competition Policy is provided. It demonstrates that the bureau is organized into four principal areas: Manufacturing, Resources, Services, and Research.

The Bureau of Consumer Affairs, under an Assistant Deputy Minister, develops programs for consumer protection and information and, in addition, insures that consumer's views are represented in all government activities that affect the marketplace. The Bureau is further subdivided into three branches: Consumer Services, Consumer Research, and the Consumer Standards Directorate.

The Consumer Services Branch directly assists consumers before and after they make purchases in the marketplace. It also supplies a broad range of information material to help consumers make choices

Figure 11:2 Organization of the Bureau of Competition Policy, Department of Consumer and Corporate Affairs

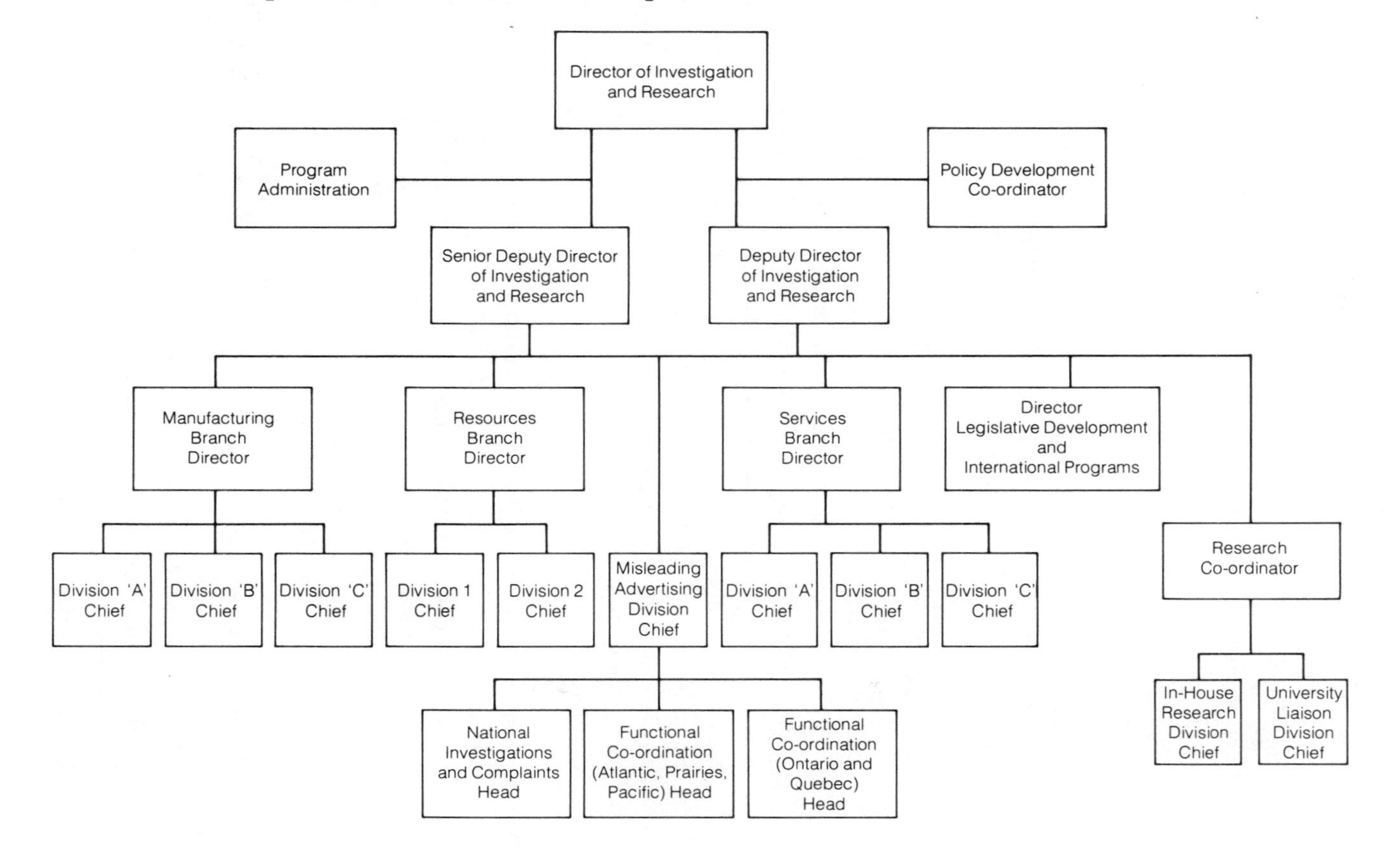

from available products. Consumer complaints and inquiries are handled through Box 99, Ottawa, the national mailing address for consumers seeking information or assistance.

The Consumer Research Branch conducts active inquiries in such far-ranging consumer problem areas as consumer credit and informative labelling, drug prices, and accident data collection. Its recommendations are then used to design new information programs and legislation. Pursuant to research conducted by the Branch, Bill C-16, an Act to provide for the protection of borrowers and depositors, to regular interest on judgment debts, to repeal the Interest Act, the Pawnbrokers Act, and the Small Loans Act, and to amend certain other statutes, was introduced in the House of Commons in October 1976.[69] The Borrowers and Depositors Protection Act was expected to delay the passage of Stage II of the Competition Act. Consistent with the experience of the competition bills the major financial institutions were strongly opposed to the passage of this bill.[70]

The Consumer Standards Directorate has a triple responsibility toward consumers. Its legal metrology division controls the types and use of measuring devices used in Canada to insure accurate measurements to protect against fraud. The Directorate develops standards for true labelling, marketing, packaging, and advertising of prepackaged consumer goods, textiles, precious metals, and food products. Safety standards are set for hazardous consumer products such as household chemicals, toys, and dangerously flammable textiles.[71]

Through Box 99 the Branch has performed an important mediating role in settling complaints. The department's officers endeavour to re-establish communication between the disputing parties so that a mutually satisfactory compromise can be reached. A communication/liaison network has been developed which embraces all levels of government, major manufacturers, retailers and trade associations, and voluntary organizations to permit the Branch to fulfill the role of mediator. In recent years complaints have been strong in areas such as foods, motor vehicles, and accessories, real estate and housing, and sales promotions. By the mid-1970s the Branch was focussed on five functional units: Travel and Transportation; Shelter; Recreation; Food, Clothing, and Textiles; and Finance. A Consumer Fraud Protection Branch consisting of three divisions, namely Agriculture, Food, and Products, performs an important advisory and regulatory role in the area of consumer protection. In this respect it co-ordinates policies with the departments of National Health and Welfare and Agriculture. The Food division participated in the preparation of revised food-labelling regulations under the Food and Drugs Act which became effective in March 1976.[72]

The Bureau of Corporate Affairs regulates aspects of the legal framework under federal jursidiction in which business operates. In short, the Bureau is concerned with much of the general legal framework that governs the orderly conduct of business under federal jurisdiction. The Bureau consists of three branches and one division: the Corporations Branch, the Bankruptcy Branch, the Corporate Research Branch, and the Registration Division.

The Corporation Branch administers the Canada Corporations Act which deals with the federal incorporation of companies, filing financial statements and annual summaries, and maintaining a register of mortgages and charges of both federally and provincially incorporated companies. Under the Corporations and Labour Unions Returns Act, the Branch also maintains an office that provides the public with information in Section "A" of the returns. The Branch also administers the Boards of Trade Act, the Trade Unions Act, and the Pension Fund Societies Act.

The Corporate Research Branch is a small group of research analysts who carry out studies to improve legislation in relation to the functioning of corporations, co-operatives, and the securities market.

The Bankruptcy Branch administers the Bankruptcy Act. The Act sets out prescribed powers of control for the Superintendent of Bankruptcy over trustees throughout Canada in the discharge of their duties. The Superintendent also investigates and reports to the minister on administrative matters. In addition, he makes inquiries into alleged offences and irregularities that occur before bankruptcy and reports his findings to the Deputy Attorney General of the province of jurisdiction. The Registration Division records such official documents as proclamations, commissions of appointment, letters patent granting lands, and corporation letters patent.

The Bureau of Intellectual Property, formed in January 1973, provides a co-ordinated approach to the department's responsibilities for patents, trademarks, copyright, and industrial design. The legislation governing these areas enables the granting of temporary legal monopolies to creators, providing protection and development incentives for inventors who disclose their ideas and knowledge. The Patent Office administers the Patent Act under which patents of inventions are granted, and each week publishes abstracts of patents granted in the Patent Office Record. The Trade Marks Office maintains a record of all registered trademarks and publishes, weekly, the *Trade Marks Journal*. The Copyright and Industrial Design Office administers the Copyright Act under which the copyright for literary, dramatic, musical, and artistic works are obtained, and the Industrial Design Act which protects original designs based on the shape, pattern, or ornamentation of a manufactured article. The Research and International Affairs Branch has been studying recommendations made in the Economic Council of Canada Report on Industrial Property. Again special mention should be made of the Field Operations Service which represents a further development of the department's effort to bring together, in a single organizational unit, all departmental employees permanently based outside Ottawa and to permit co-ordinated control and development of this large part of the department. Previously, Consumer Affairs, Corporate Affairs, and Combines Policy Programs each had separate field offices.

The field services were integrated in 1973 by the appointment of five Regional Directors and the establishment of five Regional Offices. Consequently, the Field Operations Service consists of a headquarters element and all of the staff of the department permanently located outside Ottawa which is responsible for the implementation of departmental programs and activities and the enforcement of legislation planned and developed under the Consumers Affairs, Corporate Affairs, and Combines Investigation programs.

The decentralized system operates from headquarters in Ottawa through the regional centres in Halifax, Montreal, Toronto, Winnipeg, and Vancouver down to field offices located in thirty Canadian cities. Enforcement is provided for economic fraud provisions of the Food and Drugs Act, and the Consumer Packaging and Labelling Act, the Precious Metals Marking Act, the National Trade Mark and True Labelling Act, and the Hazardous Products Act. Other legislation for which the Department of Consumer and Corporate Affairs has responsibility, in conjunction with other departments, includes the Canada Agricultural Products Standards Act, the Canada Dairy

Products Act, the Maple Products Industry Act, the Fish Inspection Act, and Provincial Agricultural Grades and Sales Act. Thus the departmental services were decentralized from headquarters to the regional office level to allow for appropriate regional variation in programs, to permit more prompt response to local demand through localized decision-making and to provide a more immediate service to Canadians. This development further reflects the trend toward decentralization identified in earlier chapters.

The Office of the Registrar General of Canada is also an important part of the department. It comprises two units, the Conflict of Interest Organization and the Registration Division.[73] The former through the office of the Assistant Deputy Registrar General (created in May 1974) administers the conflict of interest guidelines for ministers, Governor-in-Council appointees, and other individuals to whom similar guidelines are applicable. The latter Division was transferred from the Department of Registrar General to the newly-formed Department of Consumer and Corporate Affairs in December 1967.

In this chapter our objective is simply to examine the direction in which the department and its policy responsibilities have evolved. The splitting of the Competition Act into Stage I and Stage II postponed the implementation of the main regulatory components of the legislation. Stage II will introduce a fundamental change in economic philosophy because it envisages a strong role for the Tribunal which will assess the effects of mergers on competition policy and, ultimately, their effects on economic efficiency.[74] Here we are dealing in the most fundamental way with the role of the state in the management of the economy. Previously the philosophy supporting the achievement of economic efficiency identified the market system as the exclusive means by which economic efficiency is achieved. Thus the introduction of a Tribunal aimed at regulating the market signals the institutionalization of a partial rejection of the earlier philosophy. The establishment of such a tribunal means that a kind of "economic court" is making judgments on the adequacy and effectiveness of the industrial structure. It was not accidental, therefore, that the conflicting theories supporting both mergers and competition and, correspondingly, the need for regulation were discussed in the federal government's 1976 working paper *The Way Ahead*.[75] So far, our analysis has attempted merely to throw some light on the conflicting values and belief systems which partially explain the role of government in the economy and the need for a Department of Consumer and Corporate Affairs.

By the mid-1970s, the duties, powers, and functions of the minister extend to and include all matters over which the Parliament of Canada has jurisdiction, not by law assigned to any other department, branch, or agency of the Government of Canada relating to: consumer affairs; corporations and corporate securities; combines, mergers, monopolies, and restraint of trade; bankruptcy and insolvency; patents, copyrights, and trademarks; standards of identity and performance in relation to consumer goods; and legal metrology.[76]

In exercising his powers and carrying out his duties and functions in relation to consumers' affairs under the Act the minister shall: initiate, recommend, or undertake programs designed to promote the interests of the Canadian consumer; co-ordinate programs of the Government of Canada that are designed to promote the interests of the Canadian consumer; promote and encourage the institution of practices or conduct tending to the better protection of the Canadian consumer and co-operate with provincial governments or agencies thereof, or any bodies, organizations, or persons, in any programs having similar objects; and undertake, recommend, or assist in programs to assist the Canadian consumer to be more fully informed about goods and services offered to the consumer.[77]

The Government of Canada has concluded that the functioning of an effective and efficient market-economy system should be looked at as a whole rather than in a piece-meal way. The department has worked toward satisfying its conception of the public interest in at least three ways. First, it has brought together in one place and under one minister as much as was practical of general federal government law governing and regulating marketplace activities. Second, the department has attempted to work toward the development and revision of marketplace systems in a co-ordinated and harmonized way. Third, the department is concerned with the relationship between producers and consumers in the marketplace system and serves as a focal point in the federal government for the consideration of consumer concerns and needs.[78]

From a policy-making perspective, it should also be emphasized that a considerable amount of consumer and commercial legislation comes under provincial jurisdiction. To this end, a consultative process operates between the two levels of government. However, a review of the evolution of provincial consumer policies reveals significant disparities in their policy-making effectiveness.[79]

CONFLICTS IN THE MARKETPLACE AND THE CABINET

The foregoing demonstrates that the Minister of Consumer and Corporate Affairs must perform a difficult role in the political process. We have seen the political conflicts which have emerged and which are inherent in the policies formulated by ministers and which have been traced from the initial research stage through the consultation process and ultimately through the translation of the various bills into Acts.[80] Another indication of the conflicts which have affected this department may be captured through ministerial turnover. In its short history the department has been led by several ministers with fundamentally different philosophies. By way of illustration since the department crystallized, it has been headed by John Turner, Ronald Basford, Herb Gray, André Ouellet, Bryce Mackasey, and Anthony Abbott.[81] At least three ministers, namely Ronald Basford, Herb Gray, and André Ouellet, encountered significant conflicts with influential groups in the economy even though the groups had been involved previously in the consultation process.

The conflicts which must be resolved in this department were most clearly reflected in the difficulties encountered in the passage of the various competition bills and with the Borrowers and Depositors Protection Bill. The interested reader should review the passage of these bills and the group positions adopted in favour of or against the bills as one way of understanding the role of economic power in the Canadian political process.[82] The Hon. Herb Gray was most critical of the policy development especially after he left the department and could be considered as the most aggressive of the ministers particularly as his action related to the development of a food policy.[83] The Hon. Ron Basford, for a variety of reasons, may be considered as the most aggressive Consumer Affairs minister. In October 1973, Michael Pitfield, then Deputy Minister of the department, gave a presentation to the Canadian Manufacturing Association in an effort to explain the role and responsibilities of the department. The speech had the tenor of allaying business fears concerning governmental encroachment on the market.[84]

The political involvement of the department was further reflected in the area of food policy. It should be noted that the short-lived Food Prices Review Board (to be examined in Chapter 12) reported through the Minister of Consumer and Corporate Affairs. During its short existence, a major confrontation took place between the Chairman of the Food Prices Board and the Minister of Agriculture concerning the role of marketing boards. That confrontation provided further illustration of the emerging role of the department in the political process. The fact that consumers are heavily urbanized, in contrast to farmers, further reveals another dimension of the role of the department in the political process. In addition to the food-pricing problem, the department, in co-operation with the departments of Agriculture and National Health and Welfare, performs a major regulatory function with respect to food policy. In short, in order to be effective in controversial areas such as consumer policy, competition policy, credit policy, and food policy, to name a few areas, the department requires a strong minister and a militant expert group to achieve the stated objectives mentioned earlier. Yet some critics have argued that the department has lost the initial zeal displayed during Ronald Basford's leadership.[85] The Minister of Consumer and Corporate Affairs, nevertheless, must be regarded as a new but significant actor in the Cabinet.

In addition to his role within the Cabinet the incumbent minister is also placed in a unique position with respect to the development of the legal system especially as it relates to economic-policy formulation. By way of illustration, the Hon. André Ouellet was caught in one such controversy when he criticized the sugar refinery judicial decision. A significant part of the problem ensued from the fact that the relatively new department was developing a strong position on industrial and consumer policies. Thus, the Combines Investigation Act contemplates enforcement of its provisions through three institutions, the Director of Investigation and Research, the Restrictive Trade Practices Commission, and the Courts.

The foregoing demonstrates that the Minister of Consumer and Corporate Affairs is concerned with presenting to Cabinet a number of areas which previously were only of ancillary concern to other ministers. By way of illustration the Minister of Consumer and Corporate Affairs is responsible for presenting to Cabinet the political and economic issues affecting the following: the industrial structure of the economy; competitiveness in the marketplace, both domestically and internationally (hence his concern with such areas as tariffs); the maintenance of competition by avoiding undesirable mergers (hence his concern with anti-merger policy); the regulation of anti-combines practices through the enforcement of economic laws in general: presenting a contrary point of view before regulatory agencies such as the CRTC and CTC; presenting the point of view of the consumer not as a consumer advocate but through maintenance of an effective market (hence his concern with prices); providing a micro-oriented economic-research point of view by identifying and publicizing particular pricing problems after investigating specific industries in detail, in some ways, similar to the Department of Industry, Trade and Commerce; and providing an organizational structure for "modernizing legislation" affecting the marketplace. In this regard, problems emerging from the interrelationships between economics and law are most crucial.

The critical relationships between law and economics had hitherto not been adequately emphasized. The Combines Investigation Act, for example, has been under the "criminal code" for constitutional reasons. As a result, a civil law approach to combines and mergers has not emerged, a situation which led the Economic Council of Canada to recommend changes in this area. The courts have been placed in the delicate situation of having to formulate policy in an area requiring adequate information about the laws of the marketplace and on the appropriateness of monopolies to the achievement of the public interest. The large corporations have been treated as individuals. Consequently, the Minister of Consumer and Corporate Affairs has been entrusted with major long-term responsibilities for modernizing the laws affecting the marketplace. However, since concentration involves major questions impinging on societal power there are major sociological and political problems to be resolved in these areas.

The Minister of Consumer and Corporate Affairs has been delegated a number of "critical problem roles". For example, the contingency plan for wage and price controls was placed under the Minister of Consumer and Corporate Affairs following the initial measures adopted in 1968 when the Government of Canada embarked on an anti-inflation policy.[86] Similarly, the Food Prices Review Board, although independent, was made responsible to the Minister of Consumer and Corporate Affairs.

It is worth pointing out also that the presence of a minister of Consumer and Corporate Affairs has provided other ministers, such as Finance, and Industry, Trade and Commerce, with an opportunity to de-emphasize selected aspects of their departmental mandates; for example, in areas such as industrial structure and tariffs. Because of the broader concerns of the Minister of Finance (budget policy) he has not always been able to give adequate consideration to the necessity for preserving the most competitive economy. Furthermore, it is not by any means clear as to whether or not the most competitive market is always in the public interest. Consequently, a task force investigated these issues and subsequently reported to the government and a new policy is expected to be adopted.[87] The presence of a Minister of Consumer and Corporate Affairs has introduced a mediator's role in the Cabinet, involving areas such as the pricing of farm products. Most recently, we have seen intensive debates between the Chairman of the Food Prices Review Board and the Minister of Agriculture over the appropriate interpretation of data affecting the pricing of farm produce.[88]

In the "hierarchial context" of Cabinet relationships the Minister of Consumer and Corporate Affairs can be said to be delegated mainly "administrative responsibilities". In the 1973 budget, for example, he was delegated the responsibility for insuring that retail outlets dropped their prices in response to certain guidelines from the Minister of Finance.[89] Needless to say such responsibilities are sometimes frowned upon by the department since it gives the impression that there is an inner and outer Cabinet. In turn, the Department of Finance has always indicated that it has delegated several of its operational responsibilities so that it can concentrate on policy matters given its primary responsibility for formulating the budget.

The Minister of Consumer and Corporate Affairs has some responsibilities in the area of industrial structure for monitoring proceedings in the courts, consumer research, knowledge about the market, and selected aspects of the work of the Foreign Investment Review Agency.[90] Yet there are a number of controversial dimensions of policy-making which have been intensified by the presence of a Minister of Consumer and Corporate Affairs. For example, should there be a separate Department of Consumer Affairs? What policies should be adopted with respect to mergers? Other ministers in the Cabinet could effectively argue that concentration promotes efficiency. Such arguments have been made along these lines with respect to the petroleum and mining industries.[91] Given such conflicts the Minister of Consumer and Corporate Affairs must convince the Cabinet of cases which are in the public interest. Yet the public interest should be regarded as something greater than the aggregation of the particular interests or concerns of particular ministers.

This places the Minister of Consumer and Corporate Affairs in an awkward position. In one sense, he is custodian of a free and competitive market system; hence his concern with implementing the Competition Act. At the same time, the introduction of the Competition Bill provides for the establishment of a Competitive Practices Tribunal which can regulate malpractices by deciding whether or not a merger is in the public interest. Here we observe an important example of how economic management differs from economic analysis per se.

The question has certainly been raised as to whether or not the minister should perform a role in the poverty debate (e.g., consumer credit and food prices). Certainly, rising consumer prices will most adversely affect consumers in the lower income groups. A major issue here concerns the particular instrument which should be utilized to resolve this problem. The use of income support programs can provide the poorer consumers with the added purchasing power needed to maintain a basic minimum level of consumption. It appears, therefore, that the Minister of Consumer and Corporate Affairs has taken the position that the laws, in the marketplace in general, and those affecting "services" in particular, should be restructured and that these changes will ameliorate the position of the poor.

The Minister of Consumer and Corporate Affairs performs several roles ranging from more specialized research (micro-economic research), hitherto de-emphasized, to administrative regulations affecting both consumers and corporate interests. The department has taken the position, therefore, that both the corporate and the consumer interests are best served through an efficient marketplace. In this regard it has *not* adopted the direct consumer-advocate role.

We have reviewed selected changes in the philosophy and organization of the legal framework which provides support for, and compliance in, the economic system. The system is based on beliefs that a free-market economy is most efficient. However, governmental intervention has been introduced to smooth out structural imbalances which have emanated from the growth and complexity of the modern economic system; for example, undue concentration of industries.

The reform of competition law to establish some type of balance between individuals, organizations, and even multinational corporations has been mentioned and critically reviewed. The problems faced by consumers have been identified and some measures to protect the hitherto unorganized consumer have been legislated by the government. The reform of competition law has been postulated as the means by which the consumer interest can be best protected. A consumer advocate system has not been adopted. Following years of research and consultations a Competition Policy Advocate is in the process of being established.

Investors are now protected through the Business Corporation Law. The Borrowers and Depositors Protection Act regulates the credit market. On the whole, we are dealing with a mixed and regulated economy. Structural policies have been, and are being, developed to deal with imbalances in the system, some of which are caused by an economy marked by inflation. Once again, this chapter demonstrates that the economy is managed through a system of economic and legal institutions without which there would be no support and enforcement. We have identified the existence of powerful groups which can improve their position by methods other than the efficiency criteria espoused by the system. Accordingly, the state, through this department, purports to perform a type of regulatory function to establish a system of equity. As reflected in the working paper, *The Way Ahead,* the decentralization of organizational activity is being used as one method of improving accountability. Yet the economic system works only if people believe in it. The Department of Consumer and Corporate Affairs performs a most important role in insuring that the system operates in a dynamic and efficient manner.

NOTES

1. See, for example, M. Blaug, *Economic Theory in Retrospect* (Homewood, 1962), especially Chapter 2 but more generally chapters 5-11.

2. John K. Galbraith, *The New Industrial State* (New York, 1968) and his *Economics and the Public Purpose* (Boston, 1973).

3. K. Polanyi, *The Great Transformation: The Political and Economic Origins of Our Time* (Boston, 1965). Note his analysis of the social implications of the market economy and the liberal creed.

4. See Galbraith, *Economics and the Public Purpose*, especially pp. 215-324. A significant part of recent controversy impinges on the role of the state. See Polanyi, *The Great Transformation*.

5. See *Hansard*, 1st Session, 27th Parl., Vol. v, pp. 5688-90.

6. Michael Pitfield, Speech to the Canadian Manufacturers' Association in Toronto, October 2, 1973, p. 3. See also Government of Canada, *The Way Ahead: A Framework for Discussion* (Ottawa, 1976).

7. This approach has been most explicitly utilized in the French system of planning. See, for example, S. Cohen, *Modern Capitalist Planning: The French Model* (Cambridge, 1969), pp. 31-80, 157-64. The role of Crown corporations is also being affected by the new economic policy. See C. Kelf, *Twenty Years of Nationalisation: The British Experience* (London, 1969).

8. Department of Consumer and Corporate Affairs, *Annual Report, 1975-76* (Ottawa, 1976). For a penetrating discussion of these issues, although at times ideologically charged, see L. A. Skeoch, *et al.*, *Dynamic Change and Accountability in a Canadian Market Economy*. Report of an Independent Committee (Ottawa, 1976).

9. Robert A. Solo, *The Political Authority and the Market System* (Cincinnati, 1974).

10. See Galbraith, *Economics and the Public Purpose*. Here our analysis could be related to the conflict between Galbraith's "planning system" and the "public purpose". In this context the debate is also ideologically charged. Two pieces of legislation which have presented significant challenges to this department have been: the Competition Act and the Borrowers' and Depositors' Protection Act. The Canadian political process has demonstrated

strong resistance to the legislation of competition laws. On the extent to which Canadian competition laws have lagged behind other countries see Economic Council of Canada, *Interim Report on Competition Policy* (Ottawa, 1969).

11. Polanyi, *The Great Transformation*. On the evolution of issues in the Canadian system see K. J. Rea and J. T. McLeod, eds., *Business and Government in Canada*, second ed. (Toronto, 1976).

12. Economic Council of Canada, *Interim Report on Competition Policy*. See also the work of John Kenneth Galbraith.

13. This approach has been presented in various speeches late in 1976 by the Minister of Industry, Trade and Commerce.

14. Economic Council of Canada, *Competition Policy*.

15. Interviews. The positions of these groups have been reported in the press, especially in *The Financial Times*. See also *Competition Policy in the Context of a Canadian Industrial Strategy, A Commentary on Bill C-256*. Seventh McGill-Government-Industry Conference, Montebello, November 1972.

16. *Hansard*, 1st Session, 27th Parl., Vol. VI, p. 5722.

17. See Pitfield, Speech to the Canadian Manufacturers' Association, pp. 9-16. The Deputy Minister outlined the then proposed legislative timetable encompassing: Competition Policy, Intellectual Property, the Business Corporations Act, the Bankruptcy Act, and the Hazardous Products Act. As late as 1977 the Department was still experiencing difficulty getting its legislation to Parliament. The commercial and financial institutions were vehemently opposed to the various legislation.

18. Ibid., p. 2.

19. Interviews.

20. Government of Canada, *Royal Commission on the Organization of the Government of Canada* (Glassco Commission) (Ottawa, 1962); Government of Canada, *Royal Commission on Banking and Finance* (Porter Commission) (Ottawa, 1964); and Economic Council of Canada, *Interim Report on Consumer Affairs and the Department of the Registrar General* (Ottawa, 1967).

21. C. Rosenbluth and H. Thornburn, *Canadian Anti-Combines Administration, 1952-60* (Toronto, 1963). On the extent to which pluralism adversely

affects policy formulation see Rea and McLeod, eds., *Business and Government in Canada*, pp. 360-413, especially contributions by M. J. Trebilcock and Carolyn J. Tuohy.

22. *The Organization of the Government of Canada*, Vol. v, p. 41.

23. Ibid., pp. 43, 45.

24. Ibid., pp. 56, 57.

25. *Banking and Finance*.

26. On the necessity to modernize legislation affecting consumer credit see Joint Chairmen Hon. David Croll and Ron Basford, MP, *Report on Consumer Credit* (Ottawa, 1967), pp. 3-30.

27. *Hansard*, Vol. v, p. 4874.

28. Ibid., Hon. T. C. Douglas, p. 4881.

29. Ibid., Hon. L. B. Pearson, pp. 4904-05.

30. Ibid., p. 4881.

31. Ibid., Hon. Guy Favreau, pp. 5688-90.

32. Ibid.

33. *Hansard*, Hon. Guy Favreau, Vol. VI, pp. 5688-90.

34. Croll and Basford, *Report on Consumer Credit*, pp. 3-8, 14.

35. Economic Council of Canada, *Interim Report on Consumer Affairs and the Department of the Registrar General*, pp. 10-18.

36. Ibid., pp. 19-30. The department did not necessarily follow these recommendations since they were not always administratively feasible (Interviews).

37. Ibid., pp. 17, 28. It is important to note that Mrs. A. F. W. Plumptre, a former Past President of the Consumers' Association of Canada and a later Chairman of the Food Prices Review Board, was a member of the Economic Council at the time of the report.

38. *Competition Policy*, p. 19.

39. Ibid.

40. Ibid. The Council placed competition policy within the context of the economic goals outlined for Canada in its *First Annual Review*. For conflicts with goals and the Council's attempt to grapple with the goals see R. W. Phidd, "The Economic Council of Canada and Economic Policy Formulation in Canada". Unpublished PhD thesis, Queen's University, Kingston, 1972, Chapter 6 and "The Economic Council Annual Review: Whither Economic Planning in Canada?" *Canadian Public Policy*, Vol. II (1976), pp. 262-69. For comparative reference to the role of competition policy in economic management see A. Cairncross, ed., *The Managed Economy* (Oxford, 1970), Chapter 7, pp. 106-34.

41. *Competition Policy*. See Chapter 6, pp. 99-131; James Gillies, *A Review of the Economic Council's Interim Report on Competition Policy* (Montreal, 1969). For broader treatment than provided in this chapter see Phidd, "The Economic Council and Economic Policy Formulation in Canada", pp. 386-429. For later developments see Skeoch, *et al.*, *Dynamic Change and Accountability in a Canadian Market Economy*.

42. *Competition Policy*, p. 195.

43. Ibid., p. 147. On the Council approach to regulation see pp. 137-40, 159-82, and 195-98. Elsewhere we have commented on the relationship between planning and regulation. On the role which the department expects to play with respect to governmental monopolies see Department of Consumer and Corporate Affairs, *Proposals for a New Competition Policy: First Stage, Bill C-227* (Ottawa, 1973), pp. 17-34 and see also G. Bruce Doern, ed., *The Regulatory Process in Canada* (Toronto, 1978).

44. Government of Canada, Speech from the Throne, January 4, 1973, p. 1.

45. Hon. Herb Gray, quoted in Department of Consumer and Corporate Affairs, *Proposals for a New Competition Policy*, p. 2.

46. See Special Issue, *The Financial Times*, 1972.

47. Consumer and Corporate Affairs, *Proposals for a New Competition Policy*, p. 3.

48. The political advantages of incrementalism have been extensively analysed. See G. Bruce Doern and Peter Aucoin, eds., *The Structures of Policy-Making in Canada* (Toronto, 1971), Chapter 1.

49. *Annual Report, Director of Investigation and Research for the Year Ending March 31, 1976* (Ottawa, 1976), pp. 9-10.

50. Consumer and Corporate Affairs, *Proposals for a New Competition Policy*, p. 4.

51. Ibid.

52. Ibid., pp. 26-27.

53. Ibid., pp. 27-42.

54. Ibid., pp. 93-96. See *Annual Report, Director of Investigation and Research for the Year Ending March 31, 1976*, p. 14. See also Skeoch, *et al.*, *Dynamic Change and Accountability in a Canadian Market Economy*, pp. 190-97.

55. Skeoch, *et al.*, *Dynamic Change and Accountability in a Canadian Market Economy*, pp. 16-17, 116-18.

56. Solo, *The Political Authority and the Market System*.

57. Skeoch, *et al.*, *Dynamic Change and Accountability in a Canadian Market Economy*, pp. 201-25.

58. *Annual Report, Director of Investigation and Research for the Year Ending March 31, 1976*, p. 116.

59. Ibid. See also Skeoch, *et al.*, *Dynamic Change and Accountability in a Canadian Market Economy*, pp. 34-38.

60. Ibid.

61. Ibid., p. 117.

62. Ibid.

63. Ibid.

64. Ibid., p. 118. See also Skeoch, *et al.*, *Dynamic Change and Accountability*, pp. 34-38.

65. *Annual Report, Director of Investigation and Research for the Year Ending March 31, 1976*, p. 118. See also Doern, ed., *The Regulatory Process in Canada*, chapters 1, 2, and 3.

66. Skeoch, *et al.*, *Dynamic Change and Accountability*, pp. 279-352, especially

pp. 293-313. Here again we suggest reference to European developments. See J. Hayward and M. Watson, *Planning, Politics and Public Policy: The British, French and Italian Experience* (London, 1975), pp. 445-83.

67. R. W. V. Dickerson, *et al.*, *Proposals for a New Business Corporation Law for Canada*, Vol. I (Ottawa, 1971), p. 4.

68. Consumer and Corporate Affairs, *Annual Report, 1974-75*, p. 7.

69. See the Borrowers' and Depositors' Protection Act.

70. Interviews. See also Economic Council of Canada, *Efficiency and Regulation: A Study of Deposit Institutions* (Ottawa, 1976).

71. See G. Bruce Doern, *Regulatory and Jurisdictional Aspects of Regulation of Hazardous Substances in Canada*. Study for the Science Council of Canada (Ottawa, 1976).

72. Consumer and Corporate Affairs, *Annual Report, 1975-76*.

73. Consumer and Corporate Affairs, *Annual Report, 1974-75*.

74. Ibid.

75. Government of Canada, *The Way Ahead*, p. 16.

76. *Organization of the Government of Canada*.

77. Ibid.

78. Ibid.

79. Ellen Roseman, *Consumer Beware*, revised ed. (Don Mills, 1974), Chapter 9, pp. 168-81.

80. Various references presented in this chapter reflect the pluralistic nature of the Canadian political system or, at least, the power of business interests.

81. Roseman, *Consumer Beware*.

82. Ibid.

83. Ibid. This view was held by most department officials interviewed.

84. Pitfield, Speech to the Canadian Manufacturers' Association.

85. Roseman, *Consumer Beware, passim*.

86. Interviews.

87. Skeoch, *et al., Dynamic Change and Accountability*.

88. See Hon. E. Whelan, Notes for an Address to the National Farmers' Union, Leamington, March 27, 1976 and Notes for an Address to the Grocery Distributors Institute, Calgary, June 2, 1976. See also A. F. W. Plumptre, Notes for a speech to the Canadian Agricultural Economics Society, Brandon, January 27, 1975.

89. Hon. J. N. Turner, Budget Speech, February 19, 1973.

90. Skeoch, *et al., Dynamic Change and Accountability*, p. 106.

91. Solo, *The Political Authority and the Market System.*

CHAPTER TWELVE

Conflict and Consensus in Canadian Economic Management

We have now examined, in the previous chapters of Part III, specific policy elements and their organizational evolution. These include elements of both the demand and supply side of economic management and reflect a varying but persistent need to resolve conflict and achieve consensus and co-ordination among government departments, among levels of government, and between the public and private sectors. It is important to conclude this part of the book with an examination of each of the above institutional dimensions which cut across our earlier department-by-department approach.

An examination of the main interdepartmental, public sector-private sector and intergovernmental aspects of Canadian economic management will help bring us full circle to the main concerns addressed in Parts I and II, but which can now be seen in the more detailed context of the specific challenge faced by the departments of Finance, Industry, Trade and Commerce, Regional Economic Expansion, Manpower and Immigration, and Consumer and Corporate Affairs, as well as other departments and agencies just examined.

That the resolution of conflicts and the achievement of consensus and co-ordination occur is obvious. That such achievements are elusive, episodic, and difficult to politically and administratively sustain over very long periods of time is equally obvious, especially when one looks at the details of economic management as reflected in the immediately preceding five chapters. As the analysis in this book unfolds it becomes increasingly obvious that conflict resolution and consensus occur through a variety of mechanisms including: the electoral process; the raw exercise of power (and hence the political triumph—albeit usually a temporary one — of one minister and department over another or the right wing of the Cabinet over the left wing); the

Carleton University

To:

From:

Date: ______________________________

reorganization of departments and ministerial portfolios, including the creation of new departments; the sequential treatment of goals; the budgetary process itself; the use, over a longer period of time, of successive exhortative, expenditure, and regulatory instruments of governing; and finally a myriad of detailed bargaining and consultative mechanisms at the micro level in particular sectors of the economy. To these could be added the basic "appreciative system" of economic managers including their apparent consensus about the desirability of a mixed economy and a liberal democratic state, and their faith (recently shaken) in such things as the Keynesian rules of the economic-policy game.

It is in the context of these several mechanisms, and in relation to our previous analysis of the central processes of economic management, that the major and more formal channels of conflict and consensus examined in this chapter should be viewed. The chapter will offer a concluding focus on the co-ordination of departmental objectives; the use of reorganization as a device for co-ordination, the mechanisms of group consensus, including those efforts reflected in the National Productivity Council, the Economic Council of Canada, the Prices and Incomes Commission, the Food Prices Review Board, the Labour Relations Council, and the Anti-Inflation Board; and last, but certainly not least, federal-provincial co-ordination mechanisms, including the major tax agreements. It is in the context of the evolution of these formal institutions, and practices that the 1976 discussions of "tripartism" will be placed in Chapter 14.

CO-ORDINATION AS THE RESOLUTION OF CONFLICTS AMONG DEPARTMENTAL OBJECTIVES

It should be stated at the outset that in this chapter the resolution of departmental value conflicts refers primarily to issues affecting economic management. Of course, these are not the only problems which confront the Government of Canada. It is clear, however, that economic values are central to how the role of the state is viewed.[1]

In order to effectively appraise the dynamics of economic management we must identify some of the conflicting value elements underlying economic-policy objectives. We have stressed continuously that the objectives of economic policy have broadened in the postwar years and accordingly have necessitated the utilization of a wider range of instruments. In addition, the number of departments and agencies which must be mobilized, and the divergent policies which must be co-ordinated, present a special type of managerial challenge for cabinet decision-making and for the delegation and co-ordination of economic portfolios. Some governmental reorganizations merely reflect either window-dressing or mere administrative tinkering. Many others, however, are preceded by value changes which not only necessitate the creation of new departments or the consolidation of older ones but also require changes in the hierarchical structure of departmental missions and of policy-making in general.[2]

While problems of interdepartmental co-ordination can be partially corrected by mergers into a smaller number of large ministeries, this still leaves intact the difficulties associated with the problem of who should organize the co-ordination. Should the Department of Finance, for example, perform its role by merely reconciling the *ad hoc* initiatives of the spending departments or should it perform a more active role in long-term expenditure planning?[3] Whatever changes are made in this area would also require shifts in the location and implementation of government investment strategies especially in the capital-formation areas.

The establishment of the Treasury Board in 1966 as a separate department from Finance represented a change in conceptualization. The Glassco Commission implicitly suggested that the Treasury Board should be concerned with efficiency within the government. Hence the Treasury Board became the Cabinet Committee on the Expenditure Budget and the Cabinet Committee on Management, with the Department of Finance responsible for broad policy on the management of the economy. However, the Department of Finance and the Treasury Board share administrative staff and must co-operate with each other since the expenditures of the various departments must be decided in conjunction with the fiscal framework established by the Department of Finance. Furthermore, while the Treasury Board is the more administratively oriented of the two bodies, the Department of Finance is also involved with program decisions in areas such as transportation and energy which involve significant capital outlays.

At various times the feasibility of establishing an Economic Secretariat in the Privy Council Office has been discussed. Prior to his becoming Deputy Minister of Finance, Robert Bryce had performed an important role in this regard when he was on the staff of the Privy Council Office. A number of submissions to the Lamontagne Committee on Science Policy and to the Senate Committee on National Finance (Growth Employment and Price Stability) discussed the possibility of establishing a Central Economic Secretariat.[4] In some instances this structure was seen as one possible method by which an internal-policy group would utilize the work of the externally located Economic Council. The belief that there can be, and in fact should be, another centre for co-ordinating economic policy other than the Department of Finance is premised in part on the belief that financial management should be separated from broader growth questions.

Changes in departmental missions are usually in response to new problems emanating from a highly volatile domestic and international environment. As explained in earlier chapters, the aims of economic policy have been broadly defined in the postwar years to be: the maintenance of high levels of employment; the achievement of rapid and sustained economic growth; the maintenance of reasonable price stability; the achievement of equilibrium in the balance of payments; and the achievement of balanced regional development. While the objectives have been generally endorsed by most western countries, the precise application has revealed periodic shifts in the strategies adopted since the simultaneous achievement of all of the objectives represent an ideal which is difficult to achieve in practice. As a result of these challenging objectives a machinery for economic planning has been emerging in Canada. Following the expansion of the governmental bureaucracy and the growth of government expenditure, pressure for expenditure controls has led naturally to attempts to rationalize the machinery and to adopt measures for improving productivity in government. The combined efforts of the Treasury Board, the Privy Council Office, and the Department of Finance to improve the fiscal framework, to institute wage and price controls, and to devise better programs at the macro level have resulted in the need for more emphasis on the equally critical level of micro-economic management. Yet the supporters of planning have been emerging in specialized sectors where the value conflicts have been most pronounced.[5]

A comprehensive but equally pragmatic approach to formulating economic policy has supported the creation of a number of economic-policy initiatives.[6] Economic growth, especially during times of recession, depends to a considerable extent on productivity improvements. The maintenance of price stability has gone beyond dependence on market forces to the imposition of wage and price controls or prices and incomes policies. The maintenance of equilibrium in the balance of payments has led to attempts to control the supply of money and to attempts to reform the international monetary and trade systems. The failure to arrest regional disparities has led to the strengthening of the machinery for regional planning. In this regard federal-provincial pressures have impinged heavily on the type of planning which has developed.[7] The Department of Regional Economic Expansion has become a development-planning department at the federal level which in turn has led to stronger planning efforts in the provinces through the General Development Agreements. Supply-management policies in the area of energy, food, and manpower have all been given much greater emphasis in recent years.[8] These separate policy thrusts must somehow be co-ordinated; hence the emergence of varieties of co-ordinating structures. The quantification of these goals has been a major concern of the Economic Council of Canada. However it is important to stress that the goals can be viewed from different value perspectives or focal points.[9]

These issues can be seen quite concretely. The conflict between the goals of economic growth and price stability has been the central issue of continuous concern to Canadian economic-policy makers in the postwar years. In its *First Annual Review*, for example, the Economic Council of Canada observed that the goal of rapid and sustained economic growth, especially in terms of growth in productivity, does not appear to have been a consistent objective of general economic policy in Canada throughout the postwar period. Later the Council asserted that, in retrospect, it was apparent that the failure to contain price and cost increases more effectively in the early postwar period laid the basis for a subsequent accentuation of economic problems during the 1950s.[10] The question of how much relative emphasis should be placed on each goal is an issue of major importance.[11] The problem of reconciling the growth objective with price stability obviously continues to present extraordinary difficulties for Canadian economic advisors. The growth objective assumes that high employment levels can be maintained simultaneously.[12] Price stability is considered to be a major objective of the central bank. The Bank of Canada, like the Department of Finance, is under the political guidance of the Minister of Finance but the day-to-day responsibility for managing monetary policy is the responsibility of the Governor of the Bank of Canada. The Bank of Canada must take appropriate action. However the criticisms levelled against the various governors of the Bank of Canada for their management of the money supply and more specifically for their commitment to price stability clearly demonstrate the value conflicts which must be reconciled by the Minister of Finance acting alone.[13] Thus the existence of high levels of unemployment between 1975 and 1976 led to demands for more exclusive attention to the employment objective.[14] Such concerns do not only affect the Minister of Finance and his advisors but extend to relationships with other ministers such as the Minister of Labour.

Canada in the postwar years was confronted with a baby boom which, among other results, necessitated the adoption of a more active manpower policy. Yet the country has also maintained a policy of a high inflow of immigrants to meet short-term needs. These relationships subsequently encouraged the merger of manpower and immigration policies. This action was taken as part of a more encompassing labour-market policy. The relationship between the growth and employment objectives therefore permeated into immigration and labour-training and mobility policies but, important as these issues were, they still excluded other important policy areas such as energy and food policy.[15] Yet the establishment of the Department of Manpower and Immigration led to strong demands for the elevation of manpower and labour-market policies in the hierarchy of governmental policy instruments. Pursant to the hearings of the Senate Committee on Growth Employment and Price Stability, the Governor of the Bank of Canada considered the discussions so important that he cautioned the Minister of Finance and the public in general against the possibility of placing too much overt reliance on supply-management policies at the expense of the more traditional monetary and fiscal policies.[16]

These policy conflicts also present problems for specific economic sectors. Manpower policies are part of a conflict-co-operation relationship between employers and employees in deciding on the appropriate profit and wage levels which should be established. In this context, the responsibilities fall on the Minister of Labour and his responsibilities for industrial relations policies, and the Minister of Industry, Trade and Commerce and his concern with industrial and international trade policies. As we will see later in this chapter it was such considerations in the early 1960s which led to the establishment of a National Productivity Council which reported to both the ministers of Trade and Commerce and of Labour. However, the trade unions criticized the productivity objectives of the Council. In their view commitment to productivity did not place enough emphasis on wages and on broader labour-relations objectives.

In addition to the domestic price conditions there are problems with exchange rates and the demand and supply of national currencies. The Department of Finance and the Bank of Canada are involved in reconciling interest rates, prices, and productivity issues. In 1976 the Minister of Finance saw such reconciliations as a major part of his policy.[17] In addition, given the criticism of expenditure growth, the Minister of Finance together with the President of the Treasury Board have been intricately involved with the formulation of long-term expenditure controls. However, expenditure control at the macro level must be broken down into smaller and more manageable parts by viewing the problems of holding costs down and keeping productivity up. In this context the government decisions to improve productivity throughout its various institutional sectors must be carefully scrutinized along with productivity problems in the private sector in which the departments of Labour, Industry, Trade and Commerce, and Consumer and Corporate Affairs all have major interests. Consequently, the general problem of price stability in the economy goes beyond an examination and aggregation of productivity in each industrial sector and requires the formulation of some definite strategy or a set of strategies for productivity improvements. These concerns were expressed by the Hon. Donald MacDonald in his 1976 budget speech but the achievement of these objectives is certainly a problem for interdepartmental co-operation and for government-industry relations.

The creation of the Department of Consumer and Corporate Affairs was predicated on the maintenance of a competitive domestic market as an indispensable component of an efficient economy. Yet the post-war economic environment has also witnessed the advantages which flow from *economies of scale* (for example, through multinational corporations) which lends itself to technological development and the associated product differentiation. Yet there is no consensus on the relationship which should exist between the larger, concentrated industries in contrast to smaller firms which more ideally fit the model of a competitive market system.[18] The ministers of Industry, Trade and Commerce and Agriculture may be in favour of more extensive use of tariffs and subsidization policies than the Minister of Consumer and Corporate Affairs who will favour measures to encourage a highly competitive market economy, which is considered to be the *sine qua non* of a efficient economy. This was well reflected in the conflict between the ministers of Agriculture and Consumer and Corporate Affairs (and the Food Prices Review Board) over the role of marketing boards and related "supply management policies", that is, policies directed at satisfying the interest of suppliers but which may be detrimental to the interests of consumers. The issues are politically aggravated by the fact that consumers are highly urbanized while agricultural suppliers are more rurally based. This means that the demands of the cities and the demands of the rural areas are placed in conflict at least in the short run.

The protection of the income of farmers is an important responsibility of both the Minister of Finance and the Minister of Agriculture. In an attempt to formulate policies to protect rural life there existed for a few years a Department of Forestry and Rural Development. These policies were continued by the Department of Regional Economic Expansion which co-ordinated policies with the departments of Agriculture and Finance. Tariffs can be used to isolate Canadian farmers from competition from abroad. Marketing boards have been used to maintain the price of wheat, eggs, and hogs.[19] The mechanization of farms and the decline in farm labourers mean also that there are high capital costs associated with farming which makes discussion of these issues even more complex. All these discussions reveal that economic policy encompasses significant group conflicts which manifest themselves in interdepartmental relationships. The foregoing demonstrates that economic policies affect the various groups in society differently and extraordinary efforts must be made to co-ordinate them. Economic management therefore deals with the resolution of these conflicts.

As demonstrated above, the values inherent in the political system are operationally reflected in both the beliefs and normative patterns of behaviour which attempt to insure compliance in the wide ranging set of societal organizations. Understanding these belief systems is central to a more meaningful explanation of economic institutions. The debate over the efficacy of economic planning and the role of the state in economic life is directly concerned with the reconciliation of these value conflicts, most, if not all, of which are institutionalized in the cabinet system through the designation of portfolios. Reconciliation is also attempted through cabinet committees such as those on Economic and Social Policy. In 1976, a committee of ten Deputy Ministers (the so-called DM 10) was established in yet another attempt to reconcile special conflicts emerging from different departmental mandates. Furthermore, since governmental policies and programs usually develop in an *ad hoc* fashion, appropriate measures must be taken at chosen intervals to accommodate new policy initiatives and to resolve special conflicts. This arises in part from the need to relate short-term and long-term policy decisions.[20]

Another contentious issue relates to the types of supports given by government to ailing industries. At the time of writing the various tariff and incentive programs under the supervision of the Minister of Industry, Trade and Commerce were under review. Incentive programs were on the verge of being integrated, simplified, and decentralized.[21] However, if the private sector frequently criticizes government-expenditure programs then business as a whole cannot demand unreasonable forms of support from the public sector. The ministers of Finance, Industry, Trade and Commerce, Labour, and Health and Welfare would be intricately involved in the resolution of conflicts between tax incentives, industrial incentives, "prices and incomes policies", and "social-security" and "income-maintenance" policies which must be considered within the framework of the broad macro-economic stabilization policies. A new social security policy was postponed in 1975 because the Minister of Finance took the position that the economy could not afford the program at the time. Here conflicts are related to the use of the primary and secondary levers of economic policy. The Minister of Health and Welfare has indicated that because it is extremely difficult to achieve full employment, some form of income security is indispensable to the modern Canadian economy.[22]

We have chosen a selected number of ministers and their respective departments to demonstrate how economic-policy goals are allocated and what relative weights are placed on the appropriate delegation of responsibilities and the requisite need for co-ordination. These economic-policy goals, although frequently discussed by economists as technical problems, have important philosophical implications which guide "agency philosophies".[23] If a given philosophical position takes precendence then the bureaucratic structure will reflect this in a reorganization of some type. Thus the public debate on prices and incomes policies, which took place between 1966 and 1975 and which resulted in the ultimate adoption of wage and price controls, provides one example of a progressive change in governmental philosophy as reflected in the departmental and organizational reforms. These could be said to have commenced even earlier with the National Productivity Council in 1961 and culminated in the establishment of the Anti-Inflation Board in 1975.

Interdepartmental conflicts merely reflected the micro elements in this form of conflict resolution. Broader considerations of the role of monetary and fiscal policies, industrial relations policies, international trade policies, and the formulation of industrial policies ultimately reach the cabinet level where they are considered as problems of societal management. At this level, interdepartmental conflicts and business-government relations turn significantly on the role of the state in economic life. The intricacy of these numerous points of interaction show why the search for social indicators has been somewhat futile since their effective development demands more intricate analysis of a multiplicity of organizational goals and performances in the economy in general. Our brief discussion of a selected number of interdepartmental conflicts point to both the difficulties underlying economic policies and the need for the development of effective mechanisms of economic-policy co-ordination.

The Prime Minister's speech in 1975 which introduced the Anti-Inflation Program has clearly generated a heated debate on the role of the state in economic life in Canada. This debate will influence the form of economic planning which will emerge in the 1980s. That the adoption of the policy was preceded by intense political and economic controversy is clear. The resignation of John Turner, the Minister of Finance, prior to the adoption of these measures, and the public debate which followed reflected the movement of policy from the level of micro-analysis and discussion into much broader public debate. When these issues cannot be accommodated within the existing organizational structure, reorganization usually follows. From this perspective, conflicts in the bureaucracy reflect conflicts in Canadian society. The budget speeches of the Minister of Finance provide a reasonable measure of the economic management dimensions of the value conflicts which we have been discussing. It is difficult to imagine the preparation of a budget which did not disappoint a selected number of the cabinet ministers and, correspondingly, important departments and their constituencies. In relative terms, therefore, the government's expenditure budget reflects the internal conflicts within the governmental system while the economic budget reflects the broader conflicts within the economy and society and the strategies which the government considers to be an appropriate response.[24] Even without the formal publication of a plan the government's budget represents a form of planning by identifying and highlighting issues of choice and change.

CO-ORDINATION THROUGH REORGANIZATION

Our previous analysis clearly shows that, in addition to the resolution of conflict among goals by central co-ordinating bodies and by the sequential and serial treatment of goals, the federal government has increasingly used reorganization as a device for co-ordination. This has applied both to economic- and non-economic-policy fields. The degree to which reorganization has been increasingly used must be appreciated in a historical context in that, until the last decade, the major reorganization of departments and especially the creation of new portfolios was a fairly infrequent event, perhaps occurring every ten years or so.

Since the mid-1960s, however, reorganizations and the establishment of new departments have been utilized at a far greater rate both to achieve governmental co-ordination and to signal, more visibly, governmental priorities and concern about a particular problem. This process has been aided, as we pointed out in our discussion of the bases of Cabinet portfolio influence in Chapter 3, by the use of Ministers of State. Thus Ministers of State for Urban Affairs, Science and Technology, Fisheries, and Small Business have been established since 1971.

While reorganization can frequently be only window-dressing, it is important to see most of these changes as genuine problems of management, as well as in the context of the practical problems of governing and the sequential use of the instruments of governing referred to in Chapter 2. Thus in response to external criticism, or indeed to internal policy reviews, governments always face a minimum choice between doing nothing or doing something. The use of major reorganization enables governments to express, at a minimum, that they are concerned about the problems. This will not, of course, be their only motivation but it enables the presentation of a minimum position which might then, in good time, be followed by new mechanisms of consultation, new expenditure programs, and perhaps new regulations as a new consensus evolves or as support and resources (and hence other governing instruments) become politically available. In earlier decades the federal government tended to use royal commissions and then task forces to serve a similar governing function. They have increasingly added highly visible reorganization to the governing tool-kit.

Within the public services these reorganizations also have more day-to-day meaning but even internally the central agencies of government (which are invariably the enforcers of the reorganization plan, though not necessarily the source of the idea) have in mind the hopefully therapeutic effect which putting old policy wine in new organizational bottles will have. Thus through reorganization, it is hoped, not only that a political signalling of new concern will occur, but also that public servants will see and relate to their department's constituencies in new ways and with more sensitivity and responsiveness.

It is in this total context that the reorganization of economic-management portfolios should be reviewed. The reorganizations thus not only reflect new economic knowledge and criticism of past policies, and even past organizational locations, but also are part of the sequential use of governing instruments and hence of the processes through which consensus and legitimate support and compliance are sought. They therefore reflect an important form of political and organizational learning. There are of course limitations to the use of reorganization, some of which have been evident in previous chapters. We will comment more fully on these limitations in our conclusions in Chapter 13.

The reorganization of the government machinery to improve the administration of consumer policy was preceded by studies which demonstrated that the existing institutional mechanisms were outdated and should be restructured to provide a more coherent view of what constituted competition policy.[25] Thus the Economic Council recommended a more comprehensive approach which included all commercial activities including services. The Council, as we have seen in Chapter 11, had surveyed the then existing distribution of activities affecting consumers and recommended a more efficient method of co-ordinating consumer policies.[26] The Registrar General department which preceded the Department of Consumer and Corporate Affairs was formed by integrating sections from the departments of Justice, Trade and Commerce, and Health and Welfare. Similarly the formulation of a comprehensive competition policy went beyond the protection of the consumer by linking the corporate sector with consumer affairs.

Although regional development was always a major goal of the Canadian Government it was not clear what constituted a region.[27] Moreover since the concept of region is essentially a spatial approach to policy-making and involved therefore several departmental programs which cut across departmental lines, major reorganization was a prerequisite for improved regional planning.

The establishment of the Department of Regional Economic Expansion followed years of studies by the Atlantic Provinces Economic Council (APEC) and the Economic Council of Canada as well as much political criticism. Both "planning" bodies recommended improved co-ordination of policies in the regional field. Initially, the Department of Regional Economic Expansion incorporated the Department of Forestry and Rural Development, the FRED, ARDA, and MMRA programs of the Department of Agriculture, the Area Development Program (ADA) from the Department of Industry, the Atlantic Development Board, the Atlantic Development Council, and the Canadian Council on Rural Development. This extensive reorganization was intended to develop "a concerted approach" to arresting regional economic disparities which was designated as a major objective of the Trudeau government. A more sophisticated approach would have included regional stabilization and investment policies. In fact, this has been emerging with the strengthening of the Federal Business Development Bank. By 1976 DREE had developed a series of general development agreements with all provinces with the exception of Prince Edward

Island for which a plan had already existed. The development of a regional data base and the various attempts to improve planning at the provincial and regional levels reflects a much stronger regional orientation in the formulation of economic policy.

The establishment of the Department of Manpower and Immigration, as we have seen in Chapter 10, similarly followed extensive political criticism and reviews which showed the need for a more comprehensive manpower and labour-market policy and resulted in the integration of new functions with activities previously carried out in the departments of Labour and Citizenship and Immigration.

The recent amalgamation of the Unemployment Insurance Commission with the department represents the latest move to formulate a comprehensive employment policy. The department can now facilitate the demands of its various clients in a number of ways, in attaining jobs and, failing to do so, it can provide mobility grants, and training or unemployment benefits. The latest moves provide a mechanism for preventing the abuse of the unemployment insurance scheme which was very severely criticized prior to the adoption of the new approach.

One could go on and review all the changes analysed in chapters 6 to 11 as well as the process or reorganization in related fields of energy, transportation, and occupational health, but the point is clear. Reorganization has become a regular and increasingly used instrument of governing and co-ordination in the economic-management field. Reorganization of departments, moreover, requires, as we have seen, reorganization within the central agencies of government since their ability to co-ordinate these activities would be threatened without changes in their structure.

FORMAL MECHANISMS OF PUBLIC SECTOR-PRIVATE SECTOR CO-ORDINATION AND CONSENSUS

A number of formal mechanisms of public sector-private sector consensus have been attempted since 1960. These are, of course, in addition to the varying ways through which public-private relations are accommodated through political parties and electoral politics, as well as by career linkages and the relatively common value assumptions about the general desirability of the mixed economy held by Canada's most influential political leaders. In this section we will focus on the more formal attempts reflected in the establishment and functioning of the National Productivity Council (1961), the Economic Council of Canada (1963), the Prices and Incomes Commission (1968), the Food Prices Review Board (1972), the Canada Labour Relations Council (1975), and the Anti-Inflation Board (1975). Each institutional mechanism represents a particular type of conflict resolution. This interpretation provides a more sociological approach to the study of economic institutions.

These broad attempts at improving co-ordination should be seen, however, as being largely a supplement to the more regular day-to-day contact which economic-management departments have with their several industrial, labour, agricultural, and consumer clientele. As the analyses in chapters 8 to 11 in particular have shown, the Canadian processes of economic management have been characterized by a much more exclusive reliance on departmental liaison mechanisms. In contrast to British and French liaison systems with industry the Canadian mechanisms are more strictly departmental. They are part of the ministers' communication channel to industry and do not, at present, constitute a formal planning machinery. It can be said that these liaison committees were generally established to meet the needs of senior business officials who were concerned with the problems of adequate communication with government. While these micro-level mechanisms serve the particular needs of business and as such are problem-oriented they are not supported by any formal legislative structure.

The National Productivity Council (1961-63)

The National Productivity Council was established by the Diefenbaker Conservative government in 1961 to facilitate advancement in productivity as part of a strategy to improve Canada's competitive position in the realm of international trade.[28]

The National Productivity Council, in accordance with its Act, was "... to provide expanding opportunities for increased employment and trade and rising standards of living..." and in a manner consistent with "the awareness of the need for concerted actions and decisions of other entrepreneurs, of trade unions, and of public authorities", sponsored a mission to Europe, which visited Sweden, the

Netherlands, West Germany, France, Belgium, and England.[29] The mission, led by James A. Roberts, Deputy Minister of Trade and Commerce, consisted of representatives from labour, management, government, and educational institutions. The objective was to observe the operation of similar consultative bodies in Europe. The mission was impressed by the degree of consultation and co-operation which had developed in Europe and recommended further reform in those areas in Canada.[30] The Productivity Council was a mixed body which included government members; in fact, it had membership from, and reported to, both the Department of Labour and the Department of Trade and Commerce and, accordingly, was integrated into the federal bureaucracy. However, it was not primarily a research body but rather placed major emphasis on labour-management relations and on popularization as a means of improving productivity. It is important to note, however, that the Productivity Council was partially responsible for the establishment of a number of provincial planning and consultative bodies.[31] The Economic Council as we shall observe later continued some aspects of the Productivity Council's work. The National Productivity Council was a source of conflict within the bureaucracy as well as between labour and business.

The trade union members felt that the terms of reference of the Council were too narrow emphasizing, in their view, only the productivity concerns of management. The conflicts between the Department of Labour and the Department of Trade and Commerce were evident in that the former was more concerned with wages and industrial relations while the latter was more concerned with productivity and trade issues.[32]

The establishment of the National Productivity Council did however create a forum for discussion of productivity encompassing representation from business, government, labour, and education. The Council was in the process of expanding its representation when it was absorbed by the Economic Council. The Advisory Committee on Economic Studies of the National Productivity Council provided a link to the later established Economic Council.

The National Productivity Council was intricately involved with micro- or industry-oriented research. As such it was an operationally oriented agency. The Council had a very close research link with the then Department of Mines and Technical Surveys. In a sense the

Productivity Council was moving in the direction from more micro-oriented studies to macro-oriented studies with the establishment of the Advisory Committee on Economic Studies which had begun to look at broader issues such as science and economic policies. As such the National Productivity Council had initiated work in the broad field of industrial innovation.

The achievements of the National Productivity Council were modest but it did secure direct representation from major groups in the economy and government. The Council also established committees on labour-management co-operation, Work Study and Management Techniques, Training and Retraining, Economic, Industrial and Productivity Studies and Surveys, Dissemination of Information, and Matching Grants. In addition to these, plans were also made to establish an Advisory Committee on Economic Studies. The total staff of the Council numbered seventeen, which included National and Regional Officers. Finally, in the realm of applied research, the Council, with the co-operation of the Department of Mines and Technical Surveys, the Defence Research Board, the Department of Trade and Commerce, and the Department of National Defence, embarked upon a research program. Studies were carried out on the pulp and paper industry in 1961 and on the electronics, minerals and iron, and steel industries in 1962.

It is worth noting, in addition, that the Council's special Advisory Committee on Economic Studies, headed by Dr. John Deutsch, suggested a number of areas for further research which were part of the early agenda of the Economic Council subsequently headed by Deutsch. These areas included: productivity and its measurement; rationalization of industry and combines legislation; industrial research and product specialization; automation; employment; wages and price policies; management and labour training; trade and tariff policies; corporate tax levels and the taxation system; production and investment incentives; and measures to assist industry and labour with transitional problems. All of the above were considered by the Committee to be of high priority and to have a direct bearing on levels of productivity.[33]

The Committee also recommended that the Council undertake the program of proposed studies under the direction of an Advisory Committee to be established by the Council and composed of senior economists, representatives of labour, management, government, and education, and to have a leading economist as chairman. It also recommended that the Council appoint a senior economist to its staff as Director of Economic Studies. It should be noted that Dr. Deutsch was an active participant in all of the above stages. The Committee stated that the existing terms of reference of the Council were sufficiently broad to allow the Council to conduct or sponsor any economic studies related to productivity.

The Economic Council of Canada

The Economic Council of Canada was established in 1963 as a new tripartite institution intended to associate government with labour and business.[34] It is important to stress however that government was not represented on the Council. This change was most important since it has prevented an active or more direct planning role by the government. Since the debates which preceded the establishment of the Council had focussed on varieties of economic planning in different countries both the Council's senior members as well as its critics have frequently discussed its role from the perspective of a planning agency.

Many of the Council's activities can be considered to be part of a planning process.[35] The Council consists of twenty-eight members, twenty-five of whom represent different sectors of the economy and society. More specifically, the following sectors are represented on the Council: industry, labour, finance and commerce, agriculture, other primary industries, and the general public. This structure was thus intended to be representative of interests which would be affected by the policies recommended. The research component was intended to introduce an element of objectivity to offset the conflicts which the adversary system of economic-policy making would otherwise introduce. The membership therefore represented a wide range of interests from the private sectors of the economy and from different regions of the country. The members sit on the Council as individuals and not as representatives of their respective organizations from which they were appointed. This has been a difficult problem to reconcile because the trade union members have always objected to certain policy recommendations made by the Council.[36] It was felt by the creators of the Council that with objective research and analysis a broader consensus could be reached which would transcend the particularistic approach of the various sectors in the economy.

The important dimension of the Council's establishment with which we are primarily concerned here is the fact that the agency was expected to form a consensus on major issues of economic policy. It was to bring the private sector in closer harmony with the government. This was most clearly reflected in the speech by Hon. Maurice Lamontagne at the first meeting of the Economic Council when he noted:

> We have, in the government service, competent economists and well organized economic research branches, but under the pressure of the day-to-day requirements of looking after the needs of the Canadian people, there is a little time left to contemplate the future in a comprehensive way. . . . In the midst of this rapidly changing technological, commercial and political environment that we will have to provide more balanced, more stable and faster growth in order to reduce unemployment to its minimum level. It would be unrealistic to think that, under such conditions, the private sector of our economy can, in isolation, achieve the objective of full employment. Radical changes taking place in the world, and the adjustment they make necessary in our country, require not only a new association between the public and private sectors of our economy but also bolder and more dynamic government leadership. In other words, we need to plan together to make sure that the private sector can work in the same direction as the government, and that the various segments of economic policy will be well co-ordinated.[37]

The Council became a centre of controversy from its inception. First, there were the provisions in the Council's Act which suggested that it should make recommendations concerning the economy's potential. Initially, there were differences concerning the level of full employment and price stability which were feasible.[38] There were difficulties not only with the national targets but with the regional variations. The trade union members were more concerned with full employment and wage levels. The business sector was concerned with growth questions. In retrospect it appears (as we have seen in Chapter 2) that all the targets were set on the more ambitious end of the scale. It appeared also that education and manpower policies provided the greatest areas of consensus on the Council.[39]

In this regard the Council's work was heavily used by the provincial governments since it focussed on issues such as education and manpower policies which fell under provincial jurisdiction. As such the Council was also inevitably involved with federal-provincial relations. Dr. Deutsch, the Council's first Chairman, seemed to have taken the position that the Economic Council could perform a consensus-forming role in three respects. First, there were conflicts between agencies at the federal level. Since departments such as Labour, Trade and Commerce, and Agriculture, for example, have different mandates, the Council would provide more aggregative research findings and judgments which would transcend the more particularistic departmental approaches. Second, given the fact that Canada is a federal state, the Council would conduct macro-economic research which would facilitate national economic-policy making. Consequently the Council has always presented broad recommendations which would encourage compromise between the levels of government. Third, the Council was concerned primarily with long-term issues. This meant that its research findings were not primarily aimed at existing policies but at presenting broad new approaches for the future which if agreed to would, it was hoped, reduce future conflicts. Forecasting, therefore, would provide a means for improved harmonization. Dr. Deutsch saw the Council as a means for carrying on the work of earlier Royal Commissions such as the Rowell-Sirois and Gordon commissions.[40]

The actual approach to consensus-formation has been rather negative in that the Council has experienced difficulties in achieving consensus on controversial issues such as the reform of combines legislation. As indicated earlier its success has been greatest on education and manpower policies. It has been least successful on stabilization policies and with prices and incomes policies.[41]

The Council's Act also provides for the federal government to direct reference studies to the agencies. It has received three references: prices, productivity, and employment; consumer competition policies; and instability in the construction industry.

The Council experienced its greatest difficulty with the first reference on prices, productivity, and employment. This has been a difficult area for contemporary economics. There is no consensus on how to cope with high inflationary levels and high rates of unemployment simultaneously. The Council's representative composition has made it difficult to establish a consensus on issues such as wage and price controls.[42] Many of the Council's recommendations have focussed on the necessity to conduct further research before embarking on specific policies. In 1966, for example, the Council opposed the introduction of a prices and incomes policy.[43] In 1968 the federal government rejected that position and established a Prices and Incomes Commission.[44] Consequently between 1966 and 1969 the Council persistently cautioned the government about its anti-inflationary policies. In contrast, the Bank of Canada and the Department of Finance were in favour of an active anti-inflationary policy.[45] If the Bank of Canada is considered to be committed to price stability then it can be said that the Economic Council has always been committed to growth and full employment. The timing of appropriate policies to deal with the complexities of stagflation has proven to be especially difficult for both the Council and internal policy-makers.

The Economic Council has always taken the position that the various objectives of economic policy should be achieved simultaneously. However, internal policy-makers have always pointed to the difficulty of avoiding taking action on particular fronts since the government must respond to short-term requirements.[46] Between 1963 and 1976 the Council has functioned more as an external advisory body and not as a part of the governmental internal policy-making machinery. As such it has operated mainly as an agency to facilitate and encourage public debate on economic issues.

The Economic Council has definitely demonstrated a deficiency in the consensus formulation process. In order to bring the so-called broader performance goals down to more actionable steps the Council, if it is to have a role in policy-making, would have to establish at least three mechanisms. First, it must maintain some links to selected government departments. Second, it must maintain some kind of links with the various economic sectors from which it derives its members. Third, it must maintain some links with the provinces since they perform important roles in national economic-policy making.[47]

The Council has faced a dilemma with respect to its relationship with outside groups and agencies because if it focusses on broader issues, that is, on mobilizing a consensus on very general policy objectives, it cannot expect to be a major policy-advisory body on specific issues for which departments possess more expertise. This ambiguity has led to controversial positions as to whether or not the Council is primarily an economic research body as opposed to a consensus-forming body. In practice it has attempted both roles by publishing studies and by organizing conferences, the latter representing a more sporadic type of activity.

In its early years the Council participated in a number of national conferences which were intended to be types of liaison committees. These conferences included a labour management conference in 1964; a labour and industrial relations conference in 1967; a conference on stabilization policies in 1965; and a conference on international trade and agriculture in 1966. These conferences provided important information for the Council and also familiarized the various organizations with the work of the Council.

Following the development of the CANDIDE model the Council formulated a series of performance indicators which were expected to be more operationally useful than the broader performance goals which were adopted in 1964. The Council launched a series of National Economic Conferences in 1973 for which a number of industrial committees were created. It subsequently established a National Conference Secretariat which organized a second conference.[48] However, at the time of writing the series of National Conferences had been abandoned. It is worth mentioning that the Economic Council's Act prohibits the Council from indulging in continuing administrative responsibilities. Yet in most western countries arrangements have been made to incorporate industrial inputs into the planning and policy-making processes.[49] It would appear that selected government departments, given their links to particular clientele groups, must perform this type of planning role by bridging the macro and micro elements in economic-policy formulation. Consequently, the Council's planning role may be strengthened by improving liaison with various government departments and by establishing links with the groups which must implement the policies recommended. To this end, the advisory councils to the ministers of Industry, Trade and Commerce, Labour, Manpower and Immigration, Energy, Mines and Resources, Consumer and Corporate Affairs, and Regional Economic Expansion, among others, should be strengthened into a more meaningful system of economic planning.[50]

In short, the experience with the Council shows that governmental departments and agencies must perform a role in the planning and mobilization processes. Similarly, the various departments must perform a role in improving federal-provincial relationships.[51] The Economic Council has made significant recommendations for improving the consensus formulation process but our analysis suggests that several agencies are required to improve the machinery of economic planning. In fact, the establishment of the Canada Labour Relations Council has provided another example of the more active involvement of a particular department (Labour) which had fallen in stature between the mid-1960s and the mid-1970s. Thus the Minister of Labour, the Hon. John Munro, has been attempting to improve the department's image. These efforts are necessary since it is very unlikely that an effective prices and incomes policy can be formulated without the support of organized labour. The Minister of Labour is placed in a precarious position which can only be improved by reducing the adversary relationship between government and labour.[52] The creation of the Labour Relations Council therefore provides a recent example of attempts to improve interdepartmental and intersectoral co-ordination of economic policy.

The Labour Relations Council

In recent years a significant amount of unrest has affected industrial relations in Canada.[53] Industrial relations have been adversely affected by the persistence of rising prices. Organized labour has persistently argued that workers are severely and disproportionately affected by rising prices and by rising levels of taxation, and hence have experienced an erosion of their standard of living. Consequently, organized labour has made heavy demands on management in their endeavour to offset rising prices and to maintain or improve their standard of living.

These problems do not only exist at the macro level of industrial relations but affact various sectors of the labour market. If some sectors are doing well then it means that other groups will demand higher wages which could become inflationary especially if they are not accompanied by productivity improvements. Moreover, where there are a multiplicity of small sectors, the collective-bargaining process becomes unwieldly.[54]

Other factors influencing wage rates include the country's international trade position and the emergence of public-sector collective bargaining. Both the ministers of Finance and Industry, Trade and Commerce for example have frequently alerted Canadians to the gap between Canadian and American wages and productivity. These differences are most important since the United States is Canada's most important trading partner.

Finally, since the introduction of collective bargaining in the public services in the mid-1960s the public sector has become a paysetter, a development which has adversely affected the collective-bargaining process.

The foregoing concerns led the Minister of Labour in 1975 to evaluate alternative machinery[55] and to establish the Canada Labour Relations Council.[56] This is a tripartite body consisting of representatives from organized labour, management, and the federal government. More specifically, it consists of nine representatives of organized labour, nine representatives of management, and seven representatives of government departments in addition to the minister as chairman. The government departments represented are: Labour, Finance, Industry, Trade and Commerce, and Manpower and Immigration. There was also provision for a representative from the Treasury Board. The responsibilities are stated as follows:

> The Council shall consider ways and means to promote industrial peace by exploring methods and developing procedures by which labour and management may better reconcile their differences through constructive collective bargaining, thereby reducing conflict in their own and the public interest. In addition the Council shall review the role of Government in labour relations, examine existing legislation, recommend additional programs and services reducing the frequency and duration of work stoppages in Canada.[57]

The Labour Relations Council is supported by a permanent secretariat located in the Policy Group in the Department of Labour with the capacity to draw resources from within and without the department. Work has already begun on examining the feasibility of establishing a semi-autonomous agency which would provide common statistical data for collective-bargaining purposes. Another committee was examining the feasibility of developing broader based collective-bargaining units which would create a more manageable collective-bargaining process.

The creation of the Labour Relations Council provides another example of the various institutional mechanisms which are being established to try to resolve conflicts and to facilitate the process of economic management which we have outlined in this book. The mere creation of these institutions, however, does not in any way demonstrate that the problems are being solved. For example, shortly after the Labour Relations Council was established, the Canadian Labour Congress, angered by the government's anti-inflationary policies, withdrew its representatives from the Economic Council and the Labour Relations Council. We have looked at these agencies primarily to demonstrate that their functioning provides an index of the prospects for resolving group conflicts which adversely affect the management of the economy.

Late in 1976, the Canadian Labour Congress put forward proposals for the creation of a "Labour Market Board" with extensive powers to develop and administer manpower programs.[58] The Labour Market Board would perform a role in the administration of manpower-training and mobility programs, unemployment insurance, and immigration policy. Here we detect still another attempt to co-ordinate different policy sectors. The government has opposed some of these measures since it felt they would give labour too much direct power.[59]

Perhaps the most contentious issue affecting the making of economic policy is the controversy over market and administered prices. In this regard, the establishment of the Prices and Incomes Commission was most illustrative of the role of consensus institutions in economic management.

The Prices and Incomes Commission

Between 1965 and 1968 the Government of Canada became progressively more concerned with the problem of price stability. It had sought to attain vigorous economic growth and a high rate of employment while at the same time maintaining an appropriate level of price stability. Upon recognizing that demand had placed pressure on the supply capacity of the economy, monetary and fiscal mechanisms were applied to restrain the growth in demand. Consequently between 1966 and 1967 the economy grew below its potential and unemployment rose from 3.5 per cent in 1966 to 4.5 per cent in 1967.[60] As a result of these changes the federal government concluded that the then existing tools were incapable of attaining high levels of employment, price stability, and growth simultaneously.

The Government of Canada had earlier requested that the Economic Council of Canada examine the interrelationships between movements in prices, costs, productivity, and incomes, the problem of reconciling price stability with other economic goals, and the policies and experiences of other countries in this regard.[61]

The Council's report stressed the basic importance of monetary, fiscal, and commercial policies in influencing aggregate demand and maintaining a desirable balance between employment and price stability. It emphasized as well the need for complementary programs designed to increase the supply of goods and services both generally and in regard to particular pressure points. In general, the Council considered the feasibility of adopting an incomes policy for Canada. However, after careful consideration the Council recommended against the adoption of an incomes policy concluding that it would not be an effective way of "bringing about an improved reconciliation of high employment and reasonable price stability in Canada under normal peacetime conditions". In the Council's opinion, "the foundation of price stability in Canada should be the basic monetary, fiscal, commercial, and supply adjustment policies already available or in the course of being developed."[62]

The Government of Canada, however, on the recommendation of the Bank of Canada together with supporting statements from the Organization for Economic Co-operation and Development, established a Prices and Incomes Commission which consisted of "three prominent and highly qualified Canadians" who served full time, directing a professional staff. In establishing the new agency the Government of Canada asserted:

> Price stability policy involves the work of many government departments and agencies. Their activities are co-ordinated by the Cabinet Committee on Economic Policy and Programs. The Government now proposes the creation of two new bodies to focus continuing attention on the problem of rising prices:
>
> (a) A new independent public body, to be known as the Price and Incomes Commission; and
>
> (b) A new joint Senate-Commons committee to be known as the Standing Parliamentary Committee on Price Stability, Incomes and Employment.[63]

It is important to note that the federal government felt that consideration of cost and price developments should not take place only in crisis situations such as in a period of rapidly rising prices or during major collective-bargaining negotiations. It was necessary to carry out continuous analysis of price behaviour and to develop an approach to price and income problems outside of the traditional framework of government decision-making. It is important to note also that the then proposed new agency was essentially another research body to perform a more specialized economic intelligence role.[64] The Prices and Incomes Commission was charged with responsibility for conducting studies of price and income developments in Canada. It was required "to discover the facts, analyse the causes, processes, and consequences of inflation, and to inform both the public and the Government on how price stability may be achieved".[65]

The Commission had no regulatory powers in that the approach was of a "voluntary nature". As the Government stated: "It will not play the role of policeman. It will not intervene in the particular price and income decisions of individual persons, business firms, or trade unions."[66] From the perspective of this chapter, the most important provision apart from its more specialized research role was that the Commission was expected to "maintain close communication and consultation with economic groups for the purpose of obtaining information and ideas on prices and incomes, provide information and education for the public, and make policy recommendations for the achievement of greater price stability."[67]

While the Commission was empowered to make recommendations as to government policy its main function was "to rally a sense of public responsibility leading to voluntary restraint". The consensus mobilization role of the Commission was emphasized in the White Paper on Stable Prices:

> To achieve this it will be necessary for the Commission to win the continuing acceptance and co-operation of major interest groups—management in industry and commerce, trade unions, agriculture, and other organizations. It can win this support only by maintaining close consultation with such groups on a regular basis.[68]

Pursuant to the establishment of the Commission and after conducting a number of studies the government, under the aegis of the Commission, met with the leaders of various economic interest groups as part of a consultative process. Simultaneously, the various provincial governments were approached.

The various efforts between 1968 and 1972 to gain the co-operation of the functional economic groups and the provinces proved unsuccessful. Some critics argued that inflation could not be controlled by the Government of Canada acting alone in that the major pressures had come from outside. Others cited the fact that major initiatives should be taken by the provincial governments. The trade unions were not very co-operative since they felt that the program was directed at wages rather than profits. The business sector expressed the view that the government's expenditure policies were primarily responsible for inflation. Even the Economic Council of Canada was very critical of some of the government's initiatives.

However, the Prices and Incomes Commission, in its final report published in 1972, concluded:

> . . . It has seemed to us that our two main tasks were, first to explain why in recent years inflation has persisted under conditions ordinarily thought to indicate an absence of strong demand pressure on the economy and second, to consider what form of prices and incomes policy—if any—might be helpful in attempting to deal with the problem.[69]

The Commission then outlined what it considered to be the causes of inflation.[70]

The Commission's major recommendation consisted of an outline of the conditions under which "a full-fledged control system as the only form of intervention [would] likely be effective enough to be worth attempting in the near future". It suggested instead a temporary control program, but at the same time rejected the thesis of market power as the chief cause of inflation:

> The Commission's view that a temporary program of direct controls over prices, wages, and other incomes could be helpful in certain circumstances does not arise from a belief that the root of the inflation-unemployment dilemma lies in the ability of powerful unions and corporations to continue to push up costs and prices regardless of demand conditions. We do see serious difficulties, however, in trying to extricate the economy from a major inflationary outbreak originally generated by an overshoot of demand but persisting stubbornly because of widely held inflationary expectations and response lags.[71]

The strongest initiatives in support of the adoption of prices and incomes policies therefore came from the Prices and Incomes Commission. Apart from outlining what it considered to be the causes of inflation the Prices and Incomes Commission had, before its abolition, recommended stronger regulatory measures. Consequently, between 1972 and 1975, while prices continued to rise, two further initiatives followed the efforts of the Prices and Incomes Commission. These initiatives were the Food Prices Review Board, established under the Inquiries Act as a response to the uncertainties surrounding rapid food-price increases, and the Anti-Inflation Board.

These developments further illustrate a progressive utilization by the Government of Canada of stronger regulatory institutions to deal with rising prices, productivity, and employment. The Food Prices Review Board (FPRB) operated in a more specific sector of the economy and for this reason was more effective when compared to the Prices and Incomes Commission. Yet, as we will observe below, it encountered strong opposition from the Department of Agriculture within the government and from the agricultural lobby outside the government. The Anti-Inflation Board (AIB), as it extended its regulatory powers between 1975 and 1976, encountered increased opposition from the Canadian Labour Congress and from selected business sectors.

THE FOOD PRICES REVIEW BOARD AND THE ANTI-INFLATION BOARD

The Food Prices Review Board was established on May 25, 1973, by order in Council under Part I of the Inquiries Act as a response to rapid food-price increases. Initially, the Board was given a very restricted research-oriented mandate to provide "detailed and timely information and analyses with regards to price movements amongst food products". In more specific terms the Board was required:

> . . . to monitor price movements of a comprehensive series of food products and to issue reports thereon, at three-month intervals, and to inquire into the causes of particular food price increases in any class of food products, and to issue reports thereon, with all dispatch, including recommendations where the Board considers it appropriate to do so.[72]

The Board, under its initial mandate, was criticized for being somewhat "toothless" and on August 31, 1973, its duties were extended by the provision of powers "to go beyond its strict research orientation". As a result, the Board was empowered "to inquire into any increase in the price of any food item where such increase may be unwarranted, and, where the Board deems necessary, to publish a report thereon without delay".[73] The Board performed an important role in awakening public interest in food issues accompanying the escalation of prices. The upward movement of food prices beginning in 1973 created an atmosphere of public suspicion and hostility about the food system.

The Board's research has had a substantial impact in two areas in particular. First, food-policy formulation at both levels of government in Canada has long been virtually the exclusive preserve of the agriculture authorities. With the urgency surrounding food issues in 1973, many government departments turned to the Board's research as the only available independent material on current food issues which could assist them to understand, deal with, and sometimes contradict their agricultural colleagues. Second, the Board's research provided a forum for improved appraisal of the facts surrounding important policy areas such as marketing boards, egg prices, and sugar prices.[74] The Board was able to provide timely and relevant documents on the basis of which the media could base their reporting and analysis of the facts. Between 1973 and 1975 the Board was considered to have benefited from "a partnership between an independent fact-finding Board and an independent media".

The Board performed four additional functions encompassing investigation, complaints, price monitoring, and policy advocacy. First, the Board, commencing with a national survey of food prices and supermarket practices, conducted continuous investigations of food prices and pricing practices. This broad survey led to more specific analysis of food prices in specialized sectors of what it later described as the food system. As a result, governmental officials performed a type of policing role to insure compliance with major consumer-protection laws. Second, the existence of the Board provided an institutional mechanism through which consumer complaints about food prices could be presented. As a result, the Board later decided that in addition to its "ombudsman" role the complaints service should perform an educational role.[75]

Third, the Board performed a "price-monitoring" role through its weekly, national price survey. Although it relied initially on Statistics

Canada, the Board subsequently initiated a weekly national survey of food prices based on an 82-item core basket.

Fourth, the Board performed an independent advocacy role with respect to food-policy issues. Consequently, in many of its press releases and official statements, the Board took firm positions on all food-related issues. Here the specificity of the agency's mandate was most crucial. The willingness of its chairman, Beryl Plumptre, and members of the Board and its staff to speak out regularly on major issues also enhanced its effectiveness. In the opinion of the Board "the combative, advocacy function reflected the Board's policy of going beyond simply explaining food-industry problems to the active promotion of their solution."[76] Examples of this kind of activity included the Board's positions on the federal fluid milk subsidy, shoddy meat inspection services, short-sightedness on land use at the site of the proposed Pickering Airport, and labour demands in the British Columbia food industry.

The activities of the Food Prices Review Board provide a recent example of the operation of conflict-consensus resolution in economic-policy making. The definition of the problem was most important.[77] Thus the creation of a highly specialized agency focussed attention on a specific policy issue, namely food policy. Moreover, the specific orientation of the Board led to a re-evaluation of agricultural policy. Because of the widespread failure to distinguish between food and agriculture and because agriculture cuts across party lines, Canada's governmental system had encountered very significant problems in dealing effectively with food-related issues. The Board took the position that many of the policies adopted on food were "foolish and contradictory".[78] More specifically, the Board asserted:

> . . . many of the foolish and contradictory food policies now in existence reflect the marked reluctance on the part of politicians of all stripes to speak out against vested agricultural interests. During 1973-75 when a healthy political system would surely have encouraged widespread debate on food issues, Canadian politicians, with only a few exceptions, avoided these issues as much as possible and when unavoidable they discussed superficialities.[79]

The Board cited the proceedings of the special parliamentary committee, established in autumn 1974, to determine the "truth" concerning competing allegations between the Minister of Agriculture and the chairman of the Food Prices Review Board concerning the egg-marketing controversy to have been most illustrative of the inability of Canada's political groupings to critically discuss agriculture. We can deduce from the Board's research, analysis, and advocacy that "objectivity" in economic reporting is suspect inasmuch as policy is highly influenced by the organizational definition of the problem.[80] By way of illustration, the Board emphasized that two ill-defined phrases have dominated the polemics surrounding food-price developments of recent years—"fair returns" and "rip-off":

> Both terms reflect the normative equity considerations which were introduced to the debate on food prices in the period 1973-75. Though undefined, both were used to justify increased state intervention in the food system. Indeed it is truly ironic that the only widespread "rip-offs" discovered by the Food Prices Review Board were actions supported by governments in the name of "fair returns". Nonetheless, both terms were of importance in dealing with food price inflation because of the widespread public attitudes they reflected.[81]

The Board concluded that the farm-income issue should be more clearly distinguished from the food-price issue as focal points for policy-making. The Board recommended the formulation of a national food policy which would reflect intragovernmental and intergovernmental co-ordination.

> To this end, the Board is of the view that a ministry of state for food with authority to co-ordinate policies and operations in all areas affecting food would be an effective means of organizing internally within government, provided that the responsible minister were one of the three or four most powerful ministers in the government, with clear seniority over ministers responsible for agriculture, fisheries, trade, commerce and so on.[82]

This recommendation provides one method of resolving conflicts but it equally introduces new conflicts within the Cabinet. Yet the conflicts surrounding agriculture and food-policy sectors represent only a miniature of the most challenging issue affecting economic-policy making. This issue relates to the extent to which the price system efficiently and effectively allocates resources in the society in general. As discussed earlier, the Cabinet had grappled with this question long before it directed its reference on prices, productivity, and employment to the Economic Council. The extent to which economic planning can effectively cope with questions of distribution especially under no-growth conditions looms heavily in our analysis of conflict-resolution at this point.[83] It was failure to deal with this very question which led to the establishment of the Anti-Inflation Board.

The Anti-Inflation Board was established under Bill C-73 which stated that "there is hereby established a board to be known as the Anti-Inflation Board consisting of a chairman and such other members as are from time to time appointed by the Governor-in-Council". The duties of the Anti-Inflation Board are as follows:

12. (1) The Anti-Inflation Board shall (a) monitor changes in prices, profits, compensation and dividends in relation to the guidelines and the effectiveness and workability of the guidelines both in general and in their application to particular classes of businesses and groups of employees and from time to time report to the Governor-in-Council thereon recommending any modifications to the guidelines that, in its opinion, would improve the effectiveness or workability of the guidelines;
(b) identify actual and proposed changes in prices, profits, compensation and dividends that, in its opinion, contravene or, if implemented, would contravene the guidelines either in fact or in spirit;
(c) identify the causes of actual and proposed changes in prices, profits, compensation and dividends identified under paragraph (b) that are, in its opinion, likely to have a significant impact on the economy of Canada, and endeavour through consultations and negotiations with the parties involved to modify such changes so as to bring them within the limits and spirit of the guidelines or reduce or eliminate their inflationary effect;
(d) where in its opinion, consultations and negotiations under paragraph (c) have failed or are likely to fail to modify an actual or proposed change in prices, profits, compensation or dividends to bring it within the limits of the guidelines and it is not satisfied that there are circumstances that, based on the particular facts of the situation, justify the actual or proposed change in prices, profits, compensation or dividends, refer the matter to the Administrator for consideration by him; and
(e) through publication of reports, public hearings and meetings and such other methods as it considers appropriate, promote public understanding of the inflationary process, the relationships between productivity costs and prices, the various policies available to governments to deal with inflation and the advantages, effects and limitations thereof, the role to be played by businesses

and group of employees in combating inflation and the implications of the failure of governments, businesses and groups of employees to cooperate in combating inflation.[84]

The Act makes provision for the tabling of reports in Parliament and for the appointment of an administrator with powers of enforcement. Through this Act, therefore, an Anti-Inflation Appeal Tribunal was provided "with all such powers, rights and privileges as are vested in a superior court of record". Sections 3 and 5 of the Act make provision for "the Minister, with the approval of the Governor-in-Council", to enter into "an agreement with the government of a province for the application of this Act" and "for co-operation between Canada and the province with respect to the administration and enforcement of the guidelines within that province".[85] In short, the Anti-Inflation Program made provision for the establishment of an Anti-Inflation Board under the Inquiries Act, for the appointment of an administrator for the enforcement of the Anti-Inflation Act, and for an appelate body known as the Anti-Inflation Appeal Tribunal.

From the perspective of this chapter, Bill C-73 presented the most inclusive approach "for the restraint of profit margins, prices, dividends, and compensation in Canada" since the Second World War. The program was launched by the Prime Minister's speech on October 13, 1975, and sparked intense controversy between business, labour, and government and between the levels of government. The Canadian Labour Congress was the most antagonistic group to the program which it unsuccessfully challenged in the Supreme Court of Canada, and against which it organized a national day of protest or unofficial national strike.

The Minister of Finance had earlier announced stronger regulatory measures in his budget speech of May 25, 1976, in which he asserted that "within this improved framework of rules, the Anti-Inflation Board will place greater emphasis on price justification. More firms will be required to notify the Board of proposed price increases and to justify them."[86] As a result, stronger measures were adopted in July and October 1976. As the Government of Canada utilized stronger regulatory powers, the trade union and business leaders became more vociferously opposed to the measures. Notwithstanding the aggressive stands presented in public, the three sectors were actively involved in private discussions aimed at creating a series of new institutional mechanisms to combat the crisis presented by rising prices, falling productivity, and declining levels of employment.

FEDERAL-PROVINCIAL CONSENSUS AND CONFLICT

It is clearly difficult to achieve a consensus on economic policies in a federal state given the fact that "the constitution" provides for the division of responsibilities between two levels of government which are considered to be equal partners notwithstanding geographical, cultural, and economic interdependencies. Even in unitary states governmental expenditures in vital areas such as health, education, and welfare present extraordinary conflicts and controversies.[87] In addition, times and circumstances change thus creating a need for the reallocation of responsibilities between different levels of government. Accordingly analysts of federal systems have discussed these issues from the perspectives of "co-operative federalism" and, more recently, "executive federalism".[88]

The most significant problems in contemporary economic-policy making in federal systems relate to problems in taxing and spending.[89] If each level of government should raise the revenue comparable to its spending responsibilities then the structure of fiscal policy-making should reflect this ideal. This, however, would require that economic conditions determine the structure of the federal system.

Budget policies are primarily concerned with issues of taxing and spending which become more complex in a federal system because of the shared responsibilities which we have just mentioned. Consequently, a most important dimension of the politics and management of Canadian economic policies concerns the political and administrative arrangements which are developed to reconcile federal-provincial conflicts. In practice, all federal systems have established research and other policy-making structures for harmonizing economic-policy making. Since the issues which lead to the creation of these bodies are very complex we will restrict our analysis to selected questions which are most pertinent to our appraisal of conflict and consensus. These issues were perhaps first crystallized in the Canadian context in the work of the Royal Commission on Dominion-Provincial Relations (the Rowell-Sirois Commission), but they obviously extend into the controversies and proposals for reform which have been made in the 1960s and the 1970s. The Government of Ontario has been the major advocate of new economic policy-making machinery to facilitate improved federal-provincial harmonization and its relations with the federal government will be discussed as an illustrative case. However, it should be clear from the analysis in Chapters 7 and 11 that a significant portion of federal-provincial relationships occur at the agency-to-agency level between departments of both levels of governments. Notwithstanding those relationships we will be concerned here primarily with macro-level policies impinging on departments of Finance and provincial treasuries.[90]

Most discussions of Canadian federal-provincial economic-policy co-ordination go back to the inter- and postwar years, and are reflected in the Report of the Royal Commission on Dominion-Provincial Relations presented to the Prime Minister of Canada on May 3, 1940, the centralization of economic policy-making in the Department of Finance because of the needs of wartime financing, and finally, the publication of the White Paper on Employment and Income and the discussions which followed.[91]

Although the Report of the Royal Commission on Dominion-Provincial Relations had emphasized provincial autonomy, the actual approach to formulating economic policy in Canada evolved quite differently. The Commission had considered the safeguard of each province's control of the revenues necessary to meet its social and cultural development as a major condition for a healthy federal system. Thus it asserted: "Provincial autonomy to safeguard regional particularisms is more pressing in relation to health, education, and welfare services than to the regulatory activities of government."[92] Social policies loomed heavily in the discussions and federal responsibilities, from the Commission's viewpoint, should be limited to providing research, statistical and staff services, activities ancillary to other federal responsibilities, leadership to establish uniform standards, and leadership in co-ordinating provincial activities to avoid overlapping and deficiencies in health services.

Because the Commission argued that genuine provincial independence required the necessary revenues to carry out those functions for which the provincial level of government had responsibility, it was natural to conclude that priority should be given to provincial formulation of policies in the areas of health, education, and welfare. It was the view of the Commissioners also that the major strategy for the integration of the national economy existed in the provision given to the federal government for exclusive access to the major field of direct taxation with the corresponding responsibility of affecting some redistribution of financial resources among the provinces, rather than in the form of federal involvement in the areas of provincial jurisdiction. The Government of Canada therefore had priority in regard to the raising of revenue notwithstanding the spending responsibilities under provincial jurisdiction. For reasons which cannot be discussed in this chapter the major proposals of the Rowell-Sirois Commission were shelved and dominion-provincial relationships evolved quite differently.

The Dominion-Provincial Conference on Reconstruction, in May 1946, represented the second attempt to evolve a comprehensive strategy for federal-provincial economic relations. However, the philosophy espoused at that conference was the opposite of "the provincial autonomy proposals" put forward by the Rowell-Sirois Report.[93]

The Green Book proposals presented by the federal government emphasized shared-cost programs and rejected the principle of equalization. As such, the strategy of the more wealthy provinces, Ontario, Alberta, and British Columbia, first led to a system of bilateral agreements with the provinces. As a result of this development tax-sharing agreements and various shared-cost programs negotiated through structural arrangements such as the Continuing Committee on Federal-Provincial Fiscal and Economic Relations and other *ad hoc* committees have become the chief means of federal-provincial economic-policy co-ordination since the mid-1940s.[94] As Donald Smiley notes, "the formulation of economic policy has been more a matter of what the provincial cabinets and bureaucracies do rather than through the provision" of the Canadian constitution.[95] More specifically, the three principal methods of executive adjustments have been through *ad hoc* and standing committees of federal and provincial cabinet ministers and officials; the delegation of federal powers to provincial executive agencies; and the use of the federal spending power on objects usually regarded as provincial and/or local responsibilities.[96]

Because of the bilateral and multilateral systems of negotiation which developed, analysts of federal-provincial relations were frequently forced to enumerate the number of committees, meetings, and institutions to demonstrate the complexities of the harmonization process.[97].

By the mid-1960s federal-provincial economic-policy co-ordination was described as a system of co-operative relationships rather than one reflecting provincial autonomy. The federal government, through the use of devices such as shared-cost programs, and grants and loans to institutions under provincial jurisdiction, had expanded its role in the formulation of economic policy.

In reality, however, the overall management of the Canadian economy was significantly influenced by the type of economic policies pursued by all three levels of government — federal, provincial, and municipal. This is illustrated in Appendix A which shows that, in 1955, provincial and municipal governments spent about $2.7 billion while the federal government spent approximately $4.6 billion. By 1975 federal expenditures of $34.1 billion were significantly exceeded by the $40.1 billion spent by the provinces and by local governments. Hence stabilization policies had to involve all three levels of government.[98] Moreover, the emergence of the Economic Council of Canada in 1963 was accompanied by attempts to designate and quantify national economic objectives.

Edgar Gallant, commenting on the then existing structures of federal-provincial relations observed in the mid-1960s:

> In our federal-provincial relations our machinery has evolved in a reverse order. We have first developed numerous committees and conferences at a specialist level. We have not had a comparable network of intelligence concerned with the total picture of intergovernmental relations. While Canada has over 400 professionals engaged in international relations, we still have very few engaged full-time in a professional way in federal-provincial relations, and our machinery makes relatively little provision to ensure continuous liaison with respect to the overview of matters which concern both the federal and provincial governments.[99]

The Report of Intergovernmental Liaison on Fiscal and Economic Matters published in 1969 identified a number of deficiencies in the machinery of economic-policy formulation. Consequently, although it acknowledged the value of the plenary federal-provincial conference, it recommended the creation of another institution, a committee of ministers of Finance and provincial treasurers on grounds that federal and provincial departments of Finance or provincial treasurers exercised certain broadly based responsibilities which placed them apart from other ministries. The Report was particularly concerned with the inadequacy of the machinery for fiscal and economic matters:

> This committee would be concerned particularly with such matters as fiscal and monetary problems, the projection over the long-term of government revenues and expenditures, the development of long-term budgeting for both capital and current expenditure, technical methods for the control of expenditure and the more effective collection of public revenue, public borrowing, harmonizing of budgetary accounting and financial statistical practices and all matters related to the fiscal and economic problems of governments.[100]

The above-mentioned machinery which would replace the then existing Tax Structure Committee was to be supported by functional standing committees of ministers covering such areas as agriculture and rural development, labour, manpower and training, health, welfare, and natural resources.

By the mid-1970s, in addition to interdepartmental arrangements, the federal government, through its Federal-Provincial Relations Office in the Privy Council, and a number of provincial governments such as Quebec, Alberta, and Ontario had established centralized "offices" or secretariats for intergovernmental relations.[101] These offices attempt to view policy across departmental lines. However, a national research agency was still absent from the system.

A number of proposals have been made in recent years to create a new national machinery of economic advice which would transcend either federal or provincial interests. It has been argued frequently that the Economic Council of Canada as a legal creation of the federal Parliament cannot objectively represent provincial viewpoints. While several provinces possess comparable advisory bodies for economic policy they have been considered to be generally ineffective. Accordingly, the Report on Intergovernmental Liaison on Fiscal and Economic Matters noted that:

> One possible answer to the need for wider involvement in long-term economic

research commends itself to us as being worthy of greater consideration than it appears to have had. At a conference of provincial premiers in Victoria in 1962, a proposal was made by the Premier of Manitoba, Mr. Roblin, that an economic advisory council should be established representative of both levels of government. Presumably, such a council would not be directly representative of the individual provinces and Canada but would be selected from a slate of candidates put forward by the various governments. This would form a quasi-independent advisory group for all governments in much the same way as the Economic Council does for Canada. Such a council would tend to be regionally oriented rather than representative of various interests in the economy but it would serve the same basic purpose.[102]

The foregoing discussion has dealt mainly with structural changes but the various recommendations were the result of recognition of a number of deficiencies in the economic-policy-making process. The various structural changes have occurred because the provinces have always either individually or collectively objected to the dominant position taken by Ottawa in the formulation of economic policies. In the early 1960s Quebec nationalism asserted itself and a number of specific demands were made on the federal government.[103] Ontario has vehemently opposed federal policies particularly in the late 1960s and early 1970s.[104] By the mid-1970s the western provinces had emphasized even more their particular needs and their prospective views of developmental policies.[105]

The federal government has taken the position that it should perform a national redistributive role as, for example, in the payment of equalization grants and through attempts to arrest regional disparities. On such issues the federal government is usually supported by the smaller have-not provinces. More recently, the issues have become more complex since a small province like Saskatchewan has become an oil-producing province like Alberta.[106] Energy policy has provided a focal point for discussions between the provinces in recent years. Broadly speaking, industrial policies or more generally viewpoints on patterns of economic development have loomed large in federal-provincial negotiations. Ontario has evolved an economic analytical and intelligence capability equal to the federal government and has particularly urged the need for new machinery for economic-policy co-ordination.

Harmonizing Federal-Provincial Revenue and Expenditure Policies

As explained above, significant efforts have been made over the years to harmonize federal-provincial financial relations. The federal government now uses four basic methods to transfer fiscal resources to the provinces, territories, and municipalities: the reduction of federal tax in order to provide tax room for the provinces; tax abatements; unconditional grants; and conditional grants. The provinces levy their own personal income taxes, expressed as a percentage of the federal tax but this is collected by the federal government in all provinces except Quebec.

The history of Canadian federal-provincial fiscal arrangements is complex and cannot be adequately dealt with here.[107] Since the mid-1950s there have been a number of Tax-Sharing Arrangements under which agreements were made for the 1957-62, 1962-67, 1967-72, and 1972-77 periods. At the time of writing, discussions were in progress for the 1977-83 agreement. Under the Tax-Sharing Arrangements Act 1957-62, federal payments to the provinces included: a rental payment covering the personal income-tax, corporation-income-tax, and inheritance-tax fields, and calculated on the basis of the yield of specified "standard taxes" in these fields; an equalization payment, to bring a province's per-capita yield from the three standard taxes up to the weight-average per-capita yield of such taxes in the two provinces with the highest per-capita yields; and a stabilization payment to bring a province's yield from the equalization payment and standard taxes up to a minimum that was the greatest of (a) the previous financial arrangements extended into current years; (b) the last payment under the previous arrangements adjusted for population changes; or (c) 95 per cent of the average payments for the two previous years under the 1957-62 arrangements.[108]

Under the Federal-Provincial Fiscal Arrangements Act and its application for the years 1962-66, the federal government undertook to withdraw from the corporation income-tax field by 9 per cent of corporate income and from the personal income-tax field by 16 per cent in 1962 and by an additional 1 per cent in subsequent years up to 20 per cent in 1966. After further adjustments the total withdrawal amounted to 24 per cent for the 1966 tax year. Further provisions were made for the payment of 50 per cent of the federal estate-tax collections in a province to those provinces that did not impose their own succession duties. In 1964, the federal government enacted legislation, the Crown Corporations (Provincial Taxes and Fees) Act, which required approximately thirty federal Crown corporations to make payments (commencing on April 1, 1964) in respect of provincial sales taxes, gasoline taxes, and motor-vehicle licences as if they were taxable. This action placed federal corporations on an equal basis with provincial corporations.[109]

The Federal-Provincial Arrangements Act 1967 made provision for a number of significant changes in the structure of federal payments to the provinces. Essentially, the federal government increased its abatement of the personal income tax — excluding the abatements under the Established Programmes (Interim Arrangements) Act — from 24 per cent to 28 per cent of the federal-tax payable in the provinces. An extra four percentage points of personal income tax and one percentage point of corporate income tax were granted to the provinces in 1967 specifically for expenditures for post-secondary education and, in part, were a substitute for the per-capita grants for university costs. It also replaced federal operating-cost contributions to the provinces under the Technical and Vocational Training Agreements which were phased out during 1967-68.[110] A somewhat complicated form of equalization payment was introduced in the 1967-72 formula. While the 1962-67 equalization formula had been based on "three standard taxes", personal income tax, a corporation-profits tax of nine per cent, and a succession duty equivalent of fifty per cent federal duties in the province, the 1967-72 formula made provision for sixteen provincial revenue sources.[111]

After three major federal-provincial conferences held prior to 1972 the eleven governments worked out revisions to the tax-collection agreements, post-secondary education assistance, and equalization and stabilization programs. Consequently, the 1972 Federal-Provincial Fiscal Arrangements Act, and its subsequent amendment in 1973, extended the 1967 equalization system for five years ending in 1977.[112] Thus, the equalization formula adopted in 1967 which had included sixteen provincial revenue sources was increased to nineteen, incorporating the additional revenue from health insurance premiums, race track taxes, and the provincial share of income tax on power utilities. The 1973 amendment added municipal taxes imposed for local school purposes. In 1975 the Act was modified to redefine oil and natural gas revenues into basic and additional revenues.

The various tax agreements discussed above made provision for the provinces to opt out of the arrangements. For example, Quebec opted out of the 1964 youth allowance program since it had already initiated a program under the Established Program (Interim Arrangements) Act. The programs which the provinces could opt out of were divided into two categories: abatement of income tax which were offered in lieu of federal payments; and group cash compensation made available to the provinces carrying on similar programs.

The Municipal Grants Act provides for three basic types of grants: annual grants in lieu of real property taxes; transitional grants where taxable property is acquired by the federal government and withdrawn from the tax roll; and grants in lieu of special assessments for local improvements. Payments with certain exceptions are related to federal properties and federally owned and occupied buildings situated on taxable leased lands.[113]

The foregoing is illustrative of the complexities surrounding federal-provincial financial relations. At the time of writing, the major issues affecting federal-provincial arrangements were related to the anti-inflation programs and, early in 1977, to the new fiscal agreements and the consequences of the election of the separatist government in Quebec. Attempts were also being made to develop more long-term expenditure policies.

Thus in presenting their 1975 budget speeches, most provincial treasurers had anticipated a reduction and then a resurgence in economic growth for 1975.[114] While most provinces adopted policies designed to stimulate economic growth, they were generally more concerned with inflation and the unilateral actions of the federal government. On the revenue side, taxes were raised in all provinces except New Brunswick and Alberta. On the expenditure side, all provinces held themselves to a rate of growth in spending well below that experienced in recent years. Seven provinces had signed agreements with the federal government to co-operate in the national anti-inflation program prior to presenting their budgets.[115]

The intergovernmental, as well as public-private sector, relationships and consequences of inflation are usefully portrayed in Chart 12:1.[116] The chart is reproduced from the Economic Council's *Thirteenth Annual Review* and summarizes the inflation-induced gains and losses to households, business, and government in the 1969-75 period. In general it shows that middle-income groups gained at the expense of the poor and the aged, that provincial and local governments benefited from enlarged shares of transfer payments, and that, in the business sector, financial institutions gained from the manufacturing sector. Other patterns of gains and losses are also summarized thus demonstrating again the myriad pressures which such consequences will have on governments and on different regions and economic classes.[117]

As usual, the provinces were all concerned with the general state of federal-provincial relations. These concerns were intensified by the federal initiatives limiting spending in hospital- and medical-care insurance plans, changes in the Department of Regional Economic Expansion, and with the recalculation of the payments under the guarantee of income tax revenue which were all expected to have serious implications for provincial finances, especially in the Maritime provinces. In many respects the economic crisis had brought about some consistency in the policies being followed by both the federal government and the provinces. Where differences existed they were first voiced at the meeting of Finance ministers in July 1976.

In December 1976, agreement was reached on the main points for new fiscal arrangements which would apply generally for the next five years until 1982.[118] Thus, under equalization the measurement of fiscal capacity would be based on twenty-nine revenue sources and bases (as opposed to nineteen earlier). Fifty per cent of source revenues would be equalized but a 33⅓ per cent limit was placed as a cap on resource revenue as a proportion of total revenue to be equalized. The standard of equalization would be the national average.

With respect to the financing of established programs, agreement was reached to replace the then existing system with one in which federal contributions would be no longer tied to provincial expenditures. These arrangements would apply to post-secondary education, medicare, and hospital insurance, with federal contributions coming roughly half in the form of tax room and half in per-capita cash payments. The tax room would be 13.5 personal-income-tax points plus 1 corporate-income-tax point. This would include the 4.357 personal- and 1 corporate-income-tax points the provinces already had for post-secondary education. The cash portion would be based on federal contributions in 1975-76 and escalated by a three-year moving

CHART 12:1

Summary of Inflation-Induced Gains and Losses to Households, Business, and Government, 1969-75

Inflation losses by	*Inflation gains by*		
	Households	*Business*	*Governments*
Households	Debtors gained from creditors. The proportion of multi-earner families in the labour force grew, and their income increased more than single-earner families. As a result, middle-age families did better than young or old families, even though young families, more heavily in debt, were helped by inflation on both their liabilities and income. Home owners did better than renters.	Households holding short- and long-term corporate bonds, stocks, and securities lost; firms issuing liabilities gained. Pensioners lost on the eroded value of their pensions,corporate borrowers from pensions plans gained. Households with cash balances and demand deposits lost to banks.	Households lost through personal income taxes that were not fully indexed; federal and provincial governments gained. Households lost on their holdings of Canada Savings Bonds and other federal, provincial, and local debt. All levels of government gained.
Business	Corporate holders of long-term household debts, such as real estate mortgages, lost; mortgagors gained.	Financial sector gained from the manufacturing and nonmanufacturing sectors through its short-term liabilities and holdings of client demand deposits. Financial sector lost to other business sectors on its holdings of their long-term securities.	Business lost in corporate taxes because of the required use of historical cost accounting for capital cost allowances. Business also lost in corporate taxes because of the required method of accounting for inventory valuation. In both cases, the federal and provincial governments gained.

		Corporate borrowers gained from corporate contributors to private pension funds in amounts roughly equal to their unfunded pension liabilities.	Banks lost on their holdings of federal notes and reserves; the federal government gained.
Governments	Property owners gained and local governments lost because of lags in property assessment.	Corporate borrowers gained from tax allowances on their debt interest payments; federal and provincial governments lost.	Federal government lost to the provinces borrowing from the Canada Pension Plan.
	Indexation of personal income taxes and transfers represented a gain to households and a loss to the federal and provincial governments.	Corporate property holders gained and local governments lost through lags in property assessment.	Provincial governments benefited from enlarged shares of federal-provincial transfers directly attributable to extra inflation-induced revenues.
	Households gained in real terms through enriched or new expenditures or extra tax relief introduced as a direct result of the extra inflation-induced federal and provincial revenues.	Corporations gained in the same way as households, from extra government expenditures and subsidies resulting directly from the higher inflation-induced tax revenues.	Local governments benefited from similarly enlarged provincial transfers and federal expenditures.

average of nominal gross national expenditure per capita.

The attempt to limit the rate of growth of joint programs and the establishment of the incomes policy administered by the Anti-Inflation Board in the mid-1970s brought the nature of federal-provincial conflict out of its more exclusive concern in the 1960s with expenditure politics and into the realm of regulatory politics as well. As we have seen in earlier chapters this was also reflected in related concerns about the regulation of transportation, foreign investment, energy, and communications including the power of federal regulatory tribunals in these fields.[119]

Toward a New System for Co-ordination

At the federal-provincial conference of ministers of Finance and provincial treasurers in 1968, the Hon. Charles S. MacNaughton, Treasurer and Minister of Economics of the Province of Ontario, outlined a position which has been followed by that province and several others. Essentially Ontario took the position that the federal government and the provinces should approach "our financial problems in a spirit of partnership.... we must look at the structure and problems of government finance at all levels taken together."[120]

The Ontario government took the position that the federal government had time and time again introduced programs such as medicare which could ultimately place the provinces in a financial straightjacket. In addition, municipal expenditures were expanding and this placed extraordinary burdens on the provinces. In 1971, the Hon. Darcy McKeough, Treasurer of Ontario and Minister of Economics, stated even more categorically that:

> The government of Ontario believes that Canada is faced with a breakdown in the structure of economic and fiscal policy. This condition is seriously impending the ability of federal and provincial governments to deal with the economic and social problems confronting the nation. Support for this contention is provided by the current underperformance of the economy, the high level of unemployment, the lack of noticeable progress in reducing inter-regional disparities, and the absence of a national strategy to meet challenges on the international front. We believe that this breakdown can be attributed directly to a deterioration in intergovernmental fiscal and financial arrangements. It is these arrangements which determine the distribution of fiscal resources

among governments and provide the framework within which those resources are brought to bear on our problems.[121]

The government of Ontario which had drawn heavily on the work of the Economic Council of Canada asserted in 1971 that this Conference of Finance ministers should do nothing less than "lay the foundations for a fundamental reconstruction of national objectives and economic policy systems in Canada." Ontario's position which, from its perspective, represented a consensus among provincial governments was that "we do not have a co-ordinating mechanism for fiscal policy. It has also become apparent that the major initiatives and innovations are emanating from the provincial side."[122] What was even more significant in Ontario's view was the fact that the federal policy initiatives in monetary and fiscal matters in the late 1960s and early 1970s had shifted from positions of "constraint to belated expansion" and as a result were futile efforts at stabilization.

The failure of the federal stabilization initiatives led the government of Ontario to assume a major role in reinforcing the provincial economy. For example, in 1971, the province introduced a corporate income tax change in the form of a five per cent tax credit to stimulate new investment in machinery and equipment. Such measures increased the provincial deficit.[123] During the period under discussion the Ontario government also took independent initiatives on seasonal unemployment programs, an Ontario DISC program, and a full-employment budgeting system, among other changes. In the area of more long-term economic-policy formulation the province called for more comprehensive policies in the following areas: income redistribution and regional subsidization; foreign investment policies; the development of an industrial strategy; the recognition of larger industrial requirements in the development of federal competition policy; and a comprehensive look at general and specific areas of tax reform. The Ontario government completed its critique of the federal government system in 1971 by outlining an economic strategy for Ontario.

Premier Davis of Ontario demonstrated his concern for the deficiency in the then existing machinery of economic policy-making by proposing that:

The first ministers should form a national joint economic committee composed of the ministers of finance as their representatives. We envision that our terms of reference should require us to set short- and long-term economic and social goals. In addition to the use of our own research staff, we should draw on the resources of outside agencies, such as the Economic Council of Canada, to help us formulate and evaluate our objectives and progress.[124]

The introduction of the national Anti-Inflation Program in 1975 was considered as a possible means by which new national institutions would be created to harmonize economic relations between the various groups as well as between the different levels of government. While most provinces supported the program in principle they are collectively opposed to the sudden shifts in federal initiatives.

In July 1976 Ontario's Provincial Treasurer, Darcy McKeough, outlined five principles on which the provinces were in agreement on federal-provincial financial policies. The five principles further illustrate Ontario's view that there was a need for an improved system of economic harmonization.

First, the provinces thought Ottawa should share equally with the provinces the responsibility for controlling costs.

Second, the provinces did not believe that the federal contributions should be tied to the growth in the gross national product which would steadily cut the federal contributions because most of the costs involved programs — medicare, hospital insurance, post-secondary education—which were all growing, even under controls, faster than the GNP. As a result, the provinces would be more pressed for funds while the federal government had more revenue to conduct new spending.

Third, the provinces believe that any financial "benefit-of-the-doubt" should rest with them. The federal government had far greater initial taxing powers and far greater powers to change the ground rules than the provinces, so any question about the relative financial benefits should be resolved on their side.

Fourth, "the provinces believe that all matters before us should be treated as a package not as separable issues." In their view, Ottawa made medicare costly by forcing a universal program on the provinces and it subsequently failed to control the inflationary pressures which made medicare even more costly.

Fifth, the provinces insisted that "our new fiscal arrangements be made simple to both administer and understand." Because Ottawa had invaded the provincial jurisdictions the public was confused in not knowing which government taxes whom and provides which service. Thus at the time of writing, major discussions were in progress and new initiatives were being proposed to harmonize federal-provincial relationships. These issues were being discussed while efforts were being made to create new and more effective economic institutions to resolve conflicts.[125]

While the above points undoubtedly reflect a general consensus of criticism about federal-provincial relations by the provinces, it is only a consensus on principles. The translation of these into practice reflects much more severe political differences reflected in, and caused by, the existence of regional disparities, the incumbency of different governing political parties, the different basis of the several regional economies of Canada, and the varying regional strengths and electoral hopes of federal political parties.

The analysis in this chapter of efforts to secure interdepartmental, public-private, and federal-provincial consensus and co-ordination demonstrates the frequent existence of co-ordinated activity. It also shows however the elusiveness and episodic nature of the processes necessitated by the never-ending adjustments required by the concurrent pursuit of frequently conflicting economic objectives by different sectors and economic classes and groups. The chapter has focussed on the process of co-ordination achieved through the sequential treatment of interdepartmental goal conflict, on the explicit use of reorganization as a governing instrument and device for co-ordination, on the several formal institutional attempts since 1960 at public-private co-ordination, and on the evolution of federal-provincial tax agreements and related devices of intergovernmental consensus and conflict management. These macro processes reflect and represent some of the major micro-level mechanisms previously analysed and visualized in our department-by-department portrait in the previous five chapters. They again reflect in their own way the meeting of demand and supply issues, the role of economic and policy research, and the constant intermingling of politics, economics, and public administration.

NOTES

1. Pursuant to the work of Adam Smith both Marx and Weber were major thinkers who tried to explain the role of the state in economic life. They also explained the relationships between the economy and society. The extent to which different groups in society have been influenced by these values is an important factor which influences attitudes toward accumulation and legitimation. For further treatment of these issues see N. Birnbaum, "Conflicting Interpretations of the Rise of Capitalism: Marx and Weber", *The British Journal of Sociology*, Vol. VI (June 1953) and M. Hill, *The State Administration and the Individual* (Glasgow, 1976). For recent analyses focussing on Canada see D. Roussopoulos, ed., *The Political Economy of the State* (Montreal, 1973), especially pp. 18-58 and B. A. Frischke, *Inflation: It's Your Bag* (Toronto, 1976), especially pp. 96-149. The classic Canadian Socialist position is found in M. Bliss, ed., "League for Social Reconstruction for Canada", in *Planning for Canada* (Toronto, 1975). For a more up-to-date presentation of corporatism in liberal democracies see Leo Panitch, "The Development of Corporatism in Liberal Democracies". Paper presented to the Annual Meeting of the American Political Science Association in Chicago, September 2, 1976.

2. See D. Keeling, *Management in Government* (London, 1972). In the Canadian context see G. Bruce Doern and V. S. Wilson, eds., *Issues in Canadian Public Policy* (Toronto, 1974), Chapter 12.

3. Here our reference is in the realm of long-term capital expenditure planning; the use of Crown corporations in economic management and the appropriate mix between fiscal monetary and debt-management policies are most important. There is a wide-ranging set of policy mixes between the public and private sectors which necessitates more intricate analysis than that which is provided here.

4. In most instances economists have been concerned with the stabilization strategies of the Department of Finance and not with its economic-development role. For more inclusive appraisal of the role of government see *The National Finances: An Analysis of Revenue and Expenditures of the Government of Canada, 1975-76* (Toronto, 1976).

5. The following publications provide useful guidelines: Hon. J. N. Turner, Budget Speech, June 23, 1975; Hon. D. Macdonald, Budget Speech, May 25, 1976; Treasury Board, *How Your Tax Dollar is Spent* (Ottawa, 1977); Government

of Canada, *The Way Ahead: A Framework for Discussion* (Ottawa, 1976).

6. The creation of the Department of Consumer and Corporate Affairs was most significant. However, the experience of this department with the Competition Act demonstrates the power conflicts which planners encounter. See, for example, Hon. A. Abbott, Notes for Remarks to the Canadian Marketing Conference Board in Canada, Montreal, February 16, 1977. In this speech the minister reviewed the history of the Competition Act.

7. See Chapter 9. It is worth emphasizing, however, that provincial inputs have, since 1973, played an important role in economic planning. This has involved the creation of various types of central planning secretariats in the provinces and at the federal level.

8. This emphasis emerged in the 1973 budget but became more significant in the two 1974 budgets and has since continued to be dominant. We anticipate that it will continue to be so during the 1980s.

9. L. H. Officer and L. B. Smith, eds., *Issues in Canadian Economics* (Toronto, 1974), Chapter 1. See, in general, Part One, Stabilization Policy. Here again if the Department of Finance is considered to be concerned with economic management then it automatically assumes this role. The establishment of an Economic Management Board can institutionalize this dimension by providing a collective mechanism for making long-term and medium-term economic-management decisions. An agency similar to the Economic Council could provide "external" inputs into the Board.

10. Economic Council of Canada, *First Annual Review* (Ottawa, 1964).

11. See Chapter 3. However, for broader treatment, see R. W. Phidd, "The Economic Council and Economic Policy Formulation in Canada". Unpublished PhD thesis, Queen's University, Kingston, 1972. See especially chapters 6 and 9.

12. With the establishment of the Economic Council in 1963 the growth objective was considered to be the central component of its mandate. The Council also set an extraordinarily ambitious employment target. See Economic Council of Canada, *First Annual Review*. Regional variations in unemployment subsequently became an important issue.

13. It should be noted that the responsibility for the preparation of the government's budget gives the Minister of Finance extraordinary respon-

sibilities for managing the economy. These responsibilities have led to severe criticism of his management of the economy. Similar criticisms have been made against the Governor of the Bank of Canada. See Chapter 7. It should be noted, however, that most of these criticisms have been directed at stabilization policies. Very little emphasis has been given to the economic development strategy. On the relationship between development planning and stabilization or anti-cyclical planning see A. Waterston, *Development Planning: Lessons of Experience* (Baltimore, 1965).

14. E. Broadbent, Leader of the New Democratic Party, was the most outspoken advocate of this policy. The Minister of Manpower and Immigration subsequently responded to Broadbent's position. See Hon. B. Cullen, Ministry of Manpower and Immigration, Notes for an Address to the Kinsmen's Club of Sarnia, February 16, 1977.

15. Hon. J. N. Turner, Budget Speech, February 19, 1973, also Budget Speech, May 6, 1974 and November 18, 1974. With respect to food policy see Food Prices Review Board, *Final Report: Telling It Like It Is* (Ottawa, 1976).

16. Bank of Canada, *Annual Report of the Governor to the Minister of Finance 1972* (Ottawa, 1972), pp. 10-11.

17. Macdonald, Budget Speech, May 25, 1976.

18. See L. A. Skeoch, *et al.*, *Dynamic Change and Accountability in a Canadian Marketing Economy* (Ottawa, 1976), and R. MacLaren, *How to Improve Business-Government Relations in Canada* (Ottawa, 1976).

19. Consumer Research Council, *A Report on Consumer Interest in Marketing Boards* (Ottawa, 1974).

20. See, for example, the conflicts and contradictions reflected in Government of Canada, *The Way Ahead*. For comparative analysis of such issues see A. Shonfield, *Modern Capitalism: The Changing Balance of Public and Private Power* (London, 1965) and Phidd, "Economic Council and Economic Policy Formulation", especially Chapter 1, pp. 24-34.

21. See *The Globe and Mail Report on Business*, February 9, 1977, p. B13.

22. Hon. M. Lalonde, Minister of National Health and Welfare, *Working Paper on Social Security in Canada* (Ottawa, 1973).

23. There are two separate aspects to this problem. First, there is the question of ideological conflict among economists which in turn leads to varied policy recommendations. Second, there is the issue of different agency philosophies; for example, the Economic Council's position compared to the Department of Finance's and the Bank of Canada's in 1968 concerning anti-inflation policies. For further discussions of these issues see the following: A. Okun, *The Political Economy of Prosperity* (Washington, 1970), Chapter 1; L. Silk, *The Economists* (New York, 1976); and P. Self, *Administrative Theories and Politics* (Toronto, 1973).

24. Only recently have the Department of Finance and the Treasury Board been reflecting this planning orientation in their annual publications. See, for example, the Treasury Board, *How Your Tax Dollar is Spent*. See also Macdonald, Budget Speech, May 25, 1976.

25. Hon. A. Abbott, Notes for Remarks to the Canadian Marketing Conference 1977 of the Conference Board in Canada (Montreal, 1977).

26. Economic Council of Canada, *Interim Report on Competition Policy* (Ottawa, 1973).

27. For analytical discussion of regions see T. N. Brewis and G. Paquet, "Regional Development and Planning in Canada: An Exploratory Essay", *Canadian Public Administration*, Vol. XI (1968).

28. For a broader analysis of the role of the National Productivity Council, see Phidd, "Economic Council and Economic Policy Formulation".

29. *Report of the Labour-Management-Government Mission to Europe to the National Productivity Council* (Ottawa, 1962).

30. National Productivity Council, *First Annual Report, 1961-62* (Ottawa, 1962).

31. See A. H. Wilson, *Research Councils in the Provinces: A Canadian Resource* (Ottawa, 1971) and *Background to Invention* (Ottawa, 1970).

32. Interviews.

33. National Productivity Council, *First Annual Report*.

34. Phidd, "Economic Council and Economic Policy Formulation".

35. R. W. Phidd, "Economic Council of Canada: Its Establishment, Structure and Role in the Canadian Policy-Making System, 1963-74", *Canadian Public Administration*, Vol. XVIII (Fall, 1975).

36. Interviews.

37. Hon. M. Lamontagne, Statement on the Occasion of the First Meeting of the Economic Council of Canada (Ottawa, 1964).

38. Interviews.

39. Economic Council of Canada, *Sixth Annual Review* (Ottawa, 1969), see especially pp. 2-3, 6-8.

40. J. J. Deutsch, "The Current Scope of Official Planning". Speech to the Seventh Annual Seminar on Canadian-American Relations, University of Windsor, November 4, 1965.

41. Phidd, "Economic Council and Economic Policy Formulation", especially pp. 564-77.

42. Economic Council of Canada, *Third Annual Review* (Ottawa, 1966).

43. Ibid.

44. Hon. R. Basford, *Policies for Price Stability* (Ottawa, 1968).

45. *Annual Report of the Governor of the Bank of Canada to the Minister of Finance for the Year 1969* (Ottawa, 1970).

46.Economic Council of Canada, *Sixth Annual Review*. This was elaborated on in interviews.

47. The Council itself has made such recommendations on a number of occasions but it was never consistent. We see an important role in this regard for the Department of Industry, Trade and Commerce. The Hon. J. Chrétien has been emphasizing these aspects recently.

48. See, for example, *Priorities in Transition, 1974* (Ottawa, 1975), Proceedings of the National Economic Conference. The conference was sponsored by the Economic Council of Canada and held on December 2, 3, and 4, 1975. See also Hon. D. McKeough, *The Reconstruction of Economic and Fiscal Policy in Canada* (Toronto, 1971).

49. See J. Hayward and M. Watson, *Planning, Politics and Public Policy: The*

British, French, and Italian Experience (London, 1975).

50. Phidd, "Economic Council and Economic Policy Formulation", pp. 494-500, 530-613.

51. The creation of DM10 provides some indication of a possible move in this direction. See Government of Canada, *The Way Ahead*. With regard to the federal-provincial dimensions see W. Davis, Statement to the Meeting of First Ministers, Ottawa, November 15-16, 1976. Mimeo, p. 3.

52. See, for example, recent speeches by Hon. J. Munro including Address to the International Conference on Trends in Industrial and Labour Relations in Montreal, May 25, 1976.

53. See Department of Labour, *Annual Report, 1975-76* (Ottawa, 1976)

54. Economic Council of Canada, *Twelfth Annual Review* (Ottawa, 1975).

55. For examples of the manner in which the Canadian Department of Labour has been looking at labour-management relationships in other countries see C. J. Connaghan, *Partnership or Marriage of Convenience: A Critical Examination of Contemporary Labour Relations in West Germany with Suggestions for Improving the Canadian Labour-Management Relationships based on the West Coast German Experience* (Ottawa, 1976).

56. Department of Labour, "Canada Labour Relations Council Established". News Release, July 23, 1975, 21/75. Hon. J. Munro, Minister of Labour, Notes for an Address on "The Canada Labour Relations Council" at the Nova Scotia Joint Labour-Management Study Committee in Halifax, February 6, 1976. With respect to the new responsibilities of the Department of Labour see Department of Labour, *Annual Report* for the fiscal year ended March 31, 1976. Briefly, the new role was stated as follows: To promote and where necessary to protect (1) the rights of the parties involved in the world of work; (2) opportunities for work; (3) a working environment conducive to physical and social well-being; and (4) a fair return for efforts in the workplace, p. 1.

57. Ibid., p. 5.

58. See Proposals by the Canadian Labour Congress for the establishment of a Labour Market Board. See also Shirley Carr, "Replace Controls with National Forum", *The Globe and Mail*, March 5, 1977, p. 10.

59. For example, in the field of occupational health the federal proposals

early in 1977 contemplated only a tripartite research agency rather than one that had direct regulatory power over health and safety in the workplace. See G. Bruce Doern, "The Political Economy of Regulating Occupational Health: The Ham and Beaudry Reports", *Canadian Public Administration*, Vol. XX (Spring 1977), pp. 6-30.

60. Basford, *Policies for Price Stability*, p. 10. Prices and Incomes Commission, *Inflation, Unemployment and Incomes Policy*. Summary Report, J. Young, Chairman (Ottawa, 1966).

61. Economic Council of Canada, *Third Annual Report*.

62. Ibid.

63. Basford, *Policies for Price Stability*, pp. 27-33, especially p. 27.

64. Ibid.

65. Ibid., p. 28.

66. Ibid., p. 31.

67. Ibid. For trade union opposition to the program and their subsequent reiteration of this position when controls were adopted see Canadian Labour Congress memorandum to the Government of Canada, March 18, 1974, pp. 21-22. By 1976 the CLC had taken an even more antagonistic position. See Memorandum to the Government of Canada, March 22, 1976, where it stated: "The Canadian Labour Congress will never support a wage-control programme", p. 12.

68. Prices and Incomes Commission, *Inflation, Unemployment and Incomes Policy*, p. 1.

69. Ibid.

70. Ibid., pp. 2-7.

71. Ibid., pp. 7-8. On the market power thesis see also John K. Galbraith, *Economics and the Public Purpose* (New York, 1975), Chapter 30; The Fraser Institute, *The Illusion of Wage and Price Controls* (Vancouver, 1976); C. D. Goodwin, ed., *Exhortation and Controls* (Washington, 1975); and L. Panitch, *Social Democracy and Industrial Militancy, the Labour Party, the Trade Unions, and Incomes Policy* (London, 1976).

72. Food Prices Review Board, *Final Report,* p. 32.

73. Ibid., p. 29.

74. Ibid.

75. Ibid., pp. 30-32.

76. Ibid., p. 32.

77. See the analysis of Sir Geoffrey Vickers, *Value System and Social Process* (London, 1968), pp. 84, 73-95, 96-110.

78. Food Prices Review Board, *Final Report*, p. 32.

79. Ibid.

80. On the importance and significance of the organizational definition of the problems and its effect on economic management see Lawrence Pierce, *The Politics of Fiscal Policy Formation* (Pacific Palisades, Ca., 1971), especially chapters 2 and 3.

81. Food Prices Review Board, *Final Report*, p. 37 but more generally pp. 37-38.

82. Ibid., p. 63. Placed within the context of economic management we observe a problem: Can a government respond to every controversial issue by creating a new ministry or a new department? Subsequently ministries of state for sports and small business were created.

83. For discussions of such issues see A. Rotstein, ed., *Beyond Industrial Growth* (Toronto, 1976). For the manner in which the classical scholars had grappled with these issues see Frischke, *Inflation: It's Your Bag*, Part 1.

85. First Session, 13th Parl., 23-24 Elizabeth II, 1974-75. Bill C-73. An Act to provide for the restraint of profit margins, prices, dividends, and compensation in Canada. Passed by the House of Commons, December 3, 1975.

85. Ibid., ss. 3 and 5.

86. Macdonald, Budget Speech, May 25, 1976. See also Outline of Proposed Modifications in Price and Profit Guidelines under the Anti-Inflation Act, May 25, 1976, and Macdonald, Statement on Anti-Inflation Programme, September 7, 1976. On the first year of the Anti-Inflation Board see Anti-

Inflation Board, *First Year Report* (Ottawa, 1976). J. L. Pépin, Notes for a Speech to the Empire Club in Toronto, October 14, 1976, and other speeches (November 17, and October 4, 1976). For some early commentary on the controls program see Economic Council of Canada, *Thirteenth Annual Review* (Ottawa, 1976), pp. 154-65 and R. G. Lipsey, "Wage Price Controls: How To Do a Lot of Harm by Trying to Do a Little Good", *Canadian Public Policy*, Vol. III (Winter 1977), pp. 1-13.

87. J. Wilensky, *The Welfare State and Equality: Structural and Ideological Roots of Public Expenditure* (Berkeley, 1975).

88. On the United States see M. D. Reagan, *The New Federalism* (New York, 1972), especially chapter "In Praise of Permissive Federalism". On Canada see D. V. Smiley, *Canada in Question: Federalism in the Seventies*, second ed. (Toronto, 1976), chapters 3 and 5.

89. See Economic Council of Canada, *Thirteenth Annual Review*.

90. Smiley, *Canada in Question*, Chapter 5.

91. For details of this period see J. L. Granatstein, *Canada's Way: The Politics of the Mackenzie King Government* (Toronto, 1975), chapters 5 and 7, and D. Creighton, *The Forked Road: Canada, 1939-57* (Toronto, 1976), Chapter 5.

92. See J. P. Meekison, ed., *Canadian Federalism: Myth or Reality?* (Toronto, 1971) and Smiley, *Canada in Question*, p. 67.

93. Ibid., pp. 71-77.

94. Ibid.

95. D. V. Smiley, "Developments in Federal-Provincial Relations Since 1945", in Meekison, ed., *Canadian Federalism*, p. 71.

96. Ibid., pp. 72-73.

97. See, for example, E. Gallant, "The Machinery of Federal-Provincial Relations", in Meekison, ed., *Canadian Federalism*, pp. 254-65.

98. Economic Council of Canada, *Thirteenth Annual Review*, pp. 59-64.

99. Gallant, "The Machinery of Federal-Provincial Relations", p. 257.

100. Institute of Intergovernmental Relations, Queen's University Report:

Intergovernmental Liaison on Fiscal and Economic Matters (Ottawa, 1969), quoted in Meekison, ed., *Canadian Federalism*, p. 268.

101. Interviews with officials of the Federal-Provincial Relations Office. See also Smiley, *Canada in Question*, especially pp. 57-64.

102. Institute of Intergovernmental Relations, *Intergovernmental Liaison on Fiscal and Economic Matters*.

103. Smiley, *Canada in Question*.

104. McKeough, *The Reconstruction of Economic and Fiscal Policy in Canada*.

105. Government of Canada, Western Economic Opportunities Conference, Edmonton, July 1973. See Working Papers cited in Chapter 9.

106. Smiley, *Canada in Question*, pp. 143-53. Since Smiley's book was published Premier Blakeney has made some strong statements advocating that Saskatchewan benefit from its resources.

107. See Canadian Tax Foundation, *The Financing of the Canadian Federation: The First Hundred Years* (Toronto, 1966).

108. Canadian Tax Foundation, *The National Finances, 1975-76*, p. 121.

109. Ibid., pp. 121-22.

110. Ibid., pp. 122-23.

111. Ibid., pp. 123-24.

112. Ibid., pp. 124-28.

113. Ibid., p. 129.

114. See Canadian Tax Foundation, Tax Memo: Provincial Finances, 1976, no. 56 (Toronto 1976).

115. Ibid., p. 2.

116. Economic Council of Canada, *Thirteenth Annual Review*, pp. 148-49.

117. Ibid., pp. 145-49.

118. Statement by Minister of Finance Donald S. Macdonald on Fiscal Arrangements, Federal-Provincial Conference of First Ministers, Ottawa,

December 13 and 14, 1976. See also "Fiscal Arrangements". Resumé by the Prime Minister of points accepted by all provinces.

119. See Richard Schultz, "The Regulatory Process and Federal-Provincial Relations", in G. Bruce Doern, ed., *The Regulatory Process in Canada* (Toronto, 1978), Chapter 5.

120. Statement by Hon. D. McKeough, Treasurer of Ontario and Minister of Economics, to the Meeting of the Ministers of Finance in Ottawa, November 1-2, 1971: *The Reconstruction of Economic and Fiscal Policy in Canada*, p. 1.

121. Ibid., p. 2.

122. Ibid., p. 6.

123. Department of the Prime Minister, *Highlights: An Economic Strategy for Ontario: Twenty-Point Program for Progress*, October 14, 1971, p. 8.

124. Ibid.

125. McKeough, Statement to the Meeting of the Ministers of Finance in Ottawa, July 6-7, 1976: *Reforming Fiscal Arrangements and Cost-Sharing in Canada*, especially pp. 1-5.

PART FOUR

Concluding Observations

Part IV presents the authors' concluding comments and analysis, including their view of the strengths and limitations of the analysis and focus of the book.

Chapter 13 examines critically seven largely "process"-oriented issues in the politics and management of Canadian economic policy and assesses them in the light of the central concepts discussed in the book. These issues include: the growing complexity of economic variables and processes and their impact on future reform processes; the relationship between economic research and knowledge and reform processes; the emergence of new economic portfolios as a reflection of reform processes; the openness of Canadian economic-policy processes; the role of political and organizational variables as a factor in the explanation of the growth of government expenditure; the political relationship between macro- and micro-economic management; and the evolving and future roles of central Finance and Treasury ministries.

Chapter 14 relates the entire analysis in the book to the evolving debate about tripartism in Canada and to the search for new central institutions of economic management. The analysis is also tied to the major competing liberal, pluralist, and so-called "corporatist" characterizations of the modern Canadian political economy.

CHAPTER 13

Issues in the Politics and Management of Canadian Economic Policy

To analyse the politics and management of Canadian economic policy one must adopt an approach which embraces not only the broad relationships between politics and the nature of economic power, but also the intra-Cabinet, bureaucratic, and managerial dimensions of the Canadian political economy. The executive-bureaucratic arena of the Canadian political system is not a wholly accurate reflection of the realities of the Canadian political economy and hence the outputs and outcomes of Canadian economic policy cannot be fully explained by the processes that go on in that arena. Canada's market system, the federal system of government, ethnic, class, and regional divisions and the way they receive political and electoral expression, international and cultural variables, the processes of urbanization, and numerous other aggregate variables are also important.

While the executive-bureaucratic arena does not wholly reflect these factors in an even-handed way, it is an essential and critical arena in which many of them eventually come into play. Thus we have suggested that executive-bureaucratic processes have to be understood, in part at least, on their own terms. This is not to suggest that we must tolerate all that we find in the executive-bureaucratic arena, but there is an intellectual obligation to examine it and understand it thoroughly. It is also essential to recognize that mere motion and reorganization do not necessarily constitute change. At the same time, however, it is important to see the Canadian political economy through the prism of public organizational behaviour since it is a central element of political reality. Changes in organization frequently reflect a form of political learning. Economic management, moreover, is profoundly influenced by the fairly constant contradictions and alternating demands of centralization and decentralization, policy and administration, co-ordination and delegation, as well as by the temporal demands of short-run politics and the long-run physical, geographic, and production realities of the economy.

In previous chapters we have moved from the general to the relatively more specific. Part I of the book presented a broad overview of the evolving relationships between politics, economics, and management, both in an academic and, more importantly, in an applied governmental sense. These relationships were later also related to the evolution of economic research, and the gradual differentiation of new economic portfolios in government. Part II examined the central processes of economic-policy formulation including: goals and goal conflicts, the relationships, in political terms, between goals and the equally critical question of the instruments of governing available to governing politicians, the impact of cabinet government and central agencies, the political base of Cabinet portfolio influence, the relationship to the budgetary process, the dynamics of the more specific determinants of ministerial behaviour, and the roles of economic leaders in the Government of Canada. Part III described and analysed more specifically the micro-macro dimensions of economic management, examining the major economic departments in terms of the evolution of their respective policy mandates and of the relationship between the evolving mandate and the departmental structure and organization. This more detailed examination enabled us to understand the more specific multiple dimensions of consensus and conflict, both in their intra-bureaucratic sense, and in their federal-provincial and private-public sector dimensions.

We have stressed that economic management is the process through which the increasingly complex and competing goals, instruments, agencies, and research needs of economic policy are co-ordinated and controlled. Economic management is thus a broader concept than fiscal policy or even economic policy since it involves a complex interplay between policy and administration and between micro- and macro-level factors, including the successive differentiation of new economic departments in response to evolving and competing values and objectives. It involves the processes of taxing, spending, and co-ordinating the demand and supply dimensions of economic behaviour in the face of frequently conflicting short-run and longer-run political and economic demands. It involves the two-way causal relationships between new economic knowledge and research and economic policies and organization, the technical problems of acquiring and interpreting economic data, and the problems of administering economic programs in a responsive way while at the same time meeting the internal bureaucratic requirements for managerial efficiency.

We have also stressed the view that the politics of economic policy must include an understanding of both the allocation of goals and values, and the selection of the instruments of governing through which compliance and/or support is sought. In political terms, moreover, one cannot afford to assume that a tidy "means-end" relationship exists between economic goals and instruments. Although the major part of the book has been focussed on economic departments, these departments are partly a reflection of the gradual shift and evolution of Canadian economic-policy goals caused by changing group, class, and regional demands. The immediate post-Second World War need for reconstruction, the memory of the pre-war depression, and the more specific influence of the social welfare reforms in the U.K. reflected in the Beveridge Report, resulted in an early postwar emphasis on redistributive goals reflected in the growth of the Department of National Health and Welfare and in the creation of housing programs through the Central Mortgage and Housing Corporation.

In the 1950s, however, economic goals seemed to be confined to the more specific terrain of fiscal policy, price stability, economic growth, full employment, and balance-of-payments equilibrium. By the late 1950s the goals of removing regional disparities and also income disparities become more clearly and forcefully articulated resulting in the 1960s in major expenditure programs and ultimately, in the case of DREE, in a new department to express and institutionalize the regional objective. Other goals, often complementary but sometimes competing, were also articulated, not only in response to broad political pressure but also in response to change in economic knowledge. Thus, manpower policies which drew greater attention to the so-called supply side of economic management were formulated and later institutionalized in departmental form. By the early 1970s these additional goals were joined by such issues as foreign investment, energy, consumer, and also agricultural and food policy, each of which, in the presence of economic recession and inflation, made the political choices as well as the economic-management process even more difficult.

In the final two chapters we embark on two forms of summary analysis. This chapter will identify, in summary form, a number of issues in the politics and management of Canadian economic policy which arise from this book and which deserve further and continuing attention and understanding. Chapter 14 will examine the more general possibilities for the reform of central public-private sector economic-policy processes, especially as reflected in the post-1975 debate on tripartism and the post-controls period.

It is obviously important to stress that the standards against which these selected issues and reform possibilities will be assessed will vary greatly. The processes and dynamics which we have analysed have been the processes of a political system dominated by liberal-democratic governments. We will argue that a considerable amount of reform and change has occurred but obviously the adequacy of the reform can be subject to many different general and specific ideological tests and standards. For example, fundamental tests related to the questions of general and regional economic redistribution will result in views that the progress of reform has been inadequate or indeed perhaps non-existent. The multiplicity of standards is indeed a central part of the politics and management of Canadian economic policy.

Of the many issues inherent in the politics and management of Canadian economic policy seven issues seem to be especially important in the context of the analysis presented in this book. These issues deal largely with the processes involved in the politics and management of Canadian economic policy. A number of summary concluding comments will be made about each of the following issues: the growing complexity of economic variables and processes and its impact on future reform processes; the relationship between economic research and knowledge and reform processes; the emergence of new economic portfolios as a reflection of reform processes; the openness of Canadian economic policy processes; the role of political and organizational variables as a factor in the explanation of the growth of government expenditure; the political relationships between macro- and micro-economic management; and the evolving role of central Finance and Treasury ministries in the economic-management process.

THE GROWING COMPLEXITY OF ECONOMIC VARIABLES: IMPACT ON FUTURE REFORM PROCESSES

The most obvious and elementary observation about the processes analysed in this book is that economic management has become far more complex than it once was even twenty years ago. This growing complexity, brought on by the need to balance and consider a wider range of economic variables and values, is itself evidence that a considerable amount of reform has occurred. Economic-policy processes twenty-five years ago were simpler and superfically more effective, precisely because many important dimensions of economic management were ignored. Reform has occurred precisely in policy areas such as manpower, and regional development policy, among others, which now make economic management more complicated and less tidy. Economic management has been taken increasingly out of the monopoly realm of Keynesian political economy and into the muddier realm of politics and economic management. Such a process has been generally both essential and beneficial.

Economic-policy reform has been decidedly incremental in nature but it has been fairly continuous over the period examined in this book. This kind of reform process, as always, presents dilemmas both for its defenders and its critics. Radical and even moderate critics of the process will, with justification, describe these incremental reform processes as being grossly insufficient, particularly in terms of redistributive goals (both along class lines and regionally). This insufficiency can be attributed to the *modus vivendi* which exists between capitalist economic systems and liberal democratic regimes, and which is especially reinforced by the existence of federal systems of government, systems which divide and disperse governmental authority. At the same time, however, many of the reform critics have had a stake in the very reform processes of which they are critical. Many of the reforms described in this book can be traced to the influence of reform critics including those which receive their most visible political expression in the New Democratic party. Thus to criticize the current system too sharply or too radically is to criticize a system which has been shaped in part by this criticism. Therefore, to secure even more radical change inevitably requires one to overtly advocate and work toward a fundamental change in the capitalist system or the mixed economy (Canadian version).

Defenders of the reform processes will offer a generally positive assessment of the evolution of the Canadian political economy since the Second World War and will relate it positively to the necessary and desirable processes of liberal democratic "brokerage" government and politics. Such processes will achieve accommodation and a gradually evolving consensus whether consensus must be secured along French-English, federal-provincial, inter-regional, public-private, or intra-bureaucratic lines. Thus ideological models of desirable political processes implicitly or explicitly become standards against which economic-reform processes are judged. The greatest empirical evidence for the inadequacy and failure of the past reform processes is that despite the creation of new programs and new departments in important areas of economic management, the actual degree of relative economic redistribution has been either negligible or virtually non-existent. Thus, the Economic Council has observed that:

> between 1951 and 1965... there was a notable reduction in income inequality, probably in large part as a result of Canada's industrial and urban development. However, despite an impressive growth in overall average individual and family incomes from 1965 to 1971, the lowest group commanded a smaller proportion, and the highest group a larger proportion, of overall income at the end of the period. In 1973 and 1974 there was again some reduction in income inequality, but unofficial figures for 1975 suggest that at least part of this reduction may have been short-lived.[1] (See Appendix A.)

THE RELATIONSHIP BETWEEN ECONOMIC RESEARCH AND KNOWLEDGE AND THE REFORM PROCESS.

While the nature of change has been gradual and "reform-oriented" we think that the processes of reform have been greatly aided by changes in economic research and by the processes in which economic advisory intelligence and information has been disseminated in a more public way. This is not to suggest that new economic intelligence *per se* causes reform. In short, in the area of economic management, knowledge is not necessarily power. In Chapter 6, however, as well as in the rest of Part III we have stressed the importance of economic knowledge as a causal factor. Thus, for example, reforms in labour-market policies arose in part because of better research and knowledge about this area of economic management. The ability to model complex economic variables and thus to simulate better the possible consequences of different options will be increasingly important, not because the modelling provides automatic answers (far from it), but because such activity may at least avoid selecting certain options whose consequences ought to be avoided. It should be stressed that the creation of new economic departments is also frequently a stimulus for more explicit research which in turn may have a later causal effect in assisting the articulation of new economic demands.

We believe that in the general realm of the public dissemination of economic intelligence and advice through such bodies as the Economic Council of Canada and, more recently, bodies such as the Conference Board of Canada and the C. D. Howe Institute, the processes of economic management have been made more open. This is not to argue that the quality of research, as judged by professional economists or social scientists, has been uniformly good. As research, the work has ranged in quality from excellent to mediocre and poor. However, when it is compared with the total absence, as recently as in the early 1960s, of virtually any external public vehicles of economic advice and criticism, the presence of these bodies is a major improvement.

The relationships between research and economic management may best be illustrated by the role of the Economic Council of Canada. Professional economists are not normally inclined to look on the Council kindly, primarily because of a tendency to relate its role only to short-run stabilization-policy processes. It is clear that the Council's influence has been greatest precisely in these areas where it has tendered advice on both policy *and* organization, and hence on economic management. Thus its influence has been significant in areas such as labour-market policies, regional development, and consumer policies, areas which involved the need for significant reorganization as well as more intelligent articulation.

That the success or failure not only of research, but of the entire economic-management process, is profoundly influenced by "administrative lag" is obvious. Not only is the response of private organizations difficult to predict, but also the ability of government to persuade its own agencies to change their behaviour in desired directions is often quite limited. Indeed, because of the absence in the public sector of any real price signals, the latter form of administrative lag may be the most difficult to overcome.

THE EMERGENCE OF NEW ECONOMIC PORTFOLIOS AS A REFLECTION OF REFORM PROCESSES

Public bureaucracies are often portrayed as stultified, change-resistant institutions. In one sense bureaucracies are intended to be modes for delivering, in a reliable, predictable fashion, the goods and services for which they were created. They are also, as we have stressed earlier, expected to be responsive to change. Hence political ambivalence about the public service abounds. On the one hand bureaucratic power must be constrained, but at the same time politicians, through legislation and delegation, constantly give more discretionary authority to officials. Our analysis lends support to the view that the federal bureaucracy profoundly influences economic-policy choices but that it is also more capable of reflecting change than most give it credit for, and its record for responding to change is at least equal to many other sectors of Canada's economic life. Economic-policy processes reveal at least two dimensions of these patterns of change.

First, the analysis of economic-policy processes reveals the gradual appearance, in organizational form, of many economic issues, variables, and values which in successive stages emerged from being a minor component in a given department to being either a major component in a department or to being a department in its own right. Thus, concern for manpower policies emerged as a minor sub-unit of the Labour department to become a department in its own right. Regional development policies evolved from segments of the Agriculture, Forestry, and Industry departments to the status of a department (DREE) whose mission was wholly devoted to the regional dimension. Similarly consumer policies emerged from scattered locations to their current location in the Department of Consumer and Corporate Affairs.

This "bubbling up" process is important because it illustrates the ways in which various reform issues may gather some organizational momentum. The origins of the pressure for change may reside outside the bureaucracy and be reflected in political criticism by interest groups, the media, or other governments, but in recent years internal evaluation processes have helped as well. The process has been aided, as we have stressed in Chapter 12 and in the chapters on individual departments, by successive, and increasingly frequent efforts to conceptualize and reorganize old disjointed policy wine into new policy and organizational bottles. Thus essentially spatial concepts such as urban policy and regional policy have been developed, given more legitimacy, and given organizational homes. Other concepts such as an "industrial strategy", "competition" policy, and "employment" policy have been similarly concocted in an effort to reflect new or re-emerging concerns.

These efforts at recategorization are not just semantic exercises. They reflect a mixture of genuine concern and the organizational pursuit of power. There can be no doubt for example that the Department and Commission of Employment and Immigration's custody over "employment" policy will help it generate more political support than could be achieved under the more technical concept of "manpower" policy.

We have also stressed the unprecedented degree to which governments have used ministerial-level departmental reorganization and the creation of new portfolios as an explicit governing instrument to telegraph their priorities more visibly. The recent period of departmental-level organizational change has been unprecedented in Canada. That fact alone sets limits on how much more departmental-level reorganization can occur. Whereas, in the past, major reorganization occurred only every ten or fifteen years, the process of creating new departments, as described in Part III, has increased visibly in the past decade. Governments have increasingly been inclined to express and institutionalize their adoption of new priorities through departmental structures. New portfolios cannot be concocted with every new issue, however, because before long concern is expressed not only about the aggregate size of the Cabinet but also the concurrent problems of co-ordination, the consolidation of the values already institutionalized, and the micro-level problems of administering related programs in the field.

The importance of recent departmental changes which have created new economic portfolios should not, however, be underestimated. When cabinet-level portfolios are created to articulate and defend particular economic variables and values, the politics and management of Canadian economic policy becomes a greatly different process than it would be if those variables and values were merely branch plants of some other departments.

THE OPENNESS OF CANADIAN ECONOMIC-POLICY PROCESSES

The earlier comments about economic research and intelligence obviously do not do justice to all of the related questions which influence the degree of openness of Canadian economic-policy processes. While the processes appear to us to be far more open than they once were, this degree of openness must still be considered to be very limited because of the normal constraints of the Cabinet-parliamentary system of government. Cabinet systems confer power on the Cabinet with Parliament performing a legitimizing and scrutinizing role and thus the concept of openness must, to date at least, be seen in terms of general public scrutiny or analysis and the public availability of information, rather than in terms of more fundamental changes in the system of government.

The main quasi-public source of potentially countervailing economic-policy influence and power rests with provincial governments. The public services of several provincial governments have developed increasingly sophisticated economic-policy capabilities of their own. These capabilities arose out of their own intrinsic public-policy needs as well as out of a growing concern, beginning in the 1960s, that provincial economies had to gauge better, and sometimes counteract, the heavy-handed, indiscriminate effects of macro-federal fiscal and economic policies. The fact that provincial and local government expenditures greatly exceeded federal expenditures also reinforced this process. Federal policies are thus increasingly analysed and challenged by a base of expertise in provincial bureaucracies that has grown to be equal to the expertise of the federal government. This is an absolute contrast to the virtual federal monopoly of expertise that prevailed in the early Keynesian days of the 1950s.

Another, perhaps less obvious, dilemma affecting the openness of the policy process concerns the politics and strategies of giving advice.

External bodies like the Economic Council of Canada face a continuing strategical dilemma as to where they place their advisory emphasis. On the other hand, they could take a more purely public-research role in which their research plus subsequent open criticism would be relied upon to secure the desired changes in policy. Or external bodies could rely on a more quiet, consensus-oriented, behind-the-scenes, advocacy role. The latter may be less public but may have the advantage of securing access both to better information and to the real decision-making process. These twin dimensions of the public advisory role are not easily resolved and the Economic Council has been especially ambivalent about them.

The relationship between general policy openness and budgetary secrecy presents another intriguing paradox. The need to preserve budgetary secrecy at the time preceding the Minister of Finance's Budget Speech is based on the desire to insure honesty and probity in government. Individuals should not be in a position to profit from advance knowledge of tax and other financial changes. Hence the valued objectives of honesty and probity in government can conflict with the doctrine of openness. This potential conflict may increasingly arise if it is related to the widening net of ministers and officials who have a role in economic-policy processes. Maintaining budgetary secrecy may thus become increasingly difficult.

In his May 25, 1976, Budget Speech, the Minister of Finance, Donald Macdonald, drew attention to the problem of budgetary secrecy.[2] He stressed that it would be useful if he could consult with outside interests on budgetary details so that a more accurate understanding of the impact and consequences of proposals could be developed. He did not relate the secrecy issue to the growing private demands of ministers of other economic portfolios that the *internal* secrecy of the detailed budgetary process be removed, or at least lessened, so that the dominance of the Finance minister and his most senior officials in the final budget stages is reduced.

Public and parliamentary scrutiny of the economic-management process can also be aided by two possible reciprocal reforms in addition to the persistent need to strengthen the resources of the Auditor General and the Public Accounts Committee of the House of Commons. In addition to the usual budget papers, an expenditure projections white paper could be required modelled on the British expenditure review process.[3] It would require political authorities to extrapolate future expenditures and to give a public indication of their medium-term (three- to five-year) expenditure priorities. The resulting annual medium-term economic-policy debate in the House of Commons would thus complement and augment the regular budget debate on these issues. A parallel development would be the establishment of closer links between the Economic Council of Canada and Parliament through the required receipt and assessment of the Council's annual and perhaps other reports by a parliamentary committee. Such a relationship has been suggested by the late former Chairman of the Economic Council, John Deutsch.

There should be no illusions about the meaning and limitations of the kind of openness suggested by these possible reforms. Governing politicians may reject the public medium-term expenditure process because, for example, it would require them to forecast future rates of inflation and hence would be viewed, especially by their opposition critics, as tolerating an acceptance of those rates of inflation. On the other hand, opposition politicians may find such projections to their strategic disadvantage because the projections would likely illustrate the limited flexibility and room for new initiatives and thus generate greater public scepticism about their own current or future policy ideas. Despite the great difficulties and the myriad ways in which the information could be used, we think it is imperative that steps such as those suggested above be considered so as to raise both the quality and the time frame of economic-policy debates.

Canada obviously faces economic choices of great magnitude and degree of difficulty. These choices must be made in a political economy where consensus is difficult to mobilize and achieve. Economic-policy organizational and procedural variables are merely one contributing factor in a complex causal chain of behaviour. There are thus severe limitations to the reforms discussed above. Within these limitations, however, fine gradations of choice can be made to produce a system of incentives and public obligations that will require and encourage Cabinet and other political leaders to reach decisions in ways that have a higher probability of achieving beneficial results than we have known in the past.

THE ROLE OF POLITICAL AND ORGANIZATIONAL VARIABLES AS A FACTOR IN THE EXPLANATION OF THE GROWTH OF GOVERNMENT EXPENDITURES

Efforts to explain the causes of the growth in government expenditure have been fraught with problems. Explanations have included such variables as the aggregate socioeconomic processes of urbanization and industrialization; the supportive relationships between the state sector and the insatiable demands imposed on the state by the growth of monopoly capitalism; the failure to control the money supply; the laws of bureaucratic expansion; and the impact of public-sector collective bargaining.[4] No one disputes the existence of the rapid expenditure growth examined in Chapter 7. Its causes are subject, however, to the usual range of both ideological and methodological problems endemic in both politics and the social sciences. These problems are augmented by short-term cycles of expenditure change during which periods of rapid growth are followed by periods of slow growth. These fluctuations may of course themselves be either the cause of, or be affected by, the short-term Keynesian manipulation of aggregate expenditure.

We make no claims that our analysis unravels all these mysteries. We do claim, however, that any analysis of the growth of government expenditure ought to take fully into account, as *middle-level* variables, two dimensions of the politics and management of Canadian economic policy. The variables are the choice of governing instruments available to politicians, and the intra-Cabinet separation of the management of the government from the management of the economy, epitomized by the separation of the Treasury Board from the Finance Department and institutionalized and reinforced by the establishment of new spending economic portfolios.

In political terms, spending must be seen as one instrument of governing and hence must be related to the political advantages and disadvantages of other instruments such as regulation. At various times in our analysis we have stressed the importance of the existence of a continuum of governing instruments. In the most simple way, spending is a more pleasant way of governing in that it is only indirectly coercive. More directly coercive responses by way of regulation may therefore be avoided in situations where there is a choice. The spending instrument may be especially attractive to the federal government, because, generally speaking, the use of the spending power is a reasonably well-established avenue of entry into fields of mixed federal-provincial jurisdiction. Direct regulation is a far more difficult instrument both constitutionally and politically. Thus a significant portion of the marginal growth in public expenditure may be more completely explained by the alternative political value of expenditure as opposed to the regulatory and exhortative instruments of governing.

As we will stress again in Chapter 14, the instruments of governing are part of the stock in trade of governing politicians. There is a "market" for the instruments. When the supply of expenditure instruments is great, as for example in times of buoyant economic growth, they will be utilized. When supply is reduced governing politicians then will turn to other instruments. These shifts are obviously relative rather than absolute in nature, but we will illustrate in Chapter 14 how, when expenditure instruments are reduced in supply, governing politicians are likely to turn to other instruments such as regulation or perhaps exhortation.

It should also be stressed that we are using the concept of the expenditure instrument above in a general sense and in relation to other *general* instruments. *Within* each of the general instruments, however, there are finer gradations of choice. In the use of expenditure, for example, choices exist between grants, subsidies, conditional grants, loans, and capital expenditures, each of which might have different policy and hence political consequences.

Recent expenditure growth has also been reinforced by the internal changes in the organization of economic policy within the Cabinet. The separation of the Treasury Board from the Finance Department in 1966 was intended to help differentiate the management of the government from the management of the economy. It was intended to get program management away from the tight-fisted *negative* control norms which governed the pre-Glassco management system, to a system where programs would be more *positively* managed in terms of program goals and objectives. This change in emphasis has had important consequences for expenditure growth. The system is not geared, as it once was, to the relatively more exclusive control-oriented function. This initial separation was immediately reinforced by the expenditure demands of the newly institutionalized economic departments and other portfolios. These demands in turn were caused and reinforced by real economic conditions in the broader Canadian political economy. The balancing forces between expenditure control and expenditure management have perhaps, at the time of writing, come full circle. The appointment of a royal commission on financial management and accountability in November 1976 suggests a renewed concern for accountability and control, and for honesty and probity in government spending practices.

Expenditure growth is also affected by the recent tendency to use large government expenditure programs, rather than taxation, as a built-in stabilization factor. Thus, unemployment insurance, regional development grants, special employment programs, and social welfare programs have been viewed as longer-term stabilization devices. The ability to turn on and turn off expenditure instruments in the short run therefore becomes increasingly difficult both politically and economically, especially since many of the programs involve federal-provincial agreements. Beginning as early as in 1974, however, the federal government began to serve notice of its intent to put expenditure ceilings on several heretofore open-ended, joint federal-provincial programs. As Chapter 12 has shown, by the end of 1976 proposals were also made to hand several programs to the provinces in exchange for tax points. These measures, moreover, as we pointed out in Chapter 7, were being combined with a more specific search for expenditure policies (e.g., the capital sector, and government purchasing and supplies policies) which might be more explicitly used to support fiscal policy in a more flexible and effective way.

THE POLITICAL RELATIONSHIPS BETWEEN MACRO- AND MICRO-ECONOMIC MANAGEMENT

This book has drawn special attention to the importance of the complex interplay between the macro and micro dimensions of economic management. These dimensions have been examined in several different ways. They have been reflected in the gradual evolution of new economic portfolios, a development which demonstrated the first major movement away from the relatively more exclusive concern with the macro-level Keynesian manipulation of aggregate expenditure and taxation. The intra-departmental and administrative dimensions have been as important as the departmental developments. They have attempted to direct economic-management decisions into a more responsive and managerially efficient administrative mode of operation, geared to local and regional political-economic peculiarities.

The decentralization of several economic departments was analysed, especially in Part III. It would, in the long run, be misleading to view these efforts at decentralization as being merely managerial fads which will be quickly followed by some inexorable countermovement towards centralization. The administrative dimension of economic management is a critical area. Efforts to decentralize have frequently been genuine and are a product of criticism by provincial governments and clientele groups, of an evolving understanding that heavy-handed central instruments are not a sufficient condition for success, and of efforts within the bureaucracy to promote more responsive and efficient management. This is not to suggest that centralization tendencies do not exist. Public policy and administrative processes are constantly characterized by a tension between the need to treat various constituencies equally, and the concurrent need to differentiate, to be flexible, and to discriminate. There are obviously also continuing tensions between headquarters and field personnel. The history of the evolution of the politics and management of Canadian economic policy over the past twenty-five years, however, reveals an increasing need to relate the micro dimension of economic management to the major macro levers.

The politics of intergovernmental expenditures, as surveyed in Chapter 12 and as revealed in specific policy fields in Chapters 7 and 11, has also reinforced these trends. The 1950s and 1960s era of universal multi-lateral, conditional-grant, federal-provincial expenditure programs has been succeeded, though not entirely replaced, by expenditure programs which are inherently more bilateral (the federal government and one province) and which are negotiated to meet unique provincial needs.

Similarly the analysis of "industrial strategies", and "competition", "foreign investment", and "employment" policies in Chapters 8, 10, and 11 indicates the need to particularize economic-management problems on an industry-by-industry basis. Suggestions have similarly been made with regard to reorganizing collective bargaining along industry-by-industry lines. That these efforts will be resisted by groups with a contrary view of the realities of economic power is obvious. For example, labour unions are unlikely to support a further industry-by-industry *micro* approach unless it is accompanied by *macro* policy reforms in such areas as incomes policy and industrial democracy. The adoption in Canada of proposals similar to the U.K. Bullock Report on Industrial Democracy would, at one and the same time, be a major policy affecting micro *and* macro economic-management processes.[5] The Bullock proposals seek to insure parity on corporate boards of directors between shareholder-directors and worker-directors.[6] Such policies are unlikely to be adopted in Canada in the near future but they reveal the ultimate linkage of micro and macro issues which may in the mid-1970s be receiving an important, albeit more limited, reflection, in the field of occupational and industrial health and safety.[7]

Economies in general, and the Canadian economy in particular, are increasingly more difficult to manage. Economic management is more difficult because the Canadian political economy increasingly insists on the *concurrent* pursuit of several economic and social goals some of which conflict with others. In intra-Cabinet terms, the control over economic management has, of necessity, become more dispersed. The Finance Department is still the focal point for fiscal policy but the overall process has developed to the point where authority in legal terms, and influence and power in real terms, is shared relatively more among a larger number of portfolios.

One can attribute crisis proportions to the current dilemmas, for there are obviously major difficulties already apparent. Despite the current and likely future difficulties, Canada did not experience or hear the clarion call for more planning or for a planned economy until 1976. While we will discuss the tripartism debate generated by the Trudeau government's incomes policy of 1975, it is important to see it in the context of the gradual evolution of a concern for economic management and its implications for a more planned response. But planning, as such, can have a disarming and naive simplicity to it unless it is rigorously related to the determinants of governing in a liberal democratic, federal system of government in which formal political power is concentrated within cabinets in a cabinet-parliamentary system, and where great economic power resides in the corporate sector and, to a lesser extent, in the union sector. Planning, moreover, can have many different meanings, manifestations, and time frames. The annual budgetary process is clearly a form of planning. Regional policy has sought to encourage better regional planning. The five-year tax agreements are a form of planning.

While there are points where concentrations of power clearly exist, there is also an enormous number of more micro-level accommodations needed among governments, between the public and private sectors, and between departments and their several clientele groups. While examinations of the Cabinet and the bureaucratic agencies do not fully reveal all that is important about the Canadian political economy, they do suggest the need to understand these processes on their own terms. We have accordingly stressed both the rationalities and the internal contradictions of Cabinet government and of the processes that have evolved to better manage the Canadian economy. Future reform will have to come on many fronts. Because of our focus, however, we have a special obligation to examine the prospects for the future role of Finance and Treasury ministries, a task to which the final section of this chapter is devoted.

THE EVOLVING ROLE OF CENTRAL FINANCE AND TREASURY MINISTRIES

The analysis of Canadian economic management shows that any future efforts to reform the *internal* machinery of economic management, especially the main federal "Treasury" departments, will have to strike a delicate balance between a number of variables. These include the collective and representative norms of Canadian Cabinet government, the continuing managerial and political need to delegate responsibility to ministers, departments, and agencies, the need for a focussed ministerial authority and accountability for economic policy, the technical requirements of economic data and analysis, and the maximum opportunity for the full range of economic objectives and values to be considered in Cabinet deliberations.

Previous chapters have shown the extent to which the federal Department of Finance has historically evolved into an "economic affairs" department. It has done so by periodically giving up several of its more routine operational or administrative functions and by cumulatively building up analytical capability to handle, or at least monitor, the economic consequences of the major evolving priorities of government. In recent years these included regional development, health care, social security, manpower, energy, and agricultural and food policy.

In terms of the time frame of its perspective the Finance Department has evolved out of its short-term perspective into at least the medium term. This has been necessitated by a number of factors including an emerging belief that a longer-term view is necessary, the emergence of "supply" problems such as energy, manpower, and food, which are inherently less subject to manipulation in the short run, the department's responsibility for monitoring and sometimes approving the capital-investment proposals of Crown corporations, the (usually) five-year tax agreements with provincial governments, and the need to respond to the continuing, medium-term views offered by the Economic Council of Canada.

Thus, in several respects, the Finance Department has moved closer to the model of the British Department of Economic Affairs (DEA) which existed in the United Kingdom between 1964 and 1969.[8] In considering this model, it should be remembered that prior to 1964, the British Treasury, headed by the Chancellor of the Exchequer, was a more inclusive "finance" ministry than the Canadian Finance Department is now in that the British Treasury had control over both the management of the economy and the management of the expenditure process which in Canada had been delegated in the mid-1960s to the Treasury Board.

The British DEA was established by the Labour government to give a more authoritative and long- or medium-term system of economic planning. It was a government department that had no direct administrative responsibilities. It derived its authority from the leadership provided by a very senior minister who also served as Chairman of the National Economic Development Council (NEDC), the latter consisting of two other ministers, as well as representatives of labour, industry, and two academics. Most of the staff on the economic side of the Treasury was transferred to the DEA. The DEA was thus created to:

> formulate the general objectives of economic policy in its totality and act as the

coordinator of the policies of individual departments towards the achievement of these objectives.

Accordingly the DEA had to:

a) relate each departments' activities and requirements to the general objective of national economic policy, to the prospective availability of economic resources, and to the total claims upon them, and
b) provide informed advice to departments, as partners in a joint enterprise, on all aspects of economic policy, and to help them to fulfill their departmental responsibilities efficiently and economically.[9]

The British DEA was abolished in 1969 because it seriously divided responsibility between the DEA minister and the rest of the Treasury department headed by the Chancellor. Relationships between the two ministers became almost intolerable. The British economic-management system was also influenced at this time by the growing concern, expressed in the Fulton Committee reports, about the state of general management in the British civil service.[10]

A renewed debate on the role of the Treasury in the U.K. began early in 1977 when two former British prime ministers, Harold Wilson and Edward Heath, both advocated before the British House of Commons Select Committee on Expenditure that the Treasury be split. A new ministry of Budget and Manpower was suggested to handle the expenditure side in a way largely similar to the Canadian Treasury Board–Finance Department split of the early 1960s. The suggested split in the U.K. reflected the apparent frustration of two prime ministers, one Labour and one Conservative, in controlling the Treasury. It also reflected, particularly in the Labour government, the struggle between the left and right wings of the governing party over the level and composition of public spending and over the real and the perceived power of Treasury officials in the then recently concluded financial arrangements with the International Monetary Fund.[11]

Comparisons of machinery in different countries must be made with caution. While we have identified in Chapter 5 a view by officials of the Finance Department that the department is the "guardian" of the economy, our analysis indicates that the Canadian Finance Department does not have the sense of village community which Heclo and

Wildavsky ascribe to the British Treasury and its "private government of public money".[12] While in an earlier and simpler era in the 1940s and 1950s a more cohesive sense of community may have prevailed the combination of internal views which characterized Finance as the "internal opposition", as well as the emergence of new portfolios, suggests that a far less cohesive system exists in Canada.

Comparisons do indicate, however, that political conflict about machinery and positions are not to be treated lightly, and they do illustrate the existence of two main contending forces in economic management, those who see expenditure in more traditional Keynesian terms and those who see it as the main lever of economic change and, perhaps, of the redistribution of resources.

The British experience with overall governmental and civil service management has also had, as we have seen, its even earlier Canadian parallel. The Glassco Commission's concern about the management of government, and the subsequent separation of the Treasury Board under its own minister, from the more direct control of the Finance Department, shows how economic management will be affected by issues which deal with management of the government. This was the case in the early 1960s when the Glassco Commission was utterly silent about the impact of its recommendations on economic management, but it is even more true now, especially since the Treasury Board's "general manager's" role has been augmented by its overall responsibility for federal public-sector collective bargaining and language policy. Thus, on the one hand, Finance has lost direct control of managing government expenditure to the Treasury Board, while the latter has not been able to give expenditure and program management its undivided attention because of the demands placed upon it by other governmental management issues such as collective bargaining and language policy.

The above processes of delegation and allocation of responsibility, when coupled with the establishment and growth of other economic portfolios, strongly suggest that economic management under recent Liberal governments has become more pluralistic. Future advocates of internal Cabinet reform will have to contend with this reality. It may be expected, for example, that those who wish to institutionalize even more the recent evolution of new economic portfolios and mandates may want a form of economic management board which could be created by statute and which could assign more deliberately a collective responsibility for economic management to the board. Those who seek a more concerted method of controlling public expenditure and of *subordinating* the management of the government to the management of the economy will probably tend to urge the need for a strengthened central Treasury, including perhaps a much closer institutional marriage (albeit not a replica of the *pre*-Glassco variety) between Finance and the Treasury Board.

Thus in the final analysis, the internal governmental struggle for the future role of central treasuries in the federal economic-management process will at least partly reflect the larger influence of the control-versus-expenditure forces in Canadian politics, albeit moderated by the growing realization that the management of the government, and the management of the economy, though they are related, are not the same thing.

NOTES

1. Economic Council of Canada, *Thirteenth Annual Review* (Ottawa, 1977), p. 7.

2. House of Commons, *Debates*, May 25, 1976, p. 13029.

3. See Sir Samuel Goldman, *The Developing System of Public Expenditure Management and Control* (London, 1973) and R. G. S. Brown, *The Administrative Process in Britain* (London, 1971), pp. 181-84 and 311-12.

4. See R. M. Bird, *The Growth of Government Spending in Canada* (Toronto, 1970); J. O'Connor, *The Fiscal Crisis of the State* (New York, 1971); R. Deaton, "The Fiscal Crisis of the State", *Our Generation*, Vol. VIII, no. 4, pp. 11-50; and H. Wilensky, *The Welfare State and Equality: Structural and Ideological Roots of Public Expenditure* (Berkeley, 1975).

5. See *Report of the Committee of Inquiry on Industrial Democracy* (London, 1977).

6. For comparative developments in this field see Eric Batstone and P. L. Davies, *Industrial Democracy: The European Experience*. Reports prepared for the Industrial Democracy Committee (London, 1976).

7. See G. Bruce Doern, "The Political Economy of Regulating Occupational Health: The Ham and Beaudry Reports", *Canadian Public Administration*, Vol. xx, no. 1 (Spring 1977), pp. 8-28.

8. On the British DEA see A. H. Hanson and M. Walles, *Governing Britain* (London, 1970), chapters 5, 6, and 9; Samuel Brittan, *Steering the Economy: The Role of the Treasury* (London, 1970); Harold Wilson, *The Labour Government, 1964-1970* (London, 1974), pp. 544-45; Michael Stewart, *The Jekyll and Hyde Years: Politics and Economic Policy Since 1964* (London, 1977); and George Brown, *In My Way* (London, 1972).

9. Hanson and Walles, *Governing Britain*.

10. Brown, *The Administrative Process in Britain*, pp. 26-37.

11. See *The Times*, February 2, 1977, p. 2, March 3, 1977, p. 19, and March 11, 1977, pp. 4, 19. See also *The Sunday Times*, February 20, 1977, p. 14.

12. H. Heclo and A. Wildavsky, eds., *The Private Government of Public Money* (London, 1974).

CHAPTER FOURTEEN

Tripartism, Politics, and Economic Management

Until 1976 there had been little generalized and sustained political debate in Canada about the need for, or the consequences of, a more planned economy. The evolution of economic-management concepts and organization has demonstrated, however, how latent and near the political surface the "planning" issues had been. The October 1975 Anti-Inflation program promulgated by the Trudeau government brought the issues of modern economic management, its relationship to planning, and the role of the state in Canadian economic life, quickly to the surface.

Our final task is to indicate how the analysis in this book can aid in understanding the mid-1970s debate about the nature of public-private sector relations conducted under the concept of tripartism. The detailed analysis in Part III of this book as well as the more general examination in earlier parts of the book ought to leave us under no illusion that tripartism can be fully understood except in relation to the real world in which economic management and its attendent politics occur. Hence tripartism must be examined in relation to the politics and processes surrounding expenditure and taxation, demand and supply management, the conflicting pull of short-run necessities and long-run realities, centralization and decentralization, integration and delegation, and policy and administration.

Tripartism must also be seen not only in relation to the broad "isms" of contemporary political debate, liberalism, pluralism, and corporatism, but also in relation to the other conceptual categorizations in which recent economic policies have been successively put and which we have examined in great detail in Chapters 7 to 12. Thus regional policy, industrial strategy, competition policy, employment policy, and incomes policy are all variations on the same theme, in the sense that they each represent an attempt to develop a concept around which a form of public-private consensus might congeal. That these concepts have not succeeded only indicates that the task is immensely difficult. That an overall concept of tripartism is being seriously discussed indicates that the search for new organizing concepts goes on.

We have argued throughout this book that while we have focussed on the intra-governmental domain, we are cognizant of the fact that the predominant causal forces in economic management are in the total political economy of Canada of which governments and bureaucracies are only one part. Thus we have tried to demonstrate the linkage between evolving economic goals and priorities, and the nature of governmental organizational behaviour.

The formal contours of the debate begun in 1976 have been contained in the concept of tripartism which sees the future management (planning?) of the Canadian economy requiring new institutions which would bring government, business, and labour into closer, more formal, collaboration in the public interest. Tripartism, as earlier chapters have demonstrated, is not in itself new, but its characteristics must be assessed both in the light of the broadest concepts of the role of the state as discussed in Part I and in relation to the macro-micro dimensions of the economic-policy areas examined in Part III. These concepts in turn must be seen in relation to the liberal and quasi-pluralist traditions of Canadian politics and to the arguments about its relationship to corporatism. The debate about the "post-controls" society should also be tied to developments in other countries, to the realities of cabinet government and federalism, and to the concept of governing instruments and its impact on political behaviour in general and economic management in particular. The concluding analysis of tripartism and of the reform of economic policy organization will thus begin with a presentation of the 1976 tripartism debate, and then relate the debate to the liberal-pluralist and corporatist views of the role of the state and to the relationship between economic management and the instruments of governing.

THE TRIPARTISM DEBATE

While vestiges of formal tripartism have been present in earlier experiments with the National Productivity Council, the Economic Council of Canada, and the several efforts at voluntary price-and-wage guidelines, the 1976 debate can be traced more specifically to the October 1975 Anti-Inflation program and to Prime Minister Trudeau's New Year interviews and speeches in which he spoke of the inadequacy of traditional economic-management methods and of the need to rethink economic values in the coming "post-controls" society.[1] The so-called prime ministerial "musings" brought forth an immediate and frequently shrill response especially from organized labour, primarily through the Canadian Labour Congress, and from the business community and its organizations. The subsequent focus on Tripartism can best be analysed by briefly outlining the positions adopted by the CLC, by what we will call the "marketeers", and by the federal Liberal government.

The CLC Manifesto

As Chapter 2 pointed out, the CLC has been historically (and still is) a highly decentralized national federation of trade unions. Its leadership must maintain a delicate balance between powerful locals and international unions, between industrial and craft unions, between Quebec and English-Canadian unions, and more recently between rapidly growing public-sector unions and private-sector membership. It has historically sought political influence through its alliance with the New Democratic party and through indirect efforts to pressure governments into employment, labour market, occupational, health, and social policies favourable to its membership and to its view of the public interest. The CLC's *Labour's Manifesto for Canada*, adopted at its May 1976 convention in Quebec City thus marks a sharp break, at least in theory, from its traditional political strategy. Because the CLC has become the most specific proponent of a form of tripartism, its position regarding the reform of economic-policy organization should be presented first, albeit briefly.

The CLC Manifesto advocates a form of tripartism because it strongly perceives that the Trudeau government is itself moving towards such a centralized concept. Thus the Manifesto asserts:

> Logic drives us to the conclusion that the government is moving into a new era in which the institutions of this country are going to change. National planning or social and economic issues demand strong central powers. The question for

the CLC is whether it wishes to be in the forefront in planning the structure of the future in the way in which it believes will best serve the workers' interests or not. The game is dangerous but the stakes are high. It is really not a question of "co-operating" with the government but one of strength and bargaining ability—of which the labour movement has both.[2]

The CLC's concept of tripartism is based on certain conditions, namely that of a *full* partnership status (with government and business), and that business management gives up its unilateral right to determine investment and pricing policies. Without these principles the CLC argues that it "would indeed be using the union organization as an arm of both business and government to restrain the workers".[3]

The delicate balance between the CLC's desire to achieve a form of social democratic society and to avoid corporatism is revealed when the Manifesto observes:

Nevertheless, this is not to say that tripartism or the equal sharing of all powers between labour, business and government should not be an objective of labour since the wresting of power away from business and its government in the interests of labour is our legitimate goal. This is the price industry and government must pay.[4]

The CLC sees the post-controls period as being an evolution towards a kind of "liberal corporatism" in which one form of income control is merely replaced by another. It does not foresee a return to the pre-controls "normalcy" coveted by "liberal economists".[5]

In discussions in June and July 1976 with Prime Minister Trudeau and senior Cabinet ministers, the CLC proposed the creation of a new tripartite council for economic and social planning which would be responsible through a minister to Parliament.[6] The council would recommend aggregate allocations of incomes, preview draft legislation, review current practice, and recommend improvements to law and practice. In addition to the overall council there would be boards and agencies reporting to the tripartite council, including, for example, a labour market board with responsibilities for the timing of some public investment and contract allocations. A tripartite council with such administrative, regulatory, and expenditure powers would clearly go well beyond the powers of the Economic Council of Canada, or any other mechanism of mere consultation.

The Marketeers

The analysis in this book ought to make it patently obvious that it is dangerous to characterize almost any group in Canada as being a pure spokesman for the "marketeer" position. The analysis of regional policy, employment policy, competition policy, and industrial strategies in Part III shows clearly the existence in Canada of only a highly selective adherence to the market, all rhetoric to the contrary notwithstanding. Nonetheless, it is important to see the tripartism debate in relation to those whom we will call the "marketeers" in that their views lean more generally to a market-based interpretation of economic reality.

The response of the marketeers to the post-controls tripartism debate has been to call for a return not just to the trappings of the pre-control period but rather to an even earlier period where government expenditures would not be permitted to grow more rapidly than general economic productivity, where public-sector collective bargaining would be constrained, and where monetary and fiscal policy would encourage the private market economy to generate wealth, growth, jobs, and hopefully, greater price stability.

The marketeers, as we have stressed, are not a homogeneous group. They range from "monetarists" such as the newly formed Fraser Institute,[7] to the more moderate parts of the business community whose spokesmen include such former senior civil servants as D. M. Mundy, now President of the Air Industries Association, and Simon Reisman, the former Deputy Minister of Finance, who is now an Ottawa consultant. Mundy has publicly pleaded that if secondary industry

> is the foundation on which our future, including social security programs, have to be built... [the] business community doesn't see any real evidence as yet that there is recognition in Ottawa of this essential fact.[8]

Reisman called for an early end to the controls program. Attempting to refute the Galbraithian characterization of contemporary western economics, Reisman asserted that he did not believe there had been fundamental changes in the structure of the economic system over recent decades. He placed the root cause of the economic malaise to "the failure... to maintain sound economic management through the proper use of fiscal and monetary policy".[9] He also related future controls, including by inference a formal tripartite mechanism, to the basic freedoms of liberal democracy. Thus, Reisman declared:

> More important than the damage to economic efficiency is the loss of freedom which a control system entails. Over the years we have witnessed increasing state encroachment in many aspects of society. The complexity of modern living makes a larger and more ubiquitous state inevitable in certain respects. But none of these, I contend, touches the lives of ordinary people in so fundamental a manner as wage and price controls—if maintained beyond a relatively short period. Their permanent use would deliver a vital blow to the very innards of our free society. Indeed, the ultimate result would, in my view, be an authoritarian political system ruled by force.[10]

Reisman's only concession to tripartism is his suggestion that a tripartite body is needed to help control the public sector, particularly in respect of work stoppages and the remuneration of public-sector employees in essential industries.

In discussions with business leaders, the Prime Minister encountered strong opposition to the idea of a tripartite council especially one with strong administrative powers. If such mechanisms are created, business opinion was clearly of the view that they ought to be "multi-partite" reflecting such other sectors as small business, consumers, agriculture, and provincial governments. Thus the strong preference in the business community was for new consultative mechanisms but certainly not mechanisms in which power would be shared equally with labour and governments.

This "marketeer" position is quite consistent with the evolution of earlier approaches to public-private sector consultation and consensus analysed in Chapter 12 and with the department-level arrangements examined in our analysis of IT&C, DREE, CCA, and the Department and Commission of Employment and Immigration. Thus the opposition to formal entrenched tripartism by the marketeers is partly a historical reflection of the usual struggle between the power of capital and the power of labour, and partly a more pragmatic belief that a central tripartite institution could not and should not accommodate all the micro-level conflicts inherent in economic management, especially those analysed in Part III.

The Liberal View

The Liberal government's position represented an evolving compromise between Prime Minister Trudeau's original New Year's observations, the more conservative elements of the Liberal Cabinet and the internal pressures from the left wing of the Cabinet. It also reflected the growing popularity of the Progressive Conservative party in 1976. The Prime Minister's original observations, as he readily acknowledged, owed an intellectual debt to Galbraith. As pointed out in Chapter 2, Trudeau characterized the economy in ways largely similar to Galbraith's identification of the planning (non-competitive) sector and the competitive sector. In the planning sector, big industry and big labour were in league with each other at least in so far as their ability to be immune from normal market forces is concerned. Thus Trudeau agreed that a significant contributory or causal factor in contemporary inflation was the market power of big industry and big labour.[11] Even implicitly Trudeau seemed to be following Galbraith's own transformation. Galbraith had, in his earlier writings, seen the tripartite struggle between big government, labour, and industry in more benevolent terms as being a largely beneficial balance of countervailing powers.[12]

That explicit Galbraithian views should be publicly acknowledged is partly a reflection of Trudeau's habit of "thinking out loud", an almost academic-seminar style. It would be misleading, however, to confine the emergence of Galbraithian views only to the peculiar habits of the Prime Minister. They also arose, albeit much less explicitly, in other sectors of the evolving federal economic-management system which we have analysed in earlier chapters. Thus, ministers and senior officials with any experience in the recently emerging, but still subordinate, economic portfolios such as DREE, Consumer and Corporate Affairs, and Manpower and Immigration did not have to be unrepentant Galbraithians to feel that more traditional explanations of our economic malaise were simply not a full reflection of the causal factors in the Canadian political economy. Thus the evolving institutional structure and value obligations over which these ministers and officials had formal custody would help create a climate of receptivity for the Galbraithian and other related non-Keynesian and non-monetarist explanations of the economic puzzle.

No one who had been part of, or had seen, the cumulative evolution of the new economic portfolios and of the attempt to conceptualize and operationalize the regional, industrial, competition, and employment policies, not to mention the traditional levers of economic policy, could fail to see at least some truth in the Galbraithian point of view.

That these views were not adopted in their entirety became obvious as the Liberal Cabinet responded to its own internal left-wing pressures, and as it received the papers churned out by "DM Ten", the committee of ten senior deputy ministers created early in 1976 to prepare policy options for the post-controls period.

Thus the October 1976 Speech from the Throne tended to lean a little more towards the marketeers than Trudeau's January speeches had done, but it concluded with a statement which is a classic summation of both the vague Liberal governing strategy as well as of the ideological, bureaucratic, and theoretical issues which had evolved in the Canadian system of economic management:

> It is essential to the enhancement of unity, equality of opportunity and individual freedom that Canadians work together in a spirit of co-operation and mutual respect. To that end, it is important for all participants to have a well defined view of their respective roles in the pursuit of national objectives.
>
> It is appropriate therefore to define the role of government in economic and social planning and action. There are some who acknowledge only a very limited role for government, believing that the market system allocates resources most efficiently for production and growth, is least wasteful and most conducive to individual liberty and initiative.
>
> That view is vigorously opposed by those who insist on a continually expanding role for government in directing economic growth, correcting the inadequacies of the market system and assuring a socially acceptable distribution of incomes. This view asserts that government must increase to compensate for the failure of the market to serve social goals.
>
> The Government favors a middle road between those two extremes. This middle road represents a commitment to a society in which all Canadians can develop their full potential. . . .[13]

The middle-of-the-road position was more elaborately defended in the subsequent federal working paper, *The Way Ahead: A Framework For Discussion*, which the Liberal Government circulated to various interest groups, governments, and opinion leaders as a basis for consultation on the post-controls so-called "new society". Thus, on the one hand, the monetarists and related excessive government-spending advocates of the causes of inflation are viewed as extreme:

> The notion that inflation results from excessive government spending is a popular one and, indeed, there may be instances where governments must bear a large share of the responsibility for inflation. To diagnose the inflationary spiral we have recently experienced as largely attributable to a profligate government, however, is simplistic to the point that it is misleading. Such a diagnosis ignores the fact that all industrialized democracies have experienced gradually increasing inflation for at least the last three decades. Most fundamentally, it ignores the institutions that make up the Canadian economy and the complex relationships that define Canadian society.
>
> To understand the inflationary process, and the issues surrounding the role that governments play in that process, it is necessary to examine those aspects of our social and economic structure that lead to inflation directly or indirectly through demands on government—to spend money and to intervene in the economic system. The existence of market power, declining productivity growth and rising expectations, Canada's role in the world economy, economic growth itself and the issues it raises, all contribute to the nature of the role that government plays in the economy and the responsibility that the government bears for inflation.[14]

The document then goes on to stress the Galbraithian market-power thesis but concedes to the marketeers the fact that "administered prices" are also a problem in the public sector, particularly in the light of public-sector collective bargaining. Later, the Liberal government reaffirms its faith in the utility of the market:

> The market economy, and the price system on which it rests, is the most efficient allocative mechanism available. The billions of daily decisions that are freely taken by individuals and together comprise a viable, functioning economy make it obvious that any alternative to the market system would require a massive bureaucracy to administer with the unacceptable result of diminution in individual freedom of action and choice.[15]

The Liberal view thus sees the "middle-road" role of government in the post-control period after 1978 as being one which requires support policies to deal with the underlying causes of the economic malaise. It asserts that governments must fulfill their legitimate responsibilities but must do so "with less rather than more, direct intervention in the economic system".[16] Such policies, it suggests, "must provide effective alternatives to increasing expenditures and expanding bureaucracies".[17]

Two essential features follow from the above policy ambivalence: first, a commitment to a mixed economy; and second, a policy of reprivatization, i.e., a policy of shifting increased "responsibilities" from the public to the private sector. These two commitments provide the central features of the strategies outlined in the paper in (i) employment policies; (ii) social policies; (iii) labour-management relations; (iv) "social responsibility"; (v) decentralization; (vi) growth; and (vii) investment.[18]

Each component in the document reflects quite vividly the evolution of economic-management issues analysed in earlier chapters of this book. Brief concluding comments will help demonstrate the intractable dilemmas of economic management contained within the document and in the context of which the tripartism debate can be seen, and criticized, both generally and specifically.

Employment Policies Governmental involvement in the manpower field as we have examined, intensified in the early and mid-1960s in response to major technological changes and criticisms of labour-market policies. The government provided training and mobility grants to assist adversely affected workers. These expenditures together with significant increases in unemployment insurance allowances began to place severe expenditure and political strains on the government. Consequently, instead of operating on the supply side, i.e., aiding people to get jobs, the emphasis in *The Way Ahead* has now shifted to job creation particularly for specific groups such as women, students, and native peoples. The new strategy attempts to create jobs by operating through the private sector, and hence by supporting the private sector in the creation of jobs.

Social Policies The governments' 1973 position on social policy had been outlined in Marc Lalonde's proposals which advocated programs to assure minimum levels of income to those who cannot work, or whose work income is inadequate and to provide greater access to basic services. An earlier proposal to reorient social policy had tried to transfer baby bonuses from families earning over $10,000 per annum to those earning between $3,000 and $9,999 had encountered stiff criticism. Present social policies are also now being used to ameliorate regional disparities. The references in *The Way Ahead* to food and energy policies and the necessity to integrate income transfers with the tax system are indications of an attempt to mix expenditure and regulatory devices to aid social redistribution.

Labour-Management Relations Policies Governmental involvement as we have seen in Chapter 10 is now being strengthened because of rising wages and low productivity. The working paper declares a commitment to the collective-bargaining system accompanied by strong exhortations to improve productivity in Canada. The government seems, in this regard, to be directing more emphasis to the private sector. Thus employers are asked to become "more responsive to demands for high standards of industrial health and safety and to be more sensitive to the overall quality of the working environment". Employees, on the other hand, "must become more aware that continued employment opportunities depend upon the continued viability and profitability of the enterprise."

Social Responsibility In this realm the working paper emphasizes the social responsibilities of both individuals and institutions. Here the exhortations range from the development of better information and public and private accounting practices, which will hopefully make social costs more visible, to the establishment of co-operatives, voluntary organizations, and the provision that goods, which are presently provided by the public sector, be transferred to the private sector; all these endeavours are directed at achieving a greater sense of sharing, compassion, tolerance, and responsibility in Canadian society.

Decentralization The Government of Canada seems to have discovered that decentralization can be used as a device to achieve both public- and private-sector responsibility and accountability. Decentralization is seen in an economic sense when it is used for the reorganization of Canadian industries similar to the position which emerged out of the Western Economic Opportunities Conferences held in 1973. To this end, there has been an attempt to elaborate a consistent and comprehensive small-firm development strategy (a small-business policy). The approach advocates closer federal-provincial collaboration. However, when related to the employment strategy, we detect a shift toward increased involvement in community participation and decision-making. Here decentralization takes on more of a sociological approach.

Growth The 1960s saw strong emphasis on growth. While the working paper still emphasizes growth, there is some concern for the social "costs" of development. The strategy seems to be shifting toward a more "conserver society". It advocates a stronger "guidance role" for the government in the existing and emerging situation.

Investment The government seems to be supporting stronger measures to encourage domestic savings which in turn would facilitiate greater investment. Large investments are required to support the energy and transportation policies. This was reflected in changes in the anti-inflation programs to encourage new investment.

The working paper concluded with a declared need for more effective means of consultation in the decision-making process. The Liberal view did not advocate formal tripartism. The working paper was prepared after negotiations with the CLC on its tripartite proposals were well under way. In both earlier and subsequent statements government ministers and the Prime Minister were careful to reject the notion of formal tripartism, in the form advocated by the CLC, as being contrary to the basic tenets of Liberal parliamentary democracy. Only the Department of Labour has publicly been more favourably disposed to tripartism, primarily because it does not agree that labour in Canada, because of its fragmented structure, can be accurately called "big" labour.

That both the marketeers, the CLC, and the Liberal government views have been influenced by comparative developments in other countries is obvious. The social democratic, pro-tripartite, advocates see the success of the West German and Swedish systems of economic management and industrial democracy as being living proof of the proper road to economic health. The evolution of the Labour government–Trade Union Congress "social contract" in the U.K. is also seen as the way of the future despite Britain's economic woes. The marketeers see the U.K. as evidence of why a return to market incentives and forces is essential. Liberal government advisors have also been influenced not only by the evolution of the economic-management issues analysed in earlier chapters, but also by the more recent explicit exposure of senior officials to the ideas of European industrial democracy[19] and to analyses of the British economy which point out that the aggregate level of the growth of the public sector in Canada is approaching that of the U.K. presumably with all the accompanying disincentives it places on the individual's, particularly the worker's, take-home, discretionary income.[20]

Our analysis indicates that tripartism as well as other central aspects of economic management portrayed in *The Way Ahead* will have to confront a number of propositions which we think emerge from the political and organizational focus of this book. First, as noted in Chapter 13, there is a significant implementation lag in economic management. This lag has been identified by others in discussions of monetary and fiscal policy but it also applies to other aspects of economic policy. It clearly is related to the power of groups and interests which can alter significantly the intent of policy makers.

It is also caused by the fact that new policy structures and organizations have taken about ten years to mature and learn. While many policy initiatives began with apparent ambitions of comprehensiveness, the larger reality of politics and organization seems invariably to require the serial incremental treatment of problems and hence attention to the micro level detail predominates. But the most fundamental issues of economic management and planning are macro in nature, and progress, while real, has been extraordinarily slow. This proposition has been supported by comparative studies in planning and economic management. It suggests that far greater political effort must be made to understand and develop the central conflict and consensus institutions and the role governments must perform in this process.

This need is especially imposed by the realities of so-called supply management where governments have, until recently, been largely reacting to rather than anticipating problems. Weaknesses are especially apparent in longer term, capital-investment decisions both within government, and between central agencies and Crown corporations. In contrast to the thoughts expressed in *The Way Ahead*, these weaknesses suggest a far greater regulatory and interventionist role for government.

LIBERALISM, PLURALISM, CORPORATISM, AND ECONOMIC MANAGEMENT

The concepts, structures, and processes of Canadian economic management obviously reached a new plateau in the events of late 1975 and the tripartism debate which followed. It is important to relate tripartism not only to the evolving machinery of economic management but also to the broader competing concepts and characterizations of the role of the state which we discussed earlier in the book, but which emerged in many ways in Part III, in the specific policy fields encompassed by economic management. Thus the relationship of the 1976 debate and of the evolution of the organization of economic management should be examined in relation to the concepts of liberalism, pluralism, and corporatism, and to the realities and values inherent in federalism and parliamentary-Cabinet government. Efforts in the evolving process of economic management to conceptualize the regional, industrial, employment, fiscal, and competition policy fields, to name but a few, are also an inherent and increasingly explicit attempt to re-examine the contemporary meaning of these several views of the role of the state.

The controls program and the tripartism debate prompted a number of immediate academic analyses which suggested that they lead Canada on the road to corporatism. Avoiding a form of what it called "liberal corporatism" was certainly a main feature of the CLC Manifesto, but the CLC fear was also quickly articulated by scholars such as Donald Smiley and J. T. McLeod.

Smiley distinguished two alternatives which he designated as the "plebiscitary" and "corporatist" options:

> A plebiscitary regime is one in which those who wield final and authoritative political power are exclusively sustained by and restrained by the wills of individual citizens without the mediation of either private groups or of governmental institutions less immediately responsive to citizen opinion. Corporatism involves the absorption of the major social and economic institutions of the national community into the appartus of the state.[21]

For Smiley, the movement towards corporatism, Trudeau's disavowals to the contrary notwithstanding, can be traced to even earlier steps by the Trudeau government in such non-economic fields as youth-employment grants, research, and subsidies for public interest groups. He feels that as a result there are few "genuinely private varieties of associational life", and clearly prefers the plebiscitary regime.[22]

J. T. McLeod suggests that the two options may not be options but rather dual paths along which the Trudeau government might proceed concurrently at least in the short run.[23] As pointed out in Chapter 2,

McLeod tends to see a drift towards corporatism but sees this as being largely a confirmation of the historic forces of the Canadian political economy. He thus views the corporatist tendencies as being largely, though not exactly, similar to the political economic characteristics analysed earlier by Innis, S. D. Clark, and Alexander Brady, and to the more recent work of Presthus and Nelles. Thus he asserts:

> To a very considerable extent Canadians have long been familiar with a political economy which reflects the essentials of corporatism, namely state control and private ownership.[24]

As pointed out earlier Canada's political characteristics have been characterized not only as liberal democratic (or plebiscitary) and corporatist but also as being pluralist or quasi-pluralist. The latter sees the basis of politics as being considerably influenced by interest-groups bargaining. While it is clear that Canada's pluralist tendencies are not equal to those of the United States, it would be both naive and inaccurate to argue that it can be ignored as an important force. The CLC and the Canadian labour movement for example, have historically exercised influence both through the NDP and through direct representation to government. In this specific sense Smiley's plebiscitary model is an abstraction of reality and tripartism does not become such a sharp break with the characteristics of Canadian politics, since such groups have formed an intermediary layer between government and citizen.

In other respects, however, Smiley and others are right to express profound concern about the impact of tripartism, on the basic concept of Cabinet government. The CLC Manifesto and the subsequent CLC proposals virtually ignore the concept of Cabinet and parliamentary government. The Trudeau government has rejected the CLC tripartite council not only on constitutional grounds but also because of the internal realities of economic management within the Cabinet. The Social and Economic Planning Council, and its attendant agencies, would give to its minister a power which would challenge the evolving balance of departmental power and would prove intolerable to senior ministers. It is not accidental that only the Minister of Labour, the custodian of an agency which has declined in influence because of the emergence of newer economic portfolios, should be virtually the only minister who sees more advantages than disadvantages to formal tripartism.

The liberal, pluralist, and corporatist interpretation of Canadian political economy have been based on a wide variety of empirical factors, methodologies, and assumptions, including broad historical analyses, leadership studies and biographies, survey techniques, and case studies. They have not usually been developed in the light of an analysis of the evolution of government departments, organizations, and agencies, nor by looking at the processes in the context of governing. The latter approach, as adopted in this book, can distort reality, and ought not be the only perspective adopted. We think, however, that it can greatly assist analysis and understanding as a complementary approach to the study of the Canadian political economy. In the context of liberalism, pluralism, and corporatism, several implications of our analysis can be examined.

At first glance, our analysis of the evolution of economic-management portfolios and departments would suggest a gradual pluralist unfolding of the recognition and institutionalization of values and groups who have pressed their claims on successive governments. Thus regional development, industry, consumer affairs, and manpower "mandates" have gained Cabinet-level recognition. The proliferation of portfolios also suggests the existence of a more diffuse division of power and influence within the Cabinet and hence the "pluralization" of economic management. Our analysis also suggests the existence of a form of pluralism in which successive attempts at conceptualizing economic issues (e.g., regional policy, employment policy, incomes policy) not only compete in total for political attention in a highly competitive way, but also reflect *within* each category, the pluralism engendered by the public-private and intergovernmental divisions of the Canadian political economy.

While the above intra-Cabinet, organizational, and conceptual pluralism can be detected from our approach it is essential to keep in mind the hierarchical characteristics of economic management and of Cabinet government, and that this pluralism has occurred within governments that have been liberal in ideology. That the Finance department still plays the lead role in economic management is obvious. That the emergence of the PMO and the PCO helps strengthen prime-ministerial power in the management of the government is less obvious but probably true. The historic and continuing preference of Finance portfolios for basic monetary and Keynesian concepts and instruments of economic management and their preference for using the business enterprise as the focus of insuring appropriate changes in economic behaviour, provides some evidence for those who see a corporatist evolution of Canada.

The previously noted analyses by political economists, the CLC Manifesto, and even the Liberal government's 1976 Working Paper all seem to grossly under-emphasize the role of federalism as a potential counterweight to the evolution of both tripartism and corporatism. While federalism and capitalism are clearly related in that both have the effect of dividing and dispersing public power, the federal nature of Canadian politics and economic management may itself create real and desirable obstacles to corporatism, intended or unintended. Our detailed analysis of economic management shows clearly how federal-provincial conflict over revenue and expenditure decisions, supply and demand issues, foreign investment, regional development, and manpower and employment policies have pervaded the economic-policy process. Canadian political history is generally a testament to the continuing strength of provincial governments and political parties, not only those reinforced by Quebec's cultural and linguistic desire for independence and Ontario's economic hegemony, but also by the emergence of NDP governments in the west and by Alberta's growing economic power. These factors are themselves also reflected in a body like the Canadian Labour Congress. The CLC has been and still is a fragmented federation. It faces enormous difficulties and pressures from within and cannot acquire a centralized power, or wield it legitimately, over its own membership except perhaps over a very long period of time and after accumulating experience. It is not equivalent to, nor has it the political cohesiveness of, the British Trade Union Congress.

POLITICS, THE INSTRUMENTS OF GOVERNING, AND ECONOMIC MANAGEMENT

We have earlier advanced the argument that the politics of economic management, in addition to dealing with the allocation of goals and values also involved the selection by politicians of the instruments of governing through which compliance and/or support is sought. At the most general level these instruments include exhortation, expenditure incentives, and regulations. Within each of these broad categories there are of course much finer graduations of choice. We have examined these in Chapter 3 where the specific organizational reflection of the myriad detailed instruments were examined. We have also seen in several chapters in Part III, the more specific shifts that occur, for example, in expenditure policies, between grants, subsidies, conditional grants, loans, and investments. Thus the relationships between governing instruments, political and economic management must be seen in both the macro and micro contexts.

At the macro level, however, we feel there are at least three ways in which the concept of governing instruments can aid in understanding the politics and management of Canadian economic-policy processes and consequences. Each way deals with a different time dimension of political behaviour. First, in Chapters 2 and 3 we related governing instruments to the annual priority-setting process of government within which the fiscal and expenditure budget is subsumed. In Chapters 2, 8, 12, and 13 we have utilized a hypothesis of movement along a continuum of governing instruments as a way of helping to explain the evolution of a single policy field over a medium-term time frame (perhaps four or five years). Finally, we think it is helpful to suggest the existence of a *market* in governing instruments in which governing politicians trade. While the supply-and-demand configurations of the market can change in the short run it will be suggested that the market concept may help understand longer term relative shifts in the governmental preference for, need for, and supply of, the major instruments of governing. We will briefly offer some concluding observations about each of these ways, in which a general concept of governing instruments might be used.

market governing instruments

Governing Instruments and the Annual Priority-Setting Process

Governments have always had to develop ways in which their annual priorities could be determined. As we have seen in recent years, especially in the federal government, the priority-setting process has assumed somewhat more visibility and formality because of the establishment of the Cabinet Committee on Planning and Priorities chaired by the Prime Minister, the changes to the Cabinet committee system, and the designation of A, B, and X Budgets. The priority-setting process is closely tied to the budgetary process and to the central processes of economic management. These processes, as explained earlier, have the advantage of being convertible into the common coinage of money.

While the economic and budgetary processes are the most normal and visible rhythms of behaviour in government, not all of the priority-setting process can be understood or readily recognized under these processes. For example, let us assume again, as we did in Chapter 2, that the Cabinet, through its priority-setting exercises determines that the government's priorities are (hypothetically) as follows: the reduction of inflation; the promotion of national unity through language policy; the reduction of regional disparities; the re-equipment of the armed forces; and the improvement of competition in the economy.

The political realities of governing are such that not all of these priorities have equal regulatory, expenditure, or general economic consequences. For example, the first priority "might" be expressed through regulatory means by creating an Anti-Inflation Board. While the use of the regulatory instrument would have enormous *private*-expenditure impact, it would not have an impact on the government's expenditure budget, other than the increased cost of running the board. The second priority might be achieved by increasing the spending (through provincial governments) on language programs in primary and secondary schools. The third might be promoted by altering the regulation of transportation freight rates. The fourth priority would require an expenditure of, let us say, one billion dollars. The fifth priority would be recognized by creating a royal commission on corporate concentration, a kind of symbolic but fairly inexpensive governing response.

The Continuum of Governing Instruments

We have utilized a hypothesis suggested by Doern and Wilson that politically, especially in a federal, liberal democratic political system, there may be a strong tendency for the federal government to respond to a policy issue by moving successively along a continuum of governing instruments beginning with exhortation and then proceeding as and if necessary, through the use of expenditure and regulatory instruments, the latter in particular being more coercive in nature. In Chapter 12 we also related the continuum to the more visible use of reorganization as an explicit instrument of governing.

We believe that in the areas of economic management in general, but especially in the recent evolution of incomes policy, there is evidence to support this hypothesis. The Liberal government's response to inflation in the late 1960s and 1970s has been one in which a prices and incomes commission in 1969 was created and followed by at least two major efforts to exhort voluntary compliance. This was followed by, and was at times concurrent with, expenditure policies aimed at specific groups disproportionately weakened by inflation or unstable incomes, and finally, even after electoral rejection of the concepts in 1974, by direct controls (albeit confined to the largest industries, unions, and sectors of the economy).

We also advanced the argument in Chapter 13 that explanations of the growth of public spending would be politically incomplete, unless spending as a governing instrument were related to the realities of governing and to federalism. These suggest that movement along the continuum may be aided by federalism particularly in view of the comparative ease and political advantages of federal spending over other instruments of possible federal intervention. Thus the concept of a continuum was stressed as a middle-level variable, which, when combined with other macro-level variables, would offer a more satisfactory explanation of expenditure growth.

Is the hypothesis about the continuum of governing instruments and the use of instruments one which is endemic to liberal systems of government? Perhaps it is. For one thing one can apply it in Canada at the federal level only to governments which have been small "l" liberal, since liberal governments are what Canada has historically had. Others could argue that it is a behavioural tendency inherent in, and a desirable feature of, Canadian democratic, brokerage politics. Psychologically, and politically it may merely conform to a normal desire by both governors and the governed to be subject to a governing process which first tries the more pleasant means of persuasion, exhortation, and spending and only reluctantly accepts the bitter bill of direct regulation.

The hypothesis remains only a hypothesis about *single* policy fields which, in the case of recent incomes policy, seems to have been confirmed. Whether it is an accurate statement of tendency in other policy fields remains to be seen. We do strongly suggest, however, that our *political* understanding of both past and future economic management can be aided by an analysis of governing instruments and the role they play in political choice. While the use and sequential timing of governing instruments is undoubtedly influenced by the broader political ideologies of governments, we think that they have a partly *independent* causal influence of their own and that future economic management will be significantly affected by them. This independence arises from the realities of *governing*.

The Market for Governing Instruments

In governing as in other human activities there is, to borrow the economists central concept, a market. More specifically, there is an available market of governing instruments which we have simplified to include exhortation, expenditure, and regulation. Within each of these categories there are, of course, finer sub-categories of choice. When governing politicians run out of, or experience a reduced supply of, one instrument, they will turn to other instruments. Thus when the pleasant form of governing by expenditure is less readily available then governing politicians will turn to other forms, namely, exhortation and/or regulation. These choices are there primarily because the choice of doing absolutely nothing is not usually tolerated in modern politics.

Those who see the post-controls period of economic management as being ripe for the emergence of corporatism, the replacement of one form of controls with another, and a growing authoritarian presence, may find their concerns about future economic management reinforced by the concept of governing instruments enunciated above.

That the Trudeau government's 1976 Working Paper concluded with a call for systematic consultative processes is not surprising. It's declared intention to meet its priorities "in a less expenditure-oriented and interventionist manner"[25] is, however, only partly true. The use of the expenditure instrument will probably decline (although even this is debatable given the strength of the broader social and political forces which influence expenditure growth) but *intervention* will not. There is a far higher probability that the use of direct regulation will increase as the means of intervention in the post-controls period since it is more reliable than voluntary methods based on exhortation. The working paper itself gives examples of the increase in the political market for regulatory instruments. Thus as we have seen in this and earlier chapters there are clear suggestions that unemployment insurance funds rather than being merely allocated, will be tied, via new regulatory requirements, to manpower training and community employment schemes, and that income transfers will be tied more closely to the tax system.[26] Similarly more regulatory intervention is implied to constrain public-sector collective bargaining, to insure better standards of occupational health and safety in the workplace, and to decentralize public bureaucracies.[27]

The dilemmas of contemporary Canadian economic management were perhaps best summarized in a recent speech by an economist, John Helliwell, at the March 1977 Liberal party policy convention. In Helliwell's view:

> . . . no one has the power to manage the economy. Does this not conflict with the common observation that we are confronted on all sides with larger and more powerful groupings in government, industries, unions, and elsewhere in Canada and abroad? In my view, the key to this apparent contradiction lies in the increasingly complicated, specialized and interdependent nature of our economy. This interdependence means that more and more groups have the power to damage the economy in crucial ways, while fewer and fewer groups have the power to guarantee complete performance of anything. Power is increasingly defined in negative terms, and is used out of frustration. If the counterproductive results of this are not to overwhelm us, then solutions must be found that give individuals and groups more positive power (or capacity) to accomplish their jobs, and reduce their use of negative power to frustrate the legitimate aspirations of others. Governments and private groups alike must have the capacity to do what they are asked to do; must be held accountable for the use of the power they possess; and must not be held responsible for that which they have no capacity to achieve.[28]

The comment reveals some truth but greatly distorts other truths. What is "negative" or "positive" power depends greatly on the eyes of the beholder. The implication that, in an earlier era, "someone" did have the power to manage the economy can be viewed favourably or unfavourably depending upon how one viewed such persons or groups and towards what ends such power was exercised. And how can the suggested new systems of accountability, many of which are undoubtedly necessary, be arranged except through the orchestration of the state, through some mechanism of democratic politics.

As with all contemporary exercises of economic management the real point of recent history is not whether governmental intervention will occur but rather in which form, through which instruments, in the pursuit of which values, and in whose interests will the interventions occur. A decision to not act is itself a form of intervention. The politics of economic management, the evolution of economic portfolios, and the realities of governing, especially in a Cabinet-parliamentary and federal system of government, make non-intervention a non-existent option.

NOTES

1. See *The Globe and Mail*, January 8, 1976, p. 7.

2. Canadian Labour Congress, *Labour's Manifesto for Canada* (Ottawa, 1976), p. 11. See also Joseph Morris, Presidential Address to the Convention of the Canadian Labour Congress, Quebec City, May 17, 1976.

3. CLC, *Labour's Manifesto for Canada*, p. 10.

4. Ibid.

5. Ibid., p. 6.

6. *The Globe and Mail*, October 14, 1976, p. 133.

7. See the Fraser Institute, *The Illusion of Price and Wage Controls* (Vancouver, 1976).

8. Quoted in *The Globe and Mail*, September 14, 1976, p. 132.

9. *The Globe and Mail*, October 8, 1976, p. 7.

10. Ibid.

11. *The Globe and Mail*, January 8, 1976, p. 7.

12. See John K. Galbraith, *The New Industrial State* (London, 1972), *The Public Purpose* (Bergenfield, N.J., 1973), and *Money* (London, 1975).

13. Speech from the Throne, excerpted in *The Globe and Mail*, October 13, 1976, p. 7.

14. Government of Canada, *The Way Ahead: A Framework for Discussion* (Ottawa, 1976), pp. 15-16.

15. Ibid., p. 19.

16. Ibid., p. 24.

17. Ibid.

18. Ibid., pp. 24-32.

19. See *Report of the Committee of Inquiry on Industrial Democracy* (London, 1977).

20. See Robert Bacon and Walter Ellis, *Britain's Economic Problems: Too Few Producers* (London, 1976).

21. D. V. Smiley, "The Non Economics of Anti-Inflation", in K. J. Rea and J. T. McLeod, eds., *Business and Government in Canada*, second ed. (Toronto, 1976), p. 445.

22. Ibid., p. 446.

23. J. T. McLeod, "The Free Enterprise Dodo is No Phoenix", *Canadian Forum*, Vol. LVI, no. 663 (August 1976), pp. 6-10. Both Smiley and McLeod, as well as Presthus, define "corporatism" in a very general way. If corporatism is defined in more precise terms analogous to historic and some current European experience than the Canadian links to corporatism are less in evidence. See L. Panitch, "The Development of Corporatism in Liberal Democracies". Paper presented to the American Political Science Association, Chicago, September 2, 1976, p. 13.

24. Ibid., p. 8. See also Rea and McLeod, eds., *Business and Government in Canada*, pp. 334-45.

25. *The Way Ahead*, p. 32.

26. Ibid., pp. 24-26.

27. Ibid., pp. 27-29.

28. John F. Helliwell, "Managing the Economy". Speech to the Liberal Party Conference in Toronto, March 1977, p. 2.

Appendices

APPENDIX A
Primary Indicators of Canadian Economy

YEAR	*Gross Nat. Expend. in 1971 Dollars- % Change*	*Unemployment Rate* Canada	Atlantic Region	Quebec	Ontario	Prairie Region	B.C.	*Price Index*	*Fed. Exp'trs surplus or Deficit*
1947	—	2.2	—	—	—	—	—	49.0	687
1948	2.5	2.3	—	—	—	—	—	56.2	765
1949	3.8	2.8	—	—	—	—	—	57.9	484
1950	7.6	3.6	—	—	—	—	—	59.6	650
1951	5.0	2.4	—	—	—	—	—	65.9	971
1952	8.9	2.9	—	—	—	—	—	67.5	195
1953	5.1	3.0	—	—	—	—	—	66.9	151
1954	−1.2	4.6	6.6	5.9	3.8	2.5	5.2	67.3	−46
1955	9.4	4.4	6.5	6.2	3.2	3.1	3.8	67.5	202
1956	8.4	3.4	6.0	5.0	2.4	2.2	2.8	68.4	598
1957	2.4	4.6	8.4	6.0	3.4	2.6	5.0	70.6	250
1958	2.3	7.0	12.5	8.8	5.4	4.1	8.6	72.5	−767
1959	3.8	6.0	10.9	7.8	4.5	3.2	6.5	73.3	−339
1960	2.9	7.0	10.7	9.1	5.4	4.2	8.5	74.2	−229
1961	2.8	7.1	11.2	9.2	5.5	4.6	8.5	74.9	−410
1962	6.8	5.9	10.7	7.5	4.3	3.9	6.6	75.8	−507
1963	5.2	5.5	9.5	7.5	3.8	3.7	6.4	77.2	−286
1964	6.7	4.7	7.8	6.4	3.2	3.1	5.3	78.6	345
1965	6.7	3.9	7.4	5.4	2.5	2.5	4.2	80.5	544
1966	6.9	3.6	6.4	4.7	2.5	2.1	4.5	83.5	231
1967	3.3	4.1	6.6	5.3	3.1	2.3	5.1	86.5	−84
1968	5.8	4.8	7.3	6.5	3.5	3.0	5.9	90.0	−11
1969	5.3	4.7	7.5	6.9	3.1	2.9	5.0	94.1	1,021
1970	2.5	5.9	7.6	7.9	4.3	4.4	7.6	97.2	266
1971	5.7	6.4	8.6	8.2	5.2	4.5	7.0	100.0	−145
1972	6.0	6.3	9.0	8.3	4.8	4.5	7.6	104.8	−600
1973	6.9	5.6	8.9	7.4	4.0	3.9	6.5	112.7	222
1974	2.8	5.4	9.7	7.3	4.1	2.8	6.0	125.0	593
1975	0.2	7.1	11.6	8.8	6.0	3.4	8.3	138.5	−4,504

Source: Department of Finance, *Economic Review,* April 1976, pp. 112, 147, 159, and 168.

APPENDIX B
Distribution of Total Family Incomes before Taxes, Selected Years, 1965-74

	Gini	Quintiles[1]					
	coefficient	*First*	*Second*	*Third*	*Fourth*	*Fifth*	*Total*
1965	.370	4.44	11.77	17.95	24.49	41.35	100
1967	.378	4.19	11.45	17.82	24.64	41.90	100
1969	.385	4.28	11.00	17.58	24.56	42.58	100
1971	.399	3.65	10.60	17.99	24.83	42.93	100
1973	.391	3.84	10.71	17.65	25.15	42.65	100
1974	.389	4.02	10.91	17.68	24.87	42.52	100

[1] All family units are divided into five quintiles, each representing 20 per cent of the total. The first quintile comprises families with the lowest incomes, and the fifth quintile comprises families with the highest incomes.

Source: Based on data from Statistics Canada (Surveys of Consumer Finances) and estimates by the Economic Council of Canada, *Thirteenth Annual Review*, 1976, p. 7.

APPENDIX C
Federal Economic Policy Leaders: 1940-1975*

Ministers of Finance since the Second World War.

Hon. J. L. Ilsley	1940 to 1946
Hon. D. C. Abbott	1946 to 1954
Hon. W. Harris	1954 to 1957
Hon. D. M. Fleming	1957 to 1962
Hon. G. C. Nowlan	1962 to 1963
Hon. W. I. Gordon	1963 to 1965
Hon. M. W. Sharp	1965 to 1968
Hon. E. J. Benson	1968 to 1972
Hon. J. N. Turner	1972 to 1975

Ministers of Industry, Trade and Commerce since the Second World War.

Hon. J. A. Mackinnon	1940 to 1948
Hon. C. D. Howe	1948 to 1957

*This list does not reflect ministerial and other changes caused by the resignation of Hon. John Turner late in 1975.

Hon. G. Churchill	1957 to 1960
Hon. G. Hees	1960 to 1963
Hon. M. Wallace McCutcheon	1963 to 1963
Hon. M. Sharp	1963 to 1965
Hon. R. H. Winters	1966 to 1968
Hon. C. M. Drury	1968 to 1968
Hon. J. L. Pepin	1968 to 1972
Hon. A. W. Gillespie	1972 to 1975

Presidents of the Treasury Board

Hon. E. J. Benson	1966 to 1968
Hon. C. M. Drury	1968 to 1974
Hon. J. Chretien	1974 to present

Ministers of Regional Economic Expansion

Hon. J. Marchand	1969 to 1972
Hon. D. Jamieson	1972 to 1975

Ministers of Manpower and Immigration

Hon. J. Marchand	1966 to 1969
Hon. B. Mackasey	1969 to 1972
Hon. R. Andras	1972 to 1975

Ministers of Consumer and Corporate Affairs

Hon. R. Basford	1967 to 1972
Hon. H. Gray	1972 to 1974
Hon. A. Ouellet	1974 to 1975

Deputy Ministers of Finance

William Clifford Clark	1932 to 1952
Kenneth Wiffin Taylor	1953 to 1963
Robert Boughton Bryce	1963 to 1970
Simon Reisman	1970 to 1975
Tommy Shoyama	1975 to present

Deputy Ministers of Industry, Trade and Commerce

Max Weir Mackenzie	1945 to 1951
William Frederick Bull	1951 to 1957
Mitchell Sharp	1957 to 1958
John Hascoll English	1958 to 1960
James Allen Roberts	1960 to 1964
Jack Hamilton Warren	1964 to 1971
James Frederick Grandy	1971 to 1975
Gerry Stoner	1975 to 1975

Secretaries of the Treasury Board

George Davidson	1964 to 1968
Simon Reisman	1968 to 1970
A. W. Johnson	1970 to 1973
Gordon Osbaldeston	1973 to 1975

Deputy Ministers of Regional Economic Expansion

Tom Kent	1969 to 1972
Douglas Love	1972 to 1975

Deputy Ministers of Manpower and Immigration

T. Kent	1966 to 1969
L. E. Cuillard	1969 to 1972
M. Des Roches	1972 to 1974
A. Gottlieb	1974 to 1975

Deputy Ministers of Consumer and Corporate Affairs

J. Grandy	1967 to 1969
G. Osbaldeston	1969 to 1973
M. Pitfield	1972 to 1974
S. Ostry	1974 to 1975

Governors of the Bank of Canada

Graham Towers	1935 to 1954
James Coyne	1954 to 1961
Louis Rasminsky	1961 to 1973
G. W. Bouey	1973 to 1975

APPENDIX D

Public Revenues and Expenditures. All Government Levels, 1955, 1965, and 1975[1]

	1955		1965		1975	
	Millions of dollars	*Per cent*	*Millions of dollars*	*Per cent*	*Millions of dollars*	*Per cent*
Federal government						
Revenues	4,926	100.0	8,944	100.0	30,888	100.0
Direct taxes on persons		33.4		37.2		49.4
Direct taxes on corporations and government enterprises		25.3		18.5		16.4
Indirect taxes		35.5		36.3		25.5
Other items		5.8		8.0		8.7
Expenditures	4,644	100.0	8,200	100.0	34,114	100.0
Purchases of goods and services		50.9		34.6		24.3
Transfers to persons		26.5		28.2		31.2
Transfers to provinces		9.5		16.5		22.0
Interest on public debt		9.5		9.4		7.4
Subsidies and other items		3.6		11.3		15.1
Provincial governments						
Revenues	1,742	100.0	6,075	100.0	28,691	100.0
Direct taxes on persons		11.9		18.1		23.9
Indirect taxes		43.8		37.3		26.8
Transfers from federal government		25.4		22.3		26.1
Investment income		10.7		7.8		12.0
Other items		8.2		14.5		11.2

	1955		1965		1975	
	Millions of dollars	*Per cent*	*Millions of dollars*	*Per cent*	*Millions of dollars*	*Per cent*
Expenditures	1,463	100.0	5,453	100.0	28,439	100.0
Purchases of goods and services		39.5		27.7		32.5
Transfers to persons		30.7		18.8		18.7
Transfers to local governments		22.4		26.4		22.8
Transfers to hospitals				20.5		16.5
Other items		7.4		6.6		9.5
Local governments						
Revenues	1,269	100.0	3,861	100.0	12,729	100.0
Indirect taxes		71.0		57.8		45.8
Transfers from provinces		25.8		37.3		50.9
Other items		3.2		4.9		3.3
Expenditures	1,241	100.0	3,473	100.0	11,735	100.0
Purchases of goods and services		88.1		86.8		89.4
Interest on public debt		6.8		9.6		8.0
Other items		5.1		3.6		2.6

[1] The figures in this table are not directly comparable with those in Table 5-1 because of the presence of intergovernmental transfer payments in the revenues and expenditures of the different levels of government.

SOURCE Based on data from Statistics Canada reproduced in Economic Council of Canada, *Thirteenth Annual Review: The Inflation Dilemma*. Ottawa, 1976, pp. 62-63.

APPENDIX E

GROSS GENERAL EXPENDITURE BY FUNCTION

For Selected Fiscal Years Ending March 31, 1967 to 1976
($ million)

	1966-67	*1971-72*	*1972-73*	*1973-74*	*1974-75**	*1975-76**
Defence	1,549	1,872	1,909	2,123	2,261	2,601
Welfare	2,713	5,418	6,858	8,109	10,056	12,384
Health	527	1,603	1,789	1,951	2,272	2,776
Debt charges	836	1,423	1,502	1,735	2,282	2,382
General purpose transfers to other governments	563	1,546	1,640	1,883	2,688	2,790
Development of regions	37	142	140	144	186	179
Transportation and communications	1,004	1,207	1,370	1,765	2,201	2,624
Natural resources, agriculture and environment	555	841	1,070	1,526	2,602	3,153
Other—People						
Education	384	864	847	919	920	1,205
Recreation and culture	87	164	215	253	279	300
Labour, employment and immigration	71	289	489	331	474	557
Housing	12	70	99	138	149	299
	554	1,387	1,650	1,641	1,822	2,361
Other—Business and Property						
Protection	191	341	390	479	595	743
Payments to own enterprises	178	272	294	362	459	535
Trade and industry and tourism	165	356	379	435	447	556
Research	128	331	278	302	390	509
	662	1,300	1,341	1,578	1,891	2,343
Miscellaneous						
Foreign affairs and international assistance	251	312	385	439	538	743
General government	549	1,167	1,257	1,382	2,156	2,105
Other	—	—	1	1	2	—
	800	1,479	1,643	1,822	2,696	2,848
Total Gross General Expenditure	9,800	18,218	20,912	24,277	30,957	36,441

APPENDIX F
Programs to Assist Industry

ACT	*PROGRAM*	*PURPOSE*	*COMMENTS*
	Defence Industry Productivity Program (DIP)	To enhance technological competence of defence industry	Deals primarily with civilian aspects of industry. Does carry a Defence capability, *e.g.*: Aircraft Ind.
	Industrial Design Assistance Program (IDAP)	To improve the competitive position of Canadian Industry through improved designing	Deals with consumer products. Directed at people to improve designing
Industrial Research and Development Incentives Act	Industrial Research and Development Incentive Program (IRDIA)	To expand scientific research and development in Canada	(Grant) Deals with applied research along lines followed by MOST long-range research and development
	Program for the Advancement of Industrial Technology (PAIT)	To encourage industrial growth and efficiency through improved products	Assistance directed at fostering the development of a particular product to encourage follow-up
	Program to enhance Productivity (PEP)	To encourage industrial growth and productivity	This is directed at a new product. It was directed initially at small firms—assist-consulting and product imp. second phase development.

	General Adjustment Assistance Program (GAAP)	(Financing) To assist Canadian manufacturing industry to improve its position in meeting international trade competition	Loan and Grant to engage consultants to improve financial position of companies (originally automotive Industry) now includes service and manufacturing
	Pharmaceutical Industry Development Assistance (PIDA)	(Financing) To increase the efficiency of drug production and marketing in Canada	August 1967 To foster competition adopted to assist pharmaceutical industry to offset disadvantage from allowing importation of foreign drugs to lower price
	Grains and Oilseeds Marketing Incentives Program (GOMI)	To achieve a sustained expansion of the total effective market for Canadian grains and oilseeds	Directed specifically at the agricultural sector
	Agricultural and Food Products Market Development Assistance Program (MDAP)	To encourage sustained growth for the sale of Canadian agricultural and food products in export and domestic markets	Assistance to promote the sale of agricultural products—assist the agricultural sector. Export oriented
	Program for Export Market Development	To bring about a sustained increase in the export of Canadian Production	
	Promotional Projects Program	To promote the export of Canadian products and services through trade fairs and missions	Directed at any industry requiring assistance

ACT	PROGRAM	PURPOSE	COMMENTS
	Building Equipment Accessories and Materials Program (BEAM)	To increase productivity and efficiency in building operations	
	Fashion Design Assistance Program (FDAP)	To increase Canadian international competitiveness in the apparel, textile, leather and footwear industries	Designed to assist the clothing and footwear industries in particular as compared to IDAP—above
	Machinery Program (MACH)	To allow users of machinery to acquire capital equipment at the lowest possible cost	Designed to encourage productivity. Industries can import machinery at lower tariff
	Ship Construction Subsidy Regulation (SCSR)	To assist the shipbuilding industry by subsidizing construction at a level comparable to the tariff protection given to other industries	New program designed specifically for the shipping industry
	Shipbuilding Temporary Assistance Program (STAP)	To provide grants to shipbuilders	Discontinued Program
	Counselling Assistance to Small Enterprises (CASE)	Provides an opportunity for owners and managers of small businesses to benefit from managerial experience	Designed specifically for small businesses. Has been transferred recently to the Federal Business Dev. Bank
	Shipbuilding Industry Assistance Program (SIAP)	Since March (1975) provides a subsidy paid on both construction and ship conversion	Introduced after the discontinuation of STAP

Selected Bibliography

CANADIAN POLITICS, ECONOMICS, AND ECONOMIC MANAGEMENT

Books

Adams, I., *et al. The Real Poverty Report.* Edmonton: Hurtig, 1972.

Archer, M. *Introductory Macroeconomics: A Canadian Analysis.* Toronto: Macmillan, 1973.

Armitage, A. *Social Welfare in Canada.* Toronto: McClelland and Stewart, 1975.

Aucoin, Peter and R. French. *Knowledge, Power and Public Policy.* Science Council of Canada, Special Study No. 31. Ottawa: Information Canada, 1974.

Barber, C. L. *Theory of Fiscal Policy as Applied to a Province.* Ontario Committee on Taxation. Toronto: Queen's Printer, 1967.

Bird, R. M. *Charging for Public Services: A New Look at an Old Idea.* Toronto: Canadian Tax Foundation, 1976.

——.*The Growth of Government Spending in Canada.* Toronto: Canadian Tax Foundation, 1970.

Bliss, M., ed. *Planning for Canada.* Toronto: University of Toronto Press, 1975.

Brewis, T. N. *Regional Economic Policies in Canada.* Toronto: Macmillan, 1969.

Brewis, T. N., H. E. English, *et al. Canadian Economic Policy.* Toronto: Macmillan, 1965.

Bryden, K. *Old Age Pensions and Policy-Making in Canada.* Montreal: McGill-Queen's, 1974.

Burns, R. M. and L. Close. *The Winter Works Program—A Case Study in Government Expenditure Decision-Making.* Toronto: Canadian Tax Foundation, 1971.

Canadian Tax Foundation. *The Financing of the Canadian Federation: The*

First Hundred Years. Toronto: Canadian Tax Foundation, 1966.

Choddos, R. *The CPR: A Century of Corporate Welfare.* Toronto: James, Lewis and Samuel, 1973.

Clement, W. *The Canadian Corporate Elite.* Toronto: McClelland and Stewart, 1975.

Courchene, T. J. *Money, Inflation and the Bank of Canada: An Analysis of Canadian Monetary Policy From 1970 to Early 1975.* Montreal: C. D. Howe Research Institute, 1976.

Creighton, D. *The Forked Road: Canada 1939-57.* Toronto: McClelland and Stewart, 1976.

Crispo, J. H., ed. *Wages, Prices, Profits and Economic Policy.* Toronto: University of Toronto Press, 1968.

Daly, Margaret. *The Revolution Game.* Toronto: New Press, 1970.

Dawson, R. M. *The Government of Canada.* Fourth ed. Toronto: University of Toronto Press, 1975.

Doern, G. Bruce. *Science and Politics in Canada.* Montreal: McGill-Queen's, 1972.

Doern, G. Bruce, ed. *The Regulatory Process in Canada.* Toronto: Macmillan, 1978.

Doern, G. Bruce and Peter Aucoin, eds. *The Structures of Policy-Making in Canada.* Toronto: Macmillan, 1971.

Doern, G. Bruce and V. S. Wilson, eds. *Issues in Canadian Public Policy.* Toronto: Macmillan, 1974.

Doerr, Audrey. *The Role of White Papers in the Policy Process.* Unpublished Doctoral Thesis. Ottawa: Carleton University, 1975.

Dupré, J. S., *et al. Federalism and Policy Development: The Case of Adult Occupational Training in Ontario.* Toronto: University of Toronto Press, 1973.

Fayerweather, J. *Foreign Investment in Canada.* Toronto: Oxford University Press, 1973.

Foreign Direct Investment in Canada. Ottawa: Information Canada, 1972.

Foreign Ownership and the Structure of Canadian Industry. Ottawa: Privy Council Office, January 1968.

Fraser Institute. *The Illusion of Wage and Price Controls.* Vancouver: Fraser Institute, 1976.

Frischke, B. A. *Inflation, Its Your Bag.* Toronto: Simon and Pierre, 1976.

Gilles, James. *A Review of the Economic Council's Interim Report on*

Competition Policy. Montreal: Private Planning Association, 1969.

Gordon, W. *Storm Signals: New Economic Policies for Canada*. Toronto: McClelland and Stewart, 1975.

Government of Ontario. *Report of Interdepartmental Task Force on Foreign Investment*. Toronto, 1971.

Gow, Donald. *The Progress of Budgetary Reform in the Government of Canada*. Economic Council of Canada. Ottawa: Information Canada, 1973.

Granatstein, J. L. *Canada's Way: The Politics of the Mackenzie King Government*. Toronto: Oxford University Press, 1975.

Grant, George. *Empire and Technology*. Toronto: House of Anansi, 1969.

____.*Lament For A Nation*. Toronto: McClelland and Stewart, 1965.

Green, Alan G. *Immigration and the Postwar Canadian Economy*. Toronto: Macmillan, 1976.

Hawkins, Freda. *Canada and Immigration*. Montreal: McGill-Queen's, 1972.

Hockin, T., ed. *The Apex of Power*. Toronto: Prentice-Hall, 1971.

Hodgetts, J. E. *The Canadian Public Service 1867-1967: A Physiology of Government*. Toronto: University of Toronto Press, 1973.

Hodgetts, J. E., *et al*. *The Biography of an Institution*. Montreal: McGill-Queen's, 1972.

Horowitz, G. *Canadian Labour in Politics*. Toronto: University of Toronto Press, 1968.

Innis, H. *Essays in Canadian Economic History*. Toronto: University of Toronto Press, 1956.

Intergovernmental Liaison on Fiscal and Economic Matters. Queen's University Report. Institute of Intergovernmental Relations. Ottawa: Queen's Printer, 1969.

Kaliski, S. F., ed. *Economic Policy Since the War*. Montreal: Trade Committee, 1965.

Langford, John. *Transport in Transition*. Montreal: McGill-Queen's, 1976.

Lipsett, S. M. *Agrarian Socialism*. New York: Anchor Books, 1968.

MacKay, C. S. *Canadian Regionalism: The Atlantic Development Board, A Case Study*. Unpublished M.A. thesis. Montreal: McGill University, 1969.

McPherson, C. B. *Democracy in Alberta.* Toronto: University of Toronto Press, 1967.

Manzer, R. *Canada: A Socio-Political Report.* Toronto: McGraw-Hill Ryerson, 1974.

Maslove, Allan. *The Pattern of Taxation in Canada.* Ottawa: Information Canada, 1973.

Mathews, R. A. *Industrial Viability in a Free Trade Economy: A Program of Adjustment Policies for Canada.* Toronto: University of Toronto Press, 1971.

Maxwell, J. *Policy Review and Outlook 1976. Challenge to Complacency.* Montreal: C. D. Howe Research Institute, 1976.

——.*Policy Review and Outlook 1975. Restructuring the Incentive System.* Montreal: C. D. Howe Research Institute, 1975.

Meekison, J. P., ed. *Canadian Federalism: Myth or Reality.* Toronto: Methuen, 1971.

Mike, The Memoirs of the Rt. Hon. Lester B. Pearson, Vol. 3. Toronto: University of Toronto Press, 1975.

Neill, Robin. *A New Theory of Value: The Canadian Economics of H. A. Innis.* Toronto: University of Toronto Press, 1972.

Neufeld, E. P., ed. *Money and Banking in Canada.* Toronto: McClelland and Stewart, 1964.

Newman, Peter C. *Renegade in Power: The Diefenbaker Years.* Toronto: McClelland and Stewart, 1963.

——.*The Distemper of Our Times.* Toronto: McClelland and Stewart, 1968.

Officer, L. J. and L. B. Smith, eds. *Issues in Canadian Economics.* Toronto: McGraw-Hill Ryerson, 1974.

Paton, R. *The Ministry of State for Urban Affairs: The Institutional Basis of Federal Urban Policy Making.* Unpublished M. A. Research Paper. Carleton University. Institute of Canadian Studies, 1974.

Pickersgill, J. W. and D. F. Forster. *The Mackenzie King Record,* Vol. III. Toronto: University of Toronto Press, 1970.

Pinard, M. *The Rise of a Third Party: A Study of Crisis Politics.* Englewood Cliffs, N.J.: Prentice-Hall, 1971.

Phidd, Richard W. *The Economic Council and Economic Policy Formulation in Canada.* Unpublished Doctoral Dissertation, Department of Political Studies, Kingston: Queen's University, 1972.

Porter, John. *The Vertical Mosaic.* Toronto: University of Toronto Press, 1965.

Presthus, R. *Elite Accommodation in Canadian Politics*. Toronto: Macmillan, 1973.

Prince, Michael J. *A Redistributive Policy Output and its Impact on the Canadian Executive: The New Unemployment Insurance Act of 1971*. Unpublished Research Paper, Ottawa: Carleton University, School of Public Administration, 1975.

Raynauld, A. *The Canadian Economic System*. Toronto: Macmillan, 1967.

Rea, K. J. and J. T. McLeod, eds. *Business and Government in Canada*. Second edition. Toronto: Methuen, 1976.

Reid, T. E. H., ed. *Economic Planning in a Democratic Society*. Toronto: University of Toronto Press, 1963.

Report of the Commons Standing Committee on External Affairs and National Defence (Wahn Report). Ottawa: Information Canada, 1970.

Roseman, Ellen. *Consumer Beware*. Revised edition. Don Mills: New Press, 1974.

Rotstein, A., ed. *Beyond Industrial Growth*. Toronto: University of Toronto Press, 1976.

Roussopoulos, D., ed. *The Political Economy of the State*. Montreal: Black Rose Books, 1973.

Sawyer, J. A. *Macroeconomics: Theory and Policy in the Canadian Economy*. Toronto: Macmillan, 1975.

Shearer, R. and D. E. Bond. *The Economics of the Canadian Financial Systems: Theory, Practice and Institutions*. Scarborough: Prentice-Hall, 1972.

Smiley, D. *Canada in Question: Federalism in the Seventies*. Toronto: McGraw-Hill Ryerson, 1976.

Smith, Denis. *Gentle Patriot*. Edmonton: Hurtig, 1973.

Somers, G. G. and W. D. Woods, eds. *Cost-Benefit Analysis of Manpower Policies*. Kingston: Queen's University Industrial Relations Centre, 1969.

Springate, D. J. V. *Regional Development Incentive Grants and Private Investment in Canada: A Case Study of the Effect of Regional Development Incentives on the Investment Decisions of Manufacturing Firms*. Cambridge: Harvard University, 1972.

Strick, J. C. *Canadian Public Finance*. Toronto: Holt, Rinehart and Winston, 1973.

The National Finances 1970-71 to 1975-76. Toronto: Canadian Tax Foundation, 1971-76.

Trudeau, Pierre E. *Federalism and the French Canadians.* Toronto: Macmillan, 1968.

Underhill, Frank H. *In Search of Canadian Liberalism.* Toronto: Macmillan, 1960.

Van Loon, R. J. and M. Whittington. *The Canadian Political System.* Second edition. Toronto: McGraw-Hill Ryerson, 1975.

White, D. A. *Business Cycles in Canada.* Ottawa: Queen's Printer, 1967.

White, W. L. and J. C. Strick. *Policy, Politics and the Treasury Board in Canadian Government.* Don Mills: Science Research Assoc., 1970.

Wilson, W. A. *The Trudeau Question: Election 1972.* Don Mills: General Publishing, 1973.

Articles and Papers

Acheson, K. and John F. Chant. "The Bank of Canada: A Study in Bureaucracy". Manuscript. Kingston: Queen's University, 1971.

Balls, H. R. "Planning, Programming and Budgeting in Canada". *Public Administration,* Vol. 57 (Autumn 1970), p. 296.

Best, Robert. "Youth Policy" in Doern and Wilson, eds. *Issues in Canadian Public Policy.* Toronto: Macmillan, 1974, pp. 137-65.

Black, E. "The Fractured Mosaic — John Porter Revisited". Paper presented to the Canadian Political Science Association, 1974.

Breton, A. "Modelling the Behaviour of Exchequers" in Officer and Smith, eds. *Issues in Canadian Economics.* Toronto: McGraw-Hill Ryerson, 1974, pp. 110-13.

Burns, R. M. "The Operation of Fiscal and Economic Policy" in Doern and Wilson, eds. *Issues in Canadian Public Policy.* Toronto: Macmillan, 1974, pp. 286-309.

Cairns, Allan C. "The Electoral System and the Party System in Canada, 1921-1965". *Canadian Journal of Political Science,* Vol. I, No. 1 (March 1968), pp. 55-80.

____."Alternative Styles in the Study of Canadian Politics". *Canadian Journal of Political Science,* Vol. VII, No. 1 (March 1974), pp. 101-27.

Canadian Labour Congress. *Labour's Manifesto for Canada.* Ottawa: CLC, May 1976.

D'Aguino. Thomas. "The Prime Minister's Office: Catalyst or Cabal". *Canadian Public Administration,* Vol. XVII, No. 1, pp. 55-84.

Deaton, R. "The Fiscal Crisis of the State". *Our Generation,* Vol. VIII, No. 4, pp. 11-50.

Des Roches, J. M. "The Creation of New Administrative Structures: The Federal Department of Industry". *Canadian Public Administration*, Vol. VIII, pp. 285-91.

Doern, G. Bruce. "Vocational Training and Manpower Policy". *Canadian Public Administration*, Vol. XII (1969), p. 65.

——."Horizontal and Vertical Portfolios in Government", in Doern and Wilson, eds. *Issues in Canadian Public Policy*. Toronto: Macmillan, 1974, Chapter 12.

——.*Regulatory and Jurisdictional Aspects of the Regulation of Hazardous Substances in Canada*. Study for the Science Council of Canada. Ottawa: October 1976.

——."The Political Economy of Regulating Occupational Health: The Ham and Beaudry Reports." *Canadian Public Administration*, Vol. XX, No. 1, pp. 8-20.

Doern, G. Bruce, Ian A. Hunter, D. Swartz, and V. S. Wilson. "The Structure and Behaviour of Canadian Regulatory Boards and Commissions: Multidisciplinary Perspectives". *Canadian Public Administration*, Vol. XVIII, No. 2, pp. 189-215.

Drache, Daniel. "Rediscovering Canadian Political Economy". Paper presented to Canadian Political Science Association Meeting. Edmonton: June 1975.

Gartner, G. J. "A Review of Cooperation Among Western Provinces". Paper given at Annual Conference. Institute of Public Administration of Canada. Halifax: September 10, 1976.

Gillespie, W. I. "The Federal Budget as Plan, 1968-72". *Canadian Tax Journal*, Vol. XXI (1973), pp. 64-84.

Gordon, H. Scott. "A Twenty-Year Perspective: Some Reflecting on the Keynesian Revolution in Canada", in Canadian Trade Committee. *Canadian Economic Policy Since the War*. Montreal: Private Planning Association, 1966, pp. 28-46.

Green, A. G. "Regional Economic Disparities", in Officer and Smith, eds. *Issues in Canadian Economics*. Toronto: McGraw-Hill Ryerson, 1974, pp. 354-70.

Hartle, Douglas G. "The Role of the Auditor General of Canada". *Canadian Tax Journal*, Vol. XXIII, No. 3, pp. 193-204.

Helliwell, John. "Managing the Economy". Paper given to Liberal Party Conference. Toronto: March 26, 1977.

Hicks, M. "The Treasury Board of Canada and its Clients". *Canadian Public Administration*, Vol. XVI, No. 2, pp. 182-205.

Johnson, A. W. "The Treasury Board of Canada and the Machinery of Government in the 1970's". *Canadian Journal of Political Science,* Vol. IV, No. 3, pp. 346-66.

Jones, J. C. H. "The Bureaucracy and Public Policy: Canadian Merger Policy and the Combines Branch". *Canadian Public Administration,* Vol. XVIII, No. 3, pp. 269-96.

Lalonde, M. "The Changing Role of the Prime Minister's Office". *Canadian Public Administration,* Vol. XIV, No. 4, pp. 509-37.

Lipsey, R. G. "Wage Price Controls: How to do a lot of harm by trying to do a little good". *Canadian Public Policy,* Vol. III (1977), pp. 1-13.

Lomas, E. A. "The Council of Maritime Premiers: A Report and an Evaluation after Five Years". Paper given at Annual Conference. Institute of Public Administration of Canada. Halifax: September 8-10, 1976.

McCready, D., and Conrad Winn, "Redistributive Policy" in C. Winn and J. McMenemy, eds. *Political Parties in Canada.* Toronto: McGraw-Hill Ryerson, 1976, pp. 206-27.

McDonald, G. P. A. "Labour, Manpower and Government Reorganization". *Canadian Public Administration,* Vol. X, No. 4, p. 476.

McLeod, J. T. "The Free Enterprise Dodo is no Phoenix". *Canadian Forum,* Vol. LVI, No. 663 (August 1976), pp. 6-10.

Panitch, Leo. "The Development of Corporatism in Liberal Democracies". Paper presented to Annual Meeting of American Political Science Association. Chicago: September 2, 1976.

____."The Role of the Canadian State". Paper presented to Canadian Political Science Association. Quebec City: June 1976.

Phidd, Richard W. "The Economic Council of Canada, 1963-1974". *Canadian Public Administration,* Vol. XVIII, No. 3, 1975.

____."The Economic Council of Canada, 1963-1974", *Canadian Public Administration,* Vol. XVIII, No. 3, 1975.

Pitfield, M. "The Shape of Government in the 1980's". *Canadian Public Administration,* Vol. XIV, No. 1, pp. 8-14.

Rasminsky, L. "The Role of the Central Banker Today". Lecture delivered in Italy, November 9, 1956. Washington: Per Jacobson Foundation, 1956.

Robertson, Gordon. "The Changing Role of the Privy Council Office". *Canadian Public Administration,* Vol. XIV, No. 4, pp. 487-508.

Smiley, D. "Must Canadian Political Science be a Miniature Replica?"

Journal of Canadian Studies, Vol. IX, No. 1 (February 1974), pp. 31-42.
——. "The Non-Economics of Anti-Inflation" in Rea and McLeod, eds. *Business and Government in Canada,* Second edition. Toronto: Methuen, 1976, p. 445.
Trebilcock, M. "Must the Consumer Always Lose". Paper presented to the Institute of Public Administration of Canada. Ottawa: September 1975.
Watts, George S. "The Bank of Canada During the Period of Post War Adjustments". *The Bank of Canada Review* (November 1973), pp. 4-17.
——. "The Bank of Canada During the War Years". *The Bank of Canada Review* (April 1973), pp. 3-16.
——. "The Bank of Canada From 1948-1952: The Pivotal Years". *The Bank of Canada Review* (November 1974), pp. 1-16.
——. "The Legislative Birth of the Bank of Canada". *The Bank of Canada Review* (August 1972), pp. 13-26.
——. "The Origins and Background of Central Banking in Canada". *The Bank of Canada Review* (May 1972), pp. 14-25.
Wilson, V. Seymour and W. A. Mullins, "Representative Bureaucracy: Its Relevance to Canadian Public Policy". Paper presented at Carleton University. Ottawa: 1976.
Wolfe, D. "The State of Recent Economic Policy in Canada 1968-1975". Paper presented to Canadian Political Science Assoc. Quebec City: May 31, 1976.

Government Publications

Basford, Hon. R. *Policies for Price Stability.* Ottawa: Queen's Printer, 1968.
Buckley, H. and E. Tihanyi. *Canadian Policies for Rural Adjustment: A Case Study of the Economic Impact of ARDA, PFRA and MMRA.* Ottawa: Queen's Printer, 1967.
Canada. *Report of the Royal Commission on Government Organization.* Vol. I. Ottawa: Queen's Printer, 1963.
——. *Royal Commission on Banking and Finance.* Report. Ottawa: Queen's Printer, 1964.
——. *Royal Commission on Banking and Finance.* Report. Ottawa: Queen's Printer, 1964.

Canadian Council on Rural Development. *Rural Canada 1970: Prospects and Problems.* Ottawa: Information Canada, 1970.

____.*Toward a Development Strategy for Canada.* Ottawa: Information Canada, 1972.

Consumer Research Council. *A Report on Consumer Interest in Marketing Boards.* Ottawa: Consumer Research Council, 1974.

Connaghan, C. J. *Partnership or Marriage of Convenience: A Critical Examination of Contemporary Labour Relations in West Germany.* Ottawa: Labour Canada, 1976.

Committee on Government Productivity. *Interim Report Number Three.* Toronto: Queen's Printer, 1972.

Croll, Hon. David and R. Basford, MP. *Report on Consumer Credit.* Ottawa: Queen's Printer, 1967.

Department of Consumer and Corporate Affairs. *Annual Reports,* 1970-71 to 1975-76. Ottawa: Information Canada, 1971-76.

Department of Finance. *Economic Review,* 1970 to 1976. Ottawa: Information Canada, 1970-76.

____.*This is Your Department of Finance.* Ottawa: 1974.

____.*Who We Are . . . . What We Do.* Ottawa: 1973.

Department of Industry, Trade and Commerce. *Annual Report,* 1970-71 to 1975-76. Ottawa: 1970-76.

Department of Labour. *Annual Reports,* 1965 to 1976. Ottawa: Information Canada, 1965-76.

Department of Manpower and Immigration. *Annual Reports,* 1966-67 to 1975-76. Ottawa: Information Canada, 1966-76.

____.*Employment Strategy.* Ottawa: October 1976.

Department of Regional Economic Expansion. *Annual Reports,* 1969-70 to 1975-76. Ottawa: Information Canada, 1970-76.

____.*Atlantic Development Board. Annual Report 1968-69.* Ottawa: Queen's Printer, 1969.

____.*The New Approach.* Ottawa: 1976.

Department of Trade and Commerce. *History of Reconstruction in Canada.* Unpublished Paper.

Dickerson, Robert W. V., *et al. Proposals for a New Business Corporation Law for Canada.* Ottawa: Information Canada. 1971.

Director of Investigation and Research. *Annual Reports,* 1969-70 to 1975-76. Ottawa: Information Canada, 1969-76.

Economic Council of Canada. *Annual Review* (First to Thirteenth). Ottawa: Information Canada, 1964-76.

____.*Conference on Stabilization Policies.* Ottawa: Queen's Printer, 1966.

____.*Interim Report: Consumer Affairs and the Department of the Registrar General.* Ottawa: Queen's Printer, 1967.

____.*Interim Report on Competition Policy.* Ottawa: Queen's Printer, 1969.

____.*Looking Outward: A New Trade Strategy for Canada.* Ottawa: Information Canada, 1975.

____.*People and Jobs: A Study of the Canadian Labour Market.* Ottawa: Information Canada, 1976.

____.*Priorities on Transition 1974.* Proceedings of National Economic Conference. December 2-4, 1975. Ottawa: Information Canada, 1975.

____.*Regulation and Efficiency: A Study of Deposit Institutions.* Ottawa: Supply and Services, 1976.

Federal Services for Business. A Guide to Grants, Loans and Sources of Counsel Available from the Federal Government. Ottawa: Information Canada, 1974.

Francis, J. P. and N. A. Pallai. *Regional Development and Regional Policy: Some Issues and Recent Canadian Experience.* Ottawa: February 1972.

Food Prices Review Board. *Final Report: Telling It Like It Is.* Ottawa: Information Canada, February 1976.

Government of Canada. *Regional Development Opportunities: Capital Financing and Financial Institutions; Mineral Resource Development; Industrial and Trade Development.* Background Papers for Western Economic Opportunities Conference. July 24-26, 1973.

____.*The Way Ahead.* Ottawa: October 1976.

Governor of the Bank of Canada. *Annual Reports to the Minister of Finance, 1965 to 1976.* Ottawa: 1965-76.

House of Commons. *Minutes of Proceedings and Evidence of the Standing Committee on Finance, Trade and Economic Affairs,* 1965 to 1976. Ottawa: Queen's Printer, 1965-76.

____.*Minutes of Proceedings and Evidence of the Standing Committee on Regional Development Respecting Estimates,* 1973-74. Ottawa: Information Canada, April 10, 1973.

How to Improve Business-Government Relations in Canada. A Report to the Minister of Industry, Trade and Commerce. Ottawa: Department of Trade and Commerce, September 1976.

Jamieson, Hon. D. *Foreign Investment Review Act: Annual Report,* 1974-75, 1975-76. Ottawa: Information Canada, 1974-76.

Lalonde, Hon. M. *Working Papcr on Social Security in Canada.* Ottawa: Information Canada, 1973.

Macdonald, Hon. D. S. *White Paper on the Revision of Canadian Banking Legislation.* Ottawa: Supply and Services, 1976.

Mackasey, Hon. Bryce. *Unemployment Insurance in the '70's.* Ottawa: Queen's Printer, 1970.

McKeough, Hon. D. *The Reconstruction of Economic and Fiscal Policy in Canada.* Toronto: 1971.

National Productivity Council. *First Annual Report,* 1961-62. Ottawa: Queen's Printer, 1962.

Organization of the Government of Canada. Ottawa: Information Canada, 1975.

Prices and Incomes Commission. *Inflation, Unemployment and Incomes Policy.* Summary Report. Ottawa: Information Canada, 1972.

Proposals For a New Competition Policy for Canada. Ottawa: Department of Consumer and Corporate Affairs, 1973.

Report of the Standing Senate Committee on Agriculture. *Kent County Can Be Saved. An Agricultural Inquiry into the Agricultural Potential of Eastern New Brunswick.* Ottawa: Queen's Printer, 1976.

Ritchie, R. S. *An Institute for Research on Public Policy.* Ottawa: Information Canada, 1971.

Senate of Canada. *Poverty in Canada.* Ottawa: Information Canada, 1971.

____.*Proceedings of the Special Senate Committee on Science Policy,* No. 34 (March 5, 1969), Department of Finance. Ottawa: Queen's Printer, 1969.

____.*Standing Committee on National Finance, Growth, Employment and Price Stability.* Ottawa: Information Canada, 1972.

Skeoch, L. A., *et al. Dynamic Change and Accountability in a Canadian Market Economy.* Ottawa: Department of Consumer and Corporate Affairs, 1976.

Sterns, A. A. *History of the Department of Finance.* Ottawa: Department of Finance, 1965.

Treasury Board of Canada. *How Your Tax Dollar is Spent,* 1975-76. Ottawa: 1975.

Will, R. M. *The Budget as an Economic Document.* Studies of the Royal Commission on Taxation. No. 1. Ottawa: Queen's Printer, 1964.

Wilson, A. H. *Governments and Innovation.* Ottawa: Information Canada, 1973.

COMPARATIVE POLITICS, ECONOMICS, AND ECONOMIC MANAGEMENT

Beach, Y. L. *Making of Monetary and Fiscal Policies.* Washington, D.C.: The Brookings Institution, 1971.

Bacon, Robert and Walter Ellis. *Britain's Economic Problem: Too Few Producers,* London: Macmillan, 1976.

Bauchet, P. *Economic Planning: The French Experience.* London: Heinemann, 1962.

Bell, D. *The Cultural Contradictions of Capitalism.* New York: Basic Books, 1976.

Bicanie, R. *Problems of Planning: East and West.* The Hague: Mouton and Co., 1967.

Birnbaum, N. "Conflicting Interpretations of the Rise of Capitalism: Marx and Weber". *The British Journal of Sociology,* Vol. IV (June 1953).

Blaug, M. *Economic Theory in Retrospect.* Homewood: Richard D. Irwin, 1962.

Blechman, B. M., E. M. Gramlich, *et al. Setting National Priorities: The 1976 Budget.* Washington, D.C.: The Brookings Institution, 1975.

Boulding, K. *Economics as a Science.* New York: McGraw-Hill, 1970.

Breton, A. *The Economic Theory of Representative Government.* Chicago: Aldine Publishing Co., 1974.

Brittan, S. *Steering the Economy: The Role of the Treasury.* London: Allen and Unwin, 1970.

____.*The Treasury Under the Tories.* London: Allen and Unwin, 1964.

Brown, R. G. S. *The Administrative Process in Britain.* London: Methuen, 1971.

____.*The Management of Welfare.* London: Fontana, 1975.

Cairncross, A., ed. *Essays in Economic Management.* London: Allen and Unwin, 1971.

____.*The Managed Economy.* Oxford: Basil Blackwell, 1970.

Chamberlain, N. *Public and Private Planning.* Toronto: McGraw-Hill Ryerson, 1975.

Coddington, A "Keynesian Economics: The Search For First Principles". *Journal of Economic Literature,* Vol. XIV, No. 4 (December 1976), Section 1.

Cohen, S. S. *Modern Capitalist Planning: The French Model.* Cambridge: Harvard University Press, 1969.

Clower, R. and A. Leijonhufvud. "The Coordination of Economic

Activities: A Keynesian Perspective". *American Economic Review* (May 1975).

Cronin, Thomas E. "Everybody Believes in Democracy Until He Gets to the White House . . . An Examination of White House Departmental Relations", in *Papers on the Institutionalized Presidency.* Washington: The Brookings Institution, 1970.

Cross, J. A. *British Public Administration.* London: University Tutorial Press, 1970.

Dahl, Robert A. and Charles E. Lindblom. *Politics, Economics and Welfare.* New York: Harper and Row, 1956.

Davis, R. C. *Discretionary Justice.* Baton Rouge: Louisiana State Press, 1969.

Denton, G., *et al. Economic Planning and Policies in Britain, France and Germany.* London: Allen and Unwin, 1968.

Devans, Ely. *Planning and Economic Management.* Edited by Sir Alec Cairncross. Manchester: Manchester University Press, 1970.

Dror, Y. *Public Policy-Making Reexamined.* San Francisco: Chandler, 1968.

Dye, T. *Understanding Public Policy.* Englewood Cliffs, N. J.: Prentice-Hall, 1972.

Easton, David. *A Systems Analysis of Political Life.* New York: John Wiley, 1965.

Eyestone, Robert. *Political Economy.* Chicago: Markham, 1972.

Friedman, M. *Capitalism and Freedom.* Chicago: University of Chicago Press, 1962.

Friedman, M. and W. W. Heller. *Monetary vs. Fiscal Policy: A Dialogue.* New York: Norton and Co., 1969.

Galbraith, John K. *Economics and the Public Purpose.* Bergenfield, N. J.: New American Library, 1975.

_____.*Money.* London: Pelican, 1975.

_____.*The New Industrial State.* New York: Houghton and Mifflin, 1968.

Goldman, Sir Samuel. *The Developing System of Public Expenditure Management and Control.* London: H.M.S.O. 1973.

Goodwin, C. D., ed. *Exhortation and Controls.* Washington: The Brookings Institution, 1975.

Gross, Bertram. "The Managers of National Economic Change" in R. C. Martin, ed. *Public Administration and Democracy.* Syracuse: Syracuse University Press, 1965, pp. 101-28.

Hallett, G., *et al. Regional Policy for Ever?* London: Institute of Economic Affairs, 1973.

Hanson, A. H. and M. Walles. *Governing Britain.* London. Fontana, 1970.

Hayward, J. and W. Watson, eds. *Planning, Politics and Public Policy: The British, French and Italian Experience.* London: Cambridge University Press, 1975.

Heady, Bruce. *British Cabinet Ministers.* London: Allen and Unwin, 1973.

Heclo, H. *Modern Social Politics in Britain and Sweden.* New Haven: Yale University Press, 1974.

Heclo, H. and A. Wildavsky. *The Private Government of Public Money.* London: Macmillan, 1974.

Heilbroner, R. *Between Capitalism and Socialism.* New York: Random House, 1970.

Heilbroner, R., ed. *Economic Means and Social Ends.* Englewood Cliffs, N. J.: Prentice-Hall, 1969.

Henderson, H. *Emerging Synthesis in American Public Administration.* London: Asia Publishing House, 1966.

Herman, V. *et al. Cabinet Studies.* London: Macmillan, 1975.

Hill, M. *The State Administration and the Individual.* Glasgow: Fontana, 1976.

Johnson, R. A., *et al. The Theory and Management of Systems.* New York: McGraw-Hill, 1963.

Katz, D. and R. L. Kahn. *The Social Psychology of Organization.* New York: Wiley, 1966.

Keeling, Desmond. *Management in Government.* London: Allen and Unwin, 1972.

Kelf, Cohen. *Twenty Years of Nationalization: The British Experience.* London: Macmillan, 1969.

King, Anthony, ed. *The British Prime Minister.* London: Macmillan, 1969.

Kristol, I. "Taxes, Poverty and Equality". *The Public Interest,* No. 37 (Fall 1974), pp. 3-28.

Lee, Robert D. and R. W. Johnson. *Public Budgeting Systems.* Baltimore: University Park Press, 1973.

Lowi, T. "Four Systems of Policy, Politics and Choice". *Public Administration Review* (July/August, 1972), pp. 293-310.

Lutz, V. *Central Planning for the Market Economy.* London: Longmans, 1969.

McMahon, C. W. *Techniques of Economic Forecasting: Short-Term Economic Forecasting Used by the Government of Canada, France, The Netherlands, Sweden, the United Kingdom, and the United States.* Paris: OECD, 1956.

Miliband, R. *The State in Capitalist Society.* London: Weidenfeld and Nicolson, 1969.

Nourse, E. G. *Economics in the Public Service.* New York: Harcourt Brace, 1953.

O'Connor, J. *The Fiscal Crisis of the State.* New York: St. Martin's Press, 1971.

Okun, A. *The Battle Against Unemployment.* Washington: The Brookings Institution, 1970.

____.*The Political Economy of Prosperity.* Washington: The Brookings Institution, 1970.

Panitch, Leo. *Social Democracy and Industrial Militancy: The Labour Party, the Trade Unions and Incomes Policy.* Cambridge: Cambridge University Press, 1976.

Perrow, Charles. *Organizational Analysis.* Belmont, California: Brooks-Cole, 1970.

Pierce, L. *The Politics of Fiscal Policy Formation.* Pacific Palisades, Ca.: Goodyear Publishing Co., 1971.

Putnam, Robert D. *The Beliefs of Politicians: Ideology, Conflict and Democracy in Britain and Italy.* New Haven: Yale University Press, 1973.

Reagan, M. D. *The Managed Economy.* London: Oxford University Press, 1963.

____.*The New Federalism.* New York: Oxford University Press, 1972.

Redford, E.S. *Democracy in the Administrative State.* New York: Oxford University Press, 1969.

Report of the Committee of Inquiry of Industrial Democracy. London: H.M.S.O., 1977.

Self, Peter. *Administrative Theories and Politics.* Toronto: University of Toronto Press, 1973.

Selznick, P. *Leadership in Administration.* New York: Harper and Row, 1957.

Sheldon, E. B. and N. E. Freeman. "Notes on Social Indicators". *Policy Sciences,* Vol. I, No. 1, pp. 97-113.

Schultz, C. *The Politics and Economics of Public Spending.* Washington: The Brookings Institution, 1968.

Shone, Sir Robert. "The Machinery for Economic Planning: The National Economic Development Council". *Public Administration,* Vol. XLIV (Spring 1966), pp. 18-22.

Shonfield, A. *Modern Capitalism: The Changing Balance of Public and Private Power.* London: Oxford University Press, 1965.

Silk, L. *The Economists.* New York: General Publishing, 1976.

Sleeman, J. F. *The Welfare State.* London: Unwin University Books, 1973.

Smith, Brian. *Policy Making in British Government.* London: Martin Robertson, 1976.

Smith, B. L., ed. *The New Political Economy: The Public Use of the Private Sector.* New York: Macmillan, 1975.

Solo, Robert A. *The Political Authority and the Market System.* Cincinnati: Southwestern Publishing Co., 1974.

Thompson, Victor. *Bureaucracy and Innovation.* Alabama: University of Alabama Press, 1968.

Tinbergen, J. *Central Planning.* New Haven: Yale University Press, 1964.

Vickers, Sir Geoffrey. *The Art of Judgement: A Study of Policy Making.* London: Chapman and Hall, 1965.

——. *Value Systems and Social Process.* London: Tavistock, 1968.

Waldo, D. *The Administrative State.* New York: Ronald Press, 1948.

Waterston, A. *Development Planning: Lessons of Experience.* Baltimore: Johns Hopkins, 1965.

Wilensky, H. L. *The Welfare State and Equality: Structural and Ideological Roots of Public Expenditures.* Berkeley: University of California Press, 1975.

Wilson, Harold. *The Labour Government, 1964-1970.* London: Penquin, 1974.

Young, O. R. *Systems of Political Sciences.* Englewood Cliffs, N. J.: Prentice-Hall, 1968.

Index